Positive Psychology

Jan D. Sinnott
Editor

Positive Psychology

Advances in Understanding Adult Motivation

Springer

Editor
Jan D. Sinnott
Towson University,
Baltimore, Maryland, USA

ISBN 978-1-4614-7281-0 ISBN 978-1-4614-7282-7 (eBook)
DOI 10.1007/978-1-4614-7282-7
Springer New York Heidelberg Dordrecht London

Library of Congress Control Number: 2013938606

In press, Springer Publishing, New York, New York.

Printed on acid-free paper

Springer is part of Springer Science+Business Media (www.springer.com)

With gratitude to
my family,
my friends,
my colleagues
who have enriched my life and work.
We're all in this together. . . .

Preface

The search for meaning in life, for what is good, for love, for hope, and for happiness has always motivated much of adult life, whether an individual is struggling in a developing war-torn country or happily enjoying a beach vacation. Sometimes, this set of desires can be stronger than the motivations that we consider so basic such as needs for food, sex, and pleasure. The study of Positive Psychology brings a much needed fresh emphasis to the study of the cognitions, traits, and contexts of behavior that are associated with optimal development and flourishing during the entire course of life. It highlights the ways in which growth, hope, and resilience (to name just a few positive adult experiences) aid a person and motivate him or her in dealing with the inevitable challenges of life. Whether as individuals or as members of cultures and organizations, we want to optimize chances for growth and flourishing. The chapters in this book each speak to one of the major portions of adult life that can be addressed in new ways by means of the new discipline of Positive Psychology. My own Positive Psychology work now focuses on positive aspects of cognition as we pass through adulthood and aging, factors in intimate relationships that thrive, constructing the ever-changing self, and conceptualizing thriving societies.

In 2000, Seligman and Csikszentmihalyi, writing in the *American Psychologist*, offered a general introduction to a relatively new field of psychology that has been growing in popularity ever since, the field of Positive Psychology. Psychology had long been focused on pathology due, in part, to the historical events attending the founding of the field. It seemed time to study what makes individuals actually *flourish*. What individual traits or cognitions, what aspects of the environment, help a person to truly flourish, thrive and grow? When adults develop psychologically through the stages of emerging adulthood, full adulthood, middle age, and old age, they encounter numerous challenges that can "make or break" them. How do they develop resilience and a loving, caring, wise outlook on life? I have offered some ideas about Positive Psychology and adult development in two special issues of the *Journal of Adult Development* (Sinnott 2009). I also offer some of the ideas expressed by authors in this book to students when I teach courses related to Adult Development, Aging, and Positive Psychology.

Positive Psychology is defined here as the *scientific* study of aspects of the human experience that enhance the positive quality of our experience, for example, hope, joy, resilience, coping, spirituality, courage, cooperation, acceptance of diversity, workplace quality, human-enhancing economic systems, brain/body changes related to fear vs. joy, and creating personal/cultural meaning.

In this book, you will explore the ideas of 32 authors presented in 19 chapters who are active scholars and researchers in the global field of Positive Psychology. Their topics range from acceptance to teaching Positive Psychology. The book is divided into 4 Parts about research and scholarship related to the creation or existence of:

- *Positive Subjective Experiences* (Part I);
- *Positive Personality Traits* (Part II);
- *Positive Environments* (Part III); and
- *Learning to Thrive During Adulthood* (Part IV).

Of course, many chapters overlap the subfields, but this usually makes them even more interesting and useful. Within a Part, the chapters appear in alphabetical order based on the name of the lead author. Each chapter author gives a summary of the state of that part of the field at the end of the chapter.

Positive Subjective Experiences

Justin Coulson, of the School of Psychology, University of Wollongong, Australia, with coauthors Gerald Stoyles and Linsay Oades, offers ideas regarding childrearing as a "calling" or vocation. The construct of calling has received substantial attention in careers and vocational research. Recent qualitative and quantitative research also supports the prospect that people may feel called in other roles in life—specifically childrearing. This chapter will report on research that indicates that calling in childrearing is relevant to adult development, and functions in the same way that calling in the career/vocation domain does. Specifically, qualitative reports indicate that calling is relevant for parents and fits the childrearing context. Furthermore, recent research has quantitatively measured parents' subjective sense of calling in childrearing. Parental calling is positively associated with authoritative parenting style, importance of parenting, pleasure of parenting, parenting satisfaction, presence of meaning in life, satisfaction with life, and positive affect. The construct was negatively related to age and the sense that parenting is a burden. Children's well-being, positive affect, and engaged living in youth (measured through social integration and absorption in activities) are positively related to parental sense of calling in childrearing. This chapter examines the construct definition, its relation to optimizing adulthood and family life and the manner in which calling is measured. Furthermore, this chapter describes how calling facilitates flourishing through its relation to pathways to happiness most associated with a life well lived.

Sanne M. A. Lamers, Gerben J. Westerhof, and Ernst T. Bohlmeijer of the University of Twente, the Netherlands, and Corey L. M. Keyes of Emory University, explore the level and variability of mental illness and mental health across the lifespan using findings from a 9-month longitudinal Internet study. Mental health has long been defined as the absence of psychopathologies such as depression and anxiety. Although important, the absence of mental illness is a minimal outcome from a psychological perspective on lifespan development. This chapter therefore focuses on mental illness as well as on three core components of positive mental health: (1) feelings of happiness and satisfaction with life (emotional well-being), (2) positive individual functioning in terms of self-realization (psychological well-being), and (3) positive societal functioning in terms of being of social value (social well-being). The two continua model holds that mental illness and mental health are related, but have distinct dimensions. This model was studied on the basis of a representative Internet survey of Dutch adults who filled out questionnaires four times with 3-month intervals ($n = 1{,}067$). Mental illness was measured with the Brief Symptom Inventory and mental health with the Mental Health Continuum Short Form. Analyses controlled for demographic characteristics as well as personality traits. Across time, older adults score lower on psychopathological symptoms as well as on mental health. Compared with younger adults, older adults experienced less variability across time in psychopathological symptoms, but not in symptoms of positive mental health. These findings support the validity of the two continua model in adult development and illustrate that there is more to mental health development than the absence of illness.

Bryan Moore, addresses flow theory and the paradox of happiness. We all desire the experience of happiness, but happiness is not a substance in and of itself. It is a derivative, or after-effect, of something. We experience happiness through a thing that we are conscious of. The more we focus on our experience of happiness the less that it exists. A paradox arises: the only way to be truly happy is to not desire happiness. We know from personal experience that we are most satisfied when our focus is on some entity that is not directly linked to ourselves. When we savor a meal we are focused on the taste and texture of the food. When we help a needy child we are concerned only with the child's well-being. When we have sex we are enthralled with the other. Only through the relinquishment of the self does one experience happiness. Flow theory proposes that optimal experience is ascertained through a complete focus on an activity that contains clear goals, immediate feedback, and a balanced skill/challenge ratio. It has been shown that activities such as music performance, athletics, games, martial arts, and artistic expression, commonly induce flow state. By using this activity-specific model in a broader context we may be able to shed more light on what the good life is.

Grant J. Rich, of University of Alaska Southeast, explores the history and future of flow research, tracing its development from roots in related concepts such as humanistic psychologist Abraham Maslow's notion of peak experience, and the work of Mihaly Csikszentmihalyi and his colleagues on the modern flow concept. Variations of the experience in a range of populations, including students, families, athletes, musicians, and eminent elder creators are described. Special attention is given to work on flow and related mental states (such as intrinsic motivation, engagement, and effortless attention) by contemporary researchers both within and beyond the United States, including recent work on neurological correlates of the optimal state of consciousness. In addition, assessment of the flow experience is explored, including questionnaires, interviews, and ecological momentary assessment techniques such as the experience-sampling method. Implications of the flow experience for creativity, optimal development, and well-being are discussed.

Jeffrey Dean Webster, of Langara College, Vancouver, British Columbia, Canada, describes a recent empirical study investigating the relationship between identity styles and wisdom, and the possible mediating roles of empathy and attributional complexity. Despite the theoretical link between identity and wisdom, there has been no empirical work investigating this connection directly using psychometrically sound instruments. This study investigates this relationship in an ethnically diverse sample of 160 young adults. Findings are consistent with hypotheses that informational identity style correlates positively with wisdom, and suggest implications for a lifespan Positive Psychology perspective.

Evangeline A. Wheeler, of Towson University, investigates laughter, the often neglected but very important aspect of positive experiences in adulthood. She reviews current interdisciplinary literature on the psychology of laughter with the goal of explaining laughter as a positive motivator. Beginning with a presentation of some general findings on the relationship between laughter and well-being, she clarifies the distinction between laughter and humor. Subsequent sections discuss, in turn, the role of laughter in interpersonal social networks, cognition and intelligence, and pain management. A section on research suggests ways in which people may benefit from laughter as they age. This chapter ends with some cautions to consider in the conduct and application of laughter studies.

Positive Personality Traits

Monika Ardelt, Scott D. Landes, Kathryn R. Gerlach, and Leah Polkowski Fox of the University of Florida, address an important question, namely, what explains aging and dying well? Previous research primarily examined the effects of objective life conditions (e.g., physical health, finances, socioeconomic status, age, social relationships) on adults' subjective well-being, whereas their internal strengths have often been ignored. Applying theories of life-long psychosocial growth and the life-course principles of lifespan development and human agency, they argue that, contrary to situational theory and stratification theory, internal strengths (wisdom, mastery, purpose in life, and spirituality) will have a stronger positive effect on subjective well-being than objective circumstances. They use a sample of 156 older community residents, nursing home residents, and hospice patients (aged 52+) living in North Central Florida to test this hypothesis.

Leonie J. Brooks, of Towson University, examines how Black immigrants use their resilience, spirituality, hope, positive expectations, courage, and culturally influenced strategies (e.g., creating a system of pooling money and lending to each other when unable to secure loans from banks) as they adjust to living in the United

States. These traits play a role in the successful adjustment and positive functioning of Black immigrants living in the United States.

Kelly Branam Cartwright, of Christopher Newport University, addresses the role of motivation in the development of reading comprehension examining the question from a lifespan perspective. Her chapter is a review of the role of motivation and engagement (positive affective states) in successful reading comprehension development. Because of the influence of the information processing perspective in psychology and education, work in reading has focused almost exclusively on the cognitive processes involved in successful reading. However, work on the more subjective aspects of human experience and their effects on reading comprehension have been neglected. In this chapter, she argues that to have a complete picture of successful reading comprehension and its lifespan development, we must include attention to Positive Psychological variables such as motivation, engagement, and self-efficacy.

Charles H. Hackney, of Briercrest College, Saskatchewan, Canada, writes that martial arts can be a pathway to the growth of happiness and personal flourishing. Theoretical and empirical literature concerning the psychosocial correlates of training in the martial arts is reviewed in this chapter. This analysis is guided by cross-cultural research, positive psychological work on character strengths and virtues, and MacIntyre's neo-Aristotelian philosophy.

Positive Environments

Larry Froman, of Towson University, begins our consideration of positive environments with a discussion of ethical issues in the workplace. Using a Positive Psychology perspective he considers the crisis of ethics in today's workplace. He uses case studies including examples of health and safety issues, corporate corruption and greed, workplace intimidation and aggression, and corporate outsourcing and downsizing. A Positive Psychology perspective is discussed, including building effective relationships, creating cultures of virtue, trust, and social responsibility, building organizational processes including information sharing, communication patterns, and team effectiveness, and leadership development.

Sanford Lopater, of Christopher Newport University, focuses on the university as an environment and describes an upper level, undergraduate, writing-intensive seminar on Positive Psychology. A true seminar format is employed in which the instructor and students coequally share the responsibilities for teaching and learning. Several pedagogical methods are used. This format is most successful when 20 or fewer students are enrolled, and when an uninterrupted 3-h segment of time can be set aside, usually during evening hours. Introductory lecture material reviews the history of Positive Psychology and sets the stage for subsequent topics and assignments. Correlative chapters in the textbook supplement weekly topical content and discussion. Three films are presented to exemplify various attributes of individuation, personal responsibility, courage, redemption, resilience, perseverance, and the importance of sharing vulnerabilities within the context of relationships. Several movies have been employed. Students write 5–7 page reaction papers for each of the three selected films. At the beginning of the term, each student selects a research paper topic which culminates in a 20-page manuscript based on primary sources. Each student selects two others to read and write 2–3 page critiques of the research paper. Toward the end of the semester, students prepare and present a PowerPoint summary of their work, and the two critics present their analyses immediately afterward. In-depth discussion follows. Copies of all research papers and critiques are distributed to all members of the seminar. This seminar format reinforces productive, independent scholarship, critical thinking, assessment of the primary literature, and the preparation of a concise oral presentation. The student is further encouraged to appraise the cinematic arts and contemporary literature through the "lens" of a Positive Psychological perspective.

Dan P. McAdams, of Northwestern University, builds on his reviews (McAdams and Pals 2006, *American Psychologist*; McAdams and Olson 2010, *Annual Review of Psychology*), to consider what Positive Psychology is, and *should* be. He uses three different standpoints in the study of human lives: the person as a social actor, the person as a motivated agent, and the person as an autobiographical author.

Christa K. Schmidt, of Towson University, and Kathryn L. Ziemer, Sarah Piontkowski, and Trisha L. Raque-Bogdan, of the University of Maryland College Park, offer an important analysis of Positive Health Psychology looking at its history and future directions. Seligman proposed a new field of "positive health" which focuses on how optimal functioning on biological, subjective, and functional health variables promotes better overall physical and mental health. The authors have discussed the importance of advancing work on understanding how biological, psychological, and sociocultural factors work to prevent mental and physical health disorders, rather than limiting our scope to treating the problems that arise. There has been a significant increase in studying how optimal human functioning is manifested in both physiological and psychological realms, but are conclusions outpacing science? The purpose of this chapter is to examine the history of positive health in the psychological literature, identify areas of growth and understanding, and make recommendations for topics that need to be further elucidated.

Learning to Thrive During Adulthood

Michelle D. Vaughan, of Westminster College, and Eric M. Rodriguez, of the City University of New York address the influence of Erik Erikson on Positive Psychology theory, research and practice by highlighting major themes and concepts from Erik Erikson's (1959) psychosocial theory of personality development. This chapter explores the influence of his theories and research on key concepts in the discipline of Positive Psychology. Using the three pillars of positive psychology (character strengths/virtues, subjective experiences, and positive institutions) as a framework, the authors discuss those core concepts in the context of normative development.

They focus on his major contributions to the field (*Young Man Luther*; *Insight and Responsibility*; *Identity: Youth and Crisis*; *Gandhi's Truth*). Highlighting the role of developmental stress in facilitating growth and building character strengths (what Erikson termed "basic strengths"), this chapter explores the role of positive institutions in nurturing the development of these strengths. This chapter also addresses the relative lack of awareness and attention to Erikson's influence within the field and highlight how Positive Psychology can draw on the themes found throughout his work to improve theory, research, and practice with diverse populations.

Susan H. McFadden and Scott Frankowski, of the University of Texas at El Paso, Heather Flick, of the University of Wisconsin Oshkosh, and Tarynn M. Witten, of Virginia Commonwealth University, discuss *Resilience and Multiple Stigmatized Identities: Lessons from Transgender Persons' Reflections on Aging*. An international, online survey of transgender-/intersex-identified persons offers powerful evidence of the human capacity for resilience. This chapter reviews qualitative and quantitative data obtained from 141 persons living in all regions of the United States, as well as Canada, Sweden, Ireland, Denmark, Australia, Brazil, and New Zealand. Some have been closeted their whole lives; some have happily lived postoperatively as trans persons for many years; some never wanted surgery or have not been able to obtain it. Nevertheless, all have lived into older age with a nonnormative gender identity and many have experienced years of ostracism, prejudice, and hate crimes. Now they encounter another stigmatizing condition: old age and the possibility of further stigmatization due to multiple physical and/or mental challenges. Employing the constructs of Positive Psychology, this chapter reveals how many of these individuals retain generative commitments to family members and/or younger gay, lesbian, bisexual, transgender, intersex, and queer (GLBTIQ)-identified persons, demonstrate courage in facing the challenges of age, reflect with wisdom on their triumphs over the stigma elicited by gender identity, retain a sense of humor, and remain hopeful, knowing that they have gained many psychological strengths from living with multiple stigmatizing identities.

Kevin Rathunde, of the University of Utah, explores the self-regulative concept of "experiential wisdom," which is the notion that lifelong learning is enhanced by the capacity to make experiential course corrections that lead back to states of interest and flow experience. A person with experiential wisdom recognizes that optimal experiences are more likely to occur when an affectively charged intuitive mode works in synchrony with a deliberative rational mode and is better able to cultivate situations where the interrelation of these two modes is optimized. The first part of this chapter provides a framework for understanding experiential wisdom and illustrates the practice by drawing on interviews with three distinguished lifelong learners—poet Mark Strand, social scientist Donald Campbell, and medical researcher Jonas Salk. Positive styles of adult regulation and finding flow and interest are presumably formed in socialization processes children encounter in families and schools from early childhood through adolescence. The second part of this chapter explores the development of the ability to regulate experience by drawing on the developmental literature and relevant theories of self-regulation. Special attention is paid to experiences in adolescence that set the stage for adulthood.

Eric M. Rodriguez, of CUNY, and Michelle D. Vaughan, of Westminster College, write about stress-related growth in the lives of lesbian, gay, and bisexual (LGB) individuals. There is a tendency in psychological research and practice within the LGB community to focus on the negative outcomes associated with sexual minority stress without ever understanding and/or appreciating that there may also be positive outcomes. This chapter examines the importance of stress-related growth within LGB lives. Drawing from literature on stress, hardiness, and empowerment, authors explore stress-related growth as it occurs within two distinct populations of LGB individuals: LGB people of faith and lesbian and gay individuals reporting stress related to disclosing their sexual identity to others. They spotlight the unique experiences of these two groups through quantitative and qualitative research, focusing on concrete examples that illustrate this growth. This chapter provides positive psychologists the opportunity to better understand stress-related growth as embodied in LGB lives with their unique experiences of minority stress, and provides recommendations for future research and practice in this area.

Tarynn M. Witten, of the Center for the Study of Biological Complexity at Virginia Commonwealth University, gets to the underlying theoretical heart of the matter in the chapter entitled *Biological Complexity Meets Positive Psychology: What Does Nonlinear Dynamical Systems and Complexity Theory Tell Us About Positive Psychology?* Studying living systems using the traditional reductionist approaches limits our deeper understanding of their behaviors, since knowledge of the behavior of the parts does not necessarily imply any understanding of the whole. Systems biologists sought to take the pieces and glue them back together in order to understand the behavior of the whole system. Modern-day mathematical biologists and biological physicists, particularly the quantum phenomenologists, understood that any sort of damage to the system could destroy potentially important behaviors that can only appear when the system is whole and undamaged. In parallel with these developments, complexity theory and the mathematical underpinning for these concepts was developing: dynamical systems theory or nonlinear systems theory, with the constructs of catastrophes, chaos, fractals, hysteresis, attractors, networks, emergence, adaptation, evolution, and frailty. Some of the early concepts of nonlinear dynamical systems have been applied to aspects of psychological behaviors. In this chapter, we examine how the constructs of Positive Psychology can be informed by the fields of complexity theory and nonlinear dynamics.

Welcome to an innovative, exciting, and practical set of fresh ideas about Positive Psychology, and the entire study of psychology! We are just at the beginning of deeply understanding a new way of conceptualizing an important source of adult motivation.

Jan D. Sinnott

Contents

Contributors

Monika Ardelt, Ph.D. Department of Sociology and Criminology & Law, University of Florida, 3219 Turlington Hall, P. O. Box 117330, 32611-7330 Gainesville, FL, USA
e-mail: ardelt@ufl.edu

Prof. Dr. Ernst T. Bohlmeijer Department of Psychology, Health, & Technology, University of Twente, P. O. Box 217, 7500 AE Enschede, The Netherlands
e-mail: e.t.bohlmeijer@utwente.nl

Leonie J. Brooks Psychology Department, Towson University, 8000 York Road, Towson MD 21252-0001, USA
e-mail: Labrooks@towson.edu

Kelly Branam Cartwright Christopher Newport University, 1 Avenue of the Arts, Newport News, VA 23606, USA
e-mail: kewright@cnu.edu

Dr. Justin Coulson Australian Institute of Business Wellbeing, Sydney Business School, University of Wollongong, 7 Partridge Pl, Figtree, NSW 2525 Australia
e-mail: justin@happyfamilies.com.au

Heather Flick Department of Psychology, University of Wisconsin Oshkosh, 800 Algoma Blvd., Oshkosh, WI 54901, USA
e-mail: flickh18@uwosh.edu

Leah Polkowski Fox, BA University of Florida, P. O. Box 117330, 32611-7330 Gainesville, FL, USA
e-mail: leahpolk@hotmail.com

Scott Frankowski Department of Psychology, University of Texas at El Paso, Social Cognition Lab Room 311, 500 W. University Ave., El Paso, TX 79902, USA
e-mail: sdfrankowski@miners.utep.edu

Larry Froman Psychology Department, Towson University, 8000 York Road, Towson MD 21252, USA
e-mail: Lfroman@towson.edu

Kathryn R. Gerlach, M.A., M.A.M.C. Office of Technology Licensing, University of Florida, 747 SW 2nd Avenue, P. O. Box 117330, 32611-7330 Gainesville, FL, USA
e-mail: gerlach.kathryn@gmail.com

Charles H. Hackney, Ph.D. Psychology Department, Briercrest College and Seminary, 510 College Drive, Caronport, SK S0H 0S0 Canada
e-mail: chackney@briercrest.ca

Prof. Dr. Corey L. M. Keyes Department of Sociology, Emory University, Atlanta GA 30322, USA
e-mail: ckeyes@emory.edu

Dr. Sanne M. A. Lamers Department of Psychology, Health, & Technology, University of Twente, P. O. Box 217, 7500 AE Enschede, The Netherlands
e-mail: s.m.a.lamers@utwente.nl

Scott D. Landes, MDiv, MA Department of Sociology and Criminology & Law, University of Florida, 3219 Turlington Hall, P. O. Box 117330, 32611-7330 Gainesville, FL, USA
e-mail: scott.landes@ufl.edu

Sanford Lopater, Ph.D. Christopher Newport University, Newport News, VA 23606, USA
e-mail: slopater@cnu.edu

Dan P. McAdams Department of Psychology, Northwestern University, 2120 Campus Drive, Evanston, IL 60208, USA
e-mail: dmca@northwestern.edu

Susan H. McFadden Department of Psychology, University of Wisconsin Oshkosh, 800 Algoma Blvd., Oshkosh, WI 54901, USA
e-mail: mcfadden@uwosh.edu

Bryan Moore Johns Hopkins University, 550 North Broadway, Suite 506, Baltimore MD 21205, USA
e-mail: bmoore31@jhmi.edu

Dr. Lindsay Oades Australian Institute of Business Wellbeing, Sydney Business School, University of Wollongong Innovation Campus, North Wollongong, NSW 2500, Australia
e-mail: loades@uow.edu.au

Sarah Piontkowski, M.A. University of Maryland, College Park, USA
e-mail: spiontko@umd.edu

Trisha L. Raque-Bogdan, M.S. University of Maryland, College Park, USA
e-mail: tlraque@gmail.com

Kevin Rathunde, Ph.D. Department of Family and Consumer Studies, University of Utah, 225 South 1400 East, Room 228, Salt Lake City UT 84112, USA
e-mail: rathunde@fcs.utah.edu

Grant J. Rich, Ph.D. International Psychology Bulletin (APA), Juneau, Alaska
e-mail: optimalex@aol.com

Eric M. Rodriguez, Ph.D. Social Science Department, New York City College of Technology, City University of New York (City Tech, CUNY), N611, 300 Jay Street, Brooklyn, NY 11201, USA
e-mail: erodriguez@citytech.cuny.edu

Christa K. Schmidt, Ph.D. Psychology Department, Towson University, 8000 York Road, Towson 21252, USA
e-mail: ckschmidt@towson.edu

Dr. Gerald Stoyles School of Psychology, University of Wollongong Northfields Ave, Wollongong, NSW 2500, Australia
e-mail: stoyles@uow.edu.au

Michelle D. Vaughan, Ph.D. Westminster College, 2012 W. Ash Street, Apt. O 18, Columbia, MO, USA
e-mail: MichelleDV2003@hotmail.com

Jeffrey Dean Webster, M.Ed. Psychology Department, Langara College, 100 West 49th Avenue, Vancouver, BC, V5Y 2Z6, Canada
e-mail: jwebster@langara.bc.ca

Evangeline A. Wheeler, Ph.D. Department of Psychology, Towson University, 8000 York Road, Towson MD 21252, USA
e-mail: ewheeler@towson.edua

Dr. Gerben J. Westerhof Department of Psychology, Health, & Technology, University of Twente, P. O. Box 217, 7500 AE Enschede, The Netherlands
e-mail: g.j.westerhof@utwente.nl

Tarynn M. Witten, PhD, LCSW, FGSA Center for the Study of Biological Complexity, VCU, P. O. Box 842537, Suite 111, 1000 W. Cary Street, Richmond, VA 23284–2537, USA
e-mail: tmwitten@vcu.edu

Kathryn Schaefer Ziemer, M.A. University of Maryland, College Park, USA
e-mail: kschaefe@umd.edu

About the Editor

Jan D. Sinnott, PHD, is a Professor of Psychology at Towson University in Baltimore, MD. She specializes in Lifespan Positive Development and the applications of existential, transpersonal, mind-body and positive psychology. After completing a Postdoc at the National Institute on Aging, she developed her theory of Complex Problem Solving in the second half of life, and has authored or co-authored over 100 scholarly and applied books and other publications. Her research team is currently studying Complex Problem Solving, Intelligence, and Satisfaction in Intimate Relationships (book in preparation.)

Part I
Positive Subjective Experiences

Chapter 1
Calling in Childrearing: Promoting Meaningful, Purposeful Living in Family Life

Justin Coulson, Gerald Stoyles and Lindsay Oades

We should first seek to love what we're doing. That's the realisation of our highest calling.

William Frank

Your work is to discover your work and then with all your heart to give yourself to it.

Hindu Prince Gautama Siddharta, the founder of Buddhism, 563–483 B.C.

The idea that a person would view his or her work as a 'calling' has existed for centuries. This chapter will describe what a calling is, and highlight new research that expands research for calling from a purely professional/work context to the context of parenting. This chapter includes a discussion of the correlates of calling in both professional and parenting contexts, and concludes with a series of remarks designed to develop and enhance calling, specifically in family life. This chapter will also describe possibilities for future research for calling in childrearing .

Calling has a sacred history (Dreher and Plante 2007; Steger et al. 2010). In early usage, calling referred to work related to ministry or the spread of religious belief, primarily in the Christian tradition (Weber 1958). Luther is generally credited with

J. Coulson (✉)
Australian Institute of Business Wellbeing,
Sydney Business School,
University of Wollongong,
7 Partridge Pl, Figtree, NSW 2525 Australia
e-mail: justin@happyfamilies.com.au

G. Stoyles
School of Psychology,
University of Wollongong Northfields Ave,
Wollongong, NSW 2500, Australia
e-mail: stoyles@uow.edu.au

L. Oades
Australian Institute of Business Wellbeing,
Sydney Business School,
University of Wollongong Innovation Campus,
North Wollongong, NSW 2500, Australia
e-mail: loades@uow.edu.au

J. D. Sinnott (ed.), *Positive Psychology*,
DOI 10.1007/978-1-4614-7282-7_1,

broadening the meaning of having a calling from its Gospel-spreading origins to a belief that almost any work could be a calling from God (Hardy 1990). He stated that work is more than a means to obtaining our basic needs, or the accumulation of wealth. Work presents people with an opportunity to magnify their 'station' in life, utilising their God-given endowments of strength, capacity, and talent in such a way as to improve life for others. Luther effectively endowed a previously banal necessity with a God-given purpose. Work, under Luther's conceptualisation, became meaningful and gave the individual an opportunity to contribute to something greater than self. Calvinistic tenets altered this perception of calling slightly. A calling was based on one's station in life under Luther's theology of work, whereas Calvin argued for greater hierarchical movement and flexibility, not limiting a calling to one's station. In other words, one might pursue upward social mobility by following his calling. Calvin claimed that this could be done by discovering strengths, gifts, and talents. It was then up to the individual to find the best way to put those capacities to use in the service of others. Such work would provide fulfilment, enlightenment, and purpose, and be that person's calling. (More can be found on Luther and Calvin's contribution to the way we view work as a calling by reviewing Hardy 1990, and Bunderson and Thompson 2009).

Conceptions of calling have remained fairly consistent since Luther and Calvin (Hardy 1990; Weber 1958) until the past few decades where interest in having a professional calling has enjoyed renewed attention in scholarly thought and research, sparked principally by the research and case studies of Bellah et al. (1985). Since this calling revival, the attributes that comprise calling have been subject to ongoing consideration as calling has been refined and redefined (Baumeister 1991; Bunderson and Thompson 2009; Hardy 1990). The idea of having a calling to participate in work for a greater cause has, to some extent, shed its religious connotation and its notion of being God-directed (Steger et al. 2010). This has been accompanied by an increase in the secular acceptance of having a calling and a belief that one's sense of calling may being derived from alternative transcendent sources other than, though not excluding, God (Steger et al. 2010). Calling has also begun to be considered as a useful descriptor of roles outside of traditional vocational or professional pursuits (Seligman 2002; Super 1980) such as in childrearing (Baumeister 1991; Coulson 2011; Coulson et al. 2012a, 2012b; Oates et al. 2005; Sellers et al. 2005).

It should be noted that callings are considered to be universally good. By virtue of the pro-social definitions of calling and the historical roots of calling as 'God-given' (and therefore values- and virtue-laden), it is therefore argued that having evil or dysfunctional goals that would tear down what is good in society cannot be considered to be a calling. Thus, an argument that a misguided individual may feel a calling to inflict harm or damage upon an institution, a group, or anything for that matter, goes contrary to what a calling is.

Current Theoretical Positions

Certain dimensions of calling appear consistently in current theory and research (Hirschi 2010), while some components of calling are less common or are disputed. The following paragraphs briefly consider the issues related to defining calling.

There is a universal agreement that the work one feels called to, must be meaningful. Historically, fulfilling a calling was meaningful to both the individual and society because of the contribution it made to the greater good. Such contribution increased personal meaning from fulfilling calling. Some scholars retain this historical perception that the work must be meaningful to society and perform a function for enhancing the common good (Bunderson and Thompson 2009; Davidson and Caddell 1994; Dobrow 2006; Hardy 1990; Markow and Klenke 2005; Pratt and Ashforth 2003; Weiss et al. 2004) and recent evidence supports such a position. In 435 qualitative interviews, Hunter et al. (2010) found consensus in perceptions of calling among college students that a calling would require an altruistic service focus. Grant (2007) described a key aspect of calling as having a desire to improve society. Dik and Duffy's (2009) view of calling similarly invoked pro-social ends and meaningful contributions beyond the self, as did Bunderson and Thompson's (2009) qualitative research with a large sample of zookeepers.

Conversely, others indicate that personal meanings derived from one's work are sufficient to claim that one is called (Baumeister 1991). Hall and Chandler (2005) described the pursuit of one's purpose in life as a calling, arguing that personal meaning is most likely to be obtained through that pursuit. Novak (1996), Wrzesniewski and her colleagues, (Wrzesniewski and Dutton 2001; Wrzesniewski et al. 1997, 2003) and Dobrow (2004, 2006) similarly argue that personal meaningfulness is readily obtainable to those who discover their callings. Novak (1996) stipulates that a calling is unique and should fit a person's talents, but that they should receive personal enjoyment through it, be energised by it, and love to do it. Thus, while early conceptualisations of calling emphasised meaning derived from service to a greater cause, society has shifted towards individualism, self-actualising goals, and an emphasis on the self. This has led to the evolution of a more self-oriented conception of calling than theological and historical formulations (Bunderson and Thompson 2009). The moral imperatives of contribution to community and contribution to self are not mutually exclusive, but recent emphasis seems directed more towards personal meaning that is derived from making a contribution via one's calling than the community good that is provided through carrying out the calling.

A further point of contention relates to the source of the calling. Dik and Duffy (2009) differentiate between calling and vocation by stipulating that a calling must derive through a "transcendent summons" (p. 427), whereas a vocation lacks this element in its definition. Dik and Duffy's conceptualisation resonates with historical views of calling, notwithstanding the use of 'transcendent' being kept intentionally vague. The transcendent source may be God, or it may be fate, family, or perceived needs in the community. Substantial contemporary research contends that the subjective nature of calling lends itself to the secular idea that a calling is discovered with or without the presence of religious influence (Baumeister 1991; Bellah et al. 1985; Dobrow 2006; Elangovan et al. 2010; French and Domene 2010; Hall and Chandler 2005; Hirschi 2010; Steger et al. 2010; Wrzesniewski and Dutton 2001; Wrzesniewski et al. 1997, 2003).

Other Components of Calling

Although disagreement exists in relation to meaningfulness and the source of a calling, there are several elements of calling where consensus is present. Agreement on the degree of personal identity intertwined with calling is substantial (Dobrow 2006; Hirschi 2010; Wrzesniewski et al. 1997). So also is concurrence related to the sense of mission, destiny, or purpose a person feels in relation to a calling (Baumeister 1991; Dobrow 2006; Elangovan et al. 2010; Hunter et al. 2010). Researchers generally agree that finding a calling requires introspection, self-awareness, or work (Bunderson and Thompson 2009; Dobrow 2006; Hall and Chandler 2005; Novak 1996; Pratt and Ashforth 2003; Weiss et al. 2004). The use of strengths is regularly invoked in keeping with classical formulations of calling (Dreher and Plante 2007; Hunter et al. 2010; Novak 1996; Oates et al. 2005; Weiss et al. 2004) and a passion for a particular calling is commonly cited as necessary (Baumeister 1991; Dobrow 2006). There is less consistency in relation to the degree of personal sacrifice a calling might require (Baumeister 1991; Bunderson and Thompson 2009; Elangovan et al. 2010; cf. Hirschi 2010). This is to be expected, given the contrast between emphasis on personal vs. social significance of a calling in the classical and current definitions of the construct.

The lack of conceptual clarity in defining calling may partly be related to the samples used to provide qualitative data for a conceptual understanding of the construct. To illustrate this, Hirschi (2010) obtained data from undergraduate students aged 23 on average, whereas Bunderson and Thompson (2009) researched zookeepers who had many years of experience in their careers. Dobrow's (2004, 2006) longitudinal work on calling began with qualitative data obtained from aspiring musicians undergoing the transition from high school to college. Hunter et al. (2010) gathered data qualitatively from 435 undergraduate students. As a result, definitions have been derived by a combination of history, experience at work, and an arguably youthful ideology among participants. The varied sources from which the many calling definitions derive have led, unsurprisingly, to the present lack of specificity in defining calling.

Due to the ongoing conflict in relation to calling, the following definition is provided as a thorough yet concise synthesis of previous definitions of calling, representing a summary of research into the construct.

> A calling is defined as a strongly held belief that one is destined to fulfill a specific role, regardless of sacrifice, with an attitude that in so doing, his or her effort will make a meaningful contribution to the greater good. (Coulson 2011; Coulson et al. 2012b)

Calling in Childrearing

Most current research on calling has emphasised the professional context. However, there is a general acceptance that calling is a term suitably applied to domains beyond careers (Baumeister 1991; Dik and Duffy 2009; Seligman 2002; Super 1980), with some specifying the role of rearing a child as being an important and salient one in which a person might feel a sense of calling (Baumeister 1991; Seligman 2002). Baumeister (1991) highlighted the childrearing role as an example of calling beyond the traditionally researched vocational domain, indicating that a noble and respected calling is that of 'housewife and mother' (p. 126). Moreover, both quantitative (Hirschi 2010) and qualitative reports (Hunter et al. 2010; Oates et al. 2005; Sellers et al. 2005) suggest that relationships and childrearing are life roles that lend themselves to the notion of being called.

Coulson et al. (2012a) conducted a qualitative study to assess the validity of calling in a childrearing context, and to gauge parents' perceptions of how a calling would function in that role. Participants were unequivocally positive in their statements regarding calling being applicable in parenting. Participants responded to questions regarding both the definition and experience of calling in childrearing in a manner highly consistent with previous research on callings in a career context. They noted the sense of identity calling-oriented parents would assume in relation to the childrearing role, the meaningful contribution it could make in their own lives and in the lives of others, and the belief that being a parent is what they were supposed to do with their lives—that it was their destiny. Participants also highlighted the themes of awareness of the role, and their passion for doing it well. They also emphasised sacrifice as one theme that was particularly salient. That theme is less dominant in most calling research. (cf. Baumeister 1991; Bunderson and Thompson 2009). Such a potentially difficult theme suggests that calling is not a "Pollyanna"-like concept developed to enshrine positive emotions like joviality, cheer, delight, and joy as supreme. To have a calling may promote feelings of passion, meaning, and identity; it may be that such feelings are so strong and salient because of the sacrifices required for the role. A number of parents also described a calling to be a parent as a God-inspired direction for a parent's life.

It bears mention that calling may not be culturally acceptable to some people. Three participants in the study (Coulson et al. 2012a) were not comfortable with the term "calling", though they understood the concept, could talk about it, and agreed that people might claim to be called. All three cited religious antipathy as a concern. One participant also indicated strong opposition to the idea of calling due to his perception that a calling took away his ability to choose his life path, as though having a calling placed restrictions on free choice and autonomy. Therefore, the religious roots of calling may lead to some people refusing to believe that a calling is even possible, while others embrace the notion of a calling precisely because of those religious foundations.

On the surface, the various constructs that comprise a calling may be considered as simply being the constructs that comprise being a good parent. However, important differences exist. First, constructs that refer to optimal parenting generally focus on behavioural elements of parenting. The most obvious example of this is "parenting styles" (Baumrind 1991b) which refers to the degree to which parents are strict with their limits and emotionally available, warm, and engaged with their children. Calling, however, deals primarily with a parent's cognitive orientation towards the role, rather than behaviours. It examines the degree to which the parent identifies with the role, sees it as central to their sense of self, believes that it is their life's purpose, and understands the meaningful contribution their parenting has to their 'self', their child, and the greater good of the community. The passion and willingness to sacrifice also incorporate cognitive, rather than behavioural, aspects. In short, one can be a 'good parent' and even adhere to an optimal 'authoritative' parenting style without adopting a calling orientation to the role of parent. The sense of a transcendent summons, and a belief that 'this is what I'm meant to be doing with my life', make a calling unique in terms of approaches, or orientations to childrearing.

Correlates of Calling

A calling orientation correlates positively with wellbeing and satisfaction in the lives of those who hold such an orientation. Bellah et al. (1985) found that calling can yield positive life outcomes and optimal wellbeing. Wrzesniewski et al. (1997) compared participants who experienced calling in their vocation with participants who perceived their work as either a *job* (something they felt compelled to do in order to get by) or a *career* (something they did to achieve status, advancement, or extrinsic accolades and success). This study demonstrated that people who experienced calling enjoyed significantly greater life and job satisfaction in comparison to those with an alternate orientation. Seligman (2002) claimed that those who feel called are more likely to experience levels of gratification and a sense that work is satisfying, perhaps enjoying 'flow'— total absorption in a task where one loses track of anything beyond the task itself from time to time (Csikszentmihalyi 1997)—to a degree more substantial than those who do not experience calling. Recent research by Peterson et al. (2009) found moderate correlations between having a calling and possessing work zest and satisfaction with life. In their study, work satisfaction was strongly correlated with calling (see also Steger et al. 2010).

The positive correlates of a calling appear to generalise across various workplace contexts and to all levels of the organisational hierarchy (Wrzesniewski et al. 1997, 2003). Positive correlates of calling have been obtained in classroom settings, where teachers whose behaviours and attitudes were consistent with definitions of calling demonstrated elevated levels of commitment at work in comparison to those without a sense of calling (Serow et al. 1992). In an undergraduate student sample, Duffy and Sedlacek (2007) demonstrated that students who reported a sense of calling also reported higher levels of satisfaction with their choice of career, and greater clarity in that choice compared to students without a sense of calling. Compared to students without a sense of calling, these calling-oriented students were also more likely to believe that their career was important and meaningful in such a way that it might contribute to the greater good. Similarly, Duffy and Sedlacek (2010) indicated that among students, sense of calling was positively associated with life satisfaction and life meaning.

Researchers have discovered that people with a calling are less likely to suffer from stress or depression than those without a calling (Treadgold 1999). Christian mothers who felt dually called to their academic careers and their role as parent indicated that having a calling provided buffering from the stress and conflict normally associated with the challenge of finding work-life balance (Oates et al. 2005). In short, employees and others with a calling at work experience greater commitment, work and life satisfaction, wellbeing, productivity and output, and less absenteeism than those without a calling (Wrzesniewski et al. 1997).

Coulson (2011; see also Coulson et al. 2012b) developed a scale to measure calling in childrearing— the Subjective Sense of Calling in Childrearing Scale (SSCCS). The 11-item SSCCS measured calling for parents, and was comprised of three factors: Life Purpose, Awareness, and Passion. Life Purpose items reflected a sense that parenthood was the participant's *raison d'ê tre*, and that in satisfying this role, the person would experience something not just purposeful and meaningful, but would also fulfil his or her destiny. Awareness represented a mindful attention to the requirements of the childrearing role, and an alertness to what the offspring of the parent were doing at all times. Passion suggested the parent to be highly motivated to participate in the childrearing role and associated tasks.

Coulson (2011; Coulson et al. 2012b) demonstrated that calling in childrearing is correlated to optimal outcomes in the lives of parents who possess it in the same way as calling is related to optimal outcomes in a paid employment context for those who feel called to their professional lives. Significant and strong positive associations were found between having a calling and parenting satisfaction, pleasure in parenting, and parenting importance. That is, as calling increased, so did a sense that the work a person did as a parent was both satisfying and important. There was a corresponding negative relationship between feeling that parenting is a burden and having a calling.

This same research also provided further evidence that calling in childrearing is the optimal orientation to childrearing, as it is in the career context. As participants' subjective sense of calling in childrearing increased, so did their authoritative parenting style, which has been consistently described as the *ideal* parenting style (Baumrind 1991b; Bugental and Goodnow 1998; Darling and Steinberg 1993; Dornbusch et al. 1987). That is, the more a parent felt it was his or her calling to be a parent, the more likely it was that the parent practised behaviours such as showing understanding, setting firm boundaries, being emotionally available to a child, being warm and nurturing, and giving a child responsibilities. There was no relationship at all between sense of calling and authoritarian (controlling, harsh, punitive parenting), or permissive parenting (laissez-faire parenting without boundaries). This research also showed the discriminant validity of the calling construct and measure from that of other childrearing constructs and measures.

Lastly, this research showed that calling related positively to meaning in life but showed no relationship with searching for meaning. By definition, one cannot have a calling that is devoid of meaning. The fact that the SSCCS discriminated between a general measure of meaning and calling in childrearing emphasises the validity of the measure and the multi-faceted aspects of calling that stretch beyond a uni-dimensional monolithic meaning-based construct.

How Parental Calling Affects Children

Over the course of the past several decades, researchers have emphasised the important role that parents play in the wellbeing (Ben-Zur 2003; Casas et al. 2008) and socialisation of their children (Bugental and Grusec 2006; Maccoby 1992; Schneider et al. 2001). Happy parents are more likely to have happy children than are unhappy parents (Ben-Zur 2003). Those parents who practice an optimal parenting style and have positive socialisation practices are more likely to have children who experience optimal outcomes in their own lives when compared with parents who are less effective or who possess less-than-ideal parenting styles and socialisation practices.

A total of 34 early adolescents were asked about their wellbeing and engaged living (Froh et al. 2010). These were the children of approximately 800 participants described in the previous studies (Coulson 2011; Coulson et al. 2012a). As parents' sense of calling increased, so did the children's sense of personal wellbeing. This effect was found to be beyond what was predicted by the parent's own happiness and parenting style. The strongest indicator that a child would have high levels of wellbeing was the parent's sense that childrearing was his or her ultimate purpose in life, and a central component of identity. The more a parent indicated feeling as if the parenting role was a transcendent call linked with life purpose, the greater the likelihood that the child felt happy in association with health, relationships, the community, and the future.

Children's experience of positive affect was also positively related to parental calling (see also Ben-Zur 2003; Casas et al. 2008). However, this effect was significantly diminished when controlling for the happiness and parenting styles of parents. This evidence supports the view that parental attitudes and practices are clearly related to child outcomes, and in particular, that parental happiness and children's happiness are related. Furthermore, the results from the Engaged Living in Youth Scale (Froh et al. 2010) showed that calling-oriented mothers and fathers have children who are more passionate about the world around them, and who are actively engaging with both their environment and the people in it. A parent's sense of calling contributed to the teen's wellbeing beyond any contributions made by their satisfaction with life, and beyond their parenting style. Lyubomirsky (2008) and others (Seligman 2002; Snyder and Lopez 2002) have indicated that happiness is heritable to some degree. The research described here is limited in that there is no control for heritability.

Development of Calling

There is substantial research investigating calling and wellbeing correlates in personal and work-related domains. Without exception, the evidence points to calling and positive life outcomes being related. It is surprising that there have been few, if any, documented interventions aimed at helping people develop or increase their sense of calling. There are two models aimed at increasing calling in careers, but to date there is nothing published that discusses how calling in childrearing might be developed or increased. Brief attention will be given to these two models, with consideration also given to ways in which calling might be developed in parents, given the important implications associated with calling in childrearing.

The first is a model described by Dik et al. (2009) who suggested a tri-dimensional approach to creating a calling. As a foundation, this approach used Dik and Duffy's (2009) definition of a calling as

> A transcendent summons, originating beyond the self, to approach a particular life role in a manner oriented toward demonstrating or deriving a sense of purpose or meaningfulness, and that holds other-oriented values and goals as primary motivation. (p. 427)

Dik et al. (2009) suggested that in counselling sessions, clients and counsellors can explore the degree to which a person feels transcendently drawn to a particular career, and consider the meaning they experience as a result of the chosen career path. Further, people should look for ways in which their career choices provide opportunity for service to the broader community or society. In doing so, meaningful work is likely to result and employees will experience a heightened sense of calling.

An alternative model for the development of a calling orientation is that proposed by Wrzesniewski and Dutton (2010; see also Leana et al. 2009). These researchers proposed a model of job crafting that explained changes to employees' perceptions of the meaning of their work, and changes to those individuals' work-identity. Both elements are central in definitions of calling, and contribute to a person's sense of calling. According to Wrzesniewski and Dutton (2001), increase in work-identity and work-meaning can be obtained by changing three aspects of the work environment. These aspects reside in a person's capacity to change the *task*, *cognitive*, and *relational* boundaries of their work. None of these crafting opportunities is mutually exclusive. Altering one's task boundaries is likely to interact with relational and cognitive boundaries, and vice versa. Wrzesniewski and Dutton provide multiple mini case-studies as examples of how work-identity and meaning have improved as each of these boundaries has been adjusted. They also provide a comprehensive work-based literature review that offers empirical support for the various aspects of their model.

Although job crafting has been successful in the career context (Leana et al. 2009; Wrzesniewski and Dutton 2001), there is presently no evidence that such an approach will yield enhanced levels of calling in parents. Although parenting is not discussed in these models and case studies, a similar approach might also be fruitful here. Using Wrzesniewski and Dutton's (2001) model, calling may be enhanced by adjusting task boundaries in simple and practical ways that have day-to-day impact. Such changes might include reading stories to children each night rather than cleaning up the house, or eating dinner at the table together as a family rather than watching television throughout the meal, and so on. An extension to relational and cognitive boundaries may eventuate and present a profound impact on sense of calling. Such changes are consistent with changes made in job crafting, where regular routine tasks were changed in order to facilitate greater meaning, purpose, and calling at work (Wrzesniewski and Dutton 2001). Task boundary adjustment that requires parents to find ways to work with their children on a day-to-day basis—perhaps washing dishes together, reading stories together, or cooking meals together—may be more effective in producing change compared to one-off events with children. Likewise, relational boundary changes and cognitive boundary changes may similarly effect change in the sense of calling over time by associating more, and in different ways, with one's children. Time spent together communicating and sharing has the potential to increase positivity within the relationship and to be associated with a greater sense of purpose, meaning, and calling for the parent.

In aligning efforts to increase calling in parents, it might be of use to help parents see how their choices in relation to their children impact the pro-sociality of society. An awareness of the power of their contribution may be a weighty matter for some. Other ideas stemming from Dik et al. (2009) might include highlighting the pro-social aspects of childrearing, use of strengths in parenting, and cognitive reframing in terms of the banalities of the role.

Considerations

Calling is represented in a relatively recently popularised and expanding milieu of projects, focused almost exclusively in the work context. Both historical (Hardy 1990) and current descriptions (Baumeister 1991; Elangovan et al. 2010; Hunter et al. 2010) of calling acknowledge the importance of having a calling, and specific reference has been made to being called to the role of a parent. Consistently, and across contexts, calling is viewed as being positively associated with wellbeing and optimal behaviours. There are, however, several considerations that should be emphasised as research on having a calling moves forward.

The first consideration is that defining calling remains problematic. Various definitions have been put forward (Dik and Duffy 2009; Dobrow 2006; Elangovan et al. 2010; Hirschi 2010), including in this chapter, but each fails in one way or another to concisely encapsulate the complexity of this multi-faceted construct. To effectively progress calling research definitions, unanimity might be helpful. This will ensure that researchers are exploring from a mutually agreeable foundation, which will aid in the measurement attempts, validity of the construct, generalizability of findings, and research effectiveness.

A natural extension of issues with defining calling is the second challenge for researchers: the measurement of calling. Even though clear progress is being made in this area, measuring calling still remains problematic. Not described in the present chapter, there are limitations in the present commonly used measures of calling. The measurement of calling, like the defining of calling, requires ongoing refining and replication to overcome these challenges.

A third consideration relates to interventions designed to promote greater meaning, purpose, and calling. Limited data presently exist in this nascent area. It follows that challenges in defining and measuring a construct make interventions to develop that construct potentially premature. There are important practical implications associated with being able to promote conditions and decisions that will enhance a sense of calling (to be discussed in the next section), and hence, continued attention should be directed towards models and theories that provide appropriate recommendations for augmenting a sense of calling in any life domain.

Finally, the issue of a 'transcendent summons' may be a challenge for scientists, given its appeal to other-worldly forces. Moreover, as mentioned earlier in the chapter, there are many who would argue against such a phenomenon because of agnostic, atheistic, or non-spiritual/non-religious views. 'Transcendent summons' cannot be measured in any objective way. Rather, a person's subjective experience of that summons is the key criterion which delineates whether a person feels called or compelled to fulfil some kind of destiny or life purpose—their calling. Duffy et al. (2012) identify only 15 empirical research papers that have investigated callings to date, and emphasised that the subjective experience of a transcendent summons is what sets a calling apart from merely having a passion for something. The summons appears to be what imbues the 'called' with the special sense of purpose, meaning, contribution, and ultimately, calling.

Practical Implications and Applications

In appraising research on calling, the most practical application of the construct is in its relation to wellbeing (Dreher and Plante 2007; Lopez and Snyder 2003; Snyder and Lopez 2002, 2007). Put simply, having a calling is related to having a good life. It is in the interest of individuals, families, communities, and society in general to promote meaning-making and purposeful work endeavours, and to encourage exploration and internalisation of callings as broadly as possible. The promotion and increase of calling orientations in various life roles may raise the collective wellbeing of all those who experience it.

A brief caveat is noteworthy. Dobrow (2006) highlighted that calling may have a dark side. She suggested that too much passion for a role, regardless of how meaningful and pro-social it may be, may create imbalance in a person's life. A person who feels like his life's calling is in a particular vocation may sacrifice everything including his health and relationships for his calling. A parent who feels that her calling as mother supersedes any other role or commitment in life may become overprotective, over-invested, and inattentive to other priorities in life, including her own needs. To date, there does not appear to be any evidence that offers support for this contention. On the contrary, meaningfulness and purpose in one life role appear to generate a greater sense of balance and priority in other areas of life which correlates with greater wellbeing. The qualitative research by Oates et al. (2005) and Sellers et al. (2005), combined with the research described in this chapter would argue that a calling orientation appears to be a universally positive phenomenon.

Future Research

Callings-based research is a fertile field for ongoing psychological inquiry, and this is particularly true for the area of childrearing. One of the most compelling prospects for future research is a longitudinally based study that follows the trajectory of calling over time. It would be valuable to discover whether calling is a stable trait or is influenced by various developmental milestones in parents or their children. For example, does calling increase when a decision is made to have a child, when conception occurs, or when a baby is born? Are certain periods in a child's life more or less likely to enhance or reduce the sense of calling for its parents? Or does calling orientation remain stable irrespective of normal development?

Some recent findings suggest that calling is perceived differently based on gender (Phillips 2009). Research in parenting suggests some gender differences in parenting socialisation practices (Bugental and Grusec 2006; Greenberger and Goldberg 1989; Holden and Miller 1999; Maccoby 1992; Maccoby and Martin 1983). It would be valuable to discover whether these differences exist due to differences in calling conception and experience.

The role of religion may also play a part in a parent's sense of calling. Although there is a growing argument for calling as a secular construct (Steger et al. 2010), the historically religious roots of calling seem inescapable (Bunderson and Thompson 2009; Coulson et al. 2012a; Hardy 1990). Future research into the relationship between the sense of calling and religion could speak to their association. With explicit reinforcement of childrearing as a calling being found in some religious writing (Benson 1987; Fields 2008; Maggart 2003), there may be a greater disposition towards having a calling among the religious. Investigating the impact that religiosity has on parenting style and wellbeing in comparison to a non-religious population may provide a clearer picture of who has a calling in childrearing, who does not, and whether the presence of a calling in childrearing is influenced by religiosity in some way. There is clear evidence that the religious history and connotation of calling impacts some parents and discourages them from identifying with a calling in any way (Coulson et al. 2012a).

In concert with this suggestion, Duffy et al. (2012) found that religiosity was moderately correlated with calling but being a religiously oriented person did not moderate the positive association between having a calling and experiencing high levels of life satisfaction. They describe this finding as suggestive of religious belief, whether high or low, being relatively unimportant in determining relationships between sense of calling and life satisfaction. As suggested by many others, the spiritual roots of calling may impact the definition of what a calling is, but modern acceptance of the term has led to a secularisation of the construct, with a wider view of what might be considered as a 'transcendent summons' and a minimised requirement for religious or spiritual belief (Bunderson and Thompson 2009; Seligman 2002; Steger et al. 2010; Wrzesniewski et al. 1997).

Do parents who are in distress or struggling with wayward teens hold that childrearing is their life purpose and a meaningful pursuit? Some evidence (Coulson 2011) showed that calling and age are negatively related. It may happen that over time, parents become less involved with their children (Brotherson and White 2007; Noller and Callan 1991), if not emotionally then at least on a functional level. With decreased involvement in the childrearing role, there may be a sense that the childrearing is completed and the parent may become engaged and committed to alternative activities. There is evidence of dual callings for those with more than one role that provides them with purpose, meaning, and opportunities for contribution (Oates et al. 2005; Sellers et al. 2005). Alternatively, as parenting becomes harder during adolescence (Baumrind 1991a; Lieberman et al. 1999), there may be a shift in the sense of calling. Parents experiencing significant challenges in their parenting efforts combined with the adolescent's push for autonomy may diminish or at least call into question the notion that "I am doing what I am meant to be doing". If parental confidence drops, questions about identity, purpose, or meaningfulness may result. Put another way, this relationship suggests that calling is developmentally influenced. In one sense this is a healthy response to the role. It indicates, parents recognise that their participation in the role *is* time limited. Once the child reaches adulthood, a healthy childrearing process should have appropriately prepared the child to be independent. Unhealthy childrearing is displayed when the parent is unable to, or chooses not to, relinquish this role.

A salient area of investigation relates to the way calling may differ in childrearing based on the nature of the relationship between the caregiver and the child. Are adoptive parents more or less likely to feel a sense of calling than natural parents? What kind of variation in calling exists in foster parents, and do previous findings in calling research generalise into these contexts? The issue of foster parenting may be particularly interesting because this specific population is at the intersection of paid work and parenting. Foster parents are remunerated for doing the 'work' of caring for children. It would be valuable to understand the sense of calling these people feel for their work, and the meaning and purpose they put into it or derive from it. As an extension to this, can a calling to be a foster parent build the positive, engaged living, and potentially the resilience that birth children of parents with a calling experience?

Finally, what distinguishes people who develop a calling from those who do not? Further investigation into antecedents of calling should be undertaken to better understand what it is that promotes the sense of destiny and purpose, passion and meaning, identity and sacrifice that a calling connotes. Is a calling orientation due to natural biological desires to be a parent, or socialisation, or a literal transcendent summons? Or is calling a trait that people either have, or do not have? Although literature related to careers suggests that calling can be developed, future research in relation to these questions in both the professional context and the childrearing context is needed. By better understanding such antecedents, we may be better able to construct pathways and interventions to developing and building a sense of calling in parents.

References

Baumeister, R. F. (1991). *Meanings of life*. New York: The Guildford Press.

Baumrind, D. (1991a). Effective parenting during the early adolescent transition. In P. A. Cowan & M. Hetherington (Eds.), *Family transitions*. Hillsdale: Erlbaum.

Baumrind, D. (1991b). The influence of parenting style on adolescent competence and substance use. *Journal of Early Adolescence, 11,* 56–95. doi:10.1037//0003–066X.35.7.639.

Bellah, R. N., Madsen, R., Sullivan, W. M., Swidler, A., & Tipton, S. M. (1985). *Habits of the heart: Individualism and commitment in American life.* Berkeley: University of California Press.

Ben-Zur, H. (2003). Happy adolescents: The link between subjective well-being, internal resources, and parental factors. *Journal of Youth and Adolescence 32,* 67–79.

Benson, E. T. (1987). *To the fathers in Israel.* Paper presented at the Conference of the Church of Jesus Christ of Latter-Day Saints, SLC, Utah.

Brotherson, S. E., & White, J. M. (Eds.). (2007). *Why fathers count.* Harriman: Men's Studies Press.

Bugental, D. B., & Goodnow, J. J. (1998). Socialization processes. In W. Damon & N. Eisenberg (Eds.), *Handbook of child psychology, 5th ed: Vol 3 Social, emotional, and personality development* (pp. 389–462). Hoboken: Wiley.

Bugental, D. B., & Grusec, J. E. (2006). Socialization processes. In N. Eisenberg, W. Damon & R. M. Lerner (Eds.), *Handbook of child psychology: Vol 3, Social, emotional, and personality development* (6th ed., pp. 366–428). Hoboken: Wiley

Bunderson, J. S., & Thompson, J. A. (2009). The call of the wild: Zookeepers, callings, and the double-edged sword of deeply meaningful work. *Administrative Science Quarterly, 54,* 32–57.

Casas, F., Coenders, G., Cummins, R. A., Gonzalez, M., Figuer, C., & Malo, S. (2008). Does subjective wellbeing show a relationship between parents and their children? *Journal of Happiness Studies, 9,* 197–205. doi:1007/s10902–007-9044-7.

Coulson, J. C. (2011). *Parents' subjective sense of calling in childrearing.* Ph. D. Thesis. Wollongong: University of Wollongong.

Coulson, J. C., Oades, L. G., & Stoyles, G. J. (2012a). Parent's conception and experience of calling in childrearing: a qualitative analysis. *Journal of Humanistic Psychology.* doi:10.1177/0022167810382454.

Coulson, J. C., Oades, L. G., & Stoyles, G. J. (2012b). Parents' subjective sense of calling in childrearing: Measurement, development, and initial findings. *Journal of Positive Psychology.* doi:10.1080/17439760.2011.633547.

Csikszentmihalyi, M. (1997). *Finding flow: The psychology of engagement with everyday life.* New York: Basic Books.

Darling, N., & Steinberg, L. (1993). Parenting style as context: An integrative model. *Psychological Bulletin, 113,* 487–496. doi:10.1037//0033-2909.113.3.487.

Davidson, J. C., & Caddell, D. P. (1994). Religion and the meaning of work. *Journal for the Scientific Study of Religion, 33,* 135–147. doi:http://dx.doi.org/10.2307/1386600.

Dik, B. J., & Duffy, R. D. (2009). Calling and vocation at work: Definitions and prospects for research and practice. *The Counselling Psychologist, 37,* 424–450. doi:10.1177/0011000008316430.

Dik, B. J., Duffy, R. D., & Eldridge, B. M. (2009). Calling and vocation in career counselling: recommendations for promoting meaningful work. *Professional Psychology: Research and Practice, 40,* 625–632. doi:10.1037/a0015547.

Dobrow, S. R. (2004). "Extreme subjective career success: A new integrated view of having a calling". Best paper proceedings of the academy of management conference, New Orleans.

Dobrow, S. R. (2006). *Having a calling: A longitudinal study of young musicians.* Unpublished doctoral dissertation, Harvard University, Mass.

Dornbusch, S. M., Ritter, P. L., Leiderman, P., Roberts, D. F., & Fraleigh, M. J. (1987). The relation of parenting style to adolescent school performance. *Child Development, 58,* 1244–1257. doi:10.1111/j.1467-8624.1987.tb01455.x.

Dreher, D. E., & Plante, T. G. (2007). The calling protocol: Promoting greater health, joy, and purpose in life. In T. G. Plante & C. E. Thoresen (Eds.), *Spirit, science, and health: How the spiritual mind fuels physical wellness* (pp. 129–140). Westport: Praeger Publishers.

Duffy, R. D., Allan, B. A., & Bott, E. M. (2012). Calling and life satisfaction among undergraduate students: investigating mediators and moderators. *Journal of Happiness Studies, 13,* 469–479. doi:1007/s10902-011-9274-6.

Duffy, R. D., & Sedlacek, W. E. (2007). The presence of and search for a calling: connections to career development. *Journal of Vocational Behaviour, 70,* 590–601. doi:10.1016/j.jvb.2007.03.007.

Duffy, R. D., & Sedlacek, W. E. (2010). The salience of a career calling among college students: exploring group differences and links to religiousness, life meaning, and life satisfaction. *Career Development Quarterly, 59,* 27–41.

Elangovan, A. R., Pinder, C. C., & McLean, M. (2010). Callings and organizational behaviour. *Journal of Vocational Behaviour, 76,* 428–440. doi:10.1016/j.jvb.2009.10.009.

Fields, L. L. (2008). *Parenting Is your highest calling: And 8 other myths that trap us in worry and guilt.* New York: Three Rivers Press.

French, J. R., & Domene, J. F. (2010). Sense of "calling": An organizing principle for the lives and values of young women in university. *Canadian Journal of Counselling, 44,* 1–14.

Froh, J. J., Kashdan, T. B., Yurkewicz, C., Fan, J., Allen, J., & Glowacki, J. (2010). The benefits of passion and absorption in activities: engaged living in adolescents and its role in psychological well-being. *Journal of Positive Psychology, 5,* 311–322. doi:10.1080/17439760.2010.498624.

Grant, A. (2007). Relational job design and the motivation to make a prosocial difference. *Academy of Management Review, 32,* 393–417.

Greenberger, E., & Goldberg, W. A. (1989). Work, parenting, and the socialization of children. *Developmental Psychology, 25,* 22–35. doi:10.1037//0012-1649.25.1.22.

Hall, D. T., & Chandler, D. E. (2005). Psychological success: when the career is a calling. *Journal of Organizational Behaviour, 26,* 155–176. doi:http://dx.doi.org/10.1002/job.301.

Hardy, L. (1990). *The fabric of this world: Inquiries into calling, career choice, and the design of human work.* Grand Rapids: William B. Eerdmans.

Hirschi, A. (2010). Callings in career: A typological approach to essential and optional components. *Journal of Vocational Behaviour*. doi:10.1016/j.jvb.2010.11.002.

Holden, G. W., & Miller, P. C. (1999). Enduring and different: A meta-analysis of the similarity in parents' child rearing. *Psychological Bulletin, 125,* 223–254. doi:10.1037//0033-2909.125.2.223.

Hunter, I., Dik, B. J., & Banning, J. H. (2010). College students' perceptions of calling in work and life: a qualitative analysis. *Journal of Vocational Behaviour, 76,* 178–186. doi:10.1016/j/jvb.2009.10.008.

Leana, C., Appelbaum, E., & Shevchuk, I. (2009). Work process and quality of care in early childhood education: the role of job crafting. *Academy of Management Journal, 52,* 1169–1192.

Lieberman, M., Doyle, A., & Markiewicz, D. (1999). Developmental patterns in security of attachment to mother and father in late childhood and early adolescence: Associations with peer relations. *Child Development, 70,* 202–213. doi:10.1111/1467-8624.00015.

Lopez, S. J., & Snyder, C. R. (2003). *Positive psychological assessment: A handbook of models and measures*. Washington DC: American Psychological Association.

Lyubomirsky, S. (2008). *The how of happiness: A scientific approach to getting the life you want.* New York: Penguin Press.

Maccoby, E. E. (1992). The role of parents in the socialization of children: an historical overview. *Developmental Psychology, 28,* 1006–1017. doi:10.1037//0012-1649.28.6.1006.

Maccoby, E. E., & Martin, J. A. (1983). Socialization in the context of the family: Parent-child interaction. In E. M. Hetherington (Ed.), *Handbook of child psychology: Vol 4, Socialization, personality, and social development* (pp. 1–101). New York: Wiley.

Maggart, J. E. (2003). *Parenting: The highest calling: Great parents make great kids*. New York: iUniverse.com.

Markow, F., & Klenke, K. (2005). The effects of personal meaning and calling on organizational commitment: an empirical investigation of spiritual leadership. *International Journal of Organizational Analysis, 13,* 8–27.

Noller, P., & Callan, V. (1991). *The adolescent in the family*. London: Routledge.

Novak, M. (1996). *Business as a calling*. New York: Free Press.

Oates, K. L., Hall, M., & Anderson, T. L. (2005). Calling and conflict: a qualitative exploration of interrole conflict and the sanctification of work in Christian mothers in academia. *Journal of Psychology and Theology, 33,* 210–223.

Peterson, C., Park, N., Hall, N., & Seligman, M. E. P. (2009). Zest and work. *Journal of Organizational Behaviour, 30,* 161–172. doi:10.1002/job.584.

Phillips, S. L. (2009). Predictors of vocational calling in Christian college students: A structural equation model. http://udini.proquest.com/view/predictors-of-vocational-calling-in-pqid:1910938661/. Accessed 9 April 2013.

Pratt, M., & Ashforth, B. (2003). Fostering meaningfulness in working and at work. In K. Cameron, J. E. Dutton, & R. E. Quinn (Eds.), *Positive organizational scholarship* (pp. 309–327). San Francisco: Berrett-Koehler Publishers.

Schneider, B. H., Atkinson, L., & Tardif, C. (2001). Child-parent attachment and children's peer relations: A quantitative review. *Developmental Psychology, 37,* 86–100. doi:10.1037/0012-1649.37.1.86.

Seligman, M. E. P. (2002). *Authentic Happiness*. Sydney: Random House.

Sellers, T. S., Thomas, K., Batts, J., & Ostman, C. (2005). Women called: a qualitative study of Christian women dually called to motherhood and career. *Journal of Psychology and Theology, 33,* 198–209.

Serow, R. C., Eaker, D., & Ciechalski, J. (1992). Calling, service, and legitimacy: professional orientations and career commitment among prospective teachers. *Journal of Research and Development in Education, 25,* 136–141.

Snyder, C. R., & Lopez, S. J. (2002). *Handbook of positive psychology*. New York: Oxford University Press.

Snyder, C. R., & Lopez, S. J. (2007). *Positive psychology: The scientific and practical explorations of human strengths*. Thousand Oaks: Sage Publications.

Steger, M. F., Pickering, N., Shin, J. Y., & Dik, B. J. (2010). Calling in work: secular or sacred? *Journal of Career Assessment, 18,* 82–96. doi:10.1177/1069072709350905.

Super, D. E. (1980). A life-span, life-space approach to career development. *Journal of Vocational Behaviour, 16,* 282–298.

Treadgold, R. (1999). Transcendent vocations: Their relationship to stress, depression, and clarity of self-concept. *Journal of Humanistic Psychology,* 39, 81–105.

Weber, M. (1958). *The Protestant ethic and the spirit of capitalism*. New York: Scribner.

Weiss, J., Skelley, M., Haughey, J. C., & Hall, D. T. (2004). Callings, new careers, and spirituality: A reflective perspective for organizational leaders and professionals. In M. Pava & P. Primeaux (Eds.), *Spiritual intelligence at work: Meaning, metaphor, and morals* (pp. 175–201). Amsterdam: Elsevier.

Wrzesniewski, A., & Dutton, J. E. (2001). Crafting a job: revisioning employees as active crafters of their work. *Academy of Management Review, 26,* 179–201. doi:10.2307/259118.

Wrzesniewski, A., McCauley, C., Rozin, P., & Schwartz, B. (1997). Jobs, careers, and callings: People's relations to their work. *Journal of Research in Personality, 31,* 21–33. doi:10.1006/jrpe.1997.2162.

Wrzesniewski, A., Rozin, P., & Bennett, G. (2003). Working, playing, and eating: Making the most of most moments. In C. L. Keyes & J. Haidt (Eds.), *Flourishing: Positive psychology and the life well-lived* (pp. 185–204). Washington DC: American Psychological Association.

Chapter 2
Mental Health and Illness In Relation to Physical Health Across the Lifespan

Sanne M. A. Lamers, Gerben J. Westerhof, Ernst T. Bohlmeijer and Corey L. M. Keyes

The present study examines mental health differences across the adult lifespan from a positive as well as from a traditional perspective as the absence of psychopathology, including physical health as a potential confounder. Nowadays, mental health is not only regarded as the absence of psychopathology, but also as the presence of positive feelings and positive functioning in both individual and social life. According to the two continua model, psychopathology and positive mental health are related but distinct dimensions (Keyes 2005). One continuum reflects the presence or absence of psychopathology, which is only moderately related to the other continuum which reflects the presence or absence of positive mental health. The two continua model holds that an individual with few symptoms of psychopathology may experience high positive mental health with positive feelings and positive functioning in life or may experience low or no positive mental health. Confirmatory factor analyses confirm that psychopathology and mental health belong to two continua (Keyes et al. 2008; Lamers et al. 2011), which partly have independent genetic propensities (Kendler et al. 2011). Moreover, poor positive mental health as well as decrease in positive mental health are predictive of future mental disorders (Keyes et al. 2010; Wood and Joseph 2009). To examine mental health across the lifespan, assessment should not only address age differences in psychopathology but also positive mental health.

S. M. A. Lamers (✉) · G. J. Westerhof · E. T. Bohlmeijer
Department of Psychology, Health, & Technology, University of Twente, P. O. Box 217, 7500 AE Enschede, The Netherlands
e-mail: s.m.a.lamers@utwente.nl

G. J. Westerhof
e-mail: g.j.westerhof@utwente.nl

E. T. Bohlmeijer
e-mail: e.t.bohlmeijer@utwente.nl

C. L. M. Keyes
Department of Sociology, Emory University, Atlanta GA 30322, USA
e-mail: ckeyes@emory.edu

J. D. Sinnott (ed.), *Positive Psychology*,
DOI 10.1007/978-1-4614-7282-7_2, © Springer Science+Business Media, LLC 2013

The Two Continua Model of Mental Health and Illness Across the Lifespan

Most studies on the relation between age and mental health investigate mental disorders or symptoms of psychopathology. When mental health is viewed as the absence of psychopathological symptoms, several age differences are found. In general, older adults have the lowest prevalence rates for mental disorders (Bijl et al. 1998; Kessler et al. 2004; The ESEMeD/MHEDEA 2000 Investigators 2004). Minor depression, indicating the presence of depressive symptoms not fulfilling the criteria of a major depression, is more common among older adults than major depression (Beekman et al. 1999) and more common among older than younger adults (Newman and Engel 1991). However, studies including the oldest old show a curvilinear relationship between age and psychopathology, indicating an increase of the prevalence of psychopathology in the last life stage (Mirowsky and Ross 1999). Since psychopathology and positive mental health belong to two continua, the World Health Organization (2004) has argued that the assessment of psychopathology is insufficient as an indicator of mental health. With this, an important question remains: do the lower levels of psychopathology mean that older adults also have a better mental health?

Our positive approach to mental health builds on two traditions of studies in well-being, in which three types of well-being can be distinguished (Deci and Ryan 2008; Waterman 1993). Emotional well-being, corresponding to the hedonic tradition, includes the presence of feelings of happiness and life satisfaction (Diener et al. 1999). In the second tradition, the eudaimonic approach, well-being involves optimal functioning in life and consists of two types: psychological and social well-being. Psychological well-being addresses the realization of one's own potentials and is mainly focused on optimal fulfillment in individual lives (Ryff and Keyes 1995). Social well-being is directed at optimal social functioning and involvement in society (Keyes 1998). Emotional, psychological, and social well-being together form the definition of positive mental health (Keyes 2005), hence taking both traditions in well-being research into consideration.

Most studies have addressed only a few aspects of positive mental health when examining age differences. Findings differ depending on the aspects of well-being under study. In a review of international surveys on emotional well-being, Diener and Suh (1998) conclude that life satisfaction is slightly higher among older men, but there are no age differences in women. They also conclude that positive affect is lower among older age groups, although this might be a cohort effect. However, other studies reported that older adults experience more positive affect than younger adults (e.g., Mroczek and Kolarz 1998), found no relation of age to positive affect (e.g., Vaux and Meddin 1987), or found no unique effects of age after controlling for demographics, personality, health, and cognitive functioning (e.g., Isaacowitz and Smith 2003).

With respect to psychological and social well-being, older individuals do better on some aspects and worse on others than younger adults. With regard to psychological well-being, older adults experience more environmental mastery and autonomy, but less personal growth and purpose in life compared to younger adults, whereas there are no differences on self-acceptance and positive relations to others (Pinquart 2002; Ryff 1995; Ryff and Keyes 1995). Studies on social well-being (Keyes 1998; Keyes and Shapiro 2004) show that older individuals experience more social acceptance and a sense of belonging to a community, but less contribution to society than younger individuals. Moreover, older adults perceive society as less predictable, sensible, and coherent. The feeling that society is developing in a good direction was not related to age.

A broad perspective is needed to investigate whether older adults experience a better mental health than younger adults. First, there are both gains and losses across the lifespan, depending on the aspects of mental health under study. Second, aspects of well-being conceptually belong to each other from our mental health perspective and they are indeed empirically interrelated. For example, aspects of psychological well-being such as self-acceptance and environmental mastery show modest to strong correlations to emotional well-being (Ryff and Keyes 1995). To account for the diverse results and interrelations, investigations of age differences in mental health should examine overall levels of positive mental health in addition to separate aspects of well-being. A broad perspective on positive mental health will provide further insight into whether older adults generally experience better, similar, of worse well-being compared to younger adults.

Even though the two continua model indicates that positive mental health and psychopathology are complementary, there are few representative surveys which examined both positive mental health and the presence of psychopathology across the lifespan in a single study. The study on Midlife Development in the United States (Keyes 2007; Keyes and Westerhof 2012) and a previous study in the Dutch population (Westerhof and Keyes 2010) both found that a lower level of mental illness in later life was not accompanied by a higher level of mental health, thereby providing further evidence for the two continua model. However, it is important to also include physical health as a potential confounder in the relation of age to mental health and illness.

Physical Health and the Aging Paradox

The prevalence of almost every chronic illness and of the simultaneous presence of multiple chronic diseases increases with age (van den Akker et al. 1998). Older adults report more functional limitations (House et al. 1990) and lower self-evaluations of their health than younger adults (Pinquart 2001). Moreover, several studies show relations of positive mental health and psychopathology to physical health. This relation is mutual: mental health and illness influence physical health conditions, but physical health also affects mental health and illness. For example, depressive symptoms are closely related to physical health, mainly to physical disability (Kivela and Pahkala 2001) and subjective health (Beekman et al. 1997). Positive well-being is related to physical health (Lyubomirsky et al. 2005), and has a salutary impact on physical health (Howell et al. 2007; Lamers et al. 2012a). Aspects of well-being such as happiness and optimism are related to longer life, decreased risk of illness, and to increased resistance to illness (Veenhoven 2008).

Despite the increases in health problems with age and the relation of physical health to psychopathology and positive mental health, older adults do not experience higher levels of psychopathology or lower levels of well-being. This phenomenon has been labeled as the aging paradox (Staudinger et al. 1999; Westerhof et al. 2003). Adaptation theories have provided explanations for this paradox. Socioemotional selectivity theory states that perceived limitations on time remaining increase the motivation to maintain and improve emotional experiences and lead to greater complexity and better regulation of emotions in everyday life (Carstensen et al. 2003). Furthermore, older adults may have a more acceptant attitude towards health problems, because they expect to be confronted with physical problems with advancing age (Steverink et al. 2001). Moreover, older adults could be more resilient since they use other strategies, for example more readjustments of personal goals and aspirations, to regulate their development than younger adults, thereby maintaining the same level of self-integrity, self-efficacy, and meaning in life (Brandtstädter and Greve 1994; Westerhof et al. 2003).

Given the increase in physical health problems with age, physical health may act as a confounder in the relation between age and mental health: age-related increases in health problems rather than age per se may cause age differences in mental health. If physical health operates as a confounder, controlling for levels of physical health might result in similar levels of positive mental health across age groups, or even in better mental health in older adults (Kunzmann et al. 2000). Moreover, if older adults maintain their levels of mental health despite increased physical health problems in line with the aging paradox, it indicates that the relation of physical health and mental health is less strong among older than younger adults.

The Present Study

We expand current research by broadly assessing positive mental health as well as symptoms of psychopathology in the context of age differences in physical health. We include the presence of physical diseases, the maintenance of normal functioning, and self-assessments of health in the assessment of physical health. This is important as the gap between perceived and objective health status widens with age (Henchoz et al. 2008).

The aim of our study is threefold. First, we examine the relation of age to psychopathology and positive mental health, investigating both linear and curvilinear relations. We hypothesize that age is differentially associated with psychopathology and positive mental health in line with earlier studies and the two continua model (Keyes 2007; Keyes and Westerhof 2012; Westerhof and Keyes 2010). We expect that older adults experience fewer symptoms of psychopathology than younger adults, with the exception of the oldest old in accordance with the curvilinear relations reported in earlier studies. Since we examine positive mental health in a broad context including multiple dimensions of well-being, we expect that the gains will counterbalance the losses, resulting in similar levels of positive mental health across the age groups. Second, we investigate physical health as a confounder in the relation of age to psychopathology and to positive mental health. In line with earlier studies on the aging paradox, we expect that the negative relation of age with psychopathology is stronger and that the relation of age with positive mental health turns positive after controlling for physical health. Third, we assess whether the relations of physical health with positive mental health and psychopathology differ according to age. Again, in line with the aging paradox, we hypothesize that physical health shows weaker relations to psychopathology and positive mental health in older than in younger adults.

Method

Participants

A representative sample of 1,506 Dutch participants between the ages of 18 and 87 participated in this study. The sample was stratified by gender (50 % male), migration status (83 % native Dutch, versus having been born abroad, or with at least one parent born abroad), and age (23 % 18–29; 28 % 30–49; 27 % 50–64; 22 % 65+ years). The oldest age group ranged from 65 to 87, with a mean of 71.3 ($SD = 5.3$). Of the respondents, 10 % had primary education, 26 % lower vocational, 12 % secondary, 21 % middle vocational, 23 % higher vocational, and 8 % had university education. Half of the respondents (53 %) were married.

Procedure

This paper draws on data of the LISS panel of CentERdata, an internet panel for Longitudinal Internet Studies in the Social Sciences, managed by CentERdata in Tilburg, The Netherlands. The LISS panel is a representative panel of 5,000 households, which are randomly selected from the municipal registers in the Netherlands. Household members are invited to fill out online questionnaires every month and are provided with internet access and a personal computer when necessary. Compared to Dutch national statistics, the LISS panel shows a small underrepresentation of older, single, never married and widowed persons, persons living in regions with high and low levels of urbanization, and nonwestern and first generation immigrants (Knoef and De Vos, under review). In one-third of the households, one member was selected by CentERdata to fill out a module on mental health in December 2007. This module included measures of positive mental health and psychopathology, and was completed by 1,662 respondents. We also used a core module on physical health, developed by CentERdata, consisting of various health questionnaires. 1,506 participants (91 %) filled out both, the mental health module and the core module on physical health and were included in the present study.

Measurements

Demographics Questions were asked about age, gender, marital status, education, income, and migration status (Dutch versus being born abroad or having a parent born abroad).

Physical health Measures of physical health consisted of physical diseases, functional limitations, and subjective health. *Physical diseases* were measured by asking participants whether or not a doctor had told them in the past year that they had one or more of the following twelve diseases and health problems: angina, pain in the chest; heart attack including infarction or coronary thrombosis or another heart problem or failure; high blood pressure or hypertension; high cholesterol content in blood; stroke or brain infarction or a disease affecting the blood vessels in the brain; diabetes or a too high blood sugar level; chronic lung disease such as chronic bronchitis or emphysema; asthma; arthritis, including osteoarthritis, rheumatism, bone decalcification, and osteoporosis; cancer or malignant tumor, including leukemia or lymphoma, but excluding less serious forms of skin cancer; Parkinson's disease; other diseases or health problems. The number of diseases was computed as 0, 1, 2, and 3 or more physical diseases. *Functional limitations* were measured by asking the participants whether they experienced difficulties when performing nine activities of daily living (ADLs), which applied only to problems that were expected to last longer than 3 months. The questions concerned the following activities: walking a hundred meters; getting up from a chair; walking up a staircase without resting; dressing and undressing, including shoes and socks; walking across the room; bathing or showering; eating, such as cutting one's food into small bits; getting in and out of bed; using the toilet, including sitting down and standing up. The nine items were rated on a 4-point scale, indicating whether the participants could perform the activities without any trouble, with some trouble, with a lot of trouble, or only with the help of others. Cronbach's alpha was 0.86. We transformed these ratings into a dichotomous scale: no trouble when performing the activity (rated as 0) versus some or a lot of trouble or need help (rated as 1). The number of difficulties was computed, resulting in a score of 0, 1, 2, and 3 or more functional limitations. *Subjective health* was measured by asking the participants to rate their own health on a 5-point Likert scale (*poor* to *excellent*). A higher score indicated a better self-evaluated health.

Psychopathology Psychopathology was measured using the *Brief Symptom Inventory* (BSI; Dutch version: de Beurs and Zitman 2006), which is among the most commonly used instruments for screening and assessing psychopathology in mental health services in the USA. Respondents indicated the degree to which they had experienced 53 psychological symptoms in the past week using a 5-point Likert scale (*not at all* to *a lot*). An average score of psychopathology was computed, with higher scores indicating more symptoms of psychopathology. Cronbach's alpha was 0.95 in the present study.

Positive mental health Positive mental health was measured using the *Mental Health Continuum-Short Form* (MHC-SF; Keyes et al. 2008), consisting of 14 items which represent the various theoretically derived feelings of well-being. Respondents rated the frequency of each feeling in the past month on a 6-point Likert scale (*never*; *once or twice a month*; *about once a week*; *two or three times a week*; *almost every day*; *every day*). The MHC-SF is multidimensional and contains three items of emotional well-being, six items of psychological well-being, and five items of social well-being. We computed a mean score, with higher scores indicating higher levels of emotional well-being, psychological well-being, social well-being, and overall positive mental health. The Dutch version of the MHC-SF has shown good psychometric properties (Lamers et al. 2011) and stability over time (Lamers et al. 2012b). Moreover, confirmatory factor analyses confirmed the three-factor structure in emotional, psychological, and social well-being (Lamers et al. 2011). In the present study, Cronbach's alpha was 0.83 for emotional and psychological well-being, 0.74 for social well-being, and 0.89 for overall positive mental health.

Analyses

After inspecting the bivariate relations between the variables of interest, we used five hierarchical regression analyses to assess our research hypotheses: one for psychopathology and four for mental health (i.e., one for overall positive mental health, and three for the subscales emotional, psychological, and social well-being). In the first model, we entered positive mental health in the regression analysis on psychopathology, and psychopathology in the analyses on mental health. Furthermore, we controlled for demographic variables in this first model. To answer our first research question, we included age and age-squared in the second model to detect both, linear and curvilinear relations. Age was centered on the mean to avoid collinearity between age and age-squared. To investigate the second research question on physical health as a potential confounder, we added measures of physical health in the third model. To answer the third research question on age as a moderator, we examined interaction effects of age and age-squared with physical health on psychopathology and on positive mental health, by applying computational procedures in regression analysis using the Johnson–Neyman technique, as described by Hayes and Matthes (2009). The Johnson–Neyman technique computes the regression weight and explained variance of the interaction effect by identifying regions in the range of age and age-squared where the relation of physical health to psychopathology or positive mental health is statistically significant and not significant. In all analyses, we applied a p-value of 0.01 instead of the common 0.05, because of the large sample size.

Table 2.1 Descriptives and correlations of age, age-squared, physical health, psychopathology, and positive mental health

	1	2	3	4	5	6	7	8
Range	0–3	0–3	1–5	0–4	1–6	1–6	1–6	1–6
M	0.65	0.58	3.12	0.37	3.98	4.67	4.18	3.33
SD	0.89	0.98	0.76	0.33	0.84	0.94	0.99	1.01
Age[a]	0.36**	0.28**	− 0.17**	− 0.14**	− 0.06*	0.05	− 0.15**	− 0.01
Age-squared[a]	0.09**	0.11**	0.01	0.05	0.02	0.05	0.01	0.00
1. Physical diseases	–							
2. Functional limitations	0.43**	–						
3. Subjective health	− 0.41**	− 0.41**	–					
4. Psychopathology	0.18**	0.25**	− 0.29**	–				
5. Positive mental health	− 0.06	− 0.10**	0.21**	− 0.33**	–			
6. Emotional well-being	− 0.09**	− 0.13**	0.24**	− 0.47**	0.74**	–		
7. Psychological well-being	− 0.07*	− 0.11**	0.19**	− 0.27**	0.92**	0.60**	–	
8. Social well-being	− 0.01	− 0.03	0.13**	− 0.18**	0.86**	0.47**	0.64**	–

*$p < 0.01$; **$p < 0.001$

[a]Age and age-squared are controlled for each other in partial correlations

Results

Table 2.1 shows the descriptive results and bivariate correlations between age, age-squared, psychopathology, positive mental health (i.e., overall positive mental health as well as the subscales emotional, psychological, and social well-being), and physical health (i.e., physical diseases, functional limitations, and subjective health). Older adults showed less psychopathological symptoms. They also had less positive mental health than younger adults and lower levels of psychological well-being, but not of emotional and social well-being. Moreover, older adults reported lower levels of self-evaluated health than younger adults. Physical diseases and functional limitations showed both linear and curvilinear relations to age. Older adults had more physical diseases and functional limitations than younger adults, and the curvilinear relations show that the amount of diseases and limitation is disproportionally higher among older adults. Subjective health was related to lower levels of psychopathology and physical diseases and functional limitations to higher levels. The correlations of physical health to overall positive mental health as well as to the three subscales were in the opposite direction. Psychopathology and positive mental health were negatively related, with the largest correlation to emotional well-being, followed by psychological, and social well-being

Table 2.2 Hierarchical regression analysis of age and age-squared in relation to psychopathology, controlling for positive mental health, demographics, and physical health

	Psychopathology		
Model	β	β	β
Mental health			
Positive mental health	– 0.32**	– 0.33**	– 0.28**
Demographics			
Gender (high = female)	0.07*	0.06	0.03
Marital status (high = married)	– 0.13**	– 0.06	– 0.05
Education	– 0.09**	– 0.12**	– 0.07*
Income	– 0.07*	– 0.09**	– 0.08**
Migration status (high = nonnative)	0.11**	0.10**	0.09**
Age			
Age		– 0.17**	– 0.27**
Age-squared		0.02	0.00
Physical health			
Physical diseases			0.11**
Functional limitations			0.16**
Subjective health			– 0.15**
Adjusted R^2	0.15**	0.17**	0.26**

*$p < 0.01$; **$p < 0.001$

Table 2.3 Hierarchical regression analysis of age and age-squared in relation to positive mental health, controlling for psychopathology, demographics, and physical health

	Positive mental health		
Model	β	β	β
Mental health			
Psychopathology	– 0.34**	– 0.35*	– 0.33**
Demographics			
Gender (high = female)	0.05	0.04	0.04
Marital status (high = married)	– 0.06	– 0.02	– 0.02
Education	0.03	0.01	– 0.00
Income	– 0.01	– 0.02	– 0.01
Migration status (high = nonnative)	0.02	0.02	0.02
Age			
Age		– 0.11**	– 0.12**
Age-squared		0.03	0.02
Physical health			
Physical diseases			0.08*
Functional limitations			0.03
Subjective health			0.14**
Adjusted R^2	0.11**	0.12**	0.13**

*$p < 0.01$; **$p < 0.001$

Table 2.2 presents the findings of the regression analysis on psychopathology and Table 2.3 on overall positive mental health. With regard to our first research question

Table 2.4 Hierarchical regression analysis (final model) of age and age-squared in relation to emotional, psychological, and social well-being, controlling for psychopathology, demographics, and physical health

Model	Emotional well-being β	Psychological well-being β	Social well-being β
Mental health			
Psychopathology	− 0.46**	− 0.29**	− 0.18**
Demographics			
Gender (high = female)	0.06	0.05	0.00
Marital status (high = married)	0.11**	− 0.05	− 0.05
Education	− 0.06	0.01	0.02
Income	− 0.03	− 0.01	− 0.01
Migration status (high = nonnative)	− 0.03	0.02	0.03
Age			
Age	− 0.07	− 0.18**	− 0.03
Age-squared	0.10**	− 0.00	− 0.02
Physical health			
Physical diseases	0.03	0.09*	0.06
Functional limitations	0.02	0.02	0.05
Subjective health	0.14**	0.12**	0.11**
Adjusted R^2	0.26**	0.12**	0.04**

*$p < 0.01$; **$p < 0.001$

on the relation of age to psychopathology and positive mental health, we hypothesized a linear as well as a curvilinear relation of age to psychopathology, but no relation of age to positive mental health. Results on psychopathology partly confirmed our hypothesis: after controlling for positive mental health and demographics, age had a linear negative relationship with psychopathology, but no curvilinear relationship. Results on overall positive mental health differed from our hypothesis: there was a negative linear relation between age and positive mental health after controlling for psychopathology and demographics.

The second aim was to assess the relations of psychopathology and positive mental health to age after controlling for physical health. In the last model of the regression analysis, the variables accounted for 26 % of the variance in psychopathology and for 13 % of the variance in positive mental health. All three indicators of physical health were related to psychopathology, but only physical diseases and subjective health were related to positive mental health. Age remained linearly and negatively related to psychopathology. In line with our hypothesis, this correlation was stronger after physical health was added to the analysis. Although we expected age to be positively related to positive mental health when controlling for physical health, the relation of age to positive mental health remained negative after including physical health in the analysis. Table 2.4 presents the findings on the final model of the regression analyses for the three subscales: emotional, psychological, and social well-being. The results indicate that the unique negative linear relation between age and overall positive mental health only holds for psychological well-being. Moreover, physical health functioned as a confounder in the relation of age to emotional well-being. After controlling for physical health, the association of age with emotional well-being was curvilinear. Emotional well-being was higher only among older adults, after controlling for psychopathology, demographics, and physical health.

To answer the third research question on age as a moderator in the relation to psychopathology and on positive mental health, we included interactions of age and age-squared to physical diseases, functional limitations, and subjective health in the final model of the previous regression analyses. Results revealed only a linear moderating effect of age by physical diseases on psychopathology ($F(12, 1459) = 12.30$; $p < 0.01$). The relation between physical diseases and psychopathology thus varied between ages. The linear interaction effect shows that physical diseases were related to more psychopathological symptoms only in respondents between the ages of 18 and 65. In respondents aged 66 and over, the correlation between physical diseases and psychopathology was insignificant. There were no significant interaction effects for all other interactions of age and physical health on psychopathology or positive mental health. Although we expected that physical health would show weaker relations to psychopathology and positive mental health in older than in younger adults, only the age differences in the relation of physical diseases to psychopathology confirmed this hypothesis.

Discussion

The present study examined mental health differences across the lifespan from a positive as well as a traditional perspective as the absence of psychopathology, in line with the two continua model. Our hypothesis about age differences in levels of psychopathology and positive mental health is partly confirmed. In line with our expectations, older adults have fewer symptoms of psychopathology, but the findings do not confirm that levels of psychopathology are higher in the oldest old adults. Although we expected that the combination of gains and losses in aspects of well-being would result in similar levels of overall positive mental health across age groups, our findings show that older adults have a poorer psychological well-being and positive mental health than younger adults. Our hypothesis of physical health as a confounder in the relation of age to mental health is also partially confirmed. Age differences in psychopathology become stronger when taking physical health problems into account, but physical health does not confound the relation of age to overall positive mental health. However, physical health is a confounder in the relation of age to emotional well-being: emotional well-being is only higher among older adults, and only after controlling for physical health. Our last hypothesis that physical health shows weaker relations to psychopathology and positive mental health in older adults than in younger adults is not confirmed with the exception that the relation of physical diseases to psychopathology is less strong in adults over 65 years of age.

Although the relations were not always as expected, the findings provide strong support for the two continua model of mental illness and mental health. The negative relation of age to both psychopathology and positive mental health, confirms that they are two continua. The absence of psychopathology in older age groups does not necessarily imply the presence of positive mental health as would be expected from a traditional view of mental health as merely the absence of psychopathology. Furthermore, the two continua model is supported by the findings on physical health. Physical health had stronger relations to psychopathology than to positive mental health and these age differences in psychopathology became even stronger when taking physical health problems into account. Lastly, we only found age differences in the relation of physical diseases to psychopathology, but not to mental health. We conclude that psychopathology and positive mental health are more than merely opposites on one dimension and that both should be taken into account to provide a full picture of mental health in the older population.

The findings are only partly in line with previous studies on the aging paradox. The aging paradox applies more to psychopathology than to positive mental health. Older adults are capable of maintaining a relatively low level of psychopathology despite their larger number of physical diseases, functional limitations, and worse subjective health. Furthermore, physical diseases have a less stronger relation to psychopathology in older than in younger adults. However, findings on the aging paradox for positive mental health are mixed. Physical health functions as a confounder in the relation of age to emotional well-being, revealing a disproportional better emotional well-being in older than in younger adults after controlling for physical diseases, functional limitations, and subjective health. There is no confounding of physical health nor a moderating effect of age on the relation between physical health and psychological and social well-being. This is in line with previous studies on the aging paradox that mainly included measures on positive and negative affect and life satisfaction (Staudinger et al. 1999; Westerhof et al. 2003). These belong to the domain of emotional well-being, whereas our study also focused on psychological and social well-being. These evaluations of individual and social functioning may be less amenable to adaptation than emotional well-being. Westerhof and Keyes (2010) found indeed that emotional well-being is somewhat higher in older than in younger adults, whereas psychological and social well-being were not. These findings support our broad approach to positive mental health.

This study has several limitations. First, in the present study, only 13 % of the variance in positive mental health was explained as opposed to 26 % of the variance in psychopathology. Factors other than sociodemographics and health might explain levels of positive mental health, such as personality traits. For example, neuroticism discriminates strongly between individuals high and low in positive mental health (Joshanloo and Nosratabadi 2009). Furthermore, instruments for developmental regulation should be included to provide further support for the differentiated findings with regard to the aging paradox.

Second, the data are cross-sectional, which means that the results could be cohort effects and might be caused by cultural historical differences between age groups. Older adults might have had lower levels of psychopathology and positive mental health already when they were young. Due to the cross-sectional nature of our study, we can draw no causal conclusions on the development of positive mental health, psychopathology, and physical health over time. In view of the two continua model, longitudinal examination of the trajectories of positive mental health and psychopathology would be critical for future research.

A third limitation of our study is the underrepresentation of the most senior age group in the sample. With respect to psychopathology, Mirowsky and Ross (1999) showed a lower prevalence among older than younger adults, but an increasing prevalence among the oldest old. The underrepresentation of the oldest old (the oldest age group ranged from 65 to 87 with a mean age of 71.3) might be the reason that we did not find this curvilinear relationship in later life. Our results also raise questions about the prevalence of positive mental health among the oldest old. Furthermore, we measured positive mental health and psychopathology in a sample representative of the Dutch population. Hence important questions remain about positive mental health and psychopathology in clinical populations, such as physically or mentally ill patients.

Our study has important implications for both research and practice. First, future research should include psychological factors such as personality and adaptation strategies when investigating positive mental health, since our findings indicate that factors other than sociodemographics and health explain levels of positive mental health. Second, it is particularly important that physical health problems are included in the assessment of psychopathology and emotional well-being, since the presence of physical diseases might alter the relation between age with psychopathology and emotional well-being. Third, the findings confirm the two continua model and show that mental health is more than merely the absence of psychopathology. Positive mental health and psychopathology are complementary, indicating that an individual is only completely mentally healthy when the absence of psychopathology is accompanied by the presence of positive mental health. When investigating mental health across the lifespan, both psychopathology and positive mental health should be measured.

References

Beekman, A. T. F., Copeland, J. R. M., & Prince, M. J. (1999). Review of community prevalence of depression in later life. *British Journal of Psychiatry, 174,* 307–311.

Beekman, A. T. F., Penninx, B. W. J. H., Deeg, D. J. H., Ormel, J., Braam, A. W., & van Tilburg, W. (1997). Depression and physical health in later life: Results from the Longitudinal Aging Study Amsterdam. *Journal of Affective Disorders, 46,* 219–231.

Bijl, R. V., Ravelli, A., & van Zessen, G. (1998). Prevalence of psychiatric disorder in the general population: Results of the Netherlands Mental Health Survey and Incidence Study (NEMESIS). *Social Psychiatry and Psychiatric Epidemiology, 33,* 587–595.

Brandtstädter, J., & Greve, W. (1994). The aging self: Stabilizing and protective processes. *Developmental Review, 14,* 52–80.

Carstensen, L. L., Fung, H. H., & Charles, S. T. (2003). Socioemotional selectivity theory and the regulation of emotion in the second half of life. *Motivation and Emotion, 27,* 103–123.

de Beurs, E., & Zitman, F. (2006). De Brief Symptom Inventory (BSI): De betrouwbaarheid en validiteit van een handzaam alternatief. [The Brief Symptom Inventory (BSI): The reliability and validity of a practical alternative to the SCL 90]. *Maandblad Geestelijke Volksgezondheid, 61,* 120–141.

Deci, E. L., & Ryan, R. M. (2008). Hedonia, eudaimonia, and well-being: An introduction. *Journal of Happiness Studies, 9,* 1–11.
Diener, E., & Suh, E. M. (1998). Subjective well-being and age: An international analysis. *Annual Review of Gerontology and Geriatrics, 17,* 304–324.
Diener, E., Suh, E. M., Lucas, R., & Smith, H. L. (1999). Subjective well-being: Three decades of progress. *Psychological Bulletin, 125,* 276–302.
Hayes, A. F., & Matthes, J. (2009). Computational procedures for probing interactions in OLS and logistic regression: SPSS and SAS implementations. *Behavior Research Methods, 41,* 924–936.
Henchoz, K., Cavalli, S., & Girardin, M. (2008). Health perception and health status in advanced old age: A paradox of association. *Journal of Aging Studies, 22,* 282–290.
House, J. S., Kessler, R. C., & Herzog, A. R. (1990). Age, socioeconomic status, and health. *The Milbank Quarterly, 68,* 383–411.
Howell, R. T., Kern, M. L., & Lyubomirsky, S. (2007). Health benefits: Meta-analytically determining the impact of well-being on objective health outcomes. *Health Psychology Review, 1,* 83–136.
Isaacowitz, D. M., & Smith, J. (2003). Positive and negative affect in very old age. *Journal of Gerontology: Psychological Sciences, 58B,* 143–152.
Joshanloo, M., & Nosratabadi, M. (2009). Levels of mental health continuum and personality traits. *Social Indicators Research, 90,* 211–224.
Kendler, K. S., Myers, J. M., Maes, H. H., & Keyes, C. L. M. (2011, online first). The relationship between the genetic and environmental influences on common internalizing psychiatric disorders and mental well-being. *Behavior Genetics, 41*(5), 641–650.
Kessler, R. C., Mickelson, K. D., Walters, E. E., Zhao, S., & Hamilton, L. (2004). Age and depression in the MIDUS survey. In O. G. Brim, C. D. Ryff, & R. C. Kessler (Eds.), *How healthy are we: A national study of the well-being at midlife* (pp. 227–251). Chicago: University of Chicago Press.
Keyes, C. L. M. (1998). Social well-being. *Social Psychology Quarterly, 61,* 121–140.
Keyes, C. L. M. (2005). Mental illness and/or mental health? Investigating axioms of the complete state model of health. *Journal of Consulting and Clinical Psychology, 73,* 539–548.
Keyes, C. L. M. (2007). Promoting and protecting mental health as flourishing: A complementary strategy for improving national mental health. *American Psychologist, 62,* 95–108.
Keyes, C. L. M., Dhingra, S. S., & Simoes, E. J. (2010). Change in level of positive mental health as a predictor of future risk of mental illness. *American Journal of Public Health, 100,* 2366–2371.
Keyes, C. L. M., & Shapiro, A. D. (2004). Social well-being in the United States: A descriptive epidemiology. In O. G. Brim, C. D. Ryff, & R. C. Kessler (Eds.), *How healthy are we: A national study of the well-being at midlife* (pp. 350–373). Chicago: University of Chicago Press.
Keyes, C. L. M., & Westerhof, G. J. (2012). Chronological and subjective age differences in flourishing mental health and major depressive episode. *Aging and Mental Health, 16,* 67–74.
Keyes, C. L. M., Wissing, M., Potgieter, J. P., Temane, M., Kruger, A., & van Rooy, S. (2008). Evaluation of the mental health continuum-short form (MHC-SF) in Setswana-speaking South Africans. *Clinical Psychology and Psychotherapy, 15,* 181–192.
Kivela, S., & Pahkala, K. (2001). Depressive disorder as predictor of physical disability in old age. *Journal of the American Geriatrics Society, 49,* 290–296.
Knoef, M., & de Vos, K. (under review). The representativeness of LISS, an online probability panel.
Kunzmann, U., Little, T. D., & Smith, J. (2000). Is age-related stability of subjective well-being a paradox? Cross-sectional and longitudinal evidence from the Berlin Aging Study. *Psychology and Aging, 15,* 511–526.
Lamers, S. M. A., Bolier, L., Westerhof, G. J., Smit, F., & Bohlmeijer, E. T. (2012a). The impact of emotional well-being on long-term recovery and survival in physical illness: A meta-analysis. *Journal of Behavioral Medicine, 35,* 538–547.
Lamers, S. M. A., Glas, C. A. W., Westerhof, G. J., & Bohlmeijer, E. T. (2012b). Longitudinal evaluation of the Mental Health Continuum-Short Form (MHC-SF): Measurement invariance

across demographics, physical illness and mental illness. *European Journal of Psychological Assessment, 28,* 290–296.

Lamers, S. M. A., Westerhof, G. J., Bohlmeijer, E. T., ten Klooster, P. M., & Keyes, C. L. M. (2011). Evaluating the psychometric properties of the Mental Health Continuum-Short Form (MHC-SF). *Journal of Clinical Psychology, 67,* 99–110.

Lyubomirsky, S., King, L., & Diener, E. (2005). The benefits of frequent positive affect: Does happiness lead to success? *Psychological Bulletin, 131,* 803–855.

Mirowsky, J. & Ross, C. E. (1999). Well-being across the life-course. In A. V. Horwitz & T. L. Scheids (Eds.), *A handbook for the study of mental health: Social contexts, theories, and systems* (pp. 328–347). New York: Cambridge University Press.

Mroczek, D. K. & Kolarz, C. M. (1998). The effect of age on positive and negative affect: A developmental perspective on happiness. *Journal of Personality and Social Psychology, 75,* 1333–1349.

Newman, J. P., & Engel, R. J. (1991). Age differences in depressive experiences. *Journal of Gerontology, 46,* 224–235.

Pinquart, M. (2001). Correlates of subjective health in older adults: A meta-analysis. *Psychology and Aging, 16,* 414–426.

Pinquart, M. (2002). Creating and maintaining purpose in life in old age: A meta analysis. *Ageing International, 27,* 90–114.

Ryff, C. D. (1995). Psychological well-being in adult life. *Current Directions in Psychological Science, 4,* 99–104.

Ryff, C. D., & Keyes, C. L. M. (1995). The structure of psychological well-being revisited. *Journal of Personality and Social Psychology, 69,* 719–727.

Staudinger, U. M., Freund, A. M., Linden, M., & Maas, I. (1999). Self, personality and life regulation: Facets of psychological resilience in old age. In P. B. Baltes & K. U. Mayer (Eds.), *The Berlin Aging Study: Aging from 70 to 100* (pp. 302–328). New York: Cambridge University Press.

Steverink, N., Westerhof, G. J., Bode, C., & Dittmann-Kohli, F. (2001). The personal experience of aging, individual resources and subjective well-being. *Journal of Gerontology: Psychological Sciences, 56B,* 364–373.

The ESEMeD/MHEDEA 2000 Investigators (2004). Prevalence of mental disorders in Europe: Results from the European Study of the Epidemiology of Mental Disorders (ESEMeD) project. *Acta Psychiatrica Scandinavia, 109,* 21–27.

van den Akker, M., Buntinx, F., Metsemakers, J. F., Roos, S., & Knottnerus, J. A. (1998). Multimordidity in general practice: Prevalence, incidence, and determinants of co-occurring chronic and recurrent diseases. *Journal of Clinical Epidemiology, 51,* 367–375.

Vaux, A., & Meddin, J. (1987). Positive and negative life change and positive and negative affect among the rural elderly. *Journal of Community Psychology, 15,* 447–458.

Veenhoven, R. (2008). Healthy happiness: Effects of happiness on physical health and the consequences for preventive health care. *Journal of Happiness Studies, 9,* 449–469.

Waterman, A. S. (1993). Two conceptions of happiness: Contrasts of personal expressiveness (eudaimonia) and hedonic enjoyment. *Journal of Personality and Social Psychology, 64,* 678–691.

Westerhof, G. J., Dittmann-Kohli, F., & Bode, C. (2003). The aging paradox: Toward personal meaning in gerontological theory. In S. Biggs, A. Lowenstein, & J. Hendricks (Eds.), *The need for theory: Critical approaches to social gerontology* (pp. 127–143). Amityville: Baywood.

Westerhof, G. J., & Keyes, C. L. M. (2010). Mental illness and mental health: The two continua model across the lifespan. *Journal of Adult Development, 17,* 110–119.

Wood, A. M., & Joseph, S. (2009). The absence of positive psychological (eudemonic) well-being as a risk factor for depression: A ten year cohort study. *Journal of Affective Disorders, 122,* 213–217.

World Health Organization (2004). *Promoting mental health: Concepts, emerging evidence, practice* (summary report). Geneva: WHO.

Chapter 3
Flow Theory and the Paradox of Happiness

Bryan Moore

One of the overarching goals of psychology is to describe why people do what they do. This lofty pursuit has spawned an abundance of theories that attempt to explain the nature of human behavior, and how it comes into being. A commonly held assumption within many of these theories, and within psychology at large, is that a causal relationship exists between behavior and some type of antecedent. Many theories propose that there are motivational antecedents that drive people to do the things that they do (Petri and Govern 2004). In this chapter, I will explore flow theory and how it relates to adult motivation and subjective states of well-being. I will also discuss how the paradox of happiness helps to explain flow and other goal-oriented theories of motivation.

Happiness and Intrinsic Motivation

Motivation is a term that is commonly used to describe the forces that act on or within an individual to initiate and direct behavior (Petri and Govern 2004). As a concept, motivation may be one of the most elemental components of human psychology. As a field of research, it spans numerous domains and has been analyzed from a number of different theoretical perspectives; theories based on evolution (Bernard et al. 2005), learning (Dickinson and Balleine 2002), psychodynamics (Nuttin 1956), existentialism (Solomon et al. 2004), humanism (Johnson 2005; Maslow 1968), and biology (Hebb 1955) have all gained prominence in the field. In addition, psychologists have proposed cognitive and emotional theories that emphasize the central role of our conscious thoughts, feelings, and experiences in determining what we do (Eccles and Wigfield 2002; Petri and Govern 2004).

B. Moore (✉)
Johns Hopkins University, 550 North Broadway, Suite 506, Baltimore MD 21205, USA
e-mail: bmoore31@jhmi.edu

J. D. Sinnott (ed.), *Positive Psychology*,
DOI 10.1007/978-1-4614-7282-7_3, © Springer Science+Business Media, LLC 2013

In a review of modern motivational theories, Eccles and Wigfield (2002) note that, in an attempt to explain the reasons for engagement, several cognitive-based theories make a distinction between intrinsic and extrinsic types of motivation. This distinction clarifies why people partake in activities. When intrinsic motivation is involved, people engage in an activity because they are interested in, and enjoy, the activity. On the other hand, when people are extrinsically motivated, they engage in activities for instrumental or other reasons such as receiving a reward (Eccles and Wigfield 2002). From this conception, one could reasonably propose that, in both intrinsic and extrinsic types of motivation, people are driven toward an outcome that is beneficial to some type of system or entity. One of these beneficial outcomes may be happiness.

Some thinkers have proposed that happiness is an important factor in motivation (Csikszentmihalyi 1990; Waterman et al. 2008), and more specifically in intrinsic motivation (Waterman 2005). Happiness may be a motivational state (Miron et al. 2007) and it may also be one of the reasons for motivated behavior (Csikszentmihalyi 1990; Waterman et al. 2008). Though happiness has been conceptualized in many ways (e.g., Brülde 2007; Csikszentmihalyi 1990; Otake et al. 2006; Sauter and Scott 2007; Waterman et al. 2008), I will use the broad interpretation of subjective well-being as a definition for this construct (Diener and Seligman 2002; Martin 2008).

Eudaimonia and Hedonic Enjoyment

Many psychologists have conducted research following a dichotomous view of happiness where happiness is divided into two different types: eudaimonia and hedonic enjoyment (e.g., Ryan and Deci 2001; Ryan et al. 2008; Vittersø 2003; Waterman 1993; 2005; Waterman et al. 2008). This popular distinction is based on ancient Greek philosophy and has begun to generate empirical research paradigms (Waterman 1993; Waterman et al. 2008).

Both philosophical and psychological theories of happiness have traditionally differentiated higher pleasures from lower ones; this differentiation often stems from the *effort* involved in the happiness-related activities (Waterman 2005). The difference between eudaimonia and hedonic enjoyment is not necessarily based on effort level, but it appears to be based on meaning systems. Eudaimonia is characterized as the process of moving toward self-realization and performing activities that relate to personal values and virtues, whereas hedonic enjoyment is of a more episodic type and focuses on immediate pleasure (Ryan et al. 2006). See Ryan and Deci (2001) for a review of eudaimonia and hedonic enjoyment.

Some research has shown that eudaimonia and hedonic enjoyments are related, although distinguishable, types of happiness (Waterman 1993, 2005). Waterman et al. (2008) go a step further and propose that, although the two types are often thought of as separate, hedonistic enjoyment may also be experienced during feelings of eudaimonia, and that eudaimonia is a subset of hedonistic enjoyment. These ideas are not new; the third-century BCE philosopher Epicurus, who is commonly known for upholding a purely hedonistic perspective on happiness, proposed that, although pleasure does lead to happiness, happiness is not necessarily derived from lower, sensual, pleasures only (Rosenbaum 1990). With regard to motivation, Waterman et al. (2008) state that it is "...universally recognized that intrinsically motivated activities are hedonically enjoyed" (p. 47). One researcher, Csikszentmihalyi (1990) has proposed an explanatory theory of intrinsic motivation, which, indirectly, subsumes the eudaimonia and hedonic dichotomy.

Flow Theory

Flow theory (Csikszentmihalyi 1990) has been categorized as one of many types of intrinsic motivation theories (Eccles and Wigfield 2002; Waterman et al. 2008). It is based on the idea that all humans are motivated to partake in activities that elicit optimal experiences, or flow states. Flow states are what "... people report when they are intensely involved in doing something that is fun to do" (Csikszentmihalyi 2000, p. 381), and the ability to experience these states does not appear to decline with age (Payne et al. 2011). One of the key factors of flow is that a balance exists between the skill level of the individual and the challenge of the activity. Additional characteristics of flow include a distortion in one's sense of time, extreme focus or attention, and an automatic use of skills (Csikszentmihalyi 1990). In the mind of the individual, flow activities are valuable for their own sake, and they entail clear goals and performance feedback. Historically, flow research has focused on discrete flow experiences (e.g., Clarke and Haworth 1994; Fritz and Avsec 2007; Harari 2008; Jackson and Eklund 2002; Keller and Bless 2008) that, similar to hedonic enjoyment, are episodic in nature. However, Csikszentmihalyi (1990) has also proposed more global uses for the theory, which mirror more eudaimonic conceptions.

In *Flow: The Psychology of Optimal Experience*, Csikszentmihalyi (1990) alludes to the claim that flow is *the* optimal experience. Past research shows that flow is most likely one of many types of powerful positive experiences (Privette 1983), and that flow is one of many motivations (Reiss 2000). Regardless, some researchers have found positive correlations between intrinsic motivation and flow in a number of different populations: skateboarders (Seifert and Hedderson 2010), swimmers (Kowal and Fortier 1999), and architecture students (Fullagar and Mills 2008).

It should be noted that the flow and intrinsic motivation relationship may be culture-specific. At least one study supports the idea that cross-cultural differences exist (Moneta 2004). Similarly, other studies have shown that there are differences between North Americans and East Asians in the types of experiences associated with happiness; those from the West tend to experience happiness during activities related to personal achievement, whereas those from the East are more likely to experience it during social cohesion-inducing activities (Uchida et al. 2004; Uchida and Kitayama 2009).

Smith (2000) has proposed that a fundamental flaw in Csikzentmihalyi's (1990) flow theory resides in its focus on the individual rather than on interpersonal connections. Yet, Csikzentmihalyi (1990) has noted that, "...when they are treated as valuable in their own right, people are the most fulfilling source of happiness." However, Cisikzentmihalyi (1990) also recognizes a contradictory aspect of human motivation: it seems as though we yearn for connection with other people, and though they can be the source of great happiness, other people can also be the source of misery and suffering. Though the appreciation of solitude may be an important constituent of happiness, some studies show that people who are more social and have stronger social relationships tend to be happier (Diener and Seligman 2002). Most researchers in the modern field of psychology tend to dismiss such contradictory aspects of the human psyche, because these contradictions, although part of the human condition, go beyond the logic of scientific epistemologies (Koch 1981). Those who exclusively ascribe to these systems may wrongly assume that the use of scientific methods in psychological inquiry necessarily produces meaningful and complete knowledge and that contradictory findings are, by definition, lacking in value, because they cannot be fully processed by purely rational systems (Koch 1981).

It was noted previously that some studies have shown positive correlations between flow and intrinsic motivation and that intrinsically motivated activities are hedonically enjoyed. Vittersø (2003) examined the role of evaluation in hedonic enjoyment, more specifically, the process of individuals judging their experiences as either good or bad. Vittersø (2003) notes that flow does not include an evaluative element. Flow states may be evaluated later as experiences that are counter to eudaimonic goals or values, but they are not evaluated as they are happening. For example, one may experience flow during military combat (Harari 2008) and then later judge the violent combat situation to be an activity that is not consistent with one's path toward self-realization. During flow, to make a value judgment about the overall activity may disrupt the enthrallment, or high level of focused attention, that is one of the hallmarks of flow state. Similarly, Csikszentmihalyi (1999) has said that people are not necessarily happy during flow states "... because they are too involved in the task to have the luxury to reflect on their subjective states. Being happy would be a distraction, an interruption of the flow" (p. 825).

The Paradox of Happiness

According to Petri and Govern (2004), direction is a fundamental component of motivation. When one is motivated, their behavior is directed toward something. With regard to intrinsic motivation, the individual may be directed at the experience of the activity participated in. With happiness as an aim, one directs their behavior in such a way that it elicits the happiness state. Martin (2008) points out that even though individuals may be motivated to acquire happiness, this motivation may, paradoxically, be counterproductive to its realization. He states:

> …pursuing happiness directly, deliberately, and devotedly is self-defeating or otherwise problematic. Instead, we should concentrate our energies on other goals, activities, and relationships that can yield satisfactions contributing to happiness. This need for indirectness seems paradoxical because usually we assume that attentive effort is needed in pursuing important goals, in particular happiness. (Martin 2008, p. 172)

This paradox of happiness concept, not to be confused with the economic paradox of happiness (Drakopoulos 2008; Phelps 2001), may help to explain Csikszentmihalyi's (1990) flow theory and why it provides an instructive model in this domain. Csikszentmihalyi (1990) proposes that the organization of one's life around a central goal will create meaning and lead to a unified flow experience, which is something that may be construed as eudaimonic happiness.

> If a person sets out to achieve a difficult enough goal, from which all other goals logically follow, and if he or she invests all energy in developing skills to reach that goal, then actions and feelings will be in harmony, and the separate parts of life will fit together—and each activity will "make sense" in the present, as well as in view of the past and of the future. In such a way, it is possible to give meaning to one's entire life. (Csikszentmihalyi 1999, p. 214)

The importance of meaning in life has been well-documented as a factor related to happiness and well-being (Auhagen 2000; Steger and Frazier 2005; Harlow et al. 1986), but how should people chose the type of meaning-producing goal that Csikszentmihalyi (1990) describes?

Chekola (2007) proposes a theory called the *life plan view* of happiness, which may help to supplement flow theory. This concept claims that happiness stems from a global perspective of one's life. It is similar to eudaimonia, but it differs in that it focuses less on self-expression and more on an overarching plan or goal in the context of one's life story. One's life story is an autobiographical account of one's life, and the ability to create this account develops in late childhood and early adolescence (Bohn and Berntsen 2008). Happiness from this perspective is a more organized concept that includes hierarchies of global desires. According to Chekola (2007), these desires or goals should be chosen according to three criteria: firstly, they should be comprehensive and affect or incorporate many lower desires. Secondly, they should be important to the individual and cause dissatisfaction if they are not realized. Thirdly, they should be relatively permanent. If one is able to choose life goals based on these criteria and then they pursue these goals, it may be the case that a unified flow experience, or overall sense of eudaimonia may be experienced. If one is motivated by happiness, and they understand the paradox of happiness concept, they may be able to focus their attention on global life goals that will help with the realization of the initial motivation to experience happiness.

As we have seen, the current chapter described flow theory and how it attempts to explain human motivation in terms of intrinsic motivation and happiness. The research in this area has been growing and other similar theories exist (e.g., Chekola 2007; Ryan et al. 2008). Though the current chapter focused primarily on theory within the "flow" domain, a number of empirical studies have been published on the subject matter (e.g., Fullagar and Mills 2008; Kowal and Fortier 1999; Seifert and Hedderson 2010). Strong empirical evidence is important in this field of research;

however, it is crucial to be careful when operationally defining and measuring complex experiential states. Sink (2000) suggests that psychologists should not quantify subjective states of happiness or flow, but rather focus on retaining a phenomenological perspective while studying them. This recommendation may prove to be beneficial. Similarly, it may be wise for psychologists to be careful when breaking down these experiences into strict conceptualizations. As a science, psychology aims to create typologies of cognitive events, processes, and other constructs. Though many gains have been made from this act of breaking-experience-into-parts, it may be wise to keep a perspective of openness, and flexibility, when conceptualizing entities such as flow state and happiness, so that the conceptualizations may include some of the more paradoxical elements of these elusive states.

References

Auhagen, A. (2000). On the psychology of meaning of life. *Swiss Journal of Psychology, 59*(1), 34–38.

Bernard, L. C., Mills, M., Swenson, L., & Walsh, R. (2005). An evolutionary theory of human motivation. *Genetic, Social, and General Psychology Monographs, 131*(2), 129–184. doi:10.3200/MONO.131.2.129-184.

Bohn, A., & Berntsen, D. (2008). Life story development in childhood: The development of life story abilities and the acquisition of cultural life scripts from late middle childhood to adolescence. *Developmental Psychology, 44*(4), 1135–1147. doi:10.1037/0012-1649.44.4.1135.

Brülde, B. (2007). Happiness theories of the good life. *Journal of Happiness Studies, 8*(1), 15–49. doi:10.1007/s10902-006-9003-8.

Chekola, M. (2007). Happiness, rationality, autonomy and the good life. *Journal of Happiness Studies, 8*(1), 51–78. doi:10.1007/s10902-006-9004-7.

Clarke, S. G., & Haworth, J. T. (1994). 'Flow' experience in the daily lives of sixth-form college students. *British Journal of Psychology, 85,* 511–523.

Csikszentmihalyi, M. (1990). Flow: The psychology of optimal experience. New York: Harper and Rowe.

Csikszentmihalyi, M. (1999). If we are so rich, why aren't we happy? *American Psychologist, 54,* 821–827.

Csikszentmihalyi, M. (2000). *Encyclopedia of psychology* (Vol. 3). Washington: American Psychological Association.

Dickinson, A., & Balleine, B. (2002). The role of learning in the operation of motivational systems. In H. Pashler, R. Gallistel, H. Pashler, & R. Gallistel (Eds.), *Steven's handbook of experimental psychology: Learning, motivation, and emotion* (3rd ed., Vol. 3, pp. 497–533). Hoboken: Wiley. (Retrieved from EBSCO*host*).

Diener, E., & Seligman, M. P. (2002). Very happy people. *Psychological Science, 13*(1), 81–84. doi:10.1111/1467-9280.00415.

Drakopoulos, S. A. (2008). The paradox of happiness: Towards an alternative explanation. *Journal of Happiness Studies, 9*(2), 303–315. doi:10.1007/s10902-007-9054-5.

Eccles, J. S., & Wigfield, A. (2002). Motivational beliefs, values, and goals. *Annual Review of Psychology, 53*(1), 109–132. doi:10.1146/annurev.psych.53.100901.135153.

Fritz, B. S., & Avsec, A. (2007). The experience of flow and subjective well-being of music students. *Horizons of Psychology, 16*(2), 5–17.

Fullagar, C. J., & Mills, M. J. (2008). Motivation and flow: Toward an understanding of the dynamics of the relation in architecture students. *Journal of Psychology: Interdisciplinary and Applied, 142*(5), 533–553. doi:10.3200/JRLP.142.5.533-556.

Harari, Y. (2008). Combat flow: Military, political, and ethical dimensions of subjective well- being in war. *Review of General Psychology, 12*(3), 253–264. doi:10.1037/1089-2680.12.3.253.

Harlow, L. L., Newcomb, M. D., & Bentler, P. M. (1986). Depression, self-derogation, substance use, and suicide ideation: Lack of purpose in life as a mediational factor. *Journal of Clinical Psychology, 42*(1), 5–21. doi:10.1002/1097-4679(198601)42:1<5::AID-JCLP2270420102>3.0.CO;2-9.

Hebb, D. O. (1955). Drives and the conceptual nervous system. *Psychological Review, 62,* 243–253.

Jackson, S. A., & Eklund, R. C. (2002). Assessing flow in physical activity: The flow state scale- 2 and dispositional flow scale-2. *Journal of Sport & Exercise Psychology, 24,* 133–150.

Johnson, T. J. (2005). Goal theories of motivation as rigorous humanism. *Journal of Constructivist Psychology, 18*(4), 311–325. doi:10.1080/10720530500202860.

Keller, J., & Bless, H. (2008). Flow and regulatory compatibility: An experimental approach to the flow model of intrinsic motivation. *Personality and Social Psychology Bulletin, 34,* 196–209.

Koch, S. (1981). The nature and limits of psychological knowledge: Lessons of a century qua 'science'. *American Psychologist, 36*(3), 257–269. doi:10.1037/0003-066X.36.3.257.

Kowal, J., & Fortier, M. S. (1999). Motivational determinants of flow: Contributions from self- determination theory. *The Journal of Social Psychology, 139*(3), 355–368. doi:10.1080/00224549909598391.

Martin, M. W. (2008). Paradoxes of happiness. *Journal of Happiness Studies, 9*(2), 171–184. doi:10.1007/s10902-007-9056-3.

Maslow, A. H. (1968). *Toward a psychology of being* (2nd ed.). New York: Van Nostrand Reinhold.

Miron, A. M., Parkinson, S. K., & Brehm, J. W. (2007). Does happiness function like a motivational state? *Cognition and Emotion, 21*(2), 248–267. doi:10.1080/02699930600551493.

Moneta, G. B. (2004). The flow model of intrinsic motivation in Chinese: Cultural and personal moderators. *Journal of Happiness Studies, 5*(2), 181–217. doi:10.1023/B:JOHS.0000035916.27782.e4.

Nuttin, J. (1956). Human motivation and Freud's theory of energy discharge. *Canadian Journal of Psychology/Revue Canadienne De Psychologie, 10*(3), 167–178. doi:10.1037/h0083667.

Otake, K., Shimai, S., Tanaka-Matsumi, J., Otsui, K., & Fredrickson, B. L. (2006). Happy people become happier through kindness: A counting kindnesses intervention. *Journal of Happiness Studies, 7*(3), 361–375. doi:10.1007/s10902-005-3650-z.

Payne, B. R., Jackson, J. J., Noh, S., & Stine-Morrow, E. L. (2011). In the zone: Flow state and cognition in older adults. *Psychology and Aging, 26*(3), 738–743. doi:10.1037/a0022359.

Petri, H. L., & Govern, J. M. (2004). *Motivation: Theory, research, and applications* (5th ed.). Belmont: Wadsworth.

Phelps, C. D. (2001). A clue to the paradox of happiness. *Journal of Economic Behavior & Organization, 45*(3), 293. (Retrieved from EBSCO*host*).

Privette, G. (1983). Peak experience, peak performance, and flow: A comparative analysis of positive human experiences. *Journal of Personality and Social Psychology, 45*(6), 1361–1368.

Rosenbaum, S. (1990). Epicurus on pleasure and the complete life. *Monist: An International Quarterly Journal of General Philosophical Inquiry, 73*(1), 21–41.

Reiss, S. (2000). Human individuality, happiness, and flow. *American Psychologist, 55*(10), 1161–1162. doi:10.1037/0003-066X.55.10.1161.

Ryan, R. M., & Deci, E. L. (2001). On happiness and human potentials: A review of research on hedonic and eudaimonic well-being. *Annual Review of Psychology, 52,* 141–166. doi:10.1146/annurev.psych.52.1.141.

Ryan, R. M., Huta, V., & Deci, E. L. (2006). Living well: A self determination theory perspective on eudaimonia. *Journal of Happiness Studies, 9,* 139–170.

Ryan, R. M., Huta, V., & Deci, E. L. (2008). Living well: A self-determination theory perspective on eudaimonia. *Journal of Happiness Studies, 9*(1), 139–170. doi:10.1007/s10902-006-9023-4.

Sauter, D. A., & Scott, S. K. (2007). More than one kind of happiness: Can we recognize vocal expressions of different positive states? *Motivation and Emotion, 31*(3), 192–199. doi:10.1007/s11031-007-9065-x.

Seifert, T. T., & Hedderson, C. C. (2010). Intrinsic motivation and flow in skateboarding: An ethnographic study. *Journal of Happiness Studies, 11*(3), 277–292. doi:10.1007/s10902-009-9140-y.

Sink, J. R. (2000). Why can't we measure happiness? *American Psychologist, 55*(10), 1162–1163. doi:10.1037/0003-066X.55.10.1162b.

Smith, T. B. (2000). Cultural values and happiness. *American Psychologist, 55*(10), 1162. doi:10.1037/0003-066X.55.10.1162a.

Solomon, S., Greenberg, J., & Pyszczynski, T. (2004). The cultural animal: Twenty years of terror management theory and research. In J. Greenberg, S. L. Koole, & T. Pyszczynski (Eds.), *Handbook of experimental existential psychology* (pp. 13–34). New York: The Guilford Press.

Steger, M. F., & Frazier, P. (2005). Meaning in life: One link in the chain from religiousness to well-being. *Journal of Counseling Psychology, 52*(4), 574–582. doi:10.1037/0022-0167.52.4.574.

Uchida, Y., & Kitayama, S. (2009). Happiness and unhappiness in east and west: Themes and variations. *Emotion, 9*(4), 441–456. doi:10.1037/a0015634.

Uchida, Y., Norasakkunkit, V., & Kitayama, S. (2004). Cultural constructions of happiness: Theory and empirical evidence. *Journal of Happiness Studies, 5*(3), 223–239. doi:10.1007/s10902-004-8785-9.

Vittersø, J. (2003). Flow versus life satisfaction: A projective use of cartoons to illustrate the difference between the evaluation approach and the intrinsic motivation approach to subjective quality of life. *Journal of Happiness Studies, 4*(2), 141–167. doi:10.1023/A:1024413112234.

Waterman, A. S. (1993). Two conceptions of happiness: Contrasts of personal expressiveness (eudaimonia) and hedonic enjoyment. *Journal of Personality and Social Psychology, 64*(4), 678–691. doi:10.1037/0022-3514.64.4.678.

Waterman, A. S. (2005). When effort is enjoyed: Two studies of intrinsic motivation for personally salient activities. *Motivation and Emotion, 29*(3), 165–188. doi:10.1007/s11031-005-9440-4.

Waterman, A. S., Schwartz, S. J., & Conti, R. (2008). The implications of two conceptions of happiness (hedonic enjoyment and eudaimonia) for the understanding of intrinsic motivation. *Journal of Happiness Studies, 9*(1), 41–79. doi:10.1007/s10902-006-9020-7.

Chapter 4
Finding Flow: The History and Future of a Positive Psychology Concept

Grant J. Rich

This chapter examines flow, Mihaly Csikszentmihalyi's concept that defines a "state of optimal experience that people report when they are intensely involved in doing something that is fun to do" (2000a, p. 381). Flow is of considerable interest to positive psychologists, both as a temporary psychological state and as a trait that some people with what are known as autotelic personalities experience relatively frequently. Csikszentmihalyi has argued that, in keeping with flow theory, a good life is one characterized by complete absorption in what one does (Nakamura and Csikszentmihalyi 2002, p. 89). The Good Life, of course, and how to achieve it, are central concerns of the founders of the positive psychology movement (e.g., Seligman and Csikszentmihalyi 2000; Seligman 2011). Since the publication of his first book on positive psychology (2002), Seligman has continued to revise and update his conceptualization of the movement. Flow has remained a core concept in Seligman's (2011) current book on positive psychology. In fact, the second of the five pillars of Seligman's well-being theory (known by the handy mnemonic PERMA) is Engagement (the other four elements are Positive emotion, Relationships, Meaning, and Accomplishment). As Seligman notes, this element engagement, "is about flow: being one with the music, time stopping, and the loss of self-consciousness during an absorbing activity. I refer to a life lived with these aims as the 'engaged life' " (p. 11). A life worth living then, seems to involve flow. What is the background and history of this frequently studied concept? How does flow relate to similar concepts, such as peak experiences, intrinsic motivation, and effortless attention? What populations experience flow and in what activities? Does the experience of flow exist cross-culturally? Is there evidence from neuroscience in support of the concept of flow? What types of methods have been utilized to examine it? What are the implications of flow for a positive psychology of adult development? This chapter will explore these questions.

G. J. Rich (✉)
International Psychology Bulletin (APA), Juneau, Alaska
e-mail: optimalex@aol.com

J. D. Sinnott (ed.), *Positive Psychology*,
DOI 10.1007/978-1-4614-7282-7_4, © Springer Science+Business Media, LLC 2013

To begin though, it is helpful to review how Csikszentmihalyi (1990) describes the nine components of the flow experience. These components are derived from research with a range of populations—from athletes and musicians to dancers and readers of absorbing books—and with a range of methods from interviews and self-report questionnaires to experience sampling method (ESM) data and evidence from biological psychology (readers especially interested in a discussion of these techniques may read the methods section of this chapter first). These populations and methods will be described in more detail, later. In terms of the nine flow elements, first, there are clear goals every step of the way. When the rock climber senses the way, or when the author anticipates the next passage, the experience is likely to be associated with flow. In contrast, the first-year student struggling with the steps of a term paper or the marathon runner who has lost his or her way may find that attention is disrupted and distracted, and flow is less likely to occur. Second, in flow, there is immediate feedback to one's actions. For instance, on the one hand, a classical pianist hears immediately whether or not he or she has played the correct note. On the other hand, work and academic courses may not be conducive to flow if for example, performance evaluations, graduations, or grades come months or even years after a task is completed.

Third, there is a balance between challenges and skills. If perceived skills exceed perceived challenges, a person will probably experience boredom with a task. If challenges exceed skills, a person will experience anxiety. If skills and challenges are both low, a person is likely to feel apathy. However, if skills and challenges are high and approximately equal (some research suggests when challenges are slightly greater than skills), a person may experience flow. An important consideration is that flow depends on perceived, not actual challenges and skills. For instance, two musicians may have quite different experiences playing the same piece of music. A beginning Suzuki musician may experience flow when playing Twinkle, Twinkle, Little Star, as perceived skills and perceived challenges are high and in sync. In contrast, violin virtuosos like Stephane Grappelli may feel bored, as skills exceed the challenges. The fourth element in flow is that action and awareness are merged. The rower in flow feels that the oar is an extension of his arm. Likewise, a rock star musician in flow may feel a deep connection to his guitar, again feeling that he is one with his axe. Fifth, distractions are excluded from consciousness. In flow, one is not concerned with hunger pangs or irrelevant information. Instead, one is single-mindedly focused on the task at hand. Sixth, there is no worry of failure. Attention is fully focused upon the flow activity, skills and challenges are balanced and so one does not sense possible failure, and at any rate, one is immersed in the actual flow activity, not in evaluation of possible end-result outcomes. For example, the bench scientist focuses on the experiment at hand, not worrying whether the results may be published months later.

Seventh, self-consciousness disappears. Everyday worries evaporate from consciousness. The intensity of the flow experience is such that cognitive and emotional resources are fully engaged with the task at hand, leaving no resources remaining to multitask on nonessential thoughts or actions not vital to the current task. The opera singer in flow is focused on producing beautiful music, not wondering whether or not the audience finds her dress and hairstyle appealing. Eighth, sense of time becomes distorted. Often, people who have experienced flow will report that hours had passed without their knowledge, as they were so deeply engrossed in flow activity. For instance, a reader becomes completely absorbed in a book late at night, only to be surprised when the dawn light emerges, not realizing he or she has read the night away. Finally, ninth, if the previous conditions are largely met, the activity becomes autotelic, that is, it becomes an end in itself. In this sense, the flow experience has much in common with intrinsic motivation. As an example, people who tend to experience flow tend to downplay extrinsic rewards such as money, awards, or attention from others. They may report that they would continue to run, to make music, to conduct research, to keep working, and to keep doing what they were doing, even if they did not receive money, praise, or rewards. Indeed, somewhat paradoxically, people who experience flow in productive activities often develop great skill, and often do win awards. However, when asked about their work, they tend to focus upon the pleasure they receive from the experience of doing their work itself, not from the awards they receive. Such was the case with many of the Nobel Laureates interviewed by Csikszentmihalyi et al. (1996) in his study of creativity in later life.

History and Background of the Flow Concept

Although positive psychology as a formal movement is only a little over a decade old, Csikszentmihalyi (2000b, p. 387) first became interested in human psychological strengths such as hope and optimism, many years earlier, when he observed the destruction of European culture during World War II as a 10-year-old boy, and the various responses—some admirable, some not—made by adults to the situation. A desire to understand these experiences led him to psychology, where for the past 40 years, he has had an abiding interest in studying "people who appeared to like how they had chosen to live, who seemed to like what they were doing; people who were motivated by the very activities they did without much concern for rewards that they might get later on" (p. 387). In the 1960s, as part of his dissertation work studying the creative process in artists, Csikszentmihalyi noticed that when painting was going well, the artists he observed seemed single-mindedly focused on their work, ignoring hunger pangs, the time of day, and other concerns unrelated to the task at hand (Nakamura and Csikszentmihalyi 2002). This early work inspired Csikszentmihalyi's later work on what became known as flow, or autotelic experience. In his 1975 book, flow had been documented in a wide range of populations from chess players and rock climbers to dancers and surgeons. By 2011, flow has arguably become one of the most frequently studied positive psychology topics. An exploratory online search of the psychINFO database in August 2011 yielded approximately 1,230 publications on the topic "flow" by various researchers since 1975 (the search excluded the use of the term "flow" for nonrelated work, such as blood flow, cash flow, electron flow, expiratory flow, glottal flow, optic flow, laminar flow, salivary flow, traffic flow, and other irrelevant concepts).

Of course, prior to Csikszentmihalyi, other scholars researched related topics. Partly as a reaction to the deterministic nature of both Freudian and behaviorist thought in the midtwentieth century, humanistic psychologists such as Abraham Maslow and Carl Rogers developed ideas of self-determination and free will and created theories which focused on optimistic aspects of human nature which were much less evident in the work of Skinner or Freud. Rogers was a founding member of the human development program at the University of Chicago and was a faculty member there from 1945 to 1957, the same program in which Csikszentmihalyi received his BA in 1960 and his PhD in 1965, and served for many years on the faculty. Maslow had placed at least one former student on the human development faculty as well, so the influence of these humanistic psychologists was certainly part of the *zeitgeist*.

Maslow (1964) is perhaps best known for his concept of peak experiences, which are mystical or transcendent experiences linked to awe and wonder. These experiences, like flow, often involve experiencing a sense of altered time and a loss of self-consciousness. Maslow's theory of motivation (1943) with its hierarchy of human needs is also well-known, and argues that basic physiological needs such as hunger and thirst must be met before a person may meet needs higher on his pyramid, such as cognitive needs or self-actualization (theorized to be at the pinnacle of the hierarchy). Self-actualization describes the healthy psychological growth associated with movement toward reaching one's full potential. Maslow theorized that self-actualized people tend to have more frequent peak experiences than other people. In a similar way, Csikszentmihalyi theorizes that people who engage in frequent flow in productive activities will become increasingly complex in their development, an idea he expands to book length in *The Evolving Self* (1993). At any rate, Csikszentmihalyi himself (2000a, p. 381) acknowledges the influence of the humanistic psychologists, and writes that flow "includes so-called peak experiences first identified by Abraham Maslow (1965), although it does not necessarily have the intensity of the latter. Flow also overlaps with the concept of intrinsic motivation developed by Deci and Ryan (1985)." Like Maslow, the work of Rogers seems to have a bearing on the work of Csikszentmihalyi. For instance, Rogers (1961, 1980) developed the concepts of the "fully functioning person" and "the person of tomorrow" that seem to relate to Csikszentmihalyi's (1990) concept of "the autotelic personality". Furthermore, Rogers was a pioneer in applying sophisticated research methods to the problem of evaluating subjective experience. In Roger's methods, phonographic recordings and transcriptions as well as Q-sorts and other analyses were conducted in order to be as objective as possible about the subjective experience of being a client in psychotherapy. For Csikszentmihalyi (e.g., Csikszentmihalyi and Larson 1984), the spirit of being as objective as possible about subjective experience seems best illustrated by his development of the ESM, a technique that yields ample quantitative self-report data about real world phenomenological experience.

Even prior to the humanistic psychologists, however, scholars have demonstrated an interest in concepts related to flow. Dormashev (2010) writes that "in the twentieth century, autotelic activities were observed and described in detail by many prominent developmental psychologists, including Maria Montessori, Karl Buhler, and Jean

Piaget" (p. 306). One may certainly add William James (1902) to the list, because he describes numerous examples of what could be described as flow experiences as Rich (2004) amply demonstrates. If one looks at the history of certain components of flow such as attention, one may look back even further, for instance, to another work by William James (1890) and to a work by Henri Ribot (1890). Since many scholars date the birth of psychology to one of the first psychology laboratories (Wilhelm Wundt in the 1870s) or to one of the first textbooks in psychology (William James in 1890), it is clear that concepts important to, and related to flow have a long history in the field.

If one expands one's view and looks beyond the academic field of psychology, a number of descriptions of activities and people that seem to fit the flow experience may be found. For instance, Isabella Csikszentmihalyi (1988) has documented flow in a historical context, in her intriguing examination of the case of the Jesuit order of the Roman Catholic Church. Founded in 1540, the order became attractive to many men in the second half of the sixteenth century, partly because the Jesuit rules offered an optimal set of conditions that led many men to experience flow more frequently by following this challenging yet unifying life plan. Csikszentmihalyi himself (1990) notes how centuries-old Eastern traditions such as meditation can lead to the development of states of effortless attention and flow, resulting in cognitive and affective enhancements, as well as the creation of a person of greater complexity and maturity. Thus, to summarize, it is safe to say that though the formal study of flow per se dates to Csikszentmihalyi's own work beginning in the latter half of the twentieth century, related concepts have a long history in psychology and an even longer history outside of it.

The Flow Experience and Its Implications for Various Populations

The flow experience has been documented in a wide range of populations. As early as 1975, Csikszentmihalyi was able to examine its existence in groups ranging from surgeons, chess masters, and composers to rock climbers, dancers, and basketball players. These initial studies often employed smaller samples, perhaps because of the relatively time-intensive labor involved in conducting interviews as opposed to distributing surveys. For instance, Csikszentmihalyi (1975) interviewed 30 rock climbers/mountaineers, 21 surgeons, and 12 dancers. Subsequently, ample research has documented the flow experience in both talented teenagers and more typical youth and young adults in both academic and leisure activities. These studies, utilizing larger research teams, have involved ESM survey data and interviews totaling thousands of adolescents (e.g., Csikszentmihalyi et al. 1993; Csikszentmihalyi and Schneider 2000). Students who experience flow while being engaged in their talent area or in productive academic activities are apt to continue the activity in the future, thus leading to the development of greater skill complexity. Young people who do not experience flow in such activities are likely to abandon the activity as soon as they are able (such as ending math and science education when it is no longer required).

Activities that are perceived to be like both, work and play simultaneously are especially likely to be enjoyable and flow-like (Schmidt and Rich 2000). If the activity relates to a young person's future, the person is fortunate indeed, as the nature of such experiences is that one wishes to repeat them. As the old musicians' joke goes, when the young musician arrives in the big city asking for the way to get to Carnegie Hall, the taxicab driver's reply is simply one word: practice. The odds of reaching one's dream if practice is fun and flow-like are greatly improved, whether the task be persisting through completion of a PhD dissertation, achieving one's personal best time in an athletic event, or making a classical piano performance debut at a major venue.

Although flow may occur in virtually any activity, some activities seem especially conducive to the experience. For instance, many games (e.g., Csikszentmihalyi 1975) and sports (e.g., Jackson and Csikszentmihalyi 1999) are structured in such a way that there are clear goals and immediate performance feedback, which are conditions for flow. Music is also often a flow experience, as musicians can typically select pieces to optimize a match between their skills and the challenge of performing (e.g., Csikszentmihalyi and Rich 1997). Other activities may elicit boredom or apathy from most people, but may be associated with flow in others. A child learning to fold clothes, a teenager driving a car, or a mentally challenged person operating a cash register may experience flow, as challenges and skills are appropriately in sync. Even television, which is often cited as an activity that is not often associated with flow (Csikszentmihalyi and Kubey 1990), has at least one advocate. Steven Pritzker (2007), perhaps reacting from his own work as a writer for the Mary Tyler Moore show, uses personal anecdotes and a highly select literature review to argue that, at times, television can produce flow, as when educational programming challenges the skills of its viewers, or when a viewer becomes actively engaged in a well-written drama.

It is important to remember that flow is essentially an amoral psychological state. A person may find flow in volunteering at a soup kitchen or, as assessed by analyzing published accounts by veterans, in combat in the military (see, Harari 2008, on combat flow, and the ethical dimensions of subjective well-being in war). Examples of flow in activities that may be illegal or morally questionable include studies of Japanese youth in motorcycle gangs (Csikszentmihalyi and Csikszentmihalyi 1988), cannabis users (Hathaway and Sharpley 2010), exotic dancers in a strip bar (Barton and Hardesty 2010), and speeding motorists (Chen and Chen 2011). Although some of these studies rely on smaller samples (e.g., 30 interviews and surveys of motorcycle gang members or seven interviews with exotic dancers), taken as a whole, these data converge to indicate that a preponderance of the evidence supports the existence of this type of flow experience. Flow researchers and positive psychologists make important distinctions between activities which are merely pleasurable and those which are meaningful and may be part of the good life. These researchers often single out activities such as drug and alcohol use as examples of behavior that may offer simple pleasures in the short run, but over time become experientially stale, meaningless, and may lead to dire psychological and physical consequences (e.g., Csikszentmihalyi, 1990; Seligman 2011). Even activities which may be productive (such as computer use) or fun (big wave surfing) can become addictive and destructive if one becomes dependent on such activities. Several recent studies have examined the possible role of flow in exercise dependence in surfers (using 15 interviews) (Partington et al. 2009) and in problematic internet use (utilizing a survey of 1,399 users) (Thatcher et al. 2008). Parents, teachers, mentors, and societies thus ought to encourage careful selection of flow activities that are both ethical and productive. For instance, a parent may arrange for music lessons for a child that demonstrates an interest in the family's living room piano. A teacher may encourage a bored, apathetic youth to join an extracurricular group such as the chess club, or to train with a sports team. A professional mentor can steer a junior colleague to meaningful, engaging projects, providing flow-conducive goals and timely feedback. Societies can offer citizens a range of affordable, accessible options for flow in activities such as volunteer service or a midnight basketball league for community youth. Such actions may be steps to a positive psychology not only for individuals, but also for families, communities, and societies.

Cross-Cultural Research

Much of the research in psychology has been criticized for its lack of diversity. Samples, often for the sake of convenience, tend to be white Christian college students, typically young adults from the United States. Researchers themselves have also tended toward the white Christian demographic. In fact, some authors have commented that in the history of psychology, "even the lab rats were white" (Guthrie 2003).

Research on flow has been substantially more diverse in comparison. One reason may be that Csikszentmihalyi himself is multicultural and multilingual, having grown up in Hungary and Italy. This background facilitated numerous cross-national collaborations. Another reason may be that Csikszentmihalyi spent the majority of his career at the University of Chicago, where he was based in the committee on comparative human development, a program dedicated to cultural psychology and cofounded by anthropologists and psychologists. Many international doctoral students were attracted to the program and continued to write about flow professionally on their return from fieldwork or to their nations of origin. This relative abundance of international research made it possible for Csikszentmihalyi (2000b) to write that "the experience of enjoyment is described essentially in the same terms by Thai villagers, by farmers in Somalia, by Navajo shepherds, and by industrial workers in Japan, Europe, and the United States" (p. 389). Historically, across the centuries, philosophers and thinkers from a variety of belief systems and faith traditions (both Western and Eastern) have documented flow-like experiences and have theorized about the best path to happiness, and to the good life (e.g., McMahon 2006). Using modern social science methods, even earlier, flow was examined cross-culturally in groups including Japanese motorcycle gangs, Italian students, and elderly Korean immigrants (e.g., Csikszentmihalyi and Csikszentmihalyi 1988). More recent research has documented flow through statistical analysis of white-water rafting experiences in Taiwan (Wu and Liang 2011), questionnaires of 398 talented Dutch soccer players (Bakker et al. 2011), and 114 surveys of female Canadian ice hockey players (Lazarovitz 2004). Though a helpful special issue of the *Journal of Happiness Studies* was devoted to the subject of flow and its significance cross-culturally (Moneta 2004), there is ample room for further exploration that goes beyond merely documenting the existence of flow cross-nationally and cross-culturally. For instance, though the articles in the special issue do document flow in China, Italy, Japan, and the United States utilizing the ESM, research ought to more systematically examine cultural and national distinctions not only in the flow experience itself, but also in its antecedents and consequences. Moneta's own work with Hong Kong Chinese students reveals a "cultural moderation of the flow model that is partially explained by the internalization of collectivist values and self-perceptions" and the author suggests that these students may "seek a state of optimal functioning that differs from flow and is supported by Taoist and Confucianist principles prescribing prudence, attention to detail, ... and inter-connectedness with others" (p. 119). Indeed, Moneta finds that in contrast to other samples of students such as those from the majority culture in the United States, these students experience low challenge/high skill conditions as a "productive, mastery-practice orientation" (p. 119). Work such as Moneta's and work that examines differences among ethnic groups in the United States (e.g., Schmidt and Rich 2000) is much needed. Clearly, conditions that may promote flow may vary depending on sociocultural belief systems, a topic worthy of investigation because flow's implications for a life worth living are evident.

To sum up, future research ought to examine not only cross-cultural and cross-national similarities in the flow experience, but also explore possible differences. Utilizing interviews (both unstructured and semistructured) as opposed to fixed-response questionnaires may help illuminate aspects of the experiences of flow, enjoyment, and effortless attention that may vary cross-culturally. Research on related concepts such as happiness, subjective well-being, and life satisfaction (e.g., Cahn and Vitrano 2008; Diener 2009) has found both, similarities and differences cross-culturally and cross-nationally, and it seems likely that focused efforts on flow may uncover interesting and important subtleties in the experience if researchers turn their attention now to potential differences. In-depth qualitative fieldwork and ethnography (such as that conducted by anthropologists) will likely be a vital part of such work, and some such research on well-being which is relevant to flow has already been published (e.g., Mathews and Izquierdo 2009). Far from merely being ground work for future quantitative work, these studies of happiness and well-being in the Peruvian Amazon, among a group of Australian Aborigines, a group of the Cree, in a rural Indonesian village, and in China and Japan may lead researchers to expand and modify their understanding of the flow experience. Further research on cultural and national differences may also require the systematic coordination of multiple research teams internationally, to best design research that allows for meaningful quantitative comparisons, a task which requires considerable skill, time, and expense, but which is likely to yield valuable results.

Evidence from Neuroscience and Physiological Research

Although most research on flow has utilized self-reports, either via semistructured interviews or through questionnaire responses from the ESM, some scholars have investigated possible neurological and physiological correlates to the flow experience that may illuminate any underlying biological mechanisms involved. Of course, like all mental experiences, flow must have biological underpinnings. However, the flow state is not a business-as-usual state of mind, and perhaps its neuroscience may be likewise atypical. Although the search has generated considerable excitement, scholars are aware (or should be aware) that care must be taken to avoid oversimplification to the type of neophrenology that attempts to link one part of the brain in a facile manner to one experience. Previous scholars' attempts to find neurological correlates to peak religious and mystical experience have sometimes been criticized for their overly reductionistic points of view (e.g., Newberg and d'Aquili (2001). "Extraordinary claims require extraordinary evidence," the late Carl Sagan (1980) was fond of saying. Unfortunately, many studies of altered states of consciousness, particularly early ones, lacked such evidence (see Farthing 1996 for a review). A further difficulty is that the flow experience is rare, and thus typically not seen in the laboratory. Attempting to induce at least mild forms of it may be possible, but the technical gadgetry and apparatuses essential to modern neuroscience may also be likely to distract self-conscious research participants from entering a flow state in the lab.

However, in the last decade or so, promising research on the neurological correlates of the flow experience has been published by Arne Dietrich (2004) and De Manzano et al. (2010). Dietrich (2004) argues that flow is a state during which a "highly practiced skill that is represented in the implicit system's knowledge base is implemented without reference from the explicit system" (p. 746). In terms of information processing, the explicit system is conscious, and may be expressed verbally, while the implicit system is skill/experience based, and not conscious and verbalizable (p. 749). The author argues that as a prerequisite for flow, the brain must be in a state of temporary hypofrontality, which allows transient suppression of the "analytical and meta-conscious capacities of the explicit system" (p. 746). Indeed, the author notes that many people who report flow or effortless attention report automatic processing during the experience during complex tasks such as playing chess, and perceive that they are functioning without conscious thinking. This suggests that "the prefrontal cortex is not required for the successful execution of these tasks" (p. 749). Dietrich notes neuroimaging studies that indicate, acquiring a skill activates the prefrontal cortex and the premotor cortex, but practicing a skill can lead to a shift neurologically, so that a motor task becomes controlled eventually by the basal ganglia, thalamus, and hippocampus (p. 753). Dietrich notes that many times people "cannot explain why we do what we do," (p. 754), especially with motor activities, as with people unable to explain how they solved the famous Tower of Hanoi task, or how they successfully played a fiendishly difficult piano piece, or won a downhill ski race.

Dietrich offers a number of insights that seem helpful in understanding flow and related concepts such as effortless attention. However, sometimes the work does seem to reduce the complexity of the full flow experience to a point where, as he explains, it may no longer be flow. For instance, in explaining the cognitions behind free-jazz improvisation, he writes that "the musician arranges units into a flowing string... it is the number of distinct reflexive loops as well as their automatization that determines the quality of the flow experience" (p. 756). However, interviews with jazz musicians seem to indicate otherwise (e.g., Csikszentmihalyi and Rich 1997). A performance that seemed completely routinized and automatic would probably lead to boredom, not flow, as the performer's skill level would exceed the challenge of creating automized loops. At the very least, it seems that there is considerable interplay between the implicit and explicit systems, as for instance, a performer thinks about (perhaps even visualizes) the solo he or she will play at the upcoming chorus. Of course while playing a passage, the process may be largely dependent on implicit memory.

At any rate, Dietrich has provided a great service to flow research by documenting how at least certain aspects of flow may be represented by the brain. For instance, the disappearance of self-consciousness, the altered sense of time, and the sense that there is no worry of failure and no distractions are all elements of flow that Dietrich reports as being consistent with hypofrontality. In particular, he notably argues that self-consciousness is a high-order mental representation that disappears early in the flow experience, since "there are simply not enough resources left to compute this highly sophisticated feature of consciousness" (p. 758).

In addition to Dietrich's work, another research group has explored the biological psychology of the flow experience. De Manzano et al. (2010) utilized a sample of 21 professional classical pianists who played a self-selected piece five times to create variations in the flow experience. The task was an appropriate one, since previous interview data indicate that music performance is often linked with flow (e.g., Csikszentmihalyi and Rich 1997). Arterial pulse pressure waveform, respiration, head movements, and activities from the corrugator supercilii and zygomaticus major facial muscles were recorded. The researchers found significant relationships between the flow experience and blood pressure, heart rate variability, respiratory depth, heart period, and zygomaticus major muscle activity. These researchers also determined that although focused but effortless attention may seem to be a contradiction, tasks with great attentional loads may seem less effortful under a state of positive mood. They also note the fact established by research that "mental and emotional activity can alter function within the autonomic nervous system" (p. 302).

Both Dietrich and de Manzano and colleagues agree that flow may be considered a type of effortless attention and that the flow experience has a number of biological correlates. Based largely on interpreting existing research, Dietrich focused upon the role that transient hypofrontality may play in the flow experience, while de Manzano and colleagues found evidence of the fact that the EMG, cardiovascular, and respiratory measures were significantly associated with the flow experience. They argue that their findings suggest that "increased activation of the sympathetic branch of the autonomic nervous system (ANS) in combination with deep breathing and activation of the zygomaticus muscle might potentially be used as an indicator of effortless attention and flow" (p. 306).

Future research ought to seek to replicate Dietrich's work with evidence from experimentally induced flow experiences. In addition, further research should examine the role that the developing, aging brain may play in the flow experience. For instance, what are the implications for flow and attentional control that the adolescent brain is not fully developed until one's late teens and twenties? How may various dementias and conditions such as Alzheimer's disease and Parkinson's disease impact an older person's ability to experience flow (Papalia et al. 2009)? Noninvasive positive emission tomography may detect the neurofibrillary tangles and amyloid plaques in patients with Alzheimer's, and shrinkage of the hippocampus and amygdala may predict the disease. Although one suspects that changes in emotion, attention, and memory will alter the flow experience, research should be conducted to see more precisely how the flow experience is impacted by such changes. Likewise, the pruning of dendritic connections that are unused is a process that begins in the rear part of the brain, but does not reach the frontal lobes by adolescence. Although it is theorized that such changes impact the flow experience by influencing self-control, judgment, and planned behavior, researchers should examine this with evidence from neuroscience and longitudinal data. In addition, as researchers begin to find evidence for the biological mechanisms behind flow, they ought to consider the health implications of the flow experience as well, especially as health psychologists have conducted research that indicates a link between mood states and immune function, as well as enhanced self-efficacy with respect to health-promoting behaviors (e.g., Taylor 2011). Finally, researchers should expand their work to include other samples of research participants and other tasks. Although music cognition and performance is often linked to flow, one wonders how the neuroscience and biology of flow may differ in other motor tasks (such as athletics) and in nonmotor tasks (such as meditation, reading, life-review, or spiritual experience).

Methods

A variety of methods have been utilized to explore the flow experience, including interviews, questionnaires, a technique known as the ESM, and several biopsychological measures. This section of the chapter explores the strengths and weaknesses of these methods as applied to the flow experience. As this section demonstrates, there have been remarkable advances in the psychological study of the phenomenology of consciousness since the early days of psychological history in the nineteenth century, when structuralists such as Wilhelm Wundt and techniques such as introspection reigned (e.g., Shiraev 2011; Wundt 1873/1904).

The earliest work on flow utilized interviews to probe participants' experiences when given activities were going well (Csikszentmihalyi 1975). A variety of semistructured interviews have been utilized, tailored to various populations such as adolescents (Csikszentmihalyi and Schneider 2000) and eminent, highly creative older adults (e.g., Csikszentmihalyi 1996; Csikszentmihalyi and Rich 1997). These interviews have been as brief as half an hour to about an hour with the adolescents, to over an hour to several hours in the case of the creative older adults. The full semistructured interview protocol utilized in the Creativity in Later Life study of 91 creative adults over 60 years of age is published as an appendix (Csikszentmihalyi 1996) and gives a sense of what types of questions have been utilized to tap into the flow experience in this sample of eminent elders, which includes Nobel laureates and Pulitzer Prize winners. Among other things, questions ask participants to describe the project of which they have been most proud, how they became interested in their subject area, what has kept them involved for so long, when and why they have been more or less interested in their work, the tasks/challenges that they see as most important to them, the role of responsibility vs. enjoyment in the tasks to which they attend, and what determines what new projects they select once one has been completed.

Strengths of the interview approach include the opportunity to gain an insider's account of the flow experience, including potential dimensions of the experience that may be missed by fixed-question protocol questionnaires. In addition, interviews are valuable because the flow experience may be rare, and experimental induction in the lab may not be feasible for many types of flow activities. Potential weaknesses of the interview approach include memory lapses on the part of research participants for flow experiences that occurred in the past, or possible intentional deception or response bias by participants if their flow experiences occurred, for instance, during illegal or morally questionable activities, such as illicit drug use, gambling, or gang-banging. Furthermore, there could possibly be social desirability bias, as participants seek to please researchers with responses they believe the researchers wish to hear. However, it is worth noting that researchers outside of Csikszentmihalyi's University of Chicago and Claremont Graduate University labs have utilized the interview method to document the flow experience (e.g., Perry 1999). Although some psychologists are skeptical about qualitative interview work, the following quote from a review of Csikszentmihalyi's *Creativity* (1996) book is a valuable reminder of the merit of such work. Colin Martindale (1996), past-president of the *International Association for Empirical Aesthetics* and well-known for his quantitative approach, writes that "When first looking into [it], I was prepared to dislike it. There are no tables [or] statistics... I thus inferred that I was confronted with a tender-minded, qualitative book from which I would learn little. However, I was pleasantly surprised that I learned a lot from the book." Qualitative interviews, especially when documenting experiential states such as flow, have a place even in the high-technology modern era of experiments, statistical analysis, and brain science. There will always be a role for self-reports: imagine how preposterous a psychologist responding to a client or research participant would sound by saying "You may be feeling miserable, but on the basis of this physiological data, we tell you that you are in fact happy" (Davidson 2005, cited in Harari 2008, p. 258).

Of course, questionnaires have also been utilized to assess the flow experience. The Flow Questionnaire (Csikszentmihalyi and Csikszentmihalyi 1988) was based on the early interviews on flow activities (Csikszentmihalyi 1975). More recently,

Susan Jackson and colleagues (e.g., Jackson and Marsh 1999; Jackson et al. 2008) have investigated the construct validity of both long (36 item) and short (9 item) form flow scales from state and dispositional perspectives, finding with several exceptions, that both scales displayed acceptable psychometric properties.

Over the past several years, admirable attempts have been made to develop nonEnglish language versions of questionnaires that measure flow. Research has demonstrated satisfactory validity and internal consistency for a Spanish version of the Flow State Scale (Calvo et al. 2008). Kawabata et al. (2008) found strong support for the reliability and validity of Japanese versions of the Flow State Scale-2 (JFSS-2) and the Dispositional Flow Scale-2 (JDFS-2) for assessing flow in physical activities in adults. An investigation of the French translation of the Flow State Scale-2 found that results of confirmatory factor analyses replicated the structure of the original FSS-2 and the authors argue that the study supports the invariance of the flow construct across the French and English languages (Fournier et al. 2007). Future research should explore the psychometric properties of these questionnaires for populations in other regions around the globe, and for activities that are nonphysical. Of course, questionnaires do suffer from a number of the same weaknesses as interviews. For instance, memory lapses and intentional deception may occur with this method as well. However, an advantage is that questionnaires may be completed off-site and do not require the intensive labor involved when an interviewer interviews and transcribes data. In addition, the nature of questionnaires allows for extremely helpful quantitative analyses, including large samples of participants and experiences.

Perhaps the greatest innovation in flow research was the development of the ESM in the late 1970s (Csikszentmihalyi and Larson 1987; Hektner et al. 2006). Research participants are equipped with some type of alarm pager (first pagers, then programmable watches, and now personal digital assistants and smart phones have been utilized) and signaled at preprogrammed times to complete a brief questionnaire about the moment at which they were paged. Participants are asked about their moods, motivations, and cognitions, as well as about the activity they were doing and their social and physical surroundings. Since, often, the pager device is programmed to beep half a dozen to a dozen times per day for 1–2 weeks, a rich collection of experienced life results, leading toward development of a systematic phenomenology of many aspects of life as lived in the real world beyond the psychologist's laboratory. The ESM has been utilized to assess the flow experience in a range of populations, including adolescents (Csikszentmihalyi and Larson 1984), young adults (Csikszentmihalyi and Schneider 2000), couples in close relationships (Graham 2008), television viewers (Csikszentmihalyi and Kubey 1990), and marathon runners (Schuler and Brunner 2009).

A major advantage of the ESM is the large volume of data that may be collected. Furthermore, the ESM allows for everyday events and experiences to be reported in a much more naturalistic setting than a laboratory experience permits, making possible a type of real-world ecological validity that is often impossible in an artificial university lab setting. In addition, in comparison with daily dairies of experience, which are often completed as global ratings once at the end of the day, the ESM may reduce retrospective bias, because in most such studies, participants must complete questionnaires in response to the page within 15 minutes, or the questionnaire becomes unavailable. Of course, the ESM may still be subject to many of the disadvantages present in other self-report measures such as single-administration questionnaires.

In contrast to the self-reports from interview, questionnaire, and ESM data, two other forms of data collection and research design have been employed to examine flow. First, working on the assumption that all mental experience, including flow, must be represented in the brain and physiology at some point, some researchers have investigated neurological and physiological correlates of the flow experience as described in more detail earlier. Although such methods have the obvious advantage of potentially documenting the biological reality of the psychologically experienced flow events, researchers are quick to point out some of the potential disadvantages or challenges of such methods. First, invasive equipment may disrupt the flow experience and thus some researchers have opted for a trade-off in selecting their physiological measures between instrument/measure sensitivity and practical requirements. Second, although such research is valuable, this lab science requires attempts to induce flow on demand, which can be difficult to do, and requires selecting a particular sample of research participants on a particular task such as piano performance, and generating results which may or may not generalize to other populations and tasks or even beyond the lab procedure (e.g., de Manzano et al. 2010).

Finally, recently there have been some successful attempts to induce flow in a laboratory setting. Moller et al. (2010) have induced flow in the lab utilizing video games, by altering the relative skill and challenge level. Researchers have manipulated variables such as skill level in the video game and the speed of a video game to assess participant flow, apathy, boredom, and anxiety. Although such manipulations are an important tool in the methodological arsenal of flow research, there are several potential disadvantages to such approaches. As the authors note, inducing flow in a lab may be like trying to get someone to relax in a dentist's chair (p. 192). Indeed, these authors have taken care to remove distractions in the lab, such as mirrors and cameras, which may increase self-consciousness and thus diminish flow. In addition, one wonders whether results will generalize beyond video games, beyond the particular games used in this procedure or even beyond the highly controlled lab setting.

In summary, multiple methods have been utilized to examine the flow experience, each with strengths and weaknesses. Of particular interest is the recent utilization of methods from physiology and neuroscience as well as the utilization of experimental induction in the lab. One useful strategy may be to employ multiple methods in a single research project. One such case was the use of both personal interviews and the ESM in assessing flow experiences in an examination of young adults' experiences in work and play (Schmidt and Rich 2000).

Applications, Future Directions, and Conclusion

Although there has been considerable work describing the flow experience in various populations, and recent work has investigated its possible biological substrates, less work has focused on the applications of the flow. In particular, further program evaluation style research is needed to examine how flow-inspired applications and interventions may (or may not) work in real-world settings. Csikszentmihalyi (2000b) argues that the two strategies to increase flow frequency and intensity are as follows: first, change external conditions to better resemble a game (ensure clear goals, offer constructive and timely feedback, work to develop tasks that offer an optimal balance of challenges and skills); second, change one's self and one's approach (for instance, carefully select projects that are just challenging enough, clarify one's own goals, and develop needed skills). However, though research has clearly demonstrated the value of vital engagement such as flow in activities like academic work, change may be difficult to implement. In a sample of several 100 high school students, researchers found that students spent about "one-third of their time passively attending to information transmitted to the entire class (i.e., listening to a lecture, watching television or a video)" (Shernoff et al. 2003, p. 171). Utilizing ESM data, these researchers also found that students felt most engaged in nonacademic subjects such as computer science, art, and vocational education as compared to academic subjects. Thus, although research may suggest ways to improve or enhance flow, practical considerations such as rules and pressures from administrators and assessors, need to teach certain subjects, fixed school-bell structure of class periods, design of available teaching materials, and teacher training may preclude easy solutions for the classroom.

Since about one fifth of the population reports never to have felt flow (and approximately equal numbers report it several times daily), it seems crucial to develop programs that will help people find productive activities which lead to flow for them (Csikszentmihalyi (2000b)). Though limited, recent work by Walker (2010) has utilized both a survey and experiments to test the hypothesis that flow in a group is more enjoyable than solitary flow. Results confirm that college student volunteers playing paddleball games experienced more joy playing with others than alone. Given the fact, indicated by previous ESM research, that for most people solitude is rarely experienced as positively as social experiences (Csikszentmihalyi and Csikszentmihalyi 1988), perhaps future research should investigate flow interventions that are group oriented. Of course, sometimes important work must be completed while alone (such as reading or practicing some musical instruments) and thus it is also important to examine other interventions that may help people find flow in such activities.

Exciting work has recently examined how flow may predict in-role and extra-role job performance, at least for conscientious employees, in a variety of positions from a range of small and large companies of various types, including an insurance company, a dentist's practice, and the finance department of a police office (Demerouti 2006). Further research ought to work toward experimental design that includes manipulation of flow conditions in real-world settings. For instance, an experimental group may be assigned a work task with clear goals, immediate feedback, and with challenges and requiring skills appropriate to the level of the employee's training. A comparison group could be offered a similar task but without clear goals, without constructive and timely feedback, and with challenges that significantly exceed an employee's level of training. Flow is important enough to positive psychology and to the good life to demand the best from its researchers.

Although flow is not without its critics (see responses to Csikszentmihalyi 1999, in *American Psychologist* 2000, pp. 1160–1163), extensive research by Csikszentmihalyi and others has confirmed its existence in a range of populations and with a variety of methods. Applications and interventions suitable for a range of populations from students and musicians to athletes and elderly hobbyists, may be within reach. Enhanced performance in a variety of domains has been documented with interviews, questionnaires, the ESM, and several experiments. The next stage of flow research should include further explorations of its underlying neurological and physiological mechanisms, increased experimental research, as well as designs and evaluations of specific real-world interventions and applications. Far from being immaterial to a positive psychology across the lifespan, evidence from self-reports to neuroscience indicates that when understanding lives worth living, flow matters.

References

Bakker, A. B., Oerlemans, W., Demerouti, E., Slot, B. B., & Ali, D. K. (2011). Flow and performance. *Psychology of Sport and Exercise, 12*(4), 442–450.

Barton, B., & Hardesty, C. L. (2010). Spirituality and stripping. *Symbolic Interaction, 33*(2), 280–296.

Cahn, S. M., & Vitrano, C. (Eds.). (2008). *Happiness: Classic and contemporary readings in philosophy*. New York: Oxford University Press.

Calvo, T. G., Castuera, R. J., Ruano, F. J., Vaillo, R. R., & Gimeno, E. C. (2008). Psychometric properties of the Spanish version of the flow state scale. *The Spanish Journal of Psychology, 11*(2), 660–669.

Chen, C., & Chen, C. (2011). Speeding for fun. *Accident Analysis and Prevention, 43*(3), 983–990.

Csikszentmihalyi, I. (1988). Flow in a historical context. In M. Csikszentmihalyi & I. Csikszentmihalyi (Eds.), *Optimal experience* (pp. 232–248). Cambridge: Cambridge University Press.

Csikszentmihalyi, M. (1975). *Beyond boredom and anxiety*. San Francisco: Jossey-Bass.

Csikszentmihalyi, M. (1990). *Flow: The psychology of optimal experience*. New York: Harper & Row.

Csikszentmihalyi, M. (1993). *The evolving self*. New York: Collins.

Csikszentmihalyi, M. (1996). *Creativity*. New York: Collins.

Csikszentmihalyi, M. (1999). If we are so rich, why aren't we happy? *American Psychologist, 54*(10), 821–827.

Csikszentmihalyi, M. (2000a). Flow. In A. E. Kazdin (Ed.), *Encyclopedia of Psychology* Vol. *3* (pp. 381–382). Washington DC: Oxford University Press.

Csikszentmihalyi, M. (2000b). The contribution of flow to positive psychology. In J. E. Gillham (Ed.), *The science of hope and optimism* (pp. 387–395). Philadelphia: Templeton Foundation Press.

Csikszentmihalyi, M., & Csikszentmihalyi, I. (1988). *Optimal experience*. Cambridge: Cambridge University Press.

Csikszentmihalyi, M., & Kubey, R. (1990). *Television and the quality of life*. Hillsdale: Lawrence Erlbaum.

Csikszentmihalyi, M., & Larson, R. (1984). *Being adolescent*. New York: Basic Books.

Csikszentmihalyi, M., & Larson, R. (1987). Validity and reliability of the experience sampling method. *Journal of Nervous and Mental Disease, 175,* 526–536.

Csikszentmihalyi, M., Rathunde, K., & Whalen, S. (1993). *Talented teenagers*. Cambridge: Cambridge University Press.

Csikszentmihalyi, M., & Rich, G. (1997). Musical improvisation: A systems view. In K. Sawyer (Ed.), *Creativity in performance* (pp. 43–66). Greenwich: Ablex.

Csikszentmihalyi, M., & Schneider, B. (Eds.). (2000). *Becoming Adult*. New York: Basic Books.

Davidson, R. J. (2005). Well-being and affective style. In F. A. Huppert, N. Baylis, & B. Keverne (Eds.), *The science of well-being* (pp. 107–140). Oxford: Oxford University Press.

Deci, E. L., & Ryan, M. (1985). *Intrinsic motivation and self-determination in human behavior*. New York: Plenum Press.

Demerouti, E. (2006). Job characteristics, flow, and performance. *Journal of Occupational Health Psychology, 11*(3), 266–280.

Diener, E. (2009). *Culture and well-being: The collected works of Ed Diener*. New York: Springer.

Dietrich, A. (2004). Neurocognitive mechanisms underlying the experience of flow. *Consciousness and Cognition, 13,* 746–761.

Dormasev, Y. (2010). Flow experience explained on the grounds of an activity approach to attention. In B. Bruya (Ed.). *Effortless attention: A new perspective in the cognitive science of attention and action*. (pp. 287–333). Cambridge: MIT Press.

Farthing, G. W. (1996). *Psychology of consciousness*. Upper Saddle River: Prentice Hall.

Fournier, J., Gaudreau, P., Demontrond-Behr, P., Visioli, J., Forest, J., & Jackson, S. (2007). French translation of the flow state scale-2. *Psychology of Sport and Exercise, 8*(6), 897–916.

Graham, J. M. (2008). Self-expansion and flow in couple's momentary experiences. *Journal of Personality and Social Psychology, 95*(3), 679–694.

Guthrie, R. V. (2003). *Even the rat was white: A historical view of psychology* (2nd ed.). Boston: Allyn and Bacon.

Harari, Y. N. (2008). Combat flow: Military, political, and ethical dimensions of subjective well-being in war. *Review of General Psychology, 12*(3), 253–264.

Hathaway, A. D., & Sharpley, J. (2010). The cannabis experience: An analysis of "flow." In D. Jacquette (Ed.), *Cannabis* (pp. 50–61). Malden: Wiley.

Hektner, J. M., Schmidt, J. A., & Csikszentmihalyi, M. (Eds.). (2006). *Experience sampling method: Measuring the quality of everyday life*. Thousand Oaks: Sage.

Jackson, S., & Csikszentmihalyi, M. (1999). *Flow in sports*. Champaign: Human Kinetics.

Jackson, S. A., Martin, A. J., & Eklund, R. C. (2008). Long and short measures of flow. *Journal of Sport and Exercise Psychology, 30*(5), 561–587.

Jackson, M., & Marsh, S. A. (1999). Flow experience in sport. *Structural Equation Modeling, 6*(4), 343–371.

James, W. (1890). *The principles of psychology*. New York: Holt.

James, W. (1902). *The varieties of religious experience*. New York: Modern Library.

Kawabata, M., Mallett, C. J., & Jackson, S. A. (2008). The flow state scale-2 and dispositional flow scale-2: Examination of factorial validity and reliability for Japanese adults. *Psychology of Sport and Exercise, 9*(4), 465–485.

Lazarovitz, S. M. (2004). Team and individual flow in female ice hockey players. Dissertation Abstracts International: Section B: Sciences and Engineering.

McMahon, D. M. (2006). *Happiness: A history*. New York: Grove Press.

De Manzano, O., Theorell, T., Harmat, L., & Ullen, F. (2010). The psychophysiology of flow during piano playing. *Emotion, 10*(3), 301–311.

Martindale, C. (1996). Fame, fun, and flow. PsycCRITIQUES. doi:10.1037/001866.

Maslow, A. (1943). A theory of human motivation. *Psychological Review, 50*(4), 370–396.

Maslow, A. (1964). Religion, values, and peak experiences. Columbus: The Ohio State University Press.

Maslow, A. (1965). Humanistic science and transcendent experience. *Journal of Humanistic Psychology, 5*, 219–227.

Mathews, G. & Izquierdo, C. (Eds.). (2009). *Pursuits of happiness: Well-being in anthropological perspective*. New York: Berghahn Books.

Moller, A. C., Meier, B. P., & Wall, R. D. (2010). Developing an experimental induction of flow. In B. Bruya (Ed.), *Effortless attention* (pp. 191–204). Cambridge: MIT Press.

Moneta, G. B. (2004). The Flow experience across cultures. *Journal of Happiness Studies, 5*, 115–121.
Nakamura, J., & Csikszentmihalyi, M. (2002). The concept of flow. In C.R. Snyder and S.J. Lopez (Eds.), *Handbook of positive psychology* (pp. 89–105). New York: Cambridge University Press.
Newberg, A. & d'Aquili, E. (2001). *Why God won't go away: Brain science and the biology of belief*. New York: Ballantine Books.
Papalia, D. E., Olds, S. W., & Feldman, R. D. (2009). *Human development* (11th ed.). Boston: McGraw Hill.
Partington, S., Partington, E., & Olivier, S. (2009). The dark side of flow. *The Sport Psychologist, 23*(2), 170–185.
Perry, S. (1999). *Writing in flow*. Cincinnati: Writer's Digest Books.
Pritzker, S. R. (2007). Audience flow. In R. Richards (Ed.). *Everyday creativity and new views of human nature* (pp. 109–229). Washington DC: American Psychological Association.
Ribot, T. A. (1890). *The psychology of attention*. Chicago: Open Court.
Rich, G. (2004). William James and the varieties of optimal states of consciousness. *Streams of William James, 6*(2), 22–27 (Summer 2004).
Rogers, C. (1961). *On becoming a person*. London: Constable.
Rogers, C. (1980). *A way of being*. Boston: Houghton Mifflin.
Sagan, C. (1980). *Cosmos*. New York: Random House.
Schuller, J., & Brunner, S. (2009). The rewarding effect of flow experience on performance in a marathon race. *Psychology of Sport and Exercise, 10*(1), 168–174.
Schmidt, J. & Rich, G. (2000). Images of work and play. In Csikszentmihalyi, M., & Schneider, B. *Becoming Adult: How teenagers prepare for the world of work* (pp. 67–94). New York: Basic Books.
Seligman, M. E. P. (2002). *Authentic happiness*. New York: Free Press.
Seligman, M. E. P. (2011). *Flourish: A visionary new understanding of happiness and well-being*. New York: Free Press.
Seligman, M. E. P., & Csikszentmihalyi, M. (2000). Positive psychology: An introduction. *American Psychologist, 55*, 5–14.
Shernoff, D. J., Csikszentmihalyi, M., Schneider, B., & Shernoff, E. S. (2003). Student engagement in high school classrooms from the perspective of flow theory. *School Psychology Quarterly, 18*(2), 158–176.
Shiraev, E. (2011). *A history of psychology: A global perspective*. Los Angeles: Sage.
Taylor, S. E. (2011). *Health psychology* (8th ed.). Boston: McGraw Hill.
Thatcher, A., Wretschko, G., & Fridjhon, P. (2008). Online flow experiences, problematic internet use, and internet procrastination. *Computers in Human Behavior, 24*(5), 2236–2254.
Walker, C. J. (2010). Experiencing flow: Is doing it together better than doing it alone? *Journal of Positive Psychology, 5*(1), 3–11.
Wu, C. H., & Liang, R. (2011). The relationship between white-water rafting experience formation and customer reaction. *Tourism Management, 32*(2), 317–325.
Wundt, W. (1904). *Principles of physiological psychology*. (Trans: E. B. Titchener). New York: Macmillan (Original work published in 1873).

Chapter 5
Identity, Wisdom, and Critical Life Events in Younger Adulthood

Jeffrey Dean Webster

Hallmarks of positive psychology, including the motivation to reach beyond the status quo and strive for fulfillment have encouraged researchers to investigate higher-level human strengths and virtues. The search for a coherent sense of self and the pursuit of wisdom at both, the individual and societal level, are two such examples.

Younger adults today must make critical life choices about identity against a background which is potentially enabling and constricting at the same time. Myriad choices regarding leisure, education, career, lifestyle, spirituality, politics, and relationships in contemporary Western society provide many options for identity development; paradoxically, these seemingly innumerable opportunities can seem paralyzing (e.g., Schwartz 2004; Schwartz and Ward 2004). Moreover, given the rapid change in both geopolitical and sociocultural contexts, making relatively firm decisions regarding identity parameters is a complex and difficult process, partly due to the inherent uncertainty these choices entail.

The combination of overwhelming options in a dynamic social system is an excellent example of a situation which calls for wisdom (Kunzman and Baltes 2003; Webster 2010). Critical, in depth, and reflective analyses of fundamental ideological issues is a core component of both, identity (Berzonsky and Luyckx 2008; Erikson 1963; Marcia 1966) and wisdom (Ardelt 2003; Bluck and Gluck 2004; Clayton and Birren 1980; Kramer 1990, 2000; Webster 2003, 2007) development. Moreover, this type of evaluative processing often takes the form of a self-narrative (e.g., Habermas and Bluck 2000; McAdams 1993, 2003, 2006; McLean et al. 2007; Pals 2006)—a rich and powerful way of understanding ourselves and our world.

Although there are conceptual and theoretical links amongst these variables, little research on their interaction has been conducted. According to Beaumont (2009), research investigating the link between identity and wisdom "is almost nonexistent"; nor is there much empirical work investigating the link between wisdom and narrative (Bluck and Gluck 2004; Gluck et al. 2005). This study, to my knowledge, is one of

J. D. Webster (✉)
Psychology Department, Langara College, 100 West 49th Avenue,
Vancouver, BC, V5Y 2Z6, Canada
e-mail: jwebster@langara.bc.ca

J. D. Sinnott (ed.), *Positive Psychology*,
DOI 10.1007/978-1-4614-7282-7_5, © Springer Science+Business Media, LLC 2013

the first to examine the interrelationship among all three of these variables using a psychometrically sound measure of wisdom, in a methodological approach which combines quantitative and qualitative analyses.

I begin with a separate, brief discussion of identity, wisdom, and narrative. Subsequently, I briefly describe how these three domains are interrelated. Finally, I detail the specific hypotheses of this study.

Identity

Erikson (1963) postulated that the main psychosocial task of late adolescence was to establish a clearly articulated and coherent identity. Assimilating and consolidating values, aptitudes, roles, expectations, strengths, and limitations of previous psychosocial stage outcomes leads to identity achievement rather than role confusion. Marcia (1966) elaborated and extended Erikson's model by identifying two orthogonal dimensions, crisis and commitment, which when crossed, produced four identity statuses: identity achieved, moratorium, foreclosed, and identity diffusion. This typology was the dominant method of identity research for over three decades (Kroger 2000) with reviews of the area (e.g., Marcia et al. 1993) illustrating various strengths and limitations of each status (e.g., achieved status higher on measures of moral reasoning, intimacy, and achievement motivation; foreclosed low on anxiety but high on authoritarianism) as well as reporting evidence for a developmental progression from least to most mature status (i.e., diffusion to achieved), over time.

More recently, Berzonsky (1989, 2003, 2008); Berzonsky and Luyckx (2008) developed measures of identity processing styles rather than discrete identity statuses (or categories). Berzonsky (1990) defined identity as "a self-constructed cognitive representation of oneself that is used to interpret self-relevant information and to cope with personal problems and life events" (p. 156). His model consists of three social–cognitive identity styles, the informational, normative, and diffuse/avoidant, which have been differentially associated with several measures of psychosocial adjustment (Berzonsky and Kuk 2005).

The informational style involves an active search and critical evaluation of identity alternatives. These individuals process and analyze identity relevant information with the aim of eventually making firm commitments regarding fundamental identity components (e.g., sex roles, politics, and career). The informational style is consistent with the ego identity statuses of identity achieved and moratorium. Research indicates that the informational style is associated with higher levels of openness to experiences and need for cognition (Berzonsky and Sullivan 1992), transcendence and self-actualization (Beaumont 2009), future time perspective, (Luyckx et al. 2010), problem-focused coping and empathy (Soenens et al. 2005), and curiosity/exploration, proactive coping, and emotional intelligence (Seaton and Beaumont 2008).

The normative style also describes persons with strong commitments to fundamental ideological issues, but this decision closure does not follow from an active questioning, exploration, and analysis of identity alternatives. Rather, life choices are typically adopted wholesale from powerful figures (typically parents) in the adolescent's life. The normative style is consistent with Marcia's foreclosed ego identity status, and as such, has both positive and negative associated traits. In terms of the former, for instance, normative individuals typically have good relationships with parents and score low (relative to moratorium individuals) on measures of anxiety. In terms of the latter, however, normative individuals score lower, for example, on measures of empathy and openness, and higher on measures of prejudice and conservatism (Beaumont 2009; Berzonsky 1990; Soenens et al. 2005).

The diffuse-avoidant style is characteristic of persons for whom issues of identity are avoided and/or which produce feelings of confusion or anxiety. This identity style maps onto Marcia's identity diffused category. As such, individuals scoring high on the diffuse-avoidant style tend to lack introspection, conscientiousness, cognitive complexity, and emotional intelligence, and tend to be higher in neuroticism and the use of avoidant coping strategies, among other relatively negative attributes (e.g., Berzonsky et al. 2005; Seaton and Beaumont 2008).

Wisdom

Wisdom is an ancient and hallowed construct which is currently enjoying an empirical renaissance. Typically conceptualized as a cognitive–motivational–emotional capacity (e.g., Birren and Fisher 1990), wisdom is considered the acme of mature human engagement in the world, a means of pursuing a moral path to eudaimonia. Although there is no universal agreement concerning the definition of wisdom, there is a growing contemporary consensus of several of its key features, including emotional regulation, reflectiveness/introspection, openness, humor, and growth through challenging life experiences (Jeste et al. 2010).

Recent research stems from multiple perspectives (Staudinger and Gluck 2011) and employs different methods such as think aloud protocols (Baltes and Staudinger 2000), self-generated wisdom narratives (Bluck and Gluck 2004), and questionnaire measures (Ardelt 1997; Webster 2003, 2007). Converging evidence supports some assumptions about wisdom correlates (e.g., it is positively related to generativity, ego integrity, openness, empathy, and forgiveness, among others) as well as negates other assumptions (e.g., that wisdom is necessarily related to aging). Generally viewed as a positive capacity manifesting fully in older adulthood (e.g., Birren and Fisher 1990; Kramer 2000), recent indirect and direct empirical evidence suggest that vital qualities of emergent wisdom develop in late adolescence and early adulthood (e.g., Fry 1998; Pasupathi et al. 2001; Richardson and Pasupathi 2005; Webster 2010).

In terms of indirect evidence, cognitive abilities to reason dialectically (Kramer 2000; Labouvie-Vief 1990; Takahashi and Overton 2005), an appreciation of the complexity and reciprocity of family, peer, and social relationships (e.g., Damon 2000), and an increasingly sophisticated biographical understanding and narrative complexity (e.g., Habermas and Bluck 2000; Bluck and Gluck 2004; McLean 2005; McLean and Thorne 2003) all contribute to the late adolescent's capacity to nurture the seeds of wisdom. However, in terms of the latter, Richardson and Pasupathi

(2005) note that "Empirical work that directly addresses wisdom in adolescence is sparse" (p. 150). Some of the limited evidence is as discussed further.

Using the Berlin paradigm, Pasupathi, Staudinger, and Baltes (2001) showed that wisdom-related performance increased from adolescence through young adulthood, after which performance leveled out. Using participants' subjective definitions of wisdom (as assessed via remembered "wise" experiences), Bluck and Gluck (2004) found that though members from all three age groups (i.e., adolescents, young adults, older adults) were able to use experienced wisdom to transform autobiographical episodes from initially negative to positive outcomes, younger adults were more likely than adolescents or older adults to have learned valuable lessons about themselves. In a later study (Gluck et al. 2005), adolescents were shown to have a higher frequency of empathy/support forms of experienced wisdom relative to self-determination/assertion and knowledge/flexibility forms in comparison to middle-aged and older groups.

In summary, many of the putative building blocks of wisdom are developing during late adolescence and early adulthood. Certain thinking processes, ongoing emotional maturation, accumulating life experiences, and emerging biographic competencies provide opportunities for emerging adults to make sense of their lives and to discover meaning, direction, and purpose in their evolving life stories, as briefly detailed further.

Narrative

A substantial and growing body of work (e.g., Boyd 2009; Bruner 1986; Burnell et al. 2011; Freeman 1993, 2011; Fulford 1999; Jones 2010; Kenyon and Randall 1997; McAdams 1993, 2006; McLeod 1997; Ochs and Capps 2001; Randall and McKim 2008; Tedeschi and Calhoun 2004) supports the contention that the stories we construct and tell ourselves and others strongly influence myriad psychosocial outcomes. Among these possible outcomes, stories clarify goals, support existential pursuits such as the search for meaning, help identify and consolidate facets of self-knowledge into identity structures, overcome traumatic events, and enable the development of higher-level skills and virtues such as morality (e.g., Matsuba and Walker 2005) and wisdom (e.g., Mansfield et al. 2010; Randall 2011). As a natural and ubiquitous activity, therefore, narratives offer a window into the types of cognitive–emotional processes which accompany our attempts to define who we are as persons (i.e., identity) and to live a good life (i.e., wisdom).

Identity, Wisdom, and Narrative

According to McAdams (2008), the "formulation of a narrative identity is the central psychosocial challenge of emerging adults in modern societies" (p. 252). Such an enterprise places heavy cognitive, emotional, and motivational demands on late adolescents. Identifying and evaluating potential alternatives in work, relationships, and sociopolitical commitments, for instance, requires recursive analysis–synthesis cycles. Moreover, the emotional investment in trial roles, with their concomitant successes and failures can be taxing and stress-inducing. Consequently, motivational elements such as approach-avoidance conflicts, perseverance, and goal adjustment emerge as integral components of identity development. Successfully surmounting these intertwined cognitive, emotional, and motivational challenges presupposes a suite of correlated skills and personality attributes, among which may be "a general commitment to, or motivation to strive for, wisdom" (Richardson and Pasupathi 2005, p. 144).

In summary, the links between identity and wisdom are intuitive, conceptual, and theoretical. Specifically, Erikson claimed that the later phase of wisdom development is preceded by the earlier phase of identity exploration and commitment. Until very recently, however, this putative association has not been tested via direct, empirical assessment. Moreover, scholarship from a narrative approach to psychological investigation has clear links with both identity and wisdom; coherent stories about ourselves (identity) and our struggles to understand and improve our world (wisdom) evolve as we read and revise our autobiographies (Randall and Kenyon 2001; Randall and McKim 2008). This development is fostered by antecedent, concomitant, and consequent skills such as complex thinking skills and empathy. The current project assesses the theoretical link between identity and wisdom and examines the importance of cognitive (attributional complexity) and socioemotional (empathy) factors as predictors of wisdom, as well as how narratives of critical life events are associated with wisdom.

Given the discussed literature review, I hypothesized that the informational identity style would be positively correlated with wisdom, empathy, and attributional complexity; that the diffused identity style would be negatively correlated with wisdom, empathy, and attributional complexity; and that the normative identity style would be uncorrelated with wisdom, empathy, and attributional complexity. Finally, wisdom and the informational identity style would be positively correlated with the critical life narrative (CLN) scores whereas the normative identity and diffused identity scores would be uncorrelated and negatively correlated, respectively, with the CLN score. These hypotheses were initially tested with zero-order Pearson correlations and subsequently using multiple regression.

Methods

Participants

Participants included 112 women and 47 men ranging in age from 17 to 38 ($M_{age} = 20.42$, $SD = 3.62$). Participants had completed, on average, 14.01 years of total education ($SD = 1.80$) and rated their subjective health relative to persons their own age as healthy ($M = 5.03$, $SD = 1.05$) on a 7-point scale where *1 = poor* and *7 = excellent* health. Participants were primarily Caucasian (42 %) followed in descending order by Chinese (23.5 %), Indo-Canadian (8 %), Korean (2.5 %), and Japanese and African Canadian (both at 0.6 %). Finally, 22.2 % of participants rated themselves as "other". Participants were recruited from 1st and 2nd year psychology courses at a demographically diverse community college in Vancouver, Canada and were paid a $10.00 honorarium for participating.

Quantitative Measures

Identity

Identity was measured with the Identity Style Inventory, Revised (ISI3) by Berzonsky (1992). This is a 40-item inventory measuring three styles of identity processing orientation. The information style consists of 11 items (e.g., "I've spent a lot of time and talked to a lot of people trying to develop a set of values that make sense to me"); the normative style consists of 9 items (e.g., "I've more-or-less always operated according to the values with which I was brought up"); and the diffuse-avoidant style consists of 10 items (e.g., "It doesn't pay to worry about values in advance; I decide things as they happen"). An additional 10 item subscale measures commitment to identity but is not analyzed/discussed in the current study. Participants respond to all statements using a 5-point Likert scale ranging from 1 = *"not at all like me"*, to 5 = *"very much like me"*. After reverse scoring negatively worded items, total scores are composed by summing across items composing each subscale. Higher scores indicate higher levels of a particular identity processing style. Cronbach's alphas in the current study for the informational, normative, and diffuse-avoidant styles, respectively, were 0.714, 0.623, and 0.803.

Wisdom

Wisdom was measured with the Self-Assessed Wisdom Scale (SAWS; Webster 2003, 2007) a 40-item questionnaire reflecting the following five components of wisdom: Critical life experiences: "I have experienced many painful events in my life"; Reminiscence/reflectiveness: "Reviewing my past helps me gain perspective on current concerns"; Openness to experience: "I like to read books which challenge me to think differently about issues"; Emotional regulation: "I am very good about reading my emotional states"; and Humor : "Now I find that I can really appreciate life's little ironies". Participants respond to each question using a Likert type scale where 1 = "*strongly disagree*" to 6 = "*strongly agree*".

The SAWS has excellent reliability (i.e., test–retest and internal consistency) and various forms of validity. With respect to the latter, the SAWS predicts levels of foolishness (negatively), generativity, ego integrity (Webster 2007), adaptive leadership styles (e.g., Kristinsson 2005), positive psychosocial values such as personal growth and sense of coherence (Webster 2010), civic engagement and altruism (Bailey and Russell 2009), benefit finding in cancer patients (Costa and Pakenham 2011), forgiveness, psychological well-being, a lack of a socially desirable response style (e.g., Taylor et al. 2011), and mental health above and beyond personality traits (Webster et al. 2012). Cronbach's alpha for the current study is 0.869.

Empathy

Empathy was measured using the Interpersonal Reactivity Index (IRI; Davis 1983), which assesses four components of empathy including personal distress, fantasy, perspective taking, and empathic concern. The current study used only the latter two dimensions. Both empathic concern (e.g., "I often have tender, concerned feelings for people less fortunate than me") and perspective taking (e.g., " I sometimes find it difficult to see things from the 'other guy's' point of view") subscales consist of 7 items each measured on a Likert scale where *1 = "strongly disagree"* and *5 = "strongly agree"*. The empathic concern and perspective taking scales were combined with the possible total score ranging from 14 to 70. Cronbach's alpha for the current study for the IRI was 0.799.

Attributional Complexity

Attributional complexity, a measure of the attributional schemata that people use to explain human behavior, was assessed with the Attributional Complexity Scale (ACS; Fletcher et al. 1986). The scale measures seven attributional constructs: (1) a motivation component, (2) preference for complex rather than simple explanations, (3) metacognition concerning explanations, (4) awareness of the extent to which people's behavior is a function of interaction with others, (5) a tendency to infer abstract or causally complex internal attributions, (6) a tendency to infer abstract, contemporary, external causal attributions, and (7) a tendency to infer external causes operating from the past. A total of 14 items are reverse scored before summing across all items. Higher scores indicate higher levels of attributional complexity. Cronbach's alpha for the current study is 0.899.

Qualitative Measures

Critical Life Narrative

Participants provided a written narrative concerning a "critical life decision" defined as one which "had important consequences for yourself in terms of physical, emotional, or psychological health". Participants were requested to include information concerning the context, relationships, emotions, cognitions, and consequences of this critical life event. Stories were coded for insight (e.g., a person's understanding of the causes and consequences of the event, level of self responsibility, and psychological dynamics); sense of closure (i.e., evidence that the person has been able to assimilate the experience, grow from it, and move on in their life); and contextual complexity (i.e., an appreciation for the biopsychosocial constraints and opportunities within which the critical event unfolded) on a 5-point scale where 1 = *"little or no evidence"* of construct and 5 = *"very high level"* of construct. Similar types of thematic coding of narratives have been used in personality (e.g., McAdams 2006), developmental (e.g., McLean and Thorne 2003), and wisdom (e.g., Bluck and Gluck 2004) research.

The scores from insight, closure, and complexity were summed and then multiplied by an "intensity" factor. Intensity refers to the fact that some stories concerned relatively trivial decisions (e.g., pets) while others were more consequential (e.g., suicide attempts, abortion). Intensity was rated from low = 1 to high = 5. The total CLN score was thus the sum of the insight, closure, and complexity scores multiplied by the intensity factor. Scores could then theoretically range from 1 to 75. In the current study, actual scores ranged from 3 to 67.5 ($M = 28.15$, $SD = 11.36$). After training, a single coder rated all stories. Unfortunately, interrater reliability information is not available and results should therefore be treated with caution. Essentially, this aspect of the current project should be seen as pilot data, but given the importance of combining questionnaire measures of wisdom with performance measures as a validation method, it is considered important to investigate this issue at least in a preliminary and tentative way.

Results

As seen in Table 5.1, the predicted relationships for the informational and diffused identity styles, wisdom, empathy, and attributional complexity were all supported, as were all the predictions for the normative identity style with the single exception of attributional complexity in which higher normative identity scores were significantly associated with lower attributional complexity scores ($r = -0.239$, $p < 0.01$).

Based on this overall pattern of correlational findings, I conducted a multiple regression analysis in order to determine the unique predictive power of relevant variables. Specifically, the informational and diffused identity styles, empathy, attributional complexity, and the demographic variables of age and education level were selected to regress on wisdom. Due to the intercorrelation among these predictor variables, there was the possibility of multicollinearity, and hence diagnostic statistics of tolerance (a measure of variance in predictor that cannot be accounted for, by other predictors) and the variance inflation factor (VIF) were conducted. Both tests revealed values in the acceptable range and indicated that multicollinearity was unlikely to effect the reliability of the results. A further diagnostic test revealed the presence of a single outlier and hence, the regression was run with and without this

Table 5.1 Descriptive statistics and zero order correlations for demographic and main study variables

Number	Measure	M	SD	1	2	3	4	5	6	7	8	9	10	11
1	Sex			–	0.058	−0.036	0.216**	−0.063	0.018	0.046	0.048	−0.170*	−0.178*	−0.142
2	Age	20.42	3.62		–	0.567**	0.051	0.257**	0.095	−0.322**	−0.251**	0.222**	0.193*	0.268**
3	Educ	14.01	1.80			–	0.064	0.225**	0.160*	−0.055	−0.179*	0.099	0.185*	0.192*
4	Health	5.03	1.05				–	0.090	0.132	0.009	−0.164*	−0.001	0.002	0.055
5	SAWS	178.99	19.09					–	0.561**	−0.122	−0.217**	0.546**	0.455*	0.278
6	Inform	37.41	6.02						–	0.022	−0.237**	0.578**	0.454**	0.227**
7	Norm	26.9	5.02							–	−0.280**	−0.239**	−0.080	−0.097
8	Diff	27.34	6.78								–	−0.388**	−0.368**	−0.243**
9	Attrib	35.88	22.21									–	0.639**	0.326**
10	IRI	52.91	7.14										–	0.255**
11	Narr	28.15	11.36											–

Sex (Females 1; Males 2), *Educ* Years of education, *SAWS* the Self-Assessed Wisdom Scale, *Inform* Informational Identity Style, *Norm* Normative Identity Style, *Diff* Diffused Identity Style, *Attrib* Attributional Complexity Scale, *IRI* Interpersonal Reactivity Index, *Narr* Critical Life Event Narrative, *M* mean, *SD* standard deviation

N = 154–162 due to missing values

$^{*}p < 0.05$; $^{**}p < 0.01$

Table 5.2 Predictors of wisdom

Variable	*t*	*p*	B	SE	95 % CI	Beta
Constant	4.722	0.000	80.842	17.121	[46.998, 114.685]	
Informational style	4.576	0.000	1.147	0.251	[0.651, 1.642]	0.369
Diffused style	0.939	0.350	0.186	0.199	[−0.206, 0.579]	0.067
Attributional complexity	2.344	0.020	0.193	0.082	[0.030, 0.355]	0.222
Empathy	1.678	0.096	0.379	0.226	[−0.068, 0.826]	0.141
Age	1.839	0.068	0.756	0.411	[−0.057, 1.568]	0.146
Educ	0.611	0.542	0.506	0.827	[−1.129, 2.141]	0.048

B unstandardized coefficients, *SE* standard error, *Educ* total years of education

case. Results indicated that removal of the outlier had no effect on the results and therefore, the analysis reported further is based on the complete sample.

Overall, the regression model was significant, F (5, 148) = 21.92, $p < 0.000$. Collectively, the predictor variables accounted for over 40.0 % of the variance ($R^2 = 0.425$). Table 5.2 illustrates the unstandardized and standardized regression weights (β) associated with each predictor variable. As seen, the informational identity style is the strongest predictor of wisdom ($\beta = 0.369$; $t = 4.576$; $p < 0.000$) followed by attributional complexity ($\beta = 0.222$; $t = 2.344$; $p = 0.020$). None of the other variables were significant.

Finally, the qualitative narrative wisdom measure was correlated with main study variables in predicted ways. Again, due to the lack of interrater reliability for this measure, the results must be seen as tentative and treated with due caution. For this reason, I only report the bivariate correlations and do not include these values in any subsequent analyses.

Table 5.1 illustrates that the questionnaire measure of wisdom (i.e., the SAWS) is positively correlated with CLN measure ($r = 0.278$, $p < 0.01$). Further, for the rest of the main study variables, correlations follow the same pattern as the SAWS, the only difference being that the magnitude of the correlations is consistently less. Specifically, the CLN is positively correlated with the informational identity style, attributional complexity, and empathy; it is uncorrelated with the normative identity style and negatively correlated with the diffused identity style.

Finally, in terms of the demographic variables of sex and age, only the latter reached significance ($r = 0.257$, $p < 0.01$). This result is consistent with findings from Pasupathi, Staudinger, and Baltes (2001) using participants ranging in age from 14 to 37, who found an association between age and wisdom up to a point (approximately age 24) after which wisdom-related performance tended to plateau.

Discussion

The primary aim of the present study was to investigate the theoretical link between identity and wisdom, an association suggested several decades ago by Erikson (1963) but not directly and empirically investigated until very recently. Bivariate correlations were all (with one exception) consistent with predictions. Specifically, the informational identity style was positively correlated with wisdom suggesting that the types of cognitive-emotional processing capacities and behaviors associated with this identity style potentially serve as enabling conditions for wisdom. In contrast, less mature forms of identity processing involving lower empathy and openness, as well as higher prejudice and conservatism (i.e., normative identity style) and lower introspection, cognitive complexity, and use of avoidant coping strategies (i.e., diffuse identity style) are either unrelated or negatively related to wisdom. This pattern of findings maps onto recent results reported by Beaumont (2011). Using Ardelt's (2003) Three-Dimensional Wisdom Scale (3D-WS) measure of wisdom and the same identity styles questionnaire used in the present study, Beaumont found that the informational style was positively correlated, the normative style uncorrelated, and the diffused style negatively correlated with wisdom.

The current findings also augment earlier reports concerning various attributes of the three identity styles. For example, the informational, normative, and diffused identity styles are positively, uncorrelated, and negatively correlated, respectively, to empathy. This suggests that the personal struggle to evaluate options, make difficult life decisions, parse complex emotions, and overcome uncertainties about future life directions (informational style) increases one's sensitivities to others who must undergo similar trials. Consequently, empathic qualities are likely to emerge. In contrast, when such ideological struggles are not necessary (normative style) or avoided (diffuse style), an appreciation for the internal life of others is less likely to be shown.

Similarly, the informational, normative, and diffused identity styles are positively, negatively, and negatively correlated, respectively, to attributional complexity. Attributional complexity involves the recognition that the behaviors of self and others are multiply determined, and that many potential internal (e.g., traits, desires, competencies) and external (e.g., stress, environmental obstacles, social inequity) factors must be considered when making behavioral attributions. As predicted, the information style was positively, and the diffused style was negatively, correlated with attributional complexity. However, the correlation between attributional complexity and the normative style was predicted to be nonsignificant and this was not supported. Given that the normative style has both positive and negative aspects (see literature review already discussed) and that little prior research has investigated this link directly, it was difficult to make a directional hypothesis. One possible explanation for this unpredicted finding is that normative style individuals do not have to undergo the evaluative analysis and synthesis of identity components; this lack of experience with struggling to make internal identity attributions may contribute to their inability (or lack of motivation) to understand the complexities of others' motivations.

With respect to the associations among empathy, attributional complexity, and wisdom, all predictions were supported. Wisdom involves the ability to see beyond the surface, comprehend myriad, oftentimes competing motives, and understand the internal and external factors which drive persons to behave as they do (i.e., wise persons are attributionally complex). The positive association in this study between attributional complexity and wisdom ($r = 0.546$, $p < 0.01$) replicates earlier work using the same two measures (i.e., Webster 2010). Further, wisdom involves the emotional skill of "getting inside someone's head" and appreciating the rich intrapsychic life of others. Akin to Gardner's (1983) notion of interpersonal intelligence, wise persons have insight into the affective components and processes of people in general, as indicated by the association between empathy and wisdom ($r = 0.455$, $p < 0.01$) in the current study.

The already discussed correlational conclusions need to be tempered in light of the regression analysis. Of the variables meant to predict wisdom, only the informational identity style and attributional complexity achieved significance. This is not surprising given the relatively heavy cognitive emphasis of these two factors, a supposition supported by the strong bivariate association between these two variables ($r = 0.578$, $p < 0.01$).

In contrast, empathy did not contribute any additional unique variance although there was a trend in the correct direction ($\beta = 0.141$; $t = 1.678$; $p = 0.096$). This may be explained, partly by the high association between empathy and attributional complexity in this study ($r = 0.639$, $p < 0.01$). In addition to the emotional attunement aspect of the IRI (i.e., recognition of feelings and emotions in others), there is also a perspective taking element which is similar in function to attributional complexity. Hence, once the strong cognitive aspects of the informational style and attributional complexity accounted for much of the variance, there was little variance left to be accounted for by empathy.

Finally, the CLN findings provide some of the first direct evidence that the stories young adults tell about actual challenging life events (as opposed to hypothetical events as in the Berlin Wisdom paradigm) are correlated with a psychometrically sound wisdom questionnaire, indicating that wise persons tell "wise" stories. Persons higher on wisdom were more likely to describe highly stressful and/or traumatic experiences within a broader, complex context, search for life lessons learned and insights gained, and to achieve a sense of closure and move on in life.

For instance, some participants recognized highly destructive patterns of behavior and thinking which progressively spiraled out of control in terms of drug and alcohol addiction. One participant proactively, based on insight concerning her psychological state, set out on a conscious course of reflection, evaluation, planning, and action, which first removed her from damaging relationships and actions and eventually allowed her to reengage in healthy, meaningful, and nurturing relationships with her family. She developed many fundamental insights about herself, motivations, and life goals, recognizing, for instance that she became excessively angry when she drank, that her creative artistic abilities allowed her to convey her emotions in a healthy manner, and in order to change she must work through her fears and insecurities. She examined her destructive patterns and on a daily basis consciously reflected on her actions and words throughout the day in order to decide what she could do differently to correct them. This participant no longer surrenders to her fears and feelings of hopelessness and worthlessness. Instead, she currently expresses self-acceptance, even love, and recognizes her power to make healthy choices. These hard-won victories, poignant evidence of posttraumatic growth, illustrate the relationship between resilience and wisdom (e.g., Linley 2003).

These results are consistent with recent findings by Mansfield, McLean, and Lilgendahl (2010). One of the dimensions these researchers coded their narratives for, was growth, defined as experiences "... that enhance self-development and quality of one's life, by increasing clarity of identity, sense of purpose, self-efficacy, self-insight, meaningful connections with others, well-being, etc." (p. 256). As such, this measure and the current coding of the CLN share several commonalities. Mansfield et al. (2010) found that growth was positively correlated with wisdom ($r = 0.35$, $p < 0.01$) in their study but only for stories relating to transgressions, as opposed to traumas.

Limitations and Conclusion

The following limitations must be considered when drawing conclusions from the present study. First, although the link between identity and wisdom was strongly established, the correlational nature of the results precludes confirming the theoretical supposition that identity *precedes* wisdom development. It is possible that wisdom emerges before the Eriksonian stage of identity, and that wise individuals recognize the necessity, and have the skills for, developing a clearly articulated and coherent sense of self. A third, and more likely probability is that wisdom is a continuous, evolving process in which feedback from life experiences is synthesized in some dialectical fashion. Longitudinal studies are required to tease apart the temporal ambiguities inherent in the wisdom–identity relationship.

Second, although the target population of interest for this study was in fact younger adults, future studies should investigate similar issues using a greater range of ages. Erikson (1963) suggested that each psychosocial crisis can be seen in primitive forms before its critical time arrives and continues to influence development throughout life even as persons move on to higher-level stages of maturity. This means that although questions such as "Who am I" take center stage in adolescence, they continue to be of importance throughout life. Investigating identity and wisdom in middle and later adulthood, therefore, can provide some clarification about antecedents and sequalae for both these constructs.

Finally, as noted, lack of interrater reliability for the CLN is problematic. Some attenuation of this concern comes from the findings of Mansfield et al. (2010) reported earlier in the chapter, who were able to establish excellent interrater reliability for their measure of growth (i.e.,0.91). As their measure of growth shares several facets in common with the CLN, there is reason to be optimistic about the potential reliability of the CLN as well. Viewed with appropriate caution therefore, the link between critical life event narratives and wisdom point to promising new directions for research.

Answers to existential questions such as "Who am I?", and "How can I lead a 'good' life?" demand an active, persistent, and frequently taxing search for insight into identity and wisdom. These types of fundamental, ideological queries can be, and often are, framed within life stories. Writing, editing, and telling such stories allow us to see themes, motivations, and values in our evolving autobiographies which can help clarify who we are, and are becoming, as well as distilling personal insights which could contribute to wisdom development.

Perhaps achieving a consolidated sense of self enables one to develop wisdom; perhaps wise persons recognize the advantage of facing life's exigencies with a firm, hard-won sense of self. Which trait/process is antecedent and which consequent, is for future research to answer. For now, this project has illustrated in, at least, a preliminary way how identity, wisdom, and self narratives are interrelated. As such, it adds to the very limited information we have in what promises to be a very fruitful area within positive psychology.

Acknowledgements I wish to express my gratitude to Alyson Budd, Charlie Deng, and Madeline Gorman for data entry and narrative coding assistance. I also thank the Langara Research Committee for seed funding.

References

Ardelt, M. (1997). Wisdom and life satisfaction in old age. *Journal of Gerontology: Psychological Sciences, 52*(1), pp. 15–27.

Ardelt, M. (2003). Development and empirical assessment of a three-dimensional wisdom scale. *Research on Aging, 25*(3), 275–324.

Bailey, A., & Russell, K. C. (2009). Engaging youth through volunteer travel: In service of the common good. *Journal of Youth Development, 4,* 60–72.

Baltes, P. B., & Staudinger, U. M. (2000). Wisdom: A metaheuristic (pragmatic) to orchestrate mind and virtue towards excellence. *American Psychologist, 55,* 122–136.

Beaumont, S. L. (2009). Identity processing and personal wisdom: An information-oriented identity style predicts self-actualization and self-transcendence. *Identity: An International Journal of Theory and Research, 9,* 95–115.

Beaumont, S. L. (2011). Identity styles and wisdom during emerging adulthood: Relationships with mindfulness and savoring. *Identity: An International Journal of Theory and Research, 11,* 155–180.

Berzonsky, M. D. (1989). Identity style: Conceptualization and measurement. *Journal of Adolescent Research, 4,* 267–281.

Berzonsky, M. D. (1990). Self-construction over the life-span: A process perspective on identity formation. In G. J. Neimeyer & R. A. Neimeyer (Eds.), *Advances in personal construct psychology* (Vol. 1, pp. 155–186). Greenwich: JAI Press.

Berzonsky, M. D. (1992). Identity Style Inventory (ISI3): Revised version. Unpublished manuscript.

Berzonsky, M. D. (1993). Identity style, gender, and social-cognitive reasoning. *Journal of Adolescent Research, 8,* 289–296.

Berzonsky, M. D. (2003). Identity style and well-being: Does commitment matter? *Identity: An International Journal of Theory and Research, 3,* 131–142.

Berzonsky, M. D. (2008). Identity formation: The role of identity processing style and cognitive processes. *Personality and Individual Differences, 44,* 645–655.

Berzonsky, M. D., & Kuk, L. (2005). Identity style, psychosocial maturity, and academic performance. *Personality and Individual Differences, 39,* 235–247

Berzonsky, M. D., & Luyckz, K. (2008). Identity styles, self-reflective cognition, and identity processes: A study of adaptive and maladaptive dimensions of self-analysis. *Identity: An International Journal of Theory and Research, 8,* 205–219.

Berzonsky, M. D., & Sullivan, C. (1992). Social-cognitive aspects of identity style: Need for cognition, experiential openness, and introspection. *Journal of Adolescent Research, 7,* 140–155.

Birren, J. E., & Fisher, L. M. (1990). Conceptualizing wisdom: the primacy of affect-cognition relations. (pp. 317–332). In R. J. Sternberg (Ed.), *Wisdom: Its nature, origins, and development.* New York: Cambridge University Press.

Birren, J. E., & Svensson, C. M. (2005). Wisdom in history. (pp. 3–31). In R. J. Sternberg, & J. Jordan (Eds.), *A handbook of wisdom: Psychological perspectives.* New York: Cambridge University press.

Bluck, S., & Gluck, J. (2004). Making things better and learning a lesson: Experiencing wisdom across the lifespan. *Journal of Personality, 72,* 543–572.

Boyd, B. (2009). *On the origins of stories: Evolution, cognition, and fiction.* Massachusetts: Belknap Press.

Burnell, K., Coleman, P., & Hunt, N. (2011). Achieving narrative coherence following traumatic war experience: The role of social support. In G. Kenyon, E. Bohlmeijer, & W. L. Randall (Eds.), *Storying later life: Issues, investigations, and interventions in narrative gerontology* (pp. 195–212). Oxford: Oxford University Press.

Bruner, J. (1986). *Actual Minds, Possible Worlds.* Cambridge: Harvard University Press.

Clayton, V. P., & Birren, J. E. (1980). The development of wisdom across the life-span: A re-examination of an ancient topic. In P. B. Baltes & O. G. Brim, Jr (Eds.), *Life-span development and behavior* (pp. 103–135). New York: Academic Press.

Costa, R. V., & Pakenham, K. I. (2011). Associations between benefit finding and adjustment outcomes in thyroid cancer. Psycho-Oncology. doi:10.1002/pon.1960.

Damon, W. (2000). Setting the stage for the development of wisdom: Self-understanding and moral identity during adolescence. In W. S. Brown (Ed.), *Understanding wisdom: Sources, science, & society* (pp. 339–360). Philadelphia: Templeton Foundation Press.

Davis, M. H. (1983). Measuring individual differences in empathy: Evidence for a multidimensional approach. *Journal of Personality and Social Psychology, 44,* 113–126.

Erikson, E. H. (1963). *Childhood and society* (2nd edn). New York: Norton.

Fletcher, G. J. O., Danilovics, P., Fernandez, G., Peterson, D., & Reeder, G. D. (1986). Attributional complexity: An individual differences measure. *Journal of Personality and Social Psychology, 51,* 875–884.

Freeman, M. (1993). *Rewriting the self: History, memory, narrative.* New York: Routledge.

Freeman, M. (2011). Narrative foreclosure in later life: Possibilities and limits. In G. Kenyon, E. Bohlmeijer, & W. Randall (Eds.), *Storying later life: Issues, investigations, and interventions in narrative gerontology* (pp. 3–19). Oxford: Oxford University Press.

Fry, P. S. (1998). The development of personal meaning and wisdom in adolescence: A re-examination of moderating and consolidating factors and influences. In P.T.P Wong & P. S. Fry (Eds.), *The Human Quest for Meaning: A handbook of psychological research and clinical applications* (pp. 91–110). Mahwah: Lawrence Erlbaum Associates.

Fulford, R. (1999). *The triumph of narrative: Storytelling in the age of mass culture.* Toronto: House of Anansi Press.

Gardner, H. (1983). *Frames of mind: The theory of multiple intelligences.* New York: Basic Books.

Gluck, J., Bluck, S., Baron, S., & McAdams, D. P. (2005). The wisdom of experience: Autobiographical narrative across adulthood. *International Journal of Behavioral Development, 29,* 197–208.

Habermas, T., & Bluck, S. (2000). Getting a life: The emergence of the life story in adolescence. *Psychological Bulletin, 126,* 748–769.

Jeste, D. V., Ardelt, M., Blazer, D., Kraemer, H. C., Vaillant, G., & Meeks, T. W. (2010). Expert consensus on characteristics of wisdom: A Delphi method study. *The Gerontologist, 50,* 668–680.

Jones, L. (2010). Oneself as an author. *Theory, Culture & Society, 27*(5), 49–68. doi:10.1177/0263276410374629.

Kenyon, G. M., & Randall, W. L. (1997). *Restorying our lives: Personal growth through autobiographical reflection.* Westport: Praeger.

Kramer, D. A. (1990). Conceptualizing wisdom: The primacy of affect-cognition relations. In R. J. Sternberg (Ed.), *Wisdom: Its nature, origins, and development.* New York: Cambridge University Press.

Kramer, D. A. (2000). Wisdom as a classical source of human strength: Conceptualization and empirical inquiry. *Journal of Social and Clinical Psychology, 19,* 83–101.

Kristinsson, B. (2005). How are leadership styles, emotional intelligence and wisdom related? Unpublished Master's thesis, Aston Business School, London, UK.

Kroger, J. (2000). Ego identity status research in the new millennium. *International Journal of Behavioral Development, 24*(2), 145–148.

Kunzmann, U., & Baltes, P. B. (2003). Wisdom-related knowledge: Affective, motivational, and interpersonal correlates. *Personality and Social Psychology Bulletin, 29,* 1104–1119.

Labouvie-Vief, G. (1990). Wisdom as integrated thought: Historical and developmental perspectives. In R. J. Sternberg (Ed.), *Wisdom: Its nature, origins, and development* (pp. 52–83). New York: Cambridge University Press.

Linley, P. A. (2003). Positive adaptation to trauma: Wisdom as both process and outcome. *Journal of Traumatic Stress, 16,* 601–610.

Luyckx, K., Lens, W., Smits, I., & Goossens, L. (2010). Time perspective and identity formation: Short-term longitudinal dynamics in college students. *International Journal of Behavioral Development, 34,* 238–247.

Mansfield, C. D., McLean, K. C., & Lilgendahl, J. P. (2010). Narrating traumas and transgressions: Links between narrative processing, wisdom, and well-being. *Narrative Inquiry, 20*(2), 246–273.

Marcia, J. E. (1966). Development and validation of ego identity status. *Journal of Personality and social Psychology, 3,* 551–558.

Marcia, J. E., Waterman, A. S., Matteson, D. R., Archer, S. L., & Orlofsky, J. L. (1993). *Ego identity: A handbook for psychosocial research.* New York: Springer.

Matsuba, M. K., & Walker, L. J. (2005). Young adult moral exemplars: The making of self through stories. *Journal of Research on Adolescence, 15*(3), 275–297.

McAdams, D. P. (1993). *The stories we live by: Personal myths and the making of the self.* New York: Guilford Press.

McAdams, D. P. (2003). Identity and the life story. In R. Fivush & C. A. Haden (Eds.), *Autobiographical memory and the construction of a narrative self: Developmental and cultural perspectives* (pp. 187–207). Mahwah: Erlbaum.

McAdams, D. P. (2006). *The redemptive self: Stories Americans live by.* New York: Oxford University Press.

McAdams, D. P. (2008). Personal narratives and the life story. In O. P. John, R. W. Robins, & L. A. Pervin (Eds.), *Handbook of Personality: Theory and Research* (3rd edn) (pp. 242–262). New York: Guilford Press.

McLean, K. C. (2005). Late adolescent identity development: Narrative meaning making and memory telling. *Developmental Psychology, 41,* 683–691.

McLean, K. C., Pasupathi, M., & Pals, J. L. (2007). Selves creating stories creating selves: A process model of self-development. *Personality and Social Psychology Review, 11,* 262–278.

McLean, K. C., & Thorne, A. (2003). Adolescents' self-defining memories about relationships. *Developmental Psychology, 39,* 635–645.

McLeod, J. (1997). *Narrative and psychotherapy.* Thousand Oaks: Sage.

Ochs, E., & Capps, L. (2001). *Living narrative: Creating lives in everyday storytelling*. Cambridge: Harvard University Press.

Pals, J. L. (2006). Narrative identity processing of difficult life experiences: Pathways of personality development and positive self-transformation in adulthood. *Journal of Personality, 74,* 1079–1109.

Pasupathi, M., Staudinger, U. M., & Baltes, P. B. (2001). Seeds of wisdom: Adolescents' knowledge and judgment about difficult life problems. *Developmental Psychology, 37,* 351–361.

Randall, W. L. (2011). Memory, metaphor, and meaning: Reading for wisdom in the stories of our lives. In G. Kenyon, E. Bohlmeijer, & W. Randall (Eds.), *Storying later life: Issues, investigations, and interventions in narrative gerontology* (pp. 20–38). Oxford: Oxford University Press.

Randall, W. L., & McKim, A. E. (2008). *Reading our lives: The poetics of growing old*. Oxford: Oxford University Press.

Randall, W. L. & Kenyon, G. (2001). *Ordinary wisdom: Biographical aging and the journey of life.* Westport: Praeger.

Richardson, M. J., & Pasupathi, M. (2005). Young and growing wiser (pp. 139–159). In R. J. Sternberg & J. Jordan (Eds.), *A handbook of wisdom: Psychological perspectives*. New York: Cambridge University press.

Schwartz, B. (2004). The tyranny of choice. *Scientific American,* 71–75.

Schwartz, B., & Ward, A. (2004). Doing better but feeling worse: The paradox of choice. In P. A. Linley & S. Joseph (Eds.), *Positive psychology in practice* (pp. 86–104). Hoboken: Wiley.

Seaton, C. L., & Beaumont, S. L. (2008). Individual differences in identity styles predict proactive forms of positive adjustment. *Identity: An International Journal of Theory and Research, 8,* 249–268.

Soenens, B., Duriez, B., & Goossens, L. (2005). Social-psychological profiles of identity styles: Attitudinal and social-cognitive correlates in late adolescence. *Journal of Adolescence, 28,* 107–125.

Staudinger, U. M., & Gluck, J. (2011). Psychological wisdom research: Commonalities and differences in a growing field. Annual Review of Psychology, 62, 215–241. doi:10.1146/annurev.psych.121208.131659.

Takahashi, M., & Overton, W. F. (2005). Cultural foundations of wisdom: An integrated developmental approach (pp. 32–60). In R. J. Sternberg & J. Jordan (Eds.), *A handbook of wisdom: Psychological perspectives*. New York: Cambridge University Press.

Taylor, M., Bates, G., & Webster, J. D. (2011). Comparing the psychometric properties of two measures of wisdom: Predicting forgiveness and psychological well-being with the self-assessed wisdom scale (SAWS) and the three-dimensional wisdom scale (3D-WS). *Experimental Aging Research, 37*(2), 129–141.

Tedeschi, R. G., & Calhoun, L. G. (2004). A clinical approach to posttraumatic growth. In P. A. Linley & S. Joseph (Eds.), *Positive psychology in practice* (pp. 405–419). Hoboken, Wiley.

Webster, J. D. (2003). An exploratory analysis of a self-assessed wisdom scale. *Journal of Adult Development, 10,* 13–22.

Webster, J. D. (2007). Measuring the character strength of wisdom. *International Journal of Aging and Human Development, 65,* 163–183.

Webster, J. D. (2010). Wisdom and positive psychosocial values in young adulthood. Journal of Adult Development, 17(2), 70–80. doi:10.1007/s10804-009-9081-z.

Webster, J. D., Taylor, M., & Bates, G. (2011). Conceptualizing and measuring wisdom: A reply to Ardelt. *Experimental Aging Research, 37*(2), 256–259.

Webster, J. D., Westerhof, G. J., & Bohlmeijer, E. T. (2012). Wisdom and mental health across the lifespan. *Journals of Gerontology, Series B: Psychological Sciences and Social Sciences*. doi:10.1093/geronb/gbs121.

Chapter 6
Amusing Ourselves to Health: A Selected Review of Lab Findings

Evangeline A. Wheeler

Almost everyone knows the story of Norman Cousins, writer and editor, who in the 1960s transferred himself from a hospital bed to a hotel bed in order to test his theory that positive emotions would heal him better than a series of medications. He set about a program of regular hearty laughter (and large doses of vitamins), and did indeed improve his health and reduce his reliance on anesthetics. The discipline of positive psychology now identifies the propensity for laughter and sense of humor as one of the main signature strengths one can possess. It seems that modern scientific studies can now, to some extent, support a widespread cultural belief that a good laugh is good for your health (Boyle and Joss-Reid 2004; Martin 2002, 2004).

The cultural belief that laughing and humor promote physical health is nearly universal, as expressed in the Irish proverb "a good laugh and a long sleep are the best cures in the doctor's book," and humor is widely recognized as a universal phenomenon in human interaction (Lefcourt 2001). Humor is part of the class of involuntary mental mechanisms that function to distort our view of situations in order to reduce stress. Included along with humor are other high adaptive-level defense mechanisms such as anticipation, sublimation, and suppression (Valliant 2000). But Friedman et al. (1993) speculate that though sense of humor is often helpful in coping with short-term stressors, excessive humor may also lead to an unrealistic belief that things will always turn out for the best and may cause some people to underestimate the dangers of health compromising behaviors.

A growing movement among healthcare workers touts therapeutic humor through seminars, workshops, videotapes, and web sites. Recommendation of humor therapy for the relief of physical or emotional pain or stress, a recent and growing trend in mental health counseling (Vereen et al. 2006), utilizes laughter groups as a context to heal. Laughter exercises can purportedly help people to gain humorous perspectives on their lives and situations (Henderson and Rosario 2008; McCreaddie and Wiggins 2008). Today, thousands of people in over 40 countries participate in laughter groups, attesting to the popularity of this form of treatment.

E. A. Wheeler (✉)
Department of Psychology, Towson University, 8000 York Road, Towson MD 21252, USA
e-mail: ewheeler@towson.edu

J. D. Sinnott (ed.), *Positive Psychology*,
DOI 10.1007/978-1-4614-7282-7_6,

But despite the popularity of the idea that humor and laughter have associated physiological benefits that provide positive mental and physical health improvements, the current empirical evidence, far from being unequivocal, is sometimes weak and inconclusive with small effect sizes. How strong, then, is the evidence that humor and laughter are healthful? See Kuiper and Nicholl (2004) for an explanation in terms of personality differences, that people with a sense of humor may just be more inclined to report better health. But for our purposes here, we are more interested in the question of what evidence supports biological pathways through which laughter yields beneficial changes in physiology. Of the many hundreds of studies done on the topic, just a few are selected for this paper.

Physical health benefits of humor and laughter are purportedly numerous and include immunity boosts, decreased stress hormones, decreased pain, muscle relaxation, and heart disease prevention. In some studies, blood flow increased when research participants watched a funny film scene. The physiological benefits will not be undone by the many mental health benefits, which include the addition of joy and zest to life, the easing of anxiety, fear, and depression, the relief of stress (Kuhn et al. 2010; Newman and Stone 1996), improvement in mood, and enhanced resilience. Especially within the practice of psychiatry (Bell and Malhi 2009), humor has the potential to significantly influence not only general health and well-being, but also play a more specific and important role in therapeutic engagement, assessment, and diagnosis, and possibly form a component of a psychiatric management plan.

Measuring Humor and Laughter

Humor is based on a mismatch, in a safe and nonthreatening situation, between what is perceived and what is expected. For something to be humorous, we entertain two representations of the same entity that are equally plausible, and the resolution of the perceived incongruity can often result in humor and its physical expression—laughter. In lab studies, humor is assessed by any number of self-report scales. The Sense of Humor Questionnaire (Svebak 1996) provides an overall sense of humor score. The Situational Humor Response Questionnaire (SHRQ) (Martin and Lefcourt 1984) measures the degree to which a person tends to be amused and to laugh easily in a wide range of situations. The SHRQ measures an emotion-based coping mechanism whereby people reduce stress by interpreting situations with humor. In addition to an overall sense of humor score, factor analysis of the Multidimensional Sense of Humor Scale (MSHS) (Thorson and Powell 1993) indicates four principal factors: (1) humor creativity and uses of humor for social purposes, (2) uses of coping humor, (3) appreciation of humorous people, and (4) appreciation of humor.

The Coping Humor Scale (CHS) (Martin and Lefcourt 1984) measures a coping strategy aimed at changing the stressful events themselves, rather than trying to change an emotional reaction. Additionally, laughter is usually measured by observers or trained coders who watch videotapes or listen to audiotapes to count instances of overt laughing. Often, the Humor Response Scale (Bennett et al. 2003) is used to measure mirthful laughter. Finally, the Humor Styles Questionnaire (Martin et al. 2003) measures four humor styles: (1) *Affiliative* (use of humor to amuse others and facilitate relationships); (2) *Self-enhancing* (use of humor to cope with stress and maintain a humorous outlook during times of difficulty); (3) *Aggressive* (use of sarcastic, manipulative, put-down, or disparaging humor); (4) *Self-defeating* (use of humor for excessive self-disparagement, ingratiation, or defensive denial).

Humor is a complex phenomenon of human social cognition with large interindividual variability and differences in types of humor (Mahony et al. 2002). Stieger et al. (2011) established that it is a multifaceted construct that includes both adaptive and maladaptive humor styles. For instance, self-enhancing and affiliative humor styles seem to be beneficial, whereas aggressive and self-defeating humor styles may be less so or even detrimental to health. Self-defeating humor correlates positively with loneliness, shyness, depression, and negatively with self-esteem. Furthermore, research has found that people possessing damaged self-esteem have very similar characteristics to people using self-defeating humor.

Effect of Humor on Immune System and Stress

Psychoneuroimmunological research, aimed at understanding the interplay between the central nervous system and the immune system, suggests that in addition to psychological benefits, humor may have positive physiological effects on immune system functioning. How? The immune system protects the body by warding off invading bacteria, viruses, fungi, and parasites. But simple invasion of the body by disease is not sufficient to cause illness that occurs when defenses are compromised or unable to recognize invading material. Most immune system cells are located in the body in places not easily accessible, such as in the bone marrow, the thymus, lymph nodes, spleen, tonsils, appendix, and small intestines. Therefore, immune system processes are usually studied via circulating peripheral blood that transports immune system components between organs of the immune system and sites of inflammation. Components of the immune system that circulate in blood—like white blood cells and antibodies—conduct a sort of search and destroy mission against immune system invaders. Therefore, laughter may affect immunity by increasing the number of white blood cells, for example.

Researchers (for example, Berk et al. 2001) have conducted numerous clinical studies that confirm several physiological changes that happen in the immune system when we laugh, including an increase in the production of immune cells. Levels of the hormone epinephrine, which plays a role in hypertension and heart failure, decrease. Antibody levels in the blood and saliva rise, and the number of natural killer (NK) cells increases, which accelerates the body's natural anticarcinogenic response.

Also, the level of the hormone cortisol, which is chronically high when an individual is under long-term stress and which suppresses the immune system, is reduced dramatically when people laugh. Stress hormones may be the primary culprit by which negative emotions harm health. When a person is under stress, the body produces stress hormones such as adrenalin and cortisol. The hormones can have a detrimental effect on the body, including suppressing the immune system and constricting blood vessels. Laughter may have a contrasting effect, causing the body to release other natural chemicals known as endorphins that may counteract the effects of stress hormones and cause blood vessels to dilate. Laughter may also boost the immune system and reduce the amount of inflammation in the body, which has been linked to a number of health problems.

During laughter, the body increases the amount of T cells also in the blood. When we are laughing, NK cells that destroy tumors and viruses increase, as do gamma interferon (a disease-fighting protein). Laughter may lead to hiccupping and coughing, which could clear the respiratory tract of excess mucus. Laughter also increases the concentration of salivary immunoglobulin A, which defends against infectious organisms entering through the respiratory tract. Recently, researchers followed two groups of cardiac disease patients through a year-long rehabilitation program. Both randomly assigned groups received standard therapy, but one also viewed daily, self-selected humor for 30 min. Berk et al. (2001) showed that when patients experienced "eustress" or mirthful laughter, disease-related symptoms such as arrythmias occurred at lesser intervals. Another study evaluated male medical students to determine humor's effect on healthy immune systems. The students' stress levels, measured by T cell activity in the blood (which increases to jump-start the body's immune system), were significantly reduced after watching a humorous video.

Although Berk et al.'s (2001) many findings intrigue us, it is impossible to know whether the reported effects are produced by laughter, humor, or something else not considered, such as watching the video. A study about laughter should directly observe measurable levels of laughter. Several experiments have found signs that watching funny videos bolsters people's immune systems. However, other comedy-exposure studies found either no changes or even declines in immune system function. Researchers have yet to establish conclusively whether any component of immunity corresponds to how much a person laughs at funny material.

Kimata (2004), who does prodigious research on the role of laughter in various physiological responses, found that allergy patients who watched *Modern Times*, a Charlie Chaplin film, experienced reduced swelling of skin welts. Specifically, laughter caused by viewing the comic video reduced the plasma nerve growth factor, neurotrophin-3 levels, and allergic skin wheal responses in patients with atopic dermatitis, whereas viewing a nonhumorous weather video failed to do so. Also, stress induced by writing mail on a mobile phone enhanced the plasma nerve growth factor, neurotrophin-3 levels, and allergic skin wheal responses. However, previewing the comic video counteracted mobile phone-mediated enhancement of plasma neurotrophins or allergic skin wheal responses, whereas previewing the weather information failed to do so. Taken together, these results suggest that, in patients with atopic dermatitis, writing mail on a mobile phone causes stress and enhances allergic responses along with an increase in plasma neurotrophins that are counteracted by laughter.

Lai et al. (2010) examined the impact of humor on postawakening cortisol levels among a group of older men with a mean age of 73.6 years. Saliva samples were collected immediately after waking. Results indicated that higher humor scores were associated with lower cortisol levels. Findings of the present study suggest that the hypothalamic–pituitary–adrenocortical axis is the major pathway whereby positive psychological dispositions such as humor exert their health effects in the aging population. Moreover, cortisol levels in the awakening period may be particularly sensitive to the influences of psychosocial factors. Bennett et al. (2003) concluded that laughter may reduce stress and improve a type of white blood cell (Natural Killer, or NK) activity. As low NK cell activity is linked to decreased disease resistance and increased morbidity in persons with cancer and HIV disease, laughter may be a useful cognitive–behavioral intervention. To determine the effect of laughter on self-reported stress and NK cell activity, research volunteers viewed a humorous video while subjects in a distraction control group viewed a tourism video. Stress decreased for people in the humor group, compared with those in the distraction group. Amount of mirthful laughter correlated with post intervention stress measures for persons in the humor group. People who scored greater than 25 on the humor response scale had increased immune function post intervention, compared with the remaining participants. Humor response scale scores correlated with changes in NK cell activity.

Because of the central involvement of emotion regulation in psychological health and the role that implicit (largely unconscious) processes appear to play in emotion regulation, implicit emotion-regulatory processes, and perhaps a tendency to interpret events from a humorous perspective, should play a vital role in psychological health. It has been hypothesized that implicitly valuing emotion regulation translates into better psychological health in people who use adaptive emotion-regulation strategies. People who had recently experienced a stressful life event completed an implicit measure of emotion regulation valuing and reported on their habitual use of an important adaptive emotion-regulation strategy: cognitive reappraisal. People who implicitly valued emotion regulation exhibited greater levels of psychological health, but only when they were high in cognitive reappraisal use. This suggests that salutary effects of unconscious emotion-regulation processes depend on its interplay with conscious emotion-regulation processes, and implicates a role for humor (Hopp et al. 2011).

Kuiper and Martin (1998) investigated the proposal that increased laughter can serve to moderate the affective impact of negative life events. Community participants kept a record of their actual frequency of laughter for a 3-day period, and completed a measure of stressful life events each evening. Current levels of positive and negative affect were also obtained in the morning and evening of each day. A series of simple correlations, computed on a daily basis, provided little evidence for any direct relationships between amount of daily laughter and either positive or negative affect. Instead, more complex moderator analyses revealed that greater negative affect was clearly associated with a higher number of stressful life events, but only for those individuals with a lower frequency of actual laughter. In contrast, and in support of a stress buffering hypothesis, it was found that individuals with a higher frequency of laughter did not show greater levels of negative affect as stressful life events increased. When considering positive affect, it was found that only males showed a significant moderating effect of laughter. For males who laughed more frequently, a greater number of stressful life events was associated with higher levels of positive affect. These findings are discussed in terms of several possible mechanisms which may account for the moderating effects of laughter on affect, including the use of cognitive appraisals and emotion-focused coping strategies.

Gender differences in emotion processing are a common finding in functional neuroimaging studies and have been documented in behavioral studies of humor, but have received limited attention in functional neuroimaging studies on humor. Kohn et al. (2011) investigated gender differences in processing of humorous cartoons and found that brain regions were differently activated. The results indicated that women process humor though limbic reactivity, involving appraisal of its emotional features, while men apply more evaluative, executive resources to humor processing.

According to Groucho Marx, "a clown is like an aspirin, only he works twice as fast." Laughter can, at the very least, distract a person from his pain, allowing him to sleep and perform other daily activities with greater comfort. In fact, this is one of the only benefits of laughter that is not widely disputed. Lefcourt et al. (1997) found that humor may play more of a role in moderating the impact of uncontrollable and passively experienced stressors.

Effect of Humor on Pain Tolerance

Substantial research has demonstrated that cognitive psychological techniques including distraction can increase pain tolerance. In recent years, there also have been claims that humor and laughter possess unique characteristics for coping with pain and stress. Theoretically, explanations include the release of endorphins, the lowering of tension as well as the distraction that results from humor. Zweyer et al. (2004) aimed at separating three factors considered potentially essential (mood, behavior, and cognition related to humor), and examined whether they are responsible for this effect. Furthermore, they examined whether trait cheerfulness and trait seriousness moderate changes in pain tolerance. Women who volunteered for the study were assigned randomly to one of three groups, each having a different task to pursue while watching a funny film: get into a cheerful mood without smiling or laughing; smile and laugh extensively; or produce a humorous commentary to the film. Pain tolerance was measured using the cold pressor test (in which people immerse a hand or arm in ice-cold water) before, immediately after, and 20 min after the film. Results indicated that pain tolerance increased for participants from before to after watching the funny film and remained high for the 20 min. This effect was moderated by facial but not verbal indicators of enjoyment of humor. Participants low in trait seriousness had an overall higher pain tolerance. Subjects with a high score in trait cheerfulness showed an increase in pain tolerance after producing humor while watching the film whereas subjects low in trait cheerfulness showed a similar increase after smiling and laughing during the film.

A physiological view of stress is that it results from abnormal biochemical processes in the central nervous system. To the extent to which, that view is correct, laughter may benefit by shutting down the flow of excessive stress hormones which otherwise could suppress the immune system. If the physical act of laughing has similar effects on the body as other forms of exercise, then laughing will enhance blood flow to the brain, stimulate the autonomic nervous system, and trigger the release of a variety of hormones. Of all the hormones that affect our stress levels, laughter appears to reduce at least four of them: epinephrine, cortisol, DOPAC (a metabolite of the neurotransmitter dopamine) as well as growth hormones. In addition, laughter promotes muscle relaxation, which also helps our bodies alleviate stress. In one study, participants' blood vessels were monitored both, before and after being shown comedies and dramas. It was found that those who watched the comedy had blood vessels that behaved normally, whereas those who watched the dramas had vessels that tended to tense up, limiting blood flow (see Berk et al. 2001; Lefcourt et al. 1997).

Effect of Humor on Cognition

Even the simple act of chortling (making a gleeful chuckling or snorting sound) seems to improve memory. Memory is better for humorous material, as demonstrated by Carlson (2011), who read a list of 30 words to people and showed some of them a funny video clip afterward. One week later, those who had been exposed to the video within 30 min of having heard the list remembered 20 % more words than those who had not. Martin (2002, 2004), a psychologist and important laughter researcher, theorizes that laughter improves mental performance by accelerating the heartbeat, thus increasing oxygen supply to the brain.

There is some support that humor is correlated with general intelligence, as in the work of Feingold and Mazzella (1991), investigating the relationship between psychometric intelligence and humor. They found that although tests purporting to measure humor information were not highly correlated with general verbal ability or verbal creativity, tests assessing humor reasoning correlated appreciably with the verbal measures. Verbal perspicacity is usually an indicator of intelligence, and in this study, humor cognition was more strongly associated with general verbal ability than memory, for humor. Results show that humor ability can be distinguished from general intelligence and verbal ability. Consider another finding that connects humor to intelligence. Howrigan and MacDonald (2008) looked at the relationships among rater-judged humor, general intelligence, and the Big Five personality traits in a large sample of college students. General intelligence positively predicted rater-judged humor, independent of the Big Five personality traits. Extraversion also predicted rater-judged humor, although to a lesser extent than general intelligence. General intelligence did not interact with the sex of the participant in predicting rating scores on the humor production tasks. The study lends support to the prediction that effective humor production acts as an honest indicator of intelligence in humans. In addition, extraversion, and to a lesser extent, openness, may reflect motivational traits that encourage humor production.

McGhee (1971) investigated the relationship between children's level of cognitive functioning (according to Piaget's theoretical framework) and their comprehension of humor based on the notion that humor processing involves a violation of cognitive expectancies. The general hypothesis was that operational thinking is necessary for comprehension of incongruity humor but not for comprehension of novelty humor. For incongruity humor (but not novelty humor), operational thinking was found to be an important factor in the ability to give interpretive, as opposed to descriptive, explanations. Analyses of age differences indicated consistent significant increases in comprehension with increasing age. Data on typically developing children show that humor development starts from around age four or five, but studies investigating humor in children with intellectual disability are few and have generally focused on identifying differences between this population and other groups of children. Degabrielle and Walsh (2010) focused on a small sample of school-aged children with mild to moderate intellectual disability and sought to investigate what kinds of humor children with intellectual disability appreciate most in a video cartoon, and how the mode of presentation of jokes influences humor comprehension. The children rated short scenes from a video cartoon to show their appreciation for different kinds of humor. A set of video-recorded jokes with different modes of presentation were used in the comprehension task. The greatest appreciation was expressed for physical and visual humor. Nonspecific scenes with no particularly funny elements were also rated highly. Jokes presented with gesture were understood more than jokes told without supports. It seems that the context of humor (e.g., being part of a video cartoon) is important in determining what children with intellectual disabilities find funny.

To explain the pervasive role of humor in human social interaction and among mating partner preferences, Greengross and Miller (2011) proposed that intentional humor evolved as an indicator of intelligence. It could be that people seek humorousness in a mate because humor connotes intelligence (Weisfeld et al. 2011), which would be valuable in a spouse. Since males tend to be the competing sex, men may have been more strongly selected to be humorous. Cross-culturally, husbands were perceived to make wives laugh more than the reverse. Spousal humorousness was associated with marital satisfaction in all cultures, especially the wife's satisfaction. Spousal humorousness was less consistently related to spousal intelligence than to some alternative possibilities: spousal kindness, dependability, and understanding. Furthermore, the relationship between these four variables and marital satisfaction was mediated by spousal humorousness.

According to Freud, humor should be a supportive strategy for coping with experiences that threaten one's positive self-view, defending the ego's invulnerability, or humor may be a means by which the superego can be fooled into allowing the mind to express unconscious sexual and aggressive urges. This idea propelled some research by Geisler and Weber (2010) who examined the affective and cognitive impact of humor on coping with self-threat that was induced by way of a lab procedure designed to make the research participant feel unintelligent. Research was based on an incongruity concept of humor that specifies humor as a state resulting from appraising an aversive incident as both, harmful and acceptable. They investigated the consequences of humor for a self-serving interpretation of failure, the awareness of harm, and subsequent performance. Participants who were exposed to the humor induction rated their performance as poorer than the participants in the control condition, suggesting a higher awareness of harm. At the same time, the induction of humor appeared to encourage self-serving cognitive reactions, as indicated by a greater tendency for an external attribution of failure.

Clinical depression is associated with cognitive deficits affecting memory, executive functions, and affect perception, which have been linked to dysfunction of networks in the frontal lobe. It could be argued that depression affects the comprehension of humor as well, since humor processing is a complex socially relevant cognitive task. In an investigation by Uekermann et al. (2008), a computerized humor-processing task was administered to patients diagnosed with major depression. Depressed patients performed below the control group with respect to both affective and cognitive aspects of humor processing, and these were related to mentalizing and executive performance. These results suggest the existence of social cognition deficits in major depression. The ability to process humor and appreciate mentalistic perspectives may in turn influence social interactions and should be given consideration in therapeutic approaches to depression.

Teaching people with depression how to identify overly negative thought processes and then to replace them with more realistic appraisals of ongoing events is the technique of cognitive reappraisal, the *sine qua non* of cognitive behavioral therapy. Indeed, cognitive modification is hypothesized as the primary means of reducing the intensity of negative affective states. This reappraisal process is congruent with the positive psychology construct of reality negotiation, which requires a person to consider alternative interpretations of events, and oftentimes entails a modification of original appraisals in favor of slightly positively biased ones. Likewise, the cultivation of mindfulness includes an implicit element of reappraisal, in as much as it involves merely observing thoughts and feelings, without becoming attached to them, as a means of facilitating less negatively biased and distorted perspectives on events.

Cognitive behavior therapy (CBT) has received extensive empirical support as an effective intervention for the acute treatment of major depressive disorder and the prevention of depressive relapse. Nevertheless, many patients do not respond favorably to CBT, and the specific active ingredients of CBT remain unclear. With its emphasis on identifying and cultivating individual strengths, however, positive psychology appears to have considerable potential to enhance the efficacy of CBT and to help clarify the processes that mediate its salubrious effects. If humor does indeed serve as such a protective factor, as suggested by the work of Geisler and Weber (2010), one can infer that CBT might be enhanced by attending more closely to the process of increasing a depressed patient's capacities for humor.

Humor and Laughter in Interpersonal Social Networks

Substantial evidence implicates interpersonal relationships in the maintenance of good health (Kuiper and McHale 2009; Uchino et al. 2012). Benefits are partly attributed to receipt or availability of emotional support, which might be facilitated in a content of humor. Social benefits of humor and laughing are many: strengthening of relationships, attracting others to us, enhancing teamwork, defusing conflict, and promoting group bonding. People with a good sense of humor may be more socially competent, thus better able to salve social tensions, which in turn may result in more intimate relationships. Devereux and Ginsburg (2001) found that more laughter is produced when watching a funny video in the presence of others, following the earlier work of Wolosin (1975), who, in a study attempting to predict when a group atmosphere of laughter will be achieved, found that groups composed of people with similar cognitive styles will produce laughter more often, perhaps as a result of more efficient communication. Looking, laughing, and smiling are powerful nonverbal signals of warmth and attentiveness in interpersonal relationships.

When being interviewed by someone of the same sex, people highly motivated toward intimacy display significantly higher levels of eye contact, laughter, and smiling (McAdams et al. 1984). Also, the temporal pattern of laughter between social partners varies according to the sex and familiarity of the partners. Smoski (2005) examined the trajectory of antiphonal laughter (i.e., laughter between social partners that occurs in close temporal proximity) in new friendships. College students were tested in either same-sex or mixed-sex dyads, with dyads composed of people who were or were not familiar to each other. Dyads were audio-recorded while the students played brief games intended to make them laugh. New acquaintances produced more antiphonal laughter than strangers did when the antiphonal laugh pair was initiated with an unvoiced laugh, but not when initiated with a voiced laugh. Limited evidence was found to suggest that the frequency of laugh induction by a partner's laughter predicted subsequent friendship strength.

There is empirical evidence that reminiscing about positive events has positive emotional benefits, and that laughter plays a role in seemingly successful relationships. Bazzini et al. (2007) put these two findings together to ask the question of whether reminiscing about shared laughter would increase relationship satisfaction among romantic couples. They asked 52 couples to complete a questionnaire about how satisfied they were in the relationship with their romantic partner. They were then randomly assigned to one of four reminiscing conditions and completed another relationship assessment afterwards. Those couples who were assigned to reminisce about events involving shared laugher reported higher relationship satisfaction at the postmanipulation satisfaction assessment than did couples in the other three control conditions. The effect was not attributed to positive mood induction as mood scores across groups were similar. Results showed support for the notion that reminiscing about laughter may have a more potent influence on relationship well-being than reminiscing about other positive events.

Special Benefit of Laughter to Elders

The impact of positive psychological attitudes on physical health and healthy aging has been well documented through research. These benefits are some of the best kept secrets from those persons who probably have the most to gain from that information—older adults. Many of them who must live with chronic pain, arthritis, rheumatism, emphysema, memory loss, depression, and stress may be able to cope better with their conditions or find temporary relief by using humor. Berk (2001) presents an up-to-date, comprehensive synthesis of 30 years of research evidence on several psychophysiological benefits of humor and laughter with their implications for older adults. Mathieu (2008), for instance, assessed whether a therapeutic recreation program specifically addressing happiness and humor could promote life satisfaction among older adults. The Happiness and Humor Group was a 10-week program conducted once a week at an urban senior center. The Life Satisfaction Scale (LSS) was administered as a pretest and posttest to people who participated in the entire program. Scores from this self-rated assessment showed significant improvement in life satisfaction for the program participants. Anecdotal evidence also shows that participants' outlook changed significantly as a result of program participation.

The goal of Mak and Carpenter (2007) was to understand factors related to humor comprehension in old age. They proposed that in contrast to younger adults, older adults have greater difficulty with humor comprehension due to age-related cognitive decline. Tests of verbal and nonverbal humor comprehension and tests of cognitive flexibility, abstract reasoning, and short-term memory were administered to young and old adults. In general, older adults scored lower than younger adults on tests of humor and cognitive abilities. Regression analyses support the idea that cognition affects humor comprehension, but the relative contribution of each specific mechanism remains unclear. The results of this study suggest that there may be age-related deficits in humor comprehension, but more importantly, that a more sophisticated model is needed to clarify the role of cognition in humor comprehension. In a different approach, Marziali et al. (2008) examined the associations among coping humor, other personal and social factors, and the health status of community-dwelling older adults. Correlations across all variables showed coping humor to be significantly associated with social support, self-efficacy, depression, and anxiety. Forward stepwise regression analyses showed that coping humor and self-efficacy contributed to outcome variance in measures of mental health status. The importance of social support, self-efficacy, and spirituality (Wheeler 2010) in determining the quality of life of older adults is well supported in the literature. Coping humor as a mechanism for managing the inevitable health stresses of aging has received less attention. This study shows that coping humor and self-efficacy are important factors for explaining health status in older adults. Correlations among coping humor, self-efficacy, and social support suggest that a sense of humor may play an important role in reinforcing self-efficacious approaches to the management of health issues.

Finally, Svebak et al. (2010) explored the significance of sense of humor for survival over seven years. Thousands of residents in the county of Nord-Trøndelag in Norway were invited to take part in a public health survey. Sense of humor was estimated by responses to a cognitive, social, and affective item, respectively, taken from the Sense of Humor Questionnaire (SHQ). Hazard ratios (HR) were reduced with sense of humor as contrasted with increase of HR with a number of classical risk factors (e.g., cardiovascular disease, diabetes, cancer, poor subjective health). Gender proved to be of trivial importance to the effect of sense of humor in survival. Subjective health correlated positively with sense of humor and therefore might have presented a spurious relation of survival with humor, but sense of humor proved to reduce HR both in people with poor and good subjective health. However, above the age of 65, the effect of sense of humor on survival became less evident. Sense of humor appeared to increase the probability of survival into retirement, and this effect appeared independent of subjective health.

Evaluating the Evidence

Despite all the research, many experts remain dubious about claims that laughter and humor can benefit our minds and bodies to any great extent. They argue that the research is based on small-scale lab studies. They also argue that humor researchers are biased to find statistically significant results. Furthermore, for the laughter studies particularly, it is difficult to distinguish the uniqueness of laughing, as opposed to say, shouting. It is for this reason, and because reliable and valid scales are available for the measurement of humor, that in most studies, *humor*, and not *laughter*, is the important variable. More importantly, there is the difficulty of determining whether laughter is the cause or effect of good health. In other words, if people who are less likely to be sick are also found to laugh more, it is difficult to know if they are not sick because they laugh, or laughing because they are not sick.

Evidence that watching humorous videotapes boosts pain tolerance is also ambiguous. Comparable rises in pain tolerance occurred in a few studies in which people watched sad or disgusting videotapes, suggesting that various emotional states take some of the sting out of physical hurts. People with a good sense of humor, as measured on questionnaires, have yet to display any marked advantages in immunity, pain resistance, or susceptibility to physical illness over those less inclined to laugh. Published reports provide only some support for the theory that a sense of humor diminishes daily stress levels or for the notion that it increases longevity.

Kuiper et al. (2004) explored potential reasons for the continuing popularity of this viewpoint by suggesting a fundamental distinction between actual and perceived physical health. In particular, they proposed that a greater sense of humor may sometimes contribute to more positive perceptions of physical health than may actually be warranted. They investigated an alternative proposal to the view that a sense of humor improves health, which was that the distinct components of sense of humor may actually exhibit quite different relationships with psychological well-being, with only some being facilitative, and others being detrimental. This specificity hypothesis draws from contemporary multidimensional models of sense of humor, which have identified both adaptive and maladaptive components of humor (e.g., self-enhancing versus self-defeating).

Participants in their study completed measures of eight different components of sense of humor and several indices of psychological well-being, including self-esteem levels, depression, anxiety, and self-competency judgments as well as a broad range of physical health concepts pertaining to fear of death and disease, bodily focus, worry and concern about illness, frequency of treatment, decisions to seek treatment, and physical symptoms experienced. Initial analyses indicated strong support for a multidimensional approach to sense of humor that demonstrated appropriate component distinctiveness, but also with the expected degree of convergence for key elements that are either adaptive (coping, affiliative, self-enhancing, and skilled humor) or maladaptive (self-defeating, belabored, aggressive, and rude humor). In accord with the specificity hypothesis, the adaptive components of sense of humor showed facilitative effects, being associated with greater self-esteem, lower depression and anxiety levels, and more positive self-competency judgments. Higher levels on certain sense of humor components were associated with more positive health-related perceptions such as less fear of death or serious disease, less negative bodily preoccupation, and less concern about pain. It was not the case, however, that those with greater humor displayed different health habits than those with less humor.

In contrast, the maladaptive components of humor that were self-focused (e.g., self-defeating and belabored humor) showed the predicted detrimental effects, with higher levels on these specific components being associated with poorer self-esteem, greater depression and anxiety, and poorer judgments of self-competence. Also, as expected, the two maladaptive forms of sense of humor that did not focus on the self, but rather on others (i.e., aggressive and rude humor), were unrelated to personal well-being. These findings were discussed in terms of the need to identify more clearly the possible mechanisms that may result in either facilitative or detrimental effects on psychological well-being.

Psychological studies of responses to humor employ a variety of different recording methods and modes of presentation, but few have addressed whether these methodological differences affect people's responses to comedy. In a study of Martin et al. (2008), participants' expressive (laughter and smiling) and cognitive (ratings of funniness and enjoyment) responses to a popular British comedy program presented via videotape, audiotape, or in script form were measured. Behavioral response was recorded either covertly or overtly by a video camera. Mode of presentation significantly affected behavioral response: the videotape and the audiotape conditions generated significantly greater laughter and smiling than did the script condition. Although the presence of the camera was not regarded as obtrusive, its presence did inhibit laughter and depressed enjoyment (but not amusement). The findings suggest that research using humorous material should carefully consider the mode of presentation and the behavioral recording conditions employed.

Conclusion

Nonetheless, a good laugh never hurt anyone. And while considerable research with a focus on dysfunction and disease has already been done, until recently, very little was scientifically known about the physiological and psychological mechanisms of human flourishing. Humor provides at least some temporary relief from everyday problems; psychologists note that people who learn to chuckle at their own foibles, rather than letting annoyances eat at them, may find solutions to their problems easier to come by. More generally, a good guffaw is just plain healthy. People who make others laugh may make friends especially easily. If so, they probably reap the well-established health benefits of having many supportive relationships. Also, certain humor styles, such as self-deprecation, possibly improve relationships and physical health over time, while other approaches, such as sarcasm, may do the opposite. The extent of laughter's healing potential is still unclear, but researchers have yet to find any harmful side effects. So taking time to chuckle each day may keep us laughing a little longer. According to Neuhoff and Schaefer (2002), adults who act happy by smiling broadly or laughing heartily for just a minute can improve their mood for at least a few seconds. Comedian Bill Cosby said, "if you can laugh at it, you can survive it."

References

Bazzini, D. G., Stack, E. R., Martincin, P. D., & Davis, C. P. (2007). The effect of reminiscing about laughter on relationship satisfaction. *Motivation & Emotion, 31*(1), 25–34. doi:.1007/s11031-006-9045-6

Bell, D., & Malhi, G. S. (2009). Humor: Crying out to be taken seriously? *Acta Neuropsychiatrica, 21*(1), 34–35. doi:10.1111/j.1601-5215.2008.00354.x

Bennett, M. P., Zeller, J. M., Rosenberg, L., & McCann, J. (2003). The effect of mirthful laughter on stress and natural killer cell activity. *Alternative Therapies in Health & Medicine, 9*(2), 38.

Berk, R. A. (2001). The active ingredients in humor: Psychophysiological benefits and risks for older adults. *Educational Gerontology, 27*(3/4), 323–339 doi:10.1080/036012701750195021

Berk, L. S., Felten, D. L., Tan, S. A., Bittman, B. B., & Westengard, J. J. (2001). Modulation of neuroimmune parameters during the eustress of humor-associated mirthful laughter. *Advances in Mind-Body Medicine, 17*(3), 200.

Boyle, G. J., & Joss-Reid, J. (2004). Relationship of humor to health: A psychometric investigation. *British Journal of Health Psychology, 9*(1), 51–66. doi:10.1348/135910704322778722

Carlson, K. A. (2011). The impact of humor on memory: Is the humor effect about humor?. *Humor: International Journal of Humor Research, 24*(1), 21–41.

Degabriele, J., & Walsh, I. P. (2010). Humor appreciation and comprehension in children with intellectual disability. *Journal of Intellectual Disability Research, 54*(6), 525–537. doi:10.1111/j.1365-2788.2010.01277.x

Devereux, P. G., & Ginsburg, G. P. (2001). Sociality effects on the production of laughter. *Journal of General Psychology, 128*(2), 227–240. doi:10.1080/00221300109598910

Feingold, A., & Mazzella, R. (1991). Psychometric intelligence and verbal humor ability. *Personality and Individual Differences, 12*(5), 427–435. doi:10.1016/0191-8869(91)90060-O

Friedman, H. S., Tucker, J. S., Tomlinson-Keasey, C., Schwartz, J. E., Wingard, D. L., & Criqui, M. H. (1993). Does childhood personality predict longevity? *Journal of Personality & Social Psychology, 65*(1), 176–185.

Geisler, F. C. M., & Weber, H. (2010). Harm that does not hurt: Humor in coping with self-threat. *Motivation and Emotion, 34*(4), 446–456. doi:.1007/s11031-010-9185-6

Greengross, G., & Miller, G. (2011). Humor ability reveals intelligence, predicts mating success, and is higher in males. *Intelligence, 39*(4), 188–192. doi:10.1016/j.intell.2011.03.006

Henderson, S. W., & Rosario, K. (2008). But seriously: Clowning in children's mental health. *Journal of the American Academy of Child & Adolescent Psychiatry, 47*(9), 983–986. doi:10.1097/CHI.0b013e31817f1273

Hopp, H. B. (2011). The unconscious pursuit of emotion regulation: Implications for psychological health. *Cognition & Emotion, 25*(3), 532–545.

Howrigan, D. P., & MacDonald, K. B. (2008). Humor as a mental fitness indicator. *Evolutionary Psychology, 6*(4), 625–666.

Kimata, H. (2004). Reduction of allergen-specific IgE production by laughter. *European Journal of Clinical Investigation, 34*, 76–77. doi: 10.1111/j.1365-2362.2004.01294.x

Kohn, N., Kellermann, T., Gur, R. C., Schneider, F., & Habel, U. (2011). Gender differences in the neural correlates of humor processing: Implications for different processing modes. *Neuropsychologia, 49*(5), 888–897. doi:10.1016/j.neuropsychologia.2011.02.010

Kuhn, C. C., Nichols, M. R., & Belew, B. L. (2010). The role of humor in transforming stressful life events. In T. W. Miller (Ed.), *Handbook of stressful transitions across the lifespan* (pp. 653–662). New York: Springer.

Kuiper, N. A., & Martin, R. A. (1998). Laughter and stress in daily life: Relation to positive and negative affect. *Motivation & Emotion, 22*(2), 133–153.

Kuiper, N. A., & McHale, N. (2009). Humor styles as mediators between self-evaluative standards and psychological well-being. *Journal of Psychology: Interdisciplinary and Applied, 143*(4), 359–376. doi:10.3200/JRLP.143.4.359-376

Kuiper, N. A., & Nicholl, S. (2004). Thoughts of feeling better? Sense of humor and physical health. *Humor: International Journal of Humor Research, 17*(1–2), 37–66. doi:10.1515/humr.2004.007

Kuiper, N. A., Grimshaw, M., Leite, C., & Kirsh, G. (2004). Humor is not always the best medicine: Specific components of sense of humor and psychological well-being. *Humor: International Journal of Humor Research, 17*(1–2), 135–168. doi:10.1515/humr.2004.002

Lai, J. L., Chong, A. L., Siu, O. T., Evans, P., Chan, C. W., & Ho, R. H. (2010). Humor attenuates the cortisol awakening response in healthy older men. *Biological Psychology, 84*(2), 375–380. doi:10.1016/j.biopsycho.2010.03.012

Lefcourt H. M. (2001) *Humor: The psychology of living buoyantly*. New York: Kluwer Academic/Plenum Publishers.

Lefcourt, H. M., Davidson, K., Prkachin, K. M., & Mills, D. E. (1997). Humor as a stress moderator in the prediction of blood pressure obtained during five stressful tasks. *Journal of Research in Personality, 31*(4), 523–542. doi:10.1006/jrpe.1997.2191

Mahony, D. L., Burroughs, W. J., & Lippman, L. G. (2002). Perceived attributes of health-promoting laughter: A cross-generational comparison. *Journal of Psychology: Interdisciplinary and Applied, 136*(2), 171–181. doi:10.1080/00223980209604148

Mak, W., & Carpenter, B. D. (2007). Humor comprehension in older adults. *Journal of the International Neuropsychological Society, 13*(4), 606–614. doi:10.1017/S1355617707070750

Martin, R. A. (2002). Is laughter the best medicine? Humor, laughter, and physical health. *Current Directions in Psychological Science, 11*(6), 216–220. doi:10.1111/1467-8721.00204

Martin, R. A. (2004). Sense of humor and physical health: Theoretical issues, recent findings, and future directions. *Humor: International Journal of Humor Research, 17*(1–2), 1–19. doi:10.1515/humr.2004.005

Martin, R. A., & Lefcourt, H. M. (1984). Situational Humor Response Questionnaire: Quantitative measure of sense of humor. *Journal of Social and Personality Psychology, 47*, 145–155.

Martin, R. A., Puhlik-Doris, P., Larsen, G., Gray, J., & Weir, K. (2003). Individual differences in uses of humor and their relation to psychological well-being: Development of the Humor Styles Questionnaire. *Journal of Research in Personality, 37*, 48–75.

Martin, G. N., Sadler, S. J., Barrett, C. E., & Beaven, A. (2008). Measuring responses to humor: How the testing context affects individuals' reaction to comedy. *Humor: International Journal of Humor Research, 21*(2), 143–155. doi:10.1515/HUMOR.2008.007

Marziali, E., McDonald, L., & Donahue, P. (2008). The role of coping humor in the physical and mental health of older adults. *Aging & Mental Health, 12*(6), 713–718. doi:10.1080/13607860802154374

Mathieu, S. I. (2008). Happiness and humor group promotes life satisfaction for senior center participants. *Activities, Adaptation & Aging, 32*(2), 134–148. doi:10.1080/01924780802143089

McAdams, D. P., Jackson, R., & Kirshnit, C. (1984). Looking, laughing, and smiling in dyads as a function of intimacy motivation and reciprocity. *Journal of Personality, 52*(3), 261–273. doi:10.1111/1467-6494.ep7390824

McCreaddie, M., & Wiggins, S. (2008). The purpose and function of humor in health, health care and nursing: A narrative review. *Journal of Advanced Nursing, 61*(6), 584–595. doi:10.1111/j.1365-2648.2007.04548.x

McGhee, P. E. (1971). Cognitive development and children's comprehension of humor. *Child Development, 42*(1), 123–138. doi:10.2307/1127069

Newman, M., & Stone, A. A. (1996). Does humor moderate the effects of experimentally-induced stress? *Annals of Behavioral Medicine, 18*(2), 101–109. doi:10.1007/BF02909582

Neuhoff, C. C., & Schaefer, C. (2002). Effects of laughing, smiling, and howling on mood. *Psychological Reports, 91*(3), 1079.

Smoski, M. (2005). *The development of antiphonal laughter between friends and strangers*. ProQuest Information & Learning). *Dissertation Abstracts International: Section B: The Sciences and Engineering, 65*(8–). (2005-99004-228)

Stieger, S., Formann, A. K., & Burger, C. (2011). Humor styles and their relationship to explicit and implicit self-esteem. *Personality and Individual Differences, 50*(5), 747–750. doi:10.1016/j.paid.2010.11.025

Svebak, S. (1996). The development of the Sense of Humor Questionnaire: From SHQ to SHQ-6. *Humor: International Journal of Humor Research, 9,* 341–362.

Svebak, S., Romundstad, S., & Holmen, J. (2010). A 7-year prospective study of sense of humor and mortality in an adult county population: The HUNT-2 study. *International Journal of Psychiatry in Medicine, 40*(2), 125–146. doi:10.2190/PM.40.2.a

Thorson, J.A., & Powell, F.C. (1993). Development and validation of a Multidimensional Sense of Humor Scale. *Journal of Clinical Psychology, 49,* 13–23.

Uchino, B. N., Cawthon, R. M., Smith, T. W., Light, K. C., McKenzie, J., Carlisle, M., &... Bowen, K. (2012). Social relationships and health: Is feeling positive, negative, or both (ambivalent) about your social ties related to telomeres? *Health Psychology,* doi:10.1037/a0026836

Uekermann, J., Channon, S., Lehmkämper, C., Abdel-Hamid, M., Vollmoeller, W., & Daum, I. (2008). Executive function, mentalizing and humor in major depression. *Journal of the International Neuropsychological Society, 14*(1), 55–62. doi:10.1017/S1355617708080016

Vaillant, G. E. (2000). Adaptive mental mechanisms: Their role in a positive psychology. *American Psychologist, 55*(1), 89–98. doi:10.1037/0003-066X.55.1.89

Vereen, L. G., Butler, S., Williams, F. C., Darg, J. A., & Downing, T. E. (2006). The use of humor when counseling African American college students. *Journal of Counseling & Development, 84*(1), 10–15.

Weisfeld, G.E., Nowak, N.T., Lucas, T., Weisfeld, C.C., Imamoglu, E.O., Butovskaya, M., Shen, J. & Parkhill, M. R. (2011). Do women seek humorousness in men because it signals intelligence? A cross-cultural test. *Humor: International Journal of Humor Research, 24*(4), 435–462.

Wheeler, E. (2010). Life stress buffer: The salubrious role of African-centered spirituality. In T. W. Miller (Ed.), *Handbook of Stressful Transitions Across the Lifespan* (pp. 503–519). New York: Springer.

Wolosin, R. J. (1975). Cognitive similarity and group laughter. *Journal of Personality and Social Psychology, 32*(3), 503–509. doi:10.1037/h0077083

Zweyer, K., Velker, B., & Ruch, W. (2004). Do cheerfulness, exhilaration, and humor production moderate pain tolerance? A FACS study. *Humor: International Journal of Humor Research, 17*(1–2), 85–119. doi:10.1515/humr.2004.009

Part II
Positive Personality Traits

Chapter 7
Rediscovering Internal Strengths of the Aged: The Beneficial Impact of Wisdom, Mastery, Purpose in Life, and Spirituality on Aging Well

Monika Ardelt, Scott D. Landes, Kathryn R. Gerlach and Leah Polkowski Fox

A previous version of this chapter was presented at the 2001 Annual Meetings of the American Sociological Association in Anaheim, CA. The research was supported by a Brookdale National Fellowship, a grant from NIH/NIA (R03 AG14855-01), and a Research Initiation Project Award from the College of Liberal Arts and Sciences at the University of Florida.

What is the secret to a rewarding and satisfying life in old age? A vast body of literature has amassed the effects of objective life conditions such as physical health, financial situation, socioeconomic status, physical environment, and social relationships on aging well (e.g., Diener and Biswas-Diener 2002; Geerlings et al. 2000; Pinquart and Sörensen 2000; Rowe and Kahn 1998; Steverink et al. 2001). Although studies focused on objective life conditions form the majority of research in this field, the analysis of subjective conditions is not nearly as extensive (George 2010; Larson 1978). Diener et al. (1999) concluded that the approach to attribute subjective well-being to objective factors is too simplistic. They pointed to "the interaction of psychological factors with life circumstances" as one of the most fruitful areas for future research (p. 276).

Although some research has tried to integrate external and internal factors to explain subjective well-being (e.g., Kozma et al. 1991), analyses that explore the

M. Ardelt (✉) · S. D. Landes
Department of Sociology and Criminology & Law, University of Florida,
3219 Turlington Hall, P.O. Box 117330, 32611-7330 Gainesville, FL, USA
e-mail: ardelt@ufl.edu

S. D. Landes
e-mail: scott.landes@ufl.edu

K. R. Gerlach
Office of Technology Licensing, University of Florida, 747 SW 2nd Avenue,
P.O. Box 117330, 32611-7330 Gainesville, FL, USA
e-mail: gerlach.kathryn@gmail.com

L. P. Fox
University of Florida, P.O. Box 117330, 32611-7330 Gainesville, FL, USA
e-mail: leahpolk@hotmail.com

J. D. Sinnott (ed.), *Positive Psychology*,
DOI 10.1007/978-1-4614-7282-7_7,

influence of subjective elements on older adults' well-being have often taken a minor or supporting position when compared with the study of variables such as physical health, social relationships, or socioeconomic status (George 2010). The distinction between external and internal correlates of subjective well-being is echoed in past conceptual debates on "top-down" versus "bottom-up" theories of happiness. According to "bottom-up" theories such as situational theory, a happy life is "merely an accumulation of happy moments" (Diener 1984, p. 565), whereas "top-down" theories state that well-being depends more on internal psychological factors than external circumstances. A "top-down" approach to the study of subjective well-being tends to view a person's life satisfaction and positive/negative affect as originating within the individual herself, whereas a "bottom-up" approach considers a person's subjective well-being a direct result of objective life events or conditions.

For example, Veenhoven (1991, 1994) proposed that happiness is a composite of contentment and the fulfillment of basic human needs. Those who are hungry, poorly housed, and in unsafe situations are unlikely to be happy, regardless of their cognitive approach to their circumstances. However, other researchers suggested that contrary to situational theory, the internal strengths of older adults and their personality characteristics might have a greater effect on their sense of well-being than on objective circumstances (e.g., Colerick 1985; George 1990; Johnson 1995; Landau and Litwin 2001; Vaillant 2002). Spirituality, for example, often provides a sense of meaning and an alternate (and positive) perspective on difficult economic and health problems for some older individuals (Ai et al. 2010). As a consequence, the psychological impact of negative objective circumstances can be lessened, resulting in a higher-than-expected level of well-being (Black 1999). Additionally, some researchers have found that older adults who are able to extract meaning from life events are more likely to have positive mood states, regardless of health and socioeconomic status (Scioli et al. 2000). Overall, subjective factors have been shown to significantly impact well-being, and should, therefore, be taken into account when studying the elements of "successful aging."

Attitudes toward death often have been ignored as indicators of aging well, even though they may have a considerable impact on the aging experience (Kearl 1996; Scioli et al. 2000). Specifically, the death fear, often encapsulating anxieties regarding the experience of senescence, the cessation of life, loss of relationships, and the possibility of an afterlife can hamper the individual's ability to find meaning in the midst of aging (Florian and Kravetz 1983; Mikulincher and Florian 2008; Wahl 1959). Yet, previous researchers have highlighted that those adults engaged in successful aging were more likely to find existential meaning in the experience of aging and death through inner strengths such as life purpose, psychological well-being, and spirituality (Tomer et al. 2008; Van Ranst and Marcoen 2000; Wong 1998).

Following the traditions of Erikson (1982; Erikson et al. 1986), Jung (1971), and Maslow (1970, 1971) and their theories of life-long psychosocial development and growth, we propose that in a sample of 144 community residents, nursing home residents, and hospice patients between the ages of 56 and 98 years, older adults' internal strengths, consisting of their wisdom, sense of mastery, purpose in life, and spirituality, are stronger predictors of subjective well-being and death fear than their objective life conditions (Ardelt 2011b; Levenson and Crumpler 1996; McCoy et al. 2000; Nakasone 1994).

Effects of Wisdom, Mastery, and Purpose in Life on Aging Well

Erikson's (1963) theory of psychosocial growth divides a person's life into eight developmental stages or psychosocial tasks. In old age, people tend to struggle with the eighth task: the psychosocial crisis of integrity versus despair. The goal of this final stage is to acknowledge the "inalterability of the past" (Erikson et al. 1986, p. 56), and to accept the totality of one's life. Regrets over missed opportunities and past poor decisions can lead to despair when older adults realize that their time to correct mistakes and discover new opportunities is limited. Integrity, however, can be achieved if people acknowledge and embrace the lives they have lived, including their accomplishments and shortcomings. Erikson suggested that the successful resolution of this last crisis, integrity versus despair, leads to wisdom which, "... is detached concern with life itself in the face of death itself" (Erikson 1964, p. 133). Wise elders are able to confirm the importance of a continued engagement with life without ignoring or denying the realities of old age, including physical deterioration and the approach of death (Ardelt 2011b; Assmann 1994; Baltes 1993).

In this study, wisdom is defined and operationalized as an integration of cognitive, reflective, and compassionate personality characteristics (Ardelt 2004, 2008; Clayton and Birren 1980). This definition of wisdom covers the major qualities of a wise person (Ardelt 2011b; Meeks and Jeste 2009), overlaps with most layman definitions of wisdom (Bluck and Glück 2005), and is also compatible with expert theories (Jeste et al. 2010) and wisdom traditions of the East (Takahashi 2000). The *cognitive wisdom dimension* relates to the search for the true or deeper meaning of phenomena and events (Chandler and Holliday 1990; Kekes 1983; Sternberg 1990). To do this, wise individuals must look at phenomena and events from many different perspectives and engage in self-reflection (*reflective dimension*) to transcend their subjectivity and projections. Reflective thinking and the praxis of self-reflection, in turn, tend to decrease people's self-centeredness and increase their insight into the complexities of life and human nature, including their own and other people's motivations and behavior (Chandler and Holliday 1990; Csikszentmihalyi and Rathunde 1990; Kramer 1990). Finally, a better comprehension of life and the human existence together with a reduction in self-centeredness are likely to lead to greater sympathy and compassion for others (Csikszentmihalyi and Rathunde 1990; Levitt 1999; Pascual-Leone 1990), which describes the *compassionate wisdom dimension*.

Hence, wise people are expected to age well because they understand the true nature of existence, have lived a meaningful life, and therefore, are able to accept life, the realities of aging, and death (Ardelt 2000; Taranto 1989). Indeed, most but not all studies found an association between diverse measures of wisdom and aging well (Ardelt 2011b; Ardelt and Oh 2010). For example, wisdom was positively correlated with happiness in an age-diverse internet sample (Bergsma and Ardelt in press) and with life satisfaction in samples of middle-aged and older adults (Le 2011; Mickler and Staudinger 2008; Takahashi and Overton 2002). Moreover, wisdom had a stronger positive effect on life satisfaction in old age than on objective circumstances (Ardelt 1997). However, a performance measure of personal wisdom and measures of practical and transcendent wisdom were unrelated to life satisfaction in samples of age-diverse and middle-aged adults (Mickler and Staudinger 2008; Wink and Helson 1997).

Wisdom tends to be accompanied by a sense of mastery (Ardelt 2005; Glück 2011; Glück and Bluck in press) and purpose in life (Ardelt 2011a; Staudinger and Kessler 2008), which are also important predictors of aging well (Erikson 1963; Heckhausen and Schulz 1995; McCoy et al. 2000; Ryff 1989). Previous studies of older adults have found a positive association between a sense of mastery and life satisfaction (Windle and Woods 2004) and mental health (Pudrovska et al. 2005; Zautra et al. 1995), and a negative correlation with psychological distress (Comijs et al. 1999; Jang et al. 2002). Even if the loss of "primary" control in old age cannot always be avoided, it is generally possible to control the emotional adaptation to this loss, a process that is often termed "secondary control" (Heckhausen and Schulz 1993, 1995; Rothbaum et al. 1982). An acceptance of the inevitable such as physical decline and the approach of death, in turn, might be a way to gain control of the uncontrollable (Aldwin 1994; Brandtstädter and Greve 1994; McCoy et al. 2000).

There is also widespread consensus that a sense of meaning and purpose in life is essential for aging well (Erikson 1963; Hedberg et al. 2010; Ryff 1989). Wong (2000, p. 24) summarized this sentiment as follows:

> [P]ersonal meaning is the hidden dimension of successful aging ..., because having a positive meaning and purpose in life will not only add years to one's life, but also life to one's years. Without a clear sense of meaning and purpose in the face of physical decline, longevity may prove to be an unbearable burden. People need to develop a positive attitude towards life in order to maintain life satisfaction in the midst of losses and illness.

Wong's (2000) research and other studies have shown that a sense of personal meaning is strongly and positively related to happiness and subjective well-being and negatively related to psychopathology and depressive symptoms among older adults (Fry 2000; Garner et al. 2007; Hedberg et al. 2010). In line with those findings, Wong proposed "... that successful aging is 80 % attitude, and 20 % everything else" (p. 26).

Moody (1986), however, argued that a sense of meaning in old age needs to encompass a higher purpose that goes beyond the individual to alleviate the threats of physical decline, social losses, and death. In fact, most of Wong's research participants found meaning in goals that transcended self-interests and gained fulfillment and satisfaction by serving others. According to Wong (2000, p. 28).

> The untold story of successful aging is about positive attitudes towards life and death, about the spiritual and existential quest, and about personal growth in wisdom and spirituality. From this spiritual, existential perspective, successful aging is attainable for everyone with positive meanings, regardless of his or her physical condition.

Although one might suspect that older adults who feel their life is meaningless due to emotional and/or physical distress would welcome death the most, past evidence indicates that, paradoxically, those elders who have discovered meaning and purpose in their life tend to be less afraid of death and more willing to let go (Ardelt and Koenig 2007; Fortner et al. 2000; Wong 2000). It is possible that a sense of meaning and purpose in life that goes beyond the self-interests of the individual might make it easier to find meaning in death as well (Jewell 2010; Tomer and Eliason 2000).

In particular, we propose that the combination of wisdom, mastery, and purpose in life make up individuals' psychosocial strengths, which inoculate older adults from despair and death anxiety and foster subjective well-being, even under challenging objective life conditions.

Spirituality and Aging Well

Spirituality, understood as an inner strength through which the individual may move beyond self-interest and make meaning of both lived experiences and the transcendent unknown (Staton et al. 2001), provides the aging adult with another resource for finding meaning in the midst of emotional and physical distress that often accompany the aging process, including the dying experience. In the midst of the challenging existential experiences of aging, loss, disability, and dying that can work to isolate an aging adult from previous resources of support, spirituality can operate as a self-transcendent resource with which the individual can continue to grow, find meaning, and achieve a sense of completion (Byock 1996; Wong 2008). Furthermore, spirituality has been shown to be related to greater physical, psychological, and relational health (Chibnall et al. 2002) and enhanced subjective well-being (Ardelt and Koenig 2007; Fry 2000). In a qualitative longitudinal study of actively dying aging adults, spirituality, understood as an inner strength utilized to generate existential meaning in the midst of senescence and death, helped the aging adults to achieve a sense of both meaning and completion in relationship to self, others, and the transcendent realm (Staton et al. (2001). In interviews with hospice patients and their families, Hinton (1999) confirmed that spirituality frequently provided actively dying aging adults a meaning structure and/or belief system in which they constructively frame the experience of death. As highlighted in interviews with outpatients with a terminal illness, this spiritual meaning structure not only helps frame the meaning of death but can also work to "buffer" against the negative effects of death fear (Chibnall et al. (2002).

Although Wink (2006) reported no measureable effect of spirituality on death fear, some quantitative studies have found that spirituality has an inverse relationship on death anxiety in older adults (Rasmussen and Johnson 1994). Other researchers highlight the reality that belief systems might have a curvilinear relationship to death fear (McMordie 1981; Nelson and Cantrell 1980; Wink and Scott 2005) because those with either high or low religiousness or spirituality were reported to have the least death fear due to an increased consonance between their beliefs and practices, or an increased sense of expressed contentment with their spirituality. By contrast, those with a moderate level of spirituality were more likely to fear death due to a disjunction between beliefs and practices, or an expressed spiritual discontent (Landes and Ardelt 2011).

Hypotheses

To summarize, the following three hypotheses were tested:

Hypothesis 1 Psychosocial strengths, consisting of a combination of wisdom, mastery, and purpose in life, are directly related to subjective well-being and inversely to death fear in old age, even after controlling for objective circumstances such as subjective physical health, age, economic pressure, socioeconomic status, social involvement, gender, and race.

Hypothesis 2 Spirituality is directly related to subjective well-being and has a quadratic effect on death fear after controlling for objective life conditions. Although a higher level of spirituality is expected to correlate with a greater sense of subjective well-being, older adults with relatively low or relatively high spirituality scores are expected to report lower death fear than adults with moderate spirituality scores.

Hypothesis 3 Psychosocial strengths and spirituality have a stronger combined impact on subjective well-being and death fear than objective life conditions.

Method

Procedure

Community Sample

The first round of data collection for the community sample took place between December 1997 and June 1998. Respondents were drawn from 18 civic, community, or church groups of older adults located in North Central Florida. Members of the research team visited those groups to ask for volunteers, aged 55 and above, for a "Personality and Aging Well" study. Older adults who were interested in the study gave the research team member their names, phone numbers, and addresses. Shortly thereafter, a research team member contacted potential respondents to make an appointment for the delivery of the questionnaire and to give instructions for filling out the self-administered survey. The research team member also offered to conduct the interview if the respondent needed assistance in completing the questionnaire. Ten respondents accepted this offer. All other 170 questionnaires were returned by mail in stamped, preaddressed envelopes.

All respondents with known addresses were contacted by mail for a follow-up survey 10 months after the first interview. Participants who failed to return the second questionnaire within two to three weeks after its mailing were reminded by phone and asked whether they needed assistance in completing the survey. Ultimately, 123 respondents or about 70 % of the initial sample with known addresses returned the follow-up survey.

Hospice Patients and Nursing Home Residents

Between August 1999 and September 2001, 18 older hospice patients and 23 nursing home residents, who were recruited through a local hospice agency and local nursing homes participated in qualitative and quantitative face-to-face interviews as part of an "Aging and Dying Well" study. Of those 18 hospice patients, 8 resided in the community, 7 lived at a hospice care center (a residential facility operated by hospice), and 3 stayed in an assisted-living residence.

Sample

The sample included 18 hospice patients, 23 nursing home residents, and the 103 community residents with complete information on all variables, ranging in age from 56 to 98 years ($M = 74.12$; $SD = 8.49$). Of those 144 respondents, 69 % were female, 77 % were white, and 48 % were married. A total of 85 % of the respondents had at least a high school diploma and 29 % had a graduate degree.

Measures

For the community sample, objective life conditions were only assessed at baseline with the exception of subjective physical health. All other measures were taken from the second wave of data collection, which also included the spirituality measures. Hospice patients and nursing home residents were only interviewed at one point in time. Hence, the analyses to examine older people's concurrent relations between indicators of aging well and their subjective physical health and internal strengths are primarily cross-sectional rather than longitudinal.

Indicators of Aging Well

Subjective well-being was assessed as the average of general well-being during the past month and absence of depressive symptoms during the past week. The average of six items from the General Well-Being Schedule (GWBS; Fazio 1977) was taken to gauge *general well-being*. The items assessed respondents' level of life satisfaction (e.g., How happy, satisfied, or pleased have you been with your personal life during the past month?, 1 = *extremely happy* to 6 = *very dissatisfied*) and cheerfulness (e.g., How have you been feeling in general during the past month?, 1 = *in excellent spirits* to 6 = *in very low spirits*; How DEPRESSED or CHEERFUL have you been during the past month?, 0 = *very depressed* to 10 = *very cheerful*). *Absence of depressive symptoms* was calculated as the average of four items of the well-being subscale (e.g., I was happy; I enjoyed life) and the reversed seven items of the depressive affect subscale (e.g., I felt depressed; I felt sad) of the Center for Epidemiologic Studies Depression Scale (CES-D) (Radloff 1977). Respondents reported how often they had felt this way during the past week (1 = *less than 1 day* to 4 = *5–7 days*). The nine items of the CES-D that asked about perception of other people (e.g., People were unfriendly) or somatic symptoms (e.g., I could not get going) were not used in the construction of the scale because they did not measure subjective well-being, and older adults in nursing homes or under hospice care might experience somatic symptoms without being depressed. All items were transformed into 0–5 scales and reversed if necessary so that higher values reflected greater subjective well-being. The reliability coefficient Cronbach's α was 0.88 for general well-being and 0.85 for absence of depressive symptoms, and the correlation between the two variables was $r = 0.72$ ($p < 0.001$).

Death fear was assessed by one dimension of the Death Attitude Profile–Revised (Wong et al. 1994). The scale was the mean of seven items (e.g., I have an intense death fear; Death is no doubt a grim experience) with an α-value of 0.85. The scale of the items ranged from 1 (*strongly agree*) to 5 (*strongly disagree*), which was reversed for all items before the average was computed.

Internal Strengths

The Three-Dimensional Wisdom Scale (3D-WS) was administered to measure the cognitive, reflective, and compassionate indicators of *wisdom* (Ardelt 2003). The cognitive dimension of wisdom, which measures an understanding of life or the desire to know the truth, was computed as the mean of 14 items (e.g., Ignorance is bliss) with a Cronbach's α of 0.87. The reflective dimension, which taps a person's ability to look at phenomena and events from different perspectives and to avoid subjectivity and projections, was the average of 12 items (e.g., I always try to look at all sides of a problem) with an α-value of 0.70. Finally, the compassionate dimension of wisdom, which captures the extent to which an individual develops sympathy and compassion for others and the motivation to help others in need was assessed as the average of 13 items (e.g., Sometimes I feel a real compassion for everyone; If I see people in need, I try to help them one way or another) with an α-value of 0.69. All the items were measured on one of the two 5-point scales, ranging either from 1 = *strongly agree* to 5 = *strongly disagree* or from 1 = *definitely true of myself* to 5 = *not true of myself*, and all items were scored in a higher wisdom direction before the average of the items was calculated. Wisdom was measured as the average of the cognitive, reflective, and compassionate dimensions. The correlations between the three dimensions ranged from $r = 0.38$ ($p < 0.001$) between the cognitive and compassionate wisdom dimensions to $r = 0.55$ ($p < 0.001$) between the reflective and compassionate wisdom dimensions.

Mastery was assessed by Pearlin and Schooler's (1978) mastery scale. The scale consists of the average of seven items (e.g., What happens to me in the future mostly depends on me) ranging from 1 (*strongly agree*) to 5 (*strongly disagree*). The scale was reversed for the positively worded items before the average was computed. Cronbach's α was 0.72.

A sense of *purpose in life* was measured by the average of three items from Crumbaugh and Maholick's (1964) Purpose in Life Test (King and Hunt 1975). Four of the original nine items in the Purpose in Life Test assess subjective well-being and one item measures a sense of control rather than meaning and purpose in life. Hence, for this study, only the three items that refer to a sense of meaning and purpose in life were averaged (I have discovered satisfying goals and a clear purpose in life; If I should die today, I would feel that my life has been worthwhile; My personal existence often seems meaningless and without purpose) resulting in an α-value of 0.58. The scale of the items ranges from 1 (*definitely true of myself*) to 5 (*not true of myself*). The scale of the positively worded items was reversed before the average was calculated.

Psychosocial strengths were assessed by computing the average of wisdom, mastery, and purpose in life. As assumed, the associations between the three variables were relatively high, with correlations of $r = 0.57$ ($p < 0.001$) between wisdom and mastery, $r = 0.43$ ($p < 0.001$) between wisdom and purpose in life, and $r = 0.40$ ($p < 0.001$) between mastery and purpose in life.

Spirituality was measured using 13 items from one factor of the Spiritual Involvement and Beliefs Scale (Hatch et al. 1998). These items measure both spiritual involvement (e.g., frequency of prayer and spiritual activities) and beliefs (e.g., I believe there is a power greater than myself; My spiritual life fulfills me in ways that material possessions do not) in a nondenominational fashion. All items were assessed on 5-point scales (e.g., from 1 = *Always* to 5 = *Never* or from 1 = *Strongly Agree* to 5 = *Strongly Disagree*) and scored with higher values reflecting greater spiritual involvement and beliefs prior to computing the average of the 13 items. Cronbach's α for the scale was 0.92. The variable was mean-centered before the quadratic spirituality term was constructed to reduce multicollinearity.

Objective Life Conditions

Subjective physical health was assessed by two items from the GWBS to determine health concerns, worries, or distress (Have you been bothered by any illness, bodily disorder, pains, or fears about your health?, 1 = *all the time* to 6 = *none of the time;* How concerned or worried about your health have you been?, 0 = *not concerned at all* to 10 = *very concerned*). After reversing the scale of the second item and transforming both scales into 0–5 scales, the average was calculated, resulting in a Cronbach's α of 0.75.

Economic pressure was assessed by four adapted items from the Older Americans Resources and Services (OARS) Multidimensional Functional Assessment Questionnaire (Center for the Study of Aging and Human Development 1975) and the "Americans' Changing Lives" Questionnaire, Wave I (House 1994). The items measure financial situation compared to other people the respondent's age (1 = *better* to 3 = *worse*), difficulties in paying bills (1 = *not at all difficult* to 5 = *extremely difficult*), how well the respondent's amount of money takes care of his or her needs (1 = *very well* to 3 = *poorly*), and how the respondent's finances work out at the end of the month (1 = *some money left over* to 3 = *not enough money*). The 5-point scale was first transformed into a 3-point scale before all items were averaged. The combined scale had an α-value of 0.81.

Socioeconomic Status (*SES*) was the average of longest held occupation and educational degree. Longest held occupation was coded by three raters using Hollingshead's Index of Occupations (O'Rand 1982). At least two raters discussed and jointly decided all ratings for occupations whose code designation was not obvious. The scale ranged from 1 (*farm laborers, mental service workers*) to 9 (*higher executive, large business owner, major professional*). Educational degree ranged from 0 (*no high school*) to 4 (*graduate degree*) and was first transformed into a 9-point scale before it was averaged with occupation. For respondents without an occupation, SES reflected their educational degree. Cronbach's α was 0.82.

Social Involvement was the average of four adapted items from the OARS Multidimensional Functional Assessment Questionnaire (Center for the Study of Aging and Human Development 1975) and the "Americans' Changing Lives" Questionnaire, Wave I (House 1994). Items inquired how many people respondents knew well enough for visits in each others' homes (1 = *none* to 6 = *nine or more*); how many times they talked on the phone with friends, neighbors, or relatives (1 = *never or no phone* to 6 = *once a day or more*); how often they got together with friends, neighbors, or relatives to do things together or visit each other (1 = *never* to 6 = *more than once a week*); and how often they attended meetings of groups, clubs, or organizations (1 = *never* to 6 = *more than once a week*). Cronbach's α for the scale was 0.72.

Age was measured in years. Gender (0 = *male*, 1 = *female*), race (0 = *nonwhite*, 1 = *white*), marital status (0 = *unmarried*, 1 = *married*), nursing home resident (0 = *no*, 1 = *yes*), and hospice patient (0 = *no*, 1 = *yes*) were coded as dichotomous variables.

Analysis

Data were analyzed using bivariate correlation and nested multivariate ordinary least squares (OLS) regression analyses and a list wise deletion of cases. As the correlations between wisdom, mastery, and purpose in life were relatively high, all three variables were combined into a measure of psychosocial strengths to reduce multicollinearity in the regression analyses. Moreover, we assumed that the combination of these three variables had a stronger effect on subjective well-being and death fear than any of the three individual measures. To test this assumption, we entered wisdom, mastery, and purpose in life as separate independent variables in additional analyses (not shown) and report the results where appropriate.

Results

Bivariate Correlation Analyses

Bivariate correlations between the independent and dependent variables are provided in Table 7.1. The respondents' psychosocial strengths and spirituality were positively associated with subjective well-being, though the correlation was almost three times stronger for psychosocial strengths. Unlike spirituality, psychosocial strengths also had a moderately strong negative correlation with death fear. Compared with these internal strengths, the associations between objective life conditions and indicators of aging well were generally lower than psychosocial strengths, but higher than spirituality. Subjective physical health, SES, and social involvement were positively associated with subjective well-being and negatively with death fear, whereas economic pressure and being a nursing home resident were inversely related to subjective well-being and directly to greater death fear. Being a hospice patient was negatively and being married was positively correlated with subjective well-being, though both variables were unrelated to death fear. White respondents tended to have a lower level of death fear than African Americans, but there was no significant difference between the two racial groups in subjective well-being. Age and gender were not associated to either subjective well-being or death fear.

Psychosocial strengths and spirituality of the elders were only modestly positively correlated. Yet, both internal strengths measures were positively associated with subjective physical health and social involvement. In addition, SES and being married was directly related and age and economic pressure were inversely related to psychosocial strengths. Hospice patients and nursing home residents were less likely than community residents to possess psychosocial strengths, and hospice patients and men tended to be less spiritual than community and nursing home residents and the women in the sample.

The correlations of wisdom, mastery, and life purpose with indicators of aging well and objective life conditions were similar, albeit usually weaker, to the correlations with the combined psychosocial strengths measure with some notable exceptions. Only purpose in life was significantly related to spirituality, but it was unrelated to being a hospice patient or married. Advanced age was negatively related only to wisdom but had insignificant associations with mastery and life purpose.

Table 7.1 Bivariate correlation analyses between subjective well-being, death fear, internal strengths, and objective life conditions of older adults; Pearson's r

Number	Variables	1	2	3	4	5	6	7	8	9	10	11	12	13	M	SD
1	Subjective well-being														3.86	0.88
2	Death fear	−0.41**													2.47	0.85
3	Psychosocial strengths	0.70**	−0.50**												3.75	0.48
4	Spirituality	0.26**	−0.13	0.18*											3.77	0.80
5	Subjective health	0.54**	−0.27**	0.36**	0.26**										2.95	1.38
6	Economic pressure	−0.45**	0.35**	−0.42**	0.07	−0.21*									1.46	0.47
7	Socioeconomic status	0.27**	−0.20*	0.33**	−0.10	0.06	−0.42**								5.47	2.50
8	Social involvement	0.48**	−0.30**	0.46**	0.19*	0.26**	−0.48**	0.28**							4.61	1.19
9	Hospice patient	−0.22**	0.06	−0.17*	−0.18*	−0.15	0.03	−0.04	−0.08						0.13	0.33
10	Nursing home resident	−0.41**	0.17*	−0.41**	0.01	−0.14	0.47**	−0.33**	−0.53**	−0.17*					0.16	0.37
11	Age	−0.16	0.08	−0.21*	−0.15	−0.17*	0.03	0.02	−0.15	0.26**	0.03				74.12	8.48
12	Female	0.10	0.03	0.04	0.34**	0.13	0.07	−0.16	0.26**	−0.20*	−0.03	−0.10			0.69	0.47
13	White	0.03	−0.18*	0.03	−0.14	0.06	−0.21*	0.14	0.20*	0.11	−0.17*	0.19*	−0.01		0.77	0.42
14	Married	0.17*	−0.10	0.21*	−0.05	0.05	−0.34**	0.11	0.13	−0.11	−0.30**	−0.34**	−0.13	0.06	0.48	0.50

$n = 144$ *M* mean, *SD* standard deviation $^{*}p < 0.05$; $^{**}p < 0.01$

Table 7.2 Predictors of subjective well-being; hierarchical OLS regression models ($n = 144$)

	Model 1			Model 2			Model 3		
Independent variables	*b*	*β*	*SE*	*b*	*β*	*SE*	*b*	*β*	*SE*
Objective life conditions									
Subjective physical health	0.26	0.40***	0.04				0.18	0.29***	0.04
Economic pressure	− 0.33	− 0.18*	0.15				− 0.25	− 0.13	0.13
Socioeconomic status	0.02	0.05	0.03				− 0.00	− 0.01	0.02
Social involvement	0.13	0.17*	0.06				0.05	0.06	0.06
Hospice patient	− 0.45	− 0.17*	0.18				− 0.29	− 0.11	0.16
Nursing home resident	− 0.51	− 0.21*	0.19				− 0.32	− 0.13	0.17
Age	− 0.00	− 0.01	0.01				0.00	0.04	0.01
Female	− 0.04	− 0.02	0.13				− 0.04	− 0.02	0.12
White	− 0.17	− 0.08	0.14				− 0.09	− 0.04	0.12
Married	− 0.03	− 0.02	0.13				− 0.04	− 0.02	0.11
Internal strengths									
Psychosocial strengths				1.23	0.67***	0.11	0.80	0.44***	0.12
Spirituality				0.15	0.14*	0.07	0.10	0.09	0.07
Model fit									
R-squared		0.51			0.51			0.64	
R^2 change (Model 1 plus 2)								0.13***	
R^2 change (Model 2 plus 1)								0.13***	

$n = 144$ *$p < 0.05$; **$p < 0.01$; ***$p < 0.001$

Hierarchical Multivariate Regression Analyses

The results of hierarchical multivariate regression analyses of subjective well-being on predictor variables are shown in Table 7.2. Model 1 includes only the respondents' objective life conditions as predictor variables, whereas Model 2 includes only measures of internal strengths. Model 3 combines both objective life conditions and internal strengths. When only objective life conditions were included in the model (Model 1), subjective physical health and social involvement had a positive effect and economic pressure, being a hospice patient, and residing in a nursing home were negatively related to subjective well-being. Objective life conditions alone explained 51 % of the variation in subjective well-being. When only including internal strengths in the model (Model 2), both psychosocial strengths and spirituality had a positive effect on subjective well-being, also explaining 51 % of the variation in subjective well-being, yet psychosocial strengths was the main explanatory variable of the model ($\beta = 0.67, p < 0.001$).

Model 3 combined objective life conditions with internal strengths which accounted for 64 % of the variation in subjective well-being. After controlling for all variables in the model, the effects of spirituality, economic pressure, social involvement, and being a hospice patient or nursing home resident became insignificant, with only subjective physical health and psychosocial strengths remaining significantly

Table 7.3 Predictors of death fear; hierarchical OLS regression models

Predictors	Model 1			Model 2			Model 3		
Independent variables	*b*	*β*	*SE*	*b*	*β*	*SE*	*b*	*β*	*SE*
Objective life conditions									
Subjective physical health	− 0.11	− 0.18*	0.05				− 0.05	− 0.08	0.05
Economic pressure	0.40	0.22*	0.19				0.32	0.18	0.16
Socioeconomic status	− 0.02	− 0.06	0.03				0.01	0.04	0.03
Social involvement	− 0.11	− 0.16	0.08				0.01	0.02	0.07
Hospice patient	0.03	0.01	0.22				− 0.18	− 0.07	0.19
Nursing home resident	− 0.16	− 0.07	0.24				− 0.26	− 0.11	0.21
Age	0.01	0.05	0.01				− 0.00	− 0.02	0.01
Female	0.15	0.08	0.16				0.09	0.05	0.14
White	− 0.23	− 0.11	0.17				− 0.28	− 0.14	0.14
Married	0.04	0.03	0.16				0.10	0.06	0.14
Internal strengths									
Psychosocial strengths				− 0.75	− 0.43***	0.12	− 0.72	− 0.41***	0.15
Spirituality				− 0.35	− 0.33***	0.10	− 0.40	− 0.38***	0.10
Spirituality squared				− 0.33	− 0.44***	0.07	− 0.33	− 0.44***	0.07
Model fit									
R-squared		0.20			0.36			0.43	
R^2 change (Model 1 plus 2)								0.23***	
R^2 change (Model 2 plus 1)								0.06	

$n = 144$ *$p < 0.05$; **$p < 0.01$; ***$p < 0.001$

related to subjective well-being. (Although we did not hypothesize a curvilinear effect of spirituality on subjective well-being, we confirmed in separate analyses that the quadratic effect of spirituality was insignificant). The respondents' level of psychosocial strengths (combining wisdom, mastery, and purpose in life) had the strongest effect on subjective well-being ($\beta = 0.44$, $p < 0.001$). Adding either internal strengths to Model 1 or objective life conditions to Model 2 explained an additional 13 % of the variation in subjective well-being.

Entering wisdom, mastery, and purpose in life as separate variables into the regression equation in Model 2 (not shown) revealed that purpose in life had the strongest effect on subjective well-being ($\beta = 0.43, p < 0.001$), followed by wisdom ($\beta = 0.21$, $p = 0.006$) and mastery ($\beta = 0.20$, $p = 0.009$). Yet, besides subjective health, only purpose in life remained statistically significant in Model 3 ($\beta = 0.34$, $p < 0.001$), although the variance inflation factor of wisdom was 2.25, indicating the presence of multicollinearity.

The results of hierarchical multivariate regression analyses of death fear on predictor variables are reported in Table 7.3. In a modeling strategy similar to the analysis of subjective well-being, Model 1 included predictor variables of objective life conditions, Model 2 included only measures of internal strengths, and Model 3 combined objective life conditions with internal strengths. Based on previous research with this data set (Landes and Ardelt 2011), a quadratic spirituality variable was added to analyze the curvilinear effect of spirituality on death fear.

Objective life conditions (Model 1) explained 20 % of the variation in death fear with economic pressure having a direct and subjective health an inverse effect on death fear. By contrast, internal strengths alone explained 36 % of the variation in the respondent's death fear (Model 2). Psychosocial strengths were inversely related to death fear ($\beta = -0.43, p < 0.001$), whereas the effect of spirituality on death fear was curvilinear, as expected, following an upside-down u-curve. Older adults with either relatively low or high scores on spirituality tended to have less death fear than those with moderate spirituality scores. Combining both objective life conditions and internal strengths (Model 3) accounted for 43 % of the overall variation in death fear. The inclusion of internal strengths significantly increased the explanatory power of Model 1 by 23 %, whereas the explained variance of Model 2 was increased by only 6 % after all objective life conditions were added. After controlling for all predictor variables, none of the objective life conditions had a significant effect on death fear, whereas psychosocial strengths tended to have an inverse effect on the respondents' death fear that was almost equal in size ($\beta = -0.41, p < 0.001$) to the positive effect of psychosocial strengths on subjective well-being. The curvilinear relation between spirituality and death fear also remained significant, suggesting lower levels of death fear for those respondents with either a low or high level of spirituality.

Additional analyses (not shown) with wisdom, mastery, and purpose in life entered separately into Models 2 and 3, indicated inverse effects of wisdom ($\beta = -0.20$, $p = 0.025$ and $\beta = -0.21$, $p = 0.036$, respectively) and mastery ($\beta = -0.21$, $p = 0.014$ and $\beta = -0.27$, $p = 0.006$, respectively) on death fear, whereas the effect of purpose in life remained insignificant ($\beta = -0.11$, $p = 0.16$ and $\beta = -0.04$, $p = 0.62$, respectively). Wisdom was again affected by multicollinearity in Model 3 as shown by a variance inflation factor of 2.29.

Discussion

As predicted in Hypothesis 1, psychosocial strengths of the aged, consisting of a combination of wisdom, mastery, and purpose in life, were significantly and positively related to subjective well-being and negatively to death fear, even after controlling for adults' objective life conditions. In fact, contrary to situational theory and other "bottom-up" theories, psychosocial strengths had a stronger effect on subjective well-being and death fear than any of the objective life conditions. These findings corroborate and expand the previous research of Scioli et al. (2000) in examining mastery beyond SES and health levels.

Wisdom, mastery, and purpose in life were significantly correlated with each other, and the combination of those strengths appears to have a consistent benevolent effect on aging well that is not matched by the impact of the separate measures. Although purpose in life was significantly related to greater subjective well-being, it was unrelated to death fear after controlling for the other psychosocial strengths measures. By contrast, wisdom and mastery appeared to decrease death fear but did not affect subjective well-being after controlling for purpose and objective life conditions. Yet, given the relatively strong associations between wisdom, purpose in life, and mastery, which resulted in multicollinearity for wisdom in the regression models, and evidence from a short-term longitudinal study that wisdom increases purpose in life, mastery, and subjective well-being but not vice versa (Ardelt 2012), it is likely that the effects of wisdom on well-being and death fear are at least partly mediated by purpose in life and mastery, respectively. Based on the consistent impact of those combined psychosocial strengths as compared to each individual measure, we surmise that individuals who cultivate wisdom that is accompanied by a sense of purpose in life and mastery are more likely to age successfully than those who develop only one of the three psychosocial assets in isolation.

Although spirituality had a significant and direct effect on subjective well-being when objective life conditions were not included in the model, the effect became insignificant after controlling for the objective circumstances of the sample members, refuting the first part of Hypothesis 2. However, the second part of Hypothesis 2 that older adults with lower or higher levels of spirituality would report lower death fear than those with moderate spirituality was supported. Spirituality maintained a significant quadratic curvilinear effect on death fear even after controlling for objective life conditions.

It appears that a high level of spirituality is not as instrumental in maintaining subjective well-being but integral in decreasing death fear, whereas the psychosocial strengths of older adults help both, increase subjective well-being and decrease death fear. Supportive of Byock's (1996) argument of the developmental tasks necessary to facilitate a "good death," these findings reinforce the benefits of combining psychosocial and spiritual strengths in order to realize meaning and completion with the perception of self, relationships with loved ones, and conceptions of the transcendent.

Hypothesis 3, which stated that internal strengths would have a stronger impact than objective life conditions on the dependent variables, was supported for death fear but not for subjective well-being. Separately objective life conditions and internal strengths each explained 51 % of the variation in subjective well-being. When both objective life conditions and internal strengths were entered together in the regression model, they explained 64 % of the variation in subjective well-being. Hence, adding either internal strengths or objective life conditions to the model increased the explanatory power of the model by 13 %. However, the results of the combined model suggest that psychosocial strengths have the strongest impact on subjective well-being in old age, as predicted, followed by subjective physical health. In fact, subjective health has been shown to be one of the most consistent predictors of subjective well-being (Geerlings et al. 2000; Steverink et al. 2001). By contrast, the effects of economic pressure, social involvement, closeness to death (hospice patient), nursing home residency, and spirituality on subjective well-being became insignificant after controlling for all the other variables in the model.

In support of Hypothesis 3, objective life conditions alone explained only 20 % of the variation in death fear, whereas internal strengths by themselves accounted for

36 % of the variation in death fear. Combined, objective life conditions and internal strengths explained 43 % of the variation in death fear, but only the addition of internal strengths to objective life conditions significantly increased the explanatory power of the model by 23 %. Conversely, adding the effects of objective life conditions to internal strengths did not significantly improve the explanatory power of the model. Accounting for the combined effects of all predictor variables in the model resulted in a loss of significance for the effects of subjective physical health and economic pressure, whereas psychosocial strengths and spirituality maintained their significant effects on death fear.

Overall, and in accordance with Hypothesis 3, the effects of older adults' internal strengths on indicators of aging well appear to be stronger than effects of objective life conditions, illustrating that successful aging is possible even when external circumstances are difficult but also suggesting that aging well might be the result of life-long psychosocial development and growth in wisdom to discover a deeper and more mature sense of life meaning, mastery, and spirituality (Erikson 1982; Erikson et al. 1986; Jung 1971; Maslow 1970, 1971). Yet, as the significant correlations between objective life conditions and psychosocial strengths and spirituality in Table 7.1 indicate, objective life conditions might have an indirect effect on subjective well-being and death fear, mediated by psychosocial strengths and also spirituality for death fear. Therefore, improvements in the aging process need to concentrate on objective life conditions of older persons but without neglecting to attend to their internal strengths. And since the development of psychosocial strengths and a deeper sense of spirituality are likely to be time-consuming, life-long processes (Fowler 1981; Kekes 1983; Wong 2000), preparations for successful aging should be addressed long before individuals reach "old" age.

In future research, the analyses will need to be replicated with a larger and more representative data set of the older population in the United States. Yet, a number of provisional conclusions can be drawn from the current results. First, it appears that encouraging agnostic or atheist older adults to become more spiritual might not be in their best interest as less spiritual elders tended to be less afraid of death than those with medium levels of spirituality. Second, developing wisdom (Ardelt and Oh 2010) and maintaining a sense of meaning and purpose in life (Wong 1998) and control over one's environment (Schulz and Heckhausen 1996) seems to be beneficial for both, increasing subjective well-being and decreasing death fear at the later stage of life. This might be achieved by occupying meaningful roles such as giving advice and acting as mentor to the next generation, engaging in volunteer activities to improve the lives of others, or advocating for the preservation of nature and the environment (Hong and Morrow-Howell 2010; Parisi et al. 2009; Vaillant 2002). Offering these social roles to older adults would not only foster aging well but also benefit society as a whole.

References

Ai, A. L., Wink, P., & Ardelt, M. (2010). Spirituality and aging: A journey for meaning through deep interconnection in humanity. In J. C. Cavanaugh & C. K. Cavanaugh (Eds.), *Aging in America* (Vol. 3 Societal Issues, pp. 222–246). Santa Barbara: Praeger.

Aldwin, C. M. (1994). *Stress, coping, and development: An integrative perspective*. New York: Guilford Press.

Ardelt, M. (1997). Wisdom and life satisfaction in old age. *Journal of Gerontology: Psychological Sciences, 52*(1), p. 15–27.

Ardelt, M. (2000). Intellectual versus wisdom-related knowledge: The case for a different kind of learning in the later years of life. *Educational Gerontology: An International Journal of Research and Practice, 26*(8), 771–789.

Ardelt, M. (2003). Empirical assessment of a three-dimensional wisdom scale. *Research on Aging, 25*(3), 275–324.

Ardelt, M. (2004). Wisdom as expert knowledge system: A critical review of a contemporary operationalization of an ancient concept. *Human Development, 47*(5), 257–285.

Ardelt, M. (2005). How wise people cope with crises and obstacles in life. *ReVision: A Journal of Consciousness and Transformation, 28*(1), 7–19.

Ardelt, M. (2008). Being wise at any age. In S. J. Lopez (Ed.), *Positive Psychology: Exploring the Best in People* (Vol. 1: Discovering Human Strengths, pp. 81–108). Westport: Praeger.

Ardelt, M. (2011a). The measurement of wisdom: A commentary on Taylor, Bates, and Webster's comparison of the SAWS and 3D-WS. Experimental Aging Research, 37(2), 241–255. doi:10.1080/0361073X.2011.554509.

Ardelt, M. (2011b). Wisdom, age, and well-being. In K. W. Schaie & S. L. Willis (Eds.), *Handbook of the psychology of aging* (7th ed., pp. 279–291). Amsterdam: Elsevier.

Ardelt, M. (2012). Disentangling the relations between wisdom and different types of well-being: Findings from a short-term longitudinal study. Unpublished manuscript.

Ardelt, M., & Koenig, C. S. (2007). The importance of religious orientation in dying well: Evidence from three case studies. *Journal of Religion, Spirituality & Aging, 19*(4), 61–79.

Ardelt, M., & Oh, H. (2010). Wisdom: Definition, assessment, and its relation to successful cognitive and emotional aging. In D. Jeste & C. Depp (Eds.), *Successful cognitive and emotional aging* (pp. 87–113). Washington: American Psychiatric Publishing.

Assmann, A. (1994). Wholesome knowledge: Concepts of wisdom in a historical and cross-cultural perspective. In D. L. Featherman, R. M. Lerner & M. Perlmutter (Eds.), *Life-span development and behavior* (Vol. 12, pp. 187–224). Hillsdale: Lawrence Erlbaum.

Baltes, P. B. (1993). The aging mind: Potential and limits. *The Gerontologist, 33*(5), 580–594.

Bergsma, A., & Ardelt, M. (in press). Self-reported wisdom and happiness: An empirical investigation. Journal of Happiness Studies. doi:.1007/s10902-011-9275-5.

Black, H. K. (1999). Life as gift: Spiritual narratives of elderly African American women living in poverty. *Journal of Aging Studies, 13*(4), 441–455.

Bluck, S., & Glück, J. (2005). From the inside out: People's implicit theories of wisdom. In R. J. Sternberg & J. Jordan (Eds.), *A handbook of wisdom. Psychological perspectives* (pp. 84–109). New York: Cambridge University Press.

Brandtstädter, J., & Greve, W. (1994). The aging self: Stabilizing and protective processes. *Developmental Review, 14*(1), 52–80.

Byock, I. (1996). The nature of suffering and the nature of opportunity at the end of life. *Clinics in Geriatric Medicine, 12*(2), 237–252.

Center for the Study of Aging and Human Development. (1975). Multidimensional functional assessment: The OARS methodology (1st ed.). Durham: Center for the Study of Aging and Human Development.

Chandler, M. J., & Holliday, S. (1990). Wisdom in a postapocalyptic age. In R. J. Sternberg (Ed.), *Wisdom: Its nature, origins, and development* (pp. 121–141). New York: Cambridge University Press.

Chibnall, J. T., Videen, S. D., Duckro, P. N., & Miller, D. K. (2002). Psychosocial—spiritual correlates of death distress in patients with life-threatening medical conditions. *Palliative Medicine, 16*(4), 331–338. doi:10.1191/0269216302pm544oa.

Clayton, V. P., & Birren, J. E. (1980). The development of wisdom across the life-span: A reexamination of an ancient topic. In P. B. Baltes & O. G. Brim, Jr (Eds.), *Life-span development and behavior* (Vol. 3, pp. 103–135). New York: Academic Press.

Colerick, E. J. (1985). Stamina in later life. *Social Science and Medicine, 21*(9), 997–1006.

Comijs, H. C., Penninx, B. W. J. H., Knipscheer, K. P. M., & van Tilburg, W. (1999). Psychological distress in victims of elder mistreatment: The effects of social support and coping. *Journal of Gerontology: Psychological Sciences, 54B*(4), p. 240–245.

Crumbaugh, J. C., & Maholick, L. T. (1964). An experimental study in existentialism: The psychometric approach to Frankl's concept of noogenic neurosis. *Journal of Clinical Psychology, 20,* 200–207.

Csikszentmihalyi, M., & Rathunde, K. (1990). The psychology of wisdom: An evolutionary interpretation. In R. J. Sternberg (Ed.), *Wisdom: Its nature, origins, and development* (pp. 25–51). New York: Cambridge University Press.

Diener, E. (1984). Subjective Well-Being. *Psychological Bulletin, 95,* 542–575.

Diener, E., & Biswas-Diener, R. (2002). Will money increase subjective well-being? A literature review and guide to needed research. *Social Indicators Research, 57*(2), 119–169.

Diener, E., Suh, E. M., Lucas, R. E., & Smith, H. L. (1999). Subjective well-being: Three decades of progress. Psychological Bulletin, 125(2), 276–302. doi:10.1037/0033–2909.125.2.276.

Erikson, E. H. (1963). *Childhood and society*. New York: Norton.

Erikson, E. H. (1964). *Insight and responsibility. Lectures on the ethical implications of psychoanalytic insight.* New York: Norton.

Erikson, E. H. (1982). *The life cycle completed. A review.* New York: Norton.

Erikson, E. H., Erikson, J. M., & Kivnick, H. Q. (1986). *Vital involvement in old age: The experience of old age in our time*. New York: Norton.

Fazio, A. F. (1977). A concurrent validation study of the NCHS General Well-Being Schedule. (Dept. of HEW Publ. No. HRA-78-1347). Hyattsville: National Center for Health Statistics.

Florian, V., & Kravetz, S. (1983). Fear of personal death: Attribution, structure, and relation to religious belief. *Journal of Personality and Social Psychology, 44*(3), 600–607. doi:10.1037/0022-3514.44.3.600.

Fortner, B. V., Neimeyer, R. A., & Rybarczyk, B. (2000). Correlates of death anxiety in older adults: A comprehensive review. In A. Tomer (Ed.), *Death attitudes and the older adult. Theories, concepts, and applications* (pp. 95–108). Philadelphia: Brunner-Routledge.

Fowler, J. W. (1981). *Stages of faith: the psychology of human development and the quest for meaning*. (Vol. 1). San Francisco: Harper & Row.

Fry, P. S. (2000). Religious involvement, spirituality and personal meaning for life: Existential predictors of psychological wellbeing in community-residing and institutional care elders. *Aging & Mental Health, 4*(4), 375–387.

Garner, C., Bhatia, I., Dean, M., & Byars, A. (2007). Relationships between measures of meaning, well-being, and depression in an elderly sample. *International Forum for Logotherapy, 30*(2), 73–78.

Geerlings, S. W., Beekman, A. T., Deeg, D. J., & Van Tilburg, W. (2000). Physical health and the onset and persistence of depression in older adults: An eight-wave prospective community-based study. *Psychological Medicine, 30*(2), 369–380.

George, L. K. (1990). Social structure, social processes, and social-psychological states. In R. H. Binstock & L. K. George (Eds.), *Handbook of aging and the social sciences* (3rd edn., pp. 186–204). New York: Academic Press.

George, L. K. (2010). Still happy after all these years: Research frontiers on subjective well-being in later life. *The Journals of Gerontology: Series B: Psychological Sciences and Social Sciences, 65B*(3), 331–339. doi:10.1093/geronb/gbq006.

Glück, J. (2011). "She looks back without bitterness:" Wisdom as a developmental opposite of embitterment? In M. Linden & A. Maercker (Eds.), *Embitterment: Societal, psychological, and clinical perspectives* (pp. 70–82). New York: Springer.

Glück, J., & Bluck, S. (in press). The MORE life experience model: A theory of the development of wisdom. In M. Ferrari & N. Weststrate (Eds.), *Personal wisdom*. New York: Springer.

Hatch, R. L., Burg, M. A., Naberhaus, D. S., & Hellmich, L. K. (1998). The Spiritual Involvement and Beliefs Scale. *Journal of Family Practice, 46*(6), 476–486.

Heckhausen, J., & Schulz, R. (1993). Optimization by selection and compensation: Balancing primary and secondary control in life span development. *International Journal of Behavioral Development, 16*(2), 287–303.

Heckhausen, J., & Schulz, R. (1995). A life-span theory of control. *Psychological Review, 102*(2), 284–304.

Hedberg, P., Gustafson, Y., & Brulin, C. (2010). Purpose in life among men and women aged 85 years and older. *The International Journal of Aging & Human Development, 70*(3), 213–229. doi:10.2190/AG.70.3.c.

Hinton, J. (1999). The progress of awareness and acceptance of dying assessed in cancer patients and their caring relatives. *Palliative Medicine, 13*(1), 19.

Hong, S. I., & Morrow-Howell, N. (2010). Health outcomes of Experience Corps[sup] ® [/sup]: A high-commitment volunteer program. *Social Science & Medicine, 71*(2), 414–420. doi:10.1016/j.socscimed.2010.04.009.

House, J. S. (1994). Americans' Changing Lives: Wave I and Wave II, 1986 and 1989 (Computer File). ICPSR Version. Ann Arbor: University of Michigan, Survey Research Center.

Jang, Y., Haley, W. E., Small, B. J., & Mortimer, J. A. (2002). The role of mastery and social resources in the associations between disability and depression in later life. *The Gerontologist, 42*(6), 807–813.

Jeste, D. V., Ardelt, M., Blazer, D., Kraemer, H. C., Vaillant, G., & Meeks, T. W. (2010). Expert consensus on characteristics of wisdom: A Delphi method study. *The Gerontologist, 50*(5), 668–680. doi:10.1093/geront/gnq022.

Jewell, A. (2010). The importance of purpose in life in an older British Methodist sample: Pastoral implications. *Journal of Religion, Spirituality & Aging, 22*(3), 138–161. doi:10.1080/15528030903321170.

Johnson, T. F. (1995). Aging well in contemporary society. *American Behavioral Scientist, 39*(2), 120–130.

Jung, C. G. (1971). The stages of life. In J. Campbell (Ed.), *The portable Jung* (pp. 3–22). New York: Penguin Books.

Kearl, M. C. (1996). Dying well: The unspoken dimension of aging well. *American Behavioral Scientist, 39*(3), 336–360.

Kekes, J. (1983). Wisdom. *American Philosophical Quarterly, 20*(3), 277–286.

King, M. B., & Hunt, R. A. (1975). Measuring the religious variable: National replication. *Journal for the Scientific Study of Religion, 14,* 13–22.

Kozma, A., Stones, M. J., & McNeil, J. K. (1991). *Psychological well-being in later life*. Toronto: Butterworths.

Kramer, D. A. (1990). Conceptualizing wisdom: The primacy of affect-cognition relations. In R. J. Sternberg (Ed.), *Wisdom: Its nature, origins, and development* (pp. 279–313). New York: Cambridge University Press.

Landau, R., & Litwin, H. (2001). Subjective well-being among the old-old: The role of health, personality and social support. *The International Journal of Aging and Human Development, 52*(4), 265–280.

Landes, S. D., & Ardelt, M. (2011). The relationship between spirituality and death fear in aging adults. *Counseling and Spirituality, 30*(2), 87–111.

Larson, R. (1978). Thirty years of research on the subjective well-being of older Americans. *Journal of Gerontology, 33*(1), 109–125.

Le, T. N. (2011). Life satisfaction, openness value, self-transcendence, and wisdom. *Journal of Happiness Studies, 12*(2), 171–182. doi:.1007/s10902–010-9182–1.

Levenson, M. R., & Crumpler, C. A. (1996). Three models of adult development. *Human Development, 39*(3), 135–149.
Levitt, H. M. (1999). The development of wisdom: An analysis of Tibetan Buddhist experience. *Journal of Humanistic Psychology, 39*(2), 86–105.
Maslow, A. H. (1970). *Motivation and personality* (2nd edn.). New York: Harper & Row.
Maslow, A. H. (1971). *The farther reaches of human nature*. New York: The Viking Press.
McCoy, S. K., Pyszczynski, T., Solomon, S., & Greenberg, J. (2000). Transcending the self: A terror management perspective on successful aging. In A. Tomer (Ed.), *Death Attitudes and the Older Adult. Theories, Concepts, and Applications* (pp. 37–63). Philadelphia: Brunner-Routledge.
McMordie, W. R. (1981). Religiosity and fear of death: Strength of belief system. *Psychological reports, 49*(3), 921–922.
Meeks, T. W., & Jeste, D. V. (2009). Neurobiology of wisdom: A literature overview. *Archives of General Psychiatry, 66*(4), 355–365.
Mickler, C., & Staudinger, U. M. (2008). Personal wisdom: Validation and age-related differences of a performance measure. *Psychology and Aging, 23*(4), 787–799. doi:10.1037/a0013928.
Mikulincher, M., & Florian, V. (2008). The complex and multifaceted nature of The Fear of Personal Death: The multidimensional model of Victor Florian. In A. Tomer, G. T. Eliason & P. T. P. Wong (Eds.), *Existential and spiritual issues in death attitudes* (pp. 39–64). New York: Lawrence Erlbaum Associates.
Moody, H. R. (1986). Meaning of life and the meaning of old age. In T. R. Cole & S. A. Gadow (Eds.), *What does it mean to grow old? Reflections from the humanities* (pp. 9–40). Durham: Duke University Press.
Nakasone, R. Y. (1994). Spiritual journeys in aging: A Buddhist view. *Journal of Religion and Health, 33*(3), 243–251.
Nelson, L. D., & Cantrell, C. H. (1980). Religiosity and death anxiety: A multi-dimensional analysis. *Review of Religious Research, 21*(2), 148–157.
O'Rand, A. M. (1982). Socioeconomic status and poverty. In D. J. Mangen & W. A. Peterson (Eds.), *Research Instruments in Social Gerontology* (Vol. 2. Social Roles and Social Participation, pp. 281–341). Minneapolis: University of Minnesota Press.
Parisi, J. M., Rebok, G. W., Carlson, M. C., Fried, L. P., Seeman, T. E., Tan, E. J., et al. (2009). Can the wisdom of aging be activated and make a difference societally? *Educational Gerontology, 35*, 867–879. doi:10.1080/03601270902782453.
Pascual-Leone, J. (1990). An essay on wisdom: Toward organismic processes that make it possible. In R. J. Sternberg (Ed.), *Wisdom: Its nature, origins, and development* (pp. 244–278). New York: Cambridge University Press.
Pearlin, L. I., & Schooler, C. (1978). The structure of coping. *Journal of Health and Social Behavior, 19*, 2–21.
Pinquart, M., & Sörensen, S. (2000). Influences of socioeconomic status, social network, and competence on subjective well-being in later life: A meta-analysis. *Psychology and Aging, 15*(2), 187–224.
Pudrovska, T., Schieman, S., Pearlin, L. I., & Nguyen, K. (2005). The sense of mastery as a mediator and moderator in the association between economic hardship and health in late life. *Journal of Aging and Health, 17*(5), 634–660. doi:10.1177/0898264305279874.
Radloff, L. S. (1977). The CES-D Scale: A self-report depression scale for research in the general population. *Applied Psychological Measurement, 1*(3), 385–401.
Rasmussen, C. H., & Johnson, M. E. (1994). Spirituality and religiosity: Relative relationships to death anxiety. *Omega—The Journal of Death and Dying, 29*(4), 313–318.
Rothbaum, F., Weisz, J. R., & Snyder, S. S. (1982). Changing the world and changing the self: A two-process model of perceived control. *Journal of Personality and Social Psychology, 42*(1), 5–37.
Rowe, J. W., & Kahn, R. L. (1998). *Successful aging*. New York: Pantheon Books.
Ryff, C. D. (1989). Happiness is everything, or is it? Explorations on the meaning of psychological well-being. *Journal of Personality and Social Psychology, 57*(6), 1069–1081.

Schulz, R., & Heckhausen, J. (1996). A life span model of successful aging. *American Psychologist, 51*(7), 702–714.
Scioli, A., McClelland, D. C., Weaver, S. L., & Madden, E. M. (2000). Coping strategies and integrative meaning as moderators of chronic illness. *International Journal of Aging and Human Development, 51*(2), 115–136.
Staton, J., Shuy, R., & Byock, I. (2001). *A few months to live. Different paths to life's end.* Washington: Georgetown University Press.
Staudinger, U. M., & Kessler, E.-M. (2008). Adjustment and growth. Two trajectories of positive personality development across adulthood. In M. C. Smith (Ed.), *Handbook of research on adult learning and development* (pp. 239–268). New York: Routledge.
Sternberg, R. J. (1990). Wisdom and its relations to intelligence and creativity. In R. J. Sternberg (Ed.), *Wisdom: Its nature, origins, and development* (pp. 142–159). New York: Cambridge University Press.
Steverink, N., Westerhof, G. J., Bode, C., & Dittmann-Kohli, F. (2001). The personal experience of aging, individual resources, and subjective well-being. *Journals of Gerontology Series B: Psychological Sciences and Social Sciences, 56*(6), 364–373.
Takahashi, M. (2000). Toward a culturally inclusive understanding of wisdom: Historical roots in the East and West. *International Journal of Aging and Human Development, 51*(3), 217–230.
Takahashi, M., & Overton, W. F. (2002). Wisdom: A culturally inclusive developmental perspective. *International Journal of Behavioral Development, 26*(3), 269–277.
Taranto, M. A. (1989). Facets of wisdom: A theoretical synthesis. *International Journal of Aging and Human Development, 29*(1), 1–21.
Tomer, A., & Eliason, G. (2000). Beliefs about self, life, and death: Testing aspects of a comprehensive model of death anxiety and death attitudes. In A. Tomer (Ed.), *Death attitudes and the older adult. Theories, concepts, and applications* (pp. 137–153). Philadelphia: Brunner-Routledge.
Tomer, A., Eliason, G. T., & Wong, P. T. P. (Eds.). (2008). *Existential and spiritual issues in death attitudes*. New York: Lawrence Erlbaum Associates.
Vaillant, G. E. (2002). *Aging well: Surprising guideposts to a happier life from the landmark Harvard Study of Adult Development*. Boston: Little, Brown.
Van Ranst, N., & Marcoen, A. (2000). Structural components of personal meaning in life and their relationship with death attitudes and coping mechanisms in late life. In G. T. Reker & K. Chamberlain (Eds.), *Exploring existential meaning: optimizing human development across the life span* (pp. 59–74). Thousand Oaks: Sage Publications.
Veenhoven, R. (1991). Is happiness relative? *Social Indicators Research, 24*(1), 1–34.
Veenhoven, R. (1994). Is happiness a trait? Tests of the theory that a better society does not make people any happier. *Social Indicators Research, 32*(2), 101–160.
Wahl, C. W. (1959). The fear of death. In H. Feifel (Ed.), *The meaning of death* (pp. 16–29). New York: McGraw-Hill.
Windle, G., & Woods, R. T. (2004). Variations in subjective wellbeing: The mediating role of a psychological resource. *Ageing & Society, 24*(4), 583–602.
Wink, P. (2006). Who is afraid of death? Religiousness, spirituality, and death anxiety in late adulthood. *Journal of Religion, Spirituality & Aging, 18*(2), 93–110.
Wink, P., & Helson, R. (1997). Practical and transcendent wisdom: Their nature and some longitudinal findings. *Journal of Adult Development, 4*(1), 1–15.
Wink, P., & Scott, J. (2005). Does religiousness buffer against the fear of death and dying in late adulthood? Findings from a longitudinal study. *The Journals of Gerontology Series B: Psychological Sciences and Social Sciences, 60*(4), pp. 207–214. doi:10.1093/geronb/60.4.P207.
Wong, P. T. P. (1998). Spirituality, meaning, and successful aging. In P. T. P. Wong & P. S. Fry (Eds.), *The human quest for meaning: A handbook of psychological research and clinical applications* (pp. 359–394). Mahwah: Lawrence Erlbaum.
Wong, P. T. P. (2000). Meaning of life and meaning of death in successful aging. In A. Tomer (Ed.), *Death attitudes and the older adult. Theories, concepts, and applications* (pp. 23–35). Philadelphia: Brunner-Routledge.

Wong, P. T. P. (2008). *Meaning management theory and death acceptance*. New York: Lawrence Erlbaum Associates.

Wong, P. T. P., Reker, G. T., & Gesser, G. (1994). Death attitude profile-revised: A multidimensional measure of attitudes toward death. In R. A. Neimeyer (Ed.), *Death anxiety handbook. Research, instrumentation, and application* (pp. 121–148). Washington: Taylor & Francis.

Zautra, A. J., Reich, J. W., & Newsom, J. T. (1995). Autonomy and sense of control among older adults: An examination of their effects on mental health. In L. A. Bond, S. J. Cutler & A. Grams (Eds.), *Promoting Successful and Productive Aging* (pp. 153–170). Thousand Oaks: Sage.

Chapter 8
The Black Survivors: Courage, Strength, Creativity and Resilience in the Cultural Traditions of Black Caribbean Immigrants

Leonie J. Brooks

Black Caribbean immigrants have voluntarily migrated to the United States since the late nineteenth century after the abolition of slavery in 1865 (Brice-Baker, 2005). They came by thousands to New York City, Boston, and Miami seeking better opportunities for themselves and their families. Reasons for migration have been primarily economic, though increased educational opportunities in the United States, as well as political instability, prejudice (and crime) in their home countries have also been "push" factors (Holder, 2007). Caribbean immigrants also use the term "West Indian", referring to individuals from the Anglophone Caribbean region that includes Anguilla, Antigua, Bahamas, Barbados, Belize, Bermuda, Cayman Islands, Dominica, Grenada, Guyana, Jamaica, St. Kitts, St. Lucia, Montserrat, Trinidad and Tobago, St. Vincent's and the Grenadines, and the American and British Virgin Islands. There are also immigrants from the Francophone Caribbean including Guadeloupe, Martinique, and Haiti (Holder, 2007).

The rate of immigration from the region has waxed and waned in response to the increase or easing of restrictive immigration policies over time. The first wave of West Indian immigration occurred from 1900 through the early 1920s with nearly 85,000 West Indians entering the United States between 1900 and 1930. They resided throughout the East Coast, but primarily in the Black neighborhoods of Harlem and Central Brooklyn in NY. Restrictive immigration laws passed in the 1920s and the subsequent Great Depression in the 1930s slowed immigration from the Caribbean region until after World War II. Immigration increased until the early 1950s, when the McCarran-Walter Act of 1952 severely restricted legal immigration from the region. The 1965 Hart-Celler Act altered American immigration policy by removing racial quotas and establishing a visa preference system with a 120,000 annual quota for the Western Hemisphere (which included the Caribbean region) with no per country limit. Categories for immigration included family reunification or occupational

L. J. Brooks (✉)
Psychology Department, Towson University, 8000 York Road,
Towson MD 21252-0001, USA
e-mail: Labrooks@towson.edu

J. D. Sinnott (ed.), *Positive Psychology*,
DOI 10.1007/978-1-4614-7282-7_8, © Springer Science+Business Media, LLC 2013

preferences. The number of Caribbean immigrants moving to the United States after 1965 grew exponentially. By the early 1980s 50,000 legal immigrants from the Anglophone Caribbean and approximately 6,000–10,000 from Haiti were arriving annually (Waters, 1999).

Recent United States Census figures estimate that there were approximately 2,532,000 West Indian immigrants residing in the United States. An additional 950,000 of these migrants from the Caribbean region identify specifically as Jamaican, 806,000 as Haitian, 198,000 as Trinidadian and Tobagonian, and 85,000 as British West Indian (U.S. Census Bureau, 2008). The majority are located in the Northeast and South including New York, Florida, Connecticut, Massachusetts, New Jersey, and Washington DC, with growing numbers in Maryland, northern Virginia, and the Atlanta suburbs in Georgia. A significant number of immigrants have been recruited to the United States to work in the agricultural, medical, and educational sectors as well as service industries. They have harvested crops (e.g., apples, oranges, corn, and sugar cane) in the south and mid-Atlantic region, worked as nurses and other medical personnel in hospitals and clinics across the country, and have been employed as teachers in the northeast and mid-Atlantic during times of teacher shortages. Many have also been employed as domestic servants in middle- and upper class homes.

In the next section of this chapter, a description of the ethnic and cultural identities of Black Caribbean immigrants is presented. The importance of family and community is also described. Specific cultural practices and traditions that highlight the positive features, ingenuity, and resilience of this group are outlined. Anecdotal information from individual interviews with Black Caribbean immigrants and second-generation Caribbean Americans is included in this chapter to provide a more personal perspective of the experiences of members of these communities. Seventy-four Caribbean immigrants and second-generation Caribbean Americans, including 46 women and 28 men, revealed information about their racial identities, encounters with discrimination, and unique acculturation experiences as part of an unpublished sabbatical research project, which began in 2007 and continued with follow-up interviews of some participants in September 2011. Participants were recruited from Caribbean organizations in Washington DC, Maryland, New York, New Jersey, Connecticut, Georgia, and Florida. They migrated from Jamaica, Trinidad and Tobago, Barbados, Dominica, Guyana, Grenada, Haiti, Montserrat, St. Croix, St. Lucia, and St. Vincent's and the Grenadines. Ranging in age from 19 to 73 years, they shared their migration stories, cultural traditions, and coping strategies as part of the research project. Interviews were conducted in person and by telephone, and were 45–120 min in length. First-hand accounts from these "cultural brokers" who have navigated and/or continue to navigate the spaces between their "home" culture and adopted United States homeland provide important insights and rich examples of the courage, resourcefulness, and hardiness of these cultural groups.

"Out of Many, One People": Identity and Culture, Family, and Community

Black Caribbean immigrants and their American-born offspring have adopted a variety of ethnic and cultural identities that range from Americanized or American-identified, to Bicultural, Transnational, and Island identified (Waters, 1999). First-generation immigrants are more likely to maintain a stronger connection to their country of birth, and tend to identify, for example, as Jamaican, Trinidadian, Haitian, or West Indian. Immigrants from earlier periods often experienced significant isolation and disconnection from the larger society, and most of them spent long hours working in an attempt to improve their socioeconomic status. Some immigrants from earlier waves of immigration returned home to their islands after a period of time (Brice-Baker, 2005).

Subsequent groups of immigrants (particularly those who immigrated after 1965) settled into urban and suburban areas, creating sizeable West Indian communities particularly along the east coast due to the geographic proximity to their countries of birth and prior settlement patterns (Holder, 2007). They established grocery stores and other businesses, social and cultural organizations, and houses of worship. Many became successful, with relatively high levels of household income and home ownership (Kasinitz et al., 2008).

When many Black Caribbean immigrants first arrive in the United States, their most salient identity is their nationality (i.e., Jamaican) or that of an immigrant, while their racial identity is secondary. Having migrated from islands with a strong sense of empowerment as members of the racial majority and as descendants of those who successfully cast off the "mantle of colonialism," these immigrants are proud of their cultural heritage and national identity and believe that they can control their own fates and succeed in the United States, a majority White country (Brice-Baker, 2005). They have migrated from societies that are pluralistic in nature, consisting of multiple races and nationalities where they have already established their sense of a "subnational black identity." In contract to American Blacks, "... the reality of black political power, numerical dominance and relative cultural and social freedom (that Black Caribbean immigrants experience in their countries of birth) differs from the Black American experience of minority status, political and social domination by whites and relative lack of political power" (Waters, 1999, p. 91). Many Black Caribbean immigrants experience culture shock at the primary salience of race/skin color and the racism and discrimination that one encounters as a racial minority in the United States (Vickerman, 2007). One Caribbean immigrant interviewee shared the following: "... In St. Vincent's the priority is on family and community. It is more class based in St. Vincent's. Here in the US it's more about color. Institutional racism in the US is found in every facet of society..." (U. Mars, October 2007, personal communication).

Caribbean immigrants utilize a range of adaptive coping strategies including turning to family members and friends from home and in their local communities for support, becoming members of local cultural and social organizations, and relying on their religious beliefs as a source of comfort. The resilience displayed by first-generation West Indian immigrants, as well as their strong ethnic and cultural pride and determination to succeed was a common theme reflected in the stories shared by the Caribbean immigrants and Caribbean Americans interviewed by this author. "Family is important because it is my foundation. As rough as it gets when I came home, my family was there to support me, and everything is alright. . . " (D. Stewart, November 2007, personal communication).

While most first-generation immigrants maintain a strong national and immigrant identity, the identities of second (and subsequent)-generation Black immigrants are more complex. Many insist that they are both African American and West Indian and tend to be proud of their bicultural abilities (Butterfield, 2004). Many are beneficiaries of their parents' transnational practices of frequently returning home for visits and sending remittances back home to support relatives. These second-generation offspring have the opportunity to visit their parents' countries of birth and establish relationships with relatives "back home." This practice exposes the children to the values and customs of their parents, and help to preserve important cultural mores and traditions. Some children are sent back home to live with relatives at some point during their teenage years by first-generation parents who become afraid of exposing their offspring to troubled neighborhoods and less academically rigorous schools in the United States. Many of these youth frequently found their education back home created an advantage for them when applying to colleges or seeking employment in the United States (Kasinitz et al., 2008).

There are some second-generation immigrants who struggle with their identities, and reject or have difficulty integrating a bicultural frame of reference. Those who become "Americanized" may be viewed as rejecting their parent's culture and this can sometimes create intergenerational conflict. American-born children can become frustrated with their parents' high expectations for their success and what they perceive as their parents' lack of acknowledgment of the stressors of racial and ethnic minority group membership, and experiences with racism and discrimination. Families that are able to bridge this difficult cultural and generation gap tend to consist of parents who have developed "cultural understandings and strategic repertoires for responding to this set of opportunities and restraints—scripts for how to live in the world, how to decide what is important, and how to reach ones' goals" (Kasinitz et al., 2008, p. 63). One second-generation immigrant respondent fondly recalled important lessons learned from her (first-generation immigration) mother who urged her and her siblings to be humble "Humble cow suck the most milk" and when in a precarious situation to practice due diligence and extreme caution "When your hand is in the tiger's mouth, tek time fe pull it out" (M. Stephenson, September 6, 2011, personal communication). Remembering who you were and where you came from (a proud child of Caribbean heritage), that the faith and unwavering support of the family and community were with you, and that no obstacle was insurmountable as long as one was willing to work hard, were frequent lessons taught with words of encouragement and reinforced by the example of other community members who had succeeded despite the odds.

Another challenge for Black Caribbean immigrant families occurs when one family member (usually a parent and often the mother) migrates in advance of the rest of the family, a process known as serial migration. This family member makes the ultimate sacrifice of leaving home to take advantage of employment opportunities, and will leave children in the care of an extended family member, typically a grandmother or aunt who serves as a surrogate or coparent. It is often the willingness of grandparents (and other family members) to care for the children being left at home that allows for the parent to be able to migrate (Chamberlain, 2003). This flexibility in care-giving and support provided by extended family members who play a critical role in childrearing, is a strength that Black Caribbean immigrant families share with other immigrants of color (Kasinitz et al., 2008). Many of the individuals interviewed for this chapter shared fond recollections of the significant role grandmothers in particular played in their upbringing, and "the values and coping strategies learned from 'mama' were priceless" (D. Brotherton, August 25, 2011, personal communication).

School community samples from Jamaica and Trinidad and Tobago have shown prevalence rates of 35 and 10.5 %, respectively of children whose parents have migrated (Jones et al., 2004). Children often have mixed feelings about the loss of the parent including "loneliness, anger, joy, sadness and strong feelings of abandonment, despite being in regular contact with their migrating parent(s)" (Pottinger et al., 2008, p. 16). Some parents also indicate struggling with loneliness and guilt at leaving children behind. When children are reunited with their parents, usually many years after the initial separation, a difficult period of adjustment can ensue. The majority of reunifications between parents and children occur during the adolescent years, an already challenging time when teens are struggling with issues of identity and shifting roles within the family system. Studies suggest that having a parental attachment figure of the same gender as the parent who serves as the caregiver during the separation can ease the transition of the separation–reunification process (Smith et al., 2004). A caregiver environment "characterized by guidance, supervision and the presence of appropriate role models" before and after the reunion is key for successful reunification. If separations are brief and well planned, with strong, loving, and supportive caregivers in place and frequent updates about reunification, serial migration may have a minimal negative impact on children (Smith et al., 2004). Suarez-Orozco and Suarez-Orozco (2001) report that the distress associated with immigration (including serial migration) for many families is brief, and the benefits outweigh the losses in the long run.

An example of the fortitude of Black Caribbean immigrant families and communities is the practice of adopting and embracing "non-blood kin" into each other's homes; particularly, the welcoming of immigrants who have no immediate relatives nearby. Several individuals interviewed for this chapter who did not reside with or near family members revealed that they successfully navigated the transition to living in the United States in large part due to the invaluable support of friends of family members and even strangers who opened up their networks and created new families for their "adopted" kin. This was especially evident during American holidays such as Thanksgiving and July 4th when Caribbean community members put their own spin on the holidays, cooking both traditional American foods (i.e., turkey) alongside favorites from home (e.g., pelau, curry goat, jerk chicken, macaroni pie, etc.). A "liming" session, where family and friends get together and share stories and memories of growing up back home, serves to reinforce the cultural bonds and beloved national and cultural identities (C. Francis, September 6, 2011, personal communication).

Cultural Traditions and Practices

Cooperative Economics One cultural practice believed to have originated in West Africa, which was heavily incorporated among British West Indians in their home countries and practiced rigorously within the Caribbean immigrant community in the United States, is a rotating credit association known by Jamaican immigrants as "partner" and other Caribbean immigrants as "susu." These informal groups, comprised of between 5 and 20 individuals, practice a form of enforced savings, where trusted friends and family members deposit a specific sum of money weekly with a group member who serves as a designated "banker," who in turn gives all of that week's contributions to a selected group member. "The process of depositing funds ('throwing a hand') and receiving proceeds ('getting a draw') continues until each member of the group has had a chance to receive a payoff from the banker" (Vickerman, 2007, p. 482). The primary purpose of this arrangement is economic, and this allows immigrants to pool their economic resources to buy homes and start businesses. However, this practice also strengthens the cultural and ethnic bonds between members of the group, as it is wholly based on trust (Vickerman, 2007).

Collaborative Farming/Gardening Another custom that West Indians have carried from their home countries to the United States is known as "morning sport." This is a collaborative farming practice where small groups of friends and family gather at one individual's home early in the morning and spend the day working in that person's garden, planting produce (peppers, pumpkin, watermelon, tomatoes, beans, corn, herbs, etc.) and assisting with landscaping the garden and planting flowers, shrubs, and trees. This process is repeated at each group member's home and then when the crop is harvested, the bounty is shared among the group (C. Brooks, August 2011, personal communication). This practice is obviously beneficial for all participants, whose cooperative work reduces the time, expense, and effort required to grow and reap foodstuff and cultivate a garden.

Carnival and Other Cultural Celebrations In the Caribbean, there is a long tradition of celebrating carnival and other cultural festivals highlighting the music, dances, colorful costumes, comedy, foods, art and crafts, and fun and fellowship for the revelers or participants. There is usually a children's carnival as well as general carnival in which mostly adults participate in a celebration that is a family and community affair. The carnival tradition has been adapted and continued in the United States and Canada, as well as other regions including England. The largest carnival in the United States occurs on an annual basis on Labor Day in Brooklyn, NY.

At this event, Caribbean immigrants have the opportunity to celebrate and express pride in their Caribbean culture; maintain their connection to ethnic and cultural identity through dance, consuming ethnic dishes, and listening to music from home; and to expose the United States citizens to Caribbean culture and heritage in order to increase awareness and appreciation for the rich heritage from the region, and to dispel myths and negative stereotypes. Caribbean vendors and businesses are able to promote their industries, goods, and services and earn a significant profit. Immigrants often reconnect with friends and family members they have not seen for some time. Comedy performances are also associated with carnival and other cultural celebrations, as humor and satire are a significant part of Caribbean culture. A comedy festival is part of the Caribbean carnival festivities in Washington DC in June, where comics from across the Caribbean region entertain the audience with their quick wit, political satire, and a practice known as ex-tempo, where comics duel by inventing creative rhymes to music on the spot "extemporaneously" on current issues or while mocking each other. The tendency to use humor as a way of coping with stressful situations, to make light of challenging circumstances and to keep things in perspective is a common practice that reduces stress and helps to facilitate positive functioning (J. Allison, September 8, 2011, personal communication). Overall, the carnival experience creates a win-win opportunity for the Caribbean immigrant and American communities who participate, as there are prospects for bridging cultural divides and building cross-cultural coalitions that enhance the well-being for all.

Cultural/Social Organizations and School Alumni Associations Caribbean immigrants have also established a multitude of social organizations that create spaces for the development and maintenance of social cohesion within immigrant communities (Vickerman, 2007). Some associations are formed based on the country of origin (e.g., Jamaica National Association, Trinidad and Tobago Association of Baltimore), and offer the opportunity to socialize and obtain social support from individuals from their home country, a critical resource for many who experience a critical loss of support upon migrating from their home countries to the sometimes isolated cities where they resettle in the United States. The association provides a home away from home, offering a place to belong, to celebrate one's roots and heritage, and create a sense of community where one's culture and unique experiences can be affirmed and validated. Association members gain information about a range of resources including housing, the location of good schools, grocers and other retailers who sell Caribbean foods and other commodities, culturally sensitive medical treatment, and legal services regarding immigration and naturalization. These associations typically sponsor fundraisers in order to raise money to purchase supplies for schools and medical clinics back home, and are often the first to respond when their home countries experience a crisis such as the devastating earthquake in Haiti in January, 2010. They also provide the opportunity for second-generation Caribbean Americans to learn about the rich heritage and culture of their parents through cultural events including annual Independence celebrations, dance programs, steel pan lessons, and attendance at sporting events (e.g., cricket matches, football (soccer) and netball tournaments). Other institutions are more regional in nature such as the West Indian

American Day Carnival Association (WIADCA), founded in New York in the 1930s, whose main task is to plan and organize the largest annual West Indian Carnival in the United States in Brooklyn, NY.

Since its inception in 1993, the Institute of Caribbean Studies (ICS), a nonprofit, nonpartisan organization, has been at the forefront of the challenge to bring attention to the issues of critical importance to the Caribbean American community (http://www.icsdc.org retrieved September 10, 2011). This nongovernmental organization located in Washington DC advocates for the successful inclusion of Caribbean Americans in United States policy making and was the architect for the campaign that resulted in the establishment of June as National Caribbean Heritage Month in the United States. ICS is dedicated to ensuring the well-being of Caribbean Americans through building bridges between Caribbean-Americans and the larger United States population (ICS, 2011). Specific activities sponsored by the organization include an annual White House Briefing from policy makers and representatives of the Presidential administration, an annual Legislative Forum on Capitol Hill where community leaders and Congressional representatives gather to discuss critical issues affecting Caribbean American communities, and a "Respect my vote" voter education drive through a partnership with the Hip Hop Caucus.

There are a host of Caribbean high school and college/university alumni organizations throughout the United States. Individuals who have graduated from these educational institutions maintain a keen sense of pride in their identities as alumni (e.g., a "Mico man," "KC boy," or "Bishop's girl") and often welcome the chance to network and socialize with fellow graduates (C. Neslon, September 4, 2011, personal communication). The sense of self and belongingness associated with being an alumnus of these schools is evidenced by the fierce devotion and loyalty the organization members display years after their matriculation. Participation in these organizations provide a sense of safety and social connection to other people who have had similar experiences, reinforce pride in ethnic and cultural identity, and reduces the social isolation that often accompanies the complex acculturation experience of many immigrants. The alumni associations also offer the opportunity for alumni to give back to their respective institutions that they credit with shaping their values and providing a strong educational foundation during their formative years. As such, these organizations typically promote fundraisers to raise significant amounts of capital for their institutions back home (Vickerman, 2007). The University of the West Indies (UWI) at Mona in Kingston, Jamaica, sponsors an e-mentor program where alumni from the United States serve as professional mentors to current students attending the UWI campuses in Barbados, Jamaica, and Trinidad and Tobago.

Another unique organization, the West Indian American Military Members Association (WIAMMA), was established in 1996 by a group of active duty and veteran Caribbean military members who endeavor to educate others about the vast contributions members have and continue to make to the United States Armed Services, to celebrate their accomplishments, and to acknowledge the continuous sacrifices made by members and their families (M. Grant, September 6, 2011, personal communication). The term "American" was added to the association's name to reflect the patriotism of the members, as most of the participants, their spouses, and children are American citizens. The primary goals of WIAMMA are to promote awareness of the culture and history of West Indian people, to educate the general public about the significant contributions West Indians make to the United States military, and to provide an environment that encourages and supports current and retired armed services members and their families. Approximately 5000 Caribbean immigrants were actively serving in the military in 2010 (Patten, 2012). They accomplish these goals through "cultural exchanges, participating in diversity programs, sponsoring educational and artistic forums, fundraising, and honoring and celebrating the ethnic and social contributions recognized in the US during the month of June, proclaimed by the President of the United States (the group's Commander in Chief) as National Caribbean-American Heritage Month" (M. Grant, September 6, 2011, personal communication).

"We've Come This far by Faith": Religion and Spirituality No discussion of cultural strengths and traditions that facilitate optimal functioning and personal meaning among Black Caribbean immigrants would be complete without examining the significant role that religion and spirituality play in their everyday lives. All of the Caribbean cultural brokers that were consulted in the gathering of anecdotal information for this chapter identified their faith, religion, and/or spirituality as a key component of their lives. This was an important and unfailing resource that was an integral part of their upbringing, infused within the culture, and adapted and incorporated into their lives here in the United States. Researchers who have studied the role of religion and spirituality among African Americans, Black Caribbean immigrants, and non-Hispanic Whites have found that, similar to their African American counterparts, Caribbean Blacks have high levels of religious participation, will request that others pray for them, and frequently read religious and spiritual texts (Chatters et al., 2009). The religious beliefs and practices are central components of the Black Caribbean immigrants' life histories and immigration experiences (Bashi, 2007). Many of the Caribbean individuals who were interviewed quoted scriptures from the Bible including Philippians 4:13 "I can do all things through Christ who strengthens me" and "Jeremiah 29:11 "For I know the plans I have for you, says the Lord, plans to prosper you, and not to harm you, plans to give you hope and a bright future." They used these passages as sources of encouragement when faced with the challenges of acculturation (D. Jacobs, August 30, 2011, personal communication). They also report praying before undertaking major tasks including business ventures, educational pursuits, purchasing a home, or travel. Research supports the idea that Black Caribbean immigrants often look to God (or a higher power) for strength, support and guidance, and that prayer is a vital coping strategy used to deal with stress (Chatters et al., 2008).

The Black Caribbean church has been instrumental in assisting in the relocation and resettlement of immigrants to the United States (Logan and Deane, 2003). Black religious institutions and faith communities perform vital civic functions including "assisting with transnational migration, providing community resources and social capital, and facilitating immigrant adjustment" (Chatters et al., 2009, p. 1146). Immigrants who maintain and/or adapt their religious and spiritual practices are tapping into an important resource that help them to persevere during difficult times, while also preserving their connections to their home cultures and ethnic identities. The collectivistic and communal orientations that characterize their worship experience, as well as the participatory worship styles and immediate and personal connections with a divine power are common within Black Caribbean traditions (Chatters et al., 2009).

Work Ethic

> Heights by great men reached and kept
> Were not attained by sudden flight
> But they, while their companions slept
> Were toiling upward in the night
> (last verse of a Longfellow poem learned by many Caribbean youth in schools to reinforce the value of hard work; M. Hare, August 2011, personal communication).

The industriousness and strong work ethic that have characterized other immigrant groups in the United States has also been applied to Black Caribbean immigrants who are known for their hard work and determination to succeed. West Indian immigrants have high rates of labor force participation even among those with the lowest levels of education (Waters, 1999). West Indian immigrant representation in skilled, white-collar, and professional occupations has been significant (Holder, 2007). There are stereotypes of Jamaicans and other West Indian immigrants having "many jobs" and possessing a willingness to do whatever it takes to make better lives for themselves and their families. "Hard work neva kill a man" is a frequent refrain heard in many Caribbean households that underscores the importance of working hard to achieve one's goals and attaining material wealth and professional success (F. Francis, September 5, 2011, personal communication). According to the 2000 United States Census, the large majority of employed West Indians living in the United States worked in the private sector (78.6 %), with 16.5 % identified as government workers, 4.7 % self-employed, and 0.2 % as unpaid family workers (Holder, 2007). A primary reason why so few West Indians are employed by the federal and some state governments is their lack of United States citizenship. More recent estimates (2009–2011) indicate approximately 34.4 % of West Indian immigrants work in managerial, professional and related occupations, 24.2 % in service occupations, 25.9 % percent in sales and office occupations, 7.5 % in construction and maintenance occupations and 8 % in transportation (U.S. Census, 2009–2011). Holder (2007) notes that West Indians have attained better economic success in New York City than anywhere else in the country. Black Caribbean immigrants in the city have owned the majority of legitimate black businesses, and make up a sizeable percentage of "physicians, nurses and medical technicians, lawyers, teachers, managers and other business people. . . mechanics, plumbers, electricians, carpenters and masons" (Holder, 2007, p. 683). There is no doubt that this immigrant population has excelled professionally, though it is important to note that the recent recession has had a deleterious impact on wage earnings and employment in this group as it has for all racial and ethnic minority groups.

Several explanations for the relative success of Caribbean immigrants have been posited including cultural and structural hypotheses. Culturally based explanations emphasize Caribbean immigrants' Protestant work ethic developed during the formative years spent within the British educational systems. In addition, their racial majority status in the Caribbean provided role models that fostered the belief that everything is possible, and dreams can be accomplished thought hard work and effort (Waters, 1999). Structural explanations highlight the selectivity of immigration where those who migrate have traits that provide them with an advantage as compared with the native United States population (especially since immigration laws selected for literacy in earlier years and certain high-skilled occupations). Immigrants enter the country with high levels of human capital that boost their socioeconomic potential. Moreover, some employers have demonstrated a preference for foreign-born versus native-born employees. There is also the notion of white favoritism, where Black immigrants are perceived as being treated better by Whites than their African American counterparts. These hypotheses that attempt to explain the relative success and better educational and economic performance of West Indian immigrants (as compared with African Americans) have been sharply contested in the literature (Model, 2008). Waters concludes that perhaps a combination of both cultural and structural factors, as well as exaggerated cultural stereotypes play some part in explaining the success of Black Caribbean immigrants.

Anecdotal evidence gathered from those interviewed reflects themes of the importance of hard work, self-reliance, no excuses for failure or not trying your best, and nonreliance on "handouts" or government assistance. One individual described the phenomenon of a "shame tree" that accentuated the importance of working hard and making one's family proud. "Don't let your shame tree drop down" meant that upon arriving in the United States to pursue higher education and or occupational advancement, it was absolutely critical that you make something of yourself and not fail. The embarrassment of failure would not only be borne by the individual, but also that person's family and community; so, the pressure to succeed was tremendous (C. Nelson, September 4, 2011, personal communication). The expectation of success, accompanied by the support and encouragement from family and community often provided the motivation to persevere during difficult times. Another individual who migrated to the United States at age 7 recalled that her parents taught her the value of hard work and self-reliance by example. Her father worked diligently after they entered the United States, and within 6 months after migrating they were able to purchase their first home. "Every tub must sit on its own bottom" and "But by the sweat of your brow you shall eat bread" were refrains frequently cited in the household by her parents, and used to emphasize the importance of hard work, perseverance, and self-reliance (C. Brown, September 4, 2011, personal communication). "Buckle down" meaning it is time to get serious, and "free paper bun," an indication of vacation being over and it being back to school time, were reminders commonly expressed to another respondent who credits her parents staunch support and encouragement with her and her sibling's success (A. Robinson, September 6, 2011, personal communication).

Education

> Labor for learning before you grow old
> For learning is better than silver and gold
> Silver and gold will vanish away
> But a good education will never decay(verse memorized by scores of Jamaican children in primary schools; M. Hare, September 2, 2011, personal communication).

Educational attainment is highly valued among Black Caribbean immigrants, and is one of the primary reasons given for migration. Education is often viewed as a pathway for social mobility. Sociologist Douglas Massey and the *New York Times* have demonstrated that "West Indians (who have migrated to the US or who are second generation Caribbean Americans) have had noteworthy representation among Black students in some of the nation's elite private and public colleges and universities" (Holder, 2007, p. 678). A study by Bennett and Lutz (2009) found that immigrant Blacks (including Caribbean-born immigrants and their offspring) had the highest college attendance rates (75.1 %) compared with Whites (72.5 %) and native-born Blacks (60.2 %). The same study revealed that among immigrant Black students, 9.2 % were enrolled in elite institutions including Ivy League colleges and universities compared with 2.4 % of other Black students and 7.3 % of White students. A family's socioeconomic background was the major factor in creating a disadvantage for native-born Blacks' college attendance rates. No significant differences between immigrant and native-born Blacks were found in the chances of enrolling in college, if individuals were from similar socioeconomic backgrounds.

According to census data from 2009, among the nearly 3 million Caribbean immigrants in the United States ages 25 and older, approximately 900,000 were high school graduates. The remaining figures 450,000 have a Bachelor's degrees and 174,000 have obtained advanced degrees are accurate (U.S. Census Bureau, 2011). Members of the Caribbean immigrant community will often coalesce around supporting those who are pursuing higher education through formal and informal fundraising efforts to provide scholarships for tuition and fees, school supplies, housing, and transportation. When students graduate from their respective educational institutions, it is viewed as a significant accomplishment and source of pride not only for the individual, but for the larger community as well.

One interviewee described the robust sense of community present among the Caribbean immigrants at his university in the United States, and the strong desire that existed for all to succeed. He described an informal system of tutoring that existed where those who struggled with mathematics, for example, were tutored by engineering, science, and mathematics majors without financial compensation (L. Facey, August 25, 2011, personal communication). Other interviewees also described how immigrant students would share food and transportation, as well as information about internships and scholarship opportunities through their informal networks and formal Caribbean cultural organizations on campus (C. Washington, August 26, 2011, personal communication). Another interviewee shared his deep admiration and profound respect for his mother's perseverance and determination in pursuing her educational goals. She had returned to school for training as a nursing assistant and served as a primary source of motivation for him while he was pursuing his doctorate in epidemiology. He recounted fond memories of them working out mathematics problems together over the telephone. He felt that if his mother could return to school and face the challenges of obtaining advanced training as an older adult, there was no obstacle he could not overcome in earning his Ph.D. He proudly shared that he and his mother graduated in the same year (K. Brooks, September 10, 2011, personal communication). The author's father was also a key source of inspiration during her educational pursuits. Though he had already completed his education in Jamaica and had obtained numerous certifications in accounting and business in England and Canada, he returned to college after migrating to the United States, and earned both his Bachelor's degree and Masters in Business Administration while working full time. He shared numerous examples of the challenges he overcame in his quest to obtain an education both back home and in the United States. His stories of triumph over adversity and his dogged determination to attain his educational objectives were frequently recounted with the author during her own schooling. He and the author's mother (a trailblazer in her own right with a Master's degree in chemistry) imparted their strong love of learning, high expectations for educational attainment, and unwavering support during the author's successful pursuit of her doctorate in counseling psychology.

Conclusion

With its long history of migration and noteworthy contributions to the United States, the Black Caribbean immigrant population has left a lasting impression on their new homeland. The purpose of this chapter was to highlight the unique strengths, resilience, and creativity reflected in the cultural traditions and practices of these remarkable groups. It is the author's hope that meaningful lessons can be learned from these examples that enhances the well-being of all groups.

References

Bashi, V. F. (2007). *Survival of the knitted: Immigrant social networks in a stratified world*. Stanford: Stanford University Press.

Bennett, P. R., & Lutz, A. (2009). How African American is the net Black advantage? Differences in college attendance among immigrant Blacks, native Blacks and Whites. *Sociology of Education, 82I*, 70–100.

Brice-Baker, J. R. (2005). British West Indian families. In M. McGoldrick, J. Giordano, & N. Garcia-Preto (Eds.), *Ethnicity and family therapy* (3rd ed., pp. 117–126). New York: Guilford Press.

Butterfield, S-A. (2004). We're just Black: The racial and ethnic identities of second-generation West Indians in New York. In P. Kasinitz, H. H. Mollenkopf, & M. C. Waters (Eds.), *Becoming New Yorkers: Ethnographies of the new second generation* (pp. 288–312). New York: Sage.

Chamberlain, M. (2003). Rethinking Caribbean families: Extending the links. *Community, Work & Family, 6*(1), 63–76.

Chatters, L. M., Taylor, R. J., Bullard, K. M., & Jackson, J. S. (2008). Religious coping among African Americans, Caribbean Blacks and non-Hispanic Whites. *Journal of Community Psychology, 36*(3), 371–386.

Chatters, L. M., Taylor, R. J., Bullard, K. M., & Jackson, J. S. (2009). Race and ethnic differences in religious involvement: African Americans, Caribbean Blacks and non-Hispanic Whites. *Ethnic and Racial Studies Journal, 32*(7), 1143–1163.

Holder, C. B. (2007). West Indies. In M. C. Waters & R. Udea (Eds.), *The new Americans: A guide to immigration since 1965* (pp. 674–686). Cambridge: Harvard University Press.

Institute for Caribbean Studies (ICS). (2011). *Annual report 2010*. Washington: Institute for Caribbean Studies.

Jones, A., Sharpe, J., & Sogren, M. (2004). Children's experiences of separation from parents as a consequence of migration. *Caribbean Journal of Social Work, 3,* 89–109.

Kasinitz, P., Mollenkopf, J. H., Waters, M.C., & Holdaway, J. (2008). *Inheriting the city: The children of immigrants come of age*. New York: Sage.

Logan, J. R., & Deane, G. (2003). *Black diversity in metropolitan America. Report from the Mumford Center for Comparative Urban and Regional Research.* Albany: State University of New York.

Model, S. (2008). *West Indian immigrants: A Black success story?* New York: Sage.

Patten, E. (2012). *Statistical Portrait of the foreign-born population in the United States, 2010.* Washington DC: Pew Hispanic Center.

Pottinger, A. M., Stair, A. G., & Brown, S. W. (2008). A counseling framework for Caribbean children and families who have experienced migratory separation and reunion. *International Journal of Advanced Counseling, 30,* 15–24.

Smith, A., Lolonde, R. N., & Johnson, S. (2004). Serial migration and its implications for the parent-child relationship: A retrospective analysis of the experiences of the children of Caribbean immigrants. *Cultural Diversity and Ethnic Minority Psychology, 10*(2), 107–122.

Suarez-Orozco, C., & Suarez-Orozco, M. (2001). *Children of immigration.* Cambridge: Harvard University Press.

U.S. Census Bureau. (2008). American Community Survey, B04006, "People Reporting Ancestry", http://factfinder.census.gov/. Accessed Nov 2009.

U.S. Census Bureau (2009–2011). American Community Survey, S0201, "Selected Population Profile in the United States, West Indian" http://factfinder2.census.gov/faces/tableservices/jsf/pages/productview.xhtml?fpt=table. Accessed April 2013.

U.S. Census Bureau, Statistical Abstract of the United States: 2011, http://census.gov/prod/2011pubs/11statab/pop/pdf. Accessed Sept 2012.

Vickerman, M. (2007). Jamaica. In M. C. Waters & R. Udea (Eds.), *The new Americans: A guide to immigration since 1965* (pp. 479–490). Cambridge: Harvard University Press.

Waters, M. C. (1999). *Black identities, West Indian immigrant dreams and American realities.* New York: Sage.

Chapter 9
The Role of Motivation in Adults' Reading Comprehension: A Lifespan View

Kelly Branam Cartwright

As is clear from the introduction to this volume, positive aspects of individual human experience such as subjective well being, interest, and motivation, can have beneficial influences on all areas of adults' development (Seligman and Csikszentmihalyi 2000). In this chapter, I focus on the role of motivation in adults' reading comprehension. How might reading comprehension, a cognitive skill, be related to positive psychology?

A Bidirectional Relation between Positive Psychology and Reading Comprehension

Research indicates that the relation between positive psychology and reading comprehension is bidirectional. First, successful reading comprehension plays a significant role in a range of positive adult outcomes. Literacy serves social functions, aids communication, and affects relationships (see Smith 2009, for a review). According to Smith (2009, p. 604), "reading as a literacy practice is *situated* in the interactions between people, between individual readers and the texts they use or produce, and their personal literacy goals, as well as the meanings that individuals attach to their reading and writing behaviors." In addition, reading achievement affects adults' physical health: adults with low literacy have a three times greater chance of developing negative health outcomes such as low knowledge of health-related information, poor comprehension of medical discharge instructions, a greater frequency of visits to the doctor or hospital, and lower health status overall (see DeWalt et al. 2004, for a review). Furthermore, poor child health outcomes are more likely when parents are low in literacy (DeWalt and Hink 2009). Reading comprehension is required to complete job applications, understand directions on medication bottles, read road signs, enjoy a magazine or book, read the newspaper, help children with homework, and a

K. B. Cartwright (✉)
Christopher Newport University, 1 Avenue of the Arts, Newport News, VA 23606, USA
e-mail: kewright@cnu.edu

J. D. Sinnott (ed.), *Positive Psychology*,
DOI 10.1007/978-1-4614-7282-7_9,

host of other important life skills. However, the most recent National Assessment of Adult Literacy (NAAL; Institute of Education Sciences 2003) indicated that 14 % of American adults, approximately 30 million people, cannot read prose texts at a basic level; likewise, 12 % of American adults, approximately 26 million people, cannot read document texts at a basic level. These data indicate that many American adults are at risk for negative life outcomes due to low literacy.

A second way reading comprehension is related to the field of positive psychology is that motivation, a focal construct in positive psychology, plays a significant role in the development of reading comprehension. Consistent with positive psychology's examination of subjective and socio-emotional influences on other aspects of development, the field of educational psychology has recently seen calls for more integrative perspectives on educational processes such as reading, which incorporate motivational and emotional variables into what have traditionally been considered cognitive domains (Alexander et al. 1995; Alexander et al. 2004; Graesser 2009; Guthrie and Wigfield 1999). Moreover, theories of adult development have also called for integration of cognitive and subjective socio-emotional factors in conceptualizing adults' lives (Blackburn and Papalia 1992; Labouvie-Vief 1990, 1992; Sinnott 1998). The RAND Reading Study Group (RRSG 2002) recently conducted a comprehensive review of research on reading comprehension which resulted in a more integrative perspective on reading comprehension that includes three elements: reader factors, text factors, and the purposes of reading activity. Important for the discussion in this chapter, the RRSG emphasized the importance of both cognitive and motivational factors that impact the development of individuals' reading comprehension (RRSG 2002). Thus, recent cross-domain trends have called for integration of socio-emotional factors such as motivation into conceptualizations of cognitive development and reading comprehension development, across the lifespan. Yet, little work has examined the role of motivation in adults' reading comprehension; as a consequence, recent reviews have called for deeper inquiry into the role of motivational factors in adult literacy outcomes (Miller et al. 2010; U.S. Department of Health and Human Services 2004).

Why is examination of adults' reading motivation important? According to Guthrie and Wigfield (1999), "reading is a motivated act." Individuals with higher motivation read more frequently (e.g., Schutte and Malouff 2004, 2007; Wigfield and Guthrie 1997), and more frequent reading leads to better reading skill (Mol and Bus 2011). In short, motivation leads to more and better reading, which, in turn, is related to positive life outcomes. In the sections that follow, I review research on adults' reading behavior, the relation of reading behavior to reading comprehension, and the role of motivation in adults' reading comprehension.

Adults' Reading Behavior

As adults develop expertise as readers, many factors contribute to their successful development, such as knowledge of reading and of texts' content, strategic processing, as well as interest in and motivation to engage in reading tasks (Alexander 2006;

Alexander et al. 1995, 2004; Pressley and Afflerbach 1995; Pressley and Lundeberg 2008; Shanahan et al. 2011; Wyatt et al. 1993). Scholars have studied optimal adult literacy outcomes by examining the reading processes of expert readers who exhibit the cognitive skills and motivation necessary for the development and maintenance of successful reading comprehension (Pressley and Afflerbach 1995; Pressley and Lundeberg 2008; Wyatt et al. 1993). This research highlights the fact that the development of expertise in reading, or in any domain for that matter, requires deliberate practice (Alexander 2006; Ericsson et al. 1993; Feltovich et al. 2006); that is, to read well, individuals must read often.

So, how often do adults read, and what do they read? Adults spend much time reading for a variety of purposes in a variety of text types, and reading continues to be an important part of adults' recreational activities into older adulthood (Smith 1993). Kirsch and Guthrie (1984), for example, examined reading behavior in a sample of 99 employees of a Fortune 500 company who worked in a variety of occupations. Participants were interviewed about their reading habits and were told to "think of reading as gaining meaning from written messages" (p. 217). Results revealed that adults read brief documents and reference materials more frequently at work, whereas during leisure time they read other genres, such as news, science, society, recreational, and fictional texts. Types of reading at work also varied by occupation: individuals in managerial and professional positions read science and society texts more frequently, skilled workers read reference texts, and clerical workers read more brief documents. In leisure time, participants in all occupational categories read prose texts more frequently than other text types; however, individuals in managerial, professional, and clerical positions read significantly more prose texts during leisure time than individuals in skilled and semiskilled service positions (approximately 80 min versus 58 min per day, respectively). Overall, participants in this study read more at work (127 min) than in their leisure time (80 min), for an average total of about 207 min per day.

More recently, White et al. (2010) analyzed a much larger and more representative dataset gathered by the National Center for Education Statistics in the Real World Tasks Study, which used a diary method to gather data on adults' literacy behavior. This study included additional types of literacy-related activities such as computer work and quantitative reading; thus, it is not surprising that adults' average number of minutes read per day was higher than in the Kirsch and Guthrie (1984) study at 272 min per day. Overall, adults spent more time in prose reading and quantitative tasks than in other types of texts such as document reading. Of the prose texts, adults reported reading three types for at least 30 min per day: periodicals/journals/newspapers, electronic correspondence, and informational materials. Books and novels were read far less frequently at a rate of 18 min per day (see White et al. 2010, p. 295, for mean reading times by text type). In summary, adults report reading a variety of text types with the predominant text type being informational (rather than fictional) text (White et al. 2010); and adults' reading habits vary widely by type of occupation (Kirsch and Guthrie 1984).

Relation of Reading Behavior to Reading Skills and Other Cognitive Outcomes

Frequency of reading is related to a variety of cognitive outcomes, including reading skills. For example, Stanovich and Cunningham (1993) found that frequency of reading, assessed with print exposure measures, is related to knowledge in multiple domains, even when basic cognitive ability is controlled. Similarly, West et al. (1993) found adults who read more frequently, assessed with behavioral observation and print exposure measures, have greater vocabulary breadth and cultural knowledge. More recently, Kelly and Knepp (2009) showed that college students who read for pleasure more frequently outside of assigned texts showed higher scores on an assessment of creativity, including subscales that assessed creative engagement, creative cognitive style, tolerance, and fantasy. Thus, frequent reading appears to be related to positive cognitive outcomes.

Additionally, reading frequency is related to reading comprehension in high school students (Cunningham and Stanovich 1997), deaf adults (Parault and Williams 2010), and hearing adults (Grant et al. 2007; Kail et al. 1999). Recently, Mol and Bus (2011) conducted a metaanalysis which indicated that print exposure leads to improvements in reading comprehension and other reading-related and general cognitive skills across the lifespan. With respect to adults, they found that reading frequency, assessed with print exposure measures, was significantly related to oral language skills, academic achievement scores (e.g., SAT and ACT scores), spelling, word reading, and reading comprehension. Across the lifespan, those who read more, read better; however, motivation plays a significant role in individuals' reading behavior and in reading comprehension.

The Role of Motivation in Reading Comprehension

What do we know about the role of motivation in reading comprehension? In recent decades, substantial progress has been made in documenting the important role of motivation in older children's reading comprehension; however, comparatively less is known about the role of motivation in younger readers' (i.e., aged less than 8 years) and adult readers' reading comprehension (Guthrie and Humenick 2004; Miller et al. 2010). Research with older children indicates that motivation is associated with frequency of reading behavior (Wigfield and Guthrie 1997) as well as students' interest and engagement in reading tasks (Guthrie et al. 2004; Wigfield et al. 2008). Additionally, motivation contributes significantly to children's reading comprehension beyond prior knowledge and strategy use (Taboada et al. 2009), is related to reading comprehension in children of varying cultural backgrounds (Wang and Guthrie 2004), and contributes to reading comprehension in both languages for bilingual students (Lin et al. 2011). Finally, motivation contributes to growth in reading comprehension across the upper elementary grades, even beyond initial levels of students' reading comprehension (Taboada et al. 2009). In younger children (i.e., those in the early elementary grades), motivation is associated with word reading ability (Chapman and Tunmer 1995; Coddington and Guthrie 2009). And, although little work with this age group has examined the relation of motivation to reading comprehension, Cartwright et al. (2010) recently demonstrated that motivation contributes to first and second graders' reading comprehension beyond word reading ability and verbal ability.

As individuals age, motivation continues to play a significant role in reading comprehension (e.g., Mucherah and Yoder 2008). Although little research has focused on the role of motivation in adults' reading comprehension, a few studies bear on this question. For example, Walczyk et al. (1999) had adults read under time constraints. Adults who read under mild time constraints showed better comprehension than those who read under no constraints or severe time constraints. Walczyk and colleagues attributed these results to increased mindfulness, motivation, and effort, suggesting that mild time constraints produce motivation to attend to texts' meanings. However, they did not measure motivation in this study. Similarly, Lin et al. (1997) found that college students' interest in texts predicted their comprehension performance on those texts. Although they did not assess motivation in this study, interest is associated with motivation in other work (See Guthrie and Humenick 2004 for a review).

Another factor related to adults' and children's reading motivation is choice. Elementary school students who are given the option to choose texts are more interested in and motivated to read those texts (McLoyd 1979). Additionally, choice improves elementary students' ability to locate information in, and correctly answer questions about, informational texts; these results are suggestive of a relation between interest and comprehension (Reynolds and Symons 2001; see Guthrie and Humenick 2004 for a review of reading interest and motivation research with children). Finally, in a study with adults, Schraw et al. (1998) manipulated choice of texts by assigning texts or allowing college students to choose them. They found that choice affected affective responses to, and interest in the texts but not cognitive processing about or comprehension of the texts. These studies indicate that the relation between choice of texts and reading motivation seems to be robust; however, additional research is necessary to determine whether interest affects adults' comprehension of texts.

Similarly, although the relation of motivation to reading comprehension has been extensively studied in children, direct assessment of this relation in adults is rare. Recently, Parault and Williams (2010) assessed motivation in deaf and hearing adults using an adaptation of the Motivation for Reading Questionnaire (MRQ), which was originally developed for use with children (Wigfield and Guthrie 1997). They found that motivation was significantly correlated with reading comprehension in both deaf and hearing adults. Other work assessing the relation of motivation to reading comprehension has used the Need for Cognition scale, a measure of more general cognitive motivation that indicates individuals' enjoyment of effortful cognitive activities such as reading (Cacioppo et al. 1984). For example, Kardash and Noel (2000) found that cognitive motivation was significantly related to recall of text content in university students. More recently, Dai and Wang (2007) examined the contribution of cognitive motivation to adults' reading comprehension, finding that cognitive motivation made an independent contribution to reading comprehension, even when readers' beliefs about reading tasks were controlled. Recent data from my lab confirm and extend these findings; we found that cognitive motivation contributes unique variance to reading comprehension, even when verbal ability and word reading skill were controlled (Cartwright 2012). Taken together, these findings indicate that motivation plays an important role in adults' reading comprehension. However, more research is necessary to understand broader implications of motivation for adults' literacy development and positive life outcomes.

Summary and Conclusion

Reading comprehension plays a critical role in adults' daily life tasks, health status, and positive life outcomes. Yet, many American adults lack the requisite reading skills necessary for basic literacy (Institute of Education Sciences 2003). Furthermore, although research on adult literacy has traditionally focused on cognitive aspects of reading processes, the field has recently turned attention to the important role of positive, subjective factors in adults' reading comprehension development (Miller et al. 2010; RAND 2002; Smith 2009). Expert adult readers read often, with interest, and are highly motivated (Pressley and Afflerbach 1995; Pressley and Lundeberg 2008; Wyatt et al. 1993). These readers serve as models of optimal life outcomes and point to potential areas of intervention for adults with low literacy. To read well, adults must practice reading. But, to want to practice, they must be interested in, and motivated to engage in reading tasks. Future research on adults' positive life outcomes should focus on the intersection of these variables: reading frequency, reading interest, motivation, and reading comprehension as well as the effects of these variables on adults' daily health and functioning. Literacy affects all aspects of adults' lives, and a more complete picture of the role of literacy in adults' lives will ensure that optimal positive life outcomes are attainable by more individuals.

References

Alexander, P. A. (2006). The path to competence: A lifespan developmental perspective on reading. *Journal of Literacy Research, 37,* 413–436.

Alexander, P. A., Jetton, T. L., & Kulikowich, J. M. (1995). Interrelationship of knowledge, interest, and recall: Assessing a model of domain learning. *Journal of Educational Psychology, 87,* 559–575.

Alexander, P. A., Sperl, C. T., Buehl, M. M., Fives, H., & Chiu, S. (2004). Modeling domain learning: Profiles from the field of special education. *Journal of Educational Psychology, 96,* 545–557.

Blackburn, J. A., & Papalia, D. E. (1992). The study of adult cognition from a Piagetian perspective. In R. J. Sternberg & C. A. Berg (Eds.), *Intellectual development*. New York: Cambridge University Press.

Cacioppo, J. T., Petty, R. E., & Kao, C. F. (1984). The efficient assessment of need for cognition. *Journal of Personality Assessment, 48,* 306–307.

Cartwright, K. B. (2012, December). *The contribution of cognitive motivation to adults' reading comprehension: Reconsidering the simple view of reading*. Paper presented at the 62nd annual meeting of the Literacy Research Association, San Diego, CA.
Cartwright, K. B., Oliver, E., & Marshall, T. R. (2010, December). *Assessing primary students' reading engagement and its unique role in reading comprehension: Reconsidering the simple view of reading.* Paper presented at the annual meeting of the Literacy Research Association, Fort Worth, TX.
Chapman, J. W., & Tunmer, W. E. (1995). Development of young children's reading self-concepts: An examination of emerging subcomponents and their relationship with reading achievement. *Journal of Educational Psychology, 87,* 154–167.
Coddington, C. S., & Guthrie, J. T. (2009). Teacher and student perceptions of boys' and girls' reading motivation. *Reading Psychology, 30,* 225–249.
Cunningham, A. E., & Stanovich, K. E. (1997). Early reading acquisition and its relation to reading experience and ability 10 years later. *Developmental Psychology, 33,* 934–945.
Dai, D. Y., & Wang, X. (2007). The role of need for cognition and reader beliefs in text comprehension and interest development. *Contemporary Educational Psychology, 32,* 332–347.
DeWalt, D. A., & Hink, A. (2009). Health literacy and child health outcomes: A systematic review of the literature. *Pediatrics, 124,* S265–S274.
DeWalt, D. A., Berkman, N. D., Sheridan, S., Lohr, K., & Pignone, M. P. (2004). Literacy and health outcomes: A systematic review of the literature. *Journal of General Internal Medicine, 19,* 1228–1239.
Ericsson, K. A., Krampe, R. T., & Tesch-Römer, C. (1993) The role of deliberate practice in the acquisition of expert performance. *Psychological Review, 100,* 363–406.
Feltovich, P. J., Prietula, M. J., & Ericsson, K. A. (2006). Studies of expertise from psychological perspectives. In K. A. Ericsson, N. Charness, P. J. Feltovich, & R. R. Hoffman (Eds.), *The Cambridge handbook of expertise and expert performance* (pp. 41–67). Cambridge: Cambridge University Press.
Graesser, A. C. (2009). Inaugural editorial for Journal of Educational Psychology.*Journal of Educational Psychology, 101,* 259–261. doi:10.1037/a0014883.
Grant, A., Wilson, A. M., & Gottardo, A. (2007). The role of print exposure in reading skills of postsecondary students with and without reading disabilities. *Exceptionality Education Canada, 17,* 175–194.
Guthrie, J. T., & Wigfield, A. (1999). How motivation fits into a science of reading. *Scientific Studies of Reading, 3,* 199–205.
Guthrie, J. T., & Humenick, N. M. (2004). Motivating students to read: Evidence for classroom practices that increase reading motivation and achievement. In P. McCardle & V. Chhabra (Eds.), *The voice of evidence in reading research* (pp. 329–354). Baltimore: Brookes.
Guthrie, J. T., Wigfield, A., Barbosa, P., Perencevich, K. C., Taboada, A., Davis, M. H., Scafiddi, N. T., & Tonks, S. (2004). Increasing reading comprehension and engagement through concept-oriented reading instruction. *Journal of Educational Psychology, 96,* 403–423.
Institute of Education Sciences. (2003).*National assessment of adult literacy. National Center for Education Statistics*. http://nces.ed.gov/naal/kf_demographics.asp#2. Accessed 26 June 2012.
Kail, R., Hall, L. K., & Caskey, B. J. (1999). Processing speed, exposure to print, and naming speed. *Applied Psycholinguistics, 20,* 303–314.
Kardash, C. M., & Noel, L. K. (2000). How organizational signals, need for cognition, and verbal ability affect text recall and recognition. *Contemporary Educational Psychology, 25,* 317–331.
Kelly, K. E., & Knepp, L. B. (2009). Reading for pleasure and creativity among college students. *College Student Journal, 43,* 1137–1144.
Kirsch, I. S., & Guthrie, J. T. (1984). Adult reading practices for work and leisure. *Adult Education Quarterly, 34,* 213–232.
Labouvie-Vief, G. (1990). Modes of knowledge and the organization of development. In M. L. Commons, C. Armon, L. Kohlberg, F. A. Richards, T. A. Grotzer, & J. D. Sinnott (Eds.), *Adult development, Vol 2: Models and methods in the study of adolescent and adult thought* (Chapter 3, pp. 43–62). New York: Praeger.

Labouvie-Vief, G. (1992). A neo-Piagetian perspective on adult cognitive development. In R. J. Sternberg & C. A. Berg (Eds.), *Intellectual development.* New York: Cambridge University Press.

Lin, L., Zabrucky, K., & Moore D (1997). The relations among interest, self-assessed comprehension, and comprehension performance in young adults. *Reading Research and Instruction, 36,* 127–139.

Lin, D., Wong, K. K., & McBride-Chang, C. (2011). Reading motivation and reading comprehension in Chinese and English among bilingual students. *Reading and Writing, 25,* 717–737.

McLoyd, V. (1979). The effects of extrinsic rewards of differential value on high and low intrinsic interest. *Child Development, 50,* 1010–1019.

Miller, B., McCardle, P., & Hernandez, R. (2010). Advances and remaining challenges in adult literacy research. *Journal of Learning Disabilities, 43,* 101–107.

Mol, S. E., & Bus, A. G. (2011). To read or not to read: A meta-analysis of print exposure from infancy to early adulthood. *Psychological Bulletin, 137,* 267–296.

Mucherah, W., & Yoder, A. (2008). Motivation for reading and middle school students' performance on standardized testing in reading. *Reading Psychology, 29,* 214–235.

Parault, S. J., & Williams, H. M. (2010). Reading motivation, reading amount, and text comprehension in deaf and hearing adults. *Journal of Deaf Studies and Deaf Education, 15,* 120–135.

Pressley, M., & Afflerbach, P. (1995). *Verbal protocols of reading: The nature of constructively responsive reading.* Hillsdale: Erlbaum.

Pressley, M. & Lundeberg, M. (2008). An invitation to study professionals reading professional-level texts: A window on exceptionally complex, flexible reading. In K. B. Cartwright (Ed.), *Literacy processes: Cognitive flexibility in learning and teaching.* New York: Guilford.

RAND Reading Study Group. (2002). *Reading for understanding: Towards an R&D program in reading comprehension.* http://www.rand.org/content/dam/rand/pubs/monograph_reports/2005/MR1465.pdf. Accessed 8 July 2012.

Reynolds, P. L., & Symons, S. (2001). Motivational variables and children's text search. *Journal of Educational Psychology, 93,* 14–22.

Schraw, G., Flowerday, T., & Reisetter, M. F. (1998). The role of choice in reader engagement. *Journal of Educational Psychology, 90,* 705–714.

Schutte, N. S., & Malouff, J. M. (2004). University student reading preferences in relation to the big five personality dimensions. *Reading Psychology, 25,* 273–295.

Schutte, N. S., & Malouff, J. M. (2007). Dimensions of reading motivation: Development of an adult reading motivation scale. *Reading Psychology, 28,* 469–489.

Seligman, M. P., & Csikszentmihalyi, M. (2000). Positive psychology: An introduction. *American Psychologist, 55,* 5–14.

Shanahan, S., Shanahan, T., & Misischia, C. (2011). Analysis of expert readers in three disciplines: History, mathematics, and chemistry. *Journal of Literacy Research, 43,* 393–429.

Sinnott, J. D. (1998). *The development of logic in adulthood: Postformal thought and its applications.* New York: Plenum Press.

Smith, M. C. (1993). The reading abilities and practices of older adults. *Educational Gerontology, 19,* 417–432.

Smith, M. C. (2009). Literacy in adulthood. In M. C. Smith (Ed.), *Handbook of research on adult learning and development* (Chapter 21, pp. 601–635). New York: Routledge.

Stanovich, K. E., & Cunningham, A. E. (1993). Where does knowledge come from? Specific associations between print exposure and information acquisition. *Journal of Educational Psychology, 85,* 211–229.

Taboada, A., Tonks, S., Wigfield, A., & Guthrie, J. (2009). Effects of motivational and cognitive variables on reading comprehension. *Reading and Writing, 22*(1), 85–106.

U.S. Department of Health and Human Services. (2004). Adult and family literacy: *Current and future research directions—a workshop summary*. Washington, DC: US. Department of Health and Human Services, National Institutes of Health, National Institute of Child Health and Human Development. http://www.nichd.nih.gov/publications/pubs/upload/afl_workshop.pdf. Accessed 8 July 2012.

Walczyk, J. J., Kelly, K. E., Meche, S. D., & Braud, H. (1999). Time limitations enhance reading comprehension. *Contemporary Educational Psychology, 24,* 156–165.

Wang, J., & Guthrie, J. (2004). Modeling the effects of intrinsic motivation, extrinsic motivation, amount of reading, and past reading achievement on text comprehension between U.S. and Chinese students. *Reading Research Quarterly, 39*(2), 162–186.

West, R. F., Stanovich, K. E., & Mitchell, H. R. (1993). Reading in the real world and its correlates. *Reading Research Quarterly, 28,* 35–50.

White, S., Chen, J., & Forsyth, B. (2010). Reading-related literacy activities of American adults: Time spent, task types, and cognitive skills used. *Journal of Literacy Research, 42,* 276–307.

Wigfield, A., & Guthrie, J. T. (1997). Relations of children's motivation for reading to the amount and breadth of their reading. *Journal of Educational Psychology, 89,* 420–432.

Wigfield, A., Guthrie, J., Perencevich, K., Taboada, A., Klauda, S., McRae, A., & Barbosa, P. (2008). Role of reading engagement in mediating effects of reading comprehension instruction on reading outcomes. *Psychology in the Schools, 45*(5), 432–445.

Wyatt, D., Pressley, M., El-Dinary, P. B., Stein, S., Evans, P., & Brown, R. (1993). Comprehension strategies, worth and credibility monitoring, and evaluations: Cold and hot cognition when experts read professional articles that are important to them. *Learning and Individual Differences, 5,* 49–72.

Chapter 10
Martial Arts as a Pathway to Flourishing

Charles H. Hackney

The essential aim of Judo is to teach, help, and forward adult maturity.

Moshe Feldenkrais

Psychological research into the martial arts is limited at this time, but that which does exist presents us with some valuable insights which may be applied to this consideration of adult flourishing. In light of the research evidence, examples of which will be discussed below, the martial arts have been proposed as adjuncts to traditional psychotherapy (e.g., Gleser et al. 1992; Weiser et al. 1995), as a way of encouraging the reform of delinquent youth (e.g., Twemlow and Sacco 1998; Zivin et al. 2001), and fostering positive youth development (Hackney 2010a) because advancement in the warrior arts have been shown to be associated with a number of psychosocial benefits, in addition to their practical self-defense benefits (Brecklin and Ullman 2005).

Martial Arts and the Amelioration of Distress

Several researchers have found martial arts training to be associated with the reduction of negative characteristics. For example, martial training has been associated with a reduction of anxiety-related characteristics (Layton 1990; Kurian et al. 1993; Ozer and Bandura 1990) including neuroticism (Layton 1988), feelings of vulnerability (Madden 1990, 1995), nightmares (Slater and Hunt 1997), and symptoms of posttraumatic stress disorder (PTSD) (David et al. 2006). This relationship has been demonstrated in studies that are both correlational (Layton 1988, 1990; Kurian et al. 1993; Madden 1995) and experimental (Madden 1990; Slater and Hunt 1997) in nature.

C. H. Hackney (✉)
Psychology Department, Briercrest College and Seminary, 510 College Drive,
Caronport, SK S0H 0S0 Canada
e-mail: chackney@briercrest.ca

J. D. Sinnott (ed.), *Positive Psychology,*
DOI 10.1007/978-1-4614-7282-7_10, © Springer Science+Business Media, LLC 2013

The relationship between martial arts training and aggressiveness is a contentious one in the psychological literature. Bandura (1973) argues against the psychological value of martial arts training from the perspective of social learning theory. Aggressive behavior is learned by watching others be rewarded for aggression, by being rewarded oneself for it, and by rehearsing the aggressive behavior. From this perspective, the martial arts are a part of the problem, not the solution. Bandura (focusing on military training and boxing) argues that martial training should increase aggressiveness by rewarding violent behavior, by providing opportunities to observe others being rewarded for violent behavior, and by providing a venue for the rehearsal of violent behaviors (p. 82). Any talk about a defensible form of violent behavior is, according to Bandura (p. 133), nothing more than a façade of moralizing self-justification, which can itself result in a greater sense of entitlement to engage in violence. This position has received empirical support from Reynes and Lorant (2002) and Endressen and Olweus (2005), who found martial training to be associated with increase in aggressiveness.

Other empirical research on martial training and aggressiveness paints a different picture. Nosanchuk (1981) found that higher belt rank in Karate and Taekwondo was significantly associated with lower levels of aggressive fantasy. Examining Karate and Jiujitsu students, Daniels and Thornton (1990) also found a negative correlation between length of training and hostility scores, and martial arts students on the whole were no more aggressive than similar groups of either rugby or badminton players. A similar negative correlation between rank and aggressiveness was found in Skelton, Glynn, and Berta's (1991) examination of Taekwondo students. Numerous explanations have been put forward for this demonstrated relationship. Nosanchuk (1981) argues that the teachings found within the martial arts encourage conflict avoidance, self-control, and respect for others. Although sparring involves a degree of assertive physical contact, an overly-aggressive fighting style is strongly condemned. Rewarding these patterns of behavior, the author argues, may counteract the proviolence learning predicted by Bandura (1973). Twemlow and Sacco (1998) claim that a martial arts training program inculcates values such as respectful kindness, altruism, overcoming fear, and restraint in the face of provocation, and provides a socially acceptable channel for young men's needs for rough play and feelings of power.

The conclusions drawn by these researchers are weakened by the correlational nature of their studies. Without longitudinal or experimental data, the possibility exists that lower aggression scores tend to accompany higher belt rank due to attrition; that is, because highly aggressive students tend to "drop out" of martial arts training before advancing beyond an intermediate level. Two experimental studies (Delva-Tauiliili 1995; Foster 1997) found no changes in students' aggression scores following brief (2.5-week and 10-week, respectively) martial arts training programs. It can be argued, however, that such brief training is insufficient to produce any measurable changes in personality traits, leading Foster (1997) to call for studies that follow students over several years. Zivin et al.'s (2001) findings are a partial exception to this pattern. In a middle school setting, 60 boys who had been identified as being at high risk for delinquency and violence were assigned to a 10-week Kempo-based school program. Effects of the intervention indicate improvement on a wide range of variables, including a preventative buffer against expulsions and teacher-rated violence, and a reversal of the control group's downward violent trend once they were assigned to the program. An overall improvement in violent behavior, however, was not demonstrated by the intervention group. Taken together, these studies support the idea that if martial arts training is to be utilized for the purpose of counteracting aggressiveness, it is best to adopt a long-term perspective.

Martial Arts and Increases in Desirable Characteristics

Other research evidence involves the martial arts as facilitative of the development of positive characteristics. In the aforementioned study by Zivin et al. (2001), youth who participated in the Kempo program demonstrated improvement across 12 different variables, including happiness, attentive ability, and schoolwork performance. Duthie, Hope, and Barker's (1978) examination of the personalities of advanced versus average martial artists resulted in a description of the "superior" martial artist as "an outgoing extrovert somewhat aware of his social environment, looking at himself positively, and trying to get ahead in life" (p. 75), a description in line with Kurian et al.'s (1994) examination of Taekwondo practitioners' personalities, in which they conclude that "belt rank is associated with a pattern of enthusiastic optimism and self-reliance" (p. 905). Martial arts training has also been associated with increases in positive self-image (Richman and Rehberg 1986; Finkenberg 1990), and in the ability to tolerate pain (Focht et al. 2000). Of these studies, only Focht, Bouchard, and Murphey's is an experiment, the others are correlational in nature.

A Neo-Aristotelian Theory of the Martial Arts

As they work toward a description of human flourishing, with practical applications flowing from that description, several psychologists (e.g., Dueck and Reimer 2003; Fowers 2005; Tjeltveit 2003) have drawn inspiration from the work of virtue ethicists, with some drawing specifically from the approach to virtue ethics developed by Alasdair MacIntyre (1984). Inspired by MacIntyre's neo-Aristotelian virtue ethics, and by those psychologists who draw from his thought, I developed an approach to the philosophy and psychology of the martial arts grounded in MacIntyrean thought (Hackney 2009, 2010b).

In *After Virtue*, MacIntyre (1984) examines the history of philosophical ethics, and advocates a revival of the Aristotelian tradition in moral philosophy, given our current state of moral discourse. The neo-Aristotelian approach is teleological in nature, focusing on inquiry into the *telos* ("end," "goal," or "purpose") of an object or activity (e.g., the *telos* of a clock is to tell the time). Describing the *telos* of something provides a standard for describing that object as being good or bad in terms of its function. A good object fulfills its *telos* well (A good clock tells the time well) by possessing the characteristics (virtues) of a highly functioning object (A good clock will possess virtues such as precision and durability).

The *telos* of a human is a matter of some debate. Martin Seligman, for example, argues that positive psychologists should not specify a *telos* for people, preferring to focus his analysis on subjective feelings of flourishing (Seligman 2002), and cross-cultural analysis (Dahlsgaard et al. 2005). This approach has been criticized as being theoretically hollow (e.g., Sundararajan 2005) and as a disingenuous "smuggling in" of an implicit *telos* (e.g., Christopher and Hickinbottom 2008; Kristjánsson 2010). Rosalind Hursthouse (1999), by contrast, defines the human *telos* in terms of the exercise of survival-conducive adaptations involving our status as social animals, whereas MacIntyre (1999) argues that the human *telos* is to become an independent practical reasoner.

The process of flourishing, of becoming more highly functioning through growth in the virtues is referred to as *eudaimonia*, which Macintyre (1984) describes as "a complete human life lived at its best" (p. 149) by moving from one's current "untutored" state (human nature as it happens to be) toward a greater actualization of the *telos* (human nature as it could be). The influence of this kind of thinking on the positive psychology movement can be seen in the creation of the reference volume *Character Strengths and Virtues* (Peterson and Seligman 2004), often called "the *CSV*", which contains descriptions of "the strengths of character that make the good life possible" (p. 4).

One component of MacItnyre's description of eudaimonic flourishing is participation in activities that facilitate growth. MacIntyre called these activities "practices," defined as "any coherent and complex form of socially established cooperative human activity through which goods internal to that form of activity are realized in the course of trying to achieve those standards of excellence which are appropriate to, and partially definitive of, that form of activity, with the result that human powers to achieve excellence, and human conceptions of the ends and good involved, are systematically extended" (MacIntyre 1984, p. 187). Practices foster eudaimonic growth because pursuing excellence in these activities requires the cultivation of the same virtues that are necessary to be a highly functioning human. Chess (MacIntyre's favorite example) fosters virtues such as imagination, strategic intelligence, and competitive intensity. The more these virtues are cultivated, the greater the player's ability to win games and be recognized by fellow chess players as an excellent practitioner. These qualities are then transferrable to other life contexts (business, for example) and enable the individual to become a more highly functioning human (all three of these virtues would facilitate MacIntyre's description of an independent practical reasoner).

I have argued (Hackney 2009) that the martial arts fit this definition of a eudaimonic practice very well. Like chess, the martial arts are social in nature. The newcomer enters into relationships with the other members of that practice, and submits to the members' standards of value regarding excellence in the practice. Through interactions with instructors and other students, newcomers learn the skills, terminology, and values of their martial art. Benefits that accrue from the practice of the martial arts include self-defense, physical fitness, the feeling of "living history" that comes from participation in an activity with a rich tradition, enjoyable competition, and spiritual growth.

Pursuing excellence in the martial arts requires the cultivation of character traits that are deemed desirable by martial artists. Examples abound in the relevant literature, both, historical and contemporary. In Book II of *The Republic*, Plato argues that the guardians of his ideal society require speed, strength, "high spirits" (aggressive courage), and a "philosophic disposition" (gentleness and love of learning). The early fifteenth-century swordsmaster Fiore dei Liberi lists prudence, courage, strength, and swiftness as characteristics of a highly functioning practitioner of his art (Cvet 2005). Tikhonov (1998) describes the characteristics of an excellent Korean *hwarang* warrior as "mercifulness toward living creatures, indifference to material temptations, and, most importantly, a calm and optimistic attitude toward death" (p. 334). Consistent with MacIntyre's idea of a eudaimonic practice, the cultivation of these virtues will empower success in both the activity and life in general. Liberi, for example, considers "audacity" (a form of courage involving the ability to act swiftly and decisively in the face of fear) to be the crowning virtue of his art, enabling the fighter to take immediate advantage of openings in opponents' defenses. Audacity can also empower everyday acts of courage such as standing up for one's beliefs in the face of peer opposition or taking altruistic action when situations call for it (Hackney 2006).

Taking a similar approach as Dahlsgaard, Peterson, and Seligman's (2005) study of cross-cultural virtues, I engaged in a study of various literatures on warriorhood in search of ubiquitous warrior virtues (Hackney 2010b). I found that five virtues consistently emerged across history and across cultures as necessary characteristics of an excellent warrior: courage, justice, temperance, wisdom, and benevolence. Strong parallels exist between my findings and current thought on the virtues in positive psychology. The virtues that I identified are five of the six virtue categories found in the *CSV* (Peterson and Seligman 2004). These five virtues not only facilitate victory in combative encounters, but are also characteristic of highly functioning people.

Courage

Courage is the virtue most easily associated with the martial arts. Peterson and Seligman (2004) define courage as "the exercise of will to accomplish goals in the face of opposition, either external or internal" (p. 199). The most obvious example of opposition in the martial arts is one's opponent. Training in the martial arts also involves risk, and courage empowers swift action in the face of fear (Hackney 2006), and the ability to continue in spite of pain.

Failure in the face of boredom or obstacles represents a threat to one's self-concept (Peterson and Seligman 2004), and persistence, a component of what Pieper (1965) called the "statical" form of courage, involves overcoming ego-defensive fears relating to failure at a task. As an everyday example of such courage, students of the martial arts may frequently find that they "just don't feel like training today."

Training is repetitive, effortful, and sometimes painful. The temptation exists to skip training "just this one time," and self-justifying excuses are easily concocted (bad weather, other tasks requiring one's attention, etc.). The generation of these external attributions stems from a fear of seeing oneself as having failed as a martial artist, and one can courageously choose to see through the self-serving justifications and train, even if it is difficult and even if one does not feel like it.

Justice

Fives (2005) defines the virtue of justice as "the disposition to govern one's conduct according to rules of justice" (p. 123). Cupit (1996) defines an unjust act as "an unfitting act; it is an act which fails to accord with the status of the person treated" (p. 2). If a person deserves a reward, justice is ensuring that the person is rewarded; if a person deserves punishment, justice is ensuring that the person is punished. Sterba (1988) claims that all major approaches to the concept of justice within current debate agree that justice consists of giving people what they deserve. Disagreements center around exactly what people deserve and how to give it to them.

Justice can be cultivated in the martial arts through concepts such as honor (Westhusing 2003) and obligation. A highly functioning martial artist will take the obligations that come with the various roles found in the dojo seriously. For example, in some Japanese arts, the term "uke" is used to describe the one who plays the role of attacker when practicing a technique, while "tori" is used to describe the one who responds with the technique being practiced. When training in this capacity, the uke is obligated to begin with an attack that is committed and energetic, but properly controlled and without genuine intent to injure, and with the degree of severity moderated to match the skill level of the tori (Hatsumi and Cole 2001; Ledyard 2002). The tori is obligated to execute the appropriate techniques with a similar balance of intensity and gentleness.

Temperance

While Peterson and Seligman (2004) classify temperance as the category of "positive traits that protect us from excess" (p. 431), the traditional understanding of this virtue is that it is associated with balance. One who is intemperate engages in a "perversion of the true through excess *or underdevelopment*" (Jordan 1989, p. 50, italics mine), while the temperate person is able to find the healthy balance between excess and deficiency. Temperance applied to one's self-concept, for example, produces humility, a realistic assessment of one's abilities and achievements (Tangney 2000). Another character strength closely associated with temperance is self-control. In the research literature, "self-control" and "self-regulation" are often used interchangeably (Baumeister and Exline 1999), and are defined as "the exercise of control over oneself, especially with regard to bringing in the self into line with preferred (thus, regular) standards" (Vohs and Baumeister 2004, p. 2).

The martial arts provide ample opportunities for the cultivation of both humility and self-regulatory strength. Training in the martial arts will involve frequent failures and frustrations, exposure to others who are more highly skilled than oneself, and the necessity of obeying one's instructor. In the words of Judo founder Jigoro Kano, this produces a person who is "neither cocky with victory nor broken with defeat" (Kano 1986, p. 25). Lakes and Hoyt (2004) examined the possibility of martial arts training enhancing self-regulation. This study was done using traditional experimental methods, and involved a school-based Taekwondo program. Half of the 200 participants were assigned to a 4-month program of Moogong Ryu Taekwondo training, while the other half engaged in standard physical education classes. Compared to the control group, the students in the Taekwondo group demonstrated improvements in their cognitive, emotional, and behavioral self-control.

Wisdom

It is common in wisdom research to distinguish between "transcendent" and "practical" wisdom (Robinson 1990). Wink and Helson (1997) describe the transcendently wise person in terms of inner self-awareness, the ability to reconcile seemingly opposed intellectual concepts, and the search for answers to the meaning of life. Transcendently wise participants in Wink and Helson's study demonstrated elevated levels of cognitive openness, intuition, and creativity. The practically wise are described in terms of good interpersonal skills, superior decision-making ability, and expertise in giving useful advice. Variables associated with practical wisdom include greater leadership ability, empathy, and concern for making the world a better place. Fowers (2005) describes practical wisdom as a three-step process, in which the essential features of a situation are perceived, the right goal is identified, and the best strategy for attaining those goals is developed. Both, transcendant and practical wisdom play roles in Sternberg's (1998) balance theory of wisdom. Sternberg describes a wise person as being able to apply practical problem-solving skills in such a way that the person's values are employed to balance the demands of multiple interests and environmental factors toward achieving the common good. Sternberg recommends turning to religion and moral philosophy to address the nature of the common good and the values to be employed (transcendant wisdom) in solving problems (practical wisdom).

Both transcendant and practical wisdom can be found in the martial arts. One example of cultivating transcendant wisdom can be found in the traditional martial arts that maintain a strong connection to Buddhist thought and practice, including Kendo (swordfighting, see Kiyota 2002) and Kyudo (archery, see Hoff 2002). The seventeenth-century English swordmaster George Silver provides an example of practical wisdom in the martial arts. Silver's approach to training emphasizes cultivating the ability to quickly and accurately perceive situations (including the opponent's distance and position) and make use of that information in response to attacks. Silver's description of a fighter's judgments lines up well with Fowers' (2005) description of practical wisdom.

Benevolence

Livnat (2004) describes a benevolent person as "a person who tends to care about other human beings, is generally concerned about other people's well-being, and is motivated to perform acts which are aimed at doing good" (p. 304). Associated concepts within the philosophical and psychological literature include altruism (e.g., Batson 1991), compassion (e.g., Cassell 2005), love (e.g., Arman and Rehnsfeldt 2006), and care (e.g., Held 2006). These concepts are described in the *CSV* in terms of "dispositions to tend and befriend" (Peterson and Seligman 2004, p. 293).

Benevolence as a warrior virtue may strike some as odd, but it fits well with Virginia Held's description of care-based ethics: "the central focus of the ethics of care is on the compelling moral salience of attending to and meeting the needs of the particular others for whom we take responsibility" (Held 2006, p. 10). In this case, one who studies the martial arts is adopting the responsibility to protect relevant others, meeting their needs for safety and security (Hackney 2010b). Benevolence toward opponents is also found within the martial arts. One example of this is the teaching that violent force is only to be used as a last resort, which finds practical application in Karate with the requirement that the opponent be the first one to attack. "It isn't accidental," says Shotokan Karate Master Teruyuki Okazaki, "that, while training, the first move we make from shizen tai (ready/natural position) is a block, and that each kata begins with a blocking technique" (Okazaki 2006, p. 45).

One specific way in which all of these virtues are cultivated in the martial arts is in the heavy emphasis often found on politeness in the more traditional arts (Lowry 2006). Debate exists within moral philosophy over whether politeness should (e.g., Stohr 2006) or should not (e.g., Comte-Sponville 2001) be considered a virtue. I argue (Hackney 2010b) that politeness is not itself a virtue, but is instead a venue for the expression and cultivation of the virtues in everyday situations. Polite behavior has been linked to courage (Ruth 1880), temperance (Eichler 1923), justice (Buss 1999), practical wisdom (Stohr 2006), and benevolence (Young 1883), so establishing a habit of courtesy can be seen as an exercise in virtuous development.

Suggestions for Future Research

Comparisons Between Different Martial Arts and Combat Sports

There is an enormous amount of variety in the martial arts, and in the construction of training programs, and so we should not expect them to be equal in their psychological correlates. The martial arts discussed in this chapter cover a wide range of systems, including Aikido (Delva-Tauiliili 1995), Tai Chi (Slater and Hunt 1997), Judo (Gleser et al. 1992), Ninjutsu (Hatsumi 1988), and European sword-fighting (Hackney 2006). These arts vary in their relative emphases on defensive and offensive tactics, striking and grappling, and the use of weapons. Future research on this topic should include an examination of possible heterogeneity among the psychological aspects of different arts, and the question of specific arts being well-suited to certain individuals' needs. A highly aggressive individual, for example, might benefit from the near-pacifism of Aikido, while someone who lacks physical self-efficacy might benefit from the "hands on" rough-and-tumble experience of Judo.

Another source of variability in the martial arts is the division between traditional martial arts and combat sports. Traditional martial arts (Aikido would be one example) employ training methods in which techniques are practiced without active resistance, emphasize memorization of forms (kata), employ little or no sparring, and focus on learning techniques intended to be applicable in "real world" self-defense situations rather than in competitions. Combat sports (kickboxing would be one example) emphasize competitive sparring within a set of rules, focus on winning matches, train with opponents who actively resist, and employ little to no memorization of forms. Some arts combine elements of both categories. Judo, for example, has traditional roots and memorized forms, but is also an Olympic sport. Traditional and competitive versions of Karate exist. "Mixed Martial Arts" (MMA) is primarily sporting in emphasis, but is not entirely divorced from the traditional martial arts (MMA fighter Lyoto Machida has a background in Shotokan Karate).

It is reasonable to predict that the ratio of traditional to sporting elements found in a given art may have a relationship with the psychological effects of training. Using aggression as an example, in an early study (Johnson and Hutton 1955), training in a combat sport (college wrestling) was associated with an increase in aggressiveness before competing, but a reduction in aggressiveness afterward. Trulson (1986) found that Taekwondo students whose training emphasized traditional aspects demonstrated reduced aggressiveness, whereas those whose training emphasized the combative and competitive aspects demonstrated increased aggressiveness. Future research should be sensitive to the differences between martial arts, and researchers should be aware that the results of a study examining one martial art might not generalize to other arts.

The Kreese-Miyagi Effect

In addition to variability between martial arts, there can be variability within arts. Although Trulson found a difference between traditional and nontraditional versions of Taekwondo, Endressen and Olweus (2005) found positive correlations between training and antisocial violence among practitioners of both combat sports (boxing and wrestling) and martial arts (Karate, Taekwondo, Judo). Focusing specifically on

Judo, Reynes and Lorant (2002) found Judo practitioners to be more aggressive after a year of training, and Judo practitioners' heightened aggressiveness continued to be demonstrated in a follow-up study (Reynes and Lorant 2004). However, Pyecha (1970) found Judo training to be effective in cultivating a "warmhearted" and "easy-going" personality, and Lamarre and Nosanchuk (1999) found participants' years of Judo to be associated with less aggressiveness.

One possible explanation for this inconsistency in these studies might be the influence of the instructor. In the popular 1984 film *The Karate Kid*, the aggressive behavior of the Cobra Kai Karate students is shown to be the product of their authoritarian teacher, John Kreese, while the main character's instructor (Mr. Miyagi) models and teaches nonviolent values. This is in line with Barnfield's (2003) claim that martial arts instructors can reduce aggressiveness in their students by modeling self-control and moral behavior. Could some of the variability between these Judo studies be due to the instructors being either a "Kreese" or a "Miyagi" in their teaching styles? Martial arts instructors' leadership styles have been shown to influence student outcomes (e.g., Rowold 2006; Le Bars et al. 2008; Gillet et al. 2010), and athletic coaches' behaviors have been shown to influence aggression and moral behavior (e.g., Shields et al. 2007). However, the possibility that the character and leadership style of martial arts instructors could be a moderating variable in the relationship between martial arts training and positive development remains unexplored territory.

These considerations should also influence discussion of martial arts training as a possible intervention to enhance psychological functioning. Fuller (1988) and Weiser et al. (1995) consider the martial arts worthy to be included to the list of possible alternatives (e.g., art therapy, meditation, dance therapy) to traditional verbal therapy, and various pilot studies have demonstrated the potential value of the martial arts as a way of promoting the psychosocial growth of multiply handicapped children (Gleser et al. (1992), assisting sexual trauma victims (David et al. 2006), and reducing childhood disruptive behaviors (Palermo et al. 2006). Psychologists who are considering martial arts training as a venue for positive development should be sensitive to the possible differences between and within arts, as well as the character of the instructor.

Conclusion

As a eudaimonic practice, training in the martial arts may be considered a venue for the development of a more mature personality. Research in this area has generally supported the idea that training in the martial arts is associated with a range of beneficial psychosocial outcomes, apart from their utility as self-defense instruction. The results are not entirely unambiguous, however, and considerable work remains to be done as we attempt to understand possible roles for the martial arts in adult flourishing.

References

Arman, M., & Rehnsfeldt, A. (2006). The presence of love in ethical caring. *Nursing Forum, 41,* 4–12.

Bandura, A. (1973). *Aggression: A social learning analysis*. Oxford: Prentice-Hall.

Barnfield, A. M. C. (2003). Observational learning in the martial art studio: Instructors as models of positive behaviors. *Journal of Asian Martial Arts, 12(3),* 8–17.

Batson, C. D. (1991). *The altruism question: Toward a social-psychological answer*. Hillsdale: Lawrence, Erlebaum Associates.

Baumeister, R. F., & Exline, J. J. (1999). Virtue, personality, and social relations: Self-control as the moral muscle. *Journal of Personality, 67,* 1165–1194.

Brecklin, L. R., & Ullman, S. E. (2005). Self-defense or assertiveness training and women's responses to sexual attacks. *Journal of Interpersonal Violence, 20,* 738–762.

Buss, S. (1999). Appearing respectful: The moral significance of manners. *Ethics, 109,* 795–826.

Cassell, E. J. (2005). Compassion. In C. R. Snyder & S. J. Lopez (Eds.), *Handbook of positive psychology* (pp. 434–445). New York: Oxford University Press.

Christopher, J. C., & Hickinbottom, S. (2008). Positive psychology, ethnocentrism, and the disguised ideology of individualism. *Theory & Psychology, 18,* 563–589.

Comte-Sponville, A. (2001). *A small treatise on the great virtues* (C. Temerson, Trans.). New York: Henry Holt.

Cupit, G. (1996). *Justice as fittingness*. Oxford: Clarendon.

Cvet, D. M. (2005). The measure of a master swordsman. *Journal of Western Martial Art*. Retrieved from http://www.ejmas.com/jwma/articles/2005/jwmaart_cvet_0105.htm.

Dahlsgaard, K., Peterson, C., & Seligman, M. (2005). Shared virtue: The convergence of valued human strengths across culture and history. *Review of General Psychology, 3,* 203–213.

Daniels, K., & Thornton, E. W. (1990). Analysis of the relationship between hostility and training in the martial arts. *Journal of Sports Sciences, 8,* 95–101.

David, W. S., Simpson, T. L., & Cotton, A. J. (2006). Taking charge: A pilot curriculum of self-defense and personal safety training for female veterans with PTSD because of military sexual trauma. *Journal of Interpersonal Violence, 21,* 555–565.

Delva-Tauiliili, J. (1995). Does brief aikido training reduce aggression of youth? *Perceptual and Motor Skills, 80,* 297–298.

Dueck, A., & Reimer, K. (2003). Retrieving the virtues in psychotherapy: Thick and thin discourse. *American Behavioral Scientist, 47,* 427–441.

Duthie, R. B., Hope, L., & Barker, D. G. (1978). Selected personality traits of martial artists as measured by the adjective checklist. *Perceptual and Motor Skills, 47,* 71–76.

Eichler, L. (1923). *Book of etiquette*. Garden City: Nelson Doubleday.

Endressen, I. M., & Olweus, D. (2005). Participation in power sports and antisocial involvement in preadolescent and adolescent boys. *Joural of Child Psychology and Psychiatry, 64,* 468–478.

Finkenberg, M. F. (1990). Effect of participation in taekwondo on college women's self-concept. *Perceptual and Motor Skills, 71,* 891–894.

Fives, A. (2005). Virtue, justice, and the human good: Non-relative communitarian ethics and the life of religious commitment. *Contemporary Politics, 11,* 117–131.

Focht, B. C., Bouchard, L. J., & Murphey, M. (2000). Influence of martial arts training on the perception of experimentally induced pressure pain and selected psychological responses. *Journal of Sport Behavior, 23,* 232–244.

Foster, Y. A. (1997). Brief aikido training versus karate and golf training and university students' scores on self-esteem, anxiety, and expression of anger. *Perceptual and Motor Skills, 84,* 609–610.

Fowers, B. J. (2005). *Virtue and psychology: Pursuing excellence in everyday practices*. Washington: American Psychological Association.

Fuller, J. R. (1988). Martial arts and psychological health. *British Journal of Medical Psychology, 61,* 317–328.

Gillet, N., Vallerand, R. J., Amoura, S., & Baldes, B. (2010). Influence of coaches' autonomy support on athletes' motivation and sport performance: A test of the hierarchical model of intrinsic and extrinsic motivation. *Psychology of Sport and Exercise, 11,* 155–161.

Gleser, J. M., Margulies, J. Y., Nyeska, M., Porat, S., Mandelberg, H., & Wertman, E. (1992). Physical and psychosocial benefits of modified judo practice for blind, mentally retarded children: A pilot study. *Perceptual and Motor Skills, 74,* 915–925.

Hackney, C. H. (2006). Reflections on audatia as a martial virtue. *Journal of Western Martial Art.* Retrieved from http://ejmas.com/jwma/articles/2006/jwmaart_hackney_0906.htm.

Hackney, C. H. (2009). The Aristotelian philosophy of the martial arts. *Journal of Asian Martial Arts, 18*(4), 8–17.

Hackney, C. H. (2010a). A role for the martial arts in positive youth development. *PsyInsight, 1,* 38–39.

Hackney, C. H. (2010b). *Martial virtues*. North Clarendon: Tuttle.

Hatsumi, M. (1988). *The grandmaster's book of ninja training*. Chicago: Contemporary Books.

Hatsumi, M., & Cole, B. (2001). *Understand? Good. Play!* USA: Bushin Books.

Held, V. (2006). *The ethics of care: Personal, political, and global.* New York: Oxford University Press.

Hoff, F. (2002). *Kyudo: The way of the bow* (S. C. Kohn, trans). Boston: Shambhala.

Hursthouse, R. (1999). *On virtue ethics*. Oxford: Oxford University Press.

Johnson, W. R., & Hutton, D. C. (1955). Effects of a combative sport upon personality dynamics as measured by a projective test. *Research Quarterly, 26,* 49–53.

Jordan, R. D. (1989). *The quiet hero: Figures of temperance in Spenser, Donne, Milton, and Joyce.* Washington: The Catholic University of America Press.

Kano, J. (1986). *Kodokan judo*. New York: Kodansha.

Kiyota, M. (2002). *The shambhala guide to kendo*. Boston: Shambhala.

Kristjánsson, K. (2010). Positive psychology, happiness, and virtue: The troublesome conceptual issues. *Review of General Psychology, 14,* 296–310.

Kurian, M., Caterino, L. C., & Kulhavy, R. W. (1993). Personality characteristics and duration of ATA taekwondo training. *Perceptual and Motor Skills, 76,* 363–366

Kurian, M., Verdi, M. P., Caterino, L. C., & Kulhavy, R. W. (1994). Rating scales on the children's personality questionnaire to training time and belt rank in ATA taekwondo. *Perceptual and Motor Skills, 79,* 904–906.

Lakes, K. D., & Hoyt, W. T. (2004). Promoting self-regulation through school-based martial arts training. *Applied Developmental Psychology, 25,* 283–302.

Lamarre, B. W., & Nosanchuk, T. A. (1999). Judo-the gentle way: A replication of studies on martial arts and aggression. *Perceptual and Motor Skills, 88,* 992–996.

Layton, C. (1988). The personality of black-belt and nonblack-belt traditional karateka. *Perceptual and Motor Skills, 67,* 218.

Layton, C. (1990). Anxiety in black-belt and nonblack-belt traditional karateka. *Perceptual and Motor Skills, 71,* 905–906.

Le Bars, H., Gernigon, C., & Ninot, G. (2008). Personal and contextual determinants of elite young athletes' persistence or dropping out over time. *Scandinavian Journal of Medicine & Science in Sports, 19,* 274–285. doi:10.1111/j.1600–0838.2008.00786.x.

Ledyard, G. S. (2002). *Appropriate ukemi.* Retrieved from http://www.aikiweb.com/training/ledyard1.html.

Livnat, Y. (2004). On the nature of benevolence. *Journal of Social Philosophy, 35,* 304–317.

Lowry, D. (2006). *In the dojo: A guide to the rituals and etiquette of the Japanese martial arts.* Boston: Weatherhill.

MacIntyre, A. (1984). *After virtue* (2nd Edition). Notre Dame: University of Notre Dame Press.

MacIntyre, A. (1999). *Dependant rational animals: Why humans need the virtues*. Chicago: Open Court.

Madden, M. E. (1990). Attributions of control and vulnerability at the beginning and end of a karate course. *Perceptual and Motor Skills, 70,* 787–794.

Madden, M. E. (1995). Perceived vulnerability and control of martial arts and physical fitness students. *Perceptual and Motor Skills, 80,* 899–910.

Nosanchuk, T. A. (1981). The way of the warrior: The effects of traditional martial arts training on aggressiveness. *Human Relations, 34,* 435–444.

Okazaki, T. (2006). *Perfection of character: Guiding principles for the martial arts & everyday life*. Philadelphia: GMW.

Ozer, E. M., & Bandura, A. (1990). Mechanisms governing empowering effects: A self-efficacy analysis. *Journal of Personality and Social Psychology, 58,* 472–486.

Palermo, M. T., Di Luigi, M., Forno, G. D., Dominici, C., Vicomandi, D., Sambucioni, A., Proietti, L., & Pasqualetti, P. (2006). Externalizing and oppositional behaviors and karate-do: The way of crime prevention, a pilot study. *International Journal of Offender Therapy and Comparative Criminology, 50,* 654–660.

Peterson, C., & Seligman, M. E. P. (2004). *Character strengths and virtues: A handbook and classification*. Washington: American Psychological Association.

Pieper, J. (1965). *The four cardinal virtues*. New York: Harcourt.

Pyecha, J. (1970). Comparative effects of judo and selected physical education activities on male university freshman personality traits. *The Research Quarterly, 41,* 425–431.

Reynes, E., & Lorant, J. (2002). Effect of traditional judo training on aggressiveness among young boys. *Perceptual and Motor Skills, 94,* 21–15.

Reynes, E., & Lorant, J. (2004). Competitive martial arts and aggressiveness: A 2-yr longitudinal study among young boys. *Perceptual and Motor Skills, 98,* 103–115.

Richman, C. L., & Rehberg, H. (1986). The development of self-esteem through the martial arts. *International Journal of Sport Psychology, 17,* 234–239.

Robinson, D. N. (1990). Wisdom through the ages. In R. J. Sternberg (Ed.), *Wisdom: Its nature, origins, and development* (pp. 13–24). New York: Cambridge University Press.

Rowold, J. (2006). Transformational and transactional leadership in martial arts. *Journal of Applied Sport Psychology, 18,* 312–325.

Ruth, J. A. (1880). *Decorum: A practical treatise on etiquette and dress of the best American society*. New York: Union Publishing House.

Seligman, M. E. P. (2002). *Authentic happiness: Using the new positive psychology to realize your potential for lasting fulfillment*. New York: Free.

Shields, D., LaVoi, N., Bredemeier, B., Power, F. (2007). Predictors of poor sportspersonship in youth sports: Personal attitudes and social influences. *Journal of Sport & Exercise Psychology, 29,* 747–762.

Skelton, D. L., Glynn, M. A., & Berta, S. M. (1991). Aggressive behavior as a function of taekwondo ranking. *Perceptual and Motor Skills, 72,* 179–182.

Slater, J., & Hunt, H. T. (1997). Postural-vestibular integration and forms of dreaming: A preliminary report on the effects of brief t'ai chi chuan training. *Perceptual and Motor Skills, 85,* 97–98.

Sterba, J. P. (1988). *How to make people just: A practical reconciliation of alternate conceptions of justice*. Totowa: Rowman & Littlefield.

Sternberg, R. J. (1998). A balance theory of wisdom. *Review of General Psychology, 2,* 347–365.

Stohr, K. (2006). Manners, morals, and practical wisdom. In T. Chappell (Ed.), *Values and virtues: Aristotelianism in contemporary ethics* (pp. 189–211). Oxford: Clarendon.

Sundararajan, L. (2005). Happiness donut: A Confucian critique of positive psychology. *Journal of Theoretical and Philosophical Psychology, 25,* 35–60.

Tangney, J. P. (2000). Humility: Theoretical perspectives, empirical findings and directions for future research. *Journal of Social and Clinical Psychology, 19,* 70–82.

Tikhonov, V. (1998). Hwarang organization: Its function and ethics. *Korea Journal, 38,* 318–338.

Tjeltveit, A. C. (2003). Implicit virtues, divergent goods, multiple communities: Explicitly addressing virtues in the behavioral sciences. *American Behavioral Scientist, 47,* 395–414.

Trulson, M. E. (1986). Martial arts training: A novel "cure" for juvenile delinquency. *Human Relations, 39,* 1131–1140.

Twemlow, S. W., & Sacco, F. C. (1998). The application of traditional martial arts practice and theory to the treatment of violent adolescents. *Adolescence, 33,* 505–518.

Vohs, K. D., & Baumeister, R. F. (2004). Understanding self-regulation: An introduction. In R. F. Baumeister & K. D. Vohs (Eds.), *Handbook of self-regulation: Research, theory, and applications* (pp. 1–12). New York: Guilford.

Weiser, M., Kutz, I., Kutz, S. J., & Weiser, D. (1995). Psychotherapeutic aspects of the martial arts. *American Journal of Psychotherapy, 49,* 118–127.

Westhusing, T. (2003). A beguiling military virtue: Honor. *Journal of Military Ethics, 2,* 195–212.

Wink, P., & Helson, R. (1997). Practical and transcendent wisdom: Their nature and some longitudinal findings. *Journal of Adult Development, 4,* 1–15.

Young, J. H. (1883). *Our deportment: Or the manners, conduct, and dress of the most refined society*. Detroit: F. B. Dickerson & Co.

Zivin, G., Hassan, N. R., DePaula, G. F., Monti, D. A., Harlan, C., Hossain, K. D., & Patterson, K. (2001). An effective approach to violence prevention: Traditional martial arts in middle school. *Adolescence, 36,* 443–459.

Part III
Positive Environments

Chapter 11
Creating a More Ethical Workplace

Larry Froman

A Crisis in Workplace Ethics

In April 2010, the Upper Big Branch mine exploded in West Virginia resulting in the death of 29 miners. A panel of independent safety experts, using information obtained from interviews with dozens of miners, examination of the disaster site, and a review of thousands of pages of internal and public documents, concluded that the company, Massey Energy, created a culture that ignored basic safety standards and allowed its safety reports to be falsified. In its report to West Virginia Gov. Tomblin, the panel concluded that that the disaster was partly caused by a company that "put too much faith in its own mythology" (Kindy 2011, p. 3). What factors contribute to the creation of a mythology that puts the lives of workers at risk? The focus of this article will be an examination of *two pathways—individual and organizational*—that can help explain the creation of these and related mythologies that reflect workplace cultures of denial, egoism, and greed.

In December 2001, Enron, the Texas-based energy company declared bankruptcy, the largest in US history until July 2002 when WorldCom bettered Enron by 60 % (Thomas et al. 2004). Arthur Andersen, LLP, fell from being one of the largest certified public accounting firms in the world to extinction as a result of being caught in Enron's web of deceit and betrayal. These and other bankruptcies, although involving business errors and misjudgments, as noted by Schermerhorn et.al. also "involved substantial and well-documented failures of ethics" (p. 57). Ghosh (2008) refers to Enron's unethical practices that were woven into its operating norms and culture and a company that "showed little regard for ethics beyond the bottom line, using a reward system that retained only those employees who achieved target profits" (p. 69).

Enron managers created unethical and illegal accounting practices designed to hide financial losses of the company. Phony partnerships were formed to conceal debt and unprofitable investments from Enron shareholders. Kenneth Lay, the late chairman, was warned about these practices by Sherron Watkins, a company account

L. Froman (✉)
Psychology Department, Towson University, 8000 York Road, Towson MD 21252, USA
e-mail: Lfroman@towson.edu

J. D. Sinnott (ed.), *Positive Psychology*,
DOI 10.1007/978-1-4614-7282-7_11, © Springer Science+Business Media, LLC 2013

executive. Despite her warnings and concerns about the company's overall financial stability, the senior management lied to investors—telling them that the company's stock prices would continue to rise.

The managers created a culture of greed and intimidation where the means justified the ends, where success, defined by profits should be pursued at any cost, and where a corrupt system of corporate rewards and punishment was followed. For example, anyone who dared to challenge the practices of former chief operating officer Skilling and/or chief financial officer Fastow faced the prospect of reassignment, loss of bonus or termination (McLean and Elkind 2003). There was deliberate concealment of information and related motivational patterns based on employee perceptions of communicating only what the boss wants to hear, cognitive biases of belief perseverance, and group cohesion pressures resulting in "groupthink"—characterized by illusions of invulnerability, collective rationalization, and false consensus (Cohan 2002).

Ghosh (2008), referring to Enron and other corporations comments:

> Increasingly, the public perception is that too many corporate executives have directly committed flagrant breaches of trust by "cooking" the books, or shading the truth, or indirectly facilitating the process by turning a blind eye when acts of impropriety were brought to their attention. (p. 68)

Consider the following two scenarios described by Elango et al. (2010) as originally reported by Valentine and Rittenburg:

1. Driven by the need to improve sales in the United States, the C.E.O. of a British Auto firm directs its marketing department to develop a new advertising campaign. The series of ads that received the most favorable response from focus groups showed the driver surviving dramatic collisions with a tank, a locomotive, and an airplane. To achieve these results, the ads were altered (e.g., additional reinforcements to door panels, roof, and fire wall). "The C.E.O. decides to run the ads in the U.S. without disclosing that the autos in the ads have been altered for dramatic effect"(p. 556).
2. "A U.S. electronics manufactures uses a chemical solvent in its production process which results in birth defects when pregnant workers are exposed to it. Ban of the use of this chemical in the U.S. is inevitable. An economic analysis by an outside consultant indicates that it will cost three times as much for the manufactures to convert the production process to the use of a non-toxic chemical as to relocate its plant to Malaysia, where no ban on the chemical is anticipated.... The electronics manufacturer decides to relocate the plant in Malaysia" (p. 556).

Paine (1994) provides a third scenario:

3. "In the face of declining revenues, shrinking market share, and an increasingly competitive market for undercar services, Sears' management attempted to spur the performance of its auto centers by introducing new goals and incentives for employees. The company increased minimum work quotas and introduced productivity incentives for mechanics. The automotive service advisers were given product-specific sales quotas-sell so many springs, shock absorbers, alignments, or brake jobs per shift-and paid a commission based on sales. According to advisers, failure to meet quotas could lead to a transfer or a reduction in work hours.

Some employees spoke of the 'pressure, pressure, pressure' to bring in sales.... Without active management support for ethical practice and mechanisms to detect and check questionable sales methods and poor work, it is not surprising that some employees may have reacted to contextual forces by resorting to exaggeration, carelessness, or even misrepresentation" (pp. 107–108).

Finally, consider the following cheating scandal in Atlanta as reported by the PBS Newshour (2011):

A Georgia investigation report commissioned by Gov. Nathan Deal found that nearly 200 educators cheated to boost student test scores in Atlanta, a problem that has surfaced in school districts across the country. The investigation found that results were altered on state curriculum tests by district administrators, principals, and teachers for as long as a decade. Educators literally erased and corrected students' mistakes to make sure that schools met state-imposed testing standards. And it found evidence of cheating in 44 of the 56 schools examined for the 2009 school year.

These and other cases in recent years revealed fundamental lapses in ethical judgment of individuals within the context of their organizational environments. Although acknowledging the role that subtle as well as overt pressures have in explaining unethical and even illegal workplace behaviors, Paine (1994) points out that an individual's personal moral responsibility should in no way be diluted. The fear that individuals would not be held morally accountable for their actions, partly due to intense pressures emanating from their work environment, "is based on a false dichotomy between holding individual transgressors accountable and holding the 'system' accountable. Acknowledging the importance of organizational context need not imply exculpating individual wrongdoers" (p. 109).

Although holding individual employees accountable for their behavior is morally and legally imperative, the realities of management power, the values embedded in the organizational culture, and the operating norms reflecting those values can place great pressure on an individual's moral/ethical compass. As Ghosh (2008) comments, "if corporate leaders encourage rule-breaking and foster an intimidating, aggressive environment, ethical boundaries in organizations are eroded away" (p. 69). The realities of power dynamics between employers and employees coupled with the latter's concerns about keeping their jobs create a pervasive climate of fear and insecurity. Employees are presented with the proverbial "rock and hard place" squeeze: Resist the pressure with the possibility of being forced to resign or be fired; or, sweep aside one's ethical–moral compass, and continue working in an environment where one's values and ethical principles are disconnected from one's actions. Such psychological disconnection or "dissonance" can place enormous stress on employees (Abraham 1999).

Ethical Work Climates

The concept of ethical work climates refer to the perceptions that employees have of "typical organizational practices and procedures that have ethical content" (Victor and Cullen 1988, p. 101). They serve as a psychological lens in guiding employees

Table 11.1 Theoretical ethical climate types. (Adapted from Victor and Cullen (1988))

Locus of Analysis			
Ethical criterion	Individual	Organization	Society
Egoism	Self-interest[a]	Company profit	Efficiency
Benevolence	Friendship	Team interest	Social responsibility
Principle	Personal morality	Company rules and procedures	Laws and professional codes

[a]Typical decision criterion

when faced with various moral dilemmas (e.g., "What should I do?") that occur in the workplace. The existence of such climates "requires that normative systems in the organization be institutionalized . . .and that organizational members must perceive the existence of normative patterns in the organization with a measurable degree of consensus. Organizational members are asked to report not on their own behavior and values, but, rather, on the practices and procedures that they perceive to exist in their organizations" (1988, p. 103).

Victor and Cullen (1988) classify ethical climates as egoistic, benevolent, and principled. In an egoistic climate, company norms support the satisfaction of self-interest, ignoring the needs or interests of others. The egoistic climate relates directly to the norms of Enron where the environment reinforced a culture that was morally corrupt, fostering self-centered behaviors with little (if any) thought about other stakeholders in the company. In a benevolent climate, company norms maximize the interests of others, while in a principled climate, when confronted with an ethical dilemma; employees base their decisions on adherence to rules and codes.

Table 11.1 describes a conceptual model relating these categories (referred to as ethical criteria) to three levels of analysis: the individual, the organization, and society.

When considering the range of possible factors that influence employee perceptions of their organization's ethical work climate, this model can be very useful in establishing a clear and coherent road map for merging relevant levels of analysis with ethical criteria. The starting point with this model is the core assumption that rigid adherence to egoism can have far-reaching negative consequences for the well-being of others. The aforementioned examples of Enron and other organizations address this issue directly. When considering the categories of benevolence and principle, several interesting possibilities emerge. Friendship, for example, while benevolent in spirit, may not always support team, organizational, or societal interests. Indeed, much damage can be done to others in the name of "protecting friends". Following this logical progression, team and organizational interests may or may not support the broader interests of society. The horizontal pathway of principle suggests some interesting questions: To what extent do employees perceive their organizations as encouraging a personal standard of morality as the primary decision guide post—more so than company rules, or even laws and professional codes? What happens when employees perceive company policies and procedures to be the more influential factor than laws and professional codes?

Ethics and Workplace Safety

The Challenger and BP Accidents

On January 28, 1986, the space shuttle Challenger exploded shortly after liftoff, killing all seven crew members. Credo et al. (2010), referring to the commentary by Roger Biosjoly and other engineers working at Morton Thiokol, the shuttle booster contractor, describe the following:

> In the months after the disaster, the government commission created to investigate the causes of the accident concluded that cold weather caused seal failure in one of the solid rocket booster joints and led to the explosion. Testimony by Roger Biosjoly and other engineers working at Morton-Thiokol, Inc. (MTI), the booster contractor, revealed that MTI management had been alerted to the cold weather danger to the O-ring booster joints well in advance of the decision to launch Biosjoly had submitted a memo warning that the seals would not be functional in cold weather, but MTI management classified the document as *company private* so it never reached NASA. Disregard for this warning not only resulted in a disastrous breach in safety, but was also a reflection of a significant flaw in the ethical decision-making process of MTI. (pp. 325–326)

The BP Oil Spill disaster of April, 2010 did not occur overnight. Indeed, violations of regulations and disregard of employee warnings of potential consequences resulting from technical breakdowns were part of pattern of negligence occurring over a decade. BP managers were warned that the company repeatedly disregarded safety and environmental rules and that such a pattern could lead to serious accidents if it did not improve safety standards. Among the examples that employees provided in their interviews with investigators were neglect of aging equipment, being pressured not to report problems, and cutting short or delaying inspections to reduce production costs. BP systematically ignored its own safety policies across its North American operations—from Alaska to the Gulf of Mexico to California and Texas. Executives were not held accountable for the failures and some were promoted despite them (Lustgarten and Knutson 2010).

What connects the Challenger and BP tragedies is a failure of leadership—specifically, integrity-based leadership.

Integrity-Based Leadership

As part of a comprehensive safety management program, the National Safety Council identifies leadership and cultural–behavioral factors as key performance areas to leverage improvement in safety practices (National Safety Council 2011).

The starting point is commitment from the top management of the organization. The ethics message regarding safety issues must be clear and consistent permeating all levels of the organization. Although external regulation and laws play key roles in shaping safety behavior compliance, Paine (1994) points out that organizational ethics means more than avoiding illegal practice. Providing employees with a list of company policies may not address the problems underlying unlawful conduct. Compliance to policies, and indeed to regulatory codes, while necessary, is not sufficient in creating ethical cultures. Operating within a framework of integrity-based ethics management, leaders play a critical role in elevating compliance to a more comprehensive approach where ethics are infused within the organization's value system and become the governing ethics of an organization (Paine 1994; Thomas et al. 2004).

Closely related to integrity-based ethics management is the concept of transformational leadership (Barling et al. 2002). This kind of leadership emphasizes on managers becoming role models by doing what is moral or right rather than what is expedient. Such leaders do not allow safety and health of workers to be sacrificed at the altar of productivity pressures and profits. They convey occupational safety as a core value through their own personal commitment and in ways that inspire employee trust and motivation to engage in safety-related behaviors. Such leaders also inspire their employees to go beyond individual needs and self-interest to use their "ethics mindfulness"—a form of enriched awareness—(Thomas et al. 2004) towards the collective good. They challenge and motivate employees to confront long-held assumptions, and think in innovative ways that enhance information-sharing and problem-solving. Consistent with Paine's concept of integrity management, such leaders move beyond compliance with law to infuse their cultures with "reflective conduct" in which ethical thinking becomes a foundation for ethical action (Gini 1997; Thomas et al. 2004). They cultivate work environments with a "moral self-identity" that has an enduring positive influence on behavior (Aquino and Reed 2002).

Empirical Studies

Studies examining antecedents of safety-related behavior and injuries have examined leadership, safety climates, and perceived ethical work climates. For example, effective leadership practices such as those described earlier, have been found to be positively related to safety climate, safety behavior, and negatively related to safety events and injuries (Barling et al. 2002; Zohar 2002). In a study designed to examine the relationship between ethical work climates and safety, results provided support for a relationship between perceived benevolent and principled ethical work climates (refer to the previous discussion of Victor and Cullen's model) with a reduction in injuries and safety-enhancing behaviors (Parboteeah and Kapp 2008).

Legal Compliance and Ethics

The legal framework for workplace health and safety was established by the Occupational Health Safety Act (OSHA) of 1970. LaVan and Martin (2008) describe the law:

> The Occupational Safety and Health Act of 1970 was established "to assure so far as possible every working man and woman in the nation safe and healthful working conditions and to preserve human resources" (29 U.S.C. Section 651 (b)). Additionally, under the General Duty Clause, Section 5 (a) (1) of OSHA, employers are mandated to provide employees with a place of employment that "is free from recognizable hazards that are causing or likely to cause serious harm to employees."(p. 150)

However, critical as this law is in ensuring workplace health and safety, as noted earlier, compliance to law is a necessary baseline but does not necessarily lead to desired ethical–moral outcomes. As noted by Paine (1994), conduct that is lawful may still be highly problematic from an ethical perspective. For example, in some countries, hazardous products are sold without appropriate warnings. In the United States, goods are purchased from suppliers who operate inhumane sweatshops in developing countries. Companies engaged in international business often discover that conduct that infringes on recognized standards of human rights and decency is legally permissible in some jurisdictions. Defining ethics as legal compliance can lead to what Paine refers to as an implicit endorsement of "moral mediocrity" (p. 111).

A Normative Model of Ethics Applied to Workplace Health and Safety

Moving beyond legal compliance requires leadership and organizational cultures that view the health and safety of employees as a moral–ethical imperative. An example of such an approach can be found in a normative model of ethics consisting of five complementary principles: Utilitarian, moral rights, distributive justice, care ethics, and virtue ethics (Schumann 2001).

Utilitarian The focus of this principle is a concern for consequences. Schumann (2001) comments that an "action must do the most good and the least harm to be considered ethical." (p. 97). When considering accidents, be they in coal mines, space shuttles, or oil rigs, the analysis starts and ends with loss of life. Other considerations, including economic harm to organizations, impact on employee jobs, etc., though part of the ethical analysis from this perspective, pale in comparison to the safety imperative of preventing loss of life.

Moral Rights Employees' right to safety and general well-being can be viewed as moral rights (Ariss 2003; Rowan 2000). Rowan comments that the type of job, or level of responsibility within a corporation, ought not to affect the degree to which the "generic rights of freedom, well-being and equality" are held. These rights, Rowan states, "can be summarily captured under the rubric of 'respect'. . . Treating persons with respect entails not treating them as things, objects, or tools in an effort to achieve one's own goals (as a manager, say) or the goals of the corporation" (p. 357).

Regarding safety, Rowan comments that:

> Employers have a duty to provide a safe work environment and to make improvements when necessary, since failing to do so, risks the well-being of persons. There also exists the duty to inform workers of certain risks which cannot be avoided; not doing so amounts to a deliberate attempt to mislead in an effort to hold down labor costs. (p. 358)

Distributive Justice Distributive justice refers to what actions produce a fair distribution of benefits and costs for all stakeholders—defined as employees, financiers, customers, employees, and communities. Organizations ought to be managed and governed in the interest of these stakeholders (Freeman 1994).

Commenting on the need for a more pragmatic approach to business ethics, Freeman states:

> The question is less 'what is true' than 'how should we live', or better still, 'how does this narrative allow us to live,' or 'what does this way of talking allow us to do.' So, for instance, on pragmatist's grounds, the stakeholder idea is part of a narrative about how we do and could live, how we could experiment with different institutional arrangements, and how we do and could organize a sphere of our lives built mostly around something we have come to call 'work'. (p. 418)

Within this pragmatic framework, and moving beyond the narrow boundaries of legal compliance, organizations can implement health and safety policies that take into account the interests of all the stakeholders noted in this chapter. Within the context of the examples of workplace accidents described earlier—Massey Coal Mining Company, The Challenger Shuttle, and the BP oil spill—a more systematic application of this normative–pragmatic model of distributive justice could have moved these organizations through their leaders, culture, and decision-making process, towards a more ethical outcome. Such an outcome would have been guided by the paramount concerns of the health, safety, and well-being of employees, their families, and their communities.

Care Ethics Care ethics assumes that this human capacity is not situation-specific; that it applies to interpersonal relationships across the spectrum of social environments, including the workplace. As Schumann (2010) notes, the "morally correct action is the one that expresses care in protecting the special relationships that individuals have with each other" (p. 104). In the context of workplace health and safety, employers are morally obligated to ensure that their employees are not exposed to unhealthy or exceedingly dangerous conditions in their work environments. Such conditions could have been prevented had their employers at the very least, been in legal compliance; and beyond that, demonstrated a commitment to care ethics for their employees.

Virtue Ethics Virtue ethics focus on what makes a good person, as well as what makes a good action. Examples of virtue include benevolence, civility, compassion, conscientiousness, courage, fairness, honesty, and loyalty (Schumann 2001). The description of workplace accidents noted earlier, where employer actions sacrificed the safety of workers in the interest of saving money and time, clearly demonstrate how disconnected such actions can be from any semblance of virtue ethics.

Referring to the work of Velasquez, Schumann (2001) notes that "since each moral principle examines ethics from a different perspective, no one principle captures the full range of relevant issues" (p. 105). But taken together, most if not all of the relevant issues, can be considered in deciding what constitutes ethical behavior in a given situation. Using the example of workers being exposed to dangerous chemicals, Schumann states that "all five principles can be used to come to the conclusion that it is unethical for an employer to deceive employees about the true nature of hazardous chemicals in the workplace. When all five principles come to the same conclusion about the ethics of a course of action, then there is no apparent conflict about what is ethical" (p. 105).

Ethics Stress in Healthcare

The concept of ethics stress (i.e., perceived stress associated with ethical issues and/or dilemmas) can have important implications for the well-being, job satisfaction, and turnover of employees, especially for those who work in intensely stressful occupations with high levels of "emotional labor" (Grandey et al. 2007). Given the importance of nurses in providing quality patient care, an expected shortage of nurses—projected to be about 20 % by 2020—the potential negative impact of increased rates of turnover among these healthcare professionals becomes alarmingly self-evident. Regarding social workers, a 30 % increase in the need for these professionals was also projected (Ulrich et al. 2007). Given the vital role social workers have in providing outreach to families and in facilitating coordinated professional care to support the needs of patients as they transition from hospital to home or long-term care facilities, increase rates of their turnover could also have harmful consequences.

To address these issues, a study of nurses and social workers was designed to examine the relationship between ethics stress, ethical climate, job satisfaction, and intent-to-leave (Ulrich et al. 2007). The authors comment:

> As health care becomes increasingly complex, these providers encounter difficult ethical issues in patient care, perceive limited respect in their work, and are increasingly dissatisfied . . . .Urgent strategies are needed not only to recruit more nurses and social workers but also, importantly, to retain existing personnel. Economic constraints, downsizing, restructuring, and the burden of emerging and reemerging diseases on healthcare systems have created stressful working environments for many providers. Predictors of job satisfaction and intent-to-leave have mainly focused on demographics, work setting characteristics, and work attitudes, but little empirical attention has been given to their relationship with ethics-related issues within hospital and non-hospital practice settings and in different types of healthcare providers. (2007, pp. 1708–1709)

Results of the study showed that the ethical climate perceptions influenced the relationship between ethical stress and job satisfaction. Job satisfaction, perceived support, and resources were found to be critical factors in helping these professionals cope with higher levels of ethics stress. The authors suggested that respect, work autonomy, and other factors affecting job satisfaction may serve as protective factors against intent-to-leave.

Pathways to a More Ethical Workplace

Moving forward, heightened expectations need to be placed on organizations and their leaders to create a more ethical workplace—a workplace that is healthier, safer, and one that treats employees with respect and dignity. Such a workplace is also one where employees at all levels must be held accountable for their actions. Disagreements, conflicts, even formal grievances are inevitable, but hopefully, they can be dealt with, in a climate of trust, respect, and shared responsibility.

The Virtuous Organization

Virtuous organizations infuse an ethical perspective into their cultures, have multiple "bottom lines", and develop supportive leaders who empower their employees to succeed (Froman 2010). Such leaders inspire employees to give their very best, recognize and reward outstanding job performance, and build relationships based on mutual trust and respect (Cameron 2003).

In these tough economic times, such attributes of virtue can offer people hope, the resilience to overcome adversity, and the motivational capacity to engage in forward-looking behaviors. As Froman (2010) comments:

> Driven in part by the turmoil in the current economy, organizational/workplace responses often lead to job loss and other cost-cutting measures. The reality or threat of job loss swirls around the lives of many in today's workplace, affecting the hopes and dreams of thousands of workers, their families, and their communities (p. 59).... Organizations need to develop cultures of virtue, cultures built around principles of integrity, ethics, trust, and respect. Organizations bring out the best in their members by focusing on such positive psychologic concepts as strengths, hope, optimism, self-confidence, self-motivation, resilience, joy, and gratitude. Organizations of virtue strive to do well by doing good, and strive to do good by doing well. They create conditions for their members to thrive and flourish in ways that bridge economic and human development. (p. 67)

A Culture of Candor and Healthy Debate

The concept of corporate responsibility has taken on new and expanded meanings in the wake of recent business failures, scandals, and the growing income disparities between the wealthiest among us compared to the middle-class, and those on the precipice of falling into poverty and despair. It is understood that inherent in our economic system of capitalism, there will be so-called "winners" and "losers", especially in today's highly competitive global economy. There are inherent risks and inevitable losses that come with investment decisions, with creating new business ventures, and with hiring employees, particularly in times of slow economic growth and declining consumer confidence.

Commenting on corporate leaders, O'Toole and Bennis (2009) comment:

> Until recently, the yardstick used to evaluate the performance of American corporate leaders was relatively simple: *the extent to which they created wealth for investors*. But that was then. Now the forces of globalization and technology have conspired to complicate the competitive arena, creating a need for leaders who can manage rapid innovation. Expectations about the corporation's role in social issues such as environmental degradation, domestic job creation, and even poverty in the developing world have risen sharply as well. And the expedient, short-term thinking that Wall Street rewarded only yesterday has fallen out of fashion in the wake of the latest round of business busts and scandals. It's clear we need a better way to evaluate business leaders. Moving forward, it appears that the new metric of corporate leadership will be closer to this: *the extent to which executives create organizations that are economically, ethically, and socially sustainable*. (p. 54–56)

This new metric of corporate leadership requires a broader and more integrative way of defining "successful" organizations. Success, as noted before, is about doing well by doing good. Success elevates ethical and social sustainability to their rightful place in the hierarchy of core values.

O'Toole and Bennis offer the following example of an organization that bridges the pathways of ethics and success:

> …some farsighted leaders institute a "no secrets" policy designed to build trust among all corporate stakeholders. Kent Thiry, CEO of DaVita, a dialysis treatment operator, systematically collects data and solicits candid feedback from his employees, ex-employees, customers, and suppliers in order to avoid making mistakes. Thiry actively seeks out bad news and rewards employees who give it to him. To reinforce trust, he and his top managers act promptly to correct practices that employees have identified as problematic—issues that, if left unchecked, could come back to haunt the company. And historical examples of unusual displays of candor that created public trust are the stuff of legend at such diverse companies as Honeywell, Continental Airlines, Johnson & Johnson, Nordstrom, Whole Foods, and Xilinx. (p. 58)

Effective leaders are not afraid of contrarians; indeed, they seek out and embrace those who have the courage to speak their mind. They do not tolerate contrarians; they in fact reward them! Consider O'Toole and Bennis' example of Motorola's CEO:

> Companies with healthy cultures continually challenge their assumptions. That work can seldom be done by one person sitting alone in a room; it requires leaders who listen to others. An often told story about Motorola during its heyday in the 1980s concerns a young middle manager who approached then-CEO Robert Galvin and said: "Bob, I heard that point you made this morning, and I think you're dead wrong. I'm going to prove it: *I'm going to shoot you down.*" When the young man stormed off, Galvin, beaming proudly, turned to a companion and said, "That's how we've overcome Texas Instruments' lead in semiconductors!" During that period, there were no rewards at Motorola for people who supported the status quo; managers got ahead by challenging existing assumptions and by pointing out imperial nakedness. In later decades the company lost those good habits. Alas, sustaining a culture of candor is even harder than creating one. (p. 60)

By checking their egos at the door, effective leaders can create cultures of candor. Such cultures will allow for much-needed sharing of information and better decisions—decisions that are not products of the narrow confines of tunnel vision and self-interest, but rather, that reflect the input of those stakeholders inside and outside the organization whose voices need to be heard. Indeed, *such leaders seek to bridge the pathways of ethics and success.*

Extensive sharing of information, done with transparency and candor, is critical to both organizational effectiveness and ethics. Exemplary leaders not only encourage, but also reward openness and dissent. They understand that whatever discomfort they may experience is more than offset by the fact that better information helps them make better decisions. Although there is no easy way to institutionalize candor, honesty at the top is an essential first step (O'Toole and Bennis 2009).

The challenges of balancing compromise with principle, of finding ways to work effectively with one's adversaries have occupied a central place in our current politics, as evidenced by the recent firestorm over raising the debt ceiling and related issues. Moving forward, the soon-to-be-formed bicameral–bipartisan committee of legislators, charged with coming up with a longer-term plan for debt reduction, a plan that could very well include proposals for entitlement and tax reform, will need to find ways to forge principled-compromises—compromises that allow adversaries to find common ground in support of their principles.

Some lessons from history might be constructive. The brilliant and much acclaimed book by Doris Kearns Goodwin, winner of the Pulitzer Prize, *Team of Rivals: The Political Genius of Abraham Lincoln*, provides a compelling narrative of the qualities of this great leader and the intertwined relationships with his key cabinet members.

> That Lincoln, after winning the presidency, made the unprecented decision to incorporate his eminent rivals into his political family, the cabinet, was evidence of a profound self-confidence and a first indication of what would provide to others a most unexpected greatness.... Their presence in the cabinet might have threatened to eclipse the obscure prairie lawyer from Springfield.... This, then, is a story of Lincoln's political genius revealed through his extraordinary array of personal qualities that enabled him to form friendships with men who had previously opposed him; to repair injured feelings that, left untended, might have escalated into permanent hostility,... to share credit with ease; and to learn from mistakes.... His success in dealing with the strong egos of the men in his cabinet suggests that in the hands of a truly great politician the qualities we generally associate with decency and morality—kindness, sensitivity, compassion, honesty, and empathy— can also be impressive political resources. (Goodwin 2005, pp. xvi–xvii)

The takeaway point from this example is that great leaders build effective relationships around a strong ethical–moral foundation.

Identifying Values Trade-Offs

The need for greater emphasis on ethics and its connection to both, economic and social sustainability, being a central theme of this article, also requires acknowledgement of an important reality: "*All* decisions—whether judged highly ethical, grossly unethical or anywhere in between—are values-based. That is, a decision necessarily

Table 11.2 Simple confirmatory view. (Adapted from Urbany et al. 2008)

Choice options	Consequences
Implement fixed prices	Boss will be happy
Do not implement fixed prices	Boss will be angry

involves an implicit or explicit trade-off of values" (Urbany et al. 2008, p. 75). The authors comment that:

> Values, whether neutral, virtuous or not so virtuous, drive our decision making. Even unethical, illegal or dishonest decisions are "values-based"—they're just not reflective of higher-order "positive" values. For example, a decision to engage in insider trading is ultimately a choice favoring the values that hail financial gain as more important than keeping one's integrity. (p. 76)

Based on the work of Gavin's *The Price of Fixing Prices*, Urbany et al. offer the following case of John:

John's Decision "Consider the following true case, in which all names have been changed: John Taylor was a division manager at Atlantic Soda, a large bottling conglomerate that owned more than 30 companies, including a number of national-brand franchises. John was asked to meet in Tampa with George Goodwin (his boss) and Bob Miller (the regional division manager for their competitor, Mid-Major Pop). John had joined the company six months earlier, with a track record of hard work and strong results in sales and operations. He enjoyed the culture at Atlantic, which rewarded performance and talent. John had already been promoted twice in his short tenure. At the meeting, Goodwin talked about the intense price-competition problem that Atlantic Soda and Mid-Major Pop had been experiencing with each other, and the arrangement, which would be John's responsibility to implement in his region. What were John's options? What should he have done?" (p. 76).

For starters, the warning bells and siren should have swirled around John, as this practice, referred to as price fixing, is a violation of the Sherman Antitrust Act. Like previous examples covered in this chapter, where good people find themselves saying yes to unethical or even illegal actions, John—a good man with an ethical track record—chose to put the price-fixing agreement into practice. And sadly, he ultimately would go to jail for that decision.

Decision Mapping Would John have made a different decision had he used a more systematic approach? According to Urbany, et al. the answer is, maybe. The authors suggest that John might have benefited from a decision mapping process, creating a "picture" of a decision "built around *choice options*, *consequences*, *outcomes* and *values/goals*" (p. 77).

Consider the following decision maps presented in order of cognitive complexity (Table 11.2):

Using the above cognitive map, John has painted a very narrow and restrictive picture of his decision: "My job is to please the boss."

Table 11.3 An expanded confirmatory view

Choice options	Consequences	Outcomes	Values/Goals
Implement fixed prices	(+) Boss will be happy	(+) Personal achievement/promotion	(+) Financial security
Do not implement fixed prices	(−) Boss will be angry	(−) Could lose my job	(−) Jeopardize family security

Table 11.4 Expanded balanced view

Choice options	Consequences	Outcomes	Values/Goals
Implement fixed prices	(+) Boss will be happy (−) It is illegal	(+) Personal achievement/promotion (−) Risk of personal legal troubles	(+) Financial security (−) Loss of personal integrity
Do not implement fixed prices	(+) It is legal (−) Boss will be angry	(+) Business integrity (−) Could lose my job	(+) Uphold personal responsibility/integrity (−) Jeopardize family security

John's map expands when expected outcomes and values and goals are put forth. Urbany et al. comment on the importance of longer-term impacts of a decision:

> Outcomes are related to or contingent upon whatever consequences were presumed to emerge from the choice. So, for example, if John chooses to implement the fixed prices and gets positive reinforcement from his boss, he might project that his actions would ease competition, improve margins and profits, and make him a hero in the organization. The choice option of not implementing the fixed prices, which would result in John's boss getting angry, might lead to job loss or demotion.... Simply asking decision makers to consider the outcomes that follow from shorter-term consequences is a means of evoking thinking that might not have occurred otherwise. (p. 77) (Table 11.3)

The confirmation bias that can be inferred from Table 11.3 is John's tendency to focus on the positive consequences of his initially-preferred choice option and the negative consequences of the other. This narrow perspective places boundaries on John's thinking in ways that make the implementation choice easier. As noted by the authors, "John not only connects with the satisfaction of probable achievement and success within the organization but also avoids the potential loss of his job and the inability to take care of his family" (p. 77).

Essentially, this confirmation bias means that John's limited way of looking at the consequences, outcomes, and values/goals is based on restrictive positive and negative anchors in ways that move him closer to the price-fixing option. Given the pressures he was facing, John was clearly predisposed to make this choice. John thus provides a self-justifying rationale for his actions. "I have a responsibility to provide for my family and cannot risk losing my job".

To move beyond the narrow confines of the confirmatory biases shown in Tables 11.2 and 11.3, John would need to adopt a more balanced analysis where both positive and negative poles are considered for each choice option (see Table 11.4).

The takeaway points of this expanded balanced approach are:

1. A deeper discussion of consequences, outcomes, and values will position people to better understand what is the "right" thing to do.
2. Cognitive adjustments are necessary to move beyond our natural tendencies to confirm and avoid complexity.
3. By expanding our perceived choice options, decision mapping has the potential to stimulate our "*moral imagination*" (Urbany et al. 2008, p. 79).
4. John, and others in his situation, who feel torn between "a rock and hard place", who feel hemmed into a tight corner with having to choose between the "lesser of two evils", need to ask themselves questions such as: (a) Can I find a way to prevent a crime from occurring and yet salvage a working relationship with my boss? (b) Can I present some legal alternatives for enhancing market share (the driving force behind the price-fixing scheme)? (c) Can I sacrifice my integrity at the altar of (what I think will be) increased job security and a promotion? (d) Can I continue to justify working for an unethical boss and company? (e) If I resign, do I feel reasonably confident that I can find a job—comparable to my current salary and benefits—within a company that is more ethically-oriented?

John's story reflects the experiences of many in today's workplace: The narrative, reflected in the mentioned questions, is one where people feel increasingly insecure and uncertain about their future. It is a narrative of the lesser of two evils—of "damn if I do, and damn if I don't". It is a narrative of feeling pressured to cross the line into unethical and/or illegal actions. Finally, it is narrative that often defines the problem as "a few rotten apples ought not spoil the crate"—an incomplete narrative that does not consider the underlying systemic ethical failures of our organizations.

Moving Forward

A more ethical workplace requires that individuals and their organizations be held accountable for their actions. The excuse so often heard that I was simply *following my boss' orders* will not cut it. And is it not often the case, that the boss in his/her defense will simply say the same thing—that I was simply following *my boss' orders*? And so it goes up the chain of command. But today's workplace is changing in ways where traditional notions of chain of command and top-down decision-making are shifting to a more team-oriented, flatter structure designed to empower employees with the tools, resources, "voice", and opportunities to help their organizations succeed. Such organizations engage their employees to offer their insights, perspectives, skills, experience, and values—particularly on issues that directly affect them. These changes offer the promise of better days ahead, where employees working with their teams and leaders, can affirm their commitment to creating organizations of virtue—where ethical–moral concerns are infused into the culture, where leaders focus on the multiple bottom lines of ethical, social, as well as economic sustainability, and where "doing well by doing good" becomes part of the cultural fabric of the workplace.

References

Abraham, R. (1999). Emotional dissonance in organizations: Conceptualizing the roles of self-esteem and job-induced tension. *Leadership & Organization Development Journal, 20*(1), 18–25.

Aquino, K., & Reed, A., II. (2002). The self-importance of moral identity. *Journal of Personality and Social Psychology, 83*(6), 1423–1440.

Ariss, S. S. (2003). Employee involvement to improve safety in the workplace. An ethical imperative. *Mid-American Journal of Business, 18*(2), 9–16.

Barling, J., Loughlin, C., & Kelloway, E. K. (2002). Development and test of a model linking safety-specific transformational leadership and occupational safety. *Journal of Applied Psychology, 87*(3), 488–496.

Cameron, K. S. (2003). Organizational virtuousness and performance. In K. S. Cameron, J. E. Dutton, & R. E. Quinn (Eds.), *Positive organizational scholarship* (pp. 48–65). San Francisco: Berrett-Koehler.

Cohan, J. (2002). "I didn't know" and "I was only doing my job": Has corporate governance careened out of control? A case study of Enron's information myopia. *Journal of Business Ethics, 40,* 275–299.

Credo, K., Armenakis, A, Field, H., & Young, R. (2010). Organizational ethics, leader–member exchange, and organizational support: Relationships with workplace safety. *Journal of Leadership & Organizational Studies, 17*(4), 325–334.

Elango, B., Paul, K., Kundu, S., & Paudel, S. (2010). Organizational ethics, individual ethics, and ethical intentions in international decision-making. *Journal of Business Ethics, 97,* 543–561.

Freeman, R. E. (1994). The Politics of stakeholder theory: Some future directions. *Business Ethics Quarterly, 4*(4), 409–421.

Froman, L. (2010). Positive psychology in the workplace. *Journal of Adult Development, 17,* 59–69.

Ghosh, D. (2008). Corporate values, workplace decisions and ethical standards of employees. *Journal of Managerial Issues, 20*(1), 68–87.

Gini, A. (1997). Moral leadership and business ethics. *Journal of Leadership and Organization Studies, 4*(4), 64–81.

Goodwin, D. K. (2005). *Team of rivals: The political genius of Abraham Lincoln.* New York: Simon and Schuster.

Grandey, A., Kern, J., & Frone, M. (2007). Verbal abuse from outsiders versus insiders. *Journal of Occupational Health Psychology, 12,* 63–79.

Kindy, K. (2011). Report calls W.Va. mine disaster 'man-made'. *Washington Post,* (May 20), A-3.

LaVan, H., & Martin, W. (2008). Bullying in the U.S. workplace: Normative and process-oriented ethical approaches. *Journal of Business Ethics, 83,* 147–165.

Lustgarten, A., & Knutson, R. (2010). *Years of internal BP probes warned that neglect could lead to accidents.* Retrieved from www.propublica.org/bpdocs.

McLean, B., & Elkind, P. (2003). *The smartest guys in the room.* New York: Portfolio.

O'Toole, J. & Bennis, W. (2009). What's needed next: A culture of candor. *Harvard Business Review, 87,* 54–61.

Paine, L. (1994). Managing for organizational integrity. *Harvard Business Review*, March-April, 106–117.

Parboteeah, K., & Kapp, E. (2008). Ethical climates and workplace safety behaviors: An empirical investigation. *Journal of Business Ethics, 80,* 515–529.

PBS Newshour. (2011). Retrieved from www.pbs.org/newshour/bb/education/july-dec11/atlantaschools_07-06.html

Rowan, J. (2000). The moral foundation of employee rights. *Journal of Business Ethics, 24,* 355–361.

Schumann, P. (2001). A moral principles framework for human resource management ethics. *Human Resource Management Review, 11,* 93–111.

Thomas, T., Schermerhorn, J., & Dienhart, J. (2004). Strategic leadership of ethical behavior in business. *Academy of Management Executive, 18*(2), 56–66.

Ulrich, C., O'Donnell, P., Taylor, C., Farrar, A., Danis, M., & Grady, C. (2007). Ethical climate, ethics stress, and the job satisfaction of nurses and social workers in the United States. *Social Science & Medicine, 65,* 1708–1719.

Urbany, J., Reynolds, T., & Phillips, J. (2008). How to make values count in everyday decisions. *MIT Sloan Management Review, 49,* 75–80.

Victor, B., & Cullen, J. (1988). The organizational bases of ethical work climates. A*dministrative Science Quarterly, 33,* 101–125.

Zohar, D. (2002). Modifying supervisory practices to improve subunit safety: A Leadership-based intervention model. *Journal of Applied Psychology, 87*(1), 156–163.

Chapter 12
A Seminar in Positive Psychology

Sanford Lopater

The growing recognition and popularity of positive psychology provokes pedagogical questions regarding effective instructional planning and implementation for undergraduate and graduate education. This chapter addresses these issues and presents a template for a seminar in this emerging discipline. While student samples often differ significantly, this format has been developed as an upper level undergraduate strategy within a liberal arts-oriented curriculum for a relatively small group of advanced students, generally 19 or fewer. A true seminar format is employed, in which the instructor and students share coequally in their responsibilities for teaching and learning. While this particular seminar is offered at the senior level, its basic format can be adjusted to most undergraduate and graduate courses.

The seminar is comprised of undergraduate seniors who have completed all required prerequisites. These include courses in Introductory Psychology, Behavioral Statistics, and Experimental Methods in Psychology. Most students in this seminar are coenrolled in senior-level laboratory courses. All students have access to library and electronically available primary sources in the humanities and social and behavioral sciences. The seminar is designed for a 14-week semester, meets one evening each week for 3 h, and employs a writing-intensive format. While seminars frequently employ primary sources for weekly reading assignments, in this instance a textbook is required as well. Of course, the nature of the student sample will affect the text selected.

Our curriculum requires one senior seminar. In general, the seminar in positive psychology is quickly and fully enrolled, with students having numerous and diverse interests selecting it in preference to other more traditional topics. Following is a selection of the topics presented in this seminar; this list is not exhaustive: resilience, turning points in life, optimism, establishing and achieving personal goals, well-being in the occupational setting, selective optimization with compensation in the later years, subjective well-being, creativity, flow, psychological perspectives on love, spirituality and subjective well-being, character strengths, creating and maintaining physical wellness, and attributes of strong relationships. Just as wellness is

S. Lopater (✉)
Christopher Newport University, Newport News, VA 23606, USA
e-mail: slopater@cnu.edu

J. D. Sinnott (ed.), *Positive Psychology*,
DOI 10.1007/978-1-4614-7282-7_12, © Springer Science+Business Media, LLC 2013

not defined solely through the absence of disease, positive human attributes are not characterized entirely in the absence of dysphoric emotional states. An explicit attempt to avoid these artificial dichotomies is basic to seminar reading, discussion, and writing.

Seminar Objectives

From a pedagogical perspective, course objectives drive a number of fundamental organizational decisions. Specifically, course objectives determine content, instructional methods, textbook and reading selections, evaluation criteria and methods, classroom activities, and student accountability/responsibility for independent productivity, classroom participation, and cooperative learning activities. In large part, seminar objectives are also attitudinal in nature as they require a basic change in perspective regarding the content and methodologies of traditional psychological subdisciplines.

Objective 1

Historically, courses in psychology have often focused on the diagnosis and assessment of cognitive, affective, and behavioral problems among individuals in many age groups extending from prenatal development to death. These often include, but are not limited to, offerings in abnormal psychology, clinical psychology, psychopathology, the exceptional child, and the psychology of adjustment. The elucidation and classification of these dysfunctions has been an important objective in a variety of basic and applied areas of the social and behavioral sciences. Characterizing disabilities and appropriate remediation strategies often represents a substantive part of a number of traditional undergraduate offerings. Because of the vivid and sometimes bizarre behaviors associated with psychological distress and mental illness, many students are drawn to this discipline in an effort to learn the causes, manifestations, and personal and social consequences of these disorders. Further, there is much curiosity about the methods by which counseling and psychotherapy are conducted and the long-term efficacy of such interventions. Many psychology students have not been introduced to the systematic study of more optimistic, functional, happy aspects of human growth, and lifelong development.

Importantly, this more positive view has changed dramatically over the course of the last two decades, at least from an empirical/investigational perspective (Seligman and Csikszentmihalyi 2000). This seminar is often the first opportunity for undergraduates to see that a significant number of psychologists are today exploring the nature of experiences among individuals who are happy, report significant subjective well-being, optimism, self-confidence, self-esteem, wisdom, maturity, and other aspects of wellness and spiritual integrity. In recent years, there has been remarkable growth in the visibility of this perspective in the primary psychological literature, popular press, conferences, and undergraduate and graduate courses (Seligman et al. 2005). Introduction to this more contemporary perspective and demonstrated critical acumen in the recognition and measurement of positive traits in psychology, thus, comprises the first objective of the seminar.

Objective 2

One subtle feature of this seminar, and the area of positive psychology in general, regards the outcomes of counseling and psychotherapy. Many of our students have availed themselves of clinical expertise, often as children and more frequently as adolescents and young adults. Others are receiving such assistance during their collegiate years and many will be treated during adulthood and later life. Yet, the student is often left unclear regarding the specific nature of intended therapeutic benefits and the gains and enhancements they can expect over time as a result of these interventions. Students are frequently curious about the precise benefits they might expect as a result of counseling or therapy that often lasts years. A second objective of this seminar involves the students' demonstrated mastery of the timing and achievement of key socialization tasks: impulse control, delay of gratification, frustration tolerance, and the inclination and ability to live with uncertainty in the future. While developmental psychologists have explored these issues in depth throughout the lifespan, they are also plainly relevant to subjective well-being and productive functioning in the wider social milieu.

Objective 3

A third objective of this seminar requires written and oral analytic assessments of what it means to live a good life, and how this concept has been appraised historically. Notwithstanding the accidents of history, geography, and political upheaval many find a way to "... do the best you can, with what you have, where you are...," an insight sometimes attributed to Winston Churchill. The author has been consistently impressed with the degree to which this question captivates undergraduates and its powerfully provocative personal meaning.

Objective 4

Beginning with Aristotle's *Ethics*, an idea of the good life began to emerge in the Western intellectual tradition. In this work, Aristotle (1976) asserted that the good life lies in individuals taking as much of their youth as they require in order to discover the one thing they do best, and then to do that thing, only that thing, and under the guidance of virtue (Penguin Edition, 1976). This somewhat simple, straightforward view strikes a compellingly resonant chord among collegiate youth who are in the midst of planning their future with more or less certainty and self-confidence. This objective involves written and oral, independent and seminar analyses of a number of empirically based questions germane to positive psychology. These include, but are not limited to: What is happiness? What do I have to do to feel good about myself? What does it mean to demonstrate maturity in my life? Why are some people optimistic about the future? What nourishes my creativity? How is wellness different from the simple lack of disease or disorder? These questions are fundamental to virtually all reading and writing assignments in the seminar and students are encouraged to evaluate their reading and writing from the first-person perspective, although not commensurate with the APA format. In this regard, at the outset of the seminar, students are cautioned to adhere to a policy of strict confidentiality regarding peer self-disclosures during discussions, presentations, and critiques. While this seminar has no therapeutic objectives, self-assessment is basic to the students' emerging, subtle internal dialogue regarding questions of quality of life and directions of future growth.

Objective 5

The fifth objective of this seminar lies in the demonstration of the fact that these important, compelling, and personal issues can be examined meaningfully through the legitimate methodologies of traditional systematic psychology. In a very real sense, the seminar offers a review and extension of the tools and techniques learned in the students' course work in experimental methodology. The importance of subject selection, sample size, subject age, sex, race, communication capacity, socioeconomic status, nationality, educational attainment, geographic origins and residence patterns, and sampling procedures are all essential for a full understanding of the outcomes of research in positive psychology. Various techniques of statistical analysis are appraised in order to review and refresh the students' course work in behavioral statistics.

Several areas of human cognition, emotion, and behavior are explored with regard to questions of well-being, self-esteem, maturity, optimism, wisdom, creativity, and wellness. These include, but are not limited to: intimate interpersonal relationships, peer rapport, home life, the occupational setting, family functioning, child-rearing reminiscences, the educational setting, health enhancement behaviors, avocational interests, and the spiritual domain. Research techniques are examined with regard to each of these as well as data analytic methods. The strengths and drawbacks of clinical and informal interviews are examined. Questionnaire construction and interpretation receive careful assessment, and the utility of employing periodic electronic check-ins throughout the day is appraised. The rationale behind stress-management techniques and the evaluation of their comparative efficacy receive special emphasis as the alleviation of common academic and social stressors presents a recurrent problem for undergraduates (and graduate students) in institutions of higher learning of all types. Finally, the student is required to examine the scope and focus of peer-reviewed journals and assess which address the questions of positive psychology in a full and adequate fashion.

Objective 6

The seminar's sixth objective addresses the nature of the connection among theory, data, and fruitful application. Philosophers of science (including Sir Francis Bacon at the outset) have emphasized the fundamental attributes of useful theories: hypothesis generation, data collection, and rejection or conditional acceptance of the initial research question. These steps are no less basic to positive psychology than they are in sensation–perception, biopsychology, or the study of learning and motivation. Also, this process is inherent in the student's exposure to the hypothesis testing in their behavioral statistics course. Once meaningful data has been collected, their ultimate utility and application remains a priority in the assessment of their validity, and often requires further elucidation. For example, the efficacy of physical exercise in minimizing stress requires careful critical appraisal regarding the intensity, duration, and frequency of such interventions as well as their application over months and years. Another example involves the putative relationship between maturity (Allport 1961) and happiness. Students ultimately come to grasp the realization that it is possible to behave in wise, restrained, patient, and intelligent ways under horribly adverse, personal or political circumstances. The use of movies vividly illustrates this fact in often, compelling and unforgettable ways. Writing assignments assessing film content and relevance to the seminar are discussed in a later section of this chapter.

Objective 7

The final objective of this seminar involves productive, self-directed scholarship in writing a lengthy research paper and presenting its substance orally to the seminar. It is not uncommon for students to enroll in their senior seminar without having written an extensive research paper or literature review. Critical appraisal of the primary literature is a fundamental requirement of this assignment. Students are required to consult the instructor periodically while preparing their work. To ensure distributed effort in writing the research paper, the instructor requests, but does not require, interim topic and sentence outlines to assess the student's progress and make relevant editorial recommendations for refinements in content and format. Each of these objectives receives a full description below.

Seminar Format

While the instructor assumes responsibility for the seminar's structure and objectives, everyone shares in teaching and learning. Posted seminar announcements make plain the essential obligation of consistent, pertinent, and constructive classroom participation. The seminar begins with a 1-week overview of the evolution and nature of positive psychology. The diverse agendas of the discipline are introduced along with a treatment of the ancient philosophical origins of inquiries into human happiness, well-being, maturity, and wisdom. These humanistic traditions are especially relevant to the questions addressed by positive psychologists.

All sessions begin with a thorough review of the content of the previous seminar meeting. The instructor and students then raise questions regarding matters left unclear or incomplete. This review addresses previous lecture content and reading assignments. Students are encouraged to address these questions on behalf of one another with the instructor playing an observer/moderator role. It is important for students to see themselves in the role of authoritative, informed participant/contributors and to cultivate mutual respect while doing so.

A second aspect of each seminar meeting involves a show-and-tell feature. Students are requested to bring to seminar current media reports of positive relevance for sharing and discussion. These may be drawn from print, broadcasting, and electronic media and are intended to offer participants optimistic examples of human achievement, persistence, redemption, and triumph. Examples may involve cohesive family functioning, professional excellence, or personal striving and accomplishment, in most cases after long periods of adversity, failure, or obscure striving. It is common for students to become very engaged in these stories, and sometimes plainly emotional. Those who bring these contributions are generally questioned further about the stories they share and other students often seek further follow-up information at their own initiative, where it becomes a part of the following week's review discussion. At this point, the instructor offers students a 15-min break.

In the early portion of the semester, the period after break addresses the introduction of supplementary lecture material and a discussion of that week's textbook and journal reading assignments. This generally requires 60–75 min and exemplifies Maier and Hoffman's (1960) developmental discussion. Students sometimes find classroom discussions aimless and without a clear and central focus. A developmental discussion seeks to minimize these frustrations through a lucid articulation of specific, sequential objectives. These include: (1) a clear statement of relevant problems and questions, (2) the suggestion of hypotheses for addressing solutions to these problems and questions, (3) collection of information relevant to the resolution of these unanswered issues, and (4) an assessment of the validity, pertinence, and practicality of a variety of solutions for these issues. Once these steps have been articulated, there is no single, predetermined discussion objective and all seminar participants may choose to focus on one, some, or all of these points. Developmental discussion, therefore, is not overly directive, nor is there a single "correct" outcome to many diverse student contributions. This format places a premium on divergent, creating approaches to questions in positive psychology.

Films

Three or four films are shown during the course of the semester. These lend immediacy and reality to many of the virtues presented in lecture, readings, and seminar discussion. Vivid, real, and fictional characters offer students concrete depictions of the challenges inherent in the slow, and often painful process of personal growth and the attainment of wisdom and personal transcendence. Examples of human triumph, optimism, perseverance, redemption, and adherence to positive, guiding life principles consistently captivate our students (especially, because few have seen films made before 1990). The presentation of these films is one justification for holding the seminar in a single, uninterrupted 3-h evening session.

Films shown over the past several years include: *The Fountainhead*, *Gandhi*, *Schindler's List*, *Good Will Hunting*, *Rain Man*, *The Shawshank Redemption*, and *The Full Monty* (a particularly creative and timely depiction of coping with the pressures and stresses of unemployment in a depressed economy). It is important for the students to see that, positive social movements and life outcomes frequently involve periods of danger, tension, turmoil, and chaotic political upheaval. Life for heroes is often compulsive, driven, and grim. Many other films are particularly relevant to this seminar and many have been listed in Peterson's *A Primer in Positive Psychology* (2006).

Students write 5–7 page papers for each film viewed, answering a number of specific questions distributed by the instructor just before viewing. These papers address the students' perception of the personal relevance of the film to their current lives, their personal development, their dreams for the future, and their observations of others. The inspirational qualities of these movies cannot be overstated. When students cannot attend seminar screenings they are required to obtain the films independently and fulfill the writing requirement by the stated deadline.

The Research Project

At the beginning of the semester, each student selects a topic for in-depth, independent study. The seminar syllabus contains a list of 35 suggested topics, although students are free to diverge from it in pursuing their personal interests. The paper is prepared in APA format and is approximately 20 pages in length (excluding back matter). A complete bibliography is required and students are directed to cite only those sources that appear in the primary, peer-reviewed literature. The use of secondary sources, newspapers, magazines, or pop psychology is explicitly discouraged. This specific requirement is relaxed in film-related writing assignments.

One key and central requirement of the research project involves critical appraisal of the sources, most germane to the student's topic. Because many psychology students have had at least one course in statistics and an introduction to research methods in psychological science, they are required to apply the critical acumen acquired in these courses in evaluating the sources most central to their subject (not all sources cited). For example, issues such as sample size, sample selection, subject demographic attributes, and sample attributes compared with population characteristics all require assessment. Between- and within-subject designs are assessed for relevance according to author objectives and overall potential generalizability of the data is considered. The nature and appropriateness of statistical techniques are evaluated as well. Because many undergraduate seminars have capstone objectives, these requirements should pose no undue difficulties for students in a course like the one described here. The degree to which students fulfill these requirements offers other seminar participants opportunities for critical appraisal of their peers' work. As noted above, should students desire ungraded, interim instructor assessment during the development of the paper the instructor should provide guidance in evaluating topic outlines, sentence outlines, and first drafts. On completion of the research project, each seminar student will distribute copies to every other student for reasons made clear in following sections.

The Oral Presentation

Each student will present to his/her peers the fundamental features and findings of their research in oral, PowerPoint format. This presentation is allocated approximately 20 min. A simple reading, of the paper and slides is strongly discouraged. In addition to a summary of the contents of the research paper, students are required to include additional information in their oral report. These include the students' personal motivations for exploring the topic they have selected and an historical review of the subject under study. While the report may be restricted in its focus, students are required to summarize concisely our current state of knowledge of the topic. Students are required to report any conceptual and/or methodological difficulties they encountered in developing and writing their paper. Also, potential fruitful solutions to these difficulties are presented, evaluated, and discussed. Finally, some logical directions for avenues of further research conclude the oral presentation. All students therefore have a copy of the research paper and have heard the author's oral presentation. This brings us to the final, essential feature of the presentation package.

Peer Critiques

On completion of the research paper, each student selects two classmates to write critiques of their work. This is usually a student's first experience in formalizing constructive criticism of their peers' scholarly effort. The instructor actively encourages students to write critiques that are constructive and positive in their tone. Each critic receives the final research paper no less than 1 week before the oral presentation in order to assure that the critic gets ample time for thoughtful and specific remarks that are related to particular pages and passages. Critiques are 3–4 pages in length and should address certain features of the target paper. The inclusiveness and depth of the paper are examined; an analysis of the cogency of the author's analysis and synthesis are essential features of these student critiques. Critics are asked to point out conceptual, factual, or theoretical errors and to offer innovative hypotheses regarding solutions to unanswered questions and future areas of research. Students are encouraged to examine inconsistencies in data reported and interpreted by different investigators. Importantly, conformity with university-level expectations regarding grammar and spelling is assessed. Each critic presents all seminar students with a copy of their critique.

Presentation Evenings—Final 4 Weeks of the Semester

During presentation evenings students distribute copies of their research papers and make their oral, PowerPoint presentations. Each critic distributes their critique to all seminar members and orally presents the substance of their remarks. The seminar as a group then questions the author and critics and a wide-ranging discussion ensues. Two or three of these presentations occur over the course of our 3-h evening session. In brief, the seminar thus provides each student with the beginnings of a personal, professional library in positive psychology: the assigned textbook, a set of lecture notes, commentary on seminar discussions, a research paper from each member of the seminar, and two critiques of each research paper. These resources will serve well; those students who wish to pursue this discipline further, either independently or within the context of a graduate program.

Evaluation

No examinations or quizzes are conducted in this seminar. Because this is a senior-level seminar, productive work habits have generally developed in all students. The seminar format requires and reinforces distributed effort and the instructor is available throughout the term for consultation regarding the development of the research paper. The quality of the students' written work is consistently quite high. There is an explicit deemphasis on points, and a relaxed spirit of global assessment consistently emerges in the informal seminar format. The research paper and oral presentation account for about half of the student's final grade with the film analyses, weekly discussions, and critiques accounting for the other half. The degree to which a student is prepared to actively participate on the basis of having read and considered assigned materials is an important criterion in keeping with the coequal sharing of teaching and learning in this seminar. In light of the foregoing description of the assignments of this seminar, an explicit emphasis on critical thinking is fundamental to the awarding of final grades.

Summary of Pedagogical Issues

This description of a senior seminar is only an example of how a positive ambiance can be used to teach positive psychology. Of course, many of the features described here can be amended to suit diverse course requirements and different levels of an undergraduate curriculum. Certain features of this seminar enhance student interest, motivation, and involvement. Course evaluations reveal a number of consistent, qualitative assessments of this seminar. Students consistently report high enthusiasm and deep personal engagement in the topics presented. Many articulate that they would have enjoyed being introduced to positive psychology much earlier in their college careers and a few have gained entry to graduate programs in this new and exciting area. Virtually, everyone seeks sources for further reading at the conclusion of the seminar.

The writing-intensive format is a seminar requirement and creates virtually no resistance among our upper level psychology majors. Their facility in APA format is excellent. The opportunity to critique their peers' work is a responsibility that everyone takes quite seriously and with genuine constructive intent. Critical thinking is a central feature of this seminar, especially because students are required to apply their knowledge from two required prerequisites: Behavioral Statistics and Experimental Methodology in the Behavioral Sciences. This expectation reinforces the capstone nature of our senior seminars and serves to emphasize a review of two important areas which will enhance student performance on the Psychology GRE test. Importantly, the instructor has determined that student critiques are rare on our campus and this requirement affords the opportunity to constructively assess peer scholarship within well-defined parameters of appraisal. Once students begin to apply their knowledge base in statistics and experimental methodology to the analysis of the primary literature and their peers' efforts, their confidence grows significantly and rapidly.

This seminar format lends itself well to students with different learning styles. One particularly interesting distinction is between syllabus-bound and syllabus-free learners (Josephs and Smithers 1975). Syllabus-bound learners excel when course objectives are very clear, when distributed learning is required through course organization, when evaluation procedures are clearly articulated, when deadlines are known and firm, and when instructor directions and assistance is offered. In contrast, syllabus-free learners thrive, when they are free to determine the nature, pace, diversity, and depth of their academic work. Syllabus-free learners thrive on the autonomous use of personal time in the preparation of their assignments and the freedom to select topics of personal relevance for further study. They are more comfortable than their syllabus bound cohorts with relative or comparative standards of student evaluation rather than absolute performance criteria. Working with both types of students at the same time in the same classroom can be very challenging; Josephs and Smithers (1975) have created a brief, valid, and reliable questionnaire which may inform the instructor of the general nature of his or her class. The author has found this short diagnostic of high-value incourse construction and the choice of pedagogical methods. The seminar format employed here seems to work very well in meeting the dispositional preferences of both types of students. The author is not suggesting that there are only two kinds of students in the world, but any information which informs of differences in student learning styles is likely to be helpful in creating and maintaining a productive educational environment.

This seminar requires student engagement in a wide variety of learning activities: lecture, developmental discussion, independent library research, writing, critical analysis, cinematic analysis and assessment, oral presentation, and development of a PowerPoint presentation. Students consistently report enjoying this diversity of learning pursuits. Extant literature supports the importance and efficacy of student seminar presentations at both the undergraduate and graduate level (Taylor 1992; Exley and Dennick 2004; Casteel and Bridges 2007). Students share intellectual content, motivation to assume personal responsibility for learning, and affective reassurance with their peers. In addition, the use of PowerPoint presentations and cinema has been found to be a highly effective instructional strategy at the undergraduate level (Mayer and Anderson 1992; Alexander and Waxman 2000; Mayer and Johnson 2008). The format described in this chapter fosters mutual, intellectual, and affective support and peer assistance and diminishes an aggressive competitive spirit among students. Finally, each student completes the seminar with the foundation of an excellent personal, professional library in positive psychology. While no single seminar format will meet the expectations and tastes of all students and instructors, the author has enjoyed a high success rate with the template described here.

References

Alexander, M., & Waxman, D. (2000). Cinemeducation: Teaching family systems through the movies. *Families, Systems, & Health, 18*, 455–466.

Allport, G. W. (1961). *Pattern and growth in personality*. New York: Holt.

Aristotle (1976). *Ethics*. Harmondsworth: Penguin Books.

Casteel, M. A., & Bridges, K. R. (2007). Goodbye lecture: A student-led seminar approach for teaching upper division courses. *Teaching of Psychology, 34*, 107–110.

Exley, K., & Dennick, R. (2004). *Small group teaching: Tutorials, seminars, and beyond*. London: Routledge.

Josephs, A. P., & Smithers, A. G. (1975). Personality characteristics of syllabus-bound and syllabus-free sixth-formers. *British Journal of Educational Psychology, 45*, 29–38.

Maier, N. R. F., & Hoffman, L. R. (1960). Using trained "developmental" discussion leaders to improve further the quality of group decisions. *Journal of Applied Psychology, 44*, 247–251.

Mayer, R. E., & Anderson, R. B. (1992). The instructive animation: Helping students build connections between words and pictures in multimedia learning. *Journal of Educational Psychology, 84*, 444–452.

Mayer, R. E., & Johnson, C. I. (2008). Revising the redundancy principle in multimedia learning. *Journal of Educational Psychology, 100,* 380–386.
Peterson, C. (2006). *A primer in positive psychology.* New York: Oxford University Press.
Seligman, M. E. P., & Csikszentmihalyi, M. (2000). Positive psychology: An introduction. *American Psychologist, 55,* 5–14.
Seligman, M. E. P., Steen, T. A., Park, N., & Peterson, C. (2005). Positive psychology progress: Empirical validation of interventions. *American Psychologist, 60,* 410–421.
Taylor, P. (1992). Improving graduate student seminar presentations through training. *Teaching of Psychology, 19,* 236–238.

Chapter 13
The Positive Psychology of Adult Generativity: Caring for the Next Generation and Constructing a Redemptive Life

Dan P. McAdams

Fifty years before Seligman and Csikszentmihalyi (2000) introduced *positive psychology* as a breakthrough movement for psychological science and practice, Erik Erikson (1950) envisioned a positive psychology of the human life cycle, delineating fundamental strengths and virtues for each of the eight developmental stages. According to Erikson, each stage in the human life cycle is defined by a basic psychosocial challenge expressed in a polarity of human experience. In the first stage, the infant faces the challenge of establishing a secure bond of attachment with caregivers, expressed in the polarity of *trust vs. mistrust*. In the last stage, the elderly man or woman faces the challenge of accepting life as something that has been good and worthwhile, felicitously captured in Erikson's notion of *ego integrity vs. despair*. Ideally, a trusting attachment in the first stage affirms the virtue of *hope*, Erikson argued, whereas the experience of ego integrity bequeaths to the older person the virtue of *wisdom*. Between its beginning in hope and its ending in wisdom, the idealized human life—a life characterized not merely by good adjustment but also by a rich experience of flourishing— confronts a sequence of biologically and culturally induced transitions and ultimately affirms a series of corresponding life virtues. For the great seventh stage of middle adulthood, Erikson asserted that the challenge is *generativity vs. stagnation*, and the corresponding virtue is *care*.

Nearly 15 years before Seligman and Csikszentmihalyi (2000) introduced positive psychology to the world, my students and I began research on the concept of generativity, examining how the virtue of caring for the next generation plays itself out in human lives and in the stories adults construct to make sense of their lives (McAdams 1985; McAdams et al. 1986). Around the same time, the topic of generativity began to attract the attention of other investigators (e.g., Ryff and Heincke 1983; Snarey et al. 1987) because behavioral scientists sought to translate Erikson's clinical intuitions and case studies into quantitative, hypothesis-testing research. Over the past three decades, research on generativity has developed apace. The concept of generativity, however, has not typically been featured in the mainstream publications of

D. P. McAdams (✉)
Department of Psychology, Northwestern University, 2120 Campus Drive,
Evanston, IL 60208, USA
e-mail: dmca@northwestern.edu

J. D. Sinnott (ed.), *Positive Psychology*,
DOI 10.1007/978-1-4614-7282-7_13,

positive psychology such as Peterson and Seligman's (2004) handbook of character strengths and virtues. Nonetheless, research in personality, developmental, and social psychology, and in sociology has yielded an impressive corpus of findings on the meanings and manifestations of generativity in adulthood—findings that contribute an important body of knowledge and perspective to positive psychology.

My goal in this chapter is to highlight some of the central theoretical concepts and empirical findings in the positive psychology of generativity, as it has developed over the past three decades. In doing so, I will emphasize concepts and findings for which I have a special fondness, that is, those that have originated in the work conducted by my students and myself. Our research program on generativity dovetails with the study of the stories adults construct to make meaning and affirm purpose in their lives (McAdams 1985, 2006a, 2008). I will begin by describing what generativity is, the various ways in which it is expressed in the adult years, and how it is measured. I will then review behavioral studies into the origins, consequences, and correlates of generativity. Finally, I will consider the particular kinds of life stories that highly generative adults tend to tell and live by. Our research shows that a central psychological and cultural theme running through those stories is the power of human *redemption*.

What Is Generativity?

At its heart, generativity is "primarily the concern in establishing and guiding the next generation" (Erikson 1950, p. 267). As parents, teachers, mentors, role models, and leaders, generative adults aim to care for or contribute to the advancement of younger generations and thereby leave a positive legacy of the self for the future (Kotre 1984). The most obvious way in which many adults actualize their generative potential and assume generative social roles is through raising children. But adults can be generative in many other ways too, through a variety of family and work roles, friendships, volunteerism and community activity, and through a wide range of venues wherein men and women find opportunities to make productive and meaningful contributions to society—contributions that hold the promise of promoting, directly or indirectly, the survival, well-being, and/or flourishing of future generations.

In Erikson's model of the human life cycle, generativity is the psychosocial centerpiece of the seventh stage of development, the stage associated with midlife. Although young adults and older adults can certainly make important contributions to future generations, the middle adulthood years—roughly ages 35 through 65 in contemporary modern societies—typically hold out the greatest opportunities and the heaviest burdens in generativity. By the time midlife rolls around, adults have typically made psychosocial headway in consolidating identity (the fifth stage in Erikson's scheme) and establishing long-term bonds of intimacy (the sixth stage). They are now ready to devote a significant portion of their energies to taking care of young people, and taking care of the things that matter for people (young and old) in families, at the workplace, in neighborhoods and communities, and in society at large. In the midlife years, then, the object of one's generative efforts can range from a single baby to planet earth. In *Gandhi's Truth*, Erikson (1969) portrayed the Indian religious and political leader as a paragon of generativity, a man who made it his generative mission to care for an entire nation. Erikson marks a key scene in Mahatma Gandhi's midlife years when he seemed to take up the mantle of generativity:

> From the moment in January of 1915 when Gandhi set foot on a pier reserved for important arrivals in Bombay, he behaved like a man who knew the nature and the extent of India's calamity and that of his own fundamental mission. A mature man of middle age has not only made up his mind as to what, in the various compartments of his life, he does and does not *care for*, he is also firm in his vision of what he *will* and *can* take *care of*. He takes as his baseline what he irreducibly is and reaches out for what only he can, and therefore, *must do*. (Erikson 1969, p. 255, *italics* in original).

Beyond Erikson, a number of theorists have sought to describe the meaning of generativity and its place in adult life (Browning 1975; Kotre 1984; McAdams 1985; Peterson and Stewart 1990; Snarey 1993; Vaillant and Milofsky 1980). Generativity has been variously described as a biological drive to reproduce oneself, an instinctual need to care for and be needed by others, a philosophical urge for transcendence and symbolic immortality, a developmental sign of maturity and mental health in adulthood, and a social demand to create a productive niche in society. It has been identified with behavior (such as raising children), motives and values (concerns for preserving what is good and making other things better), and a general attitude about the world (having a broad perspective and understanding one's place in the sequence of generations).

Drawing from the best ideas in the theoretical literature on generativity, Ed de St. Aubin and I developed a model that delineates seven interrelated features of generativity, all oriented toward the individual and societal goal of providing for the next generation (McAdams and de St. Aubin 1992; see also McAdams 2001; McAdams et al. 1998). Generativity begins with (1) *cultural demand*. All human cultures demand that older and more experienced members provide care and guidance for younger and less experienced members. Societies provide age-graded norms regarding adult roles and responsibilities and set up institutions through which generative efforts may be channeled (Rossi 2001; Vaillant and Milofsky 1980). As men and women move toward and into their midlife years, they are increasingly expected to step up, as Gandhi did, to take care of the people and things that must be taken care of, and to assume greater responsibility in families, communities, professions, and societal institutions. As adults move through their 30s and 40s, those who are unable or unwilling to contribute to and assume responsibility for the next generation, usually through family or work, are considered "off time" and at odds with the expected "social clock" (Neugarten and Hagestad 1976). According to Erikson (1950), these adults may sink into the opposite of generativity—"stagnation."

Interacting with and reinforcing cultural demand is (2) *inner desire*. Adults often feel a "need to be needed," a communal desire to nurture others, to be of use to those who are in need (Erikson 1950; Stewart et al. 1988). Adults may also feel a strong agentic urge to extend themselves into the next generation, to leave a legacy of the self for the future and thereby attain a kind of symbolic immortality (Becker

1973; Kotre 1984; McAdams 1985). One's generative legacy can be as humble as a sage piece of advice offered to a coworker, or agreeing to chair the church's fund-raising committee. It can be as grand as raising a large family, building a business, composing a symphony, making a scientific discovery, leading a community, or even building a nation. Ideally, the product of one's generative efforts outlives the self, such that mature adults ultimately come to define themselves in terms of what they leave behind. In middle adulthood and beyond, Erikson wrote, "I am what survives me" (Erikson 1968, p. 141). At its paradoxical heart, therefore, generativity relies on both communal (selfless) and agentic (selfish) desires (Bakan 1966; Kotre 1984; McAdams 1985). To be generative is to generate something or someone in one's own image—an agentic enterprise par excellence—and to care for and nurture that something or someone in a communal way, in order to provide for the next generation. Indeed, the narrow but evolutionarily crucial task of successful biological reproduction is a primal microcosm of an agency-communion dynamic that lies at the motivational heart of all generative expressions. I create a child in my own image, and then I care for it.

Agentic and communal desires combine with and are structured by cultural norms, expectations, and influences that specify when and how adults are to engage in generative efforts in a given social milieu. Motivated by cultural demand and inner desire, adults develop (3) a conscious *concern* for the next generation. They begin to expand their purview of concern to encompass the well-being of others who will survive them. They become more interested in those institutions and cultural practices designed to promote positive functioning and social life into the future—schools, churches, charities, community organizations, professional societies, and so on. They become more concerned with intergenerational relations. They begin to see that they may have something to offer others, that the time may be right to "give something back" to society, to move from being the recipient to being the agent of care and concern.

Interacting with cultural demand, inner desire, and conscious concern are (4) *beliefs* pertaining to how advisable it may be to invest in others and in the future and how worthy others may be of one's care. Erikson (1950, p. 267) saw a "belief in the species" as a key attitudinal support for generativity. These kinds of beliefs may take many forms—faith in the goodness of humankind, hope for redemption in the future, optimism about the prospects of future prosperity for one's family, belief in a just world, and so on. By contrast, deep pessimism, cynicism, despair, and hopelessness undermine generativity, for they suggest that investments in the future are not likely to bring positive returns (Van De Water and McAdams 1989). A positive belief in the species, then, may help to buttress the adult's efforts to translate concerns into behavior through plans, goals, and other generative (5) *commitments*. Not all manifestations of generativity are planned in advance, of course. Unexpected pregnancy is the most obvious example, and in many other lives adults find that generative opportunities and challenges are as much thrust upon them as they are developed out of their own life agendas. Sooner or later, however, generativity nearly always results in some kind of commitment, entailing goals and plans. Ideally commitments lead to generative (6) *actions*. Many different kinds of actions may be construed as generative. Most common, however, are behaviors that involve creating or generating new things and people (developing an innovation, giving birth to a child), maintaining and caring for those things (and people) deemed to be good (preserving religious traditions, raising children), and passing on that which has been created or maintained as a "gift" (Becker 1973) to the next generation (teaching a skill, launching a son or daughter into the adult world).

The last feature of the theoretical model proposed by McAdams and de St. Aubin (1992) is generative (7) *narration*. As they translate their concerns and beliefs into commitment and action designed to promote the well-being of the next generation, adults construct personal narrations or stories of their generative efforts, which eventually become incorporated into the larger, autobiographical stories that come to comprise their narrative identities (McAdams 1985, 1996, 2008; McAdams and Pals 2006; McLean et al. 2007). Within a person's internalized and evolving story of his or her own life, narratives of generativity become increasingly central and salient as the adult moves into and through midlife (McAdams 1996). These narrations specify how the adult has worked and/or will continue to work to fashion a positive legacy for the future. As such a narration of generativity functions to provide a potentially satisfying "sense of an ending" (Kermode 1967) for a person's life story, in that the generativity narration anticipates how one's life may ultimately result in the generation of offspring, products, and outcomes that will outlive the self. Generative adults craft self-defining life stories whose endings defy death, in a narrative sense; even though one's own life will end, it may give birth to new beginnings.

Although some researchers have developed interview-based (Bradley and Marcia 1998), questionnaire (Ochse and Plug 1986), and Q-sort (Peterson and Klohnen 1995) measures designed to assess an Eriksonian stage of generativity as a whole, most researchers have focused on one or more of the particular features identified in the generativity model I have just described. For example, McAdams and de St. Aubin (1992) developed and validated the Loyola Generativity Scale (LGS), a 20-item self-report measure of generative *concern*. Self-report measures of generative beliefs (Van De Water and McAdams 1989), generative commitments or goals (McAdams et al. 1993), and generative actions (McAdams and de St. Aubin 1992) have also been developed and used in many studies. Researchers have also coded life narrative texts for generative themes (McAdams and de St. Aubin 1992; Stewart et al. 1988), and have developed various measures for estimating the strength of the agentic and communal desires that give rise to the inner motivations for generativity (Mansfield and McAdams 1996; Peterson 1998; Stewart and Vandewater 1998). Findings from numerous studies show that conscious generative concerns, assessed via the LGS, are positively correlated with self-report behavioral acts indicative of generativity and with generative commitments (goals) and generative themes in life stories (Cox et al. 2010; de St. Aubin and McAdams 1995; Hofer et al. 2008; McAdams and de St. Aubin 1992; McAdams et al. 1993). Research also supports the proposition that generativity may be motivated by strong inner desires or needs for agency and communion (Ackerman et al. 2000; Frimer et al. 2011; Mansfield and McAdams 1996; McAdams et al. 1986; Peterson and Stewart 1993).

The Generative Adult

Erikson situated generativity within a midlife stage of psychosocial development. But should generativity be conceived as a discrete "stage"? A considerable amount of research has tested Erikson's claim, examining relations between age and various assessments of generative desire, concern, commitment, action, and narration. Most studies have been cross-sectional, rather than longitudinal. Although a few studies find no relationship between generativity and age (e. g., Whitbourne et al. 1992), others have documented a smooth stage sequence (e. g., Snarey 1993; Vaillant and Milofsky 1980). The best estimate, however, probably lies somewhere between the two extremes.

McAdams et al. (1993) examined various features of generativity among young (age 22–27), midlife (age 37–42), and older (age 67–72) adults. The significant quadratic trend in the data showed that the midlife cohort scored markedly higher on generativity measures overall, compared to the young and older adults. However, different results were obtained for different features of generativity. McAdams et al. (1993) found that generative behaviors and narrations showed the strongest quadratic trends, with scores peaking in the midlife years. However, generative concern (assessed via the LGS) was relatively high among young adults and midlife adults, but dropped for older adults, whereas generative commitments/goals were very low for young adults but showed markedly and equally high levels for both midlife and older adults.

In a nationwide sample of over 3,000 American men and women ranging in age from 25 to 74, Keyes and Ryff (1998) showed that middle-aged and older adults provided more emotional support and unpaid assistance to others (generative actions) compared to younger adults. With respect to generative commitments/goals, midlife and older adults also showed higher levels of civic responsibility, but younger adults scored higher than the midlife and older adults, on obligations and plans to help children and other people directly. In a longitudinal study of inner desires linked to generativity, Stewart and Vandewater (1998) found that generativity motivation, assessed via Thematic Apperception Test (TAT) stories, actually *declined* from young adulthood to middle age. Young adults often feel strong urges—both agentic and communal—to make positive contributions to the next generation. But they may find it difficult to translate these urges into effective generative behavior until they have attained the status and resources that often come with middle age. Although young adults may feel strong generative desires, they look ahead to their midlife years as a time when those desires will be most effectively translated into generative commitment and action (Ryff and Heincke 1983; Peterson 1998).

The empirical findings on age and generativity seem to suggest that Erikson was broadly correct in supposing that midlife is a prime time for the expression of generativity. However, it is probably claiming too much to assert that generativity is neatly situated within a discrete, midlife stage. Different features of generativity may be differentially expressed across the adult life course. Generative desires may peak in early adult years whereas generative behaviors and commitments may increase well into and through midlife. Many older adults continue to show strong commitments to providing for younger generations. Furthermore, sociologically oriented researchers have argued that generativity is contoured by unpredictable economic and cultural changes, historical events, and sheer chance, rendering the general idea of discrete stages of adult development untenable (Cohler et al. 1998). Gender and social class may interact with age and contextual factors to shape the trajectories of generativity over time (Stewart and Ostrove 1998). Women and men may face different generative challenges and respond to different gender-based expectations regarding the timing and nature of generative expression (Miller-McLemore 2004). In a broad sense, furthermore, different cultures may comprehend generativity in different terms. For example, researchers have compared and contrasted idealized American and Japanese models regarding what constitutes a generative life and how it should unfold over the life course (de St. Aubin 2004; Yamada 2004).

Within any given society, therefore, and within any age cohort of adults, broad individual differences in generativity will reveal themselves. Simply put, some people—at any given point in time and place in society—are more generative than others. Research shows that individual differences in generativity are robustly associated with a range of psychological strengths and important life outcomes.

The prototype of generativity is the bearing and nurturing of offspring. A number of studies suggest that men and women who score high on various measures of generativity are especially effective as parents, compared to their less generative peers. In a survey study of parents whose children were enrolled in a major metropolitan school system, Lewis and Nakagawa (1995) found that mothers and fathers with high scores on a short version of the LGS tended to be more involved in their children's schooling than parents scoring lower. Parents scoring high on generativity tended to help their children with their homework more, showed higher levels of attendance at school functions, and evidenced greater knowledge about what their children were learning and doing in school, compared with parents scoring lower in generative concern. In another study of parents, researchers found that high levels of generativity were associated with valuing trust and communication with one's children and viewing parenting as an opportunity to pass on values and wisdom to the next generation (Hart et al. 2001). In a study asking adults to tell socialization stories for adolescent children, those adults scoring high on the LGS constructed narratives that manifested a strong investment in personal values and that emphasized learning important lessons from the past (Pratt et al. 1999).

Research has also connected generativity to an *authoritative* parenting style. Authoritative parenting combines an emphasis on high standards and discipline with a warm, child-centered, and caring approach to raising children. Peterson et al. (1997) found that middle-aged parents of college students expressed more authoritative attitudes about parenting if they were high in generativity. In the same study, authoritative parenting predicted attitudinal similarities between parents and their college-aged children, and it was negatively associated with parent–child conflict. Pratt et al. (2001) found that generativity among mothers of teenaged children was positively associated with authoritative parenting. Peterson (2006) examined relations between generativity in parents and the resultant personality characteristics of their children. When parents were high in generativity, their college-age offspring tended to show higher scores on personality traits related to conscientiousness and warmth, more positive emotion in everyday life, and greater levels of civic and religious involvement. Peterson (2006) argued that highly generative parents serve as role models for healthy lifestyles and engaged citizenship.

If parenting within the family is seen as the most private and local realm of generative expression, social involvements among one's peers, in churches and synagogues, and in the community offer opportunities for a more public expression of generativity. Hart et al. (2001) found that high levels of generativity were associated with more extensive networks of friends and social support in the community and greater levels of satisfaction with social relationships among both African American and white adults. In addition, generativity was positively associated with church attendance and with involvement in church activities. Adults scoring high in generativity, furthermore, were more likely to have voted in the last US Presidential election, worked for a political party or campaigned for a candidate, and called or written to a public official about a social concern or problem. Similarly, Cox et al. (2010) found that high scores on the LGS strongly predicted an index of positive societal engagement in a sample of 128 highly religious midlife American adults. Jones and McAdams (in press) found positive associations between generativity and indices of religious involvement, political participation, volunteerism, and public service motivation in a sample of 150 midlife men and women.

Cole and Stewart (1996) reported that generative concern among both, African American and Euro-American women in midlife correlated highly with measures of sense of community and political efficacy, suggesting that adults with strong generative concerns also tend to express strong feelings of attachment and belongingness in their communities and tend to view themselves as effective agents in the political process. An especially impressive documentation of generativity's positive role in both family and community life comes from Rossi's (2001) analysis of the National Survey of Midlife Development in the United States (MIDUS). After controlling for age and demographic factors in the nationwide data set, Rossi's research team found that items from the LGS were the single strongest predictor of "caring and doing for others" and "social responsibility in the domains of family, work and community" (Rossi 2001, title page). In the MIDUS study, social responsibility encompassed a wide range of prosocial behaviors, including volunteerism and contributing one's time and money to family members and to community concerns.

It is clear that by caring for the next generation, strengthening social institutions, maintaining valued cultural traditions, and working for positive social change, generative adults do a great deal of good for other people and the world around them. They also do good for themselves. Consistent with Erikson's (1950) suppositions, research shows that generativity is consistently associated with mental health and flourishing. Longitudinal investigations conducted by Vaillant (1977) and Snarey (1993) show that clinical ratings of generativity are positively associated with things such as the use of mature coping strategies during times of stress and measures of psychosocial adjustment in adulthood. A number of studies reveal consistently positive, albeit relatively modest, correlations between assessments of generative concern and generative behaviors on the one hand and self-report measures of life satisfaction, self-esteem, and psychological well-being on the other (Ackerman et al. 2000; Cox et al. 2010; de St. Aubin and McAdams 1995; Efklides et al. 2003; Grossbaum and Bates 2002; Keyes and Ryff 1998). In two longitudinal studies of graduates from the University of Michigan and Radcliffe College, Stewart and Ostrove (1998) found that the quality of midlife roles and generativity were the only significant predictors of later midlife well-being. Westermeyer (2004) found that generativity was positively associated with successful marriages, overall mental health, and a history of favorable relationships with peers across the adult life course. Peterson and Duncan (2007) reported that generativity was positively associated with a range of variables indicative of successful aging.

Researchers have also examined relationships between measures of generativity and dispositional personality traits. In general, generativity scores tend to show positive correlations with self-report indices of extraversion, agreeableness, and openness to experience, and negative associations with neuroticism (Bradley and Marcia 1998; de St. Aubin and McAdams 1995; Peterson and Duncan 2007; Van Hiel et al. 2006; Cox et al. 2010). Cox et al. (2010) conducted a fine-grained analysis of generativity's associations with personality traits by examining self-report measures of generative concern and generative actions and specific facets or components of the Big Five dispositional traits (extraversion, neuroticism, conscientiousness, agreeableness, and openness to experience). They found the strongest associations between measures of generativity on the one hand and many facets comprising the broad traits of extraversion and openness to experience on the other. For example, generativity was positively associated with the extraversion facets of warmth, assertiveness, activity, and positive emotions (but not with the extraversion facet of excitement seeking). Generativity was also strongly related to the agreeableness facet of altruism and the conscientiousness facets of achievement striving and dutifulness. For neuroticism, generativity was negatively associated with the facets of anxiety, depressiveness, and feelings of vulnerability.

Redemptive Life Stories

How do generative adults become generative in the first place? What are the developmental antecedents of generativity? The general answer is surely some complex variation on the simple idea that almost all features of an adult's personality are evolving and overdetermined products of repeated transactions between genotypes and environments. That certain features of generativity such as generative concern, may be partially determined by heredity is indirectly supported by the wealth of data showing that basic dispositional traits correlated with generative concern such as extraversion, openness, and tendencies toward altruism and dutifulness are themselves at least moderately heritable (Krueger et al. 2006). Although no prospective studies of the development of generativity from childhood into middle age are currently available, retrospective studies suggest that positive experiences with generative agents themselves (such as teachers and mentors) and with valued socializing institutions (such as schools, churches, and the military) may be partly responsible for shaping generative lives (An and Cooney 2006; Jones and McAdams in press; Rossi 2001). Nonetheless, psychologists know precious little about the developmental origins of generativity.

Despite the fact that psychologists know little, generative adults themselves have their own ideas about how they developed their strong commitments to promoting the well-being of future generations. Their own lay theories and developmental suppositions may often be found in the stories generative adults compose to make sense of their lives. In a series of qualitative and quantitative investigations conducted over the past decade and a half, my students and I have examined the life stories of highly generative adults, typically comparing their narratives to those composed by their less generative counterparts (Jones and McAdams in press; Mansfield and McAdams 1996; McAdams 2004, 2006a, b; McAdams and Albaugh 2008; McAdams and Bowman 2001; McAdams et al. 1997, 2001). The research program is based on the idea that *all* adults living in modern societies typically construct life stories, or what psychologists today often call *narrative identities*. By reconstructing the past and imagining the future as a story with plot, character, setting, scenes, and themes, adults formulate and internalize evolving stories of the self that function to provide life with some semblance of unity, meaning, and purpose (Bruner 1986; McAdams 1985, 2008; McAdams and Pals 2006; McLean et al. 2007; Singer 2004).

Generativity is tough work. In order to support one's best generative efforts and to render sensible and coherent a life given over to promoting the well-being of future generations, highly generative adults in their midlife years *need a good story*. For many highly generative adults, the story centers on the theme of *redemption*. Stripped to its psychological core, redemption is the deliverance from suffering to an enhanced status or state. Redemptive life narratives tell how protagonists invariably experience bad things in life, but bad things often lead to positive results. People overcome adversity, recover from sickness, rise above their limitations, learn positive life lessons from difficult setbacks, rehabilitate themselves, atone for their sins, and attain ultimate rewards after a life of punishment. Among the most powerful narratives of redemption in contemporary American society are stories of upward social mobility (from poverty to riches, often called "the American Dream"), personal liberation (from slavery to freedom), recovery (from sickness or addiction to health), and atonement (from sin to salvation) (McAdams 2006a). Models for these narratives can be found everywhere in American culture—from self-help books to Hollywood movies to the kinds of stories that American children learn in school about American history (McAdams 2006a).

The findings from our studies show that highly generative American adults in midlife are significantly more likely than their less generative counterparts to narrate their lives in redemptive terms. Careful content analysis of narrative data provided by hundreds of research participants shows that generativity is associated with constructing a greater number of redemption sequences (individual life episodes telling how a negative event led to a positive effect) in life narrative interviews and written autobiographical accounts. The studies also suggest that redemption sequences are accompanied by a suite of related themes that together comprise what I call *the redemptive self*. The main themes that make up the redemptive self are these: (1) the protagonist's enjoying a special advantage or blessing in childhood, or feeling that he or she has been "called" to do something good in life (the theme of *early advantage*); (2) recalling early events in which other people experienced suffering or oppression or even death (the theme of *the suffering of others*); (3) establishing strong and clear moral values, often associated with religion, by the time one has completed adolescence, and sticking with those values for the rest of life (the theme of *moral steadfastness*); (4) experiencing negative events that lead to positive outcomes or beneficial long-term effects (the theme of *redemption*); (5) struggling to reconcile competing desires/goals for agency and communion (the theme of *power vs. love*); and (6) anticipating a future in which the protagonist continues to invest in goals aimed at benefiting others and/or society at large (the theme of *prosocial goals*).

The redemptive self is a life-narrative form that is well-designed to support a generative life. The story reinforces the idea that the teller/protagonist is fortunate in some fundamental way, blessed from birth perhaps. Yet the world is full of suffering, as early memories also reinforce. "I am blessed; but others suffer." Perhaps, then, I have been called to do something good with my life, in gratitude for the blessings I have received. The juxtaposition of early advantage and the suffering of others sets up a moral challenge in the narrative. Generativity makes sense as an expression of gratitude or the pursuit of a mission in a world that really needs me. Often derived from either a faith tradition or the strong influences of family members or mentors, the protagonist develops a clear and abiding set of beliefs early on in life—typically simple ideas like the golden rule, love thy neighbor, always work for social justice, and so on. The story tells how these values continue to provide clear guidance and encouragement throughout life. The values provide a justification or rationalization for generative programs and pursuits. Bad things inevitably happen: divorce, unemployment, illness, abuse, and neglect. Family members die. Life's dreams are dashed. But good things often follow the bad in redemptive life narratives. *The tough work of generativity will pay off in the long run*, these stories say. The seeds you plant and water will eventually grow; bad children will become good; your long-term investments will yield dividends down the road.

Conclusion

In the positive psychology of generativity, the key virtue of an adult's life becomes care. Generativity is a complex arrangement of cultural demand, inner desire, concern, belief, commitment, action, and narration, constellated around the individual and collective goal of caring for and contributing to the well-being and advancement of future generations. Although generative desires may well up in adolescence and early adulthood, generative commitments and actions become especially salient in the midlife years, in keeping with Erikson's assertion that generativity vs. stagnation is the key psychosocial issue of middle adulthood. Research shows that highly generative adults prove to be more effective and engaged parents, experience broader social networks and more satisfying social support, invest themselves heavily in religious and/or civic institutions, engage in high levels of volunteer work and other behaviors aimed at improving the world they live in, and enjoy better mental health, compared to less generative adults.

Among the psychological resources upon which highly generative adults draw to support their generative activities and commitments are inspiring personal stories of redemption. Research on the life stories of highly generative American adults has identified a common form of narrative identity—called the redemptive self—that appears to sustain their efforts to care for and contribute to the well-being of future generations. The redemptive self tells the story of a blessed or gifted protagonist who journeys forth into a dangerous world, equipped with moral steadfastness and called to give something back to society for early blessings received. As the plot unfolds, the protagonist suffers greatly, but suffering is repeatedly redeemed by positive outcomes, reinforcing the protagonist's confidence and determination to make the world a better place for future generations. Strongly reinforced and shaped by a wealth of cultural narratives in American society, the redemptive self is a positive story to support a positive psychology of generativity. It is the kind of positive story you might want to construct for your own life, especially if you fancy yourself to be a highly generative adult.

References

Ackerman, S., Zuroff, D. C., & Moscowitz, D. S. (2000). Generativity in midlife and young adults: Links to agency, communion, and subjective well-being. *International Journal of Aging and Human Development, 50,* 17–41.

An, J. S., & Cooney, T. M. (2006). Psychological well-being in mid to late life: The role of generativity development across the lifespan. *International Journal of Behavioral Development, 30,* 410–421.

Bakan, D. (1966). *The duality of human existence: Isolation and communion in Western man.* Boston: Beacon Press.

Becker, E. (1973). *The denial of death.* New York: Free Press.

Bradley, C. L., & Marcia, J. E. (1998). Generativity-stagnation: A five-category model. *Journal of Personality, 66,* 39–64.

Browning, D. S. (1975). *Generative man.* New York: Dell.

Bruner, J. S. (1986). *Actual minds, possible worlds.* Cambridge, MA: Harvard University Press.

Cohler, B. J., Hostetler, A. J., & Boxer, A. M. (1998). Generativity, social context, and lived experience: Narratives of gay men in middle adulthood. In D. P. McAdams and E. de St. Aubin (Eds.), *Generativity and adult development* (pp. 265–309). Washington, DC: American Psychological Association Press.

Cole, E. R., & Stewart, A. J. (1996). Meanings of political participation among Black and White women: Political identity and social responsibility. *Journal of Personality and Social Psychology, 71,* 130–140.

Cox, K. S., Wilt, J., Olson, B., & McAdams, D. P. (2010). Generativity, the Big Five, and psychosocial adaptation in midlife adults. *Journal of Personality, 78,* 1185–1208.

De St. Aubin, E. (2004). The propagation of genes and memes: Generativity through culture in Japan and the United States. In E. de St. Aubin, D. P. McAdams, and T. C. Kim (Eds.), *The generative society* (pp. 63–82). Washington, DC: American Psychological Association Press.

De St. Aubin, E., & McAdams, D. P. (1995). The relations of generative concern and generative action to personality traits, satisfaction/happiness with life, and ego development. *Journal of Adult Development, 2,* 99–112.

Efklides, A., Kalaitzidou, M., & Chankin, G. (2003). Subjective quality of life in old age in Greece: The effect of demographic factors, emotional state and adaptation to aging. *European Psychologist, 8,* 178–191.

Erikson, E. H. (1950). *Childhood and society*. New York: Norton.

Erikson, E. H. (1968). *Identity: Youth and crisis*. New York: Norton.

Erikson, E. H. (1969). *Gandhi's truth.* New York: Norton.

Frimer, J. A., Walker, L. J., Dunlop, W. L., Lee, B. H., & Riches, A. (2011). The integration of agency and communion in moral personality: Evidence of enlightened self-interest. *Journal of Personality and Social Psychology, 101*, 149–163.

Grossbaum, M. G., & Bates, G. W. (2002). Correlates of psychological well-being at midlife: The role of generativity, agency and communion, and narrative themes. *International Journal of Behavioral Development, 26,* 120–127.

Hart, H. M., McAdams, D. P., Hirsch, B. J., & Bauer, J. J. (2001). Generativity and societal involvement among African Americans and white adults. *Journal of Research in Personality, 35,* 208–230.

Hofer, J., Bush, H., Chasiotis, A., Kartner, J., & Campos, D. (2008). Concern for generativity and its relation to implicit pro-social power motivation, generative goals, and satisfaction with life: A cross-cultural investigation. *Journal of Personality, 76,* 1–30.

Jones, B. K., & McAdams, D. P. (in press). Becoming generative: Socializing influences captured in life stories of late midlife. *Journal of Adult Development.*

Kermode, F. (1967). *The sense of an ending.* New York: Oxford University Press.

Keyes, C. L. M., & Ryff, C. D. (1998). Generativity in adult lives: Social structural contours and quality of life consequences. In D. P. McAdams and E. de St. Aubin (Eds.), *Generativity and adult development* (pp. 227-263). Washington: American Psychological Association Press.

Kotre, J. (1984). *Outliving the self: Generativity and the interpretation of lives*. Baltimore: Johns Hopkins University Press.

Krueger, R. F., & Johnson, W., & Kling, K. C. (2006). Behavior genetics and personality development. In D. K. Mroczek and T. D. Little (Eds.), *Handbook of personality development* (pp. 81–108). Mahwah: Erlbaum.

Lewis, D., & Nakagawa, K. (1995). *Race and educational reform in the American metropolis: A study of school decentralization*. Albany: SUNY Press.

Mansfield, E. D., & McAdams, D. P. (1996). Generativity and themes of agency and communion in adult autobiography. *Personality and Social Psychology Bulletin, 22,* 721–731.

McAdams, D. P. (1985). *Power, intimacy, and the life story*. Homewood: Dorsey Press.

McAdams, D. P. (1996). Narrating the self in adulthood. In J. E. Birren, G. M. Kenyon, J-E. Ruth, J. F. Schrot, and T. Svensson (Eds.), *Aging and biography* (pp. 131–148). New York: Springer.

McAdams, D. P. (2001). Generativity in midlife. In M. E. Lachman (Ed.), *Handbook of midlife development* (pp. 395–443). New York: Wiley.

McAdams, D. P. (2004). Generativity and the narrative ecology of family life. In M. W. Pratt and B. Fiese (Eds.), *Family stories and the life course* (pp. 235–257). Mahwah: Erlbaum.

McAdams, D. P. (2006a). *The redemptive self: Stories Americans live by.* New York: Oxford University Press.

McAdams, D. P. (2006b). The redemptive self: Generativity and the stories Americans live by. *Research in Human Development, 3,* 81–100.

McAdams, D. P. (2008). Personal narratives and the life story. In O. P. John, R. W. Robins, and L. A. Pervin (Eds.), *Handbook of personality: Theory and research* (3rd ed., pp. 241–261). New York: Guilford Press.
McAdams, D. P., & Albaugh, M. (2008). The redemptive self, generativity, and American Christians at midlife. In J. A. Belzen and A. Geels (Eds.), *Autobiography and the psychological study of religious lives* (pp. 255–286). Amsterdam: Rodolpi.
McAdams, D. P., & Bowman, P. J. (2001). Narrating life's turning points: Redemption and contamination. In D. P. McAdams, R. Josselson, and A. Lieblich (Eds.), *Turns in the road: Narrative studies of lives in transition* (pp. 3–34). Washington: American Psychological Association Press.
McAdams, D. P., & de St. Aubin, E. (1992). A theory of generativity and its assessment through self-report, behavioral acts, and narrative themes in autobiography. *Journal of Personality and Social Psychology, 62,* 1003–1015.
McAdams, D. P., & Pals, J. L. (2006). A new Big Five: Fundamental principles for an integrative science of personality. *American Psychologist, 61,* 204–217.
McAdams, D. P., Ruetzel, K., & Foley, J. M. (1986). Complexity and generativity at midlife: Relations among social motives, ego development, and adults' plans for the future. *Journal of Personality and Social Psychology, 50,* 800–807.
McAdams, D. P., de St. Aubin, E., & Logan, R. L. (1993). Generativity among young, midlife, and older adults. *Psychology and Aging, 8,* 221–230.
McAdams, D. P., Diamond, A., de St. Aubin, E., & Mansfield, E. D. (1997). Stories of commitment: The psychosocial construction of generative lives. *Journal of Personality and Social Psychology, 72,* 678–694.
McAdams, D. P., Hart, H. M., & Maruna, S. (1998). The anatomy of generativity. In D. P. McAdams and E. de St. Aubin (Eds.), *Generativity and adult development* (pp. 7–43). Washington: American Psychological Association Press.
McAdams, D. P., Reynolds, J., Lewis, M., Patten, A., & Bowman, P. J. (2001). When bad things turn good and good things turn bad: Sequences of redemption and contamination in life narrative, and their relation to psychological adaptation in midlife adults and in students. *Personality and Social Psychology Bulletin, 27,* 472–483.
McLean, K. C., Pasupathi, M., & Pals, J. L. (2007). Selves creating stories creating selves: A process model of self-development. *Personality and Social Psychology Review, 11,* 262–278.
Miller-McLemore, B. J. (2004). Generativity and gender: The politics of care. In E. de St. Aubin, D. P. McAdams, and T. C. Kim (Eds.), *The generative society* (pp. 175–194). Washington, DC: American Psychological Association Press.
Neugarten, B. L., & Hagestad, G. O. (1976). Aging and the life course. In R. H. Binstock and E. Shanas (Eds.), *Handbook of aging and the social sciences* (pp. 35–57). New York: D. Van Nostrand Reinhold.
Ochse, R., & Plug, C. (1986). Cross-cultural investigation of the validity of Erikson's theory of personality development. *Journal of Personality and Social Psychology, 50,* 800–807.
Peterson, B. E. (1998). Case studies of midlife generativity: Analyzing motivation and realization. In D. P. McAdams and E. de St. Aubin (Eds.), *Generativity and adult development* (pp. 101–131). Washington, DC: American Psychological Association Press.
Peterson, B. E. (2006). Generativity and successful parenting: An analysis of young adult outcomes. *Journal of Personality, 74,* 847–869.
Peterson, B. E., & Duncan, L. (2007). Midlife women's generativity and authoritarianism: Marriage, motherhood, and 10 years of aging. *Psychology and Aging, 22,* 411–419.
Peterson, B. E., & Klohnen, E. C. (1995). Realization of generativity in two samples of women at midlife. *Psychology and Aging, 10,* 20–29.
Peterson, C., & Seligman, M. E. P. (Eds.). (2004). *Character strengths and virtues: A handbook and classification.* New York: Oxford University Press.
Peterson, B. E., & Stewart, A. J. (1990). Using personal and fictional documents to assess psychosocial development: The case study of Vera Brittain's generativity. *Psychology and Aging, 5,* 400–411.

Peterson, B. E., & Stewart, A. J. (1993). Generativity and social motives in young adults. *Journal of Personality and Social Psychology, 65,* 186–198.

Peterson, B. E., Smirles, K. A., & Wentworth, P. A. (1997). Generativity and authoritarianism: Implications for personality, political involvement, and parenting. *Journal of Personality and Social Psychology, 72,* 1202–1216.

Pratt, M. W., Norris, J. E., Arnold, M. L., & Filyer, R. (1999). Generativity and moral development as predictors of value-socialization narratives for young persons across the adult life course: From lessons learned to stories shared. *Psychology and Aging, 14,* 414–426.

Pratt, M. W., Danso, H. A., Arnold, M. L., Norris, J. E., & Filyer, R. (2001). Adult generativity and the socialization of adolescents: Relations to mothers' and fathers' parenting beliefs, styles, and practices. *Journal of Personality, 69,* 89–120.

Rossi, A. S. (2001). *Caring and doing for others*. Chicago: University of Chicago Press.

Ryff, C. D., & Heincke, S. G. (1983). Subjective organization of personality in adulthood and aging. *Journal of Personality and Social Psychology, 44,* 807–816.

Seligman, M. E. P., & Csikszentmihalyi, M. (2000). Positive psychology: An introduction. *American Psychologist, 55,* 5–14.

Singer, J. A. (2004). Narrative identity and meaning making across the adult lifespan: An introduction. *Journal of Personality, 72,* 437–459.

Snarey, J., Kuehne, V. S., Son, L., Hauser, S., & Vaillant, G. E. (1987). The role of parenting in men's psychosocial development: A longitudinal study of early adulthood infertility and midlife generativity. *Developmental Psychology, 23,* 593–603.

Snarey, J. (1993). *How fathers care for the next generation: A four-decade study.* Cambridge, MA: Harvard University Press.

Stewart, A. J., & Ostrove, J. M. (1998). Women's personality in middle age: Gender, history, and midcourse corrections. *American Psychologist, 53,* 1185–1194.

Stewart, A. J., & Vandewater, E. A. (1998). The course of generativity. In D. P. McAdams and E. de St. Aubin (Eds.), *Generativity and adult development* (pp. 75–100). Washington, DC: American Psychological Association Press.

Stewart, A. J., Franz, C. E., & Layton, L. (1988). The changing self: Using personal documents to study lives. *Journal of Personality, 56,* 41–74.

Vaillant, G. E. (1977). *Adaptation to life.* Boston: Little, Brown.

Vaillant, G. E., & Milofsky, E. (1980). The natural history of male psychological health: IX. Empirical evidence for Erikson's model of the life cycle. *American Journal of Psychiatry, 137,* 1349–1359.

Van De Water, D., & McAdams, D. P. (1989). Generativity and Erikson's "belief in the species." *Journal of Research in Personality, 23,* 435–449.

Van Hiele, A., Mervielde, I., & de Fruyt, F. (2006). Stagnation and generativity: structure, validity, and differential relationships with adaptive and maladaptive personality. *Journal of Personality, 74,* 543–573.

Westermeyer, J. F. (2004). Predictors and characteristics of Erikson's life cycle model among men: A 32-year longitudinal study. *International Journal of Aging and Human Development, 58,* 29–48.

Whitbourne, S. K., Zuschlag, M. K., Elliot, L. B., & Waterman, A. S. (1992). Psychosocial development in adulthood: A 22-year sequential study. *Journal of Personality and Social Psychology, 63,* 260–271.

Yamada, Y. (2004). The generative life cycle model: Integration of Japanese folk images and generativity. In E. de St. Aubin, D. P. McAdams, and T. C. Kim (Eds.), *The generative society* (pp. 97–112). Washington, DC: American Psychological Association Press.

Chapter 14
The History and Future Directions of Positive Health Psychology

Christa K. Schmidt, Kathryn Schaefer Ziemer, Sarah Piontkowski and Trisha L. Raque-Bogdan

Positive psychology constructs have been present in physiological and mental health research for some time. From early research on the importance of social relationships to health, to the current provocative models that attempt to explain how the experience of positive emotions leads to better cardiovascular health, immune function, and slower disease progression, the field of positive health psychology has made significant contributions to our understandings of health and wellness. While many constructs related to a positive mind have been of interest to researchers in health psychology for decades, the organization and energy around investigating positive health has increased dramatically over the past decade (Schmidt et al. 2011). In this chapter, we will briefly describe the history and current status of positive health psychology before reviewing research on positive emotions, health behaviors, and social support, three well-established areas of research that exemplify positive health psychology. This overview will be followed by a look into the future directions of positive health, including emerging constructs worthy of greater exploration and the potential integration of positive health psychology and multicultural research. Finally, theoretical and methodological issues and challenges in positive health psychology will be addressed.

C. K. Schmidt (✉)
Psychology Department, Towson University, 8000 York Road, Towson 21252, USA
e-mail: ckschmidt@towson.edu

K. S. Ziemer · S. Piontkowski · T. L. Raque-Bogdan
University of Maryland, College Park, USA
e-mail: kschaefe@umd.edu

S. Piontkowski
e-mail: spiontko@umd.edu

T. L. Raque-Bogdan
e-mail: tlraque@gmail.com

J. D. Sinnott (ed.), *Positive Psychology*,
DOI 10.1007/978-1-4614-7282-7_14, © Springer Science+Business Media, LLC 2013

History and Current Status of Positive Health Psychology

Though the World Health Organization declared that the definition of health goes beyond "the absences of disease or infirmity" in 1946, it was only in the new century that the first organized effort in investigating the relationships between health and happiness took place. Ryff and Singer (2000) discussed the need for increased investigation into the neurobiological, behavioral, and psychosocial factors that lead to health benefits such as slowed disease progression and prevention of illness. The authors pointed out that positive health promotion needs to include an active examination of the positive aspects of social relationships, optimal health practices and behaviors, and psychological mechanisms such as hope, purpose, meaning, and positive emotions to more fully realize the field of positive health. The same year, the *American Psychologist* introduced a special issue on positive psychology, which included articles on the effects of positive emotions and beliefs on physical health. Salovey et al. (2000) reviewed the pathways through which positive moods may influence physical health, including enhanced immune system responding, greater self-efficacy in engaging in health-promoting behaviors, positive expectations, greater psychological resources, and enhanced social support. Taylor et al. (2000) reviewed research suggesting that the psychological beliefs of meaning, control, and optimism may be protective of physical health in the face of life-threatening illness such as HIV. Around the same time, a study on Catholic nuns analyzed the emotional content of autobiographies written early in life and found that greater positive emotion was associated with longevity six decades later (Danner et al. 2001).

Seligman (2008) built on this previous research and outlined the importance of measuring variables related to subjective, biological, and functional health in determining what constitutes positive health psychology. Subjective health includes the extent to which a person feels well and would rate their health as optimal. Variables in this realm include vigor, vitality, health-related quality of life, and physical well-being. The biological domain refers to a person's physical health and the presence or absence of disease or dysfunction. Research related to biological health includes an investigation of variables such as body mass index, blood pressure, immunology, and cardiovascular function. Finally, the functional health element refers to one's ability to function at an optimal or ideal level in terms of movement, strength, and absence of pain when meeting the demands of work, relationships, and leisure. This structure provided a map by which to begin operationalizing the variables that contribute to positive health, in order for investigations of these relationships to be on solid quantifiable footing. Seligman (2008) also suggested that researchers examine how these constructs contribute to dependent variables such as longevity, quality of life, health costs, prognosis, and mental health in the context of varying degrees of health and infirmity. While many of these variables have been investigated in the general health psychology literature for some time, Seligman (2008) believed that organization around the positive dimensions of health was warranted.

Within the past decade, there has been a dramatic increase in the number of studies exploring positive constructs within health psychology. A content analysis of three leading health psychology journals—*Health Psychology*, the *Journal of Health Psychology*, and the *International Journal of Behavioral Medicine*—revealed that there was a 227 % increase in the number of articles that included positive psychology constructs between the years of 1996–2000 and 2001–2005 (Schmidt et al. 2011). Overall, one-third of the articles published since each journal's inception mentioned at least one positive construct. While this provides encouraging evidence for the incorporation of positive psychology into health psychology, there is still much room for growth. For instance, only 3 % of the articles in the content analysis had an overtly positive focus, which suggests that while researchers are including positive constructs in health psychology, the context still remains focused on disease, dysfunction and negative effects (Schmidt et al. 2011). Moreover, several positive constructs such as social support and coping are used frequently in the health psychology literature, whereas other constructs are virtually nonexistent. For instance, the positive psychology constructs of altruism, leadership, savoring, and self-compassion were not found in any of the articles in the content analysis. Other constructs such as authenticity, courage, flow, humility, forgiveness, and mindfulness were found in only one or two articles. Thus, certain positive psychology constructs, which have been shown to be important predictors of well-being in the general positive psychology literature, remain relatively unexplored in health psychology research. In addition, there is a need to expand the populations examined by positive health psychology research, including racially and ethnically diverse individuals (Schmidt et al. 2011). To illustrate the foundation of positive health psychology research, the areas of positive emotions, health behaviors, and social support are described before introducing emerging constructs and populations that hold promise for positive health psychology.

Positive Emotions

The relationship between positive emotions and physical health has gained much attention in the past decade. Lyubormirsky et al. (2005) conducted a metaanalysis of longitudinal, cross-sectional, and experimental research examining how happiness relates to success across multiple life domains, including physical health. The authors identified 225 empirical papers that investigated the role of happiness and positive emotions in marriage, friendship, income, work performance, and health. The cross-sectional research examined in this analysis demonstrated that happy people self-report better health and fewer unpleasant physical symptoms, allergic reactions, and better quality of life when managing an illness such as cancer. This research also illustrated associations between positive affect and increased healthy behavior and immune functioning. The longitudinal research in the study, while sparser than cross-sectional designs, showed strong indicators that the experience of happiness precedes superior mental and physical health, longevity, and greater immunity to common illnesses. Finally, the experimental studies demonstrated that induced positive mood resulted in higher pain thresholds, lower blood pressure reactivity to stress, heightened willpower, and self-control over unhealthy behaviors (i.e., addictions), and a boost in immunity. Thus, in this large metaanalysis, the authors established that research is mounting regarding the influence of happiness on health. The research shows that success in life, including maintaining a healthy body and mind, does not only lead to happiness, but that the reverse is also true—individuals who experience frequent positive emotions have greater adaptability to physical health challenges.

Clearly, researchers in health psychology have heeded the call for a more succinct understanding of how positive emotions relate to, and perhaps influence, our overall health and wellness. While research had long ago established that individuals with depressed mood have more health problems than those who do not (Katon 1984; Salovey et al. 2000), understanding why individuals with a positive mood and disposition seem to be healthier has become a focus of inquiry unto itself. Several hypotheses and models have been proposed to explain this relationship.

In a review article examining the relation between positive affect and physical health, Pressman and Cohen (2005) asserted that there are multiple pathways that could explain this connection. First, the authors documented research suggesting that experiencing positive emotions for long periods of time, or maintaining a trait-like positive disposition, may have a direct influence on physical health. Specifically, enduring positivity has been associated with better health practices (e.g., exercise, sleep, nutrition), increased activation of the parasympathetic nervous system (e.g., reduced blood pressure, heart rate), reduction of stress-related hormones in the bloodstream (e.g., cortisol), increased endogenous opioids, heightened immune function (e.g., increased white blood cell activity), and enhanced social support. A second hypothesis reviewed by Pressman and Cohen (2005) discussed research that supports the notion that positive emotions buffer the deleterious effects of stress on physical health through increasing resilience, optimism, endurance, and social support. Therefore, positive emotions may be seen as a moderator of stress on health and illness. Third, positive emotions have been hypothesized to exert their influence on physical health by encouraging positive health practices such as sleep, exercise, relaxation, and proper nutrition (Smith and Baum 2003). Lastly, Pressman and Cohen (2005) suggested that individuals who have frequent positive emotions are likely to have less stress in their environments, which also factors into the relationship to physical health. Thus, there are multiple pathways that need to be examined with regard to the influence of positive emotions on physical health.

One model that has received attention from researchers is the "broaden-and-build" theory of positive emotions (Fredrickson 1998, 2001). This theory posits that the experience of positive emotions such as joy, contentment, interest, and love, while fleeting and momentary, can broaden people's thought–action repertoires and build their enduring personal resources, including resources for physical health (e.g., health behaviors; Fredrickson 2001). While thought–action repertoires tend to narrow following the experience of negative emotions such as fear or anger in the "fight-or-flight" response, the experience of positive emotions allows individuals a wider capacity for creative and inspired thoughts that can be savored and shared with others. In turn, this increased capacity leads to heightened personal resources, as the experience of positive emotions encourages people to play more, connect with others, think deeply, and create. Thus, while the experience of positive emotions is temporary, the benefits of increased resources endure well beyond the moments of joy, contentment, interest, and love. This theory has been used to examine the effect of broadened thought–action repertoires and increased personal resources on mental health outcomes such as psychological well-being, life satisfaction, and depressive symptoms (Fredrickson et al. 2008), and it is beginning to be used to understand how positive emotions may influence physical health outcomes. Drawing from the "broaden-and-build" theory, one could argue that experiencing positive emotions could lead to greater physical activity (in the form of play and exercise), more time spent building attachments with supportive others, heightened intellectual activity and mindfulness, and greater psychological well-being, all of which have implications for physical health. These possible links deserve more empirical attention to determine if theories, similar to "broaden-and-build," are relevant for understanding the role of positive emotions in health.

Another area of attention in health psychology research related to positive emotions has been the extent to which having a positive disposition, mostly defined as optimism, influences physical health outcomes. In one meta-analysis of 83 studies examining the strength of the association between optimism and physical health, Rasmussen et al. (2009) found that there was a small to moderate effect for this relation. Specifically, people who scored higher on measures of optimism also rated better physical health along a number of outcome measures including mortality, survival, immune function, cardiovascular health, cancer, pain, and pregnancy outcomes. However, the authors also found that when health outcomes were measured subjectively, the sizes of the effects of the relation between optimism and physical health were nearly double those of health outcomes measured objectively. While one would expect optimistic individuals to rate their health better in self-report measures, this finding points out a note of caution when interpreting the findings regarding positive traits and physical health outcomes: the use of self-report measures can inflate the relationship between optimism and physical health outcomes. The authors of this metaanalysis caution against relying on subjective self-report measures of physical health when examining such constructs as optimism and positive traits or states as there is likely more error in the relationship than when measured by objective measures of health.

Health Behaviors

Health behaviors involve those actions taken to maintain, attain, or regain health and prevent illness (*Mosby's Medical Dictionary* 2009). These behaviors have the potential to enhance physical and psychological health and well-being such that positive health practices are associated with living longer, healthier, and happier lives. When considering the behaviors that relate to optimal health, it is important to consider those behaviors that are associated with enhancement and flourishing physical and psychological health. Three positive health practices in particular have been identified as critical for maintaining physical well-being and quality of life (Schneider and Davidson 2003): physical exercise, restorative sleep, and nutrition.

Exercise

The beneficial effects of exercise have long been acknowledged in the literature, both through self-report and objective measures of health. Exercise has been found to affect self-reported functional health as well as overall well-being. The physiological benefits of exercise are well-documented and include improved strength and endurance (Ades et al. 1996), physical performance (Wang et al. 2011), slower cognitive decline in older adults (Deslandes et al. 2009), and a longer life (Hakim et al. 1998). Research has found that exercise can decrease risk for certain chronic diseases such as cardiovascular disease (Martel et al. 1999), osteoporosis (Tolomio et al. 2010), and diabetes (Takemura et al. 1999). The importance of exercise to maintaining physiological health is clear.

Exercise also has numerous benefits for mental health, subjective well-being, and happiness. Participation in exercise is connected to increased happiness and overall well-being (Moore and Bracegirdle 1994). Vigorous exercise such as running was found to increase positive emotions including excitement and pride (Kerr et al. 2006). Further, the association between positive emotions and exercise seems to work in the other direction as well. For instance, Baruth et al. (2011) found that men who reported a more positive outlook on life were more likely to maintain an exercise program. In addition, when exercise includes a social component such as an organized walking group, participation in the group is connected to greater exercise frequency, higher subjective well-being, greater life satisfaction, and reduced loneliness (McAuley et al. 2000). Exercise has clear implications for the field of positive health.

Sleep

Another behavior that has implications for positive physical and psychological health is the extent to which one has good sleep habits. The quality of sleep in particular seems to be an important area as it can influence daytime functioning, mood and well-being (Ancoli-Israel 1997). Improving sleep quality has been found to improve alertness, motivation, refreshment, concentration (Kohsaka et al. 1999), and activities of daily living (Tanaka and Shirakawa 2004). In addition, better sleep quality has been associated with greater positive affect (Bower et al. 2010; Norlander et al. 2005) and higher global well-being (Howell et al. 2008). Aside from the quality of sleep, the amount of sleep also seems to hold implications for health. Sleep duration has been linked with longevity (Cappuccio et al. 2010), levels of vigor (Bardwell et al. 1999), happiness (Fulgini and Hardway 2006), and psychological well-being (Hamilton et al. 2007; Ryff et al. 2004). Moreover, positive affect and well-being have been directly linked to good sleep independently of sociodemographic factors such as age, household income, and self-rated health (Steptoe et al. 2008). Earlier sleep onset has also been found to directly correlate with daily ratings of positive mood (Totterdell et al. 1994). While this represents a promising area of research, there is still insufficient evidence to draw causal conclusions about the quality or length of sleep and its impact on health (Buysse et al. 2010). The relationship between sleep and well-being may very well be bidirectional, with positive health and psychological states promoting better sleep, and better sleep leading to greater well-being.

Nutrition

In addition to exercise and sleep, nutrition can also play a role in an individual's health and well-being. Nutrition includes the minerals, vitamins, and nutrients in our diet that our body needs in order to be healthy, function optimally, and prevent illness (Thomas 2006). A literature review of observational studies found that consuming higher levels of antioxidants was associated with a lower risk for major chronic diseases (Thomas 2006) such as heart disease (Hung et al. 2004) and stroke (Sauvaget et al. 2003). Research has also shown the beneficial effects of vitamins on reducing the risk of chronic diseases such as cancer (Hercberg et al. 2004), cardiovascular disease (Moller et al. 2004; Ramos and Martinez-Castelao 2008; Yoshihara, Fujiwara, Suzuki 2010), and macular degeneration (Evans 2003). Aside from physical health, a reciprocal relationship may exist between healthy eating and positive affect. Preliminary evidence suggests that diet influences mood (Li et al. 2011; Sánchez-Villegas et al. 2006) and positive mood has been found to result in healthier eating behaviors (Turner et al. 2010).

Social Support and Relationships

The influence of social relationships on physical health may be the most researched area of positive health psychology, and investigation into this relation began long before positive health psychology was labeled a field of study. There is strong evidence that the presence of social relationships in a person's life has as much to do with her or his physical health as does exercise, diet, and smoking (House et al. 1988). Social support has been shown to play an important role in cardiovascular, endocrine, and immune system functioning (Uchino et al. 1996) such that higher levels of social support are associated with better physical health indicators (e.g., lower blood pressure, reduced cortisol in the bloodstream, greater natural killer (NK) cell lysis). Accordingly, the absence of social relationships has been shown to predict higher rates of mortality, greater morbidity (Blazer 1982), and greater risk for numerous ailments from cardiovascular disease (Grant et al. 2009) to the common cold (Cohen 2004). Further, having more supportive individuals in one's life is related to positive health practices such as exercise, maintaining a healthy diet (Yarcheski et al. 2004), and adherence to medical treatments (DiMatteo 2004). Thus, social support has received a great deal of attention from researchers in health psychology and the positive elements of relationships seem central to an understanding of what contributes to positive physical health.

Similar to positive emotions, several hypothesized mechanisms for the role of social support in physical health have been presented in the health literature. One such mechanism, known as the "buffering hypothesis," states that social support reduces stress-related hormones, which in turn has a buffering effect on the physiological consequences of stress (Cohen and Wills 1985). Thus, when a person perceives the availability of supportive resources during a stressful situation, she/he is more likely to cope effectively with the stressor. Health-related research that supports this notion includes studies that demonstrate higher levels of cortisol production in response to a stressful activity among people who report higher degrees of social isolation (e.g., Grant et al. 2009).

Another possible pathway in which social support exerts its influence on health is through its relation to better health practices (Yarcheski et al. 2004). Evidence to support this hypothesis is mixed, however, and seems to be more related to specific populations and specific behaviors. For example, there is evidence that support from family members predicts exercise behavior in adolescents (Beets et al. 2010), perceptions of social support predict treatment adherence in individuals with HIV (Gardenier et al. 2010), and quitting smoking is more likely to be successful when a person is surrounded by supportive others (Johnson et al. 2009). However, in their meta-analysis examining the potential pathways for which social support exerts its influence on physical health, Uchino et al. (1996) did not find support for the idea that social support exerts its influence on health through its effect on health behaviors. One possibility is that different types of support exert different influences on varying behaviors, and therefore cannot be considered as a broad influence. Further, as discussed earlier, the association between social support and positive emotions may contribute to enhanced physical health, as time spent with supportive others increases positive feelings, which has both direct and indirect implications for health (Pressman and Cohen 2005).

Another element of social support research that has implications for positive health psychology is the vast number of dimensions that have emerged as potentially meaningful. For instance, not only has research examined both the quantity and quality of social relationships, but social support has also been operationalized in numerous ways. Cohen and Wills (1985) made the distinction between the structure of a support network (i.e., the perception of available support) and the function (i.e., the purpose the support network serves), and demonstrated that both aspects were related to health, but via different pathways. Numerous measures of social support have operationalized support in differing ways, including global perceptions of support, sources of support (e.g., friends or family), functions of a support network (e.g., emotional vs. instrumental), and situation-specific support that arises in response to identifiable problems (e.g., coping with illness; Uchino et al. 1996). There is also some evidence that social support can have deleterious effects on health such as when the reference group models unhealthy behavior, or when the support received leads a person to feel indebted to another (Thoits 2011). Hence, the breadth of research into social support demonstrates the complexity of this construct and how complicated its relationship may be to health-related issues.

Emerging Areas of Positive Health Psychology: New Constructs

Research on positive emotions, health behaviors, and social support represent well-developed areas of positive health psychology that can serve as models as the field continues to grow. We feel that certain emerging constructs hold particular promise for positive health psychology and warrant further exploration. These constructs include self-compassion, altruism, courage, gratitude, and benefit finding.

Self-Compassion

Self-compassion has recently become a burgeoning area of research in psychology. This construct involves experiencing kindness towards oneself, being mindful of one's suffering, and recognizing one's experience as part of the common human experience (Neff 2003). Most studies on this topic have explored the relationship between self-compassion and emotional well-being; however, research is beginning to examine links to physical health as well. Preliminary evidence suggests that self-compassion may be related to health behavior and attitudes. For instance, recent studies found that self-compassion was associated with greater intrinsic motivation to exercise (Magnus et al. 2010) and less objectified body consciousness (Mosewich et al. 2011). Leary and colleagues have also found promising results in studies that have not yet been published (Weir 2011). In one study, self-compassion appeared to buffer the emotional effects of medical problems such as pain, limited mobility, and hearing loss, in the elderly. In another study, high self-compassion was associated with practicing safe sex among women with HIV. Thus, it could be that self-compassion leads to better emotional well-being which translates into good health practices and better physical well-being. Self-compassion represents a promising area for enhancing individuals health, and further research is needed to explore these links.

Altruism

Preliminary research has found strong correlations between altruism and indices of health, including well-being, happiness, and longevity (Post 2005). One way that altruism has been operationalized is by providing social support and help to others. Several studies have found that giving social support is associated with lower morbidity (Brown et al. 2003; Brown et al. 2005) and people who provide more assistance to others report significantly better physical health (Krause et al. 1999).

Another way that altruism has been operationalized is through participating in volunteer activities. Research has found that volunteering is associated with a lowered risk of death, even after controlling for confounding factors such as age, gender, chronic conditions, exercise, health habits, social support, and psychological health (Musick et al. 1999; Oman et al. 1999). These findings hold implications for public health, where nurturing helping behavior and altruistic attitudes may reduce the burden of disease within society. Altruism remains a promising area for health-related research and interventions, but consensus regarding the definition and operationalization of altruism is needed before research in this area can progress. Further, more research is needed on the physiological mediators between altruism and health and possible causal effects, and better measures of altruism need to be developed and validated (Post 2005).

Courage

Courage represents another construct that holds promise for the area of positive health psychology, but requires further definition and examination. Courage appears to be a personal strength that would likely promote health and well-being. Maddi's (2004) work on hardiness, or the attributes of people who face difficulties and stressors head-on with courage and motivation, provides a backdrop for potential research into the effect of courage on health. The quality of hardiness has been found to relate to greater participation in healthy behaviors and better indicators of physical health in the midst of stressful experiences (Maddi 2002, 2004). While the qualities of people who demonstrate courage have been investigated in this literature, courage by itself may play a role in physical health. Lopez et al. (2003) propose that psychological courage applies to situations where threat represents an illness or the side effects of medical treatment. Most of the current studies on courage have been qualitative research on individuals with long-term threats to well-being. Finfgeld (1999) conducted a metainterpretation that synthesized the findings from six qualitative studies examining courage among individuals with physical problems, HIV, terminal cancer, and experience with sexual assault. Courage in this case referred to "long-term stamina to push beyond incessant challenges" (p. 813), which seems to be particularly relevant to health psychology where threats to physical well-being often require long-term management. Results indicated that being courageous led to personal integrity and thriving, suggesting that this construct could be useful for enhancing the health of individuals. Thus, the construct of courage has potential implications for positive health, but is in need of further development and clarity in its definition (Woodard and Pury 2007).

Gratitude

Similar to courage, gratitude represents a widely experienced phenomenon that has received little attention until recently within the psychological literature (Nelson 2009). Gratitude has been linked to psychological well-being (Wood et al. 2009); however, empirical evidence exploring the link between gratitude and physical health remains limited. One study found that those high in gratitude reported fewer poor mental and physical health days as compared to those low in gratitude (Otey-Scott 2007). Another study conducted an intervention aimed at increasing gratitude and found that those who participated in the intervention reported fewer symptoms of physical illness and spent more time exercising than those in a control group (Emmons and McCullough 2003). Gratitude differs from other positive constructs in that it involves an interpersonal component, and as such, researchers have proposed that gratitude may influence physical and mental well-being through the promotion of high-quality relationships (Algoe et al. 2008; Algoe and Stanton 2011; Cohen 2004; Nelson 2009). While preliminary research has found promising results regarding the beneficial effects of gratitude on health, more studies are needed to decipher the nature of this relationship.

Benefit Finding

Benefit finding represents a construct that has received increased attention in research, but has suffered from overstated claims and requires further understanding regarding definition and measurement (Lechner et al. 2009). While many individuals who are diagnosed with a serious illness often report finding hidden benefits to their condition, the literature reveals mixed findings regarding the association between benefit finding and improvements in physical health. Several studies have demonstrated beneficial effects of benefit finding on heart-attack morbidity (Affleck et al. 1987), AIDS mortality (Bower et al. 1998; Ickovics et al. 2006), physical activity in HIV patients (Littlewood et al. 2008) and physiology in cancer patients (McGregor and Antoni 2009). However, a metaanalysis found that benefit finding was unrelated to subjective physical health and global quality of life, which included aspects of physical health (Helgeson et al. 2006). Many of the studies conducted on benefit finding suffer from small sample sizes and use retrospective, as opposed to prospective, study designs. Lechner et al. (2009) lamented that the field lacks psychometrically rigorous measurement and consensus regarding the conceptual nature of benefit finding. Moreover, much remains unknown regarding a possible link between benefit finding and physical health, including the mediating pathways (Bower et al. 2009). While there seems to be initial promise with regard to the role of benefit finding in positive health, this area requires further research before definitive claims can be made (Coyne and Tennen 2010).

Emerging Areas of Positive Health Psychology: Diverse Populations

Another area of positive health psychology that needs further investigation is the intersection between positive health and multicultural considerations. Historically, the vast majority of the literature on health in culturally diverse communities has focused on health disparities, particularly as experienced by racial and ethnic minorities (Clark et al. 1999; Davis et al. 2005; Williams and Mohammed 2009). Scholars agree that a myriad of community, economic, and social factors contribute to disparities in health (Davis et al. 2005; Herman et al. 2007). As a consequence of these factors, individuals in culturally diverse communities, as compared to the population as a whole, disproportionately experience physical and mental illness with greater frequency and severity (Davis et al. 2005). Furthermore, due to inequities related to race, poverty, class, and gender, culturally diverse individuals experience barriers to accessing health care services (both preventative and remedial), further compounding the problem (Caldwell-Colbert et al. 2009; Herman et al. 2007).

An important area of research on the topic of health disparities has focused on the consequences of racism on health. Studies have shown that perceived discrimination acts as a psychosocial stressor, and plays an important role in explaining racial and ethnic disparities in both physical and mental health outcomes (Clark et al. 1999; D'Anna et al. 2010; Williams and Mohammed 2009). For example, D'Anna et al. (2010) examined the relationship between perceived discrimination in healthcare and self-reported physical, emotional, and functional health disparities within a multiculturally diverse sample of more than 55,000 adults. Results indicated that participants who perceived racial discrimination within the healthcare system were two to three times more likely than those who did not perceive discrimination to report adverse mental and physical health symptoms. The effects of discrimination on emotional and physical health were less apparent for participants of higher socioeconomic status, suggesting that socioeconomic status may be an important mediator between perceived discrimination and health outcomes. Accordingly, one step in this line of research is to investigate additional variables that may mediate or moderate the relationship between racism-related stress and health outcomes. Researchers have begun to explore not only the association between perceived discrimination and negative health outcomes, but also the value of specific protective factors that might allow for cultural minority individuals to experience *positive* health outcomes, despite the presence of discrimination (Utsey and Constantine 2008).

There is a pronounced scarcity of literature on the health-related strengths in multicultural communities. Promisingly, scholars have noticed this paucity, resulting in an increase in the research on positive health, optimal functioning and multicultural issues in recent years. This research has focused on exploring health-related constructs and interventions that are particularly germane to multicultural populations, including resilience, hope, faith and protective factors as strength-based resources across the life span, even in the presence of health-related barriers and inequities (Caldwell-Colbert et al. 2009).

One such strengths-based resource that has received attention is the construct of perceived bicultural competence. David et al. (2009) define bicultiral competence as the belief in one's ability to function interpersonally and behaviorally in two cultures. This construct is relevant for bicultural individuals, or those who have been exposed to two different cultures and have internalized more than one cultural knowledge system, which includes cultural or ethnic minorities, multiracial individuals, and immigrants (Hong et al. 2000). Many bicultural individuals face the challenge of meeting the values and standards of both the mainstream and their heritage culture, and unsuccessful navigation of this challenging cultural landscape can result in adverse psychological outcomes such as depression and anxiety (David et al. 2009; Safdar et al. 2003). However, not all cultural or ethnic minorities experience psychological distress as research has shown that those individuals with high levels of bicultural competence can experience psychological well-being in multicultural environments (David et al. 2009). Specifically, bicultural competence has been associated with lower levels of anxiety and depression, fewer physical health symptoms, and higher life satisfaction, enculturation (a strong adherence to one's heritage culture), and levels of ethnic identity (David et al. 2009; Safdar et al. 2003). Thus, bicultural competence may have important implications for optimal health among multicultural populations, and warrants further investigation.

Ethnic identity, another variable that may be a protective factor against negative health outcomes for people of color, has been the focus of research that pertains to well-being. For instance, a meta-analysis found that ethnic identity was more strongly related to measures of positive well-being (e.g., satisfaction with life), and less strongly correlated with compromised well-being (e.g., depression and anxiety) among ethnic minorities (Smith and Silva 2010). This finding suggests that high levels of ethnic identity may be a protective factor against distress, and while its role in physical health has not been investigated, research can begin to examine this next logical connection. Promisingly, the meta-analysis found that these results held across participant race, gender, and socioeconomic status, suggesting that ethnic identity is meaningfully related to well-being, not only for a specific group, but across people of color.

Although some meaningful advances have been made in recent years in the area of multicultural health, there is much room for growth and improvement. Health disparities often are conceptualized as one of many forms of oppression for marginalized groups, and as such, scholarly and practical work in the area of reducing disparities and promoting optimal health fits in well with many psychologists' goals to champion multiculturalism, social justice and prevention (Buki 2007; Tucker et al. 2007). Accordingly, psychologists' involvement in reducing health disparities and increasing mental and physical health is an integral part of a multidisciplinary national effort, and as such, there is the potential for considerable collaboration across fields (Buki 2007). Examining health disparities through the lens of positive health also leaves room for discovering the protective factors that may play a role in reducing negative health outcomes for people of color. In a content analysis of articles in health psychology journals that maintained a positive psychological focus, only 15 % of the studies included in the analysis addressed disparities in health care and the dissemination of resources (Schmidt et al. 2011). Thus, the area of multicultural considerations in positive health is ripe for investigation.

Challenges in Positive Health Psychology: Measurement Issues and Methodology Concerns

While the intersection of positive psychology and health psychology has made strides and holds great promise, the field faces theoretical and methodological issues and challenges. As interest in the relationship between positive psychological constructs and physical health outcomes has grown in scientific communities and the popular press, many have cautioned about the claims outpacing science. Coyne and Tennen (2010) point out that many of the positive psychological constructs under investigation in health fields are in need of further development, elucidation, and measurement.

One of the biggest challenges for researchers lies in operationalizing and studying positive health in a way that actually reflects optimal functioning rather than the absence of illness or disease (Seligman 2008). Many studies claim to research positive aspects of health such as quality of life, but operationalize these variables using negative indicators of health such as the presence of physical symptoms (Schmidt et al. 2011). Ryff and Singer (2000) identified prevention as the cornerstone of good public health and viewed the use of optimal health behaviors as one of the best ways to accomplish this end. However, before this goal can be accomplished, the field requires greater clarification regarding what constitutes positive health and how it should be measured in order to conduct more rigorous research which can then inform interventions for the public.

To accurately operationalize and measure positive health, it is first necessary to define the construct of positive health in a comprehensive way. Ryff and Singer (2000) proposed that human wellness is composed of the mind, the body, and the connection between the two, concluding that comprehensive assessments of positive health then need to measure both physical and mental well-being as well as their interconnections. They also defined positive health as a multidimensional dynamic process that involves the expression of flourishing physical health and engagement in living. Seligman's (2008) model of subjective, biological, and functional health represented another approach to conceptualizing positive health in a comprehensive way.

While these conceptualizations of optimal health provide a good theoretical basis and help researchers define positive phenomena, instruments that measure positive health are still sorely lacking. As previously stated, many of the measures that intend to assess positive health actually evaluate the absence of negative health indicators such as symptoms or diseases (Schmidt et al. 2011). For instance, measures of functional health still focus largely on the impact of illness and activity limitations due to poor health (e.g., Anderson et al. 1996), rather than on positive physical capacity or optimal functioning as described by Seligman (2008). Even quality of life, which is generally associated with well-being and the capacity to engage in meaningful thoughts and behaviors (Meyers et al. 2000; Schneider and Davidson 2003), has traditionally been measured in a negative way. One example is the Health-Related

Quality of Life measure which assesses the number of days that individuals experience poor physical or mental health (CDCP 2000). As a result, Fava and Sonino (2000) called for improved quality of life assessments that measure higher levels of functioning and well-being (e.g., mastery, purpose in life). Recently, Gill et al. (2011) answered this call by developing a conceptually based and psychometrically sound quality of life measure for physical activity and health promotion that emphasizes positive well-being. The measure assesses the full range of quality of life in domains such as social, spiritual, emotional, cognitive, physical, and activities of daily living. This study provides a good model for future research that aims to develop measures assessing the optimal range of health in areas where these assessments are still lacking.

Aside from measurement issues, researchers need to be aware of possible misinterpretations of positive health research that could result in negative outcomes such as victim-blaming or prematurely developing interventions. One of the unexpected results of the positive psychology movement has been interpretation that people may be responsible for their own illness due to a lack of positive thinking (Aspinwall and Tedeschi 2010; Byrne 2006; Ehrenreich 2007). The belief that health problems can be overcome with merely a positive attitude promotes the idea that those who lack a positive attitude are to blame for their illness. Coyne and Tennen (2010) provide the example of how research related to benefit finding when living with a chronic disease has assumed that benefit finding is always a positive reaction to an illness and that something is lacking in individuals who do not find benefits in challenges to physical health. Further, benefit-finding research has jumped from trying to define the construct to creating interventions aimed at increasing benefit finding for seriously ill individuals without empirical support. Although positive health psychology research is making great advances in establishing its theoretical foundations, little has been written about its clinical application. To help prevent and diminish these misguided steps, researchers need to use restraint when making claims about the implications of their research. A focus on rigorous design and testing of interventions as well as accurate reporting is in order to prevent harm and promote good science.

There are several ways to advance our understanding of positive health, while avoiding the potential pitfalls described above. Rather than focusing solely on positive outcomes, researchers are encouraged to explore both the positive and negative outcomes of illness in order to provide a more balanced perspective (Aspinwall and Tedeschi 2010). Positive psychology has been criticized for failing to acknowledge that positive and negative experiences, emotions, and behaviors can coexist, and do not operate on a single continuum (Aspinwall and Tedeschi 2010). While research in psychology has been cited by positive psychology researchers for a focus on dysfunction, hardship, and negative emotions, positive psychology sometimes swings the pendulum too far to the other end of the spectrum by ignoring the presence of negative experiences in lieu of a focus on that which is exclusively positive. Research in positive health psychology would do best to heed these lessons and present a balanced investigation of the contributions of negative and positive constructs to physical health outcomes. Moreover, emphasis needs to be placed on prospective, process-oriented, and experimental designs in addition to cross-sectional studies or anecdotal reports in order to accurately delineate the relationship between positive constructs and health outcomes. Part of understanding this relationship involves uncovering the mechanisms through which positive phenomena influence the etiology and progression of diseases. Ryff and Singer (2000) called for more research that examines the neurobiological mechanisms through which health protection occurs, especially as it relates to different health factors. Similarly, it is important to explore cognitive, social, developmental and structural pathways that may connect positive phenomena with health (Aspinwall and Tedeschi 2010). Finally, researchers are encouraged to advance the field by challenging currently held assumptions about the effectiveness of interventions and identifying potential pitfalls in the application of research findings (Aspinwall and Tedeschi 2010). This will stimulate the creation of more effective interventions and the identification of conditions that may limit intervention success (Tennen and Affleck 2009). If future research can develop instruments that accurately define and measure positive health, incorporate positive and negative constructs and outcomes, use rigorous research designs to examine multiple pathways between positive phenomena and health, and constructively critique the findings from the field, our knowledge, understanding, and implementation of positive health will be greatly enhanced.

Conclusion

Much progress has been made in the field of positive health psychology since the turn of the century. Health-related research on positive psychological constructs has more than doubled (Schmidt et al. 2011) and multiple models for capturing the elements of positive health (e.g., subjective, biological, and functional) are in the process of being theorized and tested. Positive emotions, health behaviors, and social support have served as pioneers in this new frontier of research, and there is much room for further expansion in our empirical understanding of positive health psychology, especially in the operationalization of new constructs and in the intersection with multicultural issues. The field of positive health psychology can further advance by addressing measurement issues and methodological concerns. In doing so, positive health psychology holds great promise for expanding our understanding of physical and psychological flourishing.

References

Ades, P., Ballor, D. L., Ashikaga, T., Utton, J. L., & Nair, K. S. (1996). Weight training improves walking endurance in healthy elderly persons. *Annals of Internal Medicine, 124,* 568–572.

Affleck, G., Tennen, H., Croog, S., & Levine, S. (1987). Causal attribution, perceived benefits, and morbidity following a heart attack: An 8-year study. *Journal of Consulting and Clinical Psychology, 55,* 29–35.

Algoe, S. B., Haidt, J., & Gable, S. L. (2008). Beyond reciprocity: Gratitude and relationships in everyday life. *Emotion, 8,* 425–429.

Algoe, S. B., & Stanton, A. L. (2011). Gratitude when it is needed most: Social functions of gratitude in women with metastatic breast cancer. *Emotion, 12,* 163–168.
Ancoli-Israel, S. (1997). Sleep problems in older adults: Putting myths to bed. *Geriatrics, 52,* 20–30.
Anderson, C., Laubscher, S., & Burns, R. (1996). Validation of the Short Form 36 (SF −36) health survey questionnaire among stroke patients. *Stroke, 27,* 1812–1816.
Aspinwall, L. G., & Tedeschi, R. G. (2010). The value of positive psychology for health psychology: Progress and pitfalls in examining the relation of positive phenomena to health. *Annals of Behavioral Medicine, 39,* 4–15.
Bardwell, W. A., Berry, C. C., Ancoli-Israel, A., & Dimsdale, J. E. (1999). Psychological correlates of sleep apnea. *Journal of Psychosomatic Research, 47,* 583–596.
Baruth, M., Lee, D., Sui, X., Church, T. S., Marcus, B. H., Wilcox, S., & Blair, S. N. (2011). Emotional outlook on life predicts increases in physical activity among initially inactive men. *Health Education and Behavior, 38,* 150–158.
Beets, M. W., Cardinal, B. J., & Alderman, B. L. (2010). Parental support and the physical activity-related behaviors of youth: A review. *Health Education and Behavior, 37,* 621–644.
Blazer, D. G. (1982). Social support and mortality in an elderly community population. *American Journal of Epidemiology, 115,* 684–694.
Bower, B., Bylsma, L. M., Morris, B. H., & Rottenberg, J. (2010). Poor reported sleep quality predicts low positive affect in daily life among healthy and mood-disordered persons. *Journal of Sleep Research, 19,* 323–332.
Bower, J. E., Kemeny, M. E., Taylor, S. E., & Fahey, J. L. (1998). Cognitive processing, discovery of meaning, CD4 decline, and AIDS-related mortality among bereaved HIV-seropositive men. *Journal of Consulting and Clinical Psychology, 66,* 979–986.
Bower, J. E., Moskowitz, J. T., & Epel, E. (2009). Is benefit finding good for your health? Pathways linking positive life changes after stress and physical health outcomes. *Current Directions in Psychological Science, 18,* 337–341.
Brown, W. M., Consedine, N. S., & Magai, C. (2005). Altruism relates to health in an ethnically diverse sample of older adults. *Journal of Gerontology, 60B,* 143–152.
Brown, S. L., Nesse, R. M., Vinokur, A. D., & Smith, D. M. (2003). Providing social support may be more beneficial than receiving it: Results from a prospective study of mortality. *Psychological Science, 14,* 320–327.
Buki, L. P. (2007). Reducing health disparities: The perfect fit for counseling psychology. *The Counseling Psychologist, 35*(5), 706–715.
Buysse, D. J., Grunstein, R., Horne, J., & Lavie, P. (2010). Can an improvement in sleep positively impact on health? *Sleep Medicine Review, 14,* 405–410.
Byrne, R. (2006). *The secret.* New York: Atria Books.
Caldwell-Colbert, A. T., Parks, F. M., & Eshun, S. (2009). Positive psychology: African American strengths, resilience, and protective factors. In H. Neville, B. Tynes, & S. Utsey (Eds.), *Handbook of African American psychology* (pp. 375–384). Thousand Oaks: Sage.
Cappuccio, F. P., D'Elia, L., Strazzullo, P., & Miller, M. A. (2010). Sleep duration and all-cause mortality: A systematic review and meta-analysis of prospective studies. *Sleep, 33,* 585–592.
Centers for Disease Control and Prevention (CDCP). (2000). *Measuring healthy days.* Atlanta: Centers for Disease Control and Prevention.
Clark, R., Anderson, N. B., Clark, V. R., & Williams, D. R. (1999). Racism as a stressor for African Americans: A biopsychosocial model. *American Psychologist, 54,* 805–816.
Cohen, S. (2004). Social relationships and health. *American Psychologist, 59,* 676–684.
Cohen, S. & Wills, T. A. (1985). Stress, social support, and the buffering hypothesis. *Psychological Bulletin, 98,* 310–357.
Coyne, J. C., & Tennen, H. (2010). Positive psychology in cancer care: Bad science, exaggerated claims, and unproven medicine. *Annals of Behavioral Medicine, 39,* 16–26.
D'Anna, L. H., Ponce, N. A., & Siegel, J. M. (2010). Racial and ethnic health disparities: Evidence of discrimination's effects across the SEP spectrum. *Ethnicity & Health, 15*(2), 121–143.

Danner, D. D., Snowdon, D. A., & Friesen, W. V. (2001). Positive emotions in early life and longevity: Findings from the nun study. *Journal of Personality and Social Psychology, 80,* 804–813.
David, E. J. R., Okazaki, S., & Saw, A. (2009). Bicultural self-efficacy among college students: Initial scale development and mental health correlates. *Journal of Counseling Psychology, 56,* 211–226.
Davis, R., Cook, D., & Cohen, L. (2005). A community resilience approach to reducing ethnic and racial disparities in health. *American Journal of Public Health, 95*(12), 2168–2173.
Deslandes, A., Moraes, H., Ferreira, C., Veiga, H., Silveria, H., Mouta, R., et al. (2009). Exercise and mental health: Many reasons to move. *Neuropsychobiology, 59,* 191–198.
DiMatteo, M. R. (2004). Social support and patient adherence to medical treatment: A meta-analysis. *Health Psychology, 23,* 207–218.
Ehrenreich, B. (2007). *What causes cancer: Probably not you. Huffington Post.* Retrieved October, 1, 2011, from http://www.huffingtonpost.com/barbara-ehrenreich/what-causes-cancer-proba_b_56983.html.
Emmons, R. A., & McCullough, M. E. (2003). Counting blessings versus burdens: An experimental investigation of gratitude and subjective well-being in daily life. *Journal of Personality and Social Psychology, 84,* 377–389.
Evans, J. R. (2003). Antioxidant vitamin and mineral supplements for age-related macular degeneration. *Cochrane Database System Review,* 3. doi:10.1002/14651858.CD000253.pub3.
Fava, G. A., & Sonino, N. (2000). Psychosomatic medicine: Emerging trends and perspectives. *Psychotherapy and Psychosomatics, 69,* 184–197.
Finfgeld, D. L. (1999). Courage as a process of pushing beyond the struggle. *Qualitative Health Research, 9,* 803–814.
Fredrickson, B. L. (1998). What good are positive emotions? *Review of General Psychology, 2,* 300–319.
Fredrickson, B. L. (2001). The role of positive emotions in positive psychology: The broaden-and-build theory of positive emotions. *American Psychologist, 56,* 218–226.
Fredrickson, B. L., Cohn, M. A., Coffey, K. A., Pek, J., & Finkel, S. M. (2008). Open hearts build lives: Positive emotions, induced through loving-kindness meditation, build consequential personal resources. *Journal of Personality and Social Psychology, 95,* 1045–1062.
Fulgini, A. J., & Hardway, C. (2006). Daily variation in adolescents' sleep, activities, and psychological well-being. *Journal of Research on Adolescence, 16,* 353–378.
Gardenier, D., Andrews, C. M., Thomas, D. C., Bookhardt-Murray, L. J., & Fitzpatrick, J. J. (2010). Social support and adherence: Differences among clients in an AIDS day health care program. *JANAC: Journal of the Association of Nurses in AIDS Care, 21,* 75–85.
Gill, D. L., Chang, Y., Murphy, K. M., Speed, K. M., Hammond, C. C., Rodriguez, E. A., et al. (2011). Quality of life assessment for physical activity and health promotion. *Applied Research Quarterly Life, 6,* 181–200.
Grant, N., Hamer, M., & Steptoe, A. (2009). Social isolation and stress-related cardiovascular, lipid, and cortisol responses. *Annals of Behavioral Medicine, 37,* 29–37.
Hakim, A. A., Petrovitch, H., Burchfiel, C. M., Ross, G. W., Rodriguez, B. L., White, L. R., et al. (1998). Effects of walking on mortality among nonsmoking retired men. *New England Journal of Medicine, 338,* 94–99.
Hamilton, N. A., Nelson, C. A., Stevens, N., & Kitzman, H. (2007). Sleep and psychological well-being. *Social Indicators Research, 82,* 147–163.
Helgeson, V. S., Reynolds, K. A., & Tomich, P. L. (2006). A meta-analytic review of benefit finding and growth. *Journal of Consulting and Clinical Psychology, 74,* 797–816.
Hercberg, S., Galan, P., Preziosi, P., Bertrais, S., Mennen, L., Malvy, D., et al. (2004). The SU.VI.MAX Study: A randomized, placebo-controlled trial of the health effects of antioxidant vitamins and minerals. *Archives of Internal Medicine, 164,* 2335–2342.

Herman, K. C., Tucker, C. M., Ferdinand, L. A., Mirsu-Paun, A., Hasan, N. T., & Beato, C. (2007). Culturally sensitive health care and counseling psychology: An overview. *The Counseling Psychologist, 35*(5), 633–649.

Hong, Y., Morris, M., Chiu, C., & Benet-Martínez, V. (2000). Multicultural minds: A dynamic constructivist approach to culture and cognition. *American Psychologist, 55,* 709–720.

House, J. S., Landis, K. R., & Umberson, D. (1988). Social relationships and health. *Science, 241,* 540–545.

Howell, A. J., Digdon, N. L., Buro, K., & Sheptycki, A. R. (2008). Relations among mindfulness, well-being, and sleep. *Personality and Individual Differences, 45,* 773–777.

Hung, H. C., Joshipura, K. J., Jiang, R., Hu, F. B., Hunter, D., Smith-Warner, S. A., et al. (2004). Fruit and vegetable intake and risk of major chronic disease. *Journal of the National Cancer Institute, 96,* 1577–1584.

Ickovics, J. R., Milan, S., Boland, R., Schoenbaum, E., Schuman, P., & Vlahov, D. (2006). Psychological resources protect health: 5-year survival and immune function among HIV-infected women from four US cities. *AIDS, 20,* 1851–1860.

Johnson, D., Alexander, G., Kapke, A., McClure, J., Wiese, C., Greene, S., et al. (2009). The relationship of social support and smoking cessation among African Americans enrolled in the Project Quit Study. *Clinical Research and Medicine, 137,* 1–28.

Katon, W. (1984). Depression: Relationship to somatization and chronic medical illness. *Journal of Clinical Psychiatry, 45,* 4–11.

Kerr, J. H., Fujiyama, H., Sugano, A., Okamura, T., Chang, M., & Onouha, F. (2006). Psychological responses to exercising in laboratory and natural environments. *Psychology of Sport and Exercise, 7,* 345–359.

Kohsaka, M., Fukuda, N., Honma, H., Kobayashi, R., Sakakibara, S, Koyama, E., et al. (1999). Effects of moderately bright light on subjective evaluations in healthy elderly women. *Psychiatry and Clinical Neurosciences, 53,* 239–241.

Krause, N., Ingersoll-Dayton, B., Liang, J., & Sugisawa, H. (1999). Religion, social support, and health among the Japanese elderly. *Journal of Health and Social Behavior, 40,* 405–421.

Lechner, S. C., Tennen, H., & Affleck, G. (2009). Benefit finding and growth. In S. Lopez & C. R. Snyder (Eds.), *Oxford handbook of positive psychology* (2nd ed., pp. 633–640). New York: Oxford University Press.

Li, Y., Dai, Q., Ekperi, L. I., Dehal, A., & Zhang, J. (2011). Fish consumption and severely depressed mood, findings from the first national nutrition follow-up study. *Psychiatry Research, 190*(1), 103–109.

Littlewood, R. A., Vanable, P. A., Carey, M. P., & Blair, D. C. (2008). The association of benefit finding to psychosocial and health behavior adaptation among HIV positive men and women. *Journal of Behavioral Medicine, 31,* 145–155.

Lopez, S. J., O'Byrne, K. K., & Peterson, S. (2003). Profiling courage. In S. J. Lopez & C. R. Snyder (Eds.), *Positive psychological assessment: A handbook of models and measures* (pp. 185–198). Washington: American Psychological Association.

Lyubormirsky, S., King, L., & Diener, E. (2005). The benefits of frequent positive affect: Does happiness lead to success? *Psychological Bulletin, 131,* 803–855.

Maddi, S. R. (2002). The story of hardiness: Twenty years of research, theorizing, and practice. *Consulting Psychology Journal: Practice and Research, 54,* 175–185.

Maddi, S. R. (2004). Hardiness: An operationalization of existential courage. *Journal of Humanistic Psychology, 44,* 279–298.

Magnus, C. M. R., Kowalski, J. C., & McHugh, T. F. (2010). The role of self-compassion in women's self-determined motives to exercise and exercise-related outcomes. *Self and Identity, 9,* 363–382.

Martel, G. F., Hurlbut, D. E., Lott, M. E., Lemmer, J. T., Ivey, F. M., Roth, S. M., et al. (1999). Strength training normalizes resting blood pressure in 65- to 73-year-old men and women with high normal blood pressure. *Journal of the American Geriatrics Society, 47,* 1215–1221.

McAuley, E., Blissmer, B., Marquez, D. X., Jerome, G. J., Kramer, A. F., & Katula, J. (2000). Social relations, physical activity, and well-being in older adults. *Preventative Medicine: An International Journal Devoted to Practice and Theory, 31,* 608–617.

McGregor, B. A. & Antoni, M. H. (2009). Psychological intervention and health outcomes among women treated for breast cancer: A review of stress pathways and biological mediators. *Brain Behavior and Immunity, 23,* 159–66.

Meyers, A. R., Gage, H., & Hendricks, A. (2000). Health-related quality of life in neurology. *Archives of Neurology, 57,* 1224–1227.

Moller, P., Viscovich, M., Lykkesfeldt, J., Loft, S., & Jenson, A. (2004). Vitamin C supplementation decreases oxidative DNA damage in mononuclear blood cells of smokers. *European Journal of Nutrition, 43,* 267–274.

Moore, C. C., & Bracegirdle, H. (1994). The effects of a short-term, low-intensity exercise programme on the psychological wellbeing of community-dwelling elderly women. *British Journal of Occupational Therapy, 57,* 213–216.

Mosby. (2009). *Mosby's medical dictionary* (8th ed.). London, Elsevier.

Mosewich, A. D., Kowlaski, K. C., Sabiston, C. M., Sedgwick, W. A., & Tracy, J. L. (2011). Self-compassion: A potential resource for young women athletes. *Journal of Sport & Exercise Psychology, 33,* 103–123.

Musick, M. A., Herzog, A. R., & House, J. S. (1999). Volunteering and mortality among older adults: Findings from a national sample. *Journal of Gerontology, 54B,* S173–S180.

Neff, K. D. (2003). Self-compassion: An alternative conceptualization of a healthy attitude toward oneself. *Self and Identity, 2,* 85–102.

Nelson, C. (2009). Appreciating gratitude: Can gratitude be used as a psychological intervention to improve individual well-being? *Counseling Psychology Review, 24,* 38–50.

Norlander, T., Johansson, A., & Bood, S. A. (2005). The affective personality: Its relation to quality of sleep, well-being, and stress. *Social Behavior and Personality, 33,* 709–722.

Oman, D., Thoresen, C. E., & McMahon, K. (1999). Volunteerism and mortality among the community-dwelling elderly. *Journal of Health Psychology, 4,* 301–316.

Otey-Scott, S. (2007). *A lesson in gratitude: Exploring the salutogenic relationship between gratitude and health.* Doctoral dissertation. Retrieved from Dissertations and Thesis database. (AAT No. 3280068).

Pressman, S. D., & Cohen, S. (2005). Does positive affect influence health? *Psychological Bulletin, 131,* 925–971.

Post, S. G. (2005). Altruism, happiness, and health: It's good to be good. *International Journal of Behavioral Medicine, 12,* 66–77.

Ramos, R., & Martinez-Castelao, A. (2008). Lipoperoxidation and hemodialysis. *Metabolism, 57,* 1369–1374.

Rasmussen, H. N., Scheier, M. F., & Greenhouse, J. B. (2009). Optimism and physical health: A meta-analytic review. *Annals of Behavioral Medicine, 37,* 239–256.

Ryff, C. D., & Singer, B. (2000). Biopsychosocial challenges of the new millennium. *Psychotherapy and Psychosomatic Medicine, 69,* 170–177.

Ryff, C. D., Singer, B. H., & Love, G. D. (2004). Positive health: Connecting well-being with biology. *Philosophical Transactions of the Royal Society of London B, 359,* 1383–1394.

Safdar, S., Lay, C., & Struthers, W. (2003). The process of acculturation and basic goals: Testing a multidimensional individual difference acculturation model with Iranian immigrants in Canada. *Applied Psychology, 52*(4), 555–579.

Salovey, P., Rothman, A. J., Detweiler, J. B., & Steward, W. T. (2000). Emotional states and physical health. *American Psychologist, 55,* 110–121.

Sánchez-Villegas, A., Henríquez, P., Bes-Rastrollo, M., Doreste, J. (2006). Mediterranean diet and depression. *Public Health Nutrition, 9,* 1104–1109.

Sauvaget, C., Nagano, J., Allen, N., & Kodama, K. (2003). Vegetable and fruit intake and stroke mortality in the Hiroshima/Nagasaki life span study. *Stroke, 34,* 2355–2360.

Schmidt, C. K., Raque-Bogdan, T. L., Piontkowski, S., & Schaefer, K. L. (2011). Putting the positive in health psychology: A content analysis of three journals. *Journal of Health Psychology, 16,* 607–620.
Schneider, E. L., & Davidson, L. (2003). Physical health and adult well-being. In M. H. Bornstein, L. Davidson, C. L. M. Keyes, & K. A. Moore (Eds.), *Well-being: Positive development across the life course* (pp. 407–423). Mahwah: Lawrence Erlbaum Associates Publishers.
Seligman, M. E. P. (2008). Positive health. *Applied Psychology: An International Review, 57,* 3–18.
Smith, A. W., & Baum, A. (2003). The influence of psychological factors on restorative function in health and illness. In J. Suls & K. A. Wallston (Eds.), *Social psychological foundations of health and illness* (pp. 431–457). Malden: USishers.
Smith, T. B., & Silva, L. (2010). Ethnic identity and personal well-being of people of color: A meta-analysis. *Journal of Counseling Psychology, 58*(1), 42–60.
Steptoe, A., O'Donnell, K., Marmot, M., & Wardle, J. (2008). Positive affect, psychological well-being, and good sleep. *Journal of Psychosomatic Research, 64,* 409–415.
Takemura, Y., Kikuchi, S., Inaba, Y., Yasuda, H., & Nakagawa, K. (1999). The protective effect of good physical fitness when young on the risk of impaired glucose tolerance when old. *Preventive Medicine, 28,* 14–19.
Tanaka, H., & Shirakawa, S. (2004). Sleep health, lifestyle and mental health in the Japanese elderly: Ensuring sleep to promote a healthy brain and mind. *Journal of Psychosomatic Research, 56,* 465–477.
Taylor, S. E., Kemeny, M. E., Reed, G. M., Bower, J. E., & Gruenewald, T. L. (2000). Psychological resources, positive illusions, and health. *American Psychologist, 55,* 99–109.
Tennen, H., & Affleck, G. (2009). Assessing positive life change: In search of meticulous methods. In C. L. Park, S. C. Lechner, M. H. Antoni, & A. L. Stanton (Eds.). *Medical illness and positive life change* (pp. 31–49). Washington: American Psychological Association.
Thoits, P. A. (2011). Mechanisms linking social ties and support to physical and mental health. *Journal of Health and Social Behavior, 52,* 145–161.
Thomas, D. R. (2006). Vitamins in aging, health, and longevity. *Clinical Interventions in Aging, 1,* 81–91.
Tolomio, S., Ermolao, A., Lalli, A., & Zaccaria, M. (2010). The effect of a multicomponent dual-modality exercise program targeting osteoporosis on bone health status and physical function capacity of postmenopausal women. *Journal of Woman and Aging, 22,* 241–254.
Totterdell, P., Reynolds, S., Parkinson, B., & Briner, R. B. (1994). Associations of sleep with everyday mood, minor symptoms and social interaction experience. *Sleep, 17,* 466–475.
Tucker, C. M., Ferdinand, L. A., Mirsu-Paun, A., Herman, K. C., Delgado-Romero, E., van den Berg, J. J., & Jones, J. D. (2007). The roles of counseling psychologists in reducing health disparities. *The Counseling Psychologist, 35*(5), 650–678.
Turner, S. A., Luszczynska, A., Warner, L., & Schwarzer, R. (2010). Emotional and uncontrolled eating styles and chocolate chip cookie consumption: A controlled trial of the effects of positive mood enhancement. *Appetite, 54,* 143–149.
Uchino, B. N., Cacioppo, J. T., & Kiecolt-Glaser, J. K. (1996). The relationship between social support and physiological processes: A review with emphasis on underlying mechanisms and implications for health. *Psychological Bulletin, 119,* 488–531.
Utsey, S. O., & Constantine, M. G. (2008). Mediating and moderating effects of racism-related stress on the relation between poverty-related risk factors and subjective well-being in a community sample of African Americans. *Journal of Loss and Trauma, 13*(2–3), 186–204.
Wang, C. Y., Yeh, C. J., Wang, C. W., Wang, C. F., & Lin, Y. L. (2011). The health benefits following regular ongoing exercise lifestyle in independent community-dwelling older Taiwanese adults. *Australasian Journal on Aging, 30,* 22–26.
Weir, K. (2011). Golden rule redux. *Monitor, 42,* 42.
Williams, D. R., & Mohammed, S. A. (2009). Discrimination and racial disparities in health: Evidence and needed research. *Journal of Behavioral Medicine, 32*(1), 20–47.

Wood, A. M., Joseph, S., & Maltby, J. (2009). Gratitude predicts psychological well-being above the Big Five facets. *Personality and Individual Differences, 46,* 443–447.
Woodard, C., & Pury, C. L. S. (2007). The construct of courage: Categorization and measurement. *Consulting Psychology Journal: Practice and Research, 59,* 135–147.
Yarcheski, A., Mahon, N. E., Yarcheski, T. J., & Cannella, B. L. (2004). A meta-analysis of predictors of positive health practices. *Journal of Nursing Scholarship, 36,* 102–108.
Yoshihara, D., Fujiwara, N., & Suzuki, K. (2010). Antioxidants: Benefits and risks for long-term health. *Maturitas, 67,* 103–107.

Part IV
Learning to Thrive During Adulthood

Chapter 15
The Influence of Erik Erikson on Positive Psychology Theory and Research

Michelle D. Vaughan and Eric M. Rodriguez

> [T]he very development of psychoanalytic thought, and its present preoccupation with 'ego strength,' suggests that human strength be reconsidered, not in the sense of nobility and rectitude as cultivated by moralities, but in the sense of 'inherent strength.' (Erikson 1964, p. 111)

This chapter explores Erik Erikson's contributions throughout his major published works relevant to modern perspectives on positive psychology (PP) and related strengths-based work. Elucidating themes related to the three pillars of PP (positive subjective experiences, positive traits/virtues, and positive social institutions; Peterson and Seligman 2004) within his major published works throughout the twentieth century, this chapter serves as a primer to those wishing to better understand and apply Erikson's work to modern PP theory and research through an appreciation of his contributions to strengths-based perspectives rooted in an appreciation of culturally specific phenomena related to core developmental tasks.

Erikson's own personal journey exemplified the identity crisis as well as fruits of its resolution, lacking knowledge, or a relationship with his biological father, suffering discrimination and exclusion by his peers and exploring his vocational identity throughout his teens and twenties. Erikson's life (much like his psychohistorical biographies of Gandhi, Luther, and the Sioux of South Dakota) is simultaneously a model for the strengths and gifts to society that emerge within the context of successfully navigating the identity crisis (Table 15.1). An Ivy League professor, the creator of the first life span model of identity and personality development, Erikson's contributions to the field are particularly striking given the fact he never earned a graduate degree, and only discovered psychology in his midtwenties in the context of educating the children of Anna Freud, who also served as his analyst (Boeree 1997/2006).

M. D. Vaughan (✉)
Westminster College, 2012 W. Ash Street, Apt. O 18, Columbia, MO, USA
e-mail: MichelleDV2003@hotmail.com

E. M. Rodriguez
Social Science Department, New York City College of Technology, City University of New York (City Tech, CUNY), N611, 300 Jay Street, Brooklyn, NY 11201, USA
e-mail: erodriguez@citytech.cuny.edu

J. D. Sinnott (ed.), *Positive Psychology*,
DOI 10.1007/978-1-4614-7282-7_15, © Springer Science+Business Media, LLC 2013

Table 15.1 Erikson's psychosocial model and related character strengths

Crisis	Age (years)	Basic strength(s): related character strength(s)
Trust vs. mistrust	0–1.5	Hope, Drive: Gratitude, Hope, Integrity, Kindness, Love, Persistence, Prudence
Autonomy vs. shame/doubt	1.5–3	Willpower, Self-control: Bravery, Persistence, Self-regulation
Initiative vs. guilt	3–6	Purpose, Direction: Fidelity, Curiosity, Leadership, Vitality
Industry vs. inferiority	6–12	Competence, Method: Citizenship, Leadership, Love of Learning, Persistence, Social Intelligence
Identity vs. role confusion/diffusion	12–20	Fidelity, Devotion: Citizenship, Hope, Integrity, Leadership, Love
Intimacy vs. isolation	20–35	Love, Affiliation: Love, Kindness
Generativity vs. stagnation	35–65	Care, Production: Bravery, Citizenship, Kindness, Love, Perspective
Integrity vs. despair	65 +	Wisdom, Renunciation: Bravery, Integrity, Open-mindedness, Perspective

As a student of Anna Freud, Erikson captured the shifts in modern psychology across the twentieth century with respect to desire to incorporate the positive, the potential for growth and healthy development within Freud's rigid, pathology-focused psychosexual model of personality development. Initially seeking to expand Freud's theory to incorporate a life span perspective on development and reflect the importance of societal and cultural influences on this process and its outcomes, Erikson's contributions to early psychology are multifaceted. Hoare (2002) describes Erikson in the introduction as "the one thinker who changed our minds about what it means to live as a person who has arrived at a chronologically mature positive and yet continues to grow, to change, and to develop" (2002, p. 3), "[h]is desire was to depict mentally healthy life and health-supporting social institutions. He sometimes wrote in the style of a hopeful prophet who saw what adults, their children, and their world could yet become." (p. 5). In contrast to Freud's deterministic, downward, and backward focus on pathology, Erikson described his approach as being explicitly focused upward and forward—on the present, the future, and on the potential for healthy development (Hoare 2002). Frustrated by the limitations of psychoanalysis with respect to understanding of what has come to be known as PP (Seligman and Czsentimihalyi 2000), Erikson was unimpressed by the one-sided nature of the field during his time, noting how "[i]f, in this paper, I were to restrict myself to what is, in this sense, known about the 'healthy personality,' I would lead the reader and myself into a very honorable but very uninspiring austerity." (1950, p. 51).

Even before the first edition of *Childhood and Society* was published in 1950, Erikson's early research on child development deliberately and persistently incorporated strength-based concepts, urging the field to move beyond "our hesitation in studying human strength" (1964, p. 143), to understand the full nature of what it means to be human. Dedicating himself to filling in these gaps and advancing the study of human strengths, he worked to answer the question: "if we know what can go wrong in each stage, can we say what should have gone and can go right?" (Erikson 1997, p. 595). As discussed in *Vital Involvement in Old Age* (Erikson et al. 1986), he was also highly aware of the controversial nature of using strength-based language in his early theory and research, noting how "few, if any, other workers would have dared used such terms—and to use them both believingly and believably" (1986, p. 19).

Discussing both, the content and process by which healthy personality develops, Erikson (1950) draws an idea directly from biological principles with respect to physical growth and development (the epigenetic principle of maturation), describing how common life tasks serve as crises. Incorporating both linear and cyclical elements, the apex of each conflict is initially brought about by one's physical development and further advanced by one's internal psychological drives as well as the social and cultural institutions/rituals within one's environment. Although each of the eight stages depicted focuses on a specific task that builds upon the previous crisis, Erikson explicitly asserted the cyclical as well as linear nature of this process. Here, specific tasks coming to ascendancy during specific ages, but existing in a lesser form throughout the life span, continually emerge and reemerge within the context of other areas of foci. These highly stressful, yet inherently growth-oriented crises offer opportunities to form one's identity and personality through the development of basic virtues that bear important similarities to modern character strengths.

Erikson in Positive Psychology

Unfortunately, modern work on PP has rarely given more than a passing acknowledgement of Erikson's contributions to theory and research in these areas. Such references have been largely confined to passing mentions of his model's focus on growth/positive development (Sheldon 2006), early insights into the nature of Wisdom, and/or the concept of generativity as an expression of care/concern/love (Peterson and Seligman 2004). In the introduction to their landmark book, *Character Strengths and Virtues: A Handbook and Classification*, Peterson and Seligman devote significant attention to his contributions to the development of basic strengths as an early important perspective on systems of related character strengths/virtues (Table 15.2). Within this chapter, the authors provide an overview of his contributions regarding the social and developmental process by which virtues/strengths are forged. In their words: "Erikson's approach is an explicit reminder that strengths have a developmental trajectory and that certain strengths can lay the foundation for others" and that "cultures recognize the social nature of people's conflicts and provide their members with help to accomplish the tasks that confront them at different periods of life" (Peterson and Seligman 2004, p. 60). In fact, these authors incorporate Erikson's focus on societal support as one of the ten criteria they offer for evaluating whether a particular quality fits their definition of a character strength within PP. However, even within this discussion, Erikson's concept that specific, normative developmental tasks/crises are associated with specific strengths receives little attention in PP, other than the assertion that certain specific character strengths

Table 15.2 Virtues and character strengths adapted from Peterson and Seligman (2004)

Wisdom and knowledge—cognitive strengths to acquire and use knowledge
Creativity: producing original, adaptive ideas or behaviors that enhance self or others
Curiosity: intrinsic interest in ongoing experience via novelty, variety, challenge
Open-mindedness: utilizing flexible, broad-minded, complex, open thinking
Love of Learning: motivation to acquire or build upon skills or knowledge
Perspective: utilizing/coordinating information in ways that make sense to self/others
Courage—emotional strengths to accomplish goals in the face of opposition
Bravery: doing what needs to be done, despite fear/threat
Persistence: use of will to finish what one has started, despite obstacles
Integrity: taking responsibility for one's feelings and actions, being authentic/genuine
Vitality: feeling alive, full of zest, enthusiasm in everyday life
Humanity—interpersonal strengths regarding tending and befriending others
Love: reciprocated experiences of love, care, commitment in relationships
Kindness: expressing compassion, concern for others
Social intelligence: ability to process/use emotional information from self and others
Justice—civic strengths that underlie healthy community life
Citizenship: a sense of devotion/duty to others who share common experiences
Fairness: commitment to treating others equally and advocating for fair treatment.
Leadership: directing, inspiring others toward a shared goal
Temperance—strengths that protect against excess
Forgiveness: exhibiting mercy towards other people or situations that are transgressive
Humility: letting one's accomplishments speak for themselves
Prudence: orientation to and selection of choices based on future goals
Self-regulation: intentional control/management of one's impulses, responses, reactions
Transcendence—strengths that force connections to the universe and provide meaning
Appreciation of Beauty and Excellence: awe/wonder in the face of beauty, skill or excellence
Gratitude: recognizing and expressing thankfulness in response to a gift
Hope: focusing on the future with an expectation for good/desired outcomes
Humor: sense of playfulness, wit that serves the good of self/others
Spirituality: beliefs about higher purpose/meaning and one's place within the universe

(e.g., Open-mindedness, Appreciation of Beauty) are unlikely to develop within the context of a specific developmental stage, as they are not intrinsically tied to developmental challenges. Similarly, Lerner (2009) discusses strengths-based positive youth development. Yet, only in passing does he reference Erikson, and then only in discussing previous reductionistic, biologically deterministic models of development, wholly overlooking his direct contributions to strengths/character development.

Virtues and Basic Strengths

Consistent with current structural models of character strengths and virtues in PP (Peterson and Seligman 2004), Erikson cast virtues as the plural, overarching category under which specific strengths were embedded:

> In what follows I intend to investigate, then, first the developmental roots and later the evolutionary rationale of certain basic human qualities which I will call virtues... inherent

> strength or active quality... I will relate them to that process by which ego strength may be developed from stage to stage. (1964, p. 112–113)

Although clearly drawing on Freudian perspectives regarding the developmental process by which personality forms, Erikson consistently strived to incorporate the potential for growth in this process, describing how personality formation "leads outward from self-centeredness to the mutuality of love and communality, forward from the enslaving past to the utopian anticipation of the new potentialities, and upward from the unconscious to the enigma of consciousness" (Erikson 1975, p. 39).

Equally valuing the importance of each of the opposing, conflicting psychological forces (See Table 15.1) within each stage in shaping personality, Erikson built his model on the essential tension between what he termed syntonic and dystonic forces at each stage of development that lies at the heart of psychological growth. As quoted by Evans, Erikson argued that it is the balance between these forces that is critical for successful navigation of each stage: "a certain ratio of trust and mistrust in our basic social attitude is a critical factor. When we enter a situation, we must be able to differentiate how much we can trust and how much we must mistrust" (Evans 1981, p. 15).

The psychological pull between these contrary forces embedded within each of Erikson's developmental crises reflects as a series of highly stressful turning points that create diverse opportunities for growth, wherein "development must move one way or another, marshaling resources of growth, recovery, and further differentiation" (1968, p. 16) along the way. Those who successfully navigate a given crisis and achieve a balance between opposing forces find themselves armed with the resources and capabilities, the "inner capital" (1959, p. 89) needed to work through future developmental crises and form a maximally healthy personality. Although specific strengths identified by Erikson within his developmental model have received mention within modern PP, such references often simplify the multifaceted nature of each of his basic strengths into the more narrowly defined system of character strength and virtues initially articulated by Peterson and Seligman (2004). Although common themes and significant overlap certainly exist between the two systems of strengths, a thoughtful examination of the unique features and insights embedded within Erikson's developmentally based strengths is warranted. See Table 15.2.

Peterson and Seligman (2004) describe virtues as the six overarching, universal core characteristics valued across cultures and historical periods—Wisdom/Knowledge (encompassing cognitive strengths regarding acquiring and using knowledge); Courage (emotional strengths to exert one's will persist despite obstacles); Humanity (interpersonal strengths linked to understanding and relating to others); Justice (community-oriented strengths focused on civic values and participation); Temperance (strengths focused on protecting against excess on multiple levels); and Transcendence (strengths linked to a sense of future, meaning, and experiences beyond self). Within this designation, character strengths reflect the pathways or mechanisms by which these virtues are embodied/expressed within individuals. Within Erikson's model, the primary and secondary basic strengths that he articulated within each developmental stage span across the six virtues discussed within

PP, incorporating aspects of character strengths that emerge as a direct result of successfully navigating the specific developmental crisis at hand.

Trust vs. Mistrust

Erikson (1950) described this first stage of life as centered on the task of creating a positive relationship with one's primary caregiver, allowing self to experience the world as a safe place, while retaining a healthy degree of skepticism (incorporating aspects of the character strength of Prudence) in relationships with others. Here, establishing a balance between trust and mistrust in others and the world creates opportunities to develop the basic strength (and character strength of the same name) of Hope, supporting the development of faith in the outside world as well as faith in one's future (Peterson and Seligman 2004). Also, Hope provides the ability to trust others enough to develop loving, caring, and intimate relationships in the future and accept what is given in the context of such relationships (serving as a precursor to the character strength of Love). Peterson and Seligman (2004) also assert that a sense of Hope is integral to a sense of Gratitude, similar to how trust in the world fosters the ability to be thankful for the kindness of others, as well as provides a sense of trust in the world that allows individuals to value and systematically practice Kindness toward others (Hamacheck 1988). Hamacheck also asserts that the sense of trust in self that emerges within this stage serves as a necessary condition for expressing authenticity in adulthood by instilling the capacity to trust in one's self and act in ways consistent with one's true self (Integrity). In addition, this general sense of trust serves as the base from which individuals cultivate the secondary basic strength of Drive. Capturing the interest and ability to pursue goals in adulthood, Drive includes aspects of the character strengths of Persistence as well as Prudence (Peterson and Seligman 2004).

Autonomy vs. Shame and Doubt

For Erikson, the crisis associated with the toddler years centers on the ability to discover and exert one's Will in the face of internal and external challenges, "[b]alancing between loving good will and hateful self-insistence, between co-operation and willfulness, and between self-expression and compulsive self-restraint or meek compliance" (1968, p. 109). Building on the previously developed sense of Drive, the basic strength of Will includes both, identifying and pursuing self-selected goals incorporating aspects of the character strengths of Persistence (Peterson and Seligman 2004). This balance between autonomy and concern about the perceptions of others incorporates the new cooperative skills in relationships with others (Social Intelligence, Hamacheck 1988) as well as the initial efforts to exert the secondary basic strength of Self-control, mapping onto the character strength of Self-regulation in terms of initial efforts to manage physical impulses and responses.

For Erikson (1968), developing one's sense of autonomy or independence is a precondition for the development of Bravery with respect to the ability to assert one's self. Such themes play a central role in his psychohistorical biography of Martin Luther, highlighting his courage in questioning the Pope in the face of the threat of ostracism, excommunication, and death (Erikson 1962) "plead[ing] with the princes to permit free discussion of sectarian views; and he established the principle for a clergy man 'never to remain silent and assent to injustice, whatever the cost'." (p. 236). Similar themes emerge in Erikson's (1969) Pulitzer Prize winning work on the life of Mohandas Gandhi, highlighting Gandhi's willingness to repeatedly risk his life and liberty to improve the status and well-being of others.

Initiative vs. Guilt

As children move forward in the developmental journey into the preschool years, the crisis of Initiative vs. Guilt brings with it "a basis for a realistic sense of ambition" (Erikson 1968, p. 115), establishing an early sense of Self-regulation, of control over one's self that can become the character strength of Persistence, as individuals gain experience in working towards childhood goals. Through this basic strength of Purpose, children also experience a new sense of activation and energy "with undiminished zest" (p. 115) that accompanies new opportunities. Here, roots of the character strengths of Creativity and Vitality also take hold, while the ambition and Direction (the secondary basic strength) serve as the basis for effective Leadership in subsequent years (Hamacheck 1988).

Industry vs. Inferiority

As youth begin to explore the social world outside of their family and immerse themselves in the new opportunities afforded by formal school, their developmental crisis centers on the successful completion of tasks and goals. In the words of Erikson, the basic strength of Competence is defined as "the free exercise of dexterity and intelligence... This is the lasting basis for co-operative participation in productive adult life" (1968, p. 126). Expanding upon the underpinnings for the character strengths of Social Intelligence, Citizenship, and Leadership afforded by earlier stages, this crisis offers greater opportunities to strengthen skills related to facilitating and encouraging others in group work. For Erikson, the basic strength of Competence requires the exploration of new Methods (the secondary basic strength) that allow one to perform at a high level and become a productive member of society, building Persistence as well as Love of Learning with respect to gaining new skills (Hamacheck 1988; Peterson and Seligman 2004).

Identity vs. Role Confusion/Diffusion

Representing one of Erikson's best-known contributions to developmental psychology, the concept of the identity crisis has become relatively well-integrated into psychology, and to a lesser extent, PP. For Erikson (1959, 1974), young adulthood provides opportunities to both, explore and establish a flexible commitment to one or more positive, socially valued identities. Here, "[a] sense of identity means a sense of being at one with oneself as one grows and develops.. a sense of affinity with a community's sense of being at one with its future as well as its history" (Erikson 1974, pp. 27–28). Building upon the underpinnings for the character strengths of Integrity and Hope in others provided in Trust vs. Mistrust, Erikson defined the basic strength of Fidelity as "a renewal on a higher level of the capacity to trust (and to trust oneself), but also the claim to be trustworthy" (1997, p. 60) as well as "a persistent sharing of some kind of essential character with others" (1959, p. 102). Expanding beyond a sense of identity, Fidelity intersects rather closely with the character strength of Integrity, incorporating genuineness, authenticity, as well as a sense of personal responsibility for one's choices and behavior (Hamacheck 1988). Widely integrated into models of sexual minority identity development (Cass 1979; Coleman 1981/1982, Troiden 1979, 1989), the concept that developing a sense of self is integral to forming the most authentic, meaningful adult relationships with others has been given significant attention, although such work has rarely been connected to modern PP theory and research.

At the social level, Erikson asserts that fidelity brings with it a sense of recognition that allows individuals to form emotionally deeper, closer, more mature relationships with others (1959, 1968), supporting the character strength of Love in romantic and nonromantic relationships. In relationship to the larger world, Erikson asserted that the self-knowledge that emerges from Fidelity often brings with it "a sometimes passionate interest in ideological values of all kinds—religious, political, intellectual" (1997, p. 73), forming the basis for the character strength of Citizenship. Incorporating the secondary basic strength of Devotion, the social identities that emerge from this process allow young adults to commit their loyalty to group(s) that share their values (Peterson and Seligman 2004), giving them a sense of "collective strength" (Erikson 1950, p. 36). This allegiance to a social group brings with it the potential to serve as a facilitator, organizer, and a source of motivation to advance important shared goals. This character strength of Leadership is clearly and consistently embodied within Erikson's psychohistorical biographies of Gandhi and Luther as a product of healthy identity development, describing how these leaders struggled with stigmatized aspects of their identities in order to become transformational leaders. For Gandhi, such stories illustrate his experiences with discrimination and exclusion based on his racial/ethnic background, while within Erikson's own life, such obstacles centered on working through the negative identity he was ascribed based on his Nordic appearance and his Jewish heritage.

Intimacy vs. Isolation

As individuals begin to form close relationships with those outside of their families in young adulthood, they work to establish emotionally intimate relationships while retaining an independent sense of self. For Erikson, the further development of the basic strength (and the character strength) of Love through stages takes center stage in this crisis through committed, emotionally deep, and meaningful relationships with other adults. Building on the foundation afforded by the character strength of Kindness (Peterson and Seligman 2004) the secondary basic strength emerging from this crisis is Affiliation, capturing a sense of cooperation, belongingness, and support within one's relationships, specifically with one's significant other (Erikson 1968).

Generativity vs. Stagnation

As individuals move into middle adulthood, Erikson asserted that they are faced with a distinct opportunity to begin to Care, to contribute and give back to the next generation, nurturing the development of their own offspring or "other forms of altruistic concern and creativity which many absorb their kind of parental drive" (1968, p. 138). Although potentially including the deeper sense of care and commitment found with the character strength of Love, Peterson and Seligman (2004) equate Care with the character strength of Kindness, including general helping, providing support and empathy, "a concern with matters outside oneself and specifically the well-being of the next generation" (p. 296). Encompassing acts of mentoring and the provision of hard-won insights into the experience of being human to younger others, the character strength of Perspective is expressed, as is Erikson's secondary basic strength of Production with respect to serving as a source of support to the next generation as the cyclical nature of this developmental process emerge across generations (Peterson and Seligman 2004). Erikson's (1974) biographical work on the life of Thomas Jefferson emulated these themes regarding Care and Production, describing in rich detail how the former president "spent his last years designing, founding, and caring for the University of Virginia, providing for future generations a cupola symbolizing an Alma Mater" (p. 57).

Tapping into the civic character strengths of Citizenship (a felt sense of duty towards one's descendants) as well as Leadership (supporting and inspiring others who share one's values and goals), Erikson (1968) described generativity as a commitment to making society and the world a better place for youth and younger adults, especially in situations in which such expressions of Citizenship are intertwined with Bravery in terms of questioning existing norms and standards through political and social action, as demonstrated in Erikson's work on selfless sacrifices of Luther and Gandhi to improve the lives of those in their communities.

Integrity vs. Despair

Representing the last stage within his life span model, Erikson described the age of retirement as a time of thoughtful reflection, reconsideration, and quest to come to grips with one's life choices, "the ego's accrued assurance of its proclivity for order and meaning—an emotional integration faithful to the image-bearers of the past and ready to take, and eventually to renounce, leadership in the present" (1968, p. 139). With a focus coming to peace with the past and accepting the unavoidable ending of their lives, Erikson's basic strength of Integrity encompasses aspects of the character strengths of Integrity, Bravery, Open-mindedness, and Perspective. Staying true to one's actions and feelings in the face of opposition, Erikson described one of the key tasks of this crisis as a willingness "to defend the dignity of his own life style against all physical and economic threats" (1968, p. 140). In the context of Open-mindedness and Perspective, he saw those who were able to successfully work through this stage as demonstrating the "ripened 'wits' to accumulated knowledge, mature judgment, and inclusive understanding.... ethically concerned with the 'maintenance of the world'" (p. 140). Although the concept of Wisdom has received much attention within modern PP, such mentions are often brief, limited to ascribing credit to him for his conceptualization of Wisdom as a trait that is important to adult life (e.g., Baltes et al. 2002; Peterson and Seligman 2004; Schiebe et al. 2009).

Stress-related Growth in Positive Psychology

Consistent with the modern concept of stress-related growth (SRG: Park et al. 1996, sometimes termed posttraumatic growth or PTG : Tedeschi and Calhoun 1996), Erikson's assertions about the relationship between stressful experiences and long-term psychological growth represented an early (and decidedly rare) perspective on the process by which character strengths may develop. Described as perceived experiences of personal growth associated with a specific stressor within the domain of positive subjective experiences (Nolen-Hoeksema and Davis 2002), Erikson's early depictions of this phenomenon as a core component of his model are rarely acknowledged in the PP literature. The vast majority of the extant literature on SRG/PTG has focused on growth from traumatic and atypical life events (e.g., life-threatening illness, natural disasters, and unexpected loss of a partner/family member), based on the assumption that events/experiences must shake one's essential understandings and foundations about self and the world. As a result, work on this positive subjective experience has almost entirely neglected the study of growth from normative, developmental stresses (See Park et al. 1996; Tashiro and Frazier 2003 for notable exceptions), including experiences of growth that may emerge from each of Erikson's eight life crises. Endorsing the concept that nondevelopmental crises also serve to build character and contribute to the development of strong, healthy personalities, Erikson frequently highlighted how surviving such obstacles and traumatic experiences transformed them into sources of strength within his psychohistorical biographies, describing how Reformation leader Martin Luther "made a virtue out of what his superiors had considered a vice in him (and we, a symptom), namely the determined search for the rock bottom of his sinfulness" (Erikson 1962, p. 212). Similarly, Erikson depicted Mohandas Gandhi's experiences of discrimination based on his ethnicity while traveling in South Africa as sparking a major shift in his personality, as he "abandoned his shy self literally overnight and committed himself to his political and religious destiny as a leader" (Erikson 1969, p. 47).

Similarly, work on SRG/PTG has acknowledged the concept that the nature of the stressful event/experience may have a direct effect on the types/patterns of growth that emerge from this event, consistent with Erikson's assertions that specific developmental tasks lend themselves to the development of specific basic strengths. Schaefer and Moos (1992) postulated that event-related factors could play a major role in producing specific types or patterns of growth, describing how "[c]rises that involve a threat to life (serious illness, death of a significant person) may make one value life more; crises that test a person's physical and moral courage (combat, imprisonment) may result in increased self-reliance" (p. 160). Cohen et al. (1998), in their review of measures of SRG agreed with this concept, noting that "certain types of events and/or certain types of individuals are associated with specific types of thriving outcomes" (p. 326, emphasis added).

Social Institutions

Representing the third pillar of PP (Peterson and Seligman 2004), the concept of positive institutions, and their essential role in cultivating the development of both character traits and positive subjective experiences is embedded within Erikson's (1963) work. Representing both social and physical institutions embedded within a given culture, these structures provide "a certain well-delineated environment of care adapted to the stages of human growth." (Erikson 1974, p. 82). Embedded within such institutions are specific acts, "[r]itual confirmations, initiations, and indoctrinations [that] only enhance an indispensable process by which healthy societies bestow traditional strength on the new generation." (Erikson 1964, p. 90–91).

For Erikson, such institutions serve as broadly influential forces in the development of virtues and strengths, as "for the stage of life, then and such dispositions as faith, will power, purposefulness, competence, fidelity, love, care, wisdom— all criteria of vital individuals strength—also flow into the life of institutions. Without them, institutions wilt, but without the spirit of institutions pervading the patterns of care and love, instruction and training, no strength could emerge from the sequence of generations." (1968, p. 141). Yet, he also argued that certain social institutions may be particularly relevant at different stages, particularly early within life, as parenthood serving as a primary source of support in early childhood, schools, teachers, and one's neighborhood as influential forces in the development of Competence (Erikson 1968), as "[g]ood teachers who feel trusted and respected by the community know how to alternate play and work, games and study... They also know how to give a child time and how to handle those children to whom school, for a while, is not important and considering something to endure rather than enjoy" (1968, p. 124). The experience of religion and faith serves as a powerful source of positive identity and a facilitator of trust in others, though its ideology. Dating rituals within a culture and society, serves to support the development of Love within romantic relationships.

Erikson frames the relationship between social institutions and individual growth/development as bidirectional, as "the social process does not model a new being merely to housebreak him; it molds generations in order to be remodeled to be reinvigorated, by them" (Erikson 1962, p. 254). In other words, the support of institutions does not merely serve to reinforce and strengthen existing standards, norms, and traditions. The individuals who benefit from such institutions have the opportunity and duty to question, and challenge the then prevailing standards and norms. Although Peterson and Seligman (2004) explicitly incorporate the existence of social institutions and rituals as one of the core criteria by which their system of character strengths and virtues was measured against, discussion and research of such institutions (social or otherwise) remain rather limited within modern PP. Such supports serve as integral components in the process of formation of character strengths and virtues and serve as natural points of intervention to bolster this process in both youth and adults and further build character strengths.

Given the challenges within PP to articulate and offer models that incorporate strengths and weaknesses into a cohesive model, Erikson's insights in this area may serve as a template for work in this arena. Explorations of the levels of specific character strengths or amount of certain subjective experiences that are associated with desired adaptive outcomes have been an area of limited exploration in PP. Such work holds the promise of moving beyond overly simplistic 'more is better' assertions within PP to bring a more critical and scientific perspective to the study of strengths. Theory and research in PP may particularly benefit from exploration of the adaptive benefits of specific combinations or profiles of strengths in relation to specific tasks or challenges.

Conclusions and Recommendations

Given the emerging struggle within PP to develop a unified theoretical framework and meaningfully incorporate the influence of culture (broadly defined) (Bacigalupe 2001; Walsh 2001), Erikson's potential contributions to PP are significant. Erikson's attention to the social, cultural, and historical factors that influence the culturally specific manifestations of character strengths and related virtues that have been particularly overlooked within PP and which bear particular attention as the field seeks to break free of many of the Eurocentric and heteronormative norms and embedded within current work in the field. Sensitive to the concept that unique social contexts and cultural experiences may promote the development of culturally specific strengths (what he termed cultural virtues; Erikson 1950), his early work on the importance of cultural context serves as an important lesson for positive psychologists.

Such illustrations are evident within his ethnographic studies, describing "generosity as an outstanding virtue required in Sioux life... The companion virtue of generosity was fortitude, in Indians a quality both more ferocious and more stoical than mere bravery" (Erikson 1963, p. 137).

Although certainly a product of his own time and influences regarding endorsement of traditional gender role norms, pathological assumptions about lesbian, gay, and bisexual identities, and the endorsement of a relatively linear, stage-based models of development, Erikson's focus on the balance between psychological forces as they key to healthy personality formation addresses the existing challenges within the field regarding integrating both, strengths and weaknesses into a cohesive model. Integrating the development of basic strengths along with the potential for developing maladaptations and malignancies (Erikson and Erikson 1997), Erikson was particularly cautious of labeling certain characteristics as universally adaptive or healthy across changing social circumstances and generations, noting the importance of balance between psychological forces in psychological health. Juxtaposing strength and weakness in Erikson's clinical work with patients with schizophrenia, he noted that: "the therapist cannot be optimistic enough about the possibility of making contact with the patient's untapped inner resources; on the hand, it is also true that he cannot be pessimistic enough in the sustained apprehension that a mishap might cause the patient to remain at the rock bottom, and deplete the energy available for his re-emergence" (Erikson 1962, p. 104).

Erikson's systematic focus on describing the process by which character strengths develop across the life span also serves as an important lesson for PP, as it attempts to articulate how PP phenomena develop and offer important insights into conditions that both, facilitate and hinder the development of character traits and subjective experiences. The relative disconnect between the literature on personality development and modern PP (as noted by Leontiev 2006) serves as one such unnecessary obstacle in creating a unified explanatory paradigm for the emerging subfield that focuses on process to the same degree as content. In the recent words of Lopez and Gallagher (2009), "we must move beyond cross-sectional research designs and move toward models that account for dynamic change processes within individuals" (p. 5).

Although certainly complex and multifaceted, Erikson's contributions to understanding the development of healthy personality offer much for the future of PP. Moving beyond mere descriptions, mere taxonomies of the nature of character strengths and their associated higher virtues, the field has a duty, an obligation to focus more deliberately on describing and empirically examining the process by which such strengths may develop, testing the relationship between SRG/PTG and subsequent character strengths, the correspondence between specific developmental tasks and associated strengths, and the role of social institutions and rituals in nurturing the emergence of these positive psychological phenomena. Honoring Erikson's notable and rather innovative insights to what is now labeled as Positive Psychology is vital, the field must more deliberately explore and study these potential contributions to advance PP.

References

Bacigulupe, G. (2001). Is positive psychology only White psychology? *American Psychologist, 56*(1), 82–83. doi:10:1037/0003-066X.56.1.82b.

Baltes, P. B., Gluck, J., & Kunzmann, U. (2002). Wisdom: its structure and function in regulating successful life span development. In C. R. Snyder & S.J. Lopez, *Handbook of positive psychology* (pp. 327–347). New York: Oxford University Press.

Boeree, C. G. (1997/2006). Personality theories: Erik Erikson, 1902–1994. Available at: http://webspace.ship.edu/cgboer/erikson.html. Accessed April 2, 2013.

Cass, V. (1979). Homosexual identity formation: A theoretical model. *Journal of Homosexuality, 4*(3), 219–235.

Cohen, L., Hettler, T. & Pane, N. (1998). Assessment of post-traumatic growth. In R. Tedeschi, C. Park, & L. Calhoun (Eds.), *Post-traumatic growth: Theory and research on change in the aftermath of crisis* (pp. 23–42). Mahwah: NJ: Lawrence Erlbaum Associates.

Coleman, E. (1981/1982). Developmental stages of the coming out process. *Journal of Homosexuality, 7*(2–3), 31–43.

Erikson, E. H. (1950). *Childhood and society*. New York: Norton.

Erikson, E. H. (1962). *Young man Luther: a study of psychoanalysis and history*. New York: Norton.

Erikson, E. H. (1959). *Identity and the life cycle*. New York: Norton.

Erikson, E. H. (1963). *Childhood and society* (2nd ed.). New York: Norton.

Erikson, E. H. (1964). *Insight and responsibility*. New York: Norton.

Erikson, E. H. (1968). *Identity: youth and crisis*. New York: Norton.

Erikson, E. H. (1969). *Gandhi's truth: on the origins of militant nonviolence*. New York: Norton.

Erikson, E. H. (1974). *Dimensions of a new identity*. New York: Norton.

Erikson, E. H. (1975). *Life history and the historical moment*. New York: Norton.

Erikson, E. H., & Erikson, J. M. (1997). *The life cycle completed. Extended version with new chapters on the ninth stage of development*. New York: Norton.

Erikson, E. H., Erikson, J. M., & Kivnick, H. Q. (1986). *Vital involvement in old age*. New York: Norton.

Evans, R. I. (1981). *Dialogue with Erik Erikson*. New York: Praeger.

Hamacheck, D. E. (1988). Evaluating self-concept and ego development within Erikson's psychosocial framework: a formulation. *Journal of Counseling and Development, 66,* 354–360.

Hoare, C. H. (2002). *Erikson on development in adulthood: new insights from the unpublished papers*. New York: Oxford University Press. ISBN:978-0195131758.

Leontiev, D. (2006). Positive personality development: approaching personal autonomy. In M. Csikszentmihalyi & I. S. Csikszentmihalyi (Eds.), *A life worth living: contributions to positive psychology* (pp. 49–61). New York: Oxford University Press.

Lerner, R. M. (2009). The positive youth development perspective: theoretical and empirical basis of a strengths-based approach to adolescent development. In C. R. Snyder & S. J. Lopez (Eds.), *Handbook of positive psychology* (pp. 149–164). New York: Oxford University Press.

Lopez, S. J., & Gallagher, M. W. (2009). A case for positive psychology. In C. R. Snyder & S. J. Lopez (Eds.), *Handbook of positive psychology* (pp. 3–6). New York: Oxford University Press.

Nolen-Hoeksema S., & Davis, C. G. (2002). Positive responses to loss: perceiving benefits and growth. In C. R. Snyder & S. J. Lopez, *Handbook of positive psychology* (pp. 598–607). New York: Oxford University Press.

Park, C., Cohen, L., & Murch, R. (1996). Assessment and prediction of stress-related growth. *Journal of Personality, 64,* 71–105.

Peterson, C., & Seligman, M. E. P. (2004). *Character strengths and virtues: a handbook and classification*. New York: American Psychological Association.

Schaefer, J. & Moos, R. (1992). Life crises and personal growth. In B. Carpenter (Ed.), *Personal coping: Theory, research, and application* (pp. 149–170). Westport, CT: Praeger Publishers/Greenwood Publishing Group.

Scheibe, S., Kunzmann, U., & Baltes, P. B. (2009). New territories of positive life span development: wisdom and life-longings. In C. R. Snyder & S. J. Lopez (Eds.), *Handbook of positive psychology* (pp. 171–183). New York: Oxford University Press.

Seligman, M. E. P., & Csikszentmihalyi, M. (2000). Positive psychology: an introduction. *American Psychologist, 55,* 5–14. doi:10.1037/0003-066X.55.1.5.

Sheldon, K. (2006). Getting older, getting better? Recent psychological evidence. In M. Csikszentmihalyi & I. S. Csikszentmihalyi (Eds.), *A life worth living: contributions to positive psychology* (pp. 215–229). New York: Oxford University Press.

Tashiro, T., & Frazier, P. (2003). "I'll never be in a relationship like that again": personal growth following romantic relationship break-ups. *Personal Relationships, 10*(1), 113–128. doi:10.1111/1475-6811.00039.

Tedeschi, R. G., & Calhoun, L. G. (1996). The posttraumatic growth inventory: measuring the positive legacy of trauma. *Journal of Trauma Stress, 9*(3), 455–71.

Troiden, R. (1979). Becoming homosexual: A model of gay identity acquisition. *Psychiatry: Journal for the Study of Interpersonal Processes, 42*(4), 362–373.

Troiden, R. (1989). The formation of homosexual identities. *Journal of Homosexuality, 17*(1–2), 43–73.

Walsh, R. (2001). Positive psychology: east and west. *American Psychologist, 56*(1), 83. doi:10.1037/0003-066X.56.1.83.

Chapter 16
Resilience and Multiple Stigmatized Identities: Lessons from Transgender Persons' Reflections on Aging

Susan H. McFadden, Scott Frankowski, Heather Flick and Tarynn M. Witten

Of the many categories of diversity among older adults routinely studied by gerontologists, one that has received little attention is the group represented by the "T" in lesbian, gay, bisexual, and transgender (LGBT) studies. As Persson has written, "Transsexuals, cross-dressers, intersex, and other persons whose gender expression or identification is other than traditional represent an invisible minority within the worldwide elderly population" (2009, p. 642). In this chapter, we attempt to bring visibility to this group by presenting the results of an online study of more than 100 persons aged 61 and older who participated in the Trans Metropolitan Life Survey (Witten and Eyler 2012). Our work addresses the strengths of this group of people who live with multiple identity signifiers commonly stigmatized in our culture. Our

S. H. McFadden (✉)
Department of Psychology,
University of Wisconsin Oshkosh,
800 Algoma Blvd., Oshkosh, WI 54901, USA
e-mail: mcfadden@uwosh.edu

S. Frankowski
Department of Psychology,
University of Texas at El Paso,
Social Cognition Lab Room 311, 500 W.
University Ave., El Paso, TX 79902, USA
e-mail: sdfrankowski@miners.utep.edu

H. Flick
Department of Psychology,
University of Wisconsin Oshkosh,
800 Algoma Blvd., Oshkosh, WI 54901, USA
e-mail: flickh18@uwosh.edu

T. M. Witten
Center for the Study of Biological Complexity,
Virginia Commonwealth University,
1000 West Cary Street, Richmond, VA 23284-2030, USA
e-mail: tmwitten@vcu.edu

J. D. Sinnott (ed.), *Positive Psychology*,
DOI 10.1007/978-1-4614-7282-7_16, © Springer Science+Business Media, LLC 2013

qualitative analysis of the narrative responses given by participants provided insight into components that make up the repertoires of resilience among participants in this survey. Another paper has focused on quantitative analyses of this rich dataset, examining the religious affiliations and spiritual practices of the respondents (Porter et al. 2013).

We begin by discussing the challenges of describing the elder transgender population and we build our argument about multiple stigmatized identities by noting research on transphobia and crimes against gender-variant individuals. Next, we locate this discussion within the broader themes engaged by scholars who study intersectionality and show how research with elder transgender persons can contribute to intersectionality theory and research. Despite the fact that our respondents live at the intersection of multiple stigmatized identities, most of them told us they believe they have aged successfully. Their affirmation of successful aging requires that we inquire about resilience.

The idea of the "paradox of well-being" has been a standard observation in gerontology for several decades (e.g., Mroczek and Kolarz 1998). Despite enduring various afflictions that to younger adults are extremely negative, older people in general feel satisfied with their lives and resilient in the face of ongoing challenges. Our research inquired about how such a high percentage of persons who are the object of stigma, phobia, and sometimes hate crimes can also state that they are aging successfully.

Elder Transgender Persons

How important is an identity label? To scientists attempting to sort and interpret data, labels are critical. However, as Cook-Daniels (2006) notes, the identity question mostly serves the scientists' desire to "put everyone into neat boxes" (p. 31) and may produce spurious data because "terminology in the transgender community is hotly contested" (p. 31). As Kidd and Witten (2008a) explain, *transgender* refers "to groups such as transsexuals, cross-dressers, drag queens, drag kings, and gender queers, as well as myriad other members of the 'gender community'" (p. 36; see also Witten and Eyler 2012). However, because of this diversity of identities, as well as other markers of diversity such as age, income, race, and ethnicity, some researchers reject the notion of a transgender community (Cook-Daniels and munson 2010). Additional layers of complication are added through the use of the term *transsexual* because while it is often used to describe those who have transitioned from one gender to another through hormones and/or surgery, some people object to formulating identity in terms of biomedical procedures (Hines 2006).

Gender and sex are often conflated on medical forms and by researchers (Kidd and Witten 2008a). Gender, a psychosocial identification constructed over time through an individual's interactions with the wider culture, should be differentiated from sex, a biological description derived from anatomy, endocrinology, and/or genetics. However, things get considerably more complicated for persons identifying as transgender or intersex. The latter may be omitted when the category "birth sex" only permits two choices: male or female. The former may lie outside an essential binary system. Kidd and Witten ask, "how would one apply a binary gender system to a biologically XY-male individual who identifies as gay but who performs fulltime as a drag queen and has undergone surgery to acquire breasts and more feminine facial features?" (2008a, p. 36).

In recent years, queer theory has argued that gender binary conceptualizations are created by cultures. The postmodernist deconstruction of gender has revealed a "multiplicity of gendered identities and expressions which are unfixed to the 'sexed' body" (Hines 2006, p. 50). However, as Hines found in her research, some individuals who identify as transgender wish to retain the gender binary conceptualization and reject the notion of identity as fluid. She noted that these decisions are influenced by the individual's age and cohort location within a particular historical period, the timing of transition (if it has occurred), social and cultural messages about gender surrounding the developing individual, interactions with medical professionals, and finally, relationships with family members and friends.

Witten (2009) provided a helpful perspective on variables shaping transgender identities by pointing out that older transgender persons have reached what she calls their "elder membership state" (p. 37) in one of the three ways: (1) they have grown up in a culture that accepts nontraditional gender identities; (2) they came out and transitioned later in life and thus have had less time to live within the new gender identity; and (3) they acknowledged their gender variance earlier in life and have spent the majority of their years living with their gender of choice. An example of the latter group comes from one of the participants in our study who wrote:

> I live pretty much like any other woman in my community and I have been here over 30 years. Unless some radical outing of my gender status occurs I feel confident that no one will know or even care about my past. Essentially I am much more concerned about average aging issues than the fact that I am TS.

Similar to Hines (2006), Witten (2009) noted the influence of historical period on the experiences of transgender persons, especially in terms of when they came out to family, friends, and employers. She reminds us that the interaction between a person's age of coming out and the historical moment when that occurred can lead to people having "potentially different needs, potentially different ways of self-expression, and potentially different social support systems" (pp. 37–38). Many of our participants compared social climate experienced by younger transgender persons in the twenty-first century to their youth in the mid-twentieth century. One participant in the 70+ age group commented:

> Today there are many supports and better understanding of transsexualism. However, when I was young there were no such supports and if I had told anyone of my feelings, I'm sure I would have been put away in a mental institution. I used to feel so ashamed and deviant for wanting to be a girl.

Gender identity is unrelated to sexual orientation—the persons to whom an individual is erotically attracted. Among transgender persons, there is variability in sexual orientation as is evident in our respondents' selections from a list of possible sexual orientations (see Table 16.1). Persson agrees about this variability, stating "some

Table 16.1 Question: Given the list below, and thinking from where you are in your life right now, how would you identify yourself with respect to your sexual orientation?

Sexual orientation	Frequency
Heterosexual	39
Lesbian	28
Bisexual	26
Gay	10
Asexual	9
Celibate	7
Pan-sexual	1
Questioning	6
Omni-sexual	3
Refuse to be labeled	5

Three participants did not answer this question. Four participants listed *other*

may base their definition of sexual orientation on their gender identity; others may identify their sexual orientation based on their anatomy" (2009, p. 636).

As documented by recent studies, persons who identify as "gender variant" (Lombardi 2009) are frequently subjected to hostility (Cook-Daniels 2006), discrimination (Sánchez and Vilain 2009), sexual violence and elder abuse (Cook-Daniels and munson 2010), and hate crimes that can be classified as genocide (Kidd and Witten 2008a). If in addition to identifying as transgender or transsexual, one is also gay, lesbian, or bisexual, the risk of being the object of hate crimes may increase. Some participants in our study commented that being old added to their risk, for now they had to deal with ageism as well as prejudice, discrimination, and worse. For example, they worried that physical aging made them less able to withstand physical attack, changes in driving ability put them at risk of being stopped by police when cross-dressed, and prejudiced caregivers in nursing homes might mistreat them. These fears and concerns are not unrealistic and have been confirmed as genuine threats by a number of researchers (Cook-Daniels 2006; Kidd and Witten 2008a; Persson 2009; Witten 2002). For example, surveys of transgender adults aged 50 and older, found that one-third had experienced discrimination in health care (Cook-Daniels and munson 2010; see also Sperber 2006).

On the other hand, as we emphasize in this chapter, the majority of respondents to our survey stated they are aging successfully and many noted that their hard-won self-acceptance, desire to help others live better lives, and strong sense of agency led to good life in old age. As one respondent stated, "It gets better. Trust yourself, love yourself, and don't push the river." In other words, living at the intersection of several identities has resulted in strength and resilience.

Intersectionality

The idea of intersectionality arose in the 1990s among Black feminists, most notably from the legal analyses by Kimberlé Williams Crenshaw of cases involving discrimination due to race and gender (e.g., Crenshaw 1993). As described by Oleksy (2011), "the concept of intersectionality is used to cover the interconnections between various social differentials, such as gender, race, ethnic origin, age, disability, sexual orientation, and religion or belief" (p. 263). Intersectionality also takes into account the observation that not all group members share identity markers. Important for the study of transgender persons is what Witten (2009) describes as the "complex and broad spectrum of relationships between sex, gender, sexuality, and intimacy in these populations" (p. 38).

According to Cole (2009), psychologists have been slow to embrace intersectionality because they strive for parsimony in their models, focusing on one category (e.g., gender) while controlling for others (e.g., class), and they assume that in order to account for the dynamic relationships among categories, they would have to test huge samples. Cole argues this is not true and presents a way of incorporating intersectionality into psychological research that attends to three questions: (1) Who is included within the category? (2) What role does inequality play? and (3) How are people in the category similar? All three questions are pertinent to the current study of elder transgender persons. For example, our sample includes persons who have been "out" for many years and those who have kept their gender-variant identity hidden; some have had sexual reassignment surgery and some have not. Moreover, while psychologists might treat transgender persons as a discrete group, many of our participants refute that categorization by claiming as one person said, "being a post op transsexual person, I do not expect any other treatment than any other woman."

Intersectionality work is critical of approaches to understanding marginalization that assume, for example, an older, African American, transgender lesbian experiences discrimination in an additive fashion. Rather, according to intersectionality theorists, "such a perspective fails to address the meshing together of these or any other inequalities within everyday life and wider social and political structures" (Cronin and King 2010, p. 879). Whether intersectionality functions as a theory, a framework, or a paradigm (Syed 2010) is debated among psychologists who tend to leave analyses of "wider social and political structures" to their colleagues in other disciplines.

One area in which psychologists can contribute fresh thinking to this discussion is to observe that intersectionality like that which is evident among older transgender persons invites not only studies of the challenges of living with multiple stigmatized identities, but also research on opportunities for developing resilience in later life. According to Link and Phelan, "stigma is a persistent predicament" (2001, p. 379) consisting of "labeling, stereotyping, separation, status loss, and discrimination" (p. 363). As we will show, even though they live with the "persistent predicament" of being treated as "other," the majority of transgender elders in this study claim to be aging successfully and demonstrate various aspects of resilience. Also, they affirm and convey to others many of the virtues and character strengths noted in recent research and theorizing about positive psychology.

Resilience, Successful Aging, and Positive Psychology

The subtitle of the Trans Metropolitan Life Survey that provided data for our study—"Preparing for a Successful and Positive Later Life"—combined two references to long-held goals of gerontology. Efforts to define the parameters of successful, positive aging and to create interventions to improve the probability of this outcome recurred throughout the twentieth century (see Birren and Birren 1990, for a review). Rowe and Kahn's book summarizing their studies of successful aging appeared in 1998, making the argument that persons needed to meet three criteria in order to be deemed aging successfully: (1) having an absence of disease, disability, and risk factors for disease (such as smoking, obesity, hypertension, etc.), (2) maintaining mental and physical functioning, and (3) being actively engaged with life (Rowe and Kahn 1998).

Only 2 years after Rowe and Kahn's book appeared, Seligman and Csikszentmihalyi (2000) shook the foundations of psychology by arguing that the twenty-first century demanded a new vision for the field, one that investigated positive psychological attributes and human strengths. They envisioned positive psychology addressing individual traits (later elaborated as virtues and character strengths, Peterson and Seligman 2004), subjective experiences (e.g., of well-being and happiness), and characteristics of groups that promote and sustain positive human experience. Soon researchers from around the world launched projects addressing a number of issues related to positive psychology, including the relationship between spirituality and successful aging (Seligman et al. 2005). Thus, almost from the beginning, connections were being made between positive psychology and gerontology's focus on successful aging.

A review of the most widely studied positive psychological constructs related to psychiatric perspectives on healthy aging identified six individual traits: resilience, optimism, personal control/mastery/self-efficacy, positive attitudes toward own aging, spirituality, and wisdom (Vahia et al. 2011). The authors concluded that "positive psychological traits appear to play a greater role in cognitive and emotional functioning as one ages" (p. 232), producing longer, healthier lives and presumably, successful aging.

Along with a profusion of studies of positive psychological traits, subjective experiences, and groups, as well as research testing Rowe and Kahn's model of successful aging, critiques of each emerged. For example, Held (2004) summarized the objections of humanistic psychologists to a psychology that appeared to reject the possibility of "finding virtue in the experience of negative events and the expression of negative thoughts and feelings" (p. 19). Holstein and Minkler argued that the "new gerontology" based on the model of successful aging presents "an impoverished view of what a 'good' old age can be" (2003, p. 794) and excludes persons who by virtue of gender, race, class, genetics, or disease cannot meet Rowe and Kahn's criteria, but nevertheless proclaim their lives to have meaning and purpose. For this reason, some researchers favor the study of resilience over successful aging because "it represents a more reasonable and attainable goal for most older adults" (Clark et al. 2011, p. 51).

What is resilience? In a paper that appeared the same year as Seligman and Csikszentmihalyi's work on positive psychology, Luthar et al. (2000) carefully responded to critiques of several decades of work on children's resilience. A major problem they identified was the definitional one because researchers sometimes used "resilience" and "resiliency" interchangeably. Luthar et al. (2000, p. 543) argued that resilience is "a dynamic process encompassing positive adaptation within the context of significant adversity" and that resiliency refers to a discrete personal attribute. Although the majority of twentieth century work on resilience focused on children living under various conditions of adversity, in the late 1990s, gerontologists began to see the utility of applying the construct to their observations of older people's ability to retain or regain well-being in times of adversity (Ryff et al. 1998; Ryff 2012).

A recent book identified four domains of late life resilience—physiological, social, emotional, and spiritual—and concluded that resilience is "central to aging because adversity is inevitable at points throughout the lifespan and certainly as we age" (Resnick 2011, p. 351). Resnick, one of the book's editors, declared in her concluding chapter that "the truly successful older individual... is someone who has demonstrated resilience" (p. 352).

The "resilience repertoire" (Clark et al. 2011, p. 53) has been proposed as a metaphor to help gerontologists think about older adults' abilities to cope with adversity. As we examined the written replies of the participants in our study, we concluded that the metaphor of a resilience repertoire applies well to their lives. It offers a way of addressing their subjective experiences that might be categorized within the domains of positive psychology and successful aging without ignoring the fact that they have triumphed over many challenges, not the least of which has been the realization that their birth sex did not fit with their psychological sense of gender. The notion of a resilience repertoire also overcomes a difference of opinion among our respondents that reflects the conclusions of intersectionality researchers about the diversity found among persons grouped into identity categories. As we noted earlier, some insisted that being a trans person has no connection to their experience of aging and that they are like any other aging person who worries about developing dementia, being cared for by a relative, friend, or paid caregiver, running out of money, giving up a beloved home, and losing loved ones to death. Other persons, however, identified a long list of concerns about how they would fare in old age given their gender status.

In this study, we conducted a multimethod secondary analysis of the responses to the Trans Metropolitan Life Survey given by persons aged 61 and older. As we describe below, the survey consisted of quantitative and qualitative sections. In the former category, in response to the question "Would you say that you have aged successfully," 71 % of our sample checked "yes." Only 3 % said "no," while 13 % were unsure and for reasons unknown, another 13 % did not reply. Our sample's strong affirmation of successful aging compares with an earlier study conducted among 867 Californians aged 65–99 in which 50.3 % rated themselves as aging successfully (Strawbridge et al. 2002). We conducted a qualitative analysis of the narrative responses to try to answer the question of how these persons living with multiple stigmatized identities could affirm that they are aging successfully.

Method

Participants

More than 1,300 person aged 18 to more than 80 responded online to the Trans Metropolitan Life Survey that was adapted (with permission) by Tarynn Witten from the MetLife LGBT aging survey and was approved by the IRB of Virginia Commonwealth University (#HM12851). The current study, approved for secondary analysis by the IRB of the University of Wisconsin Oshkosh (#2045), analyzed the responses of all persons aged 61 and older ($n = 141$). Age groups were bracketed, with replies distributed as follows: 26 were 71 and older; 39 were 66–70; and 76 were 61–65. The sample was predominantly non-Hispanic White ($n = 130$). Most live in various regions of the United States ($n = 124$), although we also had replies from persons in Canada, Sweden, Ireland, Denmark, Australia, Brazil, New Zealand, and England.

Procedure

Requests for participation were posted on transrelated websites, sent to researchers and professionals working with transgender persons, and distributed through email lists maintained by Witten. Respondents could choose to link to the survey located on the VCU secure survey system. They were assured of the confidentiality provided by the Inquisite software survey program.

Measures

The survey had six sections, beginning with demographics, followed by sections addressing self-identification, hopes and concerns for the future, giving and receiving care, perceptions of aging, and end-of-life care planning. Participants checked answers to 54 questions, wrote short textual responses to ten items (e.g., "In what country do you currently reside?"), and provided narrative replies to nine questions and one request for final thoughts.

Due to an error, the first question (fears/concerns) was repeated. However, this serendipitously produced a positive result: 78 participants answered both questions, in most cases adding information the second time, 30 answered once, and 33 did not reply to either of the first two questions. The narrative items were:

- What are your worst fears/concerns about aging as a person who is gay, lesbian, bisexual, transgender, intersex, and queer (GLBTIQ)-identified? (Repeated)
- What are your worst fears/concerns about needing a caregiver as you age?
- What are your worst fears/concerns about needing to provide care for someone as you age?

- Do you think that being GLBTIQ-identified has helped you prepare for aging in any way? Tell us about how you feel that it has/has not prepared you.
- To what do you look forward as you age?
- If you feel that you have aged successfully [the checked item about successful aging preceded this question], please tell us how you managed to do so. What did you do?
- What wisdom do you have to pass on to other younger transgender/intersex-identified persons that you believe would help them to age successfully?
- What skills have you developed, approaches you have followed, paths you have taken that you believe have helped you to age in a positive fashion?
- Please provide any closing thoughts, comments, suggestions, and/or ideas here.

Analyses

Descriptive data were analyzed using PASW (SPSS) 18 software. We employed the method of interpretive phenomenological analysis in order to identify the themes conveyed in the narrative responses (Quinn and Clare 2008; Smith et al. 1999; Thomas and Pollio 2002). We coded the responses, grouped them, wrote analytic and self-reflexive memos about the groupings, compared the groupings, and checked all this using QSR NVivo-9 software for qualitative analysis. We resolved differences of opinion through discussion. To avoid inserting our preconceived ideas as much as possible, we read the literature on gender-variant aging after we had done the initial coding and categorizing. Although we were familiar with the literature on positive psychology, successful aging, and resilience, we reviewed it more carefully only after working with our data. We wanted to get to know our respondents through their answers before imposing an overlay of ideas from academic research.

Results

Descriptive Statistics

This sample is highly educated with 90 % of the sample reporting at least some education beyond high school. The modal response ($n=59$, 42.1 %) for the highest level of education completed was a graduate degree. The income level of the sample is higher than the national average with an average income between \$ 55,000 and \$ 64,000 (the national median household income in the United States in 2010 was \$ 50,046; U.S. Census Bureau 2011). The distribution of income in the sample, however, is somewhat bimodal with the most reported income on the lower end being between \$ 15,000 and \$ 24,999 ($n=24$), and on the higher end between \$ 100,000 and \$ 149,999 ($n=21$). A large majority of participants reported having been married

Table 16.2 Question: What term do you most often use to describe yourself to others?

Term	Frequency
Transgender	44
Transsexual	32
Heterosexual	23
Lesbian	8
Cross-Dresser	8
Gay	2
Straight	1
Bisexual	1
Dyke	1
Homosexual	1
Genderqueer	1

Three participants did not answer this question and 16 participants listed *other*. *Other* terms included *woman* ($n=3$), *transwoman, post-op female, gender outlaw*, and *radical liberal*

Table 16.3 Question: Which of the following, would you say, most closely describes your gender self-perception (how you see yourself)?

Gender self-perception	Frequency
Feminine	51
Transgender	29
Transwoman	21
Masculine	14
Androgynous	4
Transman	4
Two-spirited	3
Gender queer	2
Transblender	2
Gender Bender	1
Third gender	1
Questioning	1

Three participants did not answer this question and five listed *other*. *Other* responses included *crunchy dyke* and *hippie feminist*

($n=117$) and having children ($n=100$; among those who reported having children, the mean number of children reported was 2.45).

Participants were given many options to describe their gender and sexual identity. Participants were asked how they identify themselves with respect to their sexual orientation (Table 16.1), how they most often describe themselves to others (Table 16.2), their gender self-perception (Table 16.3), the sex they were assigned at birth (male, $n=125$; female, $n=13$), and the sex on their driver's license (male, $n=75$; female, $n=59$). Some persons chose not to answer these questions.

Our sample's religious identities varied as much as their gender and sexual identities (Table 16.4). The modal response was non-specific spirituality ($n=29$) followed closely by mainline Protestant ($n=21$) and agnostic ($n=20$).

Table 16.4 Question: With which particular religious/spiritual/faith tradition would you currently identify yourself?

Religious/spiritual/faith tradition	Frequency
Nonspecific spirituality	29
Mainline protestant	21
Agnostic	20
Catholic	13
Atheist	8
Jewish	6
Evangelical	5
Taoist/Buddhist/Confucianist	3
Unitarian	2
Wiccan	2
Christian scientist	1
Pentecostal/charismatic/fundamentalist	1
Muslim	1
Celtic/pagan	1
Earth goddess/sun worship/goddess worship	1

Two participants did not answer this question and 23 listed *other*. Some other responses included United Church of Christ ($n = 3$), Metropolitan Community Church ($n = 2$), Seventh Day Adventist, Wiccan Christian, esoteric Eastern Orthodox Christian, Agnostic Christian, and progressive Christian

Analyses of Narratives

We identified six components of participants' resilience repertoires that appeared to enable them to say they are aging successfully: nurturing the spiritual self, exercise of agency, self-acceptance, caring relationships, advocacy and activism, and enjoying an active, healthy life. As shown in Table 16.5, the number of times participants' responses could be categorized into one of the components varied. Among the 122 persons who wrote narrative responses, only five received no coding into any of the components of resilience. The mean number of categories was 4.17 ($SD = 1.28$; range = 1–6).

Some responses fell into more than one category and were thus counted several times. An example is a response to the question about "fears and concerns" about aging as a GLBTIQ-identified person given by an individual in the age 70 and older group. We coded it as indicating a nurturing of the spiritual self, caring relationships, and self-acceptance:

> I have come to admit that I am transgender & am not concerned really who knows except my daughter-in-law who has [medical condition deleted for confidentiality]. I do not wish to add to her condition. My remaining family can deal with it. I can deal with God as I know I have tried to help everyone in my life.... GOD BLESS.

This person is also a good example of the futility of trying to sort respondents into discrete gender identity and sexual orientation categories. In answer to the question about gender self-perception, this person checked "transwoman," but described gender identification as "mtf [male to female] transgender living as male because of my

Table 16.5 Respondents' indications of resilience categories

Category	Number/percent[a]	Codings range[b]	Total[c]	Mean/SD[d]
Nurturing the spiritual self	54 (44.26)	1–5	100	1.49 (0.80)
Exercise of agency	91 (74.59)	1–5	146	1.70 (0.84)
Self-acceptance	91 (74.59)	1–7	214	2.32 (1.32)
Caring relationships	86 (70.49)	1–4	143	1.65 (0.89)
Advocacy/activism	71 (58.19)	1–5	111	1.56 (0.93)
Enjoying an active, healthy life	96 (78.68)	1–4	224	1.59 (0.79)

[a] Number/percent of persons with narratives coded in this category
[b] Range of the number of times the category was coded for each person
[c] Total number of codings of the category
[d] Mean/SD of codings per person that met criteria of the category. Because 19 respondents completed no narrative responses, these calculations are based on $n = 122$

employment." Both birth sex and sex on driver's license are checked as male, but in response to the item asking for a description of current "sex" status, this person said "male wishing to be female." Finally, this individual checked "heterosexual" in response to the question about sexual orientation and checked "transgender" in response to the question about the terms most often used to describe the self to others.

Nurturing the Spiritual Self

As shown in the research of Witten and colleagues (Kidd and Witten 2008b; Porter et al. 2013), transgender-identified populations embrace a wide variety of spiritual beliefs and practices. This can be observed in our data as presented in Table 16.4 which resulted from responses to an item that offered 22 different options along with "not sure" and "other."

The written responses to various questions on our survey presented more complex, nuanced insights about spirituality as an important aspect of resilience. This observation is confirmed by Vahia et al. (2011) in their review of studies of resilience. Spirituality also arises in discussions of positive psychology. For example, Seligman et al. (2005) list "transcendence" as one of the six virtues identified by positive psychology and define it as "strengths that forge connections to the larger universe and provide meaning" (p. 412).

In our sample, these strengths were experienced by some persons as a sense of tranquility and peace that was sometimes combined with specific religious references as in the first two examples below, and sometimes stood alone, as in the third example. All three comments came in response to the question concerning how they have aged successfully:

> I am a Christian. I try to live my life that way. This has given me the peace and tranquility to avoid stress related issues.

> Combination of a 12-step program which allowed me to break free of addiction and fear and the Buddhism which has taken me to a new plateau of peace and serenity no matter what the situation.

> I learned to let go and live peacefully in the present moment.

Several years after Rowe and Kahn's (1998) book on successful aging appeared, a group of gerontologists published a paper arguing that the model omitted an important component: positive spirituality. They defined it as "a developing an internalized personal relation with the sacred or transcendent that is not bound by race, ethnicity, economics, or class and promotes the wellness and welfare of self and others" (Crowther et al. 2002, p. 614). Clearly, Crowther et al. (2002) were attempting to be broadly inclusive in their definition, for in addition to listing various aspects of demographic diversity, they also stated that, "positive spirituality uses aspects of both religion and spirituality" (p. 614). However, their inclusiveness did not extend to sexual orientation or gender status.

The theme of nurturing the spiritual self reinforces the necessity of listening to our respondents. Although many reported positive outcomes of their spiritual lives, and meaningful relationships with religious congregations, others noted how some persons employ religion to exclude or worse, to abuse them, because of their gender variance. Several specifically stated their fear of having a religious fanatic as a caregiver; these statements were not coded into this category. Their fears exemplify negative spirituality, when religiousness and/or spirituality are used to support stigma and oppress people, a situation that is unfortunately familiar to many trans people (Kidd and Witten 2008b). This was most strongly stated by one individual in response to the question about the worst fears/concerns regarding needing care: "That I'd have some Christer or other religious freak taking care of me."

Despite the concerns voiced by several persons about religious prejudice, we noted that spirituality was a part of the resilience repertoire for 44 % of participants who wrote narrative replies. This was most clear in their answers to three questions about what people look forward to as they age, aging successfully, and skills for positive aging. One person looks forward to "life with my family and church community and continuing with my callings from God." Another looks forward to "continued development of peace and serenity. Buddhism has allowed me to reach a level of peace without fearing the future."

Exercise of Agency

As we coded the narrative responses, we repeatedly noted respondents' statements about goal-setting and engaging in good decision-making. Many respondents spoke of being intentional about choices that enabled them to enjoy old age. Some examples are:

> Planned many years ago to have my life after retirement filled with friends and activities.
>
> I have been frugal all of my life and started preparing for my retirement at age 20. It's not been easy, but I think I have succeeded financially.
>
> I am persistent in trying to reach certain goals.

These responses reflect Emmons' findings that goal attainment is "a major benchmark for the experience of well-being" (2003, p. 106) and that goals "orient a person to what is valuable, meaningful, and purposeful" (p. 107). Emmons classified personal strivings into content categories that relate to well-being and differentiated goal orientations for “positive, desirable goals as opposed to striving to avoid negative, aversive goals” (p. 115; see also Emmons 1999).

Clearly, a major goal for many of our respondents was transition. Some regretted not making the transition earlier in life and many advised younger trans persons to transition early if possible. Respondents also noted that they had been able to age successfully because they had engaged in good financial planning earlier in their lives and now, in their 60s and beyond, felt relatively comfortable. They urged younger GLBTIQ-identified persons to be similarly careful about finances. One reason for a good financial planning is especially important related to the expenses of transition: psychotherapy required before hormone treatment and/or gender reassignment surgery, the surgery itself, and ongoing hormone treatment. In addition, several persons noted the need to have a secure cushion of financial resources in case a job change was necessary after transition.

A number responses falling under the theme of exercising agency relate to the attributes of successful aging named by Rowe and Kahn (1998). For example, having an absence of disease, disability, and risk factors for disease, and maintaining mental and physical functioning are reflected in our respondents’ statements about making good decisions about diet, exercise, alcohol and drug consumption, following doctors’ orders, getting help for depression, pursuing intellectual stimulation, and stress management. The Rowe and Kahn model described people as they are now—living well in old age. In contrast, the theme we identified of planning and decision-making—of taking control of creating and attaining goals—taps into the ways people understand that aging well is not a condition that just happens to people.

Self-Acceptance

This theme emerged in responses to many of the open-ended questions and represents a key component of the resilience repertoire. Table 16.5 shows that some persons were noted to have as many as seven different comments that we coded as referring to self-acceptance.

Psychologist Carol Ryff, whose research on psychological well-being has provided much support to the positive psychology movement, calls self-acceptance “a central characteristic of positive psychological functioning.” It is “a central feature of mental health as well as a characteristic of self-actualization, optimal functioning, and maturity” (1989, p. 1071). Standing against pervasive cultural support for stigmatizing persons with gender-variant identities, our respondents offered statements similar to these:

> I feel I have aged successfully. I believe that being open and honest about myself and really being comfortable with myself have been the most important factors.

> I learned to love myself before my transition and surgery. Since then, I have been consistently happy and content. I continue to exercise mostly to keep myself well. Having planned financially also relieves my mind.

The last statement shows the connection among parts of the resilience repertoire as we noted above. People do not split their lives into neat boxes to make it easy for researchers to analyze them. They live holistically, understanding, for example, that accepting oneself is connected with exercising agency to live well and enjoying an active, healthy life. These statements also lead us to consider one of the virtues listed by positive psychologists Peterson and Seligman (2004): courage.

Courage is defined as "emotional strengths that involve the exercise of will to accomplish goals in the face of opposition, external or internal" (Seligman et al. 2005, p. 412). Psychological studies of courage are limited primarily to persons facing the end-of-life, or those who have responded to situations with altruistic, heroic actions. However, many persons in our study needed considerable emotional strength to exercise will (or agency) in order to come out, go through transition, and radically change their own lives as well as the lives of family members and friends in order to get to a point where they could experience self-acceptance. The following response expresses this well:

> I believe the most important and significant thing that has ever happened to me is to realize and accept what I am. It has been a gradual process that only happened about 10 years ago. Before that, my life was a lie. Now, no matter what happens to me, or where I go, I am at peace with myself concerning my gender and my sexuality. Before I realized and understood what I am, I was so full of conflicts and guilt; life wasn't very comfortable. Now I am very happy just to be myself.

Caring Relationships

This facet of the resilience repertoire is not limited to caring for a dependent elder or child, although that kind of activity is certainly included in this theme. More broadly, it relates to "humanity," another virtue identified by positive psychologists and defined as "interpersonal strengths that involve 'tending and befriending' others" (Seligman et al. 2005, p. 412). Seligman et al. (2005) expanded on this idea by identifying three associated character strengths: kindness, love, and social intelligence. Similarly, Ryff (1989) included "positive relations with others" as a component of psychological well-being. A related personal trait one often finds in discussions of well-being and positive psychology (though not in the individualistic successful aging model of Rowe and Kahn) is generativity, a term Erik Erikson employed to refer to middle-aged persons actively caring for future generations.

What these terms fail to capture, however, are the blessings people experience as a result of caring relationships as described by one respondent like this:

> Providing care is no problem. I was "blessed" with that opportunity for someone who I care for just over 3 years and saw her complete decline from a brilliant [profession omitted for confidentiality] with a 140 + IQ to her being bed-ridden and holding her hand when she died. It was a true honor to help another human being through this "veil of tears!"

This theme of caring relationships with others occurred most often in response to the questions about aging successfully, wisdom to pass on to younger transgender/intersex-identified persons, and skills for positive aging. Once again, we observe the comingling of resilience themes. These individuals have consciously selected the goal of loving others and they do so out of the security rooted in their self-acceptance. Other examples of these responses are:

> Love freely; it is the one thing that if you give it away, you end up having more.
>
> In spite of how individual family members have felt at any given time, I have continued to love and to support them. Over time, this has resulted in close relationships with my parents, children, and grandchildren. These relationships will sustain me as I grow older.
>
> I have been open, giving, friendly, inquisitive, and I have tried to contribute—to my community, to the LGBT community, to my friends and family. I have not focused on myself exclusively. This has opened my world to me.

Some persons went beyond interpersonal relationships and spoke about the need to work for justice and to stop the hate. Thus, it should not be forgotten that caring relationships can involve activities that attempt to make the world a better and more just place, not only for the young as generativity would dictate, but for the old, also. This is reflected in our fifth resilience component: advocacy and activism.

Advocacy and Activism

In their extensive review of the literature on late life resilience and positive psychological well-being, Ryff et al. (1998) observed the potential for decline in a sense of purpose in life among some older people. They suggested that one way to address this would be to encourage more community voluntarism and a stronger sense of community responsibility. Since their paper appeared, there has been an outpouring of gerontological research on the connections between well-being and volunteering (e.g., George 2010; Morrow-Howell et al. 2003; Thomas 2010). However, resilience is not necessarily captured in these studies if they do take into account persons whose voluntarism reflects their experiences of maintaining or regaining well-being in the face of adversity (Ryff 2012).

Given the documentation of transphobia and discrimination against transgender-identified persons, it can be assumed that all of the persons in our sample have experienced adversity at some point in their lives as they came to terms with their gender-variant status. More than half of those who wrote narrative responses provided at least one comment that we coded as reflecting advocacy and activism. One way these comments differ from findings in the voluntarism research is that they do not necessary refer to engagement with an organization (e.g., volunteering to build houses for Habitat for Humanity). For example, one individual wrote about looking forward to aging in order to "enjoy my family and friends and educate the people who I come in contact with about being transsexual." Another wrote that an aspect of aging successfully is to "educate others about [the trans] community to make it better for the young coming up."

Another difference between the resilience category of advocacy and activism and findings from research on voluntarism is the latter does not always capture the commitment to specific causes that motivates some individuals. In other words, some people volunteer because they want to meet others, have fun, and continue to have a meaningful role in the community without a deeply held conviction about the organization or the cause. In contrast, the participants in our study whose replies we coded as indicating the resilience component of advocacy and activism expressed strong commitment to improving the lives of transgender persons. Two examples are:

> My only wish is that the public be educated and the stigma of being LGBT can be brought to light in a positive way. We did not choose to be this way nor ask for it. I would also like to see Public and/or Insurance Medical coverage for required surgeries and needed interventions.

> Our group plans to get more involved on our local level with what this survey ascribes to, that is helping folk who are current in "facilities" where they may (or may not) be hiding their "gift." We would like to seek them out and tell them it is OK to be a "senior citizen" and have the gift of "being one of us!"

In addition, some responses coded into this category were political, such as the person who wrote "Vote Democratic and put Gov. Bob on an unemployment line." More strongly, another said, "Smash the Church/smash the state. Class war... Not just for the rich any more. No god, no masters." A very different approach to social change was expressed in this reply:

> No matter what the challenge, I smile. I tried fear and hiding. Only my detractors were appeased. One I started smiling, I put a new face on transgender. I have to say that I have never been confronted by villagers marching on Frankenstein's castle, but when I came close, well, anyone would have trouble punching a face with a smile on it. Those who would are incorrigible.

Enjoyment of an Active, Healthy Life

In Peterson and Seligman's (2004) account of six virtues and their subcategories of 24 character strengths, humor is categorized as an example of a strength expressing the virtue of transcendence. Nevertheless, the literatures of positive psychology, and of successful aging, contain few references to playfulness, humor, joy, fun, or creativity.

Similarly, the literature on persons living with various forms of gender variance seldom considers how these individuals have lived with joy, playfulness, and creativity as expressed, for example, through drag shows and pride parades. Affirming this in no way eliminates the pain of being the object of transphobic behavior. However, by omitting this side of life, the literature on transgender persons is incomplete. For example, here is what one participant more than 70 years old had to say about balancing knowledge of risk with the desire to enjoy life:

> Obey the laws; dress appropriately as a female; be courteous and polite; stay out of dangerous areas and keep your head up high and enjoy the moment when you are out in public.

Among all the categories we observed in the resilience repertoires of transgender elders, the most commonly cited was what we called "enjoyment of an active and healthy life." This was most obvious in response to the question about wisdom to pass to transgender persons. Respondents urged them to enjoy the persons they are, resist what one called the "unholy Trinity" of "guilt, shame, and fear," and live proudly and honestly. As one person put it:

> Enjoy life while you can. Take it as it comes. Do something about things you can control, accept things you cannot control, and gain the good sense to know the difference. Love a lot, laugh a lot, and smile a lot. And hire a good lawyer.

A subtheme of the "enjoyment of life" aspect of the resilience repertoire is the notion that people should not allow themselves to be victims. This connects back to the theme of the exercise of agency as seen in these quotes:

> People with trans histories in particular need to give up being "other" and live a fully integrated life. Those who cannot do so will always see themselves as victims instead of having control over their lives.

> Come to terms with your gender/sex variant condition and celebrate your diversity rather than feeling sorry for yourself.

Both of these statements could easily been seen as examples of "easier said than done," but they were shared by persons aged 61 and older who have lived many years as trans persons. Despite, or perhaps because of the suffering created by stigma, they have come to the hard-won discovery that life can be lived fully with meaning, purpose, and joy.

A strong component of being able to enjoy life through activities such as travel, gardening, and pursuit of various hobbies is staying physically healthy. Thus, a number of survey participants commented on the importance of good diet, avoiding drug and alcohol abuse, engaging in safe sex, reducing stress, and exercising. Interestingly, several attributed their attention to these issues to the fact that they were more open to their feminine sides as the following quotes demonstrate:

> My feminine side helped me a lot to be a more centered and self-conscious person, which in turn made me more careful about myself and health.

> By coming out to my wife and a select few others at 48, it's allowed me to be myself in terms of "merging" my masculine and feminine sides without fear. It has completely calmed me and taken most of the stress out of my life.

Discussion

This study of the narrative responses of transgender persons aged 61 and older revealed six components of their resilience repertoires. Overall, the qualitative analyses of the narrative responses enabled us to understand the high percentage of persons who checked "yes" in response to the question about whether they considered themselves to be aging successfully. Their strengths and affirmations of successfully aging offer new light on the old question posed by the "paradox of well-being" that runs through the gerontological literature. Indeed, research with this "invisible minority within the worldwide elderly population" (Persson 2009, p. 642) may help to answer vexing questions in gerontology and more broadly in the study of human resilience (Witten and Eyler 2012).

Similar to much gerontological research, a limitation of this research was its cross-sectional design and use of self-report measures. In addition, the fourth author devised the survey and shared the data with the other authors who had no role in designing the survey and recruiting participants, but rather conducted the analyses and had IRB approval for a secondary analysis. Nevertheless, as Doolan and Froelicher (2009) have argued, secondary analysis is an important research tool. In this case, it has provided a rich array of insights into the ways persons subjected to multiple sources of stigma age well with a resilience repertoire.

More research is needed to confirm our observation that the resilience repertoires developed by persons who are stigmatized in multiple ways by the wider society support self-perceived successful aging. In a paper on LGBT aging, Sperber (2006) suggested that these persons may experience more successful aging than heterosexuals. She wrote: "Developing resilience in the face of discrimination has helped some gay and lesbian seniors become experts in dealing with adversity, facing change, and learning how to take care of themselves" (p. 252). We found that to be the case among the persons in this study. Sperber also argued that "gender-role flexibility may also add to more successful aging, as some individuals may have developed skills not developed by their heterosexual peers" (p. 253).

On this note, we close this chapter, giving the last word to one of our participants who wrote about the strengths—and resilience—gained by honestly coming to terms with a gender-variant identity. This quote movingly confirms the resilience that can emerge at the intersection of multiple stigmatized identities:

> I have been in innumerable situations where the gatekeeper I was confronting saw me as not only Trans but as "older," and possibly as "freak," and behaved toward me accordingly. The first such interactions were scary, but I quickly learned—one-trial learning, actually—to respond in the strongest terms to convey my identity and sense of my own worth to that person. Sometimes that works, and sometimes it doesn't, but whether it does or not in any individual instance must not affect one's intent to respond in identical manner the next time. On several occasions I failed the gatekeeper interaction but went off and developed ways to (metaphorically) tunnel around or climb over that particular gate. I think the attitude one cultivates in the process of doing this, over and over through the years, is like *cardiopulmonary exercise for the soul* [italics added].

Acknowledgments The authors wish to thank Samantha Hahn for assistance in organizing the qualitative responses.

References

Birren, J. E., & Birren, B. A. (1990). The concepts, models, and history of the psychology of aging. In J. E. Birren & K. W. Schaie (Eds.), *Handbook of the psychology of aging* (3rd ed., pp. 3–20). San Diego: Academic Press.

Clark, P. G., Burbank, P. M., Greene, G., Owens, N., & Riebe, D. (2011). What do we know about resilience in older adults? An exploration of some facts, factors, and facets. In B. Resnick, L. P. Gwyther, & K. A. Roberto (Eds.), *Resilience in aging: Concepts, research, and outcomes* (pp. 51–66). New York: Springer.

Cole, E. R. (2009). Intersectionality and research in psychology. *American Psychologist, 64,* 170–180.

Cook-Daniels, L. (2006). Trans aging. In D. Kimmel, R. Rose, & S. David (Eds.), *Lesbian, gay, bisexual, and transgender aging: Research and clinical perspectives* (pp. 20–35). New York: Columbia University Press.

Cook-Daniels, L., & munson, m. (2010). Sexual violence, elder abuse, and sexuality of transgender adults, age 50+: Results of three surveys. *Journal of GLBT Family Studies, 6,* 142–177.

Crenshaw, K. W. (1993). Mapping the margins: Intersectionality, identity politics, and violence against women of color. *Stanford Law Review, 43*(6), 1241–1299.

Cronin, A., & King, A. (2010). Power, inequality and identification: Exploring diversity and intersectionality amonst older LGB adults. *Sociology, 44,* 876–892.

Crowther, M. R., Parker, M. W., Achenbaum, W. A., Larimore, W. L., & Koenig, H. G. (2002). Rowe and Kahn's model of successful aging revisited: Positive spirituality—The forgotten factor. *The Gerontologist, 42,* 613–620.

Doolan, D. M., & Froelicher, E. S. (2009). Using an existing data set to answer new research questions: A methodological review. *Research and Theory for Nursing Practice: An International Journal, 23,* 203–215.

Emmons, R. A. (1999). *The psychology of ultimate concerns: Motivation and spirituality in personality*. New York: Guilford.

Emmons, R. A. (2003). Personal goals, life meaning, and virtue: Wellsprings of a positive life. In C. L. M. Keyes & J. Haidt (Eds.), *Flourishing: Positive psychology and the life well-lived* (pp. 105–128). Washington: American Psychological Association.

George, L. K. (2010). Still happy after all these years: Research frontiers on subjective well-being in later life. *Journal of Gerontology: Social Sciences, 65B,* 331–339.

Held, B. S. (2004). The negative side of positive psychology. *Journal of Humanistic Psychology, 44,* 9–46.

Hines, S. (2006). What's the difference? Bringing particularity to queer studies of transgender. *Journal of Gender Studies, 15,* 49–66.

Holstein, M. B., & Minkler, M. (2003). Self, society, and the "new gerontology." *The Gerontologist, 43,* 787–796.

Kidd, J. D., & Witten, T. M. (2008a). Transgender and transsexual identities: The next strange fruit—Hate crimes, violence and genocide against the global trans-communities. *Journal of Hate Studies, 6*(31), 31–63.

Kidd, J. D., & Witten, T. M. (2008b). Understanding spirituality and religiosity in the transgender community: Implications for aging. *Journal of Religion, Spirituality, and Aging, 20*(1–2), 29–62.

Link, B. G., & Phelan, J. C. (2001). Conceptualizing stigma. *Annual Review of Sociology, 27,* 363–385.

Lombardi, E. (2009). Varieties of transgender/transsexual lives and their relationship with transphobia. *Journal of Homosexuality, 56,* 977–992.

Luthar, S. S., Cicchetti, D., & Becker, B. (2000). The construct of resilience: A critical evaluation and guidelines for future work. *Child Development, 71,* 543–562.

Morrow-Howell, N., Hinterlong, J., Rozario, P. A., & Tang, F. (2003). Effects of volunteering on the well-being of older adults. *Journal of Gerontology: Social Sciences, 58B,* S137–S145.

Mroczek, D. K., & Kolarz, C. M. (1998). The effect of age on positive and negative affect: A developmental perspective on happiness. *Journal of Personality and Social Psychology, 75,* 1333–1349.

Oleksy, E. H. (2011). Intersectionality at the cross-roads. *Women's Studies International Forum, 34,* 263–270.

Persson, D. I. (2009). Unique challenges of transgender aging: Implications from the literature. *Journal of Gerontological Social Work, 52,* 633–646.

Peterson, C., & Seligman, M. E. P. (2004). *Character strengths and virtues: A handbook and classification*. Washington: American Psychological Association.

Porter, K. E., Oala, C. R., & Witten, T. M. (2013). Religious affiliation and successful aging among transgender older adults: Findings from the Trans MetLife Survey. *Journal of Religion, Spirituality, and Aging, 25,* 112–138.

Quinn, C., & Clare, L. (2008). Interpretive phenomenological analysis. In R. Watson, H. McKenna, S. Cowman, & J. Keady (Eds.), *Nursing research: Designs and methods* (pp. 375–384). London: Churchill Livingstone.

Resnick, B. (2011). Conclusion. In B. Resnick, L. P. Gwyther, & K. A. Roberto (Eds.), *Resilience in aging: Concepts, research, and outcomes* (pp. 351–356). New York: Springer.

Rowe, J. W., & Kahn, R. L. (1998). *Successful aging*. New York: Pantheon.

Ryff, C. D. (1989). Happiness is everything, or is it? Explorations on the meaning of psychological well-being. *Journal of Personality and Social Psychology, 57,* 1069–1081.

Ryff, C. D (2012). Existential well-being and health. In P. T. P. Wong (Ed.), *The human quest for meaning: Theories, research, and applications* (pp. 233–247). New York: Routledge.

Ryff, C. D., Singer, B., Love, G. D., & Essex, M. J. (1998). Resilience in adulthood and later life: Defining features and dynamic processes. In J. Lomranz (Ed.), *Handbook of aging and mental health: An integrative approach* (pp. 69–96). New York: Plenum.

Sánchez, F. J., & Vilain, E. (2009). Collective self-esteem as a coping resource for male-to-female transsexuals. *Journal of Counseling Psychology, 56,* 202–209.

Seligman, M. E. P., & Csikszentmihalyi, M. (2000). Positive psychology: An introduction. *American Psychologist, 55,* 5–14.

Seligman, M. E. P., Steen, T. A., Park, N., & Peterson, C. (2005). Positive psychology progress: Empirical validation of interventions. *American Psychologist, 60,* 410–421.

Smith, J. A., Jarman, M., & Osborn, M. (1999). Doing interpretative phenomenological analysis. In M. Murray & K. Chamberlain (Eds.), *Qualitative health psychology* (pp. 218–240). Thousand Oaks: Sage.

Sperber, J. B. (2006). As time goes by: An introduction to the needs of lesbian, gay, bisexual, and transgender elders. In M. D. Shankle (Ed.), *Handbook of lesbian, gay, bisexual, & transgender public health: A practitioner's guide to service* (pp. 247–260). Binghamton: Haworth.

Strawbridge, W. J., Wallhagen, M. I., & Cohen, R. D. (2002). Successful aging and well-being: Self-rated compared with Rowe and Kahn. *The Gerontologist, 42,* 727–733.

Syed, M. (2010). Disciplinarity and methodology in intersectionality theory and research. *American Psychologist, 65,* 61–62.

Thomas, P. A. (2010). Is it better to give or to receive? Social support and the well-being of older adults. *Journal of Gerontology: Social Sciences, 65B,* 351–357.

Thomas, S. P., & Pollio, H. R. (2002). *Listening to patients: A phenomenological approach to nursing research and practice*. New York: Springer.

U.S. Census Bureau. (2011). Household income for states: 2009 and 2011 (American community survey briefs). http://www.census.gov/prod/2011pubs/acsbr10-02.pdf. Accessed 3 April 2013.

Vahia, I. V., Chattillion, E., Kavirajan, H., & Depp, C. A. (2011). Psychological protective factors across the lifespan: Implications for psychiatry. *Psychiatric Clinics of North America, 34,* 231–248.

Witten, T. M. (2002). Geriatric care and management issues for the transgender and intersex populations. *Geriatric Care and Management Journal, 12*(3), 20–24.

Witten, T. M. (2009). Graceful exits: Intersection of aging, transgender identities, and the family/community. *Journal of GLBT Family Studies, 5,* 35–61.

Witten, T. M., & Eyler, A. E. (Eds.). (2012). *Gay, lesbian, bisexual, and transgender aging: Challenges in research, practice, and policy*. Baltimore: The Johns Hopkins University Press.

Chapter 17
Experiential Wisdom and Lifelong Learning

Kevin Rathunde

How does one stay on a path of interest and lifelong learning? What leads one person to stay active and absorbed in life and another to feel increasingly alienated and apathetic? These questions are obviously important for understanding an individual's development and quality of life. In addition, these questions are important for the health of a society. Enormous talent and creative potential are wasted when a person continues to age without developing new skills. In addition, when individuals stop opening themselves up to new challenges, the lack of intellectual stimulation puts them at greater risk for cognitive decline and chronic disorders such as Alzheimer's disease (Andel et al. 2005); this, in turn, places unsustainable financial burdens on nations with rapidly aging populations.

The present chapter explores how some individuals are able to stay engaged on a path of creativity and lifelong learning. It argues that staying on such a path is facilitated by the capacity to regulate optimal experience, a skill that will be referred to as *experiential wisdom*. Optimal experience is broadly defined here as experiences of interest (Renninger et al. 1992), including those occasional intense states of flow or total absorption in some activity (Csikszentmihalyi 1990). Experiential wisdom, then, presumably enhances positive learning outcomes because of the ability or "wisdom" to make experiential course corrections (e.g., to counter feelings of boredom or anxiety) that lead back to states of interest and flow. By sustaining interest, and occasionally being rewarded with experiences of flow that renew and deepen it, a person maximizes their opportunities for learning and creative insight.

This chapter is organized in three parts. Part I sets up a broad framework for thinking about experiential wisdom. It addresses the implicit assumptions of the proposed model, the role of experiential wisdom in relation to broader theories of human development, and the needed conditions for the emergence of experiential wisdom in adulthood. Part II of this chapter defines in more detail the notion of experiential wisdom. It describes the dynamics at work as a person negotiates a person–environment

K. Rathunde (✉)
Department of Family and Consumer Studies, University of Utah,
225 South 1400 East, Room 228, Salt Lake City UT 84112, USA
e-mail: rathunde@fcs.utah.edu

J. D. Sinnott (ed.), *Positive Psychology,*
DOI 10.1007/978-1-4614-7282-7_17,

fit that is more conducive to optimal experience, namely, the interrelation of a spontaneous/intuitive mode of attention with a more selective/rational mode. Experiential wisdom is presumably manifested by the flexible interoperation and synchrony of these two modes of attention. Finally, Part III of this chapter illustrates experiential wisdom by drawing on past interviews with three distinguished individuals—poet Mark Strand, social scientist Donald Campbell, and medical researcher Jonas Salk. The experiential wisdom of these three helped keep them engaged and active, setting the stage for the creative process to unfold.

The Possibility of Lifelong Learning: Assumptions, Limitations, and Prospects

Before defining in more detail the components of experiential wisdom that are postulated to help a person sustain interest and flow, it is useful to put the concept in a broader conceptual/developmental context. This introductory section of this chapter focuses on three things: (1) revealing the author's assumptions about human nature and learning that inform this chapter; (2) limiting the scope of experiential wisdom to avoid misunderstandings; and (3) briefly suggesting something about the development of experiential wisdom.

Experiential wisdom is related to lifelong learning through its capacity to help find and sustain optimal states of experience. Implicit in this claim are two assumptions: (1) intrinsically motivated states play a key role in learning and development; and (2) lifelong learning is a primary goal of human development. To researchers within the field of positive psychology (Seligman and Csikszentmihalyi 2000), these may seem to be self-evident assumptions. However, many social scientists hold a more extrinsic view of human motivation and development. In addition, many parents and teachers hold to the belief that children must be pushed, prodded, and given incentives to make them learn. It is, therefore, worthwhile to briefly address these positive assumptions before proceeding.

In contrast to a more cynical view of human motivation, this chapter is animated by the belief that continued absorption in new challenges, perpetual curiosity, and lifelong learning should not be rare outcomes for human lives; rather, they are *potentially normative ones*. This perspective on human development is related to a handful of formative ideas that have influenced my research. Abraham Maslow (1968) had an early and strong impact on this positive view through his notion of self-actualization. Maslow thought there was an inborn, intrinsic motivation to pursue self-actualization or full human development. However, this inner nature was fragile, easily dominated by more urgent physiological and psychosocial needs, and could be stifled by unhealthy family, school, and cultural contexts that operated under misguided views of human development. When the basic needs of life were met, and social contexts nurtured growth rather than suppressing it, self-actualization was manifested by more frequent peak experiences, or feelings of transcendence and complete absorption in the moment. This basic view of human motivation and potential was reinforced by my own subsequent work with Professor Csikszentmihalyi on flow, talent development, and lifelong learning (Csikszentmihalyi et al. 1997; Rathunde and Csikszentmihalyi 2006). The flow model similarly posits the importance of a play-oriented and intrinsically motivated process of learning and development that leads to more frequent episodes of flow.

Many individuals, both in academia and outside of it, are suspicious about such a positive view of human motivation and potential. Therefore, it is worth mentioning another important idea that provides a strong supporting argument for this perspective, the concept of *neoteny*. In developmental biology and evolutionary thought, neoteny refers to the unusually slow rate of human development from fetus to adulthood. As a result of this neotenous pattern, the characteristics of childhood/youth are extended into adulthood. This biologically based strategy puts a premium on learning and flexible adaptation to the environment, rather than reliance on "hardwired" instincts for survival. It elevates the importance of the characteristics of children that enable such flexibility (e.g., playfulness, curiosity, openness, intrinsic motivation to learn, and so on; Gould 1977; Lerner 1984; Montagu 1989). Lorenz (1971) maintained that these behavioral manifestations of neoteny were enormously important in the development of the species and led to the defining characteristic of humans: *an unending state of development*. Some research bears out the connection between neotenous traits and scientific and artistic creativity and achievement (Charlton 2006).

The concept of neoteny further supports the argument that lifelong learning need not be thought of as an unrealistic human outcome. In his book *Growing Young*, Ashley Montagu (1989) concurs with this view and sums it up in the following memorable phrase: "The goal of life is to die young—as late as possible" (p. 5). In other words, we are prepared by evolution, if conditions are conducive for learning and growth, to "grow young," or to utilize childlike traits as we mature. Montagu thought that the potential benefits of an applied understanding of neoteny were not fully recognized. Such an understanding would encourage the celebration and nurturance of childlike traits such as interest and intrinsic motivation, leading to significant adjustments in parenting and teaching philosophies; it would also redefine society as a support system designed to extend the neotenous traits of humankind. Another thinker who shared this radical position of redesigning schools and society to capitalize on the characteristics of the child was Maria Montessori (Standing 1984). Perhaps not surprisingly, her pedagogy was based on a fervent belief that intrinsically motivated concentration was the key to learning and, given the support of appropriate learning environments, a normal outcome for children (Montessori 1946).

To avoid misunderstandings about what is being proposed here about experiential wisdom, it is helpful to limit the scope of the concept by placing it in a broader developmental framework. Experiential wisdom is not thought of here as a trait-like characteristic that operates in a context-free way. My view of human development is consistent with contemporary trends that emphasize person–environment fit and context (Lerner 2006; Bronfenbrenner and Morris 2006). In other words, when considering an individual's developmental trajectory, it is necessary to think about interactive systems encompassing biological, psychological, sociocultural, historical, and physical contexts. Experiential wisdom, then, is best thought of as a person-level characteristic that *influences development through its effect on an evolving person–environment fit.* Seen within this broad framework, experiential wisdom is an example of what Bronfennbrenner's called a developmentally instigative characteristic. About such characteristics Bronfenbrenner (1992) commented: "When they are manifested over time in particular settings, [they] tend to evoke complementary patterns of continuing developmental feedback, creating more complex developmental trajectories that exhibit continuity through time" (pp. 219–220). In this sense, experiential wisdom is a characteristic that sets in motion *interactions* with the environment that provide feedback that can be used to negotiate a more optimally rewarding person–environment fit. Proposing that experiential wisdom is important for lifelong learning, therefore, does reduce an ecological model to the realm of personality or undermine the principle that the self-environment relationship is the primary mover of development.

Misunderstandings may also arise if experiential wisdom is not differentiated from other accounts of wisdom. The notion here has a more limited scope than descriptions that emphasize how wisdom provides a "big picture" that helps with the overall conduct of life. Baltes and Staudinger (2000), for example, emphasize how a wise individual knows what constitutes a meaningful life and knows how to plan and manage such a life. Such a wise person is thought to have a healthy combination of factual knowledge, procedural knowledge, understanding of contexts, openness to diverse values, and an awareness of the uncertainty and impermanence of life. Sternberg (2001) also utilizes the concept of wisdom to articulate the broadest possible *balance* or integration of the interests of the individual, of others, and the culture at large. Experiential wisdom does not address the overall balance of personal qualities that result in the living of a meaningful life; however, the concept is related to these and other notions of wisdom through its emphasis on process rather than outcome. Wisdom is synonymous in most definitions with the process of making good judgments; and such a process typically involves balancing contrasting views. As Sternberg (2001) suggests, wisdom is more a matter of "knowing how" rather than "knowing that." Experiential wisdom, then, is a kind of wisdom, or metacognitive knowledge about process, that is specifically related to managing one's arousal, focus, and motivation in a task at hand.

Finally, experiential wisdom should be differentiated from the positive outcomes to which it is presumably related. In other words, the perspective here is that experiential wisdom facilitates learning by keeping a person's attention engaged and highly focused. Examples provided later in this chapter suggest how experiential wisdom facilities creative insight and accomplishment, but the concept is not a substitute for a well-rounded theory of creativity. Creativity is a complex process involving the person, a social field, and a culturally based symbolic domain (Csikszentmihlayi 1996). Experiential wisdom is related to the qualities (e.g., flexibility) that may make a person creative, but it does not attempt to explain the full creative process.

Despite the human potential for experiential wisdom and lifelong learning, it must be admitted that these outcomes are not a common occurrence in later life. Rather than interpreting this fact as evidence against the possibility, the perspective here is that these positive outcomes are dependent upon an array of contextual conditions that must align appropriately. In other words, similar to Maslow's notion that self-actualization was a fragile potentiality of human development, the assumption here is that the appearance of experiential wisdom in adulthood likewise depends upon fortunate conditions in childhood that are largely outside of a person's control. It is impossible to give a full accounting in this chapter of all of the factors that might be related to the development of experiential wisdom; however, it is useful to consider a few key conditions that are likely to be related to its emergence.

By adulthood, a person has been shaped by genetic factors and socialization experiences that either build or tear down the capacity for experiential wisdom. The human organism is born with a central nervous system that is regulating optimal arousal (Berlyne 1960; Hebb 1955). For example, attempts to avoid too much or too little stimulation are apparent from the first moments of life: When a novel stimulus is introduced, infants will pay attention until they habituate to the new sight and arousal diminishes; then, attention recovers again when a novel stimulus is again introduced (Caron and Caron 1968). In terms of these early arousal dynamics, the importance of genetic predispositions and early parenting influences are evident. Temperament affects attention span, activity level, focus, persistence, and other characteristics that influence concentration (Thomas and Chess 1977). Furthermore, research has shown that the quality of early parenting affects attachment quality, which in turn affects the developing self-regulative abilities of children (Sroufe et al. 2005). Disruptions in the attachment relationship, therefore, can damage a child's capacity to regulate arousal and attention. Modifications of these early temperament and attachment influences continually take place through ongoing socialization in families and schools. Experiential wisdom, then, is more likely to emerge when there is a goodness-of-fit between genetic capacities (e.g., temperament, ability to focus attention, etc.) and the demands of parents and teachers in socializing environments (Lerner and Lerner 1987), setting in motion a cycle of optimally arousing experiences without prolonged and unresolved states of boredom and/or anxiety.

In this experiential framework on development (see Rathunde and Csikzentmihalyi 2006, for a more comprehensive discussion of the role of experience in the development of the person), one of the most important qualities of a family or school that can affect goodness-of-fit is whether or not parents are able to successfully combine support with challenge. Just as comforting and stimulating caregivers promote secure attachment by keeping infants in an optimally arousing state (Field 1985), supportive and challenging family and school contexts are optimal in terms of helping children moderate or raise their arousal level (i.e., reduce anxiety or escape boredom) and have been positively correlated with a adolescents' reports of flow and optimal experience (Rathunde 1996; Rathunde and Csikszentmihalyi 2005). A supportive and challenging family or school is also an authoritative context (Baumrind 1989); and the variety of developmental benefits associated with such a context has been widely documented in the parenting and education literatures (Steinberg et al. 1992; Wentzel 1998).

In summary, experiential wisdom, or the capacity to sustain interest and find flow, is based on the assumptions that human learning is intrinsically motivated and that lifelong learning is a biologically based goal of human development. Experiential wisdom is seen here as a person-level variable in an ecological framework on development; it instigates development by setting in motion interactions with the environment that produce feedback that can be used to negotiate a more optimal person–environment fit and thereby sustain a path of interest and optimal experience. The development of experiential wisdom in adulthood presumably depends on the appropriate conditions in infancy, childhood, and adolescence. More specifically, the capacity for regulating optimal experience depends first and foremost on having repeated optimal experiences that provide a platform for future optimal experiences. It is the infant who is kept in a state of optimal arousal who develops secure attachment and more effective self-regulative abilities in early childhood; it is the child and adolescent with supportive and challenging (authoritative) home and school environments who experiences more flow and enters adulthood with some wisdom on how to stay engaged and interested in future endeavors (see also Rathunde and Csikszentmihalyi 2006).

Navigating a Path of Abiding Interest: The Dynamics of Experiential Wisdom

If a person has experiential wisdom, and therefore the capacity to make experiential course corrections that lead back to states of interest and flow, they are more likely to stay on the path of lifelong learning (Csikszentmihalyi 1990; Dewey 1934/1980; Malsow 1968). Recurring states of interest, interspersed with renewing states of flow, are proposed here to be the best signposts and indicators that one is on such a path. In Part II of this chapter, a more detailed explanation of experiential wisdom is provided.

The Dynamics of Experiential Wisdom

A central theme of experiential wisdom is that sustained interest and flow experience are more likely to occur when two facets of attention work in synchrony: a spontaneous, affectively charged, intuitive orientation we bring to a task; and a selective, deliberate, rational focus we use to work on a task. When one or the other mode operates without the "help" of the other, staying on a path of abiding interest becomes difficult, if not impossible. That two such modes are intrinsic to human nature and important for learning is a theme that has received some attention in the adult development literature (see Hoare 2006; Kramer 2000; Labouvie-Vief 1990, 1994). Yet the latter, selective mode of attention is emphasized in most accounts of self-regulation and learning.

In these accounts, one's metacognition (i.e., thinking about thinking) allows the monitoring of ongoing activity; this monitoring leads to the use of various strategies that can enhance the mastery of a task (e.g., see Zimmerman 1990). Although experiential wisdom also implies a monitoring of ongoing cognition, and can make use of conscious strategies that can affect experience, it places an equal emphasis on the role of preconscious and intuitive modes that frame situations and *set the stage* for more conscious and selective processing. Such a view is consistent with recent perspectives in positive psychology, phenomenological philosophy, and cognitive science (Damasio 1994; Dewey 1933; Haight 2009; James 1890; Johnson 2007; Lakoff and Johnson 1999; Leder 1990; Merleau-Ponty 1962).

It is understandable that most descriptions of self-regulation and learning have focused on consciously directed attention: such processes are easier to conceive and measure. In his pioneering work on attention, William James (1890) referred to this focused and linear mode of processing as voluntary attention; others refer to this Jamesian notion as *selective attention* (see Kaplan 1995). Selective attention is obviously necessary for staying on a path of lifelong learning and must be a part of any description of experiential wisdom; however, the regulation of experience is more than a purely rational and consciously directed enterprise. Every parent and teacher knows that when one tries to force a child to pay attention, the motivation to learn often evaporates. *There is also a present-centered, spontaneous, affectively rich kind of attention that sets the stage and provides the energy for selective attention.* James (1890) referred to this kind of attention as involuntary; this chapter primarily uses the terms spontaneous or intuitive to describe this mode. Both kinds of attention—one spontaneous (involuntary and intuitive) and the other selective (voluntary and rational)—are seen here as vital for sustaining interest. When selective attention is used without the motivating energy of spontaneous attention, it results in mental fatigue and negative moods (James 1890; Kaplan and Kaplan 1989); when spontaneous attention is the only operative mode, it often results in disorganized thought and aimless distraction (Dewey 1933).

A similar theme of a preconscious frame that sets the stage for rational thought has recently been elaborated in multidisciplinary perspectives on embodied cognition (Johnson 2007; Lakoff and Johnson 1999). One key notion is the importance of an esthetic orientation emerging from bodily/sensory processes (Johnson 2007). The disembodied, scientific tradition in the West has devalued esthetic experience (and emotion) as subjective and biased. An embodied cognition approach, however, elevates such felt experience to a more prominent position. Johnson (2007) draws heavily from John Dewey's 1934/1980 book *Art as Experience* and comments: "We need a philosophy that sees aesthetics as not just about art, beauty, and taste, but rather as about how human beings experience and make meaning" (p. 212). Other perspectives on embodiment draw on the latest discoveries in neuroscience and emphasize the roles of affect and emotion in relation to rational thought. Damasio (1994) has shown that when injuries occur to areas of the brain that are important for experiencing emotion, the process of reasoning is adversely affected:

> The process of emotion and feeling are indispensable for rationality... The lower levels in the neural edifice of reason are the same ones that regulate the processing of emotions and feelings, along with the body functions necessary for an organism's survival. In turn, these lower levels maintain direct and mutual relationships with virtually every bodily organ, thus placing the body directly in the chain of operations that generate the highest reaches of reasoning, decision making, and, by extension, social behavior and creativity. (p. xiii)

Current work in positive psychology is yet another field of study that has altered the view of selective/rational processes operating in isolation. For example, Haight (2009) suggests that moral emotions have a powerful shaping effect on how a situation is framed, and reasoning is more of a "servant" than a "high priest" in the temple of morality. Such implicit frames are shaped by cultural and evolutionary forces that have been at play in the development of the human species. What has been referred to here as preconscious, spontaneous, or an esthetic grasping of a situation has been described by other positive psychologists as intuition, or the act of knowing or sensing without the use of rational processes. Myers (2004, p. 17) refers to intuition as the "automaticity of being" and has summarized the research that reveals its pervasive operation in everyday life. Intuition often reveals that there is something incomplete in a situation that needs to be made clear. In this sense, it opens the door and provides the motivational drive for the selective processing that can be used for resolving the intuited problem. Classic accounts of creativity have for many years likewise suggested a vital role for intuition in the early phases of the creative process (i.e., preparation, incubation, and insight) before selective processing takes over in the latter phases (i.e., evaluation and elaboration; Barron 1969; Csikszentmihalyi 1996; Kris 1952; Martindale 1999; Wallas 1926).

Knowing that experiential wisdom involves the interplay of spontaneous/intuitive and selective/rational modes does not bring the regulation of interest under direct control. Because spontaneous attention is involuntary, it is more accurate to consider the regulation process as *navigated* rather than self-directed. Experiential wisdom helps navigate by finding a way forward that is illuminated by preconscious intuitions, and then actively setting out on that course. In other words, it enhances the ability to find interest and flow because it helps a person "read the map" of intuition *and* make appropriate course corrections with the effort of selective attention. Because intuition operates in a preconscious way, it is not always easy to recognize its signals. To let intuition perform its necessary function, a relaxed openness, patience, and a tolerance for ambiguity—qualities that have traditionally been associated with the creative person—is required (Barron 1969; Csikszentmihalyi 1996; Sternberg 1988).

The spontaneous and selective facets of experiential wisdom work in an inseparable, dialectical fashion allowing the person to sustain interest and continually find new challenges. For instance, when a musician is inspired by a particular melody that spontaneously comes to mind, and then consciously works out the details and commits it to memory, that melody, in turn, becomes part of the musician's repertoire that provides a context for the intuition of new melodies. Dewey (1934/1980) believed that an intellectual process was no different than the artistic process and moved forward in the same way. When an author is working on a manuscript and senses that there is something important missing in the argument, intuition is at work.

The impulse to change the manuscript animates the selective focus that clarifies the problem and eventually resolves it. The amended argument in the manuscript sets the stage for the intuition of the next problem, and so it goes in dialectical fashion. More specific examples of this interplay of attentional modes are provided in the last part of this chapter.

The Role of Optimal Experience in Experiential Wisdom

As mentioned earlier, the need for optimal arousal is present at birth and is a genetically based part of human nature (Berlyne 1960; Caron and Caron 1968; Hebb 1955). Flow can be thought of as an optimal state of arousal that combines a sense of order and novelty *at the same time*. This combination is represented in the flow model by the constructs of skill and challenge, respectively, and flow is thought to occur more often when a person's skills and challenges are similarly strong and balanced (Csikszentmihalyi 1990). Such an optimally arousing condition, however, is temporary. When an activity is repeated without variation or change, it inevitably loses its intensity.

It is the short-lived and transitory nature of flow that makes it relevant to learning and development. As Piaget (1962) also observed, disequilibrium between the processes of assimilation and accommodation is inevitable; continually reestablishing equilibrium is the motor of cognitive development. In an experiential perspective, disequilibrium is subjectively signaled by boredom and anxiety—two inevitable life experiences—and flow is the feeling one has when equilibrium is reestablished (Rathunde and Csikszentmihalyi 2006).

Flow, therefore, represents a healthy solution to the inevitable problems of boredom and anxiety. To resolve boredom (i.e., low challenge with high skill), a person must raise their challenge level and initiate a feeling of change and expansion. To alleviate anxiety (i.e., high challenge with low skill), a person is required to raise skills and thereby increase a sense of order and emerging control. As skills and challenges are increased over time, a person learns and grows (Csikszentmihlayi 1990).

A person with experiential wisdom would be better equipped to respond to boredom and anxiety and make these growth-oriented adjustments. For example, if feeling bored, intuition can set in motion a challenge-finding mode. An intuited problem will introduce some directionality to the focus of attention; as selective attention fleshes out the challenge, it raises arousal and brings challenges and skills into a better balance, thereby triggering a flow experience. Conversely, when a person is anxious, intuition can set in motion a problem-solving mode. Once there is a dimly perceived direction toward resolution, selective processing can work out the details, build new skills, and thereby modulate arousal until it is again in the optimal range.

In summary, the bimodal attributes of experiential wisdom can work to differentiate and integrate knowledge and make flow more likely to reoccur (Rathunde and Csikszentmihalyi 2006). In Piagetian terms, they can help move assimilation toward accommodation and then back again, with each traverse holding the promise of equilibrium and temporary episodes of optimal experience. Depending on what adjustment to experience is needed to get back to flow, the spontaneous and selective modes of experiential wisdom can either be used to problem-find and raise arousal or problem-solve and lower arousal. In either scenario, these modes work together to intensify the present moment; and it is this total involvement and intensification of focus that triggers the subjective feeling of flow. By setting in motion a recurring cycle of optimal experience, experiential wisdom ensures an ongoing tension or rhythm in the learning process. Experiential wisdom helps coordinate the functions of spontaneous and selective attention: If the former were operating alone, the likely result will be a series of disconnected thoughts that dissipate energy; if only the latter were brought to a task, mental fatigue will eventually deaden the quality of experience.

Illustrating Experiential Wisdom: Interviews with Mark Strand, Donald Campbell, and Jonas Salk

The final part of this chapter illustrates experiential wisdom at work in the lives of three remarkable individuals who were able to navigate a path of interest and lifelong learning—the Pulitzer Prize winning poet Mark Strand, the distinguished social scientist and methodologist Donald Campbell, and the medical researcher and virologist Jonas Salk, inventor of the first successful polio vaccine. These interviews were originally collected as part of Csikszentmihalyi's (1996) study of creativity (see also Rathunde 2010, for a more comprehensive examination of the interviews). The interviews with Strand, Campbell, and Salk reveal a self-conscious understanding of the process of regulating optimal experience. It is not suggested here that such a metaawareness is a necessary condition of lifelong interest and learning; however, it is likely to be helpful to the individuals who possess it. In the excerpts from the interviews that follow, each of these distinguished individuals provide idiosyncratic descriptions with respect to how intuitive/spontaneous and rational/selective processes were coordinated to further their interest and work. Despite the uniqueness of each description, there are clear similarities that cut across the three accounts.

Making Meaning

Mark Strand is a Pulitzer Prize-winning poet and essayist and recipient of a MacArthur Fellowship ("genius award"). He served as Poet Laureate of the United States in 1990 and has taught literature and creative writing at a number of prestigious universities, including John Hopkins University and the University of Chicago. He is currently a Professor of English and Comparative Literature at Columbia University.

"Paying attention" and "witnessing" were key ideas that emerged from the Strand interview. They represent, I believe, the movement between spontaneous and selective attentional processes. Paying attention is staying acutely sensitive to the moment; witnessing is responding with thought and consciousness to what one is experiencing.

> I think that it [paying attention] grows out of a sense of mortality. I mean, we're only here for a short while on earth, and I think it's such a lucky accident, having been born, that we're almost obliged to pay attention.... We are, as far as we know, the only part of the universe that's self-conscious.... we're combined in such a way that we can describe what it's like to be alive, to be witnesses.

These same two elements emerged in his advice to an aspiring poet:

> I would say to read a great deal, withhold opinion, keep your eyes and ears open and your mouth shut for as long as possible.... be a receiver for as long as is possible until it becomes unbearable [and] you can't just receive anymore—you must produce.

Paying attention and witnessing are both part of the dynamics of Strand's poetry: one receives and pays attention as long as possible, and then one responds and produces something from that experience.

Both of these modes—one passive and the other more active—were essential according to Strand. He found it paradoxical that some young poets thought of the witnessing component to be a corruption of poetry: "You find a lot of young people... don't even want to write their poems down. [They] would rather recite them to you as if poetry were strictly performance, like it was all intuition and improvisation, nothing to do with thought or the interventions of consciousness." However, Strand recognized that the immediacy of paying attention and conscious witnessing were both important and needed to fit together in order to avoid different kinds of writer's block. For instance, Strand thought that a phase of receiving can reach a point where it becomes "unbearable," and the longer one was in this phase without reacting (i.e., witnessing), the more "frustration" one would feel. Conversely, a different impasse resulted from the overuse of selective processes. He felt that one of the "worst" mistakes a writer could make was to go back over poems and ask "How did I do that?" This urge to consciously understand the process shortchanged the holistic process of creativity and led to repeating oneself.

This dialectic of paying attention and witnessing was a process that pervaded all of Strand's life and led to a constant feeling of being "never finished." When nearing the end of a poem, he was already anticipating getting on to something new: "So you never have a feeling that you're caught up. Which is a good thing, I guess. I think if you're ever caught up... you're sort of dead." There was a continual, creative cycle: new experiences needed to be witnessed, and this witnessing set the stage for more openness to experience, even before one poem was completely finished. Through this reoccurring process, Strand manifested experiential wisdom by an ability to coordinate his spontaneous and selective modes of attention. It is interesting to note that these ideas are reflected in the titles of two of Strand's books: *Sleeping with One Eye Open* and *The Continuous Life*. The former conveys an immersion in life with a corresponding self-consciousness (presumably the one open eye that witnesses), and the latter conveys the notion of a never-ending dialectical process.

Strand knew how to cultivate spontaneity and hold off selective attention until it was more useful. For example, new ideas for a poem might occur in a variety of unpredictable ways: paying attention to language, listening to someone's use of a phrase or a word, reading, reflecting on the past, or just seeing something in a new way. Strand exercised experiential wisdom by using distractions to prolong such spontaneity and openness.

> I often, in the middle of work, play solitaire to get my mind off what I'm doing, so I [can] come back, say in 20 min or a half an hour, and approach it with a new freshness. Sometimes I'll get in the car and drive, put on music, and do meaningless errands so I can sort of forget what I'm doing but think about it at the same time—both. When you drive you have to concentrate on the road, and you have to stop at stoplights... you realize the meaninglessness of your errand all the time but yet you realize that it's getting you away from your work and you need that time away. Then you come back, and you run upstairs and work again.

These distractions as well as others such as taking a walk to the refrigerator, scanning through pictures, or even doing some other light writing, slowed down the use of rational and selective attention that might interfere with intuitive spontaneity. What is described here as selective attention Strand called "direct thinking." Direct thinking would eventually be essential to the witnessing process and the recording of a poem; however, if it occurred too early, it could be destructive. He needed sometimes to get out and get his "mind off" what he was doing: "I think I'm always thinking about what I'm writing. I think that maybe it's not always direct thinking.... I become impatient, have to get out and slow down, and think of something else." From the perspective of experiential wisdom, these distractions allowed Strand to cultivate an esthetic and immediate grasp of a situation (Johnson 2007) and continue using his intuition (Myers 2004). In Strand's view, these distractions allowed indirect thinking to run its meandering course.

After returning from various distractions, however, he might directly engage the poem: "Then I will get off alone and tune in to what's happened back there." This tuning in involved the use of voluntary and selective attention and represented the more deliberate phase of writing. In this phase he required solitude and quiet to enhance his focus and concentration. As mentioned earlier, such a working phase would be referred to as evaluation or elaboration in the creativity literature (Wallas 1926). Strand simply described it as "working hard" on the poem: "If I'm working hard on a poem, I'll keep visiting it through the afternoon and into the evening in an effort to complete it, to get rid of it. Also if I'm working on something as I've described, I'll get up very early and see if I can get rid of it." He expanded on the meaning of "getting rid" of a poem: "Finishing it. I mean, getting rid of that sort of nagging sense of responsibility I have towards finishing it, so I can begin something new."

Strand's experiential wisdom allowed him to navigate the pitfalls that could have derailed the creation of a poem, namely, the ill-timed use of spontaneity (i.e., paying attention) or selective attention (i.e., witnessing). By working to coordinate the use of these modes, the process of writing sometimes led to a flow experience, or what he called an "extended present."

> Well, you're right in the work. You lose your sense of time. You're completely enraptured. You're completely caught up in what you're doing. It's not that you're... swayed by the possibilities you see in this work, that is, the eventual end of it, although that's a little of it. If that becomes too powerful, then you get up... because the excitement is too great. You can't continue to work, or continue to see the end of the work, because you're jumping ahead of yourself all the time. The idea is to be so saturated with it that there's no future or past, it's just an extended present in which you're making meaning and dismantling meaning, and remaking it, with undue regard for the words you're using. It's meaning carried to a high order. It's not just essential communication, daily communication; it's a total communication. When you're working on something and you're working well, you have feeling that there's no other way of saying what you're saying.

There is little doubt that Strand is describing facets of a flow experience, including the loss of time, a merging of awareness with the activity, an extended present or one-pointedness of mind, and the feeling of intrinsic motivation (Csikszentmihalyi 1990). John Dewey (1910) once described the ideal mental condition as being "playful and serious at the same time" (p. 218). In this ideal state, there was a simultaneous "playful" attention to the means of an activity and a "serious" attention to its ends. One also sees this synchrony of modes in Strand's statement; he knows that if he focuses too strongly on the "eventual end" of the poem, the extended present and flow experience would be lost. These moments of optimal experience are culminating points in the process of writing and do not occur all the time. He commented that he could "never stay in that frame of mind for an entire day," and that kind of intensity "comes and goes." Nevertheless, it was clear that such subjective rewards were part of what motivated his abiding interest in poetry.

A Fringe for Exploration

Donald Campbell was writing at a time when methodology in psychology was comprised almost entirely of the inherited dogma of random assignment to treatments. His methodological innovations led to increased research outside of the laboratory and the consideration of new threats to validity and reliability that would be encountered. He was honored for these pioneering contributions by the American Psychological Association (APA; Distinguished Scientific Contribution award; APA President 1975) and the American Educational Research Association (AERA; Distinguished Contribution to Research in Education award). He died in 1996.

Campbell, similar to Strand, demonstrated experiential wisdom and the capacity to navigate a path of abiding interest. One of the most revealing ideas that emerged from the interview was the importance of preserving a "fringe" space is one's life that allowed intuition and exploration to flourish without being crushed by professional obligations and a productive frame of mind. Campbell described this in-between space in several ways. For instance, he thought it was important to have some "recreation" in one's scholarly pursuits to avoid the dead end of drudgery: "We go into academic life because we want to make a profession out of our hobby... and that is a very dangerous thing to do. If you loved taking photographs as a high school student, and you become a professional photographer, what you did enjoy becomes a drudgery." He demonstrated experiential wisdom by always making sure he had intellectual pursuits that were "not close enough to home" in terms of his major field of study. In other words, he had pursuits that he could "dabble" in, exercise choice, and feel like a "young outsider" without feeling like he had a professional obligation with respect to them. In this way, he cultivated a spontaneous openness and enjoyment of new areas.

Professors (or students) who lacked this recreational element were the most susceptible to drudgery. Campbell thought they more easily fell into the trap of thinking that "every interesting article that you see in your own field makes you anxious because you have not read it, or because they have done it before you have." Even in one's main field, he commented, "We should somehow come to grips with the fact that we are only going to dabble in the literature; keeping up with it is a sure way to become overwhelmed." He cultivated this spontaneous/recreational side of scholarship by allowing some private time each day where he did not feel anxious about being "unproductive." Campbell thought that professors who felt constantly pressured to publish in order to retain their jobs and gain promotion had the most to lose; they accommodated, but "their freedom to be creative... is being reduced by the pressure for quickness and number."

Campbell's experiential wisdom led him to understand that such freedom to dabble in a new area could be strongly affected by a social context. So, he advocated finding one that was not so competitive and work-oriented that it prematurely closed off openness to new experience. He emphasized the importance of finding a social context in which "you are being treated as a fellow explorer" and where there was "mutual encouragement, rather than competitive put down."

> You have two job offers, both of them have reasonable teaching loads. One job is going to be under high publish or parish pressure. The other job you are going to feel adequate and under less pressure. Obviously the two universities have two different national esteem levels. Which one job would you take? I say clearly take the one where you will be free of tenure anxiety and be free to intellectually explore.

As was the case in the Strand's interview, Campbell's experiential wisdom was evident in relation to protecting a space where spontaneous attention, affective immediacy, and intuition could flourish. But, there was also a purpose behind this protection: it allowed the discovery of problems and set the stage for the hard work to follow: "If you can keep this curiosity unanxious and playful... it is very clear that there is a threshold of problems. One is attracted by problems that are puzzling but seem within reach of solutions. There is a fringe there." Campbell would show patience in the exploration process until a good idea came; but once it did, it was pursued with fierce selective attention and coincided with a flow-like momentum:

> I would have... several afternoons a week in which... I could go to my carrel in the library with a view over the lake and be in solitary scholarly meditation.... Once a problem has grabbed me... then I do show an amazing ability to drag that manuscript along with me and write on it fifteen minutes here and fifteen minutes there.... I am able to keep a self-driving momentum going in spite of lots of little interruptions when I am in a flow period.

Both Strand and Campbell were rewarded with these intensive and immersive states of flow, because their experiential wisdom cultivated the best conditions for such states to emerge. Both understood that there was a time for spontaneous and selective processing, and the two modes had to be coordinated so that they worked synergistically and did not impede each other.

Going from the Intuition Department to the Reasoning Department

In 1955, Jonas Salk introduced a polio vaccine that came as an answer to one of the most terrifying public health problems in US history. He was a recipient of the prestigious Lasker Award for medical research, but never received the Nobel Prize many thought he deserved. In 1963, he founded the Salk Institute for Biological Studies in La Jolla, California. He died on June 23, 1995, at the age of 80.

My interview with Salk took place at the Salk Institute in May of 1991. The beautiful setting of the Institute, which was built in 1965 by the renowned American architect Louis I. Kahn, was an intentional part of the design; and Salk was actively involved in helping to create its feeling of space and openness. The meditative and inspirational effect of the open layout was important to Salk's goal of "making visible the invisible." The "invisible" referred to the insights he had during meditative or sleep-like states that needed to be harvested with clear and rational thinking. Salk was focused on this process of moving between preconscious and conscious states and even was aware of physiological changes that might signal more right- or left-brain activity. His conceptualization of the creative/learning process has an obvious connection to the way experiential wisdom is conceived in this chapter.

> So the intuitive realm and the rational realm... reflect both sides of the brain, separately, and by the time you're ready to write, whatever it is that is going on that I'm not aware of, that comes to which words are attached and can be expressed, is the result of the merging of the two. So that the processing on the right gets to the left and takes on words [and] form. I don't think you can dissect it because if you did, you would not see it.... You have to let it run its course, so to speak, in order to recognize it.... I see it that way, as going back and forth... I speak of going from the intuition department to the reasoning department and then back and forth to check it out to make sure it's still true, so to speak.

Salk's experiential wisdom was manifested in his cultivation of this bimodal process throughout the day. For instance, he might try to enter a more intuitive/meditative state by taking a walk on the beach, waking up very slowly from a nap, or just sitting quietly. Occasionally, he would experience "an outpouring of insights" or an "inner vision," and he tried to quietly observe what was going on in his mind: "It is as if anticipatory ideas arise to help put into the future, so to speak. It's almost as if it prepares me for what is likely to happen." After this period of observation, he would try to capture the anticipatory ideas with words.

> I'm awakened in the night and when... I don't quite know what it is that is on my mind. But it eventually surfaces, and after that point of five minutes I begin to see an unfolding, as if a poem or a painting or a story or a concept begins to have taken form.... I can't possibly

> go back to sleep. So, I will lie quietly and let things happen. And after an hour I would fall into a deep sleep unless I write, so I sit up in bed with the light on, and I might write for a half hour, 45 min. I've accumulated a considerable amount of material over the last several years that I'm now beginning to work with—actually work with me—to try to understand or see the themes that have come forth this way.

Similar to many scholars who study the creative process, Salk believed that intuitive and rational processes were both at play in his development of the polio vaccine. His intuition would frame questions, and his experimental research would help him recognize and articulate patterns. One important intuition had its origin when Salk was a young medical student. He attended two lectures with contradictory information: one suggested you could immunize against virus diseases with chemically treated toxins; the other lecture suggested a person had to experience the infection itself for immunization to occur. "Well, it struck me that both statements couldn't be true," Salk commented, and he lived for some time with this ambiguity. Later, this implicit question framed Salk's preliminary work on an influenza virus: "I then chose to see whether or not this [presumed inability to immunize] was true for flu." Salk discovered that he could introduce an inactivated virus that would stimulate the production of an antibody, without the need for the person to experience infection. This led to the development of the flu vaccine; and the polio vaccine was an extrapolation of this line of work.

> When I had an opportunity to work on polio, I just invoked the same idea, and attempted to see what could be done there and it proved to be successful. Since then, of course, all of the genetic engineering and the other things that are done to parts of the virus are continuations of the principle. So I tend to see patterns, I tend to see patterns in data when I do experiments, and I look for patterns.... I recognize patterns that become integrated and synthesized and I see meaning.

Salk was such a believer in this combination of intuition and rationality that he tried to recruit to his Institute scientists who worked in this bimodal fashion. He also tried to create social context and physical conditions at his Institute (i.e., a beautiful and open space) that were congenial to such an intuition–rationality cycle. He did not want someone who could only intuitively see the whole, or someone who was only good at dissecting the parts, he wanted individuals who could "bridge the both" or practice what he called the "art of science." Salk, in other words, was interested in attracting kindred spirits to his Institute.

> It comes through... a process of self-selection of like-minded individuals.... I can see there are some individuals who have qualities that work on both sides.... I practice the art of science, as distinct from the way science is practiced by many others. But there are many scientists... who also function that way, but I would say they're in the minority.

Salk, similar to Strand and Campbell, was fully aware that optimal experiential states sometimes occurred at culminating points in the intuition–rationality cycle. He spoke of the exhilaration involved with a "revelation," when he would "begin to see the relationships of things that I didn't see before." He remarked: "The exhilaration is more of a form of a reduction and a disappearance in the feelings... that are associated with something going on and I'm not aware of." In other words, his intuition might sense a challenge that needed resolution, as was the case with contradictory information he sensed as a medical student about the possibility of immunization. Or a half-formed idea might come to mind in the middle of the night after waking from sleep. The exhilaration he felt resulted when the tension set up by intuition was resolved with selective attention leading to clarity. It was only after beginning to write after some moment of inner vision that he would begin to say, "I see, I see, I see."

Conclusions

A central theme in this chapter is that lifelong learning is augmented by experiential wisdom, or the capacity to make experiential course corrections that lead back to states of interest and flow. These course corrections resulting in optimal experiences (e.g., escaping boredom/overcoming anxiety) are enhanced by the interoperation and coordination of spontaneous and selective modes of attention, or more generally as Jonas Salk described, the combination of intuition and rationality. That such complementary modes are intrinsic to human nature and important for lifelong learning is a theme that has received increased attention in the adult development literature (Labouvie-Vief 1990, 1994), positive psychology (Haight 2009), and contemporary philosophy and cognitive science (Damasio 1994; Johnson 2007). The notion of experiential wisdom recognizes the importance of voluntary/selective attention, but places an equal emphasis on the role of involuntary/spontaneous modes that sense new challenges and set the stage for rational processing.

Such a bimodal flexibility of attention is not only ideal for developing ideas (i.e., sensing new connections and then being able to articulate them), it is useful for self-regulating experience and putting oneself in situations where interest and flow are more likely to occur (e.g., recognizing that prolonging a state of openness to experience may be preferable, *at the moment*, to making decisions and working logically on a solution). This theme of experiential wisdom rests on key assumptions about human nature that are consistent with some perspectives in positive psychology (i.e., that intrinsically motivated states play a key role in learning and development, see Seligman and Csikszentmihalyi 2000) and evolutionary perspectives on neoteny and lifelong learning (i.e., that a defining characteristic of human development is an unending state of development fueled by childlike curiosity and openness, see Lorenz 1971; Montagu 1989).

Experiential wisdom is not an individual trait that operates in a context-free way. Rather, it is a person-level characteristic that influences development through its effect on an evolving person–environment fit (Lerner 2006). Experiential wisdom influences development by setting in motion *interactions* with the environment that generate feedback that can be used to continually negotiate a better (more optimally rewarding) person–environment fit. Moreover, in a developmental perspective, experiential wisdom is not an individual accomplishment; rather, it is presumably shaped by genetic factors and socialization conditions outside of an individual's control.

Its appearance in adulthood, if at all, depends on developmental conditions in infancy, childhood, and adolescence; in particular, parenting in infancy provides the first foundation for experiential regulation by creating an optimally arousing parent–child fit (Sroufe et al. 2005). Later, ongoing socialization in families and schools, especially in supportive and challenging (authoritative) contexts that are best for helping children to flexibly moderate or raise their arousal level (Rathunde and Csikszentmihalyi 2006), builds on the self-regulative habits established in infancy and continue to shape an person's experiential wisdom and proficiency at self-regulating interest. Simply put, repeated optimal experiences in childhood and adolescence enhance the possibility of having experiential wisdom in adulthood.

The interviews with Strand, Campbell, and Salk in Part III of this chapter do not provide empirical support for the proposed developmental history of experiential wisdom, but they do provide a compelling illustration of how such wisdom operates to sustain interest and generate flow. Although each described their experiential wisdom in unique ways, there were similarities across the three accounts.

One commonality that allowed all three to navigate a path of interest was their recognition and protection of the time it takes for spontaneous attention (intuition) to set the stage for selective attention (rationality). In order to operate effectively, intuition required a relaxed openness and a capacity to tolerate ambiguity. All three had strategies that allowed intuition to do its work without cutting it off prematurely. Strand cultivated multiple starting points for a way into a poem and used distractions such as solitaire, driving, and running errands, so that he did not rush the process of paying attention. Campbell carefully protected some "recreation" in his scholarly pursuits where he had freedom to "dabble" in areas he enjoyed; and he avoided competitive pressures that would crowd out such pursuits. Finally, Salk intentionally cultivated beautiful physical environments that inspired intuitive thoughts and learned how to sit quietly after a nap, or after waking up in the middle of the night, to see if there were any ideas to consciously cultivate.

The second commonality across all the interviews had to do with the equally important component of selective attention to work through a sensed problem or challenge. Although the interviews had less variety with respect to this widely acknowledged component of productive thought, it was clear that Strand, Campbell, and Salk all had the capacity for highly focused concentration. When it was time to "get rid" of a poem, Strand worked relentlessly on it until he could move on to something new; when it was time to write, Campbell admitted that he showed "an amazing ability" to drag a manuscript along with him and work on it continuously, even in short intervals if necessary; similarly, once a problem was caught by an intuitive insight, Salk could write in the middle of the night or work doggedly for weeks in the laboratory.

The third commonality was especially relevant to a central theme in this chapter, namely that recurring states of flow are vital for sustaining a path of lifelong learning. Each was familiar with the experience of being deeply absorbed in the moment and each recognized its significance. The experiential wisdom of Strand, Campbell, and Salk set in motion a recurring cycle of finding challenges and resolving them. Each cycle had an intrinsic rhythm that they tried to protect and enhance. As the cycle unfolded, there were apexes with moments of deep engagement and intensity. Strand referred to an "extended present," Campbell talked about a "self-driving momentum" when ideas started to "flow," and Salk used the more traditional terms of "revelation" and "exhilaration" to describe his moments of flow. The reflections of all three provide concrete illustrations of the meaning and importance of experiential wisdom to lifelong learning.

References

Andel, R., Crowe, C., Pedersen, N., Mortimer, J., Crimmins, E., Johansson, B., & Gatz, M. (2005). Complexity of work and risk of Alzheimer's disease: A population-based study of Swedish twins. *Journal of Gerontology, 60*(5), 251–258.

Baltes, P. B., & Staudinger, U. M. (2000). Wisdom: A metaheuristic (pragmatic) to orchestrate mind and virtue toward excellence. *American Psychologist, 55*, 122–136.

Barron, F. (1969). *Creative person and creative process*. New York: Holt, Rinehart and Winston.

Baumrind, D. (1989). Rearing competent children. In W. Damon (Ed.), *Child development today and tomorrow* (pp. 349–378). San Francisco: Jossey-Bass.

Berlyne, D. E. (1960). *Conflict, arousal and curiosity*. New York: McGraw-Hill.

Bronfenbrenner, U. (1992). Ecological systems theory. In R. Vasta (Ed.), *Six theories of child development* (pp. 187–249). London: Jessica Kingsley.

Bronfenbrenner, U., & Morris, P. A. (2006). The bioecological model of human development. In R. M. Lerner (Ed.), W. Damon (Series Ed.), *Handbook of Child Psychology: Vol.1. Theoretical models of human development* (6th ed.) (pp. 793–828). New York: Wiley.

Caron, R. F., & Caron, A. J. (1968). The effect of repeated exposure and stimulus complexity on visual fixation in infants. *Psychonomic Science, 10*, 207–208.

Charlton, B. G. (2006). The rise of the boy-genius: Psychological neoteny, science and modern life. *Medical Hypotheses, 67*, 679–681.

Csikszentmihalyi, M. (1990). *Flow*. New York: Harper & Row.

Csikszentmihalyi, M. (1996). *Creativity: Flow and the psychology of discovery and invention*. New York: Collins.

Csikszentmihalyi, M., Rathunde, K., & Whalen, S. (1997). *Talented teenagers: The roots of success and failure*. New York: Cambridge University Press.

Damasio, A. (1994). *Decartes' error*. New York: Penguin.

Dewey, J. (1910). *How we think*. Mineola: Dover.

Dewey, J. (1933). *How we think*. Boston: D. C. Heath & Company.

Dewey, J. (1934/1980). *Art as experience*. New York: Perigee.

Field, T. (1985). Attachment as psychobiological attunement: Being on the same wave length. In M. Reite & T. Field (Eds.), *Psychobiology of attachment* (pp. 415–454). Orlando: Academic Press.

Haight, J. (2009). The moral emotions. In R. J. Davidson, K. R. Scherer, & H. H. Goldsmith (Eds.), *Handbook of affective sciences* (pp. 852–870). New York: Oxford University Press.

Gould, S. (1977). *Ontogeny and phylogeny*. Cambridge: Harvard University Press.

Hebb, D. O. (1955). Drive and the C.N.S. (Conceptual Nervous System). *Psychological Review, 62*, 243–254.

Hoare, C. (Ed.). (2006). *Handbook of adult development and learning*. New York: Oxford University Press.

James, W. (1890). *Principles of psychology*. New York: Henry.

Johnson, M. (2007). *The meaning of the body: Aesthetics of human understanding*. Chicago: University of Chicago Press.

Kaplan, S. (1995). The restorative benefits of nature: Toward an integrative framework. *Journal of Environmental Psychology, 15*, 169–182.

Kaplan, R., & Kaplan, S. (1989). *The experience of nature: A psychological perspective*. New York: Cambridge University Press.
Kramer, D. A. (2000). Wisdom as a classical source of human strength: Conceptualization and empirical inquiry. *Journal of Social and Clinical Psychology, 19,* 83–101.
Kris, E. (1952). *Psychoanalytic explorations in art*. New York: International Universities Press.
Labouvie-Vief, G. (1990). Wisdom as integrated thought: Historical and developmental perspectives. In R. J. Sternberg (Ed.), *Wisdom: Its nature, origins, and development* (pp. 52–83). New York: Cambridge University Press.
Labouvie-Vief, G. (1994). *Psyche and eros*. New York: Cambridge University Press.
Lakoff, G., & Johnson, M. (1999). *Philosophy in the flesh*. New York: Basic Books.
Leder, D. (1990). *The absent body*. Chicago: University of Chicago Press.
Lerner, R. (2006). Developmental science, developmental systems, and contemporary theories of human development. In R. M. Lerner (Ed.), W. Damon (Series Ed.), *Handbook of Child Psychology: Vol.1. Theoretical models of human development* (6th ed.) (pp. 1–17). New York: Wiley.
Lerner, R. M. (1984). *On the nature of human plasticity*. New York: Cambridge University Press.
Lerner, R. M., & Lerner, J. (1987). Children in their contexts: A goodness-of-fit model. In J. Lancaster, J. Altmann, A. Rossi, & L. Sherrod (Eds.), *Parenting across the life span* (pp. 377–404). New York: Aldine de Gruyter.
Lorenz, K. (1971). *Studies in animal and human behavior* (Vol. 2). Cambridge: Harvard University Press.
Martindale, C. (1999). Biological bases of creativity. In R. Sternberg (Ed.), *Handbook of creativity*. New York: Cambridge University Press.
Maslow, A. (1968). *Toward a psychology of being*. New York: Van Nostrand Reinhold.
Merleau-Ponty, M. (1962). *Phenomenology of perception* (trans: Colin Smith). New York: Routledge.
Montagu, A. (1989). *Growing young*. Boston: Bergin & Garvey.
Myers, D. G. (2004). *Intuition: Its powers and perils*. New Haven: Yale University Press.
Piaget, J. (1962). *Play, dreams, and imitation in childhood*. New York: Norton.
Rathunde, K. (1996). Family context and talented adolescents' optimal experience in productive activities. *Journal of Research on Adolescence, 6,* 603–626.
Rathunde, K. (2010). Experiential wisdom and optimal experience: Interviews with three distinguished lifelong learners. *Journal of Adult Development, 17*(2), 81–93.
Rathunde, K., & Csikszetnmihalyi, M. (2005). Middle school students' motivation and quality of experience: A comparison of Montessori and traditional school environments. *American Journal of Education, 111*(3), 341–371.
Rathunde, K., & Csikszentmihalyi, M. (2006). The developing person: An experiential perspective. In R. M. Lerner (Ed.), W. Damon (Series Ed.), *Handbook of child psychology: Vol.1. Theoretical models of human development* (6th ed., pp. 465–515). New York: Wiley.
Renninger, K., Krapp, A., Hidi, S. (1992). *The role of interest in learning and development*. Mahwah: Lawrence Erlbaum Associates.
Standing, E. M. (1984). *Maria Montessori: Her life and work.* New York: Penguin Books.
Seligman, M., & Csikszentmihalyi, M. (2000). Positive psychology: An introduction. *American Psychologist, 55,* 5–14.
Sroufe, L. A., Egeland, B., Carlson, E., & Collins, W. A. (2005). Placing early attachment experiences in developmental context. In K. E. Grossmann, K. Grossmann, & E. Waters (Eds.), *Attachment from infancy to adulthood: The major longitudinal studies* (pp. 48–70). New York: Guilford.
Steinberg, L., Lamborn, S., Dornbusch, S., & Darling, N. (1992). Impact of parenting practices on adolescent achievement: Authoritative parenting, school involvement, and encouragement to succeed. *Child Development, 63,* 1266–1281.
Sternberg, R. J. (ed.). (1988). *The nature of creativity*. New York: Cambridge University Press.
Sternberg, R. J. (2001). Why schools should teach for wisdom: The balance theory of wisdom in educational settings. *Educational Psychologist, 36,* 227–245.

Thomas, A., & Chess, S. (1977). *Temperament and development.* New York: Brunner/Mazel.

Wallas, G. (1926). *The art of thought*. New York: Harcourt Brace.

Wentzel, K. (1998). Social relationships and motivation in middle school: The role of parents, teachers, and peers. *Journal of Educational Psychology, 90,* 202–209.

Zimmerman, B. J. (1990). Self-regulated learning and academic achievement: An overview. *Educational Psychologist, 25,* 3–17.

Chapter 18
Stress-Related Growth in the Lives of Lesbian and Gay People of Faith

Eric M. Rodriguez and Michelle D. Vaughan

In one of Eric's very first research projects on lesbian and gay people of faith he conducted a series of studies during the late 1990's at the Metropolitan Community Church of New York (MCCNY)—a gay-positive Christian church that continues today to minister directly to the lesbian, gay, bisexual, and transgender community (LGBT) of New York City. The purpose of Eric's research was to explore the concepts of identity conflict and identity integration between an individual's sexual orientation and religious beliefs. He used two of the quotes collected from MCCNY participants during the qualitative, semistructured interview portion of the research to start one of his very first publications on this topic (Rodriguez and Ouellette 2000a). It has been over 10 years since, those two quotes were published and yet Eric still finds himself being drawn back to these particular words over and over again. The first quote illustrated the potential for identity conflict within a gay person of faith:

> Sure, I mean [being gay and Christian] is the big thing that religious gay people grapple with isn't it? There's homophobia in there, and there's fear of divine retribution, there's all of those things. What if I'm wrong? What if there's a Hell and I'm going there because I'm a faggot, and I have sex with men? (p. 333)

The second quote, on the other hand, truly illustrated the potential for rising above the conflict and managing to integrate one's sexual orientation with one's religious and/or spiritual beliefs:

> Being lesbian and Christian is accepting the unique creation that God created me to be. Love is beautiful no matter how it's expressed. Difference doesn't have to mean sin. The Bible has been used against us and it really isn't all about what's been presented to us. The Bible is not the book that hits us in the head; it's the book that leads us into light. (p. 333)

E. M. Rodriguez (✉)
Social Science Department, New York City College of Technology, City University of New York (City Tech, CUNY), N611, 300 Jay Street, Brooklyn, NY 11201, USA
e-mail: erodriguez@citytech.cuny.edu

M. D. Vaughan
Westminster College, 2012 W. Ash Street, Apt. O 18, Columbia, MO, USA
e-mail: MichelleDV2003@hotmail.com

J. D. Sinnott (ed.), *Positive Psychology*,
DOI 10.1007/978-1-4614-7282-7_18,

These two powerful quotes illustrated both the devastating difficulties and the life-affirming joy that lesbian and gay individuals can wrestle with while trying to come to terms with the complex interaction of their sexual orientation and religious and/or spiritual beliefs—an intersection that has formed the foundation of Eric's ongoing psychological research in this area.

The reason we start this chapter by revisiting these two quotes is not to simply regurgitate Eric's old work, but to reexamine it from a completely different perspective. Currently, there is a substantial and growing body of theoretical and research literature on the intersection of sexual orientation and religious/spiritual beliefs. In Eric's recent review of the psychological research on gay and lesbian people of faith, he noted that, there is a fairly substantial amount of psychological research which explores the origins and experience of the conflict that many gays and lesbians experience between their sexual orientation and their religious and/or spiritual beliefs (see Rodriguez 2010 for more information). There are, in fact, so many studies on lesbian and gay religion and conflict—so much focus on this community's negative faith experiences—that the corresponding lack of research, or even acknowledgement, regarding potentially affirming/positive faith experiences in lesbian and gay lives is quite remarkable.

For many lesbians and gays, growing up in a religious community, while simultaneously attempting to come to terms with their burgeoning sexual orientation, can be incredibly challenging, especially if such individuals are hearing messages from the pulpit, that homosexuality is unnatural, evil, a sin, and an abomination in the eyes of both God and their faith community. Rodriguez and Ouellette (2000a) mentioned four possible pathways for dealing with the identity conflict that can potentially emerge between clashing religious beliefs and the emerging sexual orientation: remove the gay identity (i.e., via "Ex-Gay" or reparative therapy), remove the religious identity (i.e., drop out of established religion), compartmentalization (keep the two identities rigidly separate), and integration (combine the two identities into a new, positive whole). We find it interesting to note that while all four pathways are theoretically about reducing the conflict, only one of them, identity integration, can in anyway be considered to be based on the principles of positive psychology. What motivates lesbian and gay individuals to go down one path or another? Why are some individuals motivated to leave their religion behind while others instead choose to enter "ex-gay" therapy to try and abandon their gay identity? Why do others compartmentalize their two disparate identities? While some lesbians and gays leave their religion and others continue to wallow in their perceived conflict, how do others manage to integrate these two identities and rise above the antigay messages they heard from the pulpit as children? What motivates such people to integrate? The field of positive psychology suggests possibilities for addressing all of these questions and taking Eric's previous and current work on lesbian and gay people of faith into a completely different direction, asking "what if lesbian and gay religious and spiritual experience was not just studied through the lens of conflict but instead through the lens of positive psychology?" What would research in this unique direction actually look like?

Spirituality as a Character Trait/Virtue in Lesbian and Gay Lives

In their original model, that formed the foundation of early work in the field of positive psychology, Seligman and Csikzentmihalyi (2000) noted that, positive psychology contains three key pillars: (1) character traits/virtues, (2) subjective experiences, and (3) institutions. Under the first pillar, Peterson and Seligman in their (2004) book *Character Strengths and Virtues: A Handbook and Classification*, note spirituality as being a key character trait/virtue that falls under the overarching category of "strengths of transcendence" (p. 518). They in fact devote an entire chapter to the trait of spirituality in their book. According to Peterson and Seligman, the character trait of spirituality (which they alternatively refer to as religiousness, faith, and purpose) satisfies the criterion for strengths of transcendence by addressing an individual's issues of fulfillment, morality, and values. Unfortunately, while Peterson and Seligman spend a substantial amount of their chapter discussing the inclusive, multicultural aspects of spirituality from the diverse perspectives of gender, race/ethnicity, ideology, and nationality, there is absolutely no mention of sexual orientation anywhere in this chapter, not even in the section subtitled "What is Not Known?" (p. 619). Eric noted in his (Rodriguez 2010) review that:

> Only recently have psychologists begun to recognize that many gay men and lesbians ... have active religious lives as well. [We are] in the middle of a paradigm shift as social scientists begin to consider homosexuals as spiritual and religious beings in their own right, rather than merely sexual beings needing to be compared and contrasted with religious others (pp. 7–8)

While this novel idea may not have yet caught up with the field of positive psychology, we view our current book chapter as an outstanding opportunity to expand the field of positive psychology's views on the importance of the character strength/virtue of spirituality in the lives of many individuals in the lesbian and gay community.

Beyond Peterson and Seligman's (2004) book, while there have been widespread calls for the integration of cultural perspectives into the study of positive psychology, sexual and gender minority issues typically receive short shrift within this emerging body of work. Conceptualizations of multiculturalism within the broader positive psychology literature have remained narrowly focused on race/ethnicity (Lopez et al. 2002), with only passing references to faith, sexual orientation, or gender as sources of strengths (Pedrotti et al. 2009). In their discussion of faith communities as cultural groups, Lopez et al. (2002) highlights how faith/spiritual groups serve to provide an important sense of strength, meaning, and coherence in the lives of individuals that promote well-being. In their words "Drawing upon religion and/or spirituality may provide a person with the courage and strength needed to cope with everyday stressors as well as life crises" (p. 705) and that "Faith can be enlisted to prevent problems from occurring and to aid in recovery for adversity ... thus faith serves as a coping mechanism, a source of emotional and social support and a basis for help" (p. 705). Faith communities may also serve as a source of group/collective self-esteem via providing a positive social identity (Lopez et al. 2002). Lopez et al. (2002) recommends that positive psychology researchers devote more attention in "recognizing the value of religious practices, spirituality, and diverse constructions of life meaning" (p. 711). These recommendations, however, are typically given a heteronormative frame, as discussions of the role of faith/spirituality in the lives of sexual and gender minorities have almost exclusively focused on stories of loss, rejection, spiritual trauma, and exclusion from faith communities. Of course, that is when such discussions happen at all, as many in the Western world—including the larger LGBT community—rarely view sexual orientation and religious beliefs as being compatible.

The Current Chapter

When we first began discussing our respective ideas for this bookchapter, we quickly latched onto an intriguing idea that would become the foundation for this entire piece: If Eric's (Rodriguez 2006) dissertation on identity conflict and integration in lesbian and gay people of faith had sex with Michelle's (Vaughan 2007) dissertation, what would the subsequent offspring look like? This book chapter will explore this idea by examining our respective dissertations (Eric's "At the intersection of church and gay: Religion, spirituality, conflict and integration in LGB people of faith"; and Michelle's "Coming out growth: Conceptualizing and assessing experiences of stress-related growth (SRG) associated with coming out as lesbian or gay") and suggesting possibilities for a brand new area of inquiry that sits at the intersection of three disparate fields of study (positive psychology, human sexuality, and religiosity/spirituality) with the potential for a unique contribution to each.

The goal of this current book chapter is to thus, recast and reconceptualize Eric's earlier and current work on lesbian and gay people of faith (e.g., Rodriguez and Ouellette 1999, 2000a, b; Rodriguez 2010) not from a lens of conflict, but instead, from the lens of positive psychology. Here, for the very first time, we make the argument that the intersection of sexual orientation and religious/spiritual beliefs, including the experiences of lesbian and gay people of faith, can be viewed as examples of the positive psychological concepts of SRG and COG in action. We begin our chapter by exploring the concept of SRG, focusing specifically on how this construct relates to lesbian and gay life experience. We continue by discussing how Michelle's concept of COG connects to Shallenberger's (1998) work on lesbian and gay spiritual journeys. We then move onto a discussion about the importance of lesbian and gay religious institutions, before concluding with suggestions for future research and practice.

Stress Related Growth (SRG)

Self-reported experiences of growth, attributed to stressful events or experiences have been widely acknowledged within the field of psychology over the past 25 years, with over 300 articles produced on the topic. These experiences have been increasingly incorporated into positive psychology in recent years, both as an illustration of positive subjective experiences linked to psychological and physical health (Davis et al. 1998; Tennen and Affleck 1996), also, as a process by which at least some character strengths may develop in response to stress or conflict (Peterson and Seligman 2004). Theorists and researchers studying positive outcomes in the context of stressful or traumatic experiences have used a variety of terms to represent self-perceived experiences of growth associated with a stressful experience, including perceived benefits/benefit-finding (e.g., Affleck et al. 1987; McMillen et al. 1997), SRG (Park et al. 1996), and posttraumatic growth (Tedeschi and Calhoun 1996, 2004). The latter category has typically been framed as a more fundamental, pervasive growth in one's self-understanding. Worthwhile benefits and SRG focuses more specifically on shifts in behaviors, perceptions, and style of life (Janoff-Bulman 2004). Gains in more specific domains related to meaning (e.g., Janoff-Bulman and Frantz 1997) or improvements in psychosocial functioning (aka, thriving: Carver 1998; Epel et al. 1998) represent unique subcategories of these experiences.

Within the work on growth from stress and trauma, theorists have identified a number of different domains of growth, focusing on perceived gains in personal resources/new perspectives, social/relational gains, coping resources as well as positive shifts in life philosophy/spirituality (Schaefer and Moos 1992; Tedeschi and Calhoun 1996). In a review of 39 studies on the topic, Linley and Joseph (2004) found that individuals who report more growth, report better psychological health, while Tennen et al. (1992) reported that nearly three-quarters of the 20 studies on growth found evidence of a strong relationship between reports of growth and psychological health over time.

Research on Spiritual Growth from Stress As part of their review of the literature on SRG, Cohen et al. (1998) agreed with this concept, noting that "certain types of events and/or certain types of individuals are associated with specific types of thriving outcomes" (p. 326, emphasis added). Within the context of spiritual growth, there is substantial evidence that stressors that threaten one's life or the life of others may be particularly likely to produce spiritual growth (e.g., Epstein 1991; Fromm et al. 1996; Lehman et al. 1993; Parappully et al. 2002; Schaefer and Moos 1992; Schwartzberg 1993; Siegel and Schrimshaw 2000; Weiss 2002). Consistent with the concept that those who have survived a brush with death may be primed for a strengthening, renewal, or other types of positive transformation of their faith, such work has unfortunately been limited to experiences of growth in the context of life-threatening illness or death of a partner or close family member. However, the concept that stressful experiences that are perceived as challenging to one's faith or core assumptions (about self and the world) may result in spiritual growth and may be particularly relevant to experiences of growth that occur as LGBT individuals navigate the complex, developmental process of forming a healthy minority identity in the context of pervasive stigma.

Growth from Developmental and Minority Stress Despite acknowledgements that experiences of growth are shaped by the characteristics of the stressor and the context in which it occurs (e.g., Affleck et al. 1987; Roesch et al. 2004; Tennen and Affleck 1996), research on growth from developmental and/or minority stress has been limited (for exceptions see Bonet et al. 2007; Riggle et al. 2008; Savin-Williams 2001; Vaughan and Waehler 2010). However, in recent years, a number of LGBT researchers have more explicitly acknowledged how "the adversity of the process [of coming out] contributed to the formation of positive personal characteristics such as strength and introspection" (Savin-Williams 2001, p. 126) and called for research on LGBT strengths. As such, there are a host of unanswered questions about the nature of experiences of growth attributable to sexual and gender minority stress as a whole, and the potential for spiritual growth in particular.

From the perspective of growth from nontraumatic stresses, a host of theorists and researchers in the literature on SRG (Armeli et al. 2001; Collins et al. 1990; Lazarus and Folkman 1984; McMillen et al. 1997; O'Leary 1998; Parappully et al. 2002) frame growth from stress in a developmental context. Here, normative stressors (such as those involved in identity formation) promoting the growth of healthy personality are consistent with Erikson's (1959) concept of basic strengths. In the words of Schaefer and Moos (1992), "[n]ormative transitions and sudden life crises share common features that can facilitate personal growth" (p. 151). In one such example, Park and Schuster (2005) found that levels of growth from "maturation" in college freshmen were significantly higher than growth associated with the students' most recent stressful experiences. For members of minority groups (including sexual and gender minorities), such experiences "may [occur] in the context of ordinary achievement in everyday life or extraordinary achievement in the face of extreme illness, injury, or adverse social conditions" (Ickovics and Park 1998, p. 240, emphasis added). Theorists exploring the impact of minority stress in the everyday lives of individuals, including Blankenship (1998) and Poorman (2002), have described how studying the lives of individuals from minority groups may provide unique opportunities to study growth in this context.

Growth from Sexual Minority Stress The study of SRG in the lives of LGBT individuals and communities has thus far received very little attention in the positive psychology literature. Although early theories and research on gay and lesbian identity development (e.g., Berzon 1979; Cass 1979; Coleman 1981/1982; Troiden 1979) often included reports of growth that were attributed to the identity development process, this literature remained largely separate from literature on SRG and has only recently drawn connections to the emerging field of positive psychology (Riggle et al. 2008; Vaughan and Waehler 2010).

In one of the few quantitative studies on experiences of growth associated with sexual minority identity development in lesbian and bisexual (LB) women, Bonet et al. (2007) found that their participants reported levels of growth that were comparable to or were higher than averages that were typically reported using the measure to assess growth from other stresses (e.g., Park and Schuster 2005; Park and Fenster 2004; Roesch et al. 2004). Unfortunately, this measure provides little data about specific experiences of spiritual/religious growth in LB women, as only one item refers to the gains in nonspecific 'meaning' attributed to stress. Nonetheless, these results lead Bonet and colleagues to assert that:

> ... these results illustrate that coming out and/or maintaining a lesbian or bisexual identity can have positive outcomes that may buffer the negative experiences associated with this process ... Our findings reveal that the coming-out process can, in many respects, be a positive experience that fosters personal growth and development. (p. 11)

More recently, Riggle et al. (2008) provided a unique perspective on the self-described positive aspects of being gay or lesbian. Although, not explicitly framed as experiences of SRG, the authors identified similar themes regarding the strengths that commonly emerge as a result of the process of navigating a stigmatized sexual minority identity. These themes included: Social support (strong connections, sources of belongingness/community, mentoring, families of choice) related to disclosure of one's sexual orientation, insight/empathy for self/others (authenticity, honesty, stronger identity, openness, social justice /activism, and freedom from societal roles (traditional gender norms, sexuality/intimate relationships, and roles within relationships).

Coming Out Growth (COG)

The importance of coming out to others is connected to the motivation behind coming out. Building on Michelle's earlier work (i.e., Vaughan 2007; Vaughan and Waehler 2010) we define COG as the experiences of self-perceived growth directly attributed to the unique experiences and identity development processes of sexual and gender minorities. We find ourselves continually wondering, however, why coming out is typically viewed through such a traumatic and negative lens. Why is this not something that we as psychologists, and human beings, celebrate more? Why has mainstream psychology lacked strong theoretical frameworks for conceptualizing, studying, and promoting the strengths and growth possibilities found in the coming out process for lesbians and gays?

Within the context of the development of a measure of SRG specifically, for the use of sexual minority populations, Vaughan and Waehler (2010) identified five general domains of growth, of particular relevance to the process of forming a healthy sexual minority identity, referenced throughout in the theory and research of this process: (1) mental health/well-being, (2) authenticity/honesty, (3) social/relational gains, (4) identity-related growth, and (5) advocacy/generativity. First and foremost, the coming out process has been framed as offering opportunities for LGBT individuals to become more honest and authentic, both internally, and in the context of their relationships with the important others in their lives. Reports of such gains in authenticity and honesty typically represent the most common and universal experience of growth from coming out reported by sexual minorities (e.g. Ben-Ari 1995; Berzon 1979; LaSala 2000; Savin-Williams 2001; Stevens 2004). Representing the domain of identity growth, sexual minorities frequently report that the coming out process strengthened and/or promoted a greater sense of acceptance or satisfaction with their minority identities (e.g, Cass 1979; Coleman 1981/1982; LaSala 2000; McCarn and Fassinger 1996; Oswald 2000; Savin-Williams 2008; Stevens 2004; Troiden 1979). As part of the domain of mental health and resilience, sexual minorities have also commonly reported experiencing a newfound sense of strength, resilience, and enhanced coping resources, allowing them to feel more actualized and report higher levels of self-esteem, joy and life-satisfaction and reducing negative emotional states (LaSala 2000; Rosario et al. 2001; Savin-Williams 2008). In the social domain, the coming out process has been linked to a stronger, deeper relationship with others, greater access to social support and romantic partners, as well as the creation of healthy boundaries in relationships with nonaccepting others (e.g., LaSala 2000; Morris et al. 2001; Oswald 2000; Savin-Williams 2008). Extending the growth experiences into the sphere of advocacy, the last domain of growth reflects a combination of increased awareness of sexual minority prejudice along with a commitment to responding to internal and external manifestations of antiLGBT bias and providing support to other sexual and gender minorities (e.g., Monroe 2001; Oswald 2000; Stevens 2004).

Murphy (1989), in her work with coupled lesbian women, found that "being 'out' to parents allows the individual to develop an integrated self-identity without having to hide or compartmentalize herself" (p. 47). In the words of one study participant, "I became more self-confident, less afraid, more open, relieved [once I came out]" (Rhoads 1995, p. 70). Such "emotional breakthroughs" (Dank 1971, p. 192), have been widely described by participants in the qualitative literature using phrases such as "a load off your shoulders" (Monroe 2001, p. 58), becoming "liberated" (Monroe 2001, p. 114), and "at peace with myself" (p. 59). Here, disclosure to others is often seen as a conduit for growth, with participants reporting how, coming out "[has] given me courage, strength ... to confront all kinds of things in my life" (Rhoads 1995, p. 70). Berzon (1979) described how "disclosure [of a lesbian identity] ... facilitates honest communication and builds trust between people ... It is not only critical to one's social development, it is essential to the growth of intimacy in close, loving relationships" (p. 10). In his qualitative study of gay male identity development in college, Stevens (2004) described how "[d]isclosure to others also developed the immensely important support network that was integral to finding empowerment" (p. 194). "[T] he simple words, 'I am gay' are part of an affirming act that says I will no longer be silent. I will no longer be invisible. I am understandable. I am natural. I have the right to live my truth rather than living a lie to preserve someone else's fantasy of how the world should be" (Berzon 1979, p. 10). As one man in Monroe's (2001) study shared, "my coming out will always be the strongest political statement I've ever made in my life. You come out of the closet to these people, and it's like George Bailey's life in It's A Wonderful Life–you don't understand how many people you impact when you make those decisions" (p. 64).

Spiritual Journeys

In Shallenberger's (1998) work, he referred to the process of identity integration as a spiritual journey. Other researchers (e.g., Barret and Barzan 1996; Spencer 1994; and Struzzo 1989) have utilized the term "faith journey". For the purposes of this paper, no distinction is made between these two synonymous phrases as both deal with the religious and homosexual life stories of gay men and lesbians. In his narrative study of the spiritual journeys of 26 gay and lesbian people of various faiths, Shallenberger explored the intersection of community and identity and their impact on individual's sexual and religious lives. During the course of his exploratory study, he attempted to address such issues as how gay men and lesbians discover and define their spirituality, what processes lead to the construction of their spiritual identities, and how they evolve and change as gay and lesbian people of faith during the course of their spiritual journeys (Shallenberger 1998).

Discussed in detail, by both Shallenberger and several other researchers (e.g., Coleman 1981/1982; Fischer 1989; Gonsiorek and Rudolph 1991; Grant and Epp 1998) one of the most important events in any individual's spiritual journey is the process of "coming out", both to themselves and to others. The impact of coming out on an individual's spiritual journey is predicated by their religious history, i.e., how involved they and their family were in established Christian churches and religious organizations during their formative years. Shallenberger made the point that coming out is one of the most widely studied developmental constructs in the gay research literature. While recognizing that coming out is a complex theoretical construct, Shallenberger (1998) mentioned that there are several well recognized themes that cut across this particular area of the literature. These themes are "deep and often difficult self-questioning" (p. 197), growing self-recognition and self-identification with one's homosexuality in the face of prolific antigay biases from a homophobic and heterosexist culture, sudden and/or measured disclosure to loved ones, and passage into, and deeper involvement with, the gay and lesbian community (Shallenberger 1998). While the coming out process has traditionally been framed using a variety of different developmental stage models, it is important to keep in mind that coming out is a very individualized process that can be either positive or negative, but not necessarily both.

Why, therefore, is coming out such a relevant construct for a discussion of the spiritual journeys of gays and lesbians? Based on Shallenberger's ideas, it appears that coming out occurs not only when conflict between religious and homosexual identity begins, but also when an individual consciously acknowledges the inherent discrepancies between, living a gay lifestyle and remaining actively involved in organized Christian religion. This point in time potentially marks the beginning of the integration process that is central to Shallenberger's concept of a spiritual journey as it pertains to gay men and lesbians.

> Shallenberger (1998) highlighted three key issues that gay and lesbian Christians grapple with on their continuing spiritual journeys after the coming out process: questioning, reintegration, and reclaiming. In questioning, individuals engage in an extensive (mostly internal)

conversation with themselves whereby they question their own religious beliefs as they relate to their experiences as gay men or lesbians. In reintegration, they attempt to reincorporate their religious identity with their homosexual identity. This is accomplished through reading relevant literature, talking with loved ones, and identifying and approaching other gays and lesbians grappling with the same issues, to mention just a few mechanisms. During the reclaiming process, they also begin to seek out safe spaces where they can reconnect with both their gay identity and their religious identity in a community of supportive, like-minded individuals.

The Importance of Lesbian and Gay Religious Institutions

For many gays and lesbians (and as for many heterosexuals), especially in the United States which remains one of the most religious countries in the world with over 85 % of the population believing in a higher power and/or regularly attending and involving themselves with a local faith community (Pew Forum on Religion and Public Life 2012), there is a strong need to have both their gay and their religious identities in their lives. These individuals are thus motivated to find external support for this choice. This has led to the growth of both Christian and Jewish religious groups, organizations and denominations that, if not ministering directly to the LGBT community, are supportive and welcoming of their lesbian and gay congregants. With the ongoing advancement of lesbian and gay rights in the United States in areas such as adoption, gay marriage, antigay employment, and housing discrimination laws and the ending of the United States military's "Don't Ask, Don't Tell" policy, not only are lesbian and gay religious issues connected to growth at the community level but also specific community organizations have grown and developed to address these issues as well.

Rodriguez and Ouellette (2000a) made the distinction between "gay-positive" versus "gay-friendly" religious denominations. While a gay-friendly religious denomination may openly welcome the involvement of lesbians and gays, such religious spaces are not typically set up to explicitly address the specific religious and/or spiritual needs of the LGBT community. Gay-positive churches and temples, on the other hand, typically minister directly to the LGBT community and thus may provide a safe space where LGBT individuals can work on alleviating the conflict that can occur between their faith and their sexual orientation while creating the possibility of moving towards identity integration. Regardless of whether a religious space is considered to be gay-positive or gay-friendly, both forms of faith-based institutions have the potential to assist lesbians and gays turn experiences of conflict into opportunities for SRG. In the twenty-first century, many mainstream, left-leaning (i.e., those religious groups that practice liberation theology), Protestant, and Reform Judaism religious spaces have created denominational organizations (e.g., Lutheran's Concerned, Dignity in the Catholic Church, etc.) where lesbian and gay people can hear the message that God loves them regardless of their sexual orientation. Thus, providing safe spaces that can not only encourage identity integration but also SRG, especially for those lesbians and gay men who grew up internalizing the message that all dykes and fags will ultimately burn in Hell for their perverted and sinful life choices.

For example, several social science researchers have conducted studies across the United States at various Metropolitan Community Churches (MCC) which are individual gay-positive Christian denominations organized under the umbrella of an overarching federation called the United Fellowships of Metropolitan Community Churches (UFMCC). In addition to Eric's previous work (Rodriguez and Ouellette 1999, 2000a, b), several other researchers and gay-religious activists (e.g., Enroth 1974; Lukenbill 1998; Perry 1990; and Warner 1995) have all written extensively about MCC locations in California, New York, and Texas, describing how these gay-positive Christian institutions work hard to reconnect members of the LGBT community to a Christian faith that has created such conflict and ultimately driven lesbians and gays away from the church. MCC/UFMCC churches work not only as sites to alleviate identity conflict and potentially facilitate identity integration but also such spaces could be reframed entirely, from a positive psychological perspective to instead be explored as sites that promote and assist both SRG and COG processes in the LGBT community. Shokeid's (1995) work at Congregation Beth Simchat Torah, a gay-positive synagogue which ministers specifically to the LGBT Jewish community in New York City, supports these same ideas from a Jewish, as opposed to a Christian, perspective.

Suggestions for Future Research and Practice

So where do we go from here? The current chapter provides a framework that could potentially transform (Dare we say revolutionize?) the way lesbian and gay people of faith are understood via the field of psychology. The importance of this work is that, we continue to push the idea that religion and spirituality, cultural universals found across all societies on the planet, are not just issues for the heterosexual majority, but for sexual and gender minorities as well. We as psychologists need to move beyond the study of lesbian and gay people of faith as simply being conflict-based. We have a great opportunity to expand the positive psychological concepts of SRG and COG and to provide a roadmap for spiritual/religious growth—especially, how these fit on the level of spirituality as a character strength, religious experiences, and affirming religious and/or spiritual institutions. This would be a much needed addition to the work we have both read and conducted to date. This chapter serves as a call to recognize the need for more empirical research in this area. We offer the following suggestions not just to spur future qualitative and quantitative psychological research but to also encourage a different approach from a practice perspective as well.

1. **Mixed method approaches and measurement advances are both needed.** There is an ever-expanding amount of qualitative research being conducted in this area that really speaks to the human experience of lesbian and gay people of faith and has helped to greatly increase our understanding of these important

issues. However, in order for this area of inquiry to grow beyond the study of conflict, psychological researchers need to begin incorporating more quantitative and mixed methods research on how lesbian and gay people manifest both SRG and COG in relationship to their religious and/or spiritual beliefs. Spiritual development in lesbian and gay individuals becomes an important point here, as Eric was not able to operationalize spiritual growth in his previous research. To properly assess spiritual growth and development there is a need to move beyond cross-sectional studies into longitudinal research designs. Building upon Michelle's earlier work (Vaughan 2007; Vaughan and Waehler 2010), there is also a need to continue extending and refining the measurement of both SRG and COG as the use of reliable and valid scales will become more and more vital for future research.

2. **Areas of inquiry need to be expanded to include underrepresented and nontraditional populations.** The current area of inquiry needs to be expanded beyond the needs and experiences of lesbians and gay men. While Rodriguez (2006) suggested that bisexuals do not experience the same issues with religiosity and spirituality as gays and lesbians, more research is needed on this population to better understand the role that faith plays across nonheterosexual, sexual orientations. Research could be expanded into transgender and intersex communities as well. While Golub et al. (2010) article on the intersections of religiosity, social support, HIV risk and SRG is definitely a step in the right direction, at the moment there is very little research available on transgender spirituality and almost nothing on the role of faith and religion in the lives of intersex individuals. In order for this research to have the maximum possible impact moving forward, our work will need to encompass the entire lesbian, gay, bisexual, transgender, and intersex (LGBTI) community. Expanding the area of inquiry to cover people of other, nonWestern religious backgrounds would be an important next step as well. The work to date focuses predominantly on Christianity, and to a lesser extent on Judaism. What about the experiences of LGBTI individuals who practice nonWestern and nontraditional religions such as Buddhism, Daoism, Hinduism, Native American Spirituality and Wicca?
3. **Need to begin incorporating additional relevant concepts into research in this area.** There are certain key psychological theories that we see as being particularly applicable to the topic at hand and yet have received almost no attention in either the positive psychology or LGBTI people of faith literature. Two concepts that spring to our minds as being quite germane include the community psychology notion of empowerment and the personality psychology trait of hardiness. We remain puzzled why these theories have not been more heavily utilized in positive psychology. Empowerment operates on three distinct levels: individual (or psychological), organizational, and community and can be simply defined as a mechanism where people take back control of certain aspects of their lives (Perkins and Zimmerman 1995; Zimmerman 1995, 1996). Hardiness, on the other hand, is defined as a person's unique combination of personality

traits that allows them to show remarkable resilience during moments of extreme life stress (Escherman et al. 2010; Kobassa 1979; Kobassa et al. 1982; Maddi 2006). Hardiness also operates on three distinct levels, including commitment, control, and challenge (Kobassa 1979). How do the concepts of hardiness and empowerment relate to SRG and/or COG in LGBTI people of faith? SRG could be viewed as a subjective experience that could build/support new resources that enhance hardiness (growth happens in a broad array of domains; one is feeling stronger/more able to cope/bounce back). In other words, SRG as one process by which hardiness may develop, and those high in hardiness may be more likely to experience growth. A substantial amount of additional research is necessary to explore the full implications of these ideas moving forward.

4. **Where does motivation fit into all of this?** There are multiple questions that arise which speak to the motivation of LGBTI individuals who decide to either retain or remove religious and/or spiritual beliefs from their lives. Do LGBTI people of faith experience SRG as a result of their negative religious experiences? As a result of such experiences, why are some individuals motivated to leave their religion behind while others instead choose to enter "ex-gay" therapy to try and abandon their gay identity? Why are still others motivated to compartmentalize their two identities? What motivates some individuals to integrate these two seemingly disparate identities? What role does COG play in any of these personal life decisions? Significantly, more research is needed in this area to better understand the possible intersections between SRG, COG, sexual orientation, and religious and/or spiritual beliefs.
5. **Psychological practice needs to expand to cover these ideas as well.** When training in difference and when pathology becomes practice, clinicians are ultimately taught to collude with the mistaken impression that life as an LGBTI individual equates only with experiences of discrimination and oppression—especially given the negative experiences that many LGBTI individuals encounter when trying to deal with both their sexual orientation/gender identity and their religious beliefs at the same time. Clinical work with LGBTI individuals should not only take into account the need for clinicians to understand and be informed of the positive aspects of LGBTI life but also to move their clients away, from a pathology/difference model to one of strength and hope (Bieschke et al. 2007), including advocacy for LGBTI's in the larger community (Lewis and Bradley 2000). Clinicians can assist their LGBTI clients in learning to reframe negatively held beliefs and allow discussion and amplification of positively held beliefs, thoughts, and behaviors through more cognitive behaviorally based treatments such as modeling or focusing on positive, peak experiences (i.e., "Flow"; Csikszentmihalyi 2008) in the context of their same-sex attractions or positive gender experiences. It will be through this lens that clinicians can utilize and focus other modalities of treatment, into an integration of positive psychology principles and counseling psychology to help LGBTI individuals to embrace more positive and adaptive nonheteronormative beliefs and behaviors.

References

Affleck, G., Tennen, H., Croog, S., & Levine, S. (1987). Causal attribution, perceived benefits, and morbidity after a heart attack: An 8-year study. *Journal of Consulting and Clinical Psychology, 55*(1), 29–35.

Armeli, S., Gunthert, K., & Cohen, L. (2001). Stressor appraisals, coping, and post-event outcomes: The dimensionality and antecedents of stress-related growth. *Journal of Social & Clinical Psychology, 20*(3), 366–395.

Barret, R., & Barzan, R. (1996). Spiritual experiences of gay men and lesbians. *Counseling and Values, 41,* 4–15.

Ben-Ari, A. (1995). Coming out: A dialectic of intimacy and privacy. *Families in Society, 76*(5), 306–314.

Berzon, B. (1979). *Positively gay*. Millbrae: Celestial Arts.

Bieschke, K. J., Perez, R. M., & DeBord, K. A. (Eds.). (2007). *Handbook of counseling and psychotherapy with lesbian, gay, bisexual and transgender clients* (2nd ed.). Washington DC: American Psychological Association.

Blankenship, K. (1998). A race, class, and gender analysis of thriving. *Journal of Social Issues, 54*(2), 393–404.

Bonet, L., Wells, B., & Parsons, J. (2007). A positive look at a difficult time: A strength based examination of coming out for lesbian and bisexual women. *Journal of LGBT Health Research, 3*(1), 7–14.

Carver, C. S. (1998). Resilience and thriving: Issues, models, and linkages. *Journal of Social Issues, 54,* 254–266.

Cass, V. (1979). Homosexual identity formation: A theoretical model. *Journal of Homosexuality, 4*(3), 219–235.

Csikszentmihalyi, M. (2008). Flow: The psychology of optimal experience. New York: Harper Collins.

Cohen, L., Cimbolic, K., Armeli, S., & Hettler, T. (1998). Quantitative assessment of thriving. *Journal of Social Issues, 54*(2), 323–335.

Coleman, E. (1981/1982). Developmental stages of the coming out process. *Journal of Homosexuality, 7*(2–3), 31–43.

Collins, R., Taylor, S., & Skokan, L. (1990). A better world or a shattered vision? Changes in life perspectives following victimization. *Social Cognition, 8*(3), 263–285.

Dank, B. (1971). Coming out in the gay world. *Psychiatry: Journal for the Study of Interpersonal Processes, 34*(2), 180–197.

Davis, C., Nolen-Hoeksema, S., & Larson, J. (1998). Making sense of loss and benefiting from the experience: Two construals of meaning. *Journal of Personality and Social Psychology, 75*(2), 561–574.

Enroth, R. M. (1974). The homosexual church: An ecclesiastical extension of a subculture. *Social Compass, 21,* 355–360.

Eschleman, K. J., Bowling, N. A., & Alarcon, G. M. (2010). A meta-analytic examination of hardiness. *International Journal of Stress Management, 17*(4), 277–307.

Epstein, S. (1991).The self-concept, the traumatic neurosis, and the structure of personality. In D. Ozer, J. Healy, & A. Stewart (Eds.), *Perspectives in personality* (pp. 63–98). Philadelphia: Jessica Kingsley Publishers.

Erikson, E. (1959). *Identity and the life cycle*. New York: International Universities Press.

Epel, E. S., McEwen, B. S., & Ickovics, J. R. (1998). Embodying psychological thriving: Physical thriving in response to stress. *Journal of Social Issues, 54,* 301–322.

Fischer, C. B. (1989). A bonding of choice: Values and identity among lesbian and gay religious leaders. *Journal of Homosexuality, 18*(3–4), 145–174.

Fromm, K., Andrykowski, M., & Hunt, J. (1996). Positive and negative psychosocial sequelae of bone marrow transplantation: Implications for quality of life assessment. *Journal of Behavioral Medicine, 19*(3), 221–240.

Golub, S. A., Walker, J. J., Longmire-Avital, B., Bimbi, D. S., & Parsons, J. T. (2010). The role of religiosity, social support, and stress-related growth in protecting against HIV risk among transgender women. *Journal of Health Psychology, 15,* 1135–1144.

Gonsiorek, J. C., & Rudolph, J. R. (1991). Homosexual identity: Coming out and other developmental events. In J. C. Gonsiorek & J. D. Weinrich (Eds.), *Homosexuality: Research implications for public policy* (pp. 161–176). Newbury Park: Sage.

Grant, D., & Epp, L. (1998). The gay orientation: Does god mind? *Counseling and Values, 43,* 8–33.

Ickovics, J., & Park, C. (1998). Paradigm shift: Why a focus on health is important. *Journal of Social Issues, 54*(2), 237–244.

Janoff-Bulman, R. (2004). Posttraumatic growth: Three explanatory models. *Psychological Inquiry, 15*(1), 30–34.

Janoff-Bulman, R., & Frantz, C. M. (1997). The impact of trauma on meaning: From meaningless world to meaningful life. In M. Power & C. Brewin (Eds.), *The transformation of meaning in psychological therapies: Integrating theory and practice*. Sussex: Wiley.

LaSala, M. (2000). Gay male couples: The importance of coming out and being out to parents. *Journal of Homosexuality, 39*(2), 47–71.

Lazarus, R., & Folkman, S. (1984). *Stress, appraisal, and coping*. New York: Springer.

Lehman, D., Davis, C., & DeLongis, A. (1993). Positive and negative life changes following bereavement and their relations to adjustment. *Journal of Social & Clinical Psychology, 12*(1), 90–112.

Lewis, J., & Bradley, L. (Eds.). (2000). *Advocacy in counseling: Counselors, clients, and community* (pp. 5–14). Greensboro: Caps Publications.

Linley, P., & Joseph, S. (2004). Positive change following trauma and adversity: A review. *Journal of Traumatic Stress, 17*(1), 11–21.

Lopez, S. J., Prosser, E. C., Edwards, L. M., Magyar-Moe, J. L., Neufeld, J. E., & Rasmussen, H. N. (2002). Putting positive psychology in a multicultural context (pp. 700–741). In C. R. Snyder & S. J. Lopez (Eds), *Handbook of positive psychology*. New York: Oxford University Press.

Lukenbill, B. W. (1998). Observations on the corporate culture of a gay and lesbian congregation. *Journal for the Scientific Study of Religion, 37*(3), 440–452.

Kobassa, S. C. (1979). Stressful life events, personality and health: An inquiry into hardiness. *Journal of Personality and Social Psychology, 37,* 1–11.

Kobassa, S. C., Maddi, S. R., & Kahn, S. (1982). Hardiness and health: A prospective study. *Journal of Personality and Social Psychology, 42*(1), 168–177.

Maddi, S. R. (2006, July). Hardiness: The courage to grow from stresses. *The Journal of Positive Psychology, 1*(3), 160–168.

McCarn, S., & Fassinger, R. (1996). Revisioning sexual minority identity formation: A new model of lesbian identity and its implications. *Counseling Psychologist, 24*(3), 508–534.

McMillen, J., Smith, E., & Fisher, R. (1997). Perceived benefit and mental health after three types of disaster. *Journal of Consulting and Clinical Psychology, 65*(5), 733–739.

Monroe, R. (2001). *Drawing upon the experiences of those who are out: A qualitative study of the coming-out process of gays and lesbian*. Unpublished doctoral dissertation, University of Iowa.

Morris, J., Waldo, C., & Rothblum, E. (2001). A model of predictors and outcomes of outness among lesbian and bisexual women. *American Journal of Orthopsychiatry, 71*(1), 61–71.

Murphy, B. (1989). Lesbian couples and their parents: The effects of perceived parental attitudes on the couple. *Journal of Counseling & Development, 68*(1), 46–51.

O'Leary, V. (1998). Strength in the face of adversity: Individual and social thriving. *Journal of Social Issues, 54*(2), 425–446.

Oswald, R. (2000). Family and friendship relationships after young women come out as bisexual or lesbian. *Journal of Homosexuality, 38*(3), 65–83.

Parappully, J., Rosenbaum, R., Van Den Daele, L., & Nzewi, E. (2002). Thriving after trauma: The experience of parents of murdered children. *Journal of Humanistic Psychology, 42*(1), 33–70.

Park, C., & Fenster, J. (2004). Stress-related growth: Predictors of occurrence and correlates with psychological adjustment. *Journal of Social & Clinical Psychology, 23*(2), 195–215.

Park, C., & Schuster, J. (2005, August). *Influence of stress-related growth in coping with subsequent life stressors.* Paper presented at the American Psychological Association Convention, Washington DC.

Park, C., Cohen, L., & Murch, R. (1996). Assessment and prediction of stress-related growth. *Journal of Personality, 64*(1), 71–105.

Pedrotti, J. T., Edwards, L. M., & Lopez, S. J. (2009). Positive psychology within a cultural context. In C. R. Snyder & S. J. Lopez (Eds), *Oxford handbook of positive psychology* (pp. 49–57). New York: Oxford University Press.

Perkins, D. D., & Zimmerman, M. A. (1995). Empowerment theory, research, and application. *American Journal of Community Psychology, 23*(5), 569–579.

Perry, T. D. (1990). *Don't be afraid anymore: The story of reverend Troy Perry and the metropolitan community churches.* New York: St. Martin's Press.

Peterson, C., & Seligman, M. E. P. (2004). *Character strengths and virtues: A handbook and classification.* Washington DC: American Psychological Association.

Pew Forum on Religion and Public Life. (2012). *Nones on the rise: One-in-five adults have no religious affiliation.* Published by the Pew Research Center and retrieved from http://www.pewforum.org/uploadedFiles/Topics/Religious_Affiliation/Unaffiliated/NonesOnTheRise-full.pdf. Accessed 21 Oct 2012.

Poorman, P. (2002). Perceptions of thriving by women who have experienced abuse or status-related oppression. *Psychology of Women Quarterly, 26*(1), 51–62.

Rhoads, R. (1995). Learning from the coming-out experiences of college males. *Journal of College Student Development, 36*(1), 67–74.

Riggle, E. D., Whitman, J. S., Oslon, A., & Strong, S. (2008). The positive aspects of being a lesbian or gay man. *Professional Psychology: Research and Practice, 39*(2), 210–217.

Rodriguez, E. M. (2006). At the intersection of church and gay: Religion, spirituality, conflict and integration in GLB people of faith. (Doctoral dissertation, CUNY Graduate School and University Center, New York, 2006). *Dissertation Abstracts International,* 67(3B), 1742.

Rodriguez, E. M. (2010). At the intersection of church and gay: A review of the psychological research on gay and lesbian Christians. *Journal of Homosexuality, 57*(1), 5–38.

Rodriguez, E. M., & Ouellette, S. C. (1999). The metropolitan community church of New York: A gay and lesbian community. *The Community Psychologist, 32*(3), 24–29.

Rodriguez, E. M., & Ouellette, S. C. (2000a). Gay and lesbian Christians: Homosexual and religious identity integration in the members and participants of a gay-positive church. *Journal for the Scientific Study of Religion, 39*(3), 333–347.

Rodriguez, E. M., & Ouellette, S. C. (b). Religion and masculinity in Latino gay lives. In P. M. Nardi (Ed.), *Gay masculinities* (pp. 101–129). Thousand Oaks: Sage.

Roesch, S., Rowley, A., & Vaughn, A. (2004). On the dimensionality of the stress-related growth scale: One, three, or seven factors? *Journal of Personality Assessment, 82*(3), 281–290.

Rosario, M., Hunter, J., Maguen, S., Gwadz, M., & Smith, R. (2001). The coming-out process and its adaptational and health-related associations among gay, lesbian, and bisexual youths: Stipulation and exploration of a model. *American Journal of Community Psychology, 29*(1), 113–160.

Savin-Williams, R. (2001). *Mom, dad. I'm gay. How families negotiate coming out.* Washington DC: American Psychological Association.

Savin-Williams, R. C. (2008). Then and now: Recruitment, definition, diversity and positive attributes of same-sex populations. *Developmental Psychology, 44*(1), 135–138.

Schaefer, J., & Moos, R. (1992). Life crises and personal growth. In B. Carpenter (Ed.), *Personal coping: Theory, research, and application* (pp. 149–170). Westport: Praeger Publishers/Greenwood Publishing Group.

Schwartzberg, S. (1993). Struggling for meaning: How HIV-positive gay men make sense of AIDS. *Professional psychology: Research and practice, 24*(4), 483–490.

Seligman, M. E. P., & Csikzentmihalyi, M. (2000). Positive psychology: An introduction. *American Psychologist, 55*(1), 5–34.
Shallenberger, D. (1998). *Reclaiming the spirit: Gay men and lesbians come to terms with religion.* New Brunswick: Rutgers.
Shokeid, M. (1995). *A gay synagogue in New York.* New York: Columbia University.
Siegel, K., & Schrimshaw, E. (2000). Perceiving benefits in adversity: Stress-related growth in women living with HIV/AIDS. *Social Science and Medicine, 51,* 1543–1554.
Spencer, D. (1994). Church at the margins. In J. B. Nelson & S. P. Longfellow (Eds.), *Sexuality and the sacred: Sources for theological reflection* (pp. 397–401). Louisville: Westminster.
Stevens, R. (2004). Understanding gay identity development within the college environment. *Journal of College Student Development, 45*(2), 185–206.
Struzzo, J. A. (1989). Pastoral counseling and homosexuality. In R. Hasbang (Ed.), *Homosexuality and religion* (pp. 195–222). New York: Harrington Park Press.
Tedeschi, R., & Calhoun, L. (1996). The posttraumatic growth inventory: Measuring the positive legacy of trauma. *Journal of Traumatic Stress, 9*(3), 455–472.
Tedeschi, R., & Calhoun, L. (2004). Post-traumatic growth: Conceptual foundations and empirical evidence. *Psychological Inquiry, 15,* 1–18.
Tennen, H., & Affleck, G. (1996). Daily processes in coping with chronic pain. Methods and analytic strategies. In M. Zeidner & N. Endler (Eds.), *Handbook of coping* (pp. 151–177). New York: Wiley.
Tennen, H., Affleck, G., Urrows, S., Higgins, P., & Mendola, R. (1992). Perceiving control, construing benefits, and daily processes in rheumatoid arthritis. *Canadian Journal of Behavioural Science, 24*(2), 186–203.
Troiden, R. (1979). Becoming homosexual: A model of gay identity acquisition. *Psychiatry: Journal for the Study of Interpersonal Processes, 42*(4), 362–373.
Vaughan, M. D. (2007). *Coming out growth: Conceptualizing and assessing experiences of stress-related growth associated with coming out as lesbian or gay? Doctoral Dissertation.* The University of Akron, Akron OH.
Vaughan, M. D., & Waehler, C. W. (2010). Coming out growth: Conceptualizing and assessing stress-related growth associated with coming out as gay or lesbian. *Journal of Adult Development, 17*(3), 94–109.
Warner, R. S. (1995). The metropolitan community churches and the gay agenda: Power of pentecostalism and essentialism. In D. G. Bromley, M. J. Neitz, & M. S. Goldman (Eds.), *Religion and the social order: Sex, lies, and sanctity: Religion and deviance in contemporary North America* (pp. 81–108). Greenwich: Jai Press.
Weiss, T. (2002). Posttraumatic growth in women with breast cancer and their husbands: An intersubjective validation study. *Journal of Psychosocial Oncology, 20*(2), 65–80.
Zimmerman, M. A. (1995). Psychological empowerment: Issues and illustrations. *American Journal of Community Psychology, 23*(5), 581–599.
Zimmerman, M. A. (1996). Empowerment theory: Psychological, organizational, and community levels of analysis. In J. Rappaport & E. Seidman (Eds.), *The handbook of community psychology.* New York: Plenum.

Chapter 19
Biological Complexity Meets Positive Psychology: What Can Complexity Theory Tell Us About Positive Psychology?

Tarynn M. Witten

Introduction and Background

As this is an entire volume on positive psychology (PP), I will defer to the expertise of other authors for any discussion about the field of PP and its diverse content (see, for example, Fredrickson 2001; Fredrickson and Losada 2005; Seligman 2008; Seligman and Csikszentmihalyi 2000; Selgiman et al. 2005, 2006; Linley et al. 2006; Sheldon and King 2001). Instead, I am going to pursue PP from the perspective of a complexity theorist who is interested in understanding relationships between the fields of nonlinear dynamical systems (NDS) and complexity theory and the constructs arising in PP, particularly as they related to psycho-social aging processes. I am particularly interested in how those potential relationships might impact our understanding of what it means to age well, to age successfully, and to age in a positive fashion (Vahia et al. 2011), especially in the face of significant amounts of stigma, violence, loss, and abuse across the lifespan.

NDS is a large and continually growing field of research. Research areas in NDS cover such subjects as fractals, catastrophes, emergence, chaos, adaptive systems, cellular automata, and many other areas. This chapter begins with a brief review of the history of NDS and complexity, and then addresses terminology across the disciplines of psychology and dynamical systems. As I do so, I will illustrate sample conceptual applications to psychology in general and PP in particular.

Historically, the pursuit of science has taken place by breaking objects apart and subsequently trying to understand how the pieces work at increasingly smaller and smaller levels of organization, the *reductionist* methodology. It was tacitly assumed that one could just glue the pieces back together and understand the behavior of the unbroken original system. This approach worked well for centuries of scientific exploration. However, by the early 1800s, studies of biological systems, ecosystems

T. M. Witten (✉)
Center for the Study of Biological Complexity, VCU, PO Box 842537, Suite 111,
1000 W. Cary Street, Richmond, VA 23284–2537, USA
e-mail: tmwitten@vcu.edu

J. D. Sinnott (ed.), *Positive Psychology*,
DOI 10.1007/978-1-4614-7282-7_19, © Springer Science+Business Media, LLC 2013

in particular, were observed to demonstrate a variety of nonlinear behaviors; particularly oscillations, apparently chaotic time series and radical behavioral changes that could not be explained by traditional reductionist constructs. From the early work of von Bertalanffy (1950a, b) and many others emerged the concepts of systems dynamics and *systems theory* as applied to a variety of living systems. In the mid-1970s, Robert May and others began to write about simple nonlinear models with complex dynamics (May 1976, 2000; these are classic papers). Systems science looked at the parts and tried to glue them back together to understand the behavior of the system. From a systems science perspective, if I were to attempt to understand the therapist–client dyad, then I would argue that if I understand the behavior of the client and the behavior or the therapist, then if I glue those behaviors together I should be able to understand the behavior of the client–therapist dyad. While it was often possible to gain insights into the system behavior by gluing parts back together, for many systems it just did not work. This is particularly true for living systems in all of their forms and beauty. Life, it seems, was far more "complex" than had been thought (Kaneko 1998; Karakas 2011; Janecka 2007; Sole and Goodwin 2002).

As I will be making use of a large number of terms, any number of which may be unfamiliar to the readers of this book, I will begin by defining terms, so that we all begin with a uniform understanding of the chapter vocabulary. Let us begin with the two words "complex" and "complicated."

Is it Complicated or Is it Complex?

The terms "complicated" and "complex" are frequently used interchangeably in much the same way that the words "sex" and "gender" are now assumed to be linguistically equivalent, though they refer to significantly different conceptual constructs. The same can be said about the words *complicated* and *complex*. Given that a system has many parts, a system is said to be *complicated* if infinite knowledge of the behaviors of the system's components allows an experimenter to predict all possible behaviors of the system. For example, a pocket watch would satisfy the *complicated* but not *complex* criteria. We can understand the behavior of all of the cogs, wheels, and springs in the system and, with some effort, we can arrive at what would be considered reasonable inferences concerning what the watch does and how it works.

What then would be an example of a *complex* system? Consider the following examples. Infinite knowledge of a single bird or fish would not allow an experimenter to predict the phenomena of swarming or schooling or the synchronization of firefly lights (Strogatz 2003). Infinite knowledge of a single female's menstrual cycle would not predict cycle locking in a college dorm room. These systems are termed complex (Sumpter 2010). They have *emergent properties* meaning that a behavior that was not predicted from infinite knowledge of the parts emerges as part of the system's behaviors (Sulis 2010; Clarke and Hansen 2009). In a moment, we provide more details about complex system properties.

From a PP perspective, Maddi (2006) makes the argument to "... consider creativity as behavior that is innovative ..." (p. 227). We could easily argue that innovative behavior is emergent behavior and thus, creativity is an emergent and unpredictable process. Another way to think of complex systems is that they are systems in which the whole is greater than the sum of the parts (Gorban and Petrovskii 2011).

If we were to examine a large collection of different complex systems, we would find that complex systems have certain common or unifying characteristics:

- They demonstrate *emergent behavior*; behavior that cannot be inferred from a linear analysis of the behavior of the components (Clark and Hansen 2009).
- They *contain many components that are dynamically interacting* (feedback, controllers, detectors, effectors, and rules). There is no master controller. The parts interact extensively at their local level with nearest neighbors.
- The *components are diverse*, thereby leading to a significant diversity of information in the system
- The components have surrendered some of their uniqueness or identity to serve as elements of the complex system. This is called *dissolvence*.
- All interactions of the components within the system and the system acting as a component in a higher hierarchy occur locally. *There is no action at a distance*.
- These *interactions take place across a number of scale levels* and they are arranged in a *hierarchical structure* where fine structure (scale) influences large-scale behavior (Brown and West 2000).
- They are able to *self-organize* (Chow et al. 2011; Yates 1987), to *adapt* (Curtis et al. 2011; Jacobsen and Guastello 2011), and to *evolve* (Kirschner and Gerhart 1998; Miller and Page 2007).

Schuldberg (2002) discusses similar criteria in his paper on complex systems, PP, and health. However, in his paper, the approach is a bit different in that he attempts to map known nonlinear dynamical behaviors onto psychological concepts. While this is a useful approach, it limits our view of what complexity theory has to offer in terms of psychological insights. In our discussion, we will pursue some of Schuldberg's approach. However, we will also approach complexity theory's offerings from a more phenomenological perspective.

Based upon our previous discussion, it is easy to see that psycho-socio-cultural systems are, by definition, naturally occurring complex systems and that they contain many of the characteristics we just mentioned. For example, if we consider "emergence, " it is well known that individual social decision rules can develop into unpredictable social norms (Kenrick et al. 2003). Also, as we shall see in later sections of this chapter, there are many other examples of how psycho-socio-cultural systems are naturally occurring complex systems.

The language and constructs of NDS allows us to more carefully illuminate the complex concepts arising in psychology. NDS aids PP by providing the field with dynamical and mathematical constructs hypothetically analogous to those found in the general field of *psychology* (Brown and Moscowitz 1998a, b; Doba et al. 2008; Field and Schuldberg 2011; Guastello 2000, 2009; Marks-Tarlow 2008), *sociology* (Sulis and Combs 1996), *psychiatry* (Globus and Arpaia 1994; Mandell and Selz

1995), and even in some areas of *PP* (Guastello and Shissler 1994; Ho and Fung 2011; Laycraft 2011; Schuldberg 1999, 2006, 2007a, b; Schuldberg and Gottlieb 2002; Vallacher et al. 2010; Vallacher and Nowak 1997). In the upcoming discussion, we will examine a small selection of the constructs drawn from NDS and how they might be applied in psychology in general and to PP in particular. We will, however, also wax more phenomenological and examine how the more general ideas around what defines a complex system conceptually inform us with respect to the field of PP.

What Does Complexity Suggest at a Phenomenological Level?

From our list of complex system properties, one insight that immediately emerges from viewing psycho-socio-cultural systems as complex systems is that behaviors/dynamics of these systems are not necessarily linearly additive. This is an important observation in that most statistical analyses, for example, automatically assume linearity (correlation, association, regression, etc.) unless explicitly stated by the analyst. Given that complex systems are not necessarily linear, we must take this into account when we use traditional statistical methodologies to analyze complex systems data. The flaw of linearity is illustrated in the following quotation: "A simple hedonic calculus suggests that by adding up a person's positive events in consciousness, subtracting the negatives, and aggregating over time, one will get a sum that represents the person's overall well-being" (Seligman and Czikszentmihalyi 2000, p. 11). Complex systems are nonlinear and the operations of adding or subtracting are linear processes.

Systems nonlinearity suggests that PP measures (consider, for example, the idea of spiraling in the broaden and build theory of Fredrickson (2004)) may be more difficult to determine and that even if we do derive measures, the weighted linear aggregation of those measures may not represent the person's overall well-being as suggested above. Complexity of a system further suggests that the individual measures themselves may need to be nonlinear in nature. That is, simply totaling response values on a given single instrument might not necessarily provide an accurate assessment of whatever variable the instrument was intended to measure (Ramos et al. 2011).

What Does Complexity Theory Suggest from a Dynamics Perspective?

Complexity theory draws on many areas of physics and mathematics in order to form its core constructs, among them the disciplines of catastrophe theory, chaos theory, information theory, thermodynamics, network theory, NDS theory, and fractal dynamics.

NDS theory contains a bounty of interesting behaviors and offers, by means of analogy and subsequent model fitting, many possible explanations for psychological behaviors. For example, NDS suggests that small changes in one variable could lead to profound changes in another variable (magnitude changes). In addition, NDS also suggests that small changes in one variable could produce radically different outcomes (behavioral changes) in a specific variable ("sensitivity to initial conditions" as it is called in complexity theory). Danner et al. (2001) point out that "even mild and fleeting positive affect can produce large benefits in the long run." Or, as Wiese et al. (2010) put it, "A person who is insulted at time 1, for example, may experience anger or intimidation at time 2 (e.g., right away) but over time, this experience may evolve in completely different directions—diminishing, intensifying, or perhaps oscillating between these feelings" (p. 1,019). As an example, let us consider the example trajectories illustrated in Fig. 19.1.

In this illustration, we display an example of a simple simulation that has had its initial starting state changed by a value of 0.01 units. We imagine for the purposes of discussion that these data points are drawn from a hypothetical optimism variable plotted as a function of visit number. Clearly, the behavioral dynamics begins similarly between the two simulations. However, it ends up rather differently. Results such as these also suggest that understanding the dynamics of positive psychological factors may not be easily, if at all, amenable to traditional forms of reductive research and that work in understanding factors such as buffering may require new ways of looking at psycho-socio-dynamic systems (Witten 1980, 1982). For example, understanding how "courage or interpersonal skill or hope or future mindedness buffer against depression or schizophrenia or substance abuse" (Seligman and Czikszentmihalyi 2000, p. 12) may not be easily understood by attempting to create measurement/assessment scales through reductionist approaches.

In order to understand the core concepts of NDS theory and its application to psychology, there are two aspects of complexity theory that we must first address. The first of these is "time" and the second is "space." Living systems may be complex in time (Brown and Moskowitz 1998a, b; Droit-Volet and Gil 2009; Marceau et al. 2011; Nadin 2010; Perdikis et al. 2011), complex in space (pattern formation; Goldberger 1996; Bassingthwaighte et al. 1994; Iannaccone and Khokha 1996), or complex in both time and space. Conjointly, we have the concept of "being in relationship to" someone, something, some group, some other system, some other time point, etc. (Rosen 1958, 1991; Louie and Kercel 2007). Fredrickson (2004), in her discussion of the broaden and build theory of positive emotion provides numerous examples of how various actions, emotions, and physiological responses go "hand in hand" with each other (are in relation to). The idea of being in relation to is also well illustrated in the following psychological example from Seligman and Czikszentmihalhyi (2000, p. 12):

> The study of the relations between enabling conditions, individual strengths, institutions, and outcomes such as well-being or income might merely result in an empirical matrix. Such a matrix would describe, for example, what talents under what enabling conditions lead to what kinds of outcomes. This matrix would inform individuals' choices along the course of their lives, but would take no stand on the desirability of different life courses.

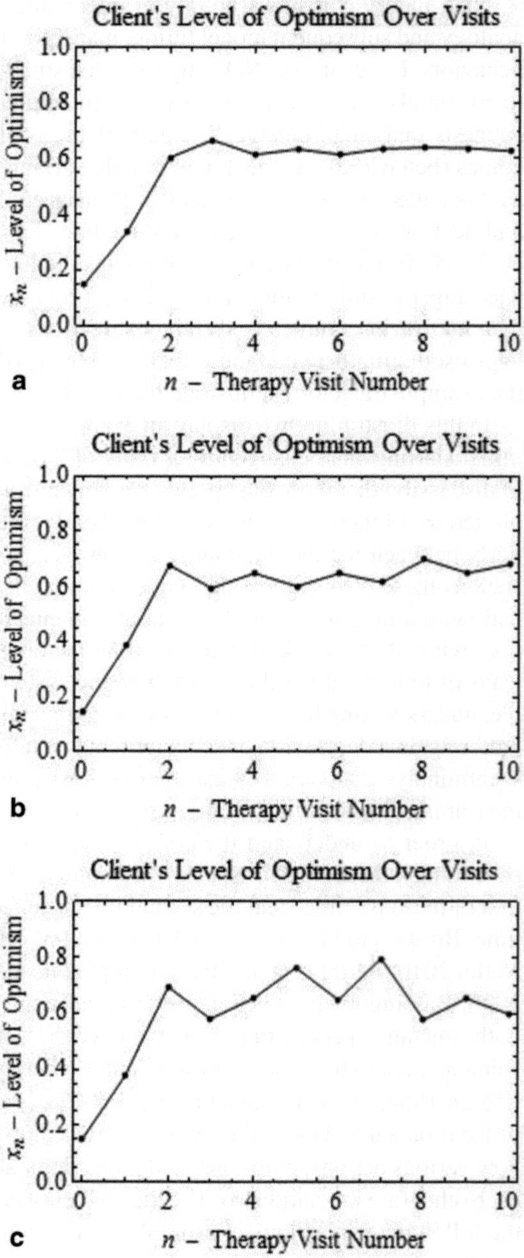

Fig. 19.1 Sample client optimism trajectories based upon the model given in equation (19.1)

We note that the authors use the important word "relations." The word "matrix" implies an underlying "structure." Structure also implies relationships and possible emergent behaviors not predicted until the matrix was created. We acknowledge that time and space can and do have interactions. However, for the purposes of our immediate discussion, we will separate them. We begin with a simple discussion of behavior in one dimension (one variable of interest). We will use this to illustrate some essential concepts of NDS and how they related to psychological ideas.

Time and Psycho-Socio-Dynamics in One Dimension

Time, similar to distance, has scales of measure from Planck time (approximately 10^{-43} s) to galactic scales of time 10^{17} s (Vrobel 2011; Perdikis et al. 2011). However, for us, time will be measured in scales relevant to a human lifespan (approximately, 10^9 s; a moment, a second, an hour, a lifetime).

Time not only has scales, it has structure. We naturally think of time as a continuum. However, we readily and quite handily use measures of time such as; last year, 2 years ago, just a moment, today, next month, etc. In these scenarios, we are discretizing time. Many life events happen in a discrete time sort of way. We have seasonal diseases (annual), we have a woman's period (monthly), we have heartbeats (seconds), etc. So, it is natural to think of biological, biomedical (did you get your annual flu shot), and even psycho-social events in terms of discrete instants in time (I get depressed just before my period begins). Moreover, the instants in time are frequently observed to be regular or patterned in time. That is, they occur at distinct intervals, every other week for example (i.e., visits to the therapist). Of course, there are many other aspects of the phenomenology of time that we cannot discuss within the limited space available. We focus on the essentials for now.

Discrete Time and Connectivity

Up to this point, there is no inherent *connectivity* between the events occurring at one time point (let us denote that time point t_{now}) and those occurring at another time point (let us denote that time point t_{next}). "The hand of the past [does not] weigh[s] heavily on the present" (Seligman and Cziksentmihalyi 2000, p. 8). We must make the temporal interplay appear if we are going to consider life course strategies. "It is impossible to describe positive psychological processes without taking a life span or at least a longitudinal approach" (2000, p. 10). If we examine the description of a complex system, we realize that we need some sort of "structure," some sort of hierarchical organization (remember the previous definition points for what makes systems complex). Somehow, we need to be able to describe "relationships" in time; a temporal hierarchy. Positive psychologists are aware of this fact, as is seen in the following quotation:

> How much delayed gratification is necessary to increase the chances of long-term well-being? Is the future mindedness necessary for serious delay of gratification antagonistic to momentary happiness, to living in the moment? What are the childhood building blocks of later happiness or of long-lasting well-being? (Seligman and Czikszentmihalhyi 2000, p. 12)

The issues illustrated in the above quotation highlight questions around the rules of relationship, relationships from future to past and from past to future. To develop our temporal relationship model, we begin as follows.

We are going to say that ρ is a rule that relates what happens at time t_{next} to what happens at time t_{now} and we will denote this mathematically as $t_{\text{next}} = f(t_{\text{now}})$. This is simply a way of writing down that I know how to predict what will happen at the next time point t_{next} based upon what has happened at the current time point t_{now}. For example, I can predict what the flu injection demand will be next year based upon what I know this year. If I know that I am having my menstrual period now, I know that in approximately 28 days, I will have another period. Both of these are simple examples. However, they introduce the importance of "being in relation to" something in time. We can now see how reductionism can break relationships and therefore yield results that are biologically or psychologically meaningless. An example of this loss of relationship leading to an incorrect conclusion is illustrated in Carnes et al. (2010, Figs. 19.1, 19.2).

The use of this discrete time approach derives from the work of the early ecologists. Far ahead of anyone else, ecologists saw the value of a "systems" approach to thinking about living systems. They noticed that they could write down mathematical equations (very simple ones as a matter of fact) that related seasonal population size at time t_{next} to what happens at time t_{now}. In particular, they noticed that they could write down equations that allowed them to predict future population sizes based upon knowledge of current population sizes. In these cases, the relationship ρ was a mathematical formula based upon the ecologist's knowledge of the system's biology. Let us construct a simple example for ourselves and see what we obtain. We begin by describing how we will track time in our simple model. We will then examine how it might be used to describe psychological constructs.

A Simple Discrete Time Model and Psychology

Developing the Hypothetical Model

The idea of using a discrete counter for time is not psychologically unreasonable. Seligman and Czikszentmihalyi (2000, p. 12) point out that "It is also necessary to realize that a person at time N is a different entity from the same person at time $N+1$." Because it is easy to visualize, we begin with a simple population model. For now, let us assume that n is our year counter (or other time unit counter). Assume that it counts $n = 0, 1, 2, \ldots$; where $n = 0$ is the current (or starting) year and each increment of n represents the next year, and the next and the next, etc. So, $n = 0, 1, 2, 3, \ldots$. Next, let us suppose that x_n represents the size of the population in year n. What May (1976), Witten (1980), and others observed was that the simplest possible nonlinear rule (because there is an x_n^2 term in the equation below) has an extremely varied set of dynamics behaviors. This equation is also known as the logistic model or logistic function. The actual model equation (relationship rule) is given as follows:

$$x_{n+1} = f(x_n) = bx_n(1 - x_n) = bx_n - bx_n^2 \quad (19.1)$$

The model simply says that the amount of insects (bugs) next season x_{n+1} is proportional to the amount of bugs there are in the population at time now minus a term that accounts for how many bugs the environment can support (the squared term x_n^2). How does such a simple model (equation) relate to psychology, much less PP? In order to make that linkage, we need just a bit more discussion and a few more definitions.

Notice that if we know the starting size x_0 of the population (time $n = 0$; start time), then using our rule that $x_{n+1} = f(x_n)$ where $f(x_n) = bx_n(1 - x_n)$, we can see that the state (size) of the population 1 year later would be written as $x_1 = f(x_0)$ and given by $x_1 = bx_0(1 - x_0)$. It should be obvious that knowing x_1 gets us the value of $x_2 = bx_1(1 - x_1)$, and so on. The set of population sizes (states) $\{x_0, x_1, x_2, \ldots, x_n\}$ is called the *trajectory* (sometimes *orbit* is used) of the initial state x_0. The fascinating thing about this very simple nonlinear model is that it turns out that trajectories, for different values of the parameter b (which we have been avoiding talking about) and different starting values of x_0 can take on a variety of different, but classifiable general behaviors as follows:

- Some trajectories will tend toward a particular point (called an *equilibrium point*) and stay there. Such points are also called *fixed points* in that once you get there, you stay there. We can think of these as steady states because we do not go anywhere once we arrive at one of these points. Trajectories may tend away from or toward other equilibria.
- Some trajectories *oscillate* back and forth between a set of points (called *periodic behavior*). The periodic behavior can be very complicated looking.
- Some trajectories appear to have *random, unpredictable* or *chaotic behavior*.

Of course, the discussion of the various types of trajectory is far more mathematically sophisticated than these three simple summaries (Baker and Gollub 1990; Gros 2008; May 1976; Nicolis 1995; Nicolis and Prigogine 1989). However, these are the general behaviors for a simple model such as our rule. Now how can we apply this to psychology?

Application to Psychology

From a psychological perspective, if we think about the previous mathematical discussion, an orbit or trajectory is nothing more than a set of discrete time point snap-shots of "states of being" in a person's life course. For example, $n = 0, 1, 2, \ldots$ might be said to represent time points such as dates of office visits for psychotherapy and the value of x_n would then represent the value of some "state of being" for the client, say degree self-confidence or degree of subjective well-being (Sheldon and King 2001) in life. Suppose we consider x_n to be a measure of well-being, then our simple model predicts that, for different values of x_0 and b a variety of dynamical behaviors can occur. These behaviors can go from behavior patterns in which the individual's sense of wellbeing tends to zero (no feelings of well-being) to behavior patterns in which the behavior pattern tends to a nonzero equilibrium (a finite positive value of well-being) to far more complex behaviors (oscillations) to trajectories in which the sense of well-being is chaotic and unpredictable.

Of course, these models ignore (oversimplify) many factors that could alter the individual client's state values. For example, random external factors are not included in the model. The time points must be equally spaced (for example, weekly or monthly or daily). The value of the parameter b does not always remain exactly the same from visit to visit. However, even with all of these assumptions, these simple nonlinear models provide us with a basic mathematical language within which we can discuss concepts in psychology in general and in PP in particular. Moreover, the dynamical behaviors have realistic analogies in psychological dynamics. We use this simple model as a mechanism by which we can illustrate some important ideas. Let us investigate this further.

More on the Model Behavior and Psychology

Let us return to our previous simple nonlinear model and examine how the parameter b affects the trajectory (the life course). First, we will ignore the effects of random factors. For the sake of the discussion, let us assume that x_n represents the client's measured level of anxiety x at time point n. After each of a sequence of office visits, you measure the client's level of anxiety and you find that x_n measures as follows: Visit $1 - x_1 = 0.65$, Visit $2 - x_2 = 0.63$, Visit $3 - x_3 = 0.62$, and Visit $4 - x_4 = 0.61$. If you were to plot this out, it would look very much similar to a horizontal line. What is interesting is that our funny little nonlinear model (Eq. 19.1) predicts that for a value of $b = 2.5$, the trajectory of the model gives almost exactly this same behavior. In other words, the trajectory tends to an equilibrium value. For our little one-dimensional model, the equilibrium is $x^* = 0.6$; very close to x_4.

Now, suppose that over a period of weeks, you implement a treatment plan that you believe will reduce the client's level of anxiety. In terms of the trajectory of the client, you hope to alter the trajectory, so that after a number of visits (and faithful homework) the anxiety level will be lower than when you started and further you hope that it will stay near that lower value. The only way to do this, in the context of our earlier simple model, is to alter the value of the parameter b. The parameter b is often called the "control parameter" as it controls the type of behavior the system expresses.

Thus, the value of the parameter b could be viewed as tuning the effect of the psychotherapeutic intervention. Suppose your anxiety measures behave as follows {Level of Anxiety = 0.65, 0.62, 0.65, 0.65, 0.62, 0.59, 0.55, 0.50, 0.48, 0.47, 0.47…}, then you have been, we might say, therapeutically successful with your client. You have reduced the level from 0.65 to 0.47. In terms of our model, you have moved the b parameter from a value of $b = 2.5$ to a value of $b = 1.886$. Perhaps at this level of anxiety, the client can manage his anxiety and potentially maintain it at the given level. However, "maintaining it" means that the client can hold the anxiety level steady over a period of time and this is conceptually mathematically equivalent to reaching a local steady state. A *steady state* (or *fixed point* if you like mathematical terms) is called an *attractive fixed point* or just an *attractor* if the trajectory tends toward that point. Other terminology calls this a *stable fixed point* or *stable attractor*. But you, as a psychologist, can think of it as a locally stable behavior pattern, where by locally we mean that behavior pattern is stable over some period of time. Similarly, the undesirable behavior pattern or life trajectory is now *unstable* (or a *repellor*). Different clients will come in with different initial levels of anxiety x_0 and you will want to reduce their current state of anxiety (a stable state in the sense of the level of anxiety, but not behaviorally stable), and you will want to move them onto a life course trajectory that (over a reasonable period of time) leads them toward a stable, less anxiety-filled state. You would do this by tuning your therapy parameter b to make the appropriate per-client adjustments. Note that when we say, "You would do this by . . ." we understand this to mean that you would alter your therapeutic intervention in such a way as to achieve the given results. When we move from one class of behavior to another, we say that there is a *bifurcation* in the behavior. For example, innovative behavior, ". . . a change from the routine or conformist . . ." (Maddi 2006, p. 227), "represents a bifurcation from one behavioral or mental trajectory to another." What the simple nonlinear model provides us with is a formal structure within which we can begin to mathematically describe the psychological dynamics. With such models we can begin to explore not only the known psycho-social behavioral dynamics, but also the ones predicted by such models.

Application to Positive Psychology (PP)

How might our simple model apply to PP? For the moment, we ignore the fact that with more of the assumptions lifted, it is possible to have multiple stable steady states (bistability/multistability; Wilhelm 2009; Frohlich et al. 2010) and save this for an upcoming point of discussion. Consider the hypothetical client in Fig. 19.2.

In Fig. 19.2, we illustrate three graphs. We have scaled the data so that all of the measures fall between 0 and 1 for ease of illustration and comparison. Figure 19.2a illustrates the data from the hypothetical client that has transferred to your practice. The previous therapist measured the level of the client's optimism over the period of a year of therapy visits (50 visits). Figure 19.2a illustrates the previous therapist's hypothetical measurements. Your new client appears to have been radically vacillating between a large amount of optimism (values near 1) and a small amount of optimism (values near 0). However, it is clear that the client has the capability of experiencing large amounts of optimism. That is, the potential for a strong optimistic outlook is there.

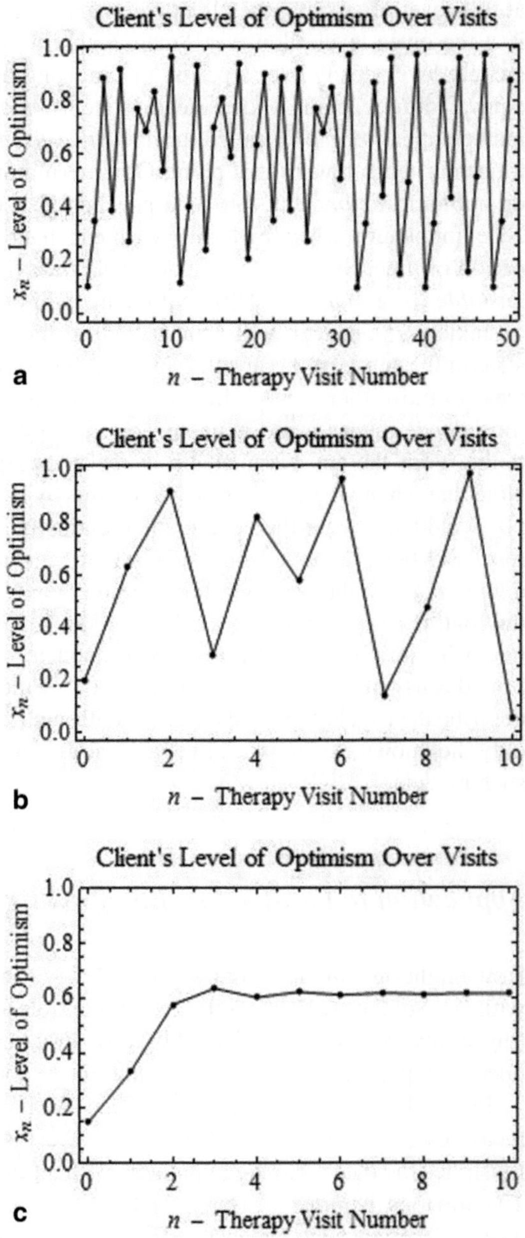

Fig. 19.2 Sample client optimism trajectories based upon the model given in equation (19.1)

You decide to measure the client's current status and you do this for ten consecutive visits (Fig. 19.2b). Again, you see that the client is capable of having a strong sense of optimism, but there remain wild oscillations in the optimism measures. Your goal is to try to assist, through therapeutic intervention, in attaining a level of optimism that is at a level and is both high and maintainable for the client. In other words, you would like to move the client's life trajectory (with respect to the level of optimism) from the vacillations of Fig. 19.2a, b to the more stable trajectory illustrated in Fig. 19.2c. While the final level of optimism may not reach the peaks seen in the client's previous data, the level is elevated to a reasonable point and is stable across time indicating that the client has been able to maintain the degree of optimism across a series of visits. Thus, we have moved the hypothetical client from a highly volatile state to a more stable state.

Nonlinear dynamics helps us to articulate the previous discussion by providing us with a theoretical construct within which we can both find similarities and notice possible dynamical nuances that we might not have otherwise suspected. We say this because Figs. 19.2a–c were actually generated using our previous simplest nonlinear model. All of the starting points had the same value x_0. The only difference between the different examples was that we altered the value of the "therapy parameter b." Of course, if life comes along and perturbs the therapeutic parameters, we hope that we have helped the client to develop a skill set that keeps his trajectory in the stable area and preferably does not move too far from the decreased level of anxiety. If this is true, then we say that our treatment is *robust* (Lenski et al. 2006) to *perturbation*. That is, we would like the client's status to be able to withstand the assortment of life perturbations that come and go with day-to-day living. We might argue as Mosca (1995) did that "the ultimate attractor relevant to human experience is what might be termed the happiness attractor." Ideally, we can imagine that we would like such a state to be an attractor, preferably stable, and certainly robust to perturbation. However, it is also possible to imagine that the happiness state is a semistable node meaning that when a client is in one life state, happiness is stable. However, if the client is moved to another domain, happiness is unstable and one moves—perhaps—toward a sad/depression state. Again, here we also see the notion of bistability appearing.

Of course, our parameter b is a lumped parameter that somehow includes buffering, resilience, evolvability, frailty, robustness, and treatment effects all in one value. Clearly, this is not very realistic. However, the fact that we can see living system behaviors similar to the previous dynamics provides us with a foundation upon which we can build our language and description of the nonlinear psychological behaviors in a more comprehensive fashion.

Randomness, Chaos, and Fractality

Again, let us consider our simple model. However, this time we will randomly perturb our "therapy parameter" in three stages: small, medium, and large perturbation. We will think of this as analogous to life forces exerting different degrees of perturbation upon our client.

For some values of the control parameter b and for certain small perturbations, the values of our client's optimism might be reasonably robust to perturbation. As we increase the degree of perturbation, the client's life trajectory is more likely to change. Based upon this ability to resist perturbation, we might say that the therapy parameter *b* is somewhat robust. However, it is hard to quantify exactly how robust because we have a composite parameter. Moreover, when a client describes his or her life as too chaotic, perhaps this is a "mathematical" way of telling the therapist that they need a way to help steer their trajectory through the chaos; that the client is not feeling robust enough in the face of the perturbations. This analysis also suggests that when perturbation undermines therapeutic intervention that perhaps the intervention strategy is not as effective as originally thought and that alternative interventions might do better.

One has to be careful about playing around with systems that exhibit *chaotic behavior* (Skarda and Freeman 1990). While too much chaos can be harmful, a little chaos can be helpful. Complexity theory teaches us that a small amount of chaos can actually stabilize a system. In fact, many biological processes can be shown to be weakened when the noise or chaotic behavior is removed or reduced too much in the system (Kang et al. 2009). When we think about the concept of noise reduction as a potentially deleterious effect, it raises important questions around how to treat individuals using positive psychological methods as this would require "perturbing" their system in a way that could potentially reduce the noise, and thereby actually hurt rather than help them. For example, Bonanno et al. (2011) examine the question of "Whether resilience building interventions can actually make people more resilient" (p. 511). In fact, the authors further point out that, "Resilience-building interventions may be ineffective and perhaps even harmful" (p. 529). This comment, in the context of NDS theory, suggests that in altering the system using a resilience-building intervention, the therapist–client dyad dynamics could generate negative results for the client even though positive psychological methods are being used. This is a counter-intuitive insight. Extrapolating from complexity theory, the reason behind this possible outcome is that alteration of the noise, chaos or fractal structure in the environment or even within the client's internal behavioral constructions might actually lead to a destabilization which would subsequently lead to some form of negative behavioral pattern, neuropsychological pattern, or physiological dynamics (Glass 1999, 2009; Goldberger 1996; Moreno-Bote et al. 2007).

Fractal patterns in time have been demonstrated to occur at many levels of the biomedical hierarchy from single cell to whole organism (Van Orden 2007). Fractal dynamics has been seen in cardiac rhythm, cognitive dynamics, and diseases such as Huntington's and Parkinson's disease (West 2006). Fractality in a signal implies that there is a certain embedded structure to the signal and that this organism (cardiac, neurological, etc.) is healthy. Goldberger (1996) and team have demonstrated that loss of fractality in cardiac signals implies an impending cardiac infarction. Similar results have been found in other biomedical signal processes. Much work has been done in this area of research and in how "variability" of a given biological signal does or does not endow the organism with a degree of wellness or unwellness (Castiglioni and Parati 2011; Karim et al. 2011; Glass 1999).

Perceived and Constructed Time

In our previous modeling discussion, we chose to treat time as a chronologically measureable entity; that is, we can actually take a clock out of our pocket and measure when various behaviors occur, various incidents happen, etc. However, similar to so many other constructs, time is not just chronological (measurable), it is also perceived and internally constructed. In addition, in some sense, time is also constructed by the observer of the system (Geoffard and Luchini 2010). Let us consider these facts, as they force us to think about nonlinear models of behavior patterns (after all behavior patterns are—in fact—patterns in time) in a different manner.

Time is constructed. In this statement we argue that individuals have internal ideas (constructions) about time flow and how living systems should be related to points in time. For example, individuals who are in their 80s should look a certain way, behave a certain way and individuals who are in their 20s should act a different way and behave in a different way. Consider the statement, "Stop behaving like a child." Or consider how, when one sees a person on the street and finds out that they are 90 years old, it is not uncommon to hear something like, "I would have never thought that you were ninety. You look like you would be in your sixties" (Nicolis and Nicolis 2010). Time flow and aging constructs raise questions around the relationships of biological and chronological time or age. These are constructed time ideas in that various exogenous factors have created an environment in which an individual observer or group of observers constructs how reality should appear or exist as a function of time.

Perceived time is a bit different. Here, as Geoffard and Luchini (2010, p. 271) state, "Impatience, in our context, implies that the experience of time up to the forthcoming event expands . . . an unpleasant event that will happen in the future triggers anxiety. This will give the experience of time contraction." It follows that perceived time is a function of emotional state. Here we are reminded of the work of Lyng (1990) who talks about time compression in what he calls "edgework." In this scenario, individuals are working on challenges of great interest to them, so that time seems to slow to a stop. Lyng's work draws on some of the concepts of Csikszentmihalyi's "flow." The philosophy of time and its construction is well beyond the scope of the material of this chapter. We simply mention a few important ideas in order to make our final point on time as a complex entity.

In both cases, perceived and constructed time, the so-called time variable is an internal construction/perception; perceived time is an assessment of personally experienced time passage and constructed time is a socially induced (though individually constructed) construction of how things should exist at certain time points. Thus, the variable that we are calling time is actually not a one-dimensional linear construct that simply flows similar to a river to the ocean. Rather, TIME is a multidimensional/higher dimensional abstraction in which what we call chronological time, perceived time, and constructed time serve as resultant "observables" in the quantum mechanical sense of operations that take the abstract higher dimensional TIME object and project it into the various perspectives of observational interest. The result of each probe, measurement/observation is the value of the particular version of time being observed. A perfect example of such a complex higher dimensional object appears on the Hofstadter's (1979) book cover. In Hofstadter's book illustration, we are shown an abstract entity that appears in the center of the page. This entity is illuminated from three different directions. When viewed from each of these different perspectives, the complex entity shows shadows of the letters G, E, or B on the projected walls. However, when we observe the central object, it embeds all of the characteristics of these letters. In this sense, the illuminated entity is a gedankt analogue to TIME itself. TIME becomes a complex abstract structure which, as we have seen, implies a collection of important properties and potential constructs. Moreover, these dynamics must be considered when one is developing clinical interventions around temporal issues. This quantum phenomenological construction may seem irrelevant to psychology much less PP. However, Fredrickson (2004, p. 1,369) points out that "Love—viewed as an amalgam of distinct positive emotions (e.g. joy, interest and contentment . . .)." Thus, the construct that Fredrickson calls love should actually be termed LOVE (in analogy with our construct of TIME). At this point, there is little empirical support in psychology for the quantum constructions. However, the door is still open.

Psychologically the idea that time is, itself, a complex object implies that it must be viewed from a complexity theoretic standpoint, just similar to any other complex object. When viewed in this fashion, complexity theory suggests that chronological measures of time are merely one facet of a potentially far more complex object TIME. Moreover, it suggests that nonlinear views of time are not only reasonable and should not be ignored, but that they are also essential. We are already aware that nonlinear temporal narratives exist. Nonlinear narratives such as flash back and flash forward are well-known temporal narratives that occur in storytelling and certainly in psychological counseling. Relativistic views of time (observer–observed) are equally nonlinear; just ask a physicist. The take home message here is that when building PP models that involve time, one must remember that TIME is also a complex variable and that, at an individual or group level, time itself can have emergent properties and nonlinear behaviors that can affect how it is seen in a particular reality, study, etc.

Resilience, Buffering, Frailty, and Robustness

Up to this point, we have discussed life trajectories in terms of local and long-term stability and outcome. We have seen how they can have different behavior patterns and different endpoints. However, complexity theory offers us other ways in which we can view a life trajectory. In the upcoming section, we examine life trajectories and their properties in much the same way that we would use theories of engineering and physics to examine a trajectory. We begin as follows.

Life is full of perturbations and rich with forces that can affect how we traverse through the potential pathways available to us. Some of these forces we are able to resist, some we are not. Those that we cannot fully resist may push us off our current life path and onto other paths. Those new paths can lead to positive or negative outcomes. When we think about life paths and trajectories, we can imagine them in much the same way we can imagine strings, springs, or rubberbands with various physical properties. Some rubberbands can resist being perturbed. Some springs can return to a natural original state. These physical properties have analogous psychological constructs. In this section, we discuss these constructs and how they apply to psycho-social dynamics. We begin with the concept of *resilience*.

Resilience

From an intuitive perspective, *resilience* can be defined as the ability of a system, when perturbed, to return to its original state of operation (Jackson 2010). Some people loosen the definition to allow the system to return to a state of operation that is close to the original state of operation, where closeness is defined in such a way that the system is still functional as if it were still in its original state. Similar to most of the terms that we have been using, resilience is a complex concept. For example, a system can take a short time or a long time to return to its operational zone. Are both of these the same degree of resilience? Surely not! A system can be perturbed for a fixed length of time and then the perturbation stops. What if the return to normalcy time depends upon the length of the perturbation? Are systems that return faster more resilient than ones that take longer to return? Can resilience be used up or built up? Thus, the term resilience encompasses a number of facets, most of which are ignored or tacitly assumed when talking about the subject of resilience.

From a psycho-social perspective, resilience (Smith et al. 2010; Bonanno et al. 2011; Lesne 2008; Luthar et al. 2000) is the ability to bounce back from a psycho-social impact of some type, a perturbation in the life course trajectory. For most psychologists, this inherently assumes that the lifecourse or life trajectory has been moved in a direction that has led to negative life experiences. Furthermore, it assumes that individuals have, within themselves, or can be shown how to gain, the capability to alter the life course; to return, not necessarily to the preperturbation state, but rather to a state that would still be considered functional in a client-based sense. Bonanno et al. (2011) state that, "...resilience can be adequately understood only when it is operationally defined as a stable trajectory of healthy adjustment across time" (p. 529). Thus, resilience is a global or systems level term that encompasses an individual's ability (a system's ability) to respond to a perturbation across the lifecourse trajectory. If you perturb the rocket on its targeted course, can it recalculate (similar to your GPS system) to arrive at the target?

Use of global terms such as resilience often implies that there is a complexity theoretic underpinning to the concept. Concepts such as entropy, information, scale, scale-freeness, and fractality (Hastings and Sugihara 1993; Iannaccone and Khokha 1996) are all global concepts that tell us something about the whole system without perturbation on our part. What we need to understand is that resilience is a system response property that allows the system to compensate after it has been perturbed.

Since it is a global system property, complexity theory teaches us that it can have unpredictable outcomes due to its inner complexity.

Bonanno et al. (2011) point out that there are many "independent predictors of resilient outcomes." This suggests two things. First, it suggests that resiliency may well be a complex concept and therefore requires nonlinear methods in order that to more effectively represent it. Second, it suggests that the human "resilience system" may be built with some form of redundancy/back-up system; some form of alternative/compensatory pathways in case some portion of the resilience system fails. This type of organizational structure suggests that the human "resilience system" may have a fractal dimension that lies in what is often called the "robust to attack" domain. That is, the resilience system may have evolved in such a way that it is not *frail*; not easily vulnerable to attack/perturbation. If the system is fractal in nature, then this also suggests that the various paths to prototypical outcome trajectories (Bonanno et al. 2011, p. 515) are connected in some form of what we can call a network (Kepes 2007; Barabasi 2002) that is complex.

The work of Bonanno et al. (2011) makes use of latent growth mixture (LGM) modeling, thereby opening up the concept of looking at the whole trajectory as a means of understanding resilience. While LGM models are not strictly NDS, they do involve looking at the whole trajectory. Looking at the trajectory as a whole entity reinforces the idea that the complexity theoretic approach of nonreduction may offer information that is otherwise not available. Their approach also suggests that patterns generated by the individual trajectories might fall into clusters of identifiable patterns in time and space. These clusters could represent classes of similar outcome behaviors based upon the variables used to derive the original clusters. The use of pattern identification methods is a natural way to address complex systems as it does not involve reductionist methodologies. One simply measures the system trajectory and uses that as the input data to some form of clustering algorithm. From a complexity theoretic perspective, this represents the most natural way to analyze the system as you are examining the whole system without dissecting it and attempting to understand how the pieces interact. Resilience must then be understood as a catch-all label for a complex internal system that carries out certain functions for the living system within which it resides. The caveat here is that this discussion is very dependent upon how one defines resilience. It is possible, in some cases, to capture resilience using catastrophe modeling (Pincus and Metten 2010; Thompson 2010; Guastello 2011a, b)

Robustness, Buffering, and Frailty

In the previous section, we talked about the idea of resilience and pointed out that it is, in some sense, a measure of the system's ability to return to an operational space upon perturbation. The fact that the system was able to be perturbed indicates that it was not able to resist the forces of perturbation. This brings us to the concept of *robustness*.

There are many definitions for "robustness" and they are all context dependent. In one sense, robustness and resilience are opposite concepts. Robustness can be viewed as resistance to perturbation and resilience is ability to return to one's original state, or—in the case of PP—to subsequently "[achieve a] positive adaptation despite major assaults on the developmental process (Luthar et al. 2000)" after a perturbation (see also Huang et al. 2010). Thus, robustness to stress implies that it is hard for stress to move a person off their current trajectory (life course), while resilience says that if the individual is moved away from the life course trajectory then how long, if you will, does it take to get back to the original trajectory or to a trajectory that will serve as an acceptable surrogate for the original trajectory (Wagner 2008).

Systems that are robustly designed are often more difficult to study because they have built in ability to resist perturbation and, if they blow a circuit or an operational unit, they often have backup systems that can keep the living system (or nonliving system) operating in a functional way (Gao et al. 2010; Pradhan et al. 2011; Schneider et al. 2011; Srinivasan and Stevens 2011). Robustness, from a psychological perspective, implies that a system is hard to move from one psychological state to another. For example, a client who has robust internal constructs is likely to be more difficult to work with and likely to be more difficult to develop a change plan than one who is less robust. On the other hand, a client who has developed a robust sense of self (positive robustness) may be more resistant to external perturbations that assault their sense of self. Thus, similar to resilience, robustness is a global catchall term designed to describe a system's ability to defend itself against perturbation.

Robustness, or *resistance to perturbation* (Wagner 2005; Bedau and Humphreys 2008; Lesne 2008) can be enhanced by developing the client's strengths. "... there are human strengths that act as buffers against mental illness : courage, future mindedness, optimism ... to name several" (Seligman and Csikszentmihalyi 2000, p. 7). Thus, the construct of robustness may be seen as an emergent consequence of a system design that has built in buffers against assaultative pressures.

Because robustness represents a system's ability to resist perturbation, robustness could also represent a threat to evolvability and adaptability (Wagner and Altenberg 1996). If we consider Guastello et al.'s (1999) discussion on motivational flow, we find an excellent example of how all of these concepts (as well as the upcoming concept of evolvability) fit together. We can view motivation as a precursor to executing some action. Thus, motivation could be considered as a driving force. The force acts on the lifecourse trajectory (think of a force perturbing a rubberband). Depending upon how strong the force and how robust the system, the motivational force will perturb the system. If the perturbation is strong enough, the system trajectory will change (bifurcate) to a different path. It is presumed that this path is the path for positive change. If, for some reason, the system is either overly robust (perturbation does not affect the system enough to induce change) or overly resilient (system returns to original unperturbed state), then the motivational process has not been effective and needs to be reconsidered. A more recent discussion of motivation may be found in Navaro et al. (2007). The literature on motivation is fairly large and beyond the possibility of review here.

Evolvability is the system's ability to alter itself in response to changes in external forces in such a way as to allow the system to continue to function; adaptive evolution (Daniels et al. 2008; Kirschner and Gerhart 1998). A living system is said to be evolvable if it can acquire novel functions through genetic change, functions that help the organism survive and reproduce. Because the concept of evolvability originally arose in the field of organismal evolution, it carries with it the ideas associated with genetic evolution in the face of exogenous pressures. However, it is not unreasonable to think of living systems such as organizations as having constructs that are equivalent to genes and to ask how an organization might evolve in the face of external pressures such as economic stress. Complex systems such as organizations, groups, crowds, etc. have a topology of connections (organization chart, group structure, etc.; Barabasi 2002). These important nodes in the hierarchy can change as can the connections (Greenbury et al. 2010; Whitacre and Bender 2010a, b). These changes can lead to new emergent dynamics that could be considered adaptations to the exogenous stressors or forces (Jensen 1998). This leads us to addressing systems with more than one lifecourse trajectory. It should be made clear that not every resilience model must be a logistic function (Pincus and Metten 2010; Thompson 2010; Guastello et al. 2011a, b). Rather, I am using the simple nonlinear model to illustrate NDS concepts.

Typology of Trajectory Behavior Patterns

In the previous section, we discussed global dynamical features of trajectories (life histories). However, there is another aspect of trajectories that is also of importance and that aspect is the "orbital pattern" or "orbital form"; the topology of the trajectory itself. As Wiese et al. (2010) point out, "emphasis on temporal patterns and the complex interplay of influences on these patterns represents a dramatic change in the way social psychological processes are conceptualized and investigated" (p. 1019). Sometimes, for example, it is not necessary to obtain a certain specific "magnitude" (degree of creative mastery, sense of well-being) rather, it is simply necessary to instill the needed behavior patterns so that the individual is in the right ballpark. Fredrickson (2004) points out, that "positive emotions broaden an individual's momentary thought-action repertoire . . ." (p. 1367). What she is saying is that positive emotions actually expand the available state space, both in terms of possible states through which trajectories can pass as well as possible outcomes. In other words, it is the pattern that is important rather than the final magnitude of a given psychological measure. As we will continue to see, patterns (dynamical behaviors) play an important role in complexity theory (particularly emergent patterns). Moreover, they are an important part of psychology as well.

By considering a simple, discrete, and one-dimensional model we have generated a large vocabulary by which we can describe psycho-socio-behavioral phenomena. We have seen how the concepts can be applied to psychological phenomena. While a simple one-dimensional model can generate quite a number of simple and interesting dynamical behaviors, as we increase the dimensions of the model, the dynamical system (model, living system) has many more potential behaviors available to it. One of the challenges in working in NDS is the meaning of the words being used. For example, applied mathematicians might say that our simple mapping f is one-dimensional in that it has only one dependent measure. However, topologists might say otherwise in that it is quadratic in degree. Thus, terminology is frequently context-dependent and this should be something of which the reader of this literature should be aware.

Higher Dimensional Dynamical Systems Models in Psychology

Clearly, the ideas and language of nonlinear dynamics have given us a useful means by which we may describe behaviors occurring in psycho-socio-cultural systems. However, it is also obvious that we are limited in our ability to describe many behaviors due to the fact that we have, so far, considered only a very simple model. We accepted the argument that the model parameter b represented the overall effects of therapy and from a qualitative perspective that argument was reasonable. However, if we really wished to model the therapeutic interaction with a client, we would need at least two equations (see, for example, the springs and blocks discussion in Schuldberg 2002): one describing the behavior of the therapist, and one describing the behavior of the client, and each containing a term that describes their cross interactions. This leads us into the area of dyadic dynamics (Rivera et al. 2010). However, I would caution the reader to be aware that the number of equations is not necessarily equal to the number of dimensions, as the number of dimensions is very much dependent upon the complexity subdiscipline being used to make the model.

Dyadic Models

Dyadic dynamical models (models containing two dependent variables) provide a variety of new collection of equilibria that are typically classified as *node*, *saddle point*, *center or focus, and limit cycle*. These equilibria can be stable (meaning that the behavioral trajectory is attracted toward the node), unstable (meaning that the behavioral trajectory tends away from the node), or semi-stable (meaning that in one direction, the node is stable and in another it is not). One might imagine a psychotherapeutic equilibrium where the client comes for therapy each week, but simply talks about subject matter irrelevant to the problem he or she is trying to address. The therapist listens, comments, and may attempt to have the client discuss problem-related topics. However, nothing happens in terms of client movement toward improvement. This could go on for some period of time and might be considered a "local equilibrium" in the therapeutic dyad. We use the word local equilibrium because there may be other possible equilibria for a given system.

Two-dimensional models of interactive social behaviors have been around for a while. For example, the Lancaster war models describe the arms escalation/deescalation between two countries (Bellany 1999). One can make an initial argument that escalation/deescalation is correlated with fear and aggression in the system. The Romeo and Juliet model of love and hate between two individuals has also been around for some time (Strogatz 1994) and is more exhaustively studied in Gottman et al. (2002). A more recent excellent example of dyadic modeling is illustrated in Guastello et al. (2006), who discuss electro-dermal arousal between participants in a conversation. Here, the investigators studied pairs of students engaged in brief 20-min conversations while they were connected to electrodes that measured their skin response. The nonlinear modeling results supported the fact that empathy acted as a moderator of the underlying nonlinear dynamics that moderates to electrodermal response. Mathematically, models of this type are often represented either as a system of discrete (iterative) equations or as a system of ordinary differential equations. In the previous discussion, we have mentioned pretty typical behaviors of simple two-dimensional systems. However, there are many other possible behaviors that nonlinear systems may demonstrate. However, remember that there other forms of modeling that do not use discrete or differential equation systems and yet can be applied to modeling these types of behaviors. In order to see these more exciting features, we will increase our system of equations to at least three equations (three dependent variables of interest) describing our system.

Higher Dimensional Behaviors

We have already seen that two-dimensional models can give rise to stable periodic behaviors and other phenomena such as semistable foci. However, higher dimensional models can also give rise to more interesting dynamics such as bursting phenomena (Izhikevich 2000; Sorribes et al. 2011), strange attractors, bistability and multistability (Deco et al. 2007), and many other interesting behaviors (Baker and Gollub 1990; Bar-Yam 1997). Consider the following quotation:

> Enjoyment, on the other hand, refers to the good feelings people experience when they break through the limits of homeostasis—when they do something that stretches them beyond what they were—in an athletic event, an artistic performance, a good deed, a stimulating conversation.

Notice that breaking through the limits implies a change in behavior, which could be viewed as a "bifurcation" in behavior. It could also be seen as a bursting behavior or as a possible catastrophe (momentarily, we will see catastrophes).

Bursting Phenomena

Bursting behavior can occur in a variety of physical and biomedical systems. Here, we will focus on the generic idea of bursting, particularly as it applies to neural systems. Without getting into too much detail about how neural systems function, we can say that a neuron fires a spike (action potential) and then rests before it can fire again. Bursting is a different state. Here, the neuron repeatedly fires discrete sequences or groups of spikes. Once the group has finished there is a period of rest (also called quiescence) before the next group of spikes fires. Bursting is a very important phenomenon in neuroscience as it is related to interneuron communication, motor pattern generation and neural synchronization. However, bursting can actually have psychological analogies.

Many bursting phenomena are governed by algorithms of priority-driven behavioral choice such as those that we have seen in our previous discussion. However, if the bursting through is priority driven, then part of the PP approach is to change the individual's behavior cues from solely environmental (in which case the behaviors would be more random) to more decision-based priority oriented in which case this is a change that can lead to the bursting through behaviors we have mentioned. Moreover, it also has the tone and tenor of a "bursting" phenomenon; the individual's state has reached a point where they have reached a "firing threshold" and with the correct supportive environment burst through to a new state of awareness of being. This state could be a momentary existential illumination or a more transformative state; one that we hope will continue to persist. Maddi (2006) provides us with another excellent example of bursting behavior when he points out that, "A good example of such conceptualizing would be to consider creativity as behavior that is innovative rather than routine or conformist." However, innovation can be viewed as either a bifurcation to a new form of behavior trajectory (dynamics) or it can be seen as a bursting behavior that lasts for a period of time before the system falls back to its preinnovative dynamical trajectory. If, however, the system is sensitive to perturbation or is subject to sensitivity to initial conditions, we have a system behavior that is isomorphic to chaotic dynamics. Zausner (2011) notes that creativity can be seen as a nonlinear behavior, arguing that it can generate either positive or negative experiences that can be modeled by "limit cycle" behavior.

One of the challenges of using NDS analogies is that oftentimes more than one analogy may apply to a given behavioral process requiring the psychologist to attempt to unify the processes with a higher level analogy or else to understand that the two analogies may be psychological equivalents of the quantum projections we discussed earlier in this chapter, again requiring the psychologist to attempt to understand the higher dimensional object from which the analogies were derived. An excellent discussion on these topics may be found in Arrechi (2011). It is also important to realize that while NDS offers us conceptual and linguistic analogies that may lead to interesting insights, it is also a discipline that is rich with analytical models that can be applied to the various psychological behaviors we have been discussing.

Bistability and Multistability

In an earlier part of our discussion, we observed that it was possible to have different stability configurations for a higher dimensional system based upon the particular parameter set values. In other words, depending upon the values of the model (control) parameters, one dynamical behavior might be stable whereas another dynamical behavior might be stable for a different set of parameters.

In the case where there are only two possible stable states for the system, we call this bistability. *Bistability* is the ability of a system to live in one of two different states depending upon the system parameters (Moreno-Bote et al. 2007; Wilhelm 2009). Bistability in perceptual systems has been around since the early work of Poston and Stewart (1978) and Stewart and Peregoy (1983); who used catastrophe modeling to describe the perceptual systems dynamics. As the parameters change from one domain to another, the system moves from one equilibrium position to another. This type of behavior is also illustrated by the following quotation:

> When cultures face military threat, shortages of goods, poverty or instability, they may most naturally concerned with defense and damage control. Cultures may turn their attention to creativity, virtue and the highest qualities in life only when they are stable, prosperous and at peace (Seligman and Csikszentmihalyi 2000, p. 12).

Observe that, in the preceding example, it is possible for the "culture" to reside in either of the two wells (defense vs. creativity) and that the resting place of that culture can change over time depending upon changes in the parameter values of the system as well as the particulars of any external forces that might perturb the system. More recent work in the field argues that innovation can occur in situations where the culture is dealing with significant angst and unhappy situations; a case in point is the innovations arising out of World War II.

The higher the dimensionality (number of variables) of the system, the more possibilities are there for the dynamical system to have more than two possible equilibria (and also a larger potential for different dynamical behaviors). Systems with more than two possible equilibria are called *multistable systems*. One example of a multistable system is the developmental dynamics of a multicellular organism. Each well (or attractor state) represents a particular cell type and transitions from attractor to attractor correspond to different cell differentiation paths. Ecosystems can also exhibit multistable states (Dublin et al. 1990). Leopold and Logothetis (1999) discuss the phenomenon of multistable visual phenomena such as ambiguous figures and perceptual rivalry. It is interesting to note that gravitation theorists have a concept called an "egg-crate." The egg-crate is represented by a potential surface that looks similar to a traditional egg-crate in that there are many equilibria (wells) in which a system may reside. Thus, higher dimensional systems may have not only an increasing number of possible equilibria, but also a more complex surface on which those equilibria might lie.

Bistability can serve as a switching mechanism so that when certain conditions are true, the system resides in one state and when they are not true, the system resides in another. From a psychological perspective, bipolar behavior could be viewed as a bistable switching mechanism that flips back and forth between two states in an unpredictable fashion. Biologists have recognized that two important criteria for bistability are (1) ultrasensitivity and (2) positive feedback in the system. The spiraling nature of Fredrickson's (2004) broaden and build argument is an excellent example of a system that meets criteria (2) above. Positive feedback implies that the rate of change of a particular variable is proportional (positive constant) to the value of the variable. Thus, the system grows rapidly.

It is not unreasonable to imagine that there might be behavioral analogies to these constructs and therefore that bistability could be viewed as a possible dynamical systems analogy for bipolar class behaviors. Our bistable analogy suggests that when dealing with bipolar class behaviors, it may be important to examine how such qualities as ultrasensitivity in the client might be important to the treatment protocol where we view ultrasensitivity as a global measure of the "client system."

Bistability arguments have also been used to model perception (Moreno-Bote et al. 2007; DeMaris 2011) and the effects of noise on perception. Optical illusions that contain two different possible visual outcomes serve as an illustration of what we might call perceptive bistability. Here, one views one form of the illusion and then, by some perturbation of the visual system, is able to view the other form. If bistability is an important aspect of mental and visual status, then this can clearly impact the psychology of the individual. Since bistability is a nonlinear phenomenon, this reinforces the need to pursue psychological research with an eye toward thinking in a complexity theoretic, NDS fashion.

Strange, Lorentz, and Other Attractors

Higher dimensional systems can exhibit behaviors that appear to orbit around an equilibrium for a time and then, for no apparent reason, move to an orbit around another equilibrium. The system will orbit around the second equilibrium for an equally unpredictable period of time and then revert to orbiting around the first equilibrium. This is a particular class of systems. They have sensitivity to initial conditions and, in many cases, sensitivity to parameter values. They have positive feedback components as well. The class of systems that contains these behaviors may also contain attractors such the Lorentz and strange attractors. These systems typically have three or more dependent variables. In such systems, the system orbits around one equilibrium during which it is sTable (in the sense that it will orbit around that equilibrium for a period of time) and then it switches to another equilibrium around which it will orbit. The switching can be viewed as a switching in a bistable system (one state to another). However, in the case of the Lorentz and other attractors, parameter sensitivity is often great and therefore slight parametric perturbations can cause the system to bifurcate into a nonchaotic dynamics.

Strange attractors and similar behavior classes have analogies in stream of consciousness dialogue, dynamic reconfiguration of the self-identity, struggles around changing one's life path as these attractors can flip back and forth unpredictably between states much as an individual with attention disorder can flip back and forth between subjects. While the analogy is not perfect, it shows us another window into describing psychological behaviors via NDS analogues.

A fascinating application of NDS constructs to PP may be found in the work of Losada (1999) and Losada and Heaphy (2004). Losada constructs a fascinating model that describes a relationship between network connectivity and positivity. Figure 5 of Losada and Heaphy (2004) illustrates the basic structural form of the model while multiple figures in Losada (1999) illustrate with discussion how the model can lead to complex dynamics such as chaotic behavior and strange attractors. What is interesting is that we see the actual emergence of a complexity-based PP construct that actually both illustrates and actually correctly predicts PP dynamics. What is also important to note is that this model provides strong support for our earlier mentioned statement that network structure influences possible network dynamics. What we see in the Losada modeling effort is the integration of many facets of complexity theory applied to PP. We continue our exploration by exploring the "broaden" component of Fredrickson's broaden and build model of PP. To do this, we begin by discussing the idea of outcome surfaces.

Outcome Surfaces and Psychological Dynamics

What are Outcome Surfaces?

Up to this point, we have examined the life course trajectory as a series of states that occur across a continuum timeline. We discretized time in some meaningful way for the problem under discussion and we then looked at how we can create relationships in time, thereby creating our life course trajectory. This perspective is useful when one is examining an individual trajectory or treating a group of individual trajectories as some sort of average (envelope) trajectory over the group. We discussed concepts of trajectory dynamics and trajectory behavior. We also mentioned that it is possible to examine the overall form of the trajectory and to categorize behavior based upon that form. Let us further examine the form of trajectories as related to what we call the outcome space.

The *outcome space* (space of all possible outcomes) describes the topology of possible system outcomes in a given model space. For example, suppose that we are examining the problem of understanding the catharsis of self-pity (Zeeman 1977, p. 15) or conflicting judgments caused by stress (1977, p. 363). It is natural, in the case of self-pity, to label the outcomes in the outcome space and then to examine how they cover the space. By covering the space, we mean how the different possible outcomes sit next to each other; what is their topology or layout? Is frustration next to "anxiety" or is it next to "lose temper" (1977, p. 16; Fig. 10). If we think of our outcome space as a surface in three dimensions, and if we color the surface regions representing different degrees of outcome or state of being, then we can also ask whether or not our surface has hills and valleys, folds and bends and how does the location of the possible outcomes on the surface potentially affect the potential flow and final outcome of our trajectories? It is interesting to note that bending and folding of space is not an unknown concept. Large planetary masses have been shown to bend space and that the bent space is experienced as gravitational attraction by nearby bodies.

Folded Spaces, Hysteresis, Catastrophes, Outcomes, and Psychological Dynamics

How do these concepts apply to psychology in general and to PP in particular? Spaces have a structure/shape/form. In some cases, the space can fold over on itself (see Fig. 12, Stewart and Peregoy 1983). In this case, depending upon where one starts out on the surface, the trajectory can travel through a variety of different outcome possibilities, the endpoint dependent solely upon the starting point. In his classic book, Zeeman (1977) took the concept of a catastrophe, as originally developed by Thom (1975) and demonstrated how the concepts of the different types of catastrophes could be applied to various life processes; many of them psychological processes. Applications of catastrophe theoretic approaches have found success in a number of psychological areas such as neo-Piagetian theories (Stamovlasis 2011), diffusion models for innovation (Jacobsen and Guastello 2011), smoking prevention (Byrne et al. 2001), drug addiction (Guastello 1984), leadership emergence (Guastello and Bond 2007), as well as the examples of Zeeman (1976, 1977) and many others. But what do we mean when we say "catastrophe?" What does a catastrophe look like mathematically?

Catastrophe theory approaches to dynamical systems processes give rise to the concept of hysteresis (Hysteresis 2011; Kopfova 2006) and reinforce the idea of bifurcation (called a catastrophe because of the sudden change in dynamical behaviors of the system). For example, let us consider Fig. 12 of Stewart and Peregoy (1983). The vertical or z axis represents the viewer's perception (across a scale from -10 to 10) as to whether or not an image looks "a lot like a woman" to "looks a lot like a man." Observe that if we project the three dimensional surface down into the two dimension xy-plane (labeled D and R in this figure), we see a simple cusp catastrophe.

A system is said to exhibit hysteresis "when it responds differently to identical inputs depending upon the direction in which the system is being driven" (Farrell 1999, p. 226). In a different way, hysteresis is the dependence of the state of the system on the history of the given state. Hysteresis, similar to entropy, is a term that has different definitions depending upon the field in which it is being used. Hysteresis-like behavior occurs at all levels of biological organization. Hysteresis has been documented at subcellular biochemical levels all the way through single human dynamics (Haken-Kelso-Bunz Model 2011). A simple illustration of hysteresis-like behavior is illustrated in Fig. 1 of Wikipedia (2012). Observe that hysteresis pathways, while different, have nearly—if not exactly—the same start and end points. Farrell (1999, Fig. 1) provides a simple example of hysteresis when he demonstrates how the shape of a human information processing curve changes during increasing and decreasing demand.

Revisiting the Broaden and Build Theory of Positive Psychology (PP)

In Fredrickson (2004) and related papers, Fredrickson lays out major constructs of her broaden and build theory. One of the chief arguments she makes is summed up in her statement "I call this the broaden and build theory of positive emotions because positive emotions appear to broaden peoples' momentary thought-action repertoires and build their enduring personal resources" (Fredrickson 2004, p. 1369). When we look more closely at this statement we realize that it very much relates to outcome spaces. What Fredrickson is saying is that the initial increase in positive emotions activates a process that broadens the outcome space by making more options for final outcomes possible. In broadening the potential outcomes, it implicitly argues for a larger variety of potential trajectories from a given point into the space of possible outcomes, thereby enhancing pathways to the added outcome space options. By adding potential trajectories we are, in a sense providing the individual with more options; we are building their resources by adding additional pathways to the new outcomes. Thus, we can see that the NDS constructs provide us with a mathematical realization of Fredrickson's broaden and build theory.

Spatial Constructs and Psychological Dynamics

Temporal relationships are not the only way in which we can establish the construct of "being in relation to". We can also look at how our objects of interest are interconnected. For example, we can derive a network that illustrates how different people are connected through Facebook connections or through other friendships. We can also look at "who knew whom" networks. Networks are a common way to illustrate relationships between objects in a set of objects; the objects themselves can be complex networks. For example, we can have interpersonal relationships such as social support networks and healthcare support networks. Our bodies contain numerous networks. We have neural networks, cellular signaling networks, biochemical networks and myriad of other networks that "live" within our bodies and many others that exist outside our bodies. We have friendship networks, social support networks, healthcare networks. Our social support network can and often probably does overlap our healthcare network, as does our friendship network. These overlaps can often create new, more complex linkages between members of the networks. These linkages can lead to emergent network properties. Moreover, emotions, similar to viruses can spread across these networks (Fowler and Christakis 2008). As the old saying goes, "If Momma's not happy, ain't no one that's happy." Similarly, these networks can contribute to positive psychological dynamics (Schwartz 2000). For example, strong social support networks have been shown to reduce morbidity and to decrease rates of depression in the elderly (Cornwell and Waite 2009; Walter-Ginzberg et al. 2002).

The idea of networks in PP is not new although it is not directly mentioned in that way. For example, Maddi (2006) mentions networks in multiple ways throughout this paper. "Now that a number of variables have surfaced as relevant, more attention needs to be given to how they fit together in some overall way of understanding admirable human functioning." This statement is about how nodes (variables) are linked (fit together) and this is network theory. If we are given a set of nodes and a set of connections, we say that we have a graph or a network.

However, connection is not the only feature of a network (graph). Connections can have direction. Node 1 is connected to Node 2 but it feeds Node 2. That is, Node 2 is dependent upon Node 1. We would express this as Node 1 $\rightarrow$ Node 2. These are called *directed networks* or graphs. Maddi (2006) points out that "advocates of each relevant variable [node in the network] need to identify whether it is an independent (causative) or dependent (resultant) factor." Independence and dependence signify a direction in the connections between the nodes (factors) in the network. We can also have nodes that depend upon each other. That is, the two nodes feed back and forth to each other denoted Node 1 $\leftrightarrow$ Node 2. As Maddi (2006) again says, "…is optimism an independent variable (in the sense of being an outlook that provokes admirable performance and health)? Or a dependent variable (in the sense of being the admirable result of whatever leads one to have a successful life), or is it both?" Here, we see the idea of directionality in one, or the other, or both directions. Diagrams of this sort are also known as *causal* or *relational diagrams* and are really quite essential to understanding the dynamics of living systems (Louie and Kercel 2007 and work of Rosen 1985, 1999 and Witten 1982, 1983, 1984, 1985). Seligman and Csikszentmihalyi (2000, p. 10) bring these constructs into PP when they observe that:

> The study of relations among enabling conditions, individual strengths, institutions, and outcomes such as well-being or income might merely result in an empirical matrix. Such a matrix would describe, for example, what talents under what enabling conditions lead to what kinds of outcomes. This matrix would inform individuals' choices along the course of their lives, but would take no stand on the desirability of different life courses.

Notice that this quotation contains the essential concepts of relationship, structure, dynamical trajectory as a function of an initial condition all of which are essential concepts in NDS theory.

Networks can often be represented by graphs. Moreover, if the data is available, they can be said to contain flows. In fact, there are direct relationships between networks and differential equation models (linear and/or nonlinear) that allow us to infer behaviors such as oscillations in a network based upon the connectivities of the graph representation of the network. Thus, graphs are important as they can also tell us about dynamical behaviors in the system between the different nodes. If we have an undirected graph (a network with no arrows on the edges so that we do not know in which direction things flow), we can look for pathways from one node to another (assuming that there could be flow along the given pathway) and this tells us about the redundancy of given pathways. Redundant pathways are backup systems and backup systems in an organism make the system more robust to assault and therefore provide increased fault tolerance. As Srinivasan and Stevens (2011, p. 3) point out, "The logic behind using redundant neurons to produce fault tolerance is that the overall pattern generated does not depend on any single connection being present. No two of these networks have exactly the same connections, but they still work as they need to, and they continue working even when connections or cells are eliminated (up to a point)." Witten (1983, 1984) used the same arguments to show how mortality curves could be affected by critical elements in networks and how redundant elements could be used to prolong longevity. For PP, this suggests that one way to build robustness is to build redundant pathways into the individual or group system. These pathways may not be exactly identical to each other as long as they perform a certain function. A simple analogy is the ability to be able to write. If we are right-handed and we lose use of our right hand, then if we have not trained to use our left hand in advance, we lose the ability to write clearly. We may be able to write slowly and with some degree of skill; however, it will not be nearly as effective as if we had built up the skill of writing with both hands and done so in advance. Consequently, teaching individuals different coping strategies or different positive measure for handling the same challenge could easily be considered as building up robustness in an individual.

Anticipation and Self-Organization

An anticipatory system is one which can encode and build models of self and environment for the purposes of system guidance and control, and can utilize those models in order to change behavior in the present according to predicted future events or conditions. Anticipatory behavior is an innate property of the human existence. We develop, over time, models of the world that become our instinctive models against which we anticipate future dynamics and subsequently make our decisions for present behavior patterns. Some of these instinctive models may well be somatically encoded as survival mechanisms while others may be encoded as "learning" and can be more easily adapted via external influence.

Conclusions

As we have observed, human systems are complex and demonstrate many of the properties we have previously discussed (Guastello and Gregson 2011a; West 2006). They are composed of numerous elements that relate to each other in hierarchies across scale (Brown and West 2000). They can evolve, adapt, and often anticipate. They have emergent properties and through their evolution and internal structures adapt, evolve, and generate new emergent properties as required. They are nonlinear, illustrating such phenomena as chaos, hysteresis, and bursting behaviors (Gros 2008). They can have properties that are fractal in nature, some are fragile, they can self-organize, and they may show symmetry and scale laws themselves. NDS theory and its component disciplines provide us with a language, methodologies, and analogies that can be used to describe psychological systems behaviors, model them and through the use of analogies and models develop insights into psychological behavior in general and PP in particular.

Quantum mechanical constructions of observation and reality have been used to discuss how measurements of complex systems may simply be projections from a higher dimensional object into a reality constructed by the individual making the measurements and that multiple measuring instruments may be related in nonlinear ways. We have seen many examples of how these NDS ideas can be shown to map onto psychological constructs and how these mappings can lead to potential new paths of insight and study. Moreover, we have seen how NDS theory can provide us with both a language for discussion as well as potential explanations for psychological behavior that is not readily explainable in other ways.

Duckworth et al. (2005, p. 646) state that their "final recommendation concerns the collection and testing of new positive psychology interventions . . . An important task is for positive psychologists to collect and consolidate ideas about how to build positive emotion, engagement and meaning . . . and then put them to rigorous empirical test." This statement still smacks of a reductionist perspective in that what individuals are attempting to do is to develop measures for different projections of a more complex entity. Rather, we should—perhaps—look to the domain of complexity theory for some new ideas; ways, perhaps to reverse engineer without perturbation (or minimal perturbation) what we are trying to study. Complexity theory can be used to analyze the structure of PP itself, thereby offering entirely new suggestions as to how the field ought to develop itself.

For example, the requirements of scale imply that for PP to be effective there must be a match between the scale and the complexity of the various functional capabilities of PP and the complexity of the tasks performed. If we accept the initial premise that PP is a complex entity (read discipline/organization), an argument that seems plausible based upon our previous discussion, then it suggests that the discipline of PP must have certain overall structural behaviors in terms of how subdisciplines and sub-subdisciplines (etc.) must interact. For example, we speak of a discipline being robust. This implies certain connectivity relationships between the different subcomponent disciplines of PP. It suggests that different components of PP should be organized in different ways so that they can carry out their functions. As Bar-Yam (2006) points out, "Turbulence occurs when a simple coherent flow is broken up into many smaller flows" (p. 461). Also, as he further points out, the problem is not that the complex flows exist, but how does one control them? We are currently seeing in PP is turbulence as it struggles to emerge and to define itself, its measures, and its playing field. Complexity theory suggests ways in which to work with this emerging organization so at to improve its overall effectiveness. As we have discussed, setting up a graph (think organizational chart) of PP and its flows can help to understand challenges based upon complexity analysis of the graph. It can also allow us to make suggestions that can control the flows in such a way as to enhance the overall effectiveness of the discipline of PP as a member of the overall field of psychology.

Acknowledgments Many people have contributed to my ongoing interest in looking at sociodynamics through the lens of mathematical physics. When I was 13 years old, I came across a paper written by the great cosmologist John Wheeler. Contained within its pages were some astounding ideas about the flow of time. I did not understand them and I wanted to have them explained to me. I wrote Wheeler a letter. You know, on 3-hole notebook paper with the blue lines! My father mailed the letter, but remarked that I probably should not expect a response. A few weeks later, a response came. And it was addressed to me. The great cosmologist had sent a letter from Princeton! Wheeler treated me as if I was a young budding scientist sending along a hand-typed letter (we used typewriters then) and some of his reprints of more advanced articles on the subject about which I had inquired. He told me that I would probably first have to teach myself calculus to really understand what was going on. I spent that summer trying to learn calculus and John is the reason that I am able to write this chapter today.

I would like to thank my doctoral dissertation advisor Robert Rosen for introducing me to the concepts of abstract algebra and its relationship to the dynamics of living (M,R)—systems and for introducing me to the use of quantum phenomenology in the field of theoretical biology. Howard Pattee and the members of the then Center for Theoretical Biology at SUNY Stonybrook opened the philosophical doorways of information theory and the interface of living systems to complexity theory as we tried to tackle the difficult question: "What is life?"

I would also like to thank Stephen Guastello who has been a constant source of support and resource.

Lastly, I would like to thank the referees of this chapter. The reviews were comprehensive and very illuminating and contributed significant improvements in this chapter.

My arrival here is built upon some of the great players in multiple fields of research. There is no way that I could have written this chapter without their shoulders raising me up to the light.

References

Arrechi, F. T. (2011). Phenomenology of consciousness from apprehension to judgment. *Nonlinear Dynamics, Psychology, and Life Sciences, 15,* 377–388.

Baker, G. L., & Gollub, J. P. (1990). *Chaotic dynamics: An introduction*. Cambridge: Cambridge University Press.

Balazs, A. C., & Epstein, I. R. (2009). Emergent or just complex? *Science, 325,* 1632–1634. doi:10.1126/science.1178323.

Bar-Yam, Y. (1997). *Dynamics of complex systems*. Reading: Perseus Books.

Bar-Yam, Y. (2006). Improving the effectiveness of health care and public health: A multiscale complex systems analysis. *American Journal of Public Health, 96*(3), 459–466.

Barabasi, A.-L. (2002). *Linked*. New York: Plume.

Bassingthwaighte, J. B., Liebovitch, L. S., & West, B. J. (1994). *Fractal physiology*. New York: Oxford University Press.

Bedau, M. A., & Humphreys, P. (2008). *Emergence: Contemporary readings in philosophy and science*. Boston: MIT.

Bellany, I. (1999). Modeling war. *Journal of Peace Research, 36*(6), 729–739. http://dx.doi.org/10.1177/0022343399036006008.

Bonanno, G. A., Westphal, M., & Mancini, A. D. (2011). Resilience to loss and potential trauma. *Annual Review of Clinical Psychology, 7,* 511–535. doi:10.1146/annurev-clinpsy-032210-104526.

Brown, J., & West, G. B. (Eds.). (2000). *Scaling in biology*. Oxford: Oxford University Press.

Brown, K. W., & Moscowitz, D. S. (1998a). It's a function of time: A review of the process approach to behavioral medicine research. *Annals of Behavioral Medicine, 20*(2), 109–117.

Brown, K. W., & Moscowitz, D. S. (1998b). Dynamic stability of behavior: The rhythms of our interpersonal lives. *Journal of Personality, 66*(1), 105–134.

Byrne, D. G., Mazanov, J., & Gregson, R. A. M. (2001). A cusp catastrophe analysis of changes to adolescent smoking behavior in response to smoking prevention programs. *Nonlinear Dynamics, Psychology and Life Sciences, 5*(2), 115–137.

Carnes, B., Staats, D., Vaughn, M., & Witten, T. M. (2010). An organismal view of cellular aging. *Médicine et Longévité, 2,* 141–150.

Castiglioni, P., & Parati, G. (2011). Present trends and future directions in the analysis of cardiovascular variability. *Journal of Hypertension, 29,* 1285–1288.

Chow, J. Y., Davids, K., Hristovski, R., Araujo, D., & Passos, P. (2011). Nonlinear pedagogy: Learning design for self-organizing neurobiological systems. *New Ideas in Psychology, 29,* 189–200. doi:10.1016/j.newideapsych.2010.10.001.

Clarke, B., & Hansen, M. B. N. (2009). *Emergence & embodiment: New essays on second-order systems theory*. Durham: Duke University Press.

Cornwell, E. Y., & Waite, L. J. (2009). Social disconnectedness, perceived isolation, and health among older adults. *Journal of Health and Social Behavior, 50*(3), 31–48.

Curtis, V. B., de Barra, M., & Aunger, R. (2011). Disgust as an adaptive system for disease avoidance behavior. *Philosophical Transactions of the Royal Society B, 366,* 389–401. doi:10.1098/rstb.2010.0117.

Daniels, B. C., Chen, Y.-J., Sethna, J. P., Gutenjunst, R. N., & Myers, C. R. (2008). Sloppiness, robustness and evolvability in systems biology. *Current Opinion in Biotechnology, 19,* 389–395.

Deco, G., Perez-Sanagustin, M., de Lafuente, V., & Romo, R. (2007). Perceptual detection as a dynamical bistability phenomenon: A neurocomputational correlate of sensation. *Proceedings of the National Academy of Science, 104*(50): 20073–20077. doi:10.1073/pnas.0709794104.

DeMaris, D. (2011). Dynamic symbolism, chaos and perception. http://www.well.com/~demaris/einmag.html. Accessed 19 Aug 2011.

Doba, K., Nandrino, J-L., Lesne, A., Humez, C. & Pezard, L. (2008). Organization of the narrative components in autobiographical speech of anorexic adolescents: a statistical and non-linear dynamical analysis. New Ideas in Psychology, 26: 295–308. doi: 10.1016/j.newideapsych.2007.07.004.

Droit-Volet, S., & Gil, S. (2009). The time-emotion paradox. *Philosophical Transactions of the Royal Society B, 364,* 1943–1953. doi:10.1098/rtsb.2009.0013.

Dublin, H. T., Sinclair, A. R. E., & McGlade, J. (1990). Elephants and fire are causes of multiple stable states in the Serengeti-Mara woodlands. *Journal of Animal Ecology, 59,* 1147–1164.

Duckworth, A. L., Steen, T. A., & Seligman, M. E. P. (2005). Positive psychology in clinical practice. *Annual Reviews of Clinical Psychology, 1,* 621–651. doi:10.1146/annurev.clinpsy.1.102803.144154.

Farrell, P. S. E. (1999). The hysteresis effect. *Human Factors: The Journal of the Human Factors and Ergonomics Society, 41,* 226–240.

Field, R., & Schuldberg, D. (2011). Social-support moderated stress: A nonlinear dynamical model and stress-buffering hypothesis. *Nonlinear Dynamics, Psychology and Life Sciences, 15*(1), 53–85.

Fourie, M. M., Rauch, H. G. L., Morgan, B. E., Ellis, G. F., Jordaan, E. R., & Thomas, K. G. F. (2011). Guilt and pride are heartfelt, but not equally so. *Psychophysiology, 48,* 888–899.

Fowler, J. H., & Christakis, N. A. (2008). Dynamic spread of happiness in a large social network: Longitudinal analysis over 20 years in the Framingham heart study. *British Medical Journal, 337,* a2338. doi:10.1136/bmj.a2338.

Fredrickson, B. L. (2001). The role of positive emotions in positive psychology: The broaden and build theory of positive emotions. *American Psychologist, 56*(3), 218–226.

Fredrickson, B. L. (2004). The broaden-and-build theory of positive emotions. *Philosophical Transactions of the Royal Society of London B, 39,* 1367–1377. doi:10.1098/rstb.2004.1512.

Fredrickson, B. L., & Losada, M. F. (2005). Positive affect and the complex dynamics of human flourishing. *American Psychologist, 60*(7), 678–686. doi:10.1037/0003-066X.60.7.678.

Frohlich, F., Sejnowski, T. J., & Bazhenov, M. (2010). Network bistability mediates spontaneous transitions between normal and pathological brain states. *The Journal of Neuroscience, 30*(32), 10734–10743.

Galazter-Levy, R. M. (2009). Finding your way through chaos, fractals and other exotic mathematical objects: A guide for the complex. *Journal of the American Psychoanalytic Association, 57,* 1227–1249.

Gao, J., Buldyreve, S. V., Havlin, S., & Stanley, H. E. (2010). Robustness of a network of networks. http://arxiv.org/abs/1010.5829v1.

Garland, E. L., Fredrickson, B., Kring, A. M., Johnson, D. P., Meyer, P. S., & Penn, D. L. (2010). Upward spirals of positive emotions counter downward spirals of negativity: Insights from the broaden-and-build theory and affective neuroscience on the treatment of emotion dysfunctions and deficits in psychopathology. *Clinical Psychology Review, 30,* 849–864.

Geoffard, P. -Y., & Luchini, S. (2010). Changing time and emotions. *Philosophical Transactions of the Royal Society B, 365,* 271–280.

Glass, L. (1999). Chaos and heart rate variability. *Journal of Cardiovascular Electrophysiology, 10,* 1358–1360.

Glass, L. (2009). Introduction to controversial topics in nonlinear science: Is the normal heart rate chaotic? *Chaos, 19,* 028501. doi:10.1063/1.3156832.

Globus, G. G., & Arpaia, J. P. (1994). Psychiatry and the new dynamics. *Biological Psychiatry, 35,* 352–364.

Goldberger, A. L. (1996). Nonlinear dynamics for clinicians: Chaos theory, fractals and complexity at the bedside. *The Lancet, 347,* 1312–1314.

Gorban, A., & Petrovskii, S. (2011). Collective dynamics: When one plus one does not make two. *Mathematical Medicine and Biology, 28,* 85–88. doi:10.1093/imammb/dqr003.

Gottman, J. M., Murray, J. D., Swanson, C. C., Tyson, R., & Swanson, K. R. (2002). *The mathematics of marriage: Dynamic nonlinear models*. Cambridge: MIT.

Greenbury, S. F., Johnston, I. G., Smith, M. A., Doye, J. P. K., & Louis, A. A. (2010). The effect of scale free topology on the robustness and evolvability of genetic regulatory networks. http://arxiv.org/PS_cache/arxiv/pdf/1005/1005.4342v1.pdf.

Gros, C. (2008). *Complex and adaptive dynamical systems: A primer*. Berlin: Springer.

Guastello, S. J. (1984). Cusp and butterfly catastrophe modeling of two opponent process models: Drug addiction and work performance. *Behavioral Science, 29,* 258–262.

Guastello, S. J. & Shissler, J. E. (1994). A two -factor taxonomy of creative behavior. *Journal of Creative Behavior, 28*(3): 211–221.

Guastello, S. J. (2000). Nonlinear dynamics in psychology. *Discrete Dynamics in Nature and Society, 00,* 1–20.

Guastello, S. J. (2009). Chaos as a psychological construct: Historical roots, principal findings and current growth directions. *Nonlinear Dynamics, Psychology and Life Sciences, 13*(3), 289–310.

Guastello, S. J., Boeh, H., Shumaker, C., & Schimmels, M. (2011a). Catastrophe models for cognitive workload and fatigue. *Theoretical Issues in Ergonomic Sciences, 12* (ahead of print).

Guastello, S. J., & Bond, R. W. (2007). A swallowtail catastrophe model for the emergence of leadership in coordination-intensive groups. *Nonlinear Dynamics, Psychology and Life Sciences, 11*(2), 235–251.

Guastello, S. J., & Gregson, R. A. M. (2011). *Nonlinear dynamical systems analysis for the behavioral sciences using real data*. Boca Raton: CRC.

Guastello, S. J., Johnson, E. A., & Rieke, M. L. (1999). Nonlinear dynamics of motivational flow. *Nonlinear Dynamics, Psychology and Life Sciences, 3*(3), 259–273.

Guastello, S. J., Koopmans, M., & Pincus, D. (Eds.). (2011b). *Chaos and complexity in psychology: Theory of nonlinear dynamical systems*. Cambridge: Cambridge University Press.

Guastello, S. J., Pincus, D., Gunderson, P. R. (2006). Electrodermal arousal between participants in a conversation. *Nonlinear Dynamics, Psychology and Life Sciences, 10,* 365–399.

Haken-Kelso-Bunz Model for Bimanual Handed Coordination. (2011). http://www.scholarpedia.org/article/Haken-Kelso-Bunz_model. Accessed 29 Nov 2011.

Hastings, H. M., & Sugihara, G. (1993). *Fractals: A user's guide for the natural sciences*. Oxford: Oxford University Press.

Ho, M. Y., & Fung, H. H. (2011). A dynamic process model of forgiveness: A cross-cultural perspective. *Review of General Psychology, 15*(1), 77–84.

Hofstadter, D. (1979). *Goedel, Escher, Bach: An eternal golden braid*. New York: Basic Books.

Huang, X., Gao, J., Buldyrev, S. V., Havlin, S., & Stanley, H. D. (2010). Robustness of interdependent networks under targeted attack. http://arxiv.org/abs/1010.5829v1.

Hysteresis. (2011) http://en.wikipedia.org/wiki/Hysteresis. Accessed 29 Nov 2011.

Iannaccone, P. M., & Khokha, M. (1996). *Fractal geometry in biological systems: An analytical approach*. Boca Raton: CRC.

Izhikevich, E. M. (2000). Neural excitability, spiking and bursting. *International Journal of Bifurcation and Chaos, 10*(6), 1171–1266.

Jackson, S. (2010). *Architecting resilient systems*. Hoboken: Wiley.

Jacobsen, J. J., & Guastello, S. J. (2011). Diffusion models for innovation: S-curves, networks, power laws, catastrophes, and entropy. *Nonlinear Dynamics, Psychology, and Life Sciences, 15*(2), 307–333.

Janecka, I. P. (2007). Cancer control through principles of systems science, complexity and chaos theory: A model. *International Journal of Medical Sciences, 4*(3), 164–173.

Jensen, H. J. (1998). *Self-organized criticality: Emergent complex behavior in physical and biological systems*. Cambridge: Cambridge University Press.

Kaneko, K. (1998). Life as complex systems: Intra-inter dynamics, isologous diversification and emergence of recursivity. *Physica A, 254,* 73–76.

Kang, H. G., Costa, M. D., Priplata, A. A., Starobinets, O. V., Goldberger, A. L., Peng, C. -K., Kiely, D. K., Cupples, L. A., & Lipsitz, L. A. (2009). Frailty and the degradation of complex balance dynamics during a dual-task protocol. *Journal of Gerontology: Biological Science Medical Science, 64A,* 1304–1311.

Karakas, F. (2011). Positive management education: Creating creative minds, passionate hearts and kindred spirits. *Journal of Management Education, 35*(2), 198–226.

Karim, N., Hasan, J. A., & Ali, S. S. (2011). Heart rate variability—A review. *Journal of Basic and Applied Sciences, 7*(1), 71–77.

Kenrick, D. T., Li, N. P., & Butner, J. (2003). Dynamical evolutionary psychology: Individual decision rules and emergent social norms. *Psychological Review, 110*(1), 3–28. doi:10.1037/0033-295X.110.1.3.

Kepes, F. (2007). (Ed.). *Biological networks*. Singapore: World Scientific.

Kidd, J., & Witten, T. M. (2008a). Assessing spirituality, religiosity and faith in the transgender community: A case study in violence and abuse—Implications for the aging transgender community and for gerontological research. *Journal of Religious Gerontology, 20*(1–2), 29–62.

Kidd, J., & Witten, T. M. (2008b). Transgender and transsexual identities: The next strange fruit—Hate crimes, violence and genocide against trans-communities. *Journal of Hate Studies, 6*(1), 31–63.

Kirschner, M., & Gerhart, J. (1998). Evolvability. *Proceedings of the National Academy of Science USA, 95,* 8420–8427.

Knutson, B., & Greer, S. M. (2008). Anticipatory affect: Neural correlates and consequences for choice. *Philosophical Transactions of the Royal Society, 363,* 3771–3786. doi:10.1098/rstb.2008.0155.

Kopfova, J. (2006). Hysteresis in biological models. *Journal of Physics: Conference Series, 55,* 130–134. doi:10.1088/1742-6596/55/1/012.

Laycraft, K. (2011). The theory of positive disintegration as a model of adolescent development. *Nonlinear Dynamics, Psychology and Life Sciences, 15*(1), 29–52.

Laing, R. D. (1970). *Knots*. New York: Vintage Books.

Lenski, R. E., Barrick, J. E., & Ofria, C. (2006). Balancing robustness and evolvability. *PLOS Biology, 4*(12), e428.

Leopold, D. A., & Logothetis, N. K. (1999). Multistable phenomena: Changing views in perception. *Trends in Cognitive Sciences, 3*(7), 254–264.

Lesne, A. (2008). Robustness: Confronting lessons from physics and biology. *Biological Reviews, 83,* 509–532. doi:10.1111/j.1469-185X.2008.00052.x.

Levy, B. R., Slade, M. D., Kunkel, S. R., & Kasl, S. V. (2002). Longevity increased by positive perceptions of aging. *Journal of Personality and Social Psychology, 83*(2), 262–270.

Linley, P. A., Joseph, S., Harrington, S., & Wood, A. M. (2006). Positive psychology: Past, present and (possible) future. *Journal of Positive Psychology, 1*(1), 3–16. doi:10.1080/17439760500372796.

Losada, M. (1999). The complex dynamics of high performance teams. *Mathematics and Computers in Modeling, 30,* 179–192.

Losada, M., & Heaphy, E. (2004). The role of positivity and connectivity in the performance of business teams a nonlinear dynamics model. *American Behavioral Scientist, 47,* 740–765.

Louie, A. H., & Kercel, S. W. (2007). Topology and life redux: Robert Rosen's relational diagrams of living systems. *Axiomathes, 17,* 109–136.

Luthar, S. S., Cicchetti, D., & Becker, B. (2000). The construct of resilience: A critical evaluation and guidelines for future work. *Child Development, 71*(3), 543–562.

Lyng, S. (1990). Edgework: A social psychological analysis of voluntary risk taking. *American Journal of Sociology, 95*(4), 851–886.

Maddi, S. R. (2006). Building an integrated positive psychology. *The Journal of Positive Psychology, 1*(4), 226–229.

Mandell, A. J., & Selz, K. A. (1995). Nonlinear dynamical patterns as personality theory for neurobiology and psychiatry. *Psychiatry, 58*(4), 371–390.

Marceau, K., Ram, N., Houts, R. M., Grim, K. J., & Susman, E. J. (2011). Individual differences in boy's and girl's timing and tempo of puberty: Modeling development with nonlinear growth models. *Developmental Psychology, 45*(5), 1389–1409. doi:10.1037/a0023838.

Marks-Tarlow, T. (2008). *Psyche's veil: Psychotherapy, fractals and complexity*. London: Routledge.

May, R. M. (1976). Simple mathematical models with very complicated dynamics. *Nature, 261,* 459–467.

May, R. M. (2000). Simple rules with complex dynamics. *Science, New Series, 287* (5453), 601–602.

Miller, J. H., & Page, S. E. (2007). *Complex adaptive systems: An introduction to computational models of social life*. Princeton: Princeton University Press.

Mitina, O. V., & Abraham, D. F. (2011). The use of fractals for the study of the psychology of perception. http://www.blueberry-brain.org/dynamics/nitina-fractal-perception.htm

Moreno-Bote, R., Rinzel, J., & Rubin, N. (2007). Noise-induced alternans in an attractor network model of perceptual bistability. *Journal of Neurophysiology, 98,* 1124–1139. doi:10.1152/jn.00116.2007.

Mosca, F. (1995). Freedom in chaos theory: A case for choice in a universe without a bottom line. In F. D. Abraham & A. R. Gilgen (Eds.), *Chaos theory in psychology* (pp. 181–191). Westport: Praeger.

Nadin, M. (2010). Anticipation and dynamics: Rosen's anticipation in the perspective of time. *International Journal of General Systems, 39*(1), 3–33. doi:10.1080/03081070903453685.

New testament social networks. (2011). http://davewainscott.blogspot.com/2011/01/new-testament-social-networks.html. Accessed 29 Nov 2011.

Nicolis, G. (1995). *Introduction to nonlinear science*. Cambridge: Cambridge University Press.

Nicolis, G., & Prigogine, I. (1989). *Exploring complexity*. New York: Freeman and Company.

Nicolis, H., & Nicolis, S. C. (2010). The selfish to egalitarian transition in young children: Developmental processes versus cooperative interactions. *Nonlinear Dynamics, Psychology and Life Sciences, 14*(3), 257–264.

Ostir, G. V., Ottenbacher, K. J., Markides, K. S. (2004). Onset of frailty in older adults and the role of positive affect. *Psychology & Aging, 19*(3), 402–408.

Perdikis, D., Huys, R., & Jirsa, V. K. (2011). Time scale hierarchies in the functional organization of complex behaviors. *PLOS Computational Biology, 7*(9), e1002198. doi:10.1371/journal.pcbi.1002198.

Pincus, D., & Metten, A. (2010). Nonlinear dynamics in biopsychosocial resilience. *Nonlinear Dynamics, Psychology and Life Sciences, 14,* 353–380.

Poston, T., & Stewart, I. N. (1978). Nonlinear modeling of multistable perception. *Behavioral Science, 23,* 318–334.

Pradhan, N., Dasgupta, S., & Sinha S. (2011). Modular organization enhances the robustness of attractor network dynamics. http://arxiv.org/abs/1101.5853v1.

Ramos, R. T., Sassi, R. B., & Piqueira, J. R. C. (2011). Self-organized criticality and the predictability of human behavior. *New Ideas in Psychology, 29,* 38–48. doi:10.1016/j.newideapsych.2009.12.001.

Rivera, T., Soderstrom, S. B., & Uzzi, B. (2010). Dynamics of dyads in social networks: Assertive, relational and proximity mechanisms. *Annual Reviews of Sociology, 36,* 91–115. doi:10.1146/annurev.soc.34.040507.134743.

Rosen, R. (1958). A relational theory of biological systems. *Bulletin of Mathematical Biophysics, 20,* 245–260.

Rosen, R. (1985). *Anticipatory systems: Philosophical, mathematical and methodological foundations*. New York: Pergamon.

Rosen, R. (1991). *Life itself: A comprehensive inquiry into the nature, origin, and fabrication of life*. New York: Columbia University Press

Rosen, R. (1999). *Essays on life itself.* New York: Columbia University Press.

Sakhanenko, N. A., & Galas, D. J. (2011). Complexity of networks I: The set-complexity of binary graphs. *Complexity, 17*(2), 51–64. doi:10.1002/cplx.20382.

Sambrook, R. C. (2008). Spatial behavior analysis at the global level using fractal geometry. *Nonlinear Dynamics, Psychology and Life Sciences, 12*(1), 3–14.

Schiepek, G., Fartacek, C., Sturm, J. Kralovec, D., Fartacek, R., & Ploderl, M. (2011). Nonlinear dynamics: Theoretical perspectives and application to suicidology. *Suicide and Life-Threatening Behavior, 46*(6), 661–675.

Schneider, C. M., Araujo, N. A. M., Havlin, S., & Herrmann, H. J. (2011). Towards designing robust coupled networks. http://arxiv.org/abs/1106.3234

Schuldberg, D. (1999). Chaos theory and creativity. *Encyclopedia of Creativity, 1,* 259–272.

Schuldberg, D. (2002). Theoretical contributions of complex systems to positive psychology and health: A somewhat complicated affair. *Nonlinear Dynamics, Psychology and Life Sciences, 6*(4), 335–350.

Schuldberg, D. (2006). Complicato, ma non troppo: A small nonlinear model and the good life. In A. Delle Fave (Ed.), *Dimensions of well-being: Research and intervention.* Milano: FrancoAngeli.

Schuldberg, D. (2007a). Nonlinear dynamics of positive psychology: Parameters, models and searching for a systems summum bonum. In A. D. Ong & M. H. M. van Dulmen (Eds.), *Oxford handbook of methods in positive psychology*. Oxford: Oxford University Press.

Schuldberg, D. (2007b). Living well creatively: What's chaos got to do with it? In R. Richards (Ed.), *Everyday creativity and new views of human nature: Psychological, social and spiritual perspectives*. Washington: American Psychological Association.

Schuldberg, D., & Gottlieb, J. (2002). Dynamics and correlates of microscopic changes in affect. *Nonlinear Dynamics, Psychology and Life Sciences, 6*(3), 231–257.

Schwartz, B. (2000). Self-determination: The tyranny of freedom. *American Psychologist, 55,* 79–88.

Seligman, M. E. P. (2008). Positive health. *Applied Psychology: An International Review, 57,* 3–18. doi:10.1111/j.1464-0597.2008.0351.x.

Seligman, M. E. P., & Csikszentmihalyi, M. (2000). Positive psychology: An introduction. *American Psychologist, 55*(1), 5–14.

Seligman, M. E. P., Rashid, T., & Parks, A. C. (2006). Positive psychotherapy. *American Psychologist, 8*(61), 774–788.
Seligman, M. E. P., Steen, T. A., Park, N., & Peterson, C. (2005). Positive psychology progress: Empirical validation of interventions. *American Psychologist, 60*(5), 410–421. doi:10.1037/0003-66X.60.5.410.
Sheldon, K. M., & King, L. (2001). Why positive psychology is necessary. *American Psychologist, 56*(3), 216–217.
Skarda, C. A., & Freeman, W. J. (1990). Chaos and the new science of the brain. *Concepts in Neuroscience, 1*(2), 275–285.
Smith, B. W., Tooley, E. M., Christopher, P. J., & Kay, V. S. (2010). Resilience as the ability to bounce back from stress: A neglected personal resource? *Journal of Positive Psychology, 5*(3), 166–176. doi:10.1080/17439760.2010.482186.
Sole, R., & Goodwin, B. (2002). *Signs of life: How complexity pervades biology*. New York: Perseus.
Sorribes, A., Armendariz, B. G., Lopez-Pigozzi, D., Murga, C., & de Polavieja, G. G. (2011). The origin of behavioral bursts in decision-making circuitry. *PLOS Computational Biology, 7*(6), e1002075. doi:10.1371/journal.pcbi.1002075.
Srinivasan, S., & Stevens, C. F. (2011). Robustness and fault tolerance make brains harder to study. *BMC Biology, 9,* 46. http:///www.biomedcentral.com/1741-7007/9/46.
Stamovlasis, D. (2011). Nonlinear dynamics and neo-Piagetian theories in problem solving: Perspectives on a new epistemology and theory development. *Nonlinear Dynamics, Psychology and Life Sciences, 15*(2), 145–173.
Stephen, D. G., Boncoddo, R. A., Magnusun, J. S., & Dixon, J. A. (2009). The dynamics of insight: Mathematical discovery as a phase transition. *Memory & Cognition, 37*(8), 1132–1149.
Stewart, I. N., & Peregoy, P. L. (1983). Catastrophe theory modeling in psychology. *Psychology Bulletin, 94*(2), 336–362.
Strogatz, S. H. (1994). *Nonlinear dynamics and chaos*. New York: Addison-Wesley.
Strogatz, S. H. (2003). *Sync: How order emerges from chaos in the universe, nature and daily life*. New York: Hyperion.
Sulis, W. (2010). Archetypal dynamics, emergent situations and the reality game. *Nonlinear Dynamics, Psychology and Life Sciences, 14*(3), 209–238.
Sulis, W., & Combs, A. (Eds.). (1996). *Nonlinear dynamics in human behavior*. Singapore: World Scientific.
Sumpter, D. J. T. (2010). *Collective animal behavior*. Princeton: Princeton University Press.
Thom, R. (1975). *Structural stability and morphogenesis*. Reading: W.A. Benjamin.
Thompson, H. L. (2010). *The stress effect: Why smart leaders make dumb decisions*. San Francisco: Jossey-Bass.
Tschacher, W., & Dauwalder, J.-P. (2003). *The dynamical systems approach to cognition: Concepts and empirical paradigms based on self-organization, embodiment and coordination dynamics. Studies in nonlinear phenomena in life science. V10*. Singapore: World Scientific.
Vahia, I. V., Chattillion, E., Kaviraja, H., & Depp, C. A. (2011). Psychological protective factors across the lifespan: Implications for psychiatry. *Psychiatric Clinics of North America, 34,* 231–248. doi:10.1016/j.psc.2010.11.011.
Vallacher, R. R., Coleman, P. T., Nowak, A., & Bui-Wrzosinska, L. (2010). Rethinking intractable conflict: The perspective of dynamical systems. *American Psychologist, 65*(4), 262–278. doi:10.1037/a0019290.
Vallacher, R. R., & Nowak, A. (1997). Dynamical social psychology: The next iteration. *Psychological Inquiry, 8*(2), 152–160.
Van Orden, G. C. (2007). The fractal picture of health and well-being. *Scientific Briefs*. http://www.apa.org/science/about/psa/2007/02/van-ordern.aspx
Von Bertalanffy, L. (1950a). The theory of open systems in physics and biology. *Science New Series, 111*(2872), 23–29.
Von Bertalanffy, L. (1950b). An outline of general system theory. *The British Journal for the Philosophy of Science, 1*(2), 134–165.

Vrobel, S. (2011). *Fractal time: Why a watched kettle never boils*. Singapore: World Scientific

Wagner, A. (2005). *Robustness and evolvability in living systems*. Princeton: Princeton University Press.

Wagner, A. (2008). Robustness and evolvability: A paradox resolved. *Proceedings of the Royal Society B, 275,* 91–100.

Wagner, G. P., & Altenberg, L. (1996). Perspective: Complex adaptation and the evolution of adaptability. *Evolution, 50*(3), 967–976.

Walter-Ginzberg, A., Blumstein, T., Chetrit, A., & Modan, B.(2002). Social factors and mortality in the old-old in Israel: The CALAS study. *Journals of Gerontology: Social Sciences, 57B,* S308–S318.

Ward, L. M. (2002). *Dynamical cognitive science*. Cambridge: MIT.

West, B. J. (2006). *Where medicine went wrong: Rediscovering the path to complexity*. Singapore: World Scientific.

Whitacre, J. M., & Bender, A. (2010a). Degeneracy: A design principle for achieving robustness and evolvability. *Journal of Theoretical Biology, 263,* 143–153.

Whitacre, J. M., & Bender, A. (2010b). Networked buffering: A basic mechanism for distributed robustness in complex adaptive systems. *Theoretical Biology and Medical Modeling, 7,* 20. http://www.tbiomed.com/content/7/1/20.

Whitfield, K. E., Bromwell, L., Bennett, G., & Edwards, C. L. (2011). *Biobehavioral aspects on late-life morbidities. Annual review of gerontology and geriatrics* (pp. 57–74). New York: Springer. doi:10.1891/0198-8794.29.57.

Wiese, S. L., Vallacher, R. R., & Strawinska, U. (2010). Dynamical social psychology: Complexity and coherence in human experience. *Social and Personality Psychology Compass, 4*(11), 1018–1030. doi:10.1111/j.1751-9004.2010.00319.x.

Wikipedia. (2012). http://en.wikipedia.org/wiki/Hysteresis. Accessed 30 May 2012.

Wilhelm, T. (2009). The smallest chemical reaction with bistability. *BMC Systems Biology, 3,* 90. doi:10.1186/1752-0509-3-90.

Witten, T. M. (1980). A note on the structure of system state spaces and its implications on the existence of non-repeatable experiments. *Bulletin of Mathematical Biology, 42,* 267–272.

Witten, T. M. (1982). Some thoughts on quantum non-demolition experiments in biological systems. *Bulletin of Mathematical Biology, 44,* 572–584.

Witten, T. M. (1983). A return to time, cells, systems, and aging: I. Rethinking the concepts of senescence in mammalian systems. *Mechanisms of Aging and Development, 21:* 69–81.

Witten, T. M. (1984a). Time aberration in living organisms: Stochastic effects. *Mathematical Modeling, 5:* 97–101.

Witten, T. M. (1984b). A return to time, cells, systems, and aging: II. Relational and reliability theoretic aspects of senescence in mammalian systems. *Mechanisms of Aging and Development, 27:* 323–340.

Witten, T. M. (1985). A return to time, cells, systems and aging: III. Critical elements, hierarchies, and Gompertzian dynamics, *Mechanisms of Aging and Development, 32:* 141–177.

Witten, T. M. (2007). (M, R)-systems, (P, M, C)-nets, hierarchical decay and biological aging: Reminiscences of Robert Rosen. *Chemistry and Biodiversity, 4*(10), 2332–2344.

Yates, F. E. (Ed.). (1987). *Self-organizing systems: The emergence of order*. New York: Plenum.

Zausner, T. (2011). Chaos, creativity, and substance abuse: The nonlinear dynamics of choice. *Nonlinear Dynamics, Psychology and Life Sciences, 15*(2), 207–227.

Zeeman, E. C. (1976). Catastrophe theory. *Scientific American, 234,* 65–70. (Continued on pages 75–83).

Zeeman, E. C. (1977). *Catastrophe theory: Selected papers: 1972–1977*. Reading: Addison-Wesley.

Index

J. D. Sinnott (ed.), *Positive Psychology*,
DOI 10.1007/978-1-4614-7282-7, © Springer Science+Business Media, LLC 2013

MIX
Papier aus verantwortungsvollen Quellen
Paper from responsible sources
FSC® C105338

If you have any concerns about our products,
you can contact us on
ProductSafety@springernature.com

In case Publisher is established outside the EU,
the EU authorized representative is:
Springer Nature Customer Service Center GmbH
Europaplatz 3, 69115 Heidelberg, Germany

Printed by Libri Plureos GmbH
in Hamburg, Germany